Econometric Exercises, Volume 7

Bayesian Econometric Methods

SECOND EDITION

Bayesian Econometric Methods examines principles of Bayesian inference by posing a series of theoretical and applied questions and providing detailed solutions to those questions. This second edition adds extensive coverage of models popular in finance and macroeconomics, including state space and unobserved components models, stochastic volatility models, ARCH, GARCH, and vector autoregressive models. The authors have also added many new exercises related to Gibbs sampling and Markov Chain Monte Carlo (MCMC) methods.

The text includes regression-based and hierarchical specifications, models based upon latent variable representations, and mixture and time series specifications. MCMC methods are discussed and illustrated in detail – from introductory applications to those at the current research frontier – and MATLAB computer programs are provided on the website accompanying the text. Suitable for graduate study in economics, the text should also be of interest to students studying statistics, finance, marketing, and agricultural economics.

Joshua Chan is Professor of Economics at Purdue University. He is interested in building flexible models for large datasets and developing efficient estimation methods. His favorite applications include trend inflation estimation and macroeconomic forecasting. He has co-authored the textbook *Statistical Modeling and Computation*.

Gary Koop is a professor in the Department of Economics at the University of Strathclyde. He received his Ph.D. at the University of Toronto in 1989. His research work in Bayesian econometrics has resulted in numerous publications in top econometrics journals such as the *Journal of Econometrics*. He has also published several textbooks, including *Bayesian Econometrics*, and *Bayesian Econometric Methods*, and is co-editor of *The Oxford Handbook of Bayesian Econometrics*. He is on the editorial board of several journals, including the *Journal of Business and Economic Statistics* and the *Journal of Applied Econometrics*.

Dale J. Poirier is Emeritus Professor of Economics and Statistics at the University of California–Irvine. He is a fellow of the Econometric Society, the American Statistical

Association, the International Society for Bayesian Analysis, and the *Journal of Econometrics*. He has been on the editorial boards of the *Journal of Econometrics* and *Econometric Theory*, and was the founding editor of *Econometric Reviews*. His previous books include *Intermediate Statistics and Econometrics: A Comparative Approach*, and *The Econometrics of Structural Change*.

Justin L. Tobias is Professor and Head of the Economics Department at Purdue University. He received his Ph.D. from the University of Chicago in 1999, and has contributed to and served as an Associate Editor for several leading econometrics journals, including the *Journal of Applied Econometrics* and *Journal of Business and Economic Statistics*. His work focuses primarily on the development and application of Bayesian microeconometric methods.

Econometric Exercises

Editors:

The volumes in Econometric Exercises are intended to be much more than a collection of several hundred solved exercises. Each book has a coherent and well-organized sequence of exercises in a specific field or sub-field of econometrics. Every chapter of a volume begins with a short technical introduction that emphasizes the main ideas and overviews the most relevant theorems and results, including applications and occasionally computer exercises. They are intended for undergraduates in econometrics with an introductory knowledge of statistics, for first and second year graduate students of econometrics, and for students and instructors from neighboring disciplines (e.g., statistics, political science, psychology and communications) with interests in econometric methods.

Titles in the Series (* = planned):

1 Matrix Algebra (K. M. Abadir and J. R. Magnus)
2 Statistics (K. M. Abadir, R. D. H. Heijmans, and J. R. Magnus)*
3 Econometric Theory, I (P. Paruolo)
4 Empirical Applications, I (A. van Soest and M. Verbeek)*
5 Econometric Theory, II*
6 Empirical Applications, II*
7 Bayesian Econometric Methods (G. Koop, D. J. Poirier, and J. L. Tobias)
7 Bayesian Econometric Methods 2nd edition (J. Chan, G. Koop, D. J. Poirier, and J. L. Tobias)
* Time Series Econometrics, I
* Time Series Econometrics, II
* Microeconometrics
* Panel Data
* Nonlinear Models
* Nonparametrics and Semiparametrics
* Simulation-Based Econometrics
* Computational Methods
* Financial Econometrics
* Robustness
* Econometric Methodology

Website: www.cambridge.org/ECEX

Bayesian Econometric Methods

SECOND EDITION

Joshua Chan
Purdue University, Indiana

Gary Koop
University of Strathclyde

Dale J. Poirier
University of California–Irvine

Justin L. Tobias
Purdue University, Indiana

CAMBRIDGE
UNIVERSITY PRESS

CAMBRIDGE
UNIVERSITY PRESS

University Printing House, Cambridge CB2 8BS, United Kingdom

One Liberty Plaza, 20th Floor, New York, NY 10006, USA

477 Williamstown Road, Port Melbourne, VIC 3207, Australia

314-321, 3rd Floor, Plot 3, Splendor Forum, Jasola District Centre, New Delhi - 110025, India

79 Anson Road, #06-04/06, Singapore 079906

Cambridge University Press is part of the University of Cambridge.

It furthers the University's mission by disseminating knowledge in the pursuit of education, learning and research at the highest international levels of excellence.

www.cambridge.org
Information on this title: www.cambridge.org/9781108423380
DOI: 10.1017/9781108525947

First published 2007
Second edition 2020

A catalogue record for this publication is available from the British Library

ISBN 978-1-108-42338-0 Hardback
ISBN 978-1-108-43749-3 Paperback

Additional resources for this publication at www.cambridge.org/Chan2ed

To Bettina

To Lise

To the Reverend but not the Queen

To Melissa, Madeline, and Drew: Still, and Always.

Contents

List of Exercises

Preface to the Series

The past two decades have seen econometrics grow into a vast discipline. Many different branches of the subject now happily coexist with one another. These branches interweave econometric theory and empirical applications and bring econometric method to bear on a myriad economic issues. Against this background, a guided treatment of the modern subject of econometrics in volumes of worked econometric exercises seemed a natural and rather challenging idea.

The present series, *Econometric Exercises*, was conceived in 1995 with this challenge in mind. It has since become an exciting reality with the publication of the first installment of a series of volumes of worked econometric exercises. How can these volumes work as a tool of learning that adds value to the many existing textbooks of econometrics? What readers do we have in mind as benefiting from this series? What format best suits the objective of helping these readers learn, practice, and teach econometrics? These questions we now address, starting with our overall goals for the series.

Econometric Exercises is published as an organized set of volumes. Each volume in the series provides a coherent sequence of exercises in a specific field or subfield of econometrics. Solved exercises are assembled together in a structured and logical pedagogical framework that seeks to develop the subject matter of the field from its foundations through to its empirical applications and advanced reaches. As the Schaum series has done so successfully for mathematics, the overall goal of *Econometric Exercises* is to develop the subject matter of econometrics through solved exercises, providing a coverage of the subject that begins at an introductory level and moves through to more advanced undergraduate- and graduate-level material.

Problem solving and worked exercises play a major role in every scientific subject. They are particularly important in a subject like econometrics in which there is a rapidly growing literature of statistical and mathematical technique and an ever-expanding core to the discipline. As students, instructors, and researchers, we all benefit by seeing carefully worked-out solutions to problems that develop the subject and illustrate its methods and workings. Regular exercises and problem sets consolidate learning and reveal applications of textbook material. Clearly laid out solutions, paradigm answers, and alternate routes to solution all develop problem-solving skills. Exercises train students in clear analytical thinking and help them in preparing for tests and exams. Teachers, as well as students, find solved exercises useful in their classroom preparation and in designing problem sets, tests, and examinations. Worked problems and illustrative empirical applications appeal to researchers and professional economists wanting to learn about specific econometric techniques. Our intention for the *Econometric Exercises* series is to appeal to this wide range of potential users.

Each volume of the series follows the same general template. Chapters begin with a short outline that emphasizes the main ideas and provides an overview of the most relevant theorems and results. The introductions are followed by a sequential development of the material by solved examples and applications, and by computer exercises when appropriate. All problems are solved and they are graduated in difficulty with solution techniques evolving in a logical, sequential fashion. Problems are asterisked when they require more creative solutions or reach higher levels of technical difficulty. Each volume is self-contained. There is some commonality in material across volumes to reinforce learning and to make each volume accessible to students and others who are working largely, or even completely, on their own.

Content is structured so that solutions follow immediately after the exercise is posed. This makes the text more readable and avoids repetition of the statement of the exercise when it is being solved. More importantly, posing the right question at the right moment in the development of a subject helps to anticipate and address future learning issues that students face. Furthermore, the methods developed in a solution and the precision and insights of the answers are often more important than the questions being posed. In effect, the inner workings of a good solution frequently provide benefit beyond what is relevant to the specific exercise.

Exercise titles are listed at the start of each volume, following the table of contents, so that readers may see the overall structure of the book and its more detailed contents. This organization reveals the exercise progression, how the exercises relate to one another, and where the material is heading. It should also tantalize readers with the exciting prospect of advanced material and intriguing applications.

The series is intended for a readership that includes undergraduate students of econometrics with an introductory knowledge of statistics, first- and second-year graduate students of econometrics, as well as students and instructors from neighboring disciplines (such as statistics, psychology, or political science) with interests in econometric methods. The volumes generally increase in difficulty as the topics become more specialized.

The early volumes in the series (particularly those covering matrix algebra, statistics, econometric models, and empirical applications) provide a foundation to the study of econometrics. These volumes will be especially useful to students who are following the first-year econometrics course sequence in North American graduate schools and need to prepare for graduate comprehensive examinations in econometrics and to write an applied econometrics paper. The early volumes will equally be of value to advanced undergraduates studying econometrics in Europe, to advanced undergraduate and honors students in the Australasian system, and to masters and doctoral students in general. Subsequent volumes will be of interest to professional economists, applied workers, and econometricians who are working with techniques in those areas, as well as students who are taking an advanced course sequence in econometrics and statisticians with interests in those topics.

The *Econometric Exercises* series is intended to offer an independent learning-by-doing program in econometrics and it provides a useful reference source for anyone wanting to learn more about econometric methods and applications. The individual volumes can be used in classroom teaching and examining in a variety of ways. For instance, instructors can work through some of the problems in class to demonstrate methods as they are introduced; they can illustrate theoretical material with some of the solved examples; and they can show real data applications of the methods by drawing on some of the empirical examples. For examining purposes, instructors may draw freely from the solved exercises in test preparation. The systematic development of the subject in individual volumes will make the material easily accessible both for students in revision and for instructors in test preparation.

In using the volumes, students and instructors may work through the material sequentially as part of a complete learning program, or they may dip directly into material in which they are experiencing difficulty, to learn from solved exercises and illustrations. To promote intensive study, an instructor might announce to a class in advance of a test that some questions in the test will be selected from a certain chapter of one of the volumes. This approach encourages students to work through most of the exercises in a particular chapter by way of test preparation, thereby reinforcing classroom instruction.

Further details and updated information about individual volumes can be obtained from the *Econometric Exercises* website:

www.cambridge.org/ECEX

As series editors, we welcome comments, criticisms, suggestions, and, of course, corrections from all our readers on each of the volumes in the series as well as on the series itself. We bid you as much happy reading and problem solving as we have had in writing and preparing this series.

York, Tilburg, New Haven
June 2005

Karim M. Abadir
Jan R. Magnus
Peter C. B. Phillips

Preface

Bayesian econometrics has enjoyed an increasing popularity in many fields. This popularity has been evidenced through the recent publication of several textbooks at the advanced undergraduate and graduate levels, including those by Poirier (1995), Bauwens, Lubrano, and Richard (1999), Koop (2003), Lancaster (2004), Geweke (2005), and Greenberg (2013). The purpose of the present volume is to provide a wide range of exercises and solutions suitable for students interested in Bayesian econometrics at the level of these textbooks.

The Bayesian researcher should know the basic ideas underlying Bayesian methodology (i.e., Bayesian theory) and the computational tools used in modern Bayesian econometrics (i.e., Bayesian computation). The Bayesian should also be able to put the theory and computational tools together in the context of substantive empirical problems. We have written this book with these three activities – theory, computation, and empirical modeling – in mind. We have tried to construct a wide range of exercises on all of these aspects.

Loosely speaking, Chapters 1 through 9 focus on Bayesian theory, whereas Chapters 11 and 12 focus primarily on recent developments in Bayesian computation. The remaining chapters focus on particular models (usually regression-based). Inevitably, these chapters combine theory and computation in the context of particular models. Although we have tried to be reasonably complete in terms of covering the basic ideas of Bayesian theory and the computational tools most commonly used by the Bayesian, there is no way we can cover all the classes of models used in econometrics. Accordingly, we have selected a few popular classes of models (e.g., regression models with extensions and panel data models) to illustrate how the Bayesian paradigm works in practice. Particularly in Chapters 12 through 20 we have included substantive empirical exercises – some of them based closely on journal articles. We hope that the student who works through these chapters will have a good feeling for how serious Bayesian empirical work is done and will be well placed to write a Ph.D. dissertation or a journal article using Bayesian methods.

For the student with limited time, we highlight that a division in this book occurs between the largely theoretical material of Chapters 1 through 9 and the computational and model-specific material in Chapters 10 through 20. A student taking a course on Bayesian statistical theory could focus on Chapters 1 through 9, whereas a student taking a Bayesian econometrics course (or interested solely in empirical work) could focus more on Chapters 10 through 20 (skimming through the more methodologically oriented material in the early chapters).

Although there have been some attempts to create specifically Bayesian software, in our estimation, most Bayesians still prefer to create their own programs using software such as MATLAB, R, Python, or Julia. We have used MATLAB to create answers to the empirical problems in this book. Our code for various exercises is provided on the following web site:

http://web.ics.purdue.edu/~jltobias/bem.html

While we use MATLAB in our own coding we wish to note that, at least at the time of this writing, a free alternative is available called Octave, which can be downloaded from:

www.gnu.org/software/octave/

The statistics package within Octave and a number of other useful packages can also be freely installed, and we highly encourage those interested in pursuing this option to do so. In our own experimentation, much of the code we provide can be executed without difficulty within Octave with the support of these additional packages and our supporting m-files.

A few notational conventions are applied throughout the book, and it is worthwhile reviewing some of these prior to diving into the exercises. In regression-based problems, which constitute the majority of the exercises in the later chapters, lowercase letters such as y and x_i are reserved to denote scalar or vector quantities whereas capitals such as X or X_j are used to denote matrices. In cases for which the distinction between vectors and scalars is critical, this will be made clear within the exercise. In the regression-based problems, y is assumed to denote the $n \times 1$ vector of stacked responses for the dependent variable, y_i the ith element of that vector, x_i a k-vector of covariate data, and X the $n \times k$ matrix obtained from stacking the x_i over i. Latent variables, which are often utilized in the computational chapters of the book, are typically designated with a "*" superscript, such as y_i^*. In Chapters 1 through 9, many exercises are presented that are not directly related to linear regression models or models that can be viewed as linear on suitably defined latent data. In these exercises, the distinction between random variables and realizations of those variables is sometimes important. In such cases, we strive to use capital letters to denote random variables, which are unknown *ex ante*, and lowercase letters to denote their realizations, which are known *ex post*. So, in the context of discussing a posterior distribution (which conditions on the data), we will use $\overline{y}$, but if we are interested in discussing the sampling properties of the sample mean, $\overline{Y}$ would be the appropriate notation. In multiline derivations, "$\times$" is used to denote multiplication, and we will also use $=$ and $\propto$ to refer to the preceding line of the derivation so that, for example, the third line may be equal to the second, while the fourth line is proportional to the third. We will also use iid throughout to denote independent and identically distributed random variables, "pdf" to denote a probability density function and "cdf" to denote the cumulative distribution function. In the later chapters of the book, we will also frequently use the abbreviation "M–H" algorithm to refer to the Metropolis–Hastings algorithm. Finally, specific parameterizations of various densities are provided in the Appendix.

On the issue of parameterization, the reader who is somewhat familiar with the Bayesian literature may realize that researchers often employ different parameterizations for the same model, with no particular choice being "correct" or "ideal." A leading example is the linear regression model, in which the researcher can choose to parameterize this model in terms of the error variance or the error precision (the reciprocal of the variance). In this book, we try to remain consistent in terms of parameterization within individual chapters, though some departures from this trend do exist. These differences arise from our own individual tastes and styles toward approaching these models, and they are superficial rather than substantive. In our view it is quite valuable to expose the student to the use of different parameterizations, since this is the reality that he or she will face when exploring the Bayesian literature in more detail. In all cases, the parameterization employed is clearly delineated within each exercise.

We would like to thank the editors of the *Econometrics Exercises* series – Karim Abadir, Jan Magnus, and Peter Phillips – for their helpful comments and support during the planning and writing of this book. Hoa Jia, Babatunde Abidoye, Jingtao Wu, and Dimitris Korobilis deserve special recognition for reviewing numerous exercises and helping to reduce the number of typographical errors in the first edition. Jiang Huang provided helpful support in the typesetting of several exercises in the second edition and Daniel Kebede provided valuable assistance in reviewing several of the exercises new to this edition. Tim Bond and Kevin Mumford kindly shared American Community Survey (ACS) data for use in some exercises. The list of other colleagues and students who have helped us – through designing, solving, and pointing out errors in our problems or solutions – is too long to enumerate here. We would, however, like to thank our students at the Australian National University; University of California, Irvine; Purdue University; Iowa State University; Leicester University; Scottish Graduate Programme in Economics; University of Toronto; and the University of Technology Sydney for their participation, wise insights, and enthusiasm.

1

The Subjective Interpretation of Probability

Reverend Thomas Bayes (born circa 1702; died 1761) was the oldest son of Reverend Joshua Bayes, who was one of the first ordained nonconformist ministers in England. Relatively little is known about the personal life of Thomas Bayes. Although he was elected a Fellow of the Royal Society in 1742, his only known mathematical works are two articles published posthumously by his friend Richard Price in 1763. The first dealt with the divergence of the Stirling series, and the second, "An Essay Toward Solving a Problem in the Doctrine of Chances," is the basis of the paradigm of statistics named for him. His ideas appear to have been independently developed by James Bernoulli in 1713, also published posthumously, and later popularized independently by Pierre Laplace in 1774. In their comprehensive treatise, Bernardo and Smith (1994, p. 4) offer the following summarization of *Bayesian statistics*:

> Bayesian Statistics offers a rationalist theory of personalistic beliefs in contexts of uncertainty, with the central aim of characterizing how an individual should act in order to avoid certain kinds of undesirable behavioral inconsistencies. The theory establishes that expected utility maximization provides the basis for rational decision making and that Bayes' Theorem provides the key to the ways in which beliefs should fit together in the light of changing evidence. The goal, in effect, is to establish rules and procedures for individuals concerned with disciplined uncertainty accounting. The theory is not descriptive, in the sense of claiming to model actual behavior. Rather, it is prescriptive, in the sense of saying "if you wish to avoid the possibility of these undesirable consequences you must act in the following way."

Bayesian econometrics consists of the tools of Bayesian statistics applicable to the models and phenomena of interest to economists. There have been numerous axiomatic formulations leading to the central unifying Bayesian prescription of maximizing subjective utility as the guiding principle of Bayesian statistical analysis. Bernardo and Smith (1994, Chapter 2) is a valuable segue into this vast literature. Deep issues are involved regarding meaningful separation of probability and utility assessments, and we do not address these here.

Non-Bayesians, who we hereafter refer to as *frequentists*, argue that situations not admitting repetition under essentially identical conditions are not within the realm of statistical enquiry, and hence "probability" should not be used in such situations. Frequentists define the probability of an event as its long-run relative frequency. This frequentist interpretation cannot be applied to (i) unique, once-and-for-all phenomena, (ii) hypotheses, or (iii) uncertain past events. Furthermore, this definition is nonoperational since only a finite number of trials can ever be conducted. In contrast, the desire to expand the set of relevant events over which the concept of probability can be applied, and the willingness to entertain formal introduction of "nonobjective" information into the analysis, led to the subjective interpretation of probability.

Definition 1.1 (Subjective interpretation of probability) Let κ denote the body of knowledge, experience, or information that an individual has accumulated about the situation of concern, and let A denote an uncertain event (not necessarily repetitive). The *probability of A afforded by κ* is the "degree of belief" in A held by an individual in the face of κ.

Since at least the time of Ramsey (1926), such degrees of belief have been operationalized in terms of agreed upon reference lotteries. Suppose you seek your degree of belief, denoted $p = P(A)$, that an event A occurs. Consider the following two options:

1. Receiving a small reward $\$r$ if A occurs, and receiving \$0 if A does not occur.
2. Engaging in a lottery in which you win $\$r$ with probability p, and receiving \$0 with probability $1 - p$.

If you are indifferent between these two choices, then your degree of belief in A occurring is p. Requiring the reward to be "small" is to avoid the problem of introducing utility into the analysis; that is, implicitly assuming utility is linear in money for small gambles.

Bruno de Finetti considered the interesting situation in which an individual is asked to quote betting odds (ratios of probabilities) on a set of uncertain events and accept any wagers others may decide to make about these events. According to de Finetti's *coherence principle*, the individual should never assign "probabilities" so that someone else can select stakes that guarantee a sure loss *(Dutch book)* for the individual whatever the eventual outcome. A sure loss amounts to the "undesirable consequences" contained in the earlier quote of Bernardo and Smith. This simple principle implies the axioms of probability discussed in Abadir, Heijmans, and Magnus (2006, Chapter 1), except that the additivity of probability of intersections for disjoint events is required to hold only for *finite* intersections. Nonetheless, for purposes of convenience, we consider only countably additive probability in this volume.

De Finetti's Dutch book arguments also lead to the standard rule for conditional probability. Consider two events, A and B. By using the *factorization rule for conditional probability* (Abadir et al. 2006, p. 5),

$$P(A \text{ and } B) = P(A)P(B|A) = P(B)P(A|B),$$

the simplest form of Bayes' theorem follows immediately:

$$P(B|A) = \frac{P(B)P(A|B)}{P(A)}.$$

In words, we are interested in the event B to which we assign the *prior* probability $P(B)$ for its occurrence. We observe the occurrence of the event A. The probability of B occurring given that A has occurred is the *posterior* probability $P(B|A)$. More generally, we have the following result.

Theorem 1.1 (Bayes' theorem for events) Consider a probability space $[S, \tilde{A}, P(\cdot)]$ and a collection $B_n \in \tilde{A}$ $(n = 1, 2, \ldots, N)$ of mutually disjoint events such that $P(B_n) > 0$ $(n = 1, 2, \ldots, N)$ and $B_1 \cup B_2 \cup \cdots \cup B_N = S$. Then

$$P(B_n|A) = \frac{P(A|B_n)P(B_n)}{\sum_{j=1}^{N} P(A|B_j)P(B_j)} \quad (n = 1, 2, \ldots, N) \tag{1.1}$$

for every $A \in \tilde{A}$ such that $P(A) > 0$.

Proof The proof follows directly upon noting that the denominator in (1.1) is $P(A)$.

An important philosophical topic is whether the conditionalization in Bayes' theorem warrants an unquestioned position as the model of learning in the face of knowledge of the event A. Conditional probability $P(B|A)$ refers to *ex ante* beliefs on events not yet decided. *Ex post* experience of an event can sometimes have a striking influence on the probability assessor (e.g., experiencing unemployment, stock market crashes, etc.), and the experience can bring with it more information than originally anticipated in the event. Nonetheless, we adopt such conditionalization as a basic principle.

The subjective interpretation reflects an individual's personal assessment of the situation. According to the subjective interpretation, probability is a property of an individual's perception of reality, whereas according to classical and frequency interpretations, probability is a property of reality itself. For the subjectivist there are no "true unknown probabilities" in the world out there to be discovered. Instead, "probability" is in the eye of the beholder.

Bruno de Finetti assigned a fundamental role in Bayesian analysis to the concept of *exchangeability*, defined as follows.

Definition 1.2 A finite sequence Y_t $(t = 1, 2, \ldots, T)$ of events (or random variables) is *exchangeable* iff the joint probability of the sequence, or any subsequence, is invariant under permutations of the subscripts, that is,

$$P(y_1, y_2, \ldots, y_T) = P(y_{\pi(1)}, y_{\pi(2)}, \ldots, y_{\pi(T)}), \tag{1.2}$$

where $\pi(t)$ $(t = 1, 2, \ldots, T)$ is a permutation of the elements in $\{1, 2, \ldots, T\}$. An infinite sequence is exchangeable iff any finite subsequence is exchangeable.

Exchangeability provides an operational meaning to the weakest possible notion of a sequence of "similar" random quantities. It is "operational" because it only requires probability assignments of *observable* quantities, although admittedly this becomes problematic in the case of infinite exchangeability. For example, a sequence of Bernoulli trials is *exchangeable* iff the probability assigned to particular sequences does not depend on the order of "successes" (S) and "failures" (F). If the trials are exchangeable, then the sequences FSS, SFS, and SSF are assigned the same probability.

Exchangeability involves recognizing symmetry in beliefs concerning only observables, and presumably this is something about which a researcher may have intuition. Ironically, subjectivists emphasize observables (data) and objectivists focus on unobservables (parameters). Fortunately, Bruno de Finetti provided a subjectivist solution to this perplexing state of affairs. De Finetti's representation theorem and its generalizations are interesting because they provide conditions under which exchangeability gives rise to an isomorphic world in which we have iid observations conditional on a mathematical construct, namely, a parameter. These theorems provide an interpretation of parameters that differs substantively from the interpretation of an objectivist.

As in the case of iid sequences, the individual elements in an exchangeable sequence are identically distributed, but they are *not* necessarily independent, and this has important predictive implications for learning from experience. The importance of the concept of exchangeability is illustrated in the following theorem.

Theorem 1.2 (de Finetti's representation theorem) Let Y_t $(t = 1, 2, \ldots)$ be an infinite sequence of Bernoulli random variables indicating the occurrence (1) or nonoccurrence (0) of some event of interest. For any finite sequence Y_t $(t = 1, 2, \ldots, T)$, define the average number of occurrences as

$$\overline{Y}_T = \frac{1}{T}\sum_{t=1}^{T} Y_t. \tag{1.3}$$

Let $h(y_1, y_2, \ldots, y_T) = \Pr(Y_1 = y_1, Y_2 = y_2, \ldots, Y_T = y_T)$ denote a probability mass function (pmf) reflecting *exchangeable* beliefs for an arbitrarily long finite sequence Y_t $(t = 1, 2, \ldots, T)$, and let $H(y) = \Pr(Y \leq y)$ denote its associated cumulative distribution function (cdf). Then $h(\cdot)$ has the representation

$$h(y_1, y_2, \ldots, y_T) = \int_0^1 L(\theta)dF(\theta), \tag{1.4}$$

where

$$L(\theta) = \prod_{t=1}^{T} \theta^{y_t}(1-\theta)^{(1-y_t)}, \tag{1.5}$$

$$F(\theta) = \lim_{T\to\infty} P_H(\overline{Y}_T \leq \theta), \tag{1.6}$$

and $P_H(\cdot)$ denotes probability with respect to the cdf $H(\cdot)$ corresponding to the pmf (1.4).

Proof See de Finetti (1937) or the simpler exposition of Heath and Sudderth (1976).

Theorem 1.1 implies that it is *as if*, given θ, Y_t $(t = 1, 2, \ldots, T)$ are iid Bernoulli trials where the probability of a success is θ, and the "parameter" θ is assigned a probability distribution with cdf $F(\cdot)$ that can be interpreted as belief about the long-run relative frequency of $\overline{Y}_T \leq \theta$ as $T \to \infty$. From de Finetti's standpoint, both the quantity θ and the notion of independence are "mathematical fictions" implicit in the researcher's subjective assessment of arbitrarily long *observable* sequences of successes and failures. The parameter θ is of interest primarily because it constitutes a limiting form of predictive inference about the observable $\overline{Y}_T$ via (1.6). The mathematical construct θ may nonetheless be useful. However, Theorem 1.2 implies that the subjective probability distribution need not apply to the "fictitious θ" but only to the *observable* exchangeable sequence of successes and failures. When the cdf is absolutely continuous, so that $f(\theta) = \partial F(\theta)/\partial\theta$ exists, then (1.4) becomes

$$h(y_1, y_2, \ldots, y_T) = \int_0^1 \prod_{t=1}^{T} \theta^{(y_t)}(1-\theta)^{(1-y_t)} f(\theta)d\theta. \tag{1.7}$$

It is clear from (1.4) and (1.7) that exchangeable beliefs assign probabilities acting as if the Y_t are iid Bernoulli random variables given θ, and then average over values of θ using the weight $f(\theta)$ to obtain a marginal density for the Y_t. Let $S_T = T\overline{Y}_T$ be the number of successes in T trials. Since there are $\binom{T}{r}$ ways in which to obtain $S_T = r$ successes in T trials, it follows immediately from (1.4) and (1.5) that

$$\Pr(S_T = r) = \binom{T}{r} \int_0^1 \theta^r(1-\theta)^{T-r} dF(\theta) \quad (r = 0, 1, \ldots, T), \tag{1.8}$$

where

$$F(\theta) = \lim_{T\to\infty} \Pr(T^{-1}S_T \leq \theta). \tag{1.9}$$

Thus, given θ, it follows from (1.8) that exchangeable beliefs assign probabilities acting as if S_T has a binomial distribution given θ, and then average over values of θ using the weight $f(\theta) = \partial F(\theta)/\partial\theta$. Bayes and Laplace suggest choosing the "mixing" distribution $F(\theta)$ for θ to be uniform over $[0, 1]$, in which case (1.8) reduces to

$$\Pr(S_T = r) = (T+1)^{-1}, \quad r = 0, 1, \ldots, T. \tag{1.10}$$

In words, (1.10) describes beliefs that in T trials, any number r of successes are equally likely. In the degenerate case in which the distribution of θ assigns probability one to some value θ_0, then de Finetti's theorem implies that S_T follows the standard binomial distribution

$$\Pr(S_T = r) = \binom{T}{r} \theta_0^r (1 - \theta_0)^{T-r}, \tag{1.11}$$

and (1.9) implies that

$$\lim_{T\to\infty} \overline{Y}_T = \theta_0 \tag{1.12}$$

with "probability one." This last result, as a special case of de Finetti's theorem, is equivalent to the *strong law of large numbers*.

De Finetti's representation theorem has been generalized by seeking more stringent forms of "symmetry" than simple exchangeability, in the process rationalizing sampling models other than the binomial (see Bernardo and Smith 1994, Chapter 4; Poirier 2011). Although these theorems do not hold exactly for infinite sequences, they hold approximately for sufficiently large finite sequences.

The pragmatic value of de Finetti's theorem depends on whether it is easier to assess the left-hand side of (1.8), which involves only observable quantities, or instead, the integrand on the right-hand side of (1.8), which involves two distributions and the mathematical fiction θ. Most statisticians think in terms of the right-hand side. Frequentists implicitly do so with a degenerate distribution for θ that in effect treats θ as a constant, and Bayesians do so with a nondegenerate "prior" distribution for θ. What is important to note here, however, is the isomorphism de Finetti's theorem suggests between two worlds, one involving only observables and the other involving the parameter θ. De Finetti put parameters in their proper perspective: (i) they are mathematical constructs that provide a convenient index for a probability distribution, and (ii) they induce conditional independence for a sequence of observables.

Exercise 1.1 (*Let's Make a Deal*) Consider the television game show *Let's Make a Deal* in which the host Monty Hall asks contestants to choose the prize behind one of three curtains. Behind one curtain lies the grand prize; the other two curtains conceal only relatively small gifts. Assume that Monty knows what is behind every curtain. Once the contestant has made a choice, Monty Hall reveals what is behind one of the two curtains that were not chosen. Having been shown one of the lesser prizes, the contestant is offered a chance to switch curtains. Should the contestant switch?

Solution

Let C denote which curtain hides the grand prize. Let $\hat{C}$ denote the curtain the contestant chooses first, and let M denote the curtain Monty shows the contestant. Assume that $\Pr(C = i) = 1/3$, $i = 1, 2, 3$, $\Pr(\hat{C} = k|C) = 1/3$, $k = 1, 2, 3$, and that C and $\hat{C}$ are independent. Without loss of generality, suppose $C = 1$ and $M = 2$. Then use Bayes' theorem for events to compute the numerator and denominator of the following ratio:

$$\begin{aligned}
\frac{\Pr(C = 3|M = 2, \hat{C} = 1)}{\Pr(C = 1|M = 2, \hat{C} = 1)} &= \frac{\frac{\Pr(M=2,\hat{C}=1|C=3)\Pr(C=3)}{\Pr(M=2,\hat{C}=1)}}{\frac{\Pr(M=2,\hat{C}=1|C=1)\Pr(C=1)}{\Pr(M=2,\hat{C}=1)}} \\
&= \frac{\Pr(M = 2, \hat{C} = 1|C = 3)}{\Pr(M = 2, \hat{C} = 1|C = 1)} \\
&= \frac{\Pr(M = 2|\hat{C} = 1, C = 3)\Pr(\hat{C} = 1|C = 3)}{\Pr(M = 2|\hat{C} = 1, C = 1)\Pr(\hat{C} = 1|C = 1)} \\
&= \frac{\Pr(M = 2|\hat{C} = 1, C = 3)}{\Pr(M = 2|\hat{C} = 1, C = 1)}. \qquad (1.13)
\end{aligned}$$

The numerator of the last line of (1.13) is one because Monty has no choice but to choose $M = 2$ when $\hat{C} = 1$ and $C = 3$. The denominator of (1.13), however, is ambiguous because when $\hat{C} = 1$ and $C = 1$, Monty can choose either $M = 2$ or $M = 3$. The problem formulation does not contain information on Monty's choice procedure in this case. But since this probability must be less than or equal to one, the ratio (1.13) can never be less than one. Unless $\Pr(M = 2|\hat{C} = 1, C = 1) = 1$, the contestant is better off switching curtains. If $\Pr(M = 2|\hat{C} = 1, C = 1) = \Pr(M = 3|\hat{C} = 1, C = 1) = 1/2$, then the contestant doubles the probability of winning the grand prize by switching.

Exercise 1.2 (Making Dutch book) Consider a horse race involving N horses. Suppose a bettor's beliefs are such that he believes the probability of horse n winning is p_n, where $p_1 + p_2 + \cdots + p_N < 1$. Show how to make Dutch book with such an individual.

Solution

Consider a bet with this person of p_n dollars that pays one dollar if horse n wins, and place such a bet on each of the N horses. Then you are guaranteed winning one dollar (since one of the horses has to win) and earning a profit of $1 - (p_1 + p_2 + \cdots + p_N) > 0$.

Exercise 1.3 (Independence and exchangeability) Suppose $Y = [Y_1\ Y_2\ \cdots\ Y_T]' \sim N(0_T, \Sigma)$, where $\Sigma = (1 - \alpha)I_T + \alpha\iota_T\iota_T'$ is positive definite for some scalar α and ι is a $T \times 1$ vector with each element equal to unity. Let $\pi(t)$ $(t = 1, 2, \ldots, T)$ be a permutation of $\{1, 2, \ldots, T\}$ and suppose that $[Y_{\pi(1)}, Y_{\pi(2)}, \ldots, Y_{\pi(T)}] = AY$, where A is a $T \times T$ selection matrix such that, for $t = 1, 2, \ldots, T$, row t in A consists of all zeros except column $\pi(t)$, which is unity. Show that these beliefs are exchangeable.

Solution
Note that $AA' = I_T$ and $A\iota_T = \iota_T$. Then, $AY \sim N(0_T, \Omega)$, where

$$\begin{aligned}\Omega &= A\Sigma A' \\ &= A[(1-\alpha)I_t + \alpha\iota_T\iota_T']A' \\ &= (1-\alpha)AA' + \alpha A\iota_T\iota_T'A' \\ &= (1-\alpha)I_T + \alpha\iota_T\iota_T' \\ &= \Sigma.\end{aligned}$$

Hence, beliefs regarding $Y_t (t = 1, 2, \ldots, T)$ are exchangeable. Despite this exchangeability, it is interesting to note that if $\alpha \neq 0$, Y_t $(t = 1, 2, \ldots, T)$ are *not independent*.

Exercise 1.4 (Predicted probability of success of a Bernoulli random variable)
Suppose a researcher makes a coherent probability assignment to an infinite sequence Y_t $(t = 1, 2, 3, \ldots)$ of exchangeable Bernoulli random variables. Given an observed sequence of T trials with r successes, find the probability that the next outcome, Y_{T+1}, is y_{T+1}.

Solution
Applying the definition of conditional probability and then Theorem 1.2 to both the numerator and denominator yields

$$\begin{aligned}\Pr(Y_{T+1} = y_{T+1}|T\overline{Y}_T = r) &= \frac{\Pr(T\overline{Y}_T = r, Y_{T+1} = y_{T+1})}{\Pr(T\overline{Y}_T = r)} \\ &= \frac{\int_0^1 \theta^{(r+y_{T+1})}(1-\theta)^{(T+1-r-y_{T+1})}p(\theta)d\theta}{\int_0^1 \theta^r(1-\theta)^{(T-r)}p(\theta)d\theta} \\ &= \frac{\int_0^1 \theta^{(y_{T+1})}(1-\theta)^{(1-Y_{T+1})}p(\theta)L(\theta)d\theta}{\int_0^1 L(\theta)p(\theta)d\theta} \\ &= \int_0^1 \theta^{(y_{T+1})}(1-\theta)^{(1-y_{T+1})}p(\theta|y)d\theta, \qquad (1.14)\end{aligned}$$

where

$$p(\theta|y) = \frac{p(\theta)L(\theta)}{p(y)}. \qquad (1.15)$$

Therefore, $\Pr(Y_{T+1} = y_{T+1}|T\overline{Y}_T = r)$ is simply

$$E(\theta|y) \text{ if } y_{T+1} = 1,$$

or

$$1 - E(\theta|y) \text{ if } y_{T+1} = 0.$$

The simplicity of this exercise hides its importance because it demonstrates most of the essential operations that characterize the Bayesian approach to statistics. First, the existence of the density $p(\theta)$ is a result of Theorem 1.2, *not* an assumption. Second, the updating of prior beliefs captured in (1.15) amounts to nothing more than Bayes' theorem. Third, although Y_t $(t = 1, 2, \ldots, T)$ are independent conditional on θ, unconditional on θ they are dependent. Finally, the parameter θ is merely a mathematical entity indexing the integration in (1.14). Its "real-world existence" is a question only of metaphysical importance.

Exercise 1.5 (Independence and conditional independence) Consider three events A_i $(i = 1, 2, 3)$, where $\Pr(A_i) = p_i$, $i = 1, 2, 3$. Show that the following statements are totally unrelated: (a) A_1 and A_2 are independent; (b) A_1 and A_2 are conditionally independent given A_3.

Solution

There are $2^3 = 8$ possible three-element strings that can occur when considering A_i $(i = 1, 2, 3)$ and their complements A_i^c $(i = 1, 2, 3)$. This leaves assessment of $7 = 8 - 1$ probabilities since the eighth is determined by the adding-up condition. These can be assessed in terms of the following probabilities: $\Pr(A_1 \cap A_2) = q_{12}$, $\Pr(A_1 \cap A_3) = q_{13}$, $\Pr(A_2 \cap A_3) = q_{23}$, and $\Pr(A_1 \cap A_2 \cap A_3) = s$. Independence of A_1 and A_2 places a restriction on $\Pr(A_1 \cap A_2)$, namely $q_{12} = p_1 p_2$. Conditional independence places a restriction on the remaining probabilities q_{13}, q_{23}, p_3, and s. To see this, note that $\Pr(A_1 \cap A_2 | A_3) = s/p_3$ by simply expressing the conditional as the joint divided by the marginal, and conditional independence implies $\Pr(A_1 \cap A_2 | A_3) = \Pr(A_1 | A_3)\Pr(A_2 | A_3) = (q_{13}/p_3)(q_{23}/p_3)$. Putting these equalities together implies $s = q_{13} q_{23}/p_3$. Note that the restrictions implied by independence and conditional independence share no common probabilities.

2

Bayesian Inference

In this chapter we extend Chapter 1 to cover the case of random variables. By *Bayesian inference* we mean the updating of prior beliefs into posterior beliefs conditional on observed data. This chapter covers a variety of standard sampling situations in which prior beliefs are sufficiently regular that the updating can proceed in a fairly mechanical fashion. Details of point estimation, interval estimation, hypothesis testing, and prediction are covered in subsequent chapters. We remind the reader that the definitions of many common distributions are provided in the Appendix. Further details on the underlying probability theory are available in Chapters 1 and 2 of Poirier (1995).

One of the appealing things about Bayesian analysis is that it requires only a few general principles that are applied over and over again in different settings. Bayesians begin by writing down a joint distribution of all quantities under consideration (except known constants). Quantities to become known under sampling are denoted by the T-dimensional vector y, and remaining unknown quantities by the K-dimensional vector $\theta \in \Theta \subseteq \mathbb{R}^K$. Unless noted otherwise, we treat θ as a continuous random variable. Working in terms of densities, consider

$$p(y, \theta) = p(\theta)p(y|\theta) = p(y)p(\theta|y), \tag{2.1}$$

where $p(\theta)$ is the *prior density* and $p(\theta|y)$ is the *posterior density*. Viewing $p(y|\theta)$ as a function of θ for known y, any function proportional to it is referred to as a *likelihood function*. We will denote the likelihood function as $L(\theta)$. Unless noted otherwise, we will work with $L(\theta) = p(y|\theta)$ and thus include the integrating constant for $y|\theta$ in our description of the likelihood. We also note that

$$p(y) = \int_{\Theta} p(\theta)L(\theta)d\theta \tag{2.2}$$

is the *marginal density of the observed data* (also known as the *marginal likelihood*).

From (2.1), Bayes' *theorem for densities* follows immediately:

$$p(\theta|y) = \frac{p(\theta)L(\theta)}{p(y)} \propto p(\theta)L(\theta). \tag{2.3}$$

The shape of the posterior can be learned by plotting the right-hand side of (2.3) when $k = 1$ or 2. Obtaining moments or quantiles, however, requires the integrating constant (2.2). Fortunately, in some situations the integration in (2.2) can be performed analytically, in which case the updating of prior beliefs $p(\theta)$ in light of the data y to obtain the posterior beliefs $p(\theta|y)$ is straightforward. These situations correspond to cases where $p(\theta)$ and $L(\theta)$ belong to the *exponential family* of densities (see Exercise 2.13). In this case the prior density can be chosen so that the posterior density falls within the same elementary family of distributions as the prior. These families are called *conjugate families*.

The denominator in (2.3) serves as a factor of proportionality (not involving θ) that ensures that the posterior density integrates to unity. To simplify much of the analysis that follows, we calculate a posterior density by dropping all factors of proportionality from the prior density and the likelihood function, concentrating attention on the resulting posterior kernel, and then compute the required posterior integrating constant at the end. This works particularly well when using easily recognized conjugate families. Note also that this implies that when considering experiments employing the same prior, and that yield proportional likelihoods for the observed data, identical posteriors will emerge. This reflects the important fact that Bayesian inference is consistent with the *likelihood principle* (see Berger and Wolpert 1988).

In most practical situations, not all elements of θ are of direct interest. Let $\theta_1 \in \Theta_1$, $\theta_2 \in \Theta_2$, and $\theta = [\theta_1, \theta_2] \in \Theta_1 \times \Theta_2$ be partitioned into *parameters of interest* θ_1 and *nuisance parameters* θ_2 not of direct interest. For example, θ_1 may be the mean and θ_2 the variance of some sampling distribution. Nuisance parameters are well named for frequentists, because dealing with them in a general setting is one of the major problems frequentist researchers face. In contrast, Bayesians have a universal approach to eliminating nuisance parameters from the problem: they are integrated out of the posterior density, yielding the marginal posterior density for the parameters of interest, that is,

$$p(\theta_1|y) = \int_{\Theta_2} p(\theta_1, \theta_2|y)\, d\theta_2, \quad \theta_1 \in \Theta_1. \tag{2.4}$$

Many of the following exercises involve particular distributions. The Appendix contains definitions and properties of many common distributions. It is worth noting that there are two common parameterizations of the gamma distribution and we use both in this chapter (see Definition A.2).

Exercise 2.1 (Conjugate Bernoulli analysis) Given the parameter θ, where $0 < \theta < 1$, consider T *iid* Bernoulli random variables Y_t $(t = 1, 2, \ldots, T)$, each with pmf

$$p(y_t|\theta) = \begin{cases} \theta & \text{if } y_t = 1, \\ 1 - \theta & \text{if } y_t = 0. \end{cases} \tag{2.5}$$

The likelihood function is

$$L(\theta) = \theta^m (1 - \theta)^{T-m}, \tag{2.6}$$

where $m = T\overline{y}$ is the number of successes (i.e., $y_t = 1$) in T trials. Suppose prior beliefs concerning θ are represented by a beta distribution with pdf

$$p_B(\theta|\underline{\alpha}, \underline{\delta}) = [\mathcal{B}(\underline{\alpha}, \underline{\delta})]^{-1} \theta^{\underline{\alpha}-1} (1 - \theta)^{\underline{\delta}-1}, \quad 0 < \theta < 1, \tag{2.7}$$

where $\underline{\alpha} > 0$ and $\underline{\delta} > 0$ are known, and $\mathcal{B}(\underline{\alpha}, \underline{\delta}) = \Gamma(\underline{\alpha})\Gamma(\underline{\delta})/\Gamma(\underline{\alpha} + \underline{\delta})$ is the beta function defined in terms of the gamma function $\Gamma(\alpha) = \int_0^\infty t^{\alpha-1} \exp(-t) dt$. This class of priors can represent a wide range of prior opinions. Find the posterior density of θ.

Solution

The denominator (2.2) of the posterior (2.3) density is easy to compute. Define

$$\overline{\alpha} = \underline{\alpha} + m, \tag{2.8}$$
$$\overline{\delta} = \underline{\delta} + T - m, \tag{2.9}$$

and consider

$$\begin{aligned} p(y) &= \int_0^1 [\mathcal{B}(\underline{\alpha}, \underline{\delta})]^{-1} \theta^{\underline{\alpha}-1} (1 - \theta)^{\underline{\delta}-1} \theta^m (1 - \theta)^{T-m} d\theta \\ &= \left[\frac{\mathcal{B}(\overline{\alpha}, \overline{\delta})}{\mathcal{B}(\underline{\alpha}, \underline{\delta})}\right] \int_0^1 [\mathcal{B}(\overline{\alpha}, \overline{\delta})]^{-1} \theta^{\overline{\alpha}-1} (1 - \theta)^{\overline{\delta}-1} d\theta \\ &= \left[\frac{\mathcal{B}(\overline{\alpha}, \overline{\delta})}{\mathcal{B}(\underline{\alpha}, \underline{\delta})}\right], \end{aligned} \tag{2.10}$$

where the integral in (2.10) equals unity because the integrand is a beta pdf for θ. From (2.3) and (2.8)–(2.10) it follows that the posterior density of θ is

$$\begin{aligned} p(\theta|y) &= \frac{[\mathcal{B}(\underline{\alpha}, \underline{\delta})]^{-1} \theta^{\underline{\alpha}-1} (1 - \theta)^{\underline{\delta}-1} \theta^m (1 - \theta)^{T-m}}{\mathcal{B}(\overline{\alpha}, \overline{\delta})/\mathcal{B}(\underline{\alpha}, \underline{\delta})} \\ &= [\mathcal{B}(\overline{\alpha}, \overline{\delta})]^{-1} \theta^{\overline{\alpha}-1} (1 - \theta)^{\overline{\delta}-1}, \quad 0 < \theta < 1. \end{aligned} \tag{2.11}$$

Therefore, because the posterior density (2.11) is itself a beta pdf with parameters $\overline{\alpha}$ and $\overline{\delta}$ given by (2.8) and (2.9), it follows that the conjugate family of prior distributions for a Bernoulli likelihood is the beta family of pdfs.

Exercise 2.2 (Application of Bayes' theorem) A laboratory blood test is 95% effective in detecting a certain disease when it is, in fact, present. However, the test also yields a "false positive" result for 1% of the healthy people tested. If 0.1% of the population actually has the disease, what is the probability that a person has the disease given that her test result is positive?

Solution

Let D denote the presence of the disease, D^c denote its absence, and $+$ denote a positive test result. Then $\Pr(+|D) = .95$, $\Pr(+|D^c) = .01$, and $P(D) = .001$. Then, according to Bayes' theorem,

$$P(D|+) = \frac{P(D)P(+|D)}{P(+)} = \frac{.001(.95)}{.001(.95) + .999(.01)} = .0868.$$

Exercise 2.3 (Conjugate normal analysis with unknown mean and known variance) Given $\theta = [\theta_1 \ \theta_2]' \in \mathbb{R} \times \mathbb{R}^+$, consider a random sample Y_t $(t = 1, 2, \ldots, T)$ from an $N(\theta_1, \theta_2^{-1})$ population. For reasons that will become clear as we proceed, it is convenient to work in terms of θ_2, the reciprocal of the variance (called the *precision*). (In later exercises, however, particularly those in the computational chapters, we will work directly with the error variance. Both approaches are commonly employed in the literature.)

Assume θ_2 is known. Suppose prior beliefs for θ_1 are represented by the normal distribution

$$\theta_1 \sim N(\underline{\mu}, \underline{h}^{-1}), \tag{2.12}$$

where $\underline{\mu}$ and $\underline{h} > 0$ are given. Find the posterior density of θ_1 and marginal likelihood $p(y)$.

Solution

For later notational convenience, let

$$h = [\theta_2^{-1}/T]^{-1} = T\theta_2, \tag{2.13}$$
$$\overline{h} = \underline{h} + h, \tag{2.14}$$

and

$$\overline{\mu} = \overline{h}^{-1}(\underline{h}\underline{\mu} + h\overline{y}). \tag{2.15}$$

It is useful to employ two identities. The first identity is

$$\sum_{t=1}^{T}(y_t - \theta_1)^2 = \sum_{t=1}^{T}(y_t - \overline{y})^2 + T(\overline{y} - \theta_1)^2 = \nu s^2 + T(\overline{y} - \theta_1)^2, \tag{2.16}$$

for all θ_1, where

$$\nu = T - 1 \tag{2.17}$$

and

$$s^2 = \nu^{-1} \sum_{t=1}^{T} (y_t - \overline{y})^2. \tag{2.18}$$

The second identity is

$$\underline{h}(\theta_1 - \underline{\mu})^2 + h(\overline{y} - \theta_1)^2 = \overline{h}(\theta_1 - \overline{\mu})^2 + (\underline{h}^{-1} + h^{-1})^{-1}(\overline{y} - \underline{\mu})^2, \tag{2.19}$$

for all θ_1, $\underline{h}$, and h.

Now we apply Bayes' theorem to find the posterior density of θ_1. Using identities (2.13) and (2.16), we write the likelihood function as

$$\begin{aligned} L(\theta_1) &= \prod_{t=1}^{T} \phi(y_t|\theta_1, \theta_2^{-1}) \\ &= (2\pi\theta_2^{-1})^{-T/2} \exp\left(-\frac{\theta_2}{2} \sum_{t=1}^{T} (y_t - \theta_1)^2 \right) \\ &= (2\pi\theta_2^{-1})^{-T/2} \exp\left(-\frac{h}{2T} \left[\nu s^2 + T(\overline{y} - \theta_1)^2 \right] \right) \\ &= c_1 \phi(\overline{y}|\theta_1, h^{-1}), \end{aligned} \tag{2.20}$$

where

$$c_1 = (2\pi)^{-\nu/2} T^{(-1/2)} \theta_2^{\nu/2} \exp\left(-\frac{1}{2} \theta_2 \nu s^2 \right) \tag{2.21}$$

does *not* depend on θ_1. Note that the factorization in (2.20) demonstrates that $\overline{y}$ is a sufficient statistic for θ_1. Also note that the density $\phi(\overline{y}|\theta_1, h^{-1})$ corresponds to the sampling density of the sample mean, given θ_1.

Using identity (2.19) and factorization (2.20), the numerator of (2.3) is

$$\begin{aligned} p(\theta_1)L(\theta_1) &= \phi(\theta_1|\underline{\mu}, \underline{h}^{-1}) c_1 \phi(\overline{y}|\theta_1, h^{-1}) \\ &= c_1 (2\pi)^{-1} (\underline{h}h)^{1/2} \exp\left(-\frac{1}{2} \left[\underline{h}(\theta_1 - \underline{\mu})^2 + h(\overline{y} - \theta_1)^2 \right] \right) \\ &= c_1 (2\pi)^{-1} (\underline{h}h)^{1/2} \exp\left(-\frac{1}{2} \left[\overline{h}(\theta_1 - \overline{\mu})^2 + (\underline{h}^{-1} + h^{-1})^{-1}(\overline{y} - \underline{\mu})^2 \right] \right) \\ &= c_1 \phi\left(\overline{y}|\underline{\mu}, \underline{h}^{-1} + h^{-1} \right) \phi(\theta_1|\overline{\mu}, \overline{h}^{-1}). \end{aligned} \tag{2.22}$$

Bayes' theorem tells us that the posterior distribution of θ_1 is proportional to (2.22). Thus, all terms not involving θ_1 that enter (2.22) multiplicatively are absorbed in the normalizing constant, allowing us to focus on the posterior kernel. When looking at the final line of (2.22), we immediately see that

$$p(\theta_1|y) = \phi\left(\theta_1|\overline{\mu}, \overline{h}^{-1} \right). \tag{2.23}$$

The interpretations of quantities (2.14) and (2.15) are now clear from (2.23): they are the posterior precision and posterior mean, respectively. Note that it is the additivity of precisions in (2.14) that motivates working with precisions rather than variances. Because posterior density (2.23) and prior density (2.12) are both members of the normal family, it follows that the conjugate prior for the case of random sampling from a normal population with *known* variance is itself a normal density.

The marginal density of the data – i.e., the denominator of (2.3) – can be obtained from (2.22):

$$\begin{aligned} p(y) &= \int_{-\infty}^{\infty} p(\theta_1)L(\theta_1)d\theta_1 \\ &= c_1\phi\left(\overline{y}|\underline{\mu}, \underline{h}^{-1} + h^{-1}\right)\int_{-\infty}^{\infty}\phi(\theta_1|\overline{\mu}, \overline{h}^{-1})d\theta_1 \\ &= c_1\phi\left(\overline{y}|\underline{\mu}, \underline{h}^{-1} + h^{-1}\right). \end{aligned} \tag{2.24}$$

Alternatively, we can represent the regression model in the following way. The sampling assumptions regarding y_t imply $y = \iota_T\theta_1 + \epsilon$, where $y = [y_1\ y_2\ \cdots\ y_T]'$, ι_T is a $T \times 1$ vector of ones, and $\epsilon \sim N(0, \theta_2^{-1}I_T)$. Similarly, the prior for θ_1 in (2.12) can be written as $\theta_1 = \underline{\mu} + \eta$, where $\eta \sim N(0, \underline{h}^{-1})$. Substituting the equation for our prior into the equation for y gives $y = \iota_T\underline{\mu} + \epsilon + \iota_T\eta$, which implies $y \sim N\left(\iota_T\underline{\mu}, \left[\theta_2^{-1}I_T + \underline{h}^{-1}\iota_T\iota_T'\right]\right)$, or equivalently,

$$p(y) = \phi\left(y|\iota_T\underline{\mu}, [\theta_2^{-1}I_T + \underline{h}^{-1}\iota_T\iota_T']\right). \tag{2.25}$$

At first glance, it is not at all obvious that the expressions in (2.24) and (2.25) are in agreement, though if we have done our derivations correctly, they must agree. To show that these expressions are, in fact, the same, we expand (2.25). To fix ideas, we focus on reproducing the portion of (2.24) involving the normal density for $\overline{y}$. The remaining terms in (2.24) will also fall out of this derivation, though we suppress them here for clarity.

The kernel of (2.25) involves a term of the form

$$\exp\left[-[1/2](y - \iota_T\underline{\mu})'[\theta_2^{-1}I_T + \underline{h}^{-1}\iota_T\iota_T']^{-1}(y - \iota_T\underline{\mu})\right].$$

To simplify this quadratic form, we use the result

$$\begin{aligned} [\theta_2^{-1}I_T + \underline{h}^{-1}\iota_T\iota_T']^{-1} &= \theta_2\left[I_T - [\underline{h}^{-1}/(\theta_2^{-1} + T\underline{h}^{-1})]\iota_T\iota_T'\right] \\ &= hT^{-1}\left[I_T - [\underline{h}^{-1}/(Th^{-1} + T\underline{h}^{-1})]\iota_T\iota_T'\right] \\ &= hT^{-1}\left[I_T - (\beta/T)\iota_T\iota_T'\right], \end{aligned}$$

where $\beta \equiv \underline{h}^{-1}/(\underline{h}^{-1}+h^{-1})$, and, again, we have made use of the definition of h in (2.13). [The expression for this inverse is actually a commonly used formula in longitudinal data models with random effects, as the covariance matrix in such models has an identical structure to the covariance matrix in (2.25).]

Using this result, we can write the quadratic form in our exponential kernel as

$$\exp\left[-[1/2](hT^{-1})(y-\iota_T\underline{\mu})'[I_T-(\beta/T)\iota_T\iota_T'](y-\iota_T\underline{\mu})\right].$$

With a little work, one can show that this quadratic form can be expressed as

$$(y-\iota_T\underline{\mu})'[I_T-(\beta/T)\iota_T\iota_T'](y-\iota_T\underline{\mu})=\sum_t(y_t-\underline{\mu})^2-(\beta/T)\left[\sum_t(y_t-\underline{\mu})\right]^2.$$

Following (2.16), and in the spirit of getting (2.25) to look like (2.24), we can also write

$$\sum_t(y_t-\underline{\mu})^2=\nu s^2+T(\overline{y}-\underline{\mu})^2,$$

and similarly,

$$\sum_t(y_t-\underline{\mu})=T(\overline{y}-\underline{\mu}).$$

Putting these results together gives

$$(y-\iota_T\underline{\mu})'[I_T-(\beta/T)\iota_T\iota_T'](y-\iota_T\underline{\mu})=vs^2+T(\overline{y}-\underline{\mu})^2-\beta T(\overline{y}-\underline{\mu})^2.$$

The kernel of the density in (2.25) can thus be expressed as

$$\begin{aligned}&\exp\left(-(1/2)[T^{-1}h][\nu s^2+T(1-\beta)(\overline{y}-\underline{\mu})^2]\right)\\&=\exp\left(-(1/2)\theta_2\nu s^2\right)\exp\left(-(1/2)h(1-\beta)(\overline{y}-\underline{\mu})^2\right).\end{aligned}$$

Note that the first term on the right-hand side of this equation reproduces the corresponding term in the definition of c_1 in (2.21). As for the last term, by using our definition of β, it follows that

$$h(1-\beta)=h\left(\frac{h^{-1}+\underline{h}^{-1}}{h^{-1}+\underline{h}^{-1}}-\frac{\underline{h}^{-1}}{h^{-1}+\underline{h}^{-1}}\right)=(h^{-1}+\underline{h}^{-1})^{-1}.$$

Thus, we are indeed left with a term of the form $\phi(\overline{y}|\underline{\mu},h^{-1}+\underline{h}^{-1})$, as in (2.24). Including the normalizing constant of (2.25) into this derivation will show that (2.24) and (2.25) are identical.

Exercise 2.4 (Conjugate normal analysis with unknown mean and variance) Consider Exercise 2.3, but with the precision θ_2 also unknown. Suppose the joint prior distribution for $\theta=[\theta_1\ \theta_2]'$ is the normal-gamma distribution, denoted $\theta\sim NG(\underline{\mu},\underline{q},\underline{s}^{-2},\underline{\nu})$

(see Definition A.5 for details) with density

$$\begin{aligned} f_{NG}(\theta|\underline{\mu}, \underline{q}, \underline{s}^{-2}, \underline{\nu}) &= \phi(\theta_1|\underline{\mu}, \theta_2^{-1}\underline{q}) f_\gamma(\theta_2|\underline{s}^{-2}, \underline{\nu}) \\ &= \left((2\pi\theta_2^{-1}\underline{q})^{-1/2} \exp\left[-\frac{1}{2}\theta_2 \underline{q}^{-1}(\theta_1 - \underline{\mu})^2\right]\right) \\ &\times \left[\left(\left[\frac{2}{\underline{\nu}\underline{s}^2}\right]^{\underline{\nu}/2} \Gamma(\underline{\nu}/2)\right)^{-1} \theta_2^{(\underline{\nu}-2)/2} \exp\left(-\frac{1}{2}\theta_2 \underline{\nu}\underline{s}^2\right)\right] \\ &\propto \theta_2^{(\underline{\nu}-1)/2} \exp\left(-\frac{1}{2}\theta_2[\underline{\nu}\underline{s}^2 + \underline{q}^{-1}(\theta_1 - \underline{\mu})^2]\right), \end{aligned} \tag{2.26}$$

where $\underline{\mu} \in \mathbb{R}$, $\underline{q}$, $\underline{s}^2$, and $\underline{\nu}$ are known positive constants, and "$\times$" has been used to denote multiplication in multiline equations. Find the posterior density of θ.

Solution

Dropping irrelevant constants not depending on θ_1 and θ_2, (2.3) implies the posterior density $p(\theta|y)$ is proportional to the product of the kernels (2.26) and (2.20):

$$\begin{aligned} p(\theta|y) &\propto p(\theta)L(\theta) \\ &\propto \left[\phi(\theta_1|\underline{\mu}, \theta_2^{-1}\underline{q}) f_\gamma(\theta_2|\underline{s}^{-2}, \underline{\nu})\right] \left[c_1(\theta_2)\phi(\overline{y}|\theta_1, h^{-1})\right] \\ &\propto \theta_2^{(\underline{\nu}-1)/2} \exp\left(-\frac{\theta_2}{2}[\underline{\nu}\underline{s}^2 + \underline{q}^{-1}(\theta_1 - \underline{\mu})^2]\right) \theta_2^{T/2} \exp\left(-\frac{\theta_2}{2}[\nu s^2 + T(\overline{y} - \theta_1)^2]\right) \\ &\propto \theta_2^{(\overline{\nu}-1)/2} \exp\left(-\frac{\theta_2}{2}[\underline{\nu}\underline{s}^2 + \nu s^2 + \underline{q}^{-1}(\theta_1 - \underline{\mu})^2 + T(\overline{y} - \theta_1)^2]\right), \end{aligned} \tag{2.27}$$

where

$$\overline{\nu} = \underline{\nu} + T. \tag{2.28}$$

Using identity (2.19) with $\underline{h} = \underline{q}^{-1}$ and $h = T$, we can write the last two terms in the square brackets in (2.27) as

$$\underline{q}^{-1}(\theta_1 - \underline{\mu})^2 + T(\overline{y} - \theta_1)^2 = \overline{q}^{-1}(\theta_1 - \overline{\mu})^2 + (\underline{q} + T^{-1})^{-1}(\overline{y} - \underline{\mu})^2, \tag{2.29}$$

where

$$\overline{q} = (\underline{q}^{-1} + T)^{-1} \tag{2.30}$$

and

$$\overline{\mu} = \overline{q}(\underline{q}^{-1}\underline{\mu} + T\overline{y}). \tag{2.31}$$

Then, by letting

$$\overline{s}^2 = [\overline{\nu}]^{-1}\left[\underline{\nu}\underline{s}^2 + \nu s^2 + (\underline{q} + T^{-1})^{-1}(\overline{y} - \underline{\mu})^2\right] \tag{2.32}$$

$$= [\overline{\nu}]^{-1}\left[\underline{\nu}\underline{s}^2 + \nu s^2 + \underline{q}^{-1}\overline{q}T(\overline{y} - \underline{\mu})^2\right], \tag{2.33}$$

it follows from (2.27)–(2.33) that the posterior density (2.27) can be written

$$p(\theta|y) \propto \theta_2^{(\overline{\nu}-1)/2} \exp\left(-\frac{\theta_2}{2}[\overline{q}^{-1}(\theta_1 - \overline{\mu})^2 + \overline{\nu}\overline{s}^2]\right) \tag{2.34}$$

$$\propto \theta_2^{1/2} \exp\left[-\frac{\theta_2}{2}\overline{q}^{-1}(\theta_1 - \overline{\mu})^2\right] \theta_2^{(\overline{\nu}-2)/2} \exp\left[-\frac{\theta_2}{2}\overline{\nu}\overline{s}^2\right]. \tag{2.35}$$

Comparing (2.26) and (2.35), it is seen that the posterior density $p(\theta|y)$ corresponds to the kernel of an $NG(\overline{\mu}, \overline{q}, \overline{s}^{-2}, \overline{\nu})$ distribution, with updating formulas (2.28)–(2.33). Because both (2.26) and (2.35) are proportional to normal-gamma densities, the prior density (2.26) is the natural conjugate prior for random sampling from a normal population with unknown mean and variance.

Exercise 2.5 (Properties of a normal-gamma distribution) Consider the normal-gamma prior density in Exercise 2.4 for θ_1 and θ_2 with hyperparameters $\underline{\mu}$, $\underline{q}$, $\underline{s}^{-2}$, and $\underline{\nu} > 2$.
(a) Are θ_1 and θ_2 independent?
(b) Is θ_1 mean-independent of θ_2 (i.e., is the mean of θ_1 independent of θ_2)?
(c) Are θ_1 and θ_2 uncorrelated?

Solution
(a) No, because $\theta_1|\theta_2 \sim N(\underline{\mu}, \underline{q}/\theta_2)$ clearly depends on θ_2.
(b) Yes, because $E(\theta_1|\theta_2) = \underline{\mu}$ does not depend on θ_2.
(c) Yes, because mean-independence implies zero covariance.

Exercise 2.6 (Fictitious sample interpretation of natural conjugate priors)
Natural conjugate priors have the desirable feature that prior information can be viewed as "fictitious sample information" in that it is combined with the sample in exactly the same way that additional sample information would be combined. The only difference is that the prior information is "observed" in the mind of the researcher, not in the real world. To clarify this point, reconsider Exercises 2.1, 2.3, and 2.4.
(a) Using the setup of Exercise 2.1, show that a beta prior distribution with parameters $\underline{\alpha}$ and $\underline{\delta}$ can be interpreted as the information contained in a sample of size $\underline{T} = \underline{\alpha}+\underline{\delta}-2$ with $\underline{\alpha} - 1$ successes from the Bernoulli process of interest. (Of course, if $\underline{\alpha}$ and $\underline{\delta}$ are not integers, then this interpretation must be loosely made.) This does not mean that the researcher has actually observed such a sample, but rather only that the researcher imagines his or her prior information as being from such a sample.
(b) Using the setup of Exercise 2.3 (known variance), show that a normal prior distribution (2.12) can be interpreted in terms of equivalent sample information.

Solution

(a) Such an interpretation follows directly from the form of the Bernoulli likelihood in (2.6). In this case, the likelihood for $\underline{\alpha}-1$ successes in $\underline{T}$ trials is

$$L(\theta) = \theta^{\underline{\alpha}-1}(1-\theta)^{\underline{T}-(\underline{\alpha}-1)}$$
$$= \theta^{\underline{\alpha}-1}(1-\theta)^{\underline{\delta}-1},$$

using the definition of $\underline{T}$. This is proportional to the beta prior in (2.7), and thus the prior can be given this fictitious sample interpretation.

(b) Define

$$\underline{T} \equiv \frac{\theta_2^{-1}}{\underline{h}^{-1}} = \frac{\underline{h}}{\theta_2}, \tag{2.36}$$

and write the prior variance as

$$\underline{h}^{-1} = \frac{\theta_2^{-1}}{\underline{T}}. \tag{2.37}$$

Now, consider the likelihood for θ_1 obtained from a sample of size $\underline{T}$ from the population distribution $N(\theta_1, \theta_2^{-1})$ yielding a sample mean $\underline{\mu}$. With θ_2 known, from (2.20) the likelihood for this "sample" is proportional to

$$L(\theta_1) \propto \exp\left(-\frac{\theta_2 \underline{T}}{2}(\theta_1 - \underline{\mu})^2\right),$$

which forms the kernel of a normal prior for θ_1 with mean $\underline{\mu}$ and variance $\underline{T}^{-1}\theta_2^{-1} = \underline{h}^{-1}$, as in (2.12).

Similarly, using (2.14), we can define

$$\overline{T} \equiv \frac{\theta_2^{-1}}{\overline{h}^{-1}} = \frac{\overline{h}}{\theta_2} = \underline{T} + T, \tag{2.38}$$

and note that posterior mean (2.15) can be written

$$\overline{\mu} = \frac{\underline{T}\underline{\mu} + T\overline{y}}{\overline{T}}. \tag{2.39}$$

Given this interpretation, (2.38) and (2.39) can be viewed as formulas for pooling the information from the actual sample and the fictitious prior sample.

This updating can also be extended to the more general case of Exercise 2.4. Let

$$\underline{T} = \frac{1}{\underline{q}} \tag{2.40}$$

represent the prior sample size and let

$$\overline{T} = \frac{1}{\overline{q}} = \underline{T} + T \tag{2.41}$$

represent the "total" sample size. Then, again, the posterior mean (2.31) can be written as the weighted average (2.39).

Exercise 2.7 (Conjugate normal analysis with known mean and unknown variance) Consider Exercise 2.3 but with the mean θ_1 known and the population precision $\theta_2 \equiv \sigma^{-2}$ unknown. Suppose a prior density of the form $\sigma^{-2} \sim \gamma(\underline{s}^{-2}, \underline{\nu})$ is employed. Find the posterior for σ^{-2}.

Solution
Using the identity in (2.16) gives the likelihood function

$$L(\sigma^{-2}) = (2\pi)^{-T/2}(\sigma^{-2})^{T/2} \exp\left(-\frac{1}{2}\sigma^{-2}[\nu s^2 + T(\overline{y} - \theta_1)^2]\right),$$

and the prior density is

$$p(\sigma^{-2}) \propto (\sigma^{-2})^{(\underline{\nu}-2)/2} \exp\left(-\frac{1}{2}\sigma^{-2}\underline{\nu}\underline{s}^2\right).$$

Using Bayes' theorem gives the posterior density

$$\begin{aligned} p(\sigma^{-2}|y) &\propto p(\sigma^{-2})L(\sigma^{-2}) \\ &\propto (\sigma^{-2})^{(\underline{\nu}+T-2)/2} \exp\left(-\frac{\sigma^{-2}}{2}[\underline{\nu}\underline{s}^2 + \nu s^2 + T(\overline{y} - \theta_1)^2]\right) \\ &\propto (\sigma^{-2})^{(\overline{\nu}-2)/2} \exp\left(-\frac{\sigma^{-2}}{2}\overline{\nu}\overline{s}^2\right). \end{aligned}$$

Therefore, $\sigma^{-2}|y \sim \gamma([\overline{s}]^{-2}, \overline{\nu})$, with $\overline{\nu}$ defined in (2.28) and $\overline{s}^2 = \overline{\nu}^{-1}[\underline{\nu}\underline{s}^2 + \nu s^2 + T(\overline{y} - \theta_1)^2]$.

Exercise 2.8 (Marginal distribution of θ_1 when $\theta_1, \theta_2 \sim NG$) Consider the normal-gamma prior density of (2.26). Find the marginal distribution of θ_1.

Solution
The marginal pdf of θ_1 is obtained by integrating out θ_2 from the joint pdf (2.26). Note that the last line of (2.26) is the kernel of a $\gamma(a, b)$ distribution for θ_2 given all other quantities, where

$$\begin{aligned} a &= \frac{\underline{\nu}+1}{\underline{\nu}\underline{s}^2}\left[1 + \frac{1}{\underline{\nu}}\left(\frac{(\theta_1 - \underline{\mu})^2}{\underline{s}^2\underline{q}}\right)\right]^{-1}, \\ b &= \underline{\nu} + 1. \end{aligned}$$

Thus, integrating (2.26) with respect to θ_2 is proportional to the integrating constant of a $\gamma(a,b)$ distribution, namely

$$p(\theta_1|\underline{\mu},\underline{q},\underline{s}^2,\underline{\nu}) \propto \Gamma(b/2)\left(\frac{2a}{b}\right)^{b/2} \propto \left[1+\frac{1}{\underline{\nu}}\left(\frac{(\theta_1-\underline{\mu})^2}{\underline{s}^2\underline{q}}\right)\right]^{-(\underline{\nu}+1)/2}, \qquad (2.42)$$

which is the kernel of a $t(\underline{\mu},\underline{s}^2\underline{q},\underline{\nu})$ distribution.

Exercise 2.9 (Conditional distribution of $\theta_2|\theta_1$ when $\theta_1,\theta_2 \sim NG$) Consider the normal-gamma prior of (2.26). Find the conditional distribution of θ_2 given θ_1.

Solution

Consider (2.26). Discarding any constants of proportionality (including factors involving θ_1) yields

$$p(\theta_2|\theta_1,\underline{\mu},\underline{q},\underline{s}^{-2},\underline{\nu}) \propto \theta_2^{[(\underline{\nu}+1)-2]/2}\exp\left(-\frac{1}{2}\theta_2(\underline{\nu}+1)\left[\frac{\underline{\nu}\underline{s}^2+\underline{q}^{-1}(\theta_1-\underline{\mu})^2}{\underline{\nu}+1}\right]\right),$$

which is recognized as the kernel of a $\gamma[(\underline{\nu}+1)/[\underline{\nu}\underline{s}^2+\underline{q}^{-1}(\theta_1-\underline{\mu})^2],\underline{\nu}+1]$ distribution.

Exercise 2.10 (Conjugate exponential analysis) Suppose Y_t $(t=1,2,\ldots,T)$ is a random sample from an exponential distribution $f_{EXP}(y_t|\theta)=\theta\exp(-\theta y_t)$, which has mean θ^{-1}, and that the prior distribution of θ is the gamma distribution $G(\underline{\alpha},\underline{\beta})$, where $\underline{\alpha}>0$ and $\underline{\beta}>0$. (See Definition A.2 for this parameterization of the gamma density.) Find the posterior distribution of θ.

Solution

The likelihood function is

$$L(\theta)=\prod_{t=1}^{T} f_{EXP}(y_t|\theta)=\prod_{t=1}^{T}\theta\exp(-\theta y_t)=\theta^T\exp(-T\overline{y}\theta).$$

Define $\overline{\alpha}=\underline{\alpha}+T$ and $\overline{\beta}=(\underline{\beta}^{-1}+T\overline{y})^{-1}$. Using (2.3) gives the posterior density

$$\begin{aligned} p(\theta|y) &\propto p_G(\theta|\underline{\alpha},\underline{\beta})L(\theta)\\ &\propto \theta^{\underline{\alpha}-1}\exp(-\theta/\underline{\beta})\theta^T\exp(-T\overline{y}\theta)\\ &\propto \theta^{T+\underline{\alpha}-1}\exp\left[-(\underline{\beta}^{-1}+T\overline{y})\theta\right]\\ &= \theta^{\overline{\alpha}-1}\exp(-\theta/\overline{\beta}). \end{aligned}$$

Therefore, $\theta|y \sim G(\overline{\alpha},\overline{\beta})$.

Exercise 2.11 (Conjugate uniform analysis) Suppose Y_t $(t=1,2,\ldots,T)$ is a random sample from a $U(0,\theta)$ distribution, where θ is unknown, and suppose the prior distribution for θ is Pareto with parameters $\underline{\gamma} > 0$ and $\underline{\lambda} > 0$ (see Definition A.11). Find the posterior distribution of θ.

Solution

Let $\overline{\gamma} = \max\{\underline{\gamma}, y_1, y_2, \ldots, y_T\}$ and $\overline{\lambda} = \underline{\lambda} + T$. The likelihood function is $L(\theta) = \theta^{-T}$ for $\theta \geq \max\{y_1, y_2, \ldots, y_T\}$, and the prior density for θ is

$$f_{Pa}(\theta|\underline{\gamma}, \underline{\lambda}) = \frac{\underline{\lambda}\underline{\gamma}^{\underline{\lambda}}}{\theta^{\underline{\lambda}+1}} I(\theta > \underline{\gamma}) \propto \theta^{-(\underline{\lambda}+1)} I(\theta > \underline{\gamma}).$$

Using (2.3) gives the posterior density

$$p(\theta|y) \propto \left(\frac{\underline{\lambda}\underline{\gamma}^{\underline{\lambda}}}{\theta^{\underline{\lambda}+1}}\right) \theta^{-T} I(\theta > \overline{\gamma}) \propto \theta^{-(\overline{\lambda}+1)} I(\theta > \overline{\gamma}),$$

which forms the kernel of a Pareto density with parameters $\overline{\gamma}$ and $\overline{\lambda}$.

Exercise 2.12 (Conjugate Poisson analysis) Suppose Y_t $(t = 1, 2, \ldots, T)$ is a random sample from a Poisson distribution (see Definition A.8) with mean θ and that the prior distribution of θ is the gamma distribution $G(\underline{\alpha}, \underline{\beta})$, where $\underline{\alpha} > 0$ and $\underline{\beta} > 0$. Find the posterior distribution of θ.

Solution

The likelihood function is

$$L(\theta) = \prod_{t=1}^{T} f_{Po}(y_t|\theta) = \prod_{t=1}^{T} \frac{\theta^{y_t} \exp(-\theta)}{y_t!} = \frac{\theta^{T\overline{y}} \exp(-T\theta)}{\prod_{t=1}^{T} y_t!}.$$

Define $\overline{\alpha} = \underline{\alpha} + T\overline{y}$ and $\overline{\beta} = (\underline{\beta}^{-1} + T)^{-1}$. Using (2.3) gives the posterior density

$$\begin{aligned}
p(\theta|y) &\propto f_G(\theta|\underline{\alpha}, \underline{\beta}) L(\theta) \\
&\propto \theta^{\underline{\alpha}-1} \exp(-\theta/\underline{\beta}) \theta^{T\overline{y}} \exp(-T\theta) \\
&\propto \theta^{[T\overline{y}+\underline{\alpha}-1]} \exp[-(\underline{\beta}^{-1} + T)\theta] \\
&\propto \theta^{\overline{\alpha}-1} \exp(-\theta/\overline{\beta}).
\end{aligned}$$

Therefore, $\theta|y \sim G(\overline{\alpha}, \overline{\beta})$.

Exercise 2.13 (Conjugate exponential family analysis) Suppose Y_t $(t = 1, 2, \ldots, T)$ comprise a random sample from an *exponential family* distribution with density

$$p(y_t|\theta) = a(\theta) b(y_t) \exp\left[\sum_{j=1}^{J} c_j(\theta) d_j(y_t)\right], \tag{2.43}$$

where $\theta = [\theta_1\ \theta_2\ \cdots\ \theta_k]'$ and $a(\theta)$, $b(y)$, $c_j(\theta)$, and $d_j(y)$ $(j = 1, 2, \ldots, J)$ are suitably chosen functions. Consider a prior density of the form

$$p(\theta) = p(\theta|\underline{\alpha}, \underline{\delta}) = [a(\theta)]^{\underline{\alpha}} g(\underline{\alpha}, \underline{\delta}) \exp\left[\sum_{j=1}^{J} c_j(\theta)\underline{\delta}_j\right], \tag{2.44}$$

where $\underline{\alpha} > 0$ and $\underline{\delta} = [\underline{\delta}_1\ \underline{\delta}_2\ \cdots\ \underline{\delta}_J]'$ are given and $g(\underline{\alpha}, \underline{\delta})$ is chosen so that (2.44) integrates to unity with respect to θ.

(a) Show that the posterior distribution is of the form $p(\theta|\overline{\alpha}, \overline{\delta})$, where

$$\overline{\alpha} = \underline{\alpha} + T, \tag{2.45}$$

$$\hat{d}_j \equiv \hat{d}_j(y) = \sum_{t=1}^{T} d_j(y_t), \quad j = 1, 2, \ldots, J, \tag{2.46}$$

$$\overline{\delta}_j = \underline{\delta}_j + \hat{d}_j(y), \quad j = 1, 2, \ldots, J. \tag{2.47}$$

(b) Consider a mixture prior of the form

$$g(\theta) = \sum_{m=1}^{M} \underline{w}_m p(\theta|\underline{\alpha}_m, \underline{\delta}_m), \tag{2.48}$$

where $\underline{w}_m \geq 0$ $(m = 1, 2, \ldots, M)$ are known weights satisfying $\sum_m \underline{w}_m = 1$, $p(\theta|\underline{\alpha}_m, \underline{\delta}_m)$ retains the form of (2.44) for each m, and $\underline{\alpha}_m$, $\underline{\delta}_m$ $(m = 1, 2, \ldots, M)$ are given. Find the posterior density based on this prior.

Solution

(a) The likelihood function corresponding to (2.43) is

$$\begin{aligned} L(\theta) &= \prod_{t=1}^{T} a(\theta) b(y_t) \exp\left[\sum_{j=1}^{J} c_j(\theta) d_j(y_t)\right] \\ &= [a(\theta)]^T b_T(y) \exp\left[\sum_{t=1}^{T}\sum_{j=1}^{J} c_j(\theta) d_j(y_t)\right] \\ &\propto [a(\theta)]^T \exp\left[\sum_{j=1}^{J} c_j(\theta)\hat{d}_j(y)\right], \end{aligned} \tag{2.49}$$

where $b_T(y) = \prod_{t=1}^{T} b(y_t)$ and $\hat{d}_j(y)$ is defined in (2.46). Using Bayes' theorem, the posterior density of θ is

$$\begin{aligned} p(\theta|y) &\propto p(\theta)L(\theta) \\ &\propto [a(\theta)]^{\underline{\alpha}} g(\underline{\alpha}, \underline{\delta}) \exp\left[\sum_{j=1}^{J} c_j(\theta)\underline{\delta}_j\right] [a(\theta)]^T b_T(y) \exp\left[\sum_{j=1}^{J} c_j(\theta)\hat{d}_j(y)\right] \\ &\propto [a(\theta)]^{\underline{\alpha}+T} \exp\left[\sum_{j=1}^{J} c_j(\theta)[\underline{\delta}_j + \hat{d}_j(y)]\right] \\ &\propto [a(\theta)]^{\overline{\alpha}} \exp\left[\sum_{j=1}^{J} c_j(\theta)\overline{\delta}_j\right], \end{aligned}$$

with $\overline{\alpha}$ and $\overline{\delta}_j$ defined in (2.45) and (2.47), respectively. Therefore, the posterior density is of the form $p(\theta|\overline{\alpha}, \overline{\delta})$.

(b) Using the mixture prior (2.48) together with likelihood (2.49) yields the posterior density

$$\begin{aligned} p(\theta|y) &\propto p(\theta)L(\theta) \\ &= \left[\sum_{m=1}^{M} \underline{w}_m [a(\theta)]^{\underline{\alpha}_m} g(\underline{\alpha}_m, \underline{\delta}_m) \exp\left[\sum_{j=1}^{J} c_j(\theta)\underline{\delta}_{mj}\right]\right] \\ &\quad \times [a(\theta)]^T b_T(y) \exp\left[\sum_{j=1}^{J} c_j(\theta)\hat{d}_j(y)\right] \\ &\propto \sum_{m=1}^{M} \underline{w}_m [a(\theta)]^{\underline{\alpha}_m+T} g(\underline{\alpha}_m, \underline{\delta}_m) \exp\left[\sum_{j=1}^{J} c_j(\theta)[\underline{\delta}_{mj} + \hat{d}_j(y)]\right] \\ &= \sum_{m=1}^{M} \underline{w}_m [a(\theta)]^{\overline{\alpha}_m} g(\underline{\alpha}_m, \underline{\delta}_m) \exp\left[\sum_{j=1}^{J} c_j(\theta)\overline{\delta}_{mj}\right], \end{aligned}$$

where $\overline{\alpha}_m$ and $\overline{\delta}_{mj}$ are defined analogously to (2.45)–(2.47). This shows that the posterior is a mixture of the same form as the prior.

Exercise 2.14 (Conjugate multivariate normal analysis) Consider a random sample Y_t $(t = 1, 2, \ldots, T)$ from an $N(\mu, \Sigma)$ distribution, where μ is $M \times 1$ and Σ is an $M \times M$ positive definite matrix. Define

$$\overline{y} = \frac{1}{T}\sum_{t=1}^{T} y_t$$

and

$$S = \sum_{t=1}^{T} (y_t - \overline{y})(y_t - \overline{y})'.$$

Suppose $\underline{m}$ and $\underline{\mu}$ are both $M \times 1$, $\underline{T} > 0$ and $\underline{\omega} > M$ are both scalars, and $\underline{S}$ is an $M \times M$ positive definite matrix. Consider the natural conjugate priors for the following three cases.

(a) Suppose μ is unknown, Σ^{-1} is known, and the prior distribution for μ is multivariate normal with prior density $p(\mu) = \phi(\mu|\underline{\mu}, \underline{\Sigma})$. Find the posterior distribution for μ.

(b) Suppose μ is known, Σ^{-1} is unknown, and the prior for Σ^{-1} is the Wishart distribution (see Definition A.6), $\Sigma^{-1} \sim W(\underline{S}, \underline{\omega})$. Find the posterior distribution for Σ^{-1}.

(c) Suppose both μ and Σ^{-1} are unknown with prior distribution

$$\begin{aligned} p(\mu, \Sigma^{-1}) &= p(\mu|\Sigma^{-1})p(\Sigma^{-1}) \\ &= \phi(\mu|\underline{\mu}, \underline{T}^{-1}\Sigma) f_W(\Sigma^{-1}|\underline{S}, \underline{\omega}). \end{aligned}$$

Find the posterior distribution for μ and Σ^{-1}.

Solution

The likelihood function is

$$\begin{aligned} L(\mu, \Sigma^{-1}) &= \prod_{t=1}^{T} (2\pi)^{-M/2} |\Sigma^{-1}|^{(1/2)} \exp\left[-\frac{1}{2}(y_t - \mu)'\Sigma^{-1}(y_t - \mu)\right] \\ &= (2\pi)^{-TM/2} |\Sigma^{-1}|^{(T/2)} \exp\left[-\frac{1}{2}\sum_{t=1}^{T}(y_t - \mu)'\Sigma^{-1}(y_t - \mu)\right] \\ &= (2\pi)^{-TM/2} |\Sigma^{-1}|^{(T/2)} \exp\left[-\frac{1}{2}\sum_{t=1}^{T} \mathrm{tr}\left[\Sigma^{-1}(y_t - \mu)(y_t - \mu)'\right]\right] \\ &= (2\pi)^{-TM/2} |\Sigma^{-1}|^{(T/2)} \exp\left[-\frac{1}{2}\mathrm{tr}\left(\Sigma^{-1}\sum_{t=1}^{T}(y_t - \mu)(y_t - \mu)'\right)\right], \end{aligned} \quad (2.50)$$

where “tr” denotes the trace operator. Noting the identity

$$\sum_{t=1}^{T}(y_t - \mu)(y_t - \mu)' = S + T(\overline{y} - \mu)(\overline{y} - \mu)',$$

we can write the likelihood (2.50) as

$$L(\mu, \Sigma^{-1}) = (2\pi)^{-TM/2} |\Sigma^{-1}|^{(T/2)} \exp\left[-\frac{1}{2}\mathrm{tr}\left(\Sigma^{-1}[S + T(\overline{y} - \mu)(\overline{y} - \mu)']\right)\right]. \quad (2.51)$$

(a) With Σ known, combining the multivariate normal prior density $p(\mu) = \phi(\mu|\underline{\mu}, \underline{\Sigma})$ with likelihood (2.51) yields

$$\begin{aligned} p(\mu|y) &\propto \exp\left[-\frac{1}{2}(\mu - \underline{\mu})'\underline{\Sigma}^{-1}(\mu - \underline{\mu})\right] \\ &\quad \times \exp\left[-\frac{1}{2}\text{tr}\left(\Sigma^{-1}[S + T(\overline{y} - \mu)(\overline{y} - \mu)']\right)\right] \\ &\propto \exp\left[-\frac{1}{2}\left((\mu - \underline{\mu})'\underline{\Sigma}^{-1}(\mu - \underline{\mu}) + (\mu - \overline{y})'(T\Sigma^{-1})(\mu - \overline{y})\right)\right]. \end{aligned} \tag{2.52}$$

By completing the square on μ, that is, by writing

$$\begin{aligned} &(\mu - \underline{\mu})'\underline{\Sigma}^{-1}(\mu - \underline{\mu}) + (\mu - \overline{y})'(T\Sigma^{-1})(\mu - \overline{y}) \\ &= (\mu - \overline{\mu})'(\underline{\Sigma}^{-1} + T\Sigma^{-1})(\mu - \overline{\mu}) + (\underline{\mu} - \overline{y})'[\underline{\Sigma}^{-1}(\underline{\Sigma}^{-1} + T\Sigma^{-1})^{-1}T\Sigma^{-1}](\underline{\mu} - \overline{y}), \end{aligned} \tag{2.53}$$

where

$$\overline{\mu} = (\underline{\Sigma}^{-1} + T\Sigma^{-1})^{-1}(\underline{\Sigma}^{-1}\underline{\mu} + T\Sigma^{-1}\overline{y}), \tag{2.54}$$

the posterior kernel (2.52) simplifies to

$$p(\mu|y) \propto \exp\left[-\frac{1}{2}(\mu - \overline{\mu})'(\underline{\Sigma}^{-1} + T\Sigma^{-1})(\mu - \overline{\mu})\right], \tag{2.55}$$

which is immediately recognized as a multivariate normal kernel. Therefore,

$$\mu|y \sim N\left(\overline{\mu}, [\underline{\Sigma}^{-1} + T\Sigma^{-1}]^{-1}\right). \tag{2.56}$$

(b) When μ is known, combining the Wishart prior $W(\underline{S}, \underline{\omega})$ for Σ^{-1} with likelihood (2.51) yields the posterior distribution for Σ^{-1}:

$$\begin{aligned} p(\Sigma^{-1}|y) &\propto |\Sigma^{-1}|^{(\underline{\omega}-M-1)/2} \exp\left[-\frac{1}{2}\text{tr}(\underline{S}^{-1}\Sigma^{-1})\right] \\ &\quad \times \left[|\Sigma^{-1}|^{(T/2)} \exp\left(-\frac{1}{2}\text{tr}([S + T(\overline{y} - \mu)(\overline{y} - \mu)']\Sigma^{-1})\right)\right] \\ &\propto |\Sigma^{-1}|^{(T+\underline{\omega}-M-1)/2} \exp\left[-\frac{1}{2}\text{tr}\left([\underline{S}^{-1} + S + T(\overline{y} - \mu)(\overline{y} - \mu)']\Sigma^{-1}\right)\right]. \end{aligned} \tag{2.57}$$

The density given in the last line of (2.57) is the kernel of a Wishart distribution $W(\overline{S}^{-1}, \overline{\omega})$, where

$$\overline{\omega} = \underline{\omega} + T$$

and

$$\overline{S} = \underline{S}^{-1} + S + T(\overline{y} - \mu)(\overline{y} - \mu)'. \tag{2.58}$$

(c) The posterior for μ and Σ^{-1} is

$$p(\mu, \Sigma^{-1}|y) \propto |\underline{T}\Sigma^{-1}|^{(1/2)} \exp\left[-\frac{1}{2}(\mu - \underline{\mu})'\underline{T}\Sigma^{-1}(\mu - \underline{\mu})\right] \tag{2.59}$$

$$\times |\Sigma^{-1}|^{(\underline{\omega}-M-1)/2} \exp\left[-\frac{1}{2}\text{tr}\left(\underline{S}^{-1}\Sigma^{-1}\right)\right] \tag{2.60}$$

$$\times \left(|\Sigma^{-1}|^{(T/2)} \exp\left[-\frac{1}{2}\text{tr}\left([S + T(\overline{y} - \mu)(\overline{y} - \mu)']\Sigma^{-1}\right)\right]\right)$$

$$\propto |\Sigma^{-1}|^{(1/2)} \exp\left[-\frac{1}{2}(\mu - \underline{\mu})'\underline{T}\Sigma^{-1}(\mu - \underline{\mu})\right]$$

$$\times \exp\left[-\frac{1}{2}(\mu - \overline{y})'T\Sigma^{-1}(\mu - \overline{y})\right]$$

$$\times \left(|\Sigma^{-1}|^{(T+\underline{\omega}-M-1)/2} \exp\left[-\frac{1}{2}\text{tr}\left([\underline{S}^{-1} + S]\Sigma^{-1}\right)\right]\right). \tag{2.61}$$

Analogous to (2.53) and (2.54) we have

$$(\mu - \underline{\mu})'\underline{T}\Sigma^{-1}(\mu - \underline{\mu}) + (\mu - \overline{y})'(T\Sigma^{-1})(\mu - \overline{y})$$
$$= (\mu - \overline{\mu})'[(\underline{T} + T)\Sigma^{-1}](\mu - \overline{\mu}) + (\underline{\mu} - \overline{y})'[\underline{T}T(\underline{T} + T)^{-1}\Sigma^{-1})](\underline{\mu} - \overline{y}), \tag{2.62}$$

where

$$\overline{\mu} = \frac{\underline{T}\underline{\mu} + T\overline{y}}{\underline{T} + T}. \tag{2.63}$$

Using (2.60) and (2.61) simplifies posterior (2.59) to

$$p(\mu, \Sigma^{-1}|y) \propto |\overline{T}\Sigma^{-1}|^{(1/2)} \exp\left[-\frac{1}{2}(\mu - \overline{\mu})'\overline{T}\Sigma^{-1}(\mu - \overline{\mu})\right]$$

$$\times \left(|\Sigma^{-1}|^{(\overline{\omega}-M-1)/2} \exp\left[-\frac{1}{2}\text{tr}\left(\tilde{S}^{-1}\Sigma^{-1}\right)\right]\right), \tag{2.64}$$

where $\overline{T} = \underline{T} + T$, $\overline{\omega} = T + \underline{\omega}$, and

$$\tilde{S}^{-1} = \underline{S}^{-1} + S + \frac{\underline{T}T}{\underline{T} + T}(\underline{\mu} - \overline{y})(\underline{\mu} - \overline{y})'. \tag{2.65}$$

These provide updating equations for the hyperparameters of our prior.

Exercise 2.15 (Conjugate gamma distribution) Suppose that Y_t $(t = 1, 2, \ldots, T)$ is a random sample from a distribution for which the pdf is $p(y|\theta) = \theta y^{\theta-1}$ for $0 < y < 1$, and $p(y|\theta) = 0$, otherwise. Suppose also that the prior distribution of θ is the gamma distribution $G(\underline{\alpha}, \underline{\beta})$ with $\underline{\alpha} > 0$ and $\underline{\beta} > 0$. Determine the mean and variance of the posterior distribution of θ.

Solution

Let $x = -\sum_{t=1}^{T} \ln(y_t)$. Then the likelihood function is

$$L(\theta; y) = \theta^T \left[\prod_{t=1}^{T} y_t\right]^{\theta-1} = \theta^T [\exp(-x)]^{\theta-1} = \theta^T \exp(-x\theta)\exp(x).$$

The prior density is

$$p_G(\theta|\underline{\alpha}, \underline{\beta}) = [c_G(\underline{\alpha}, \underline{\beta})]^{-1} \theta^{\underline{\alpha}-1} \exp(-\theta/\underline{\beta}), \quad \theta > 0.$$

Define $\bar{\alpha} = T + \underline{\alpha}$ and $\bar{\beta} = \left(\underline{\beta}^{-1} + x\right)^{-1}$. Then the posterior density of θ is

$$\begin{aligned} p(\theta|y) &\propto p_G(\theta|\underline{\alpha}, \underline{\beta}) L(\theta; y) \\ &\propto \theta^{\underline{\alpha}-1} \exp(-\theta/\underline{\beta}) \theta^T \exp(-x\theta) \\ &\propto \theta^{\bar{\alpha}-1} \exp\left(-\theta/\bar{\beta}\right), \end{aligned}$$

which is immediately recognized as the kernel of the density of the gamma distribution $G\left(\bar{\alpha}, \bar{\beta}\right)$. Hence, using Theorem A.2, the posterior mean and variance are $\bar{\alpha}\bar{\beta}$ and $\bar{\alpha}\bar{\beta}^2$.

Exercise 2.16 (Identification) Let $\theta = [\theta_1\ \theta_2]' \in \mathbb{R}^2$. Consider a prior density $p(\theta_1, \theta_2)$. Suppose the likelihood function for the observed data y depends on θ_1 and not θ_2, that is,

$$L(\theta_1, \theta_2) = L(\theta_1).$$

In other words, θ_2 is *not identified*.

(a) Find the conditional posterior density of θ_2 given θ_1.

(b) Find the marginal posterior density of θ_2.

(c) Do you learn anything about θ_2? Discuss.

Solution

(a) The joint posterior density

$$p(\theta_1, \theta_2|y) = \frac{p(\theta_1)p(\theta_2|\theta_1)L(\theta_1)}{p(y)}$$

implies the marginal posterior density

$$p(\theta_1|y) = \frac{p(\theta_1)L(\theta_1)}{p(y)},$$

and hence the conditional posterior density is

$$\begin{aligned} p(\theta_2|\theta_1, y) &= \frac{p(\theta_1, \theta_2|y)}{p(\theta_1|y)} \\ &= \frac{[p(\theta_1)p(\theta_2|\theta_1)L(\theta_1)]/[p(y)]}{[p(\theta_1)L(\theta_1)]/[p(y)]} \\ &= p(\theta_2|\theta_1). \end{aligned}$$

(b) The marginal posterior density of θ_2 is

$$\begin{aligned} p(\theta_2|y) &= \int_{\mathbb{R}} p(\theta_1, \theta_2|y) d\theta_1 \\ &= \int_{\mathbb{R}} \frac{p(\theta_1)p(\theta_2|\theta_1)L(\theta_1)}{p(y)} d\theta_1 \\ &= \int_{\mathbb{R}} p(\theta_2|\theta_1)p(\theta_1|y) d\theta_1 \\ &= E_{\theta_1|y}[p(\theta_2|\theta_1)], \end{aligned}$$

and thus $p(\theta_2|y) = p(\theta_2)$ if θ_1 and θ_2 are independent *a priori*. In the case of prior dependence, however, $p(\theta_2|y) \neq p(\theta_2)$.

(c) From (a) we see that conditional on θ_1 we do not learn about θ_2 – the conditional posterior is identical to the conditional prior. Noting that $p(\theta_2) = E_{\theta_1}[p(\theta_2|\theta_1)]$, we see from (b) that we learn marginally about θ_2, provided θ_1 and θ_2 are *dependent*.

3

Point Estimation

Frequentist point estimation techniques are typically based on the choice of an intuitively sensible criterion (e.g., method of moments), and the statistical properties of the resulting estimators are addressed after the fact. In contrast, Bayesian point estimation begins by announcing a criterion for determining what constitutes a good point estimate, and a method for producing an "optimal" point estimate given the data at hand is then derived.

The Bayesian begins by specifying a *loss (cost) function* $C(\hat{\theta}, \theta)$, that is, a non-negative function satisfying $C(\theta, \theta) = 0$, which measures the consequences of using $\hat{\theta} = \hat{\theta}(Y)$ (i.e., a particular function of the data) as an estimate when the "state of nature" is θ. Usually, $C(\hat{\theta}, \theta)$ is a non-decreasing function of the *sampling error* $\hat{\theta} - \theta$. Frequentists sometimes argue that the need to specify a loss function is one of the shortcomings of the Bayesian approach. However, there is usually a frequentist analogue to the Bayesian choice of loss function. For instance, the familiar concept of mean squared error (defined in the following) simply corresponds to a particular type of loss function, namely quadratic loss.

A good estimate is one that "minimizes" $C(\hat{\theta}, \theta)$ in some sense, but its randomness must first be eliminated. From the frequentist sampling theory point of view, θ is non-stochastic but $C(\hat{\theta}, \theta)$ is nonetheless stochastic because the estimator $\hat{\theta} = \hat{\theta}(Y)$ is a random variable (i.e., $\hat{\theta}$ depends on the random variable Y). An obvious way to circumscribe the randomness of $C(\hat{\theta}, \theta)$ is to focus attention on its expected value, assuming it exists. Frequentists consider the *risk function*, that is, the non-stochastic function

$$R(\hat{\theta}|\theta) = E_{Y|\theta}[C(\hat{\theta}(Y), \theta)], \tag{3.1}$$

where the expectation (assumed to exist) is taken with respect to the sampling probability function $p(y|\theta)$.

In contrast, the Bayesian perspective is entirely *ex post* (i.e., it conditions on the observed data y).[1] That is, the Bayesian uses $\hat{\theta} = \hat{\theta}(y)$ as a point estimate of the unknown parameter θ. Unlike the frequentist approach, no role is provided for data that could have been observed but were not observed. Since θ is unknown, the Bayesian perspective suggests treating it as a random variable with a distribution reflecting all the information at hand. Such information is fully contained in the posterior distribution of θ: it reflects both prior and sample information.

In contrast to the frequentist approach, the randomness in the loss function $C(\hat{\theta}, \theta)$ from the Bayesian perspective arises because θ is an unknown random variable. From the frequentist perspective, although θ is unknown, it is treated as a fixed constant. The *ex ante* perspective of the frequentist view implies that $C(\hat{\theta}, \theta)$ is random because $\hat{\theta}$ is viewed as a random variable with a sampling distribution in repeated samples. The Bayesian solution to the randomness of the loss function is similar to the frequentist solution: take its expectation before minimization. The expectation, however, is with respect to the posterior distribution $\theta|y$, and not the sampling distribution $y|\theta$ used to obtain the risk function. The Bayesian prescription is equivalent to the principle usually advocated for economic agents acting in a world of uncertainty: Using all available information, choose actions so as to maximize expected utility, or equivalently, minimize expected loss. The prescription is formalized in the following definition.

Definition 3.1 Given the posterior density $p(\theta|y)$ and the cost function $C(\hat{\theta}, \theta)$, the *Bayes estimate* (i.e., the Bayesian point estimate) is defined as the solution (assuming the expectation exists) to the following problem:

$$\min_{\hat{\theta}} E_{\theta|y}[C(\hat{\theta}, \theta)], \tag{3.2}$$

where

$$c(\hat{\theta}) = E_{\theta|y}[C(\hat{\theta}, \theta)] = \int_{\Theta} C(\hat{\theta}, \theta) p(\theta|y) d\theta. \tag{3.3}$$

Most importantly, note that the posterior expectation in (3.3) removes θ from the criterion function (3.2), unlike the case of risk function (3.1). Also note that if the researcher is interested only in a subset θ_1 of the parameter vector $\theta = [\theta_1, \theta_2]'$, where $\Theta = \Theta_1 \times \Theta_2$ and the elements of θ_2 are regarded as nuisance parameters, then this preference can be reflected in the loss function specification: $C(\hat{\theta}, \theta) = C(\hat{\theta}_1, \theta_1)$. In this case the expected loss in (3.3) reduces to

[1] We remind the reader that we are using capital (small) letters to denote a random variable (its realization). Hence, Y is a random variable and y a particular data realization.

$$
\begin{aligned}
E_{\theta|y}[C(\hat{\theta},\theta)] &= \int_{\Theta_1}\int_{\Theta_2} C(\hat{\theta},\theta)p(\theta|y)d\theta_2 d\theta_1 \\
&= \int_{\Theta_1} C(\hat{\theta}_1,\theta_1)\left[\int_{\Theta_2} p(\theta_1,\theta_2|y)d\theta_2\right]d\theta_1 \\
&= \int_{\Theta_1} C(\hat{\theta}_1,\theta_1)p(\theta_1|y)d\theta_1. \qquad (3.4)
\end{aligned}
$$

Thus, nuisance parameters are simply marginalized out of the problem.

Definition 3.2 Consider the case of a single parameter of interest θ. Let c, c_1, and c_2 be known constants. The loss (cost) function

$$
C(\hat{\theta},\theta) = c(\hat{\theta}-\theta)^2 \qquad (3.5)
$$

is known as a *quadratic loss function*. The loss function

$$
C(\hat{\theta},\theta) = \begin{cases} c_1|\hat{\theta}-\theta| & \text{if } \hat{\theta} \le \theta, \\ c_2|\hat{\theta}-\theta| & \text{if } \hat{\theta} > \theta, \end{cases} \qquad (3.6)
$$

is known as an *asymmetric linear loss function*. In the case $c_1 = c_2$, (3.6) is known as a *symmetric linear loss function*. Given constants $c > 0$ and $d > 0$, the loss function

$$
C(\hat{\theta},\theta) = \begin{cases} c & \text{if } |\hat{\theta}-\theta| > d, \\ 0 & \text{if } |\hat{\theta}-\theta| \le d, \end{cases} \qquad (3.7)
$$

is known as an *all-or-nothing loss function* over $|\hat{\theta}-\theta| \le d$.

When there are several parameters of interest, the most popular loss functions are the *weighted squared error* generalization of (3.5):

$$
C(\hat{\theta},\theta) = (\hat{\theta}-\theta)'Q(\hat{\theta}-\theta), \qquad (3.8)
$$

where Q is a positive definite matrix.

Bayesian point estimates corresponding to the loss functions defined in Definition 3.2 are given in the following exercises.

Exercise 3.1 (Point estimation under quadratic loss) Let $\hat{\theta}$ denote the Bayesian point estimates obtained by solving (3.2) for quadratic loss function (3.5). Show that $\hat{\theta} = E(\theta|y)$.

Solution

Consider

$$
\begin{aligned}
(\hat{\theta}-\theta)^2 &= \left[\hat{\theta} - E(\theta|y) + E(\theta|y) - \theta\right]^2 \\
&= [\hat{\theta} - E(\theta|y)]^2 + 2[\hat{\theta} - E(\theta|y)][E(\theta|y) - \theta] + [E(\theta|y) - \theta]^2. \qquad (3.9)
\end{aligned}
$$

Note that only the last two terms of (3.9) involve θ. Then

$$\begin{aligned} c(\hat{\theta}) &= E_{\theta|y}[c(\hat{\theta}-\theta)^2] \\ &= c\left[[\hat{\theta}-E(\theta|y)]^2 + 2[\hat{\theta}-E(\theta|y)]E_{\theta|y}[E(\theta|y)-\theta] + E_{\theta|y}[E(\theta|y)-\theta]^2\right] \\ &= c[\hat{\theta}-E(\theta|y)]^2 + 0 + c\text{Var}(\theta|y), \end{aligned} \tag{3.10}$$

which is minimized by setting the first term to zero – i.e., $\hat{\theta} = E(\theta|y)$.

Exercise 3.2 (Point estimation under asymmetric linear loss) Let $\hat{\theta}$ denote the Bayesian point estimates obtained by solving (3.2) for asymmetric linear loss function (3.6). Show that $\hat{\theta} = \zeta_q$, where $q = c_1/(c_1 + c_2)$ and ζ_q denotes the qth quantile of the posterior density $p(\theta|y)$.

Solution

The expected posterior loss is

$$\begin{aligned} E_{\theta|y}[C(\hat{\theta},\theta)] &= c_2\int_{-\infty}^{\hat{\theta}}(\hat{\theta}-\theta)p(\theta|y)d\theta + c_1\int_{\hat{\theta}}^{\infty}-(\hat{\theta}-\theta)p(\theta|y)d\theta \\ &= c_2\hat{\theta}P(\hat{\theta}|y) - c_2\int_{-\infty}^{\hat{\theta}}\theta p(\theta|y)d\theta - c_1\hat{\theta}[1-P(\hat{\theta}|y)] + c_1\int_{\hat{\theta}}^{\infty}\theta p(\theta|y)d\theta, \end{aligned} \tag{3.11}$$

where $P(\cdot)$ denotes the cdf corresponding to $p(\cdot)$. Differentiating (3.11) with respect to $\hat{\theta}$ yields

$$\begin{aligned} \frac{\partial E_{\theta|y}[C(\hat{\theta},\theta)]}{\partial\hat{\theta}} &= c_2P(\hat{\theta}|y) + c_2\hat{\theta}p(\hat{\theta}|y) - c_2\hat{\theta}p(\hat{\theta}|y) \\ &\quad - c_1[1-P(\hat{\theta}|y)] + c_1\hat{\theta}p(\hat{\theta}|y) - c_1\hat{\theta}p(\hat{\theta}|y) \\ &= -c_1 + (c_1+c_2)P(\hat{\theta}|y). \end{aligned} \tag{3.12}$$

Equating (3.12) to zero and solving for $\hat{\theta}$ yields

$$\hat{\theta} = P_{\theta|y}^{-1}\left(\frac{c_1}{c_1+c_2}\right),$$

that is, the $c_1/(c_1+c_2)$ posterior quantile of θ.

Exercise 3.3 (Point estimation under all-or-nothing loss) Let $\hat{\theta}$ denote the Bayesian point estimate obtained by solving (3.2) for the all-or-nothing loss function (3.7). Show that $\hat{\theta}$ is the center of an interval of width $2d$ having maximum posterior probability.

Solution
The expected posterior loss is

$$E_{\theta|y}[C(\hat{\theta},\theta)] = c\left[1 - \int_{\hat{\theta}-d}^{\hat{\theta}+d} p(\theta|y)d\theta\right] = c[1 - (P(\hat{\theta}+d|y) - P(\hat{\theta}-d|y))]. \quad (3.13)$$

Minimizing (3.13) corresponds to picking $\hat{\theta}$ to be the center of an interval of width $2d$ having maximum posterior probability. Differentiating (3.13) with respect to $\hat{\theta}$ yields

$$\frac{\partial E_{\theta|y}[C(\hat{\theta},\theta)]}{\partial\hat{\theta}} = c\left[p(\hat{\theta}-d|y) - p(\hat{\theta}+d|y)\right]. \quad (3.14)$$

Equating (3.14) to zero and solving for $\hat{\theta}$ implies that the end points of this interval have equal posterior density. Also note that as $d \to 0$, $\hat{\theta}$ becomes the mode of $p(\theta|y)$.

Exercise 3.4 (Point estimation under quadratic loss for conjugate Bernoulli analysis) Consider the Bernoulli sampling problem considered in Exercise 2.1 with posterior pdf given by (2.11). Find the Bayesian point estimate of θ under quadratic loss.

Solution
Exercise 3.1 implies that the Bayesian point estimate is the posterior mean:

$$\hat{\theta} = \frac{\overline{\alpha}}{\overline{\alpha}+\overline{\delta}} = \frac{m+\underline{\alpha}}{T+\underline{\alpha}+\underline{\delta}} = \frac{T\overline{y}+\underline{T}(\underline{T}^{-1}\underline{\alpha})}{T+\underline{T}},$$

where the second equality follows by using the definitions in (2.8) and (2.9). In the final equality, $\underline{T} \equiv \underline{\alpha}+\underline{\delta}$. Thus, the posterior mean can be interpreted as a weighted average of the sample mean $\overline{y} = T^{-1}m$ and the effective prior mean $\underline{T}^{-1}\underline{\alpha}$.

Exercise 3.5 (Point estimation under asymmetric linear loss for conjugate Bernoulli analysis) Consider the Bernoulli sampling problem considered in Exercise 2.1 with posterior pdf given by (2.11). Find the Bayesian point estimate of θ under the asymmetric linear loss function (3.6).

Solution
Exercise 3.2 implies that the Bayesian point estimate of θ is the qth posterior quantile, where $q = c_1/(c_1+c_2)$, that is, the value $\hat{\theta}$ that solves

$$\frac{c_1}{c_1+c_2} = \int_0^{\hat{\theta}} \frac{\theta^{\overline{\alpha}-1}(1-\theta)^{\overline{\delta}-1}}{\mathcal{B}(\overline{\alpha},\overline{\delta})}d\theta.$$

If $c_1 = c_2$ then $\hat{\theta}$ equals the posterior median.

Exercise 3.6 (Point estimation under all-or-nothing loss for conjugate Bernoulli analysis) Consider the Bernoulli sampling problem considered in Exercise 2.1 with posterior pdf (2.11). Find the Bayesian point estimate of θ under the all-or-nothing loss function (3.7) as $d \rightarrow 0$.

Solution

Exercise 3.3 implies that, under loss function (3.7), the Bayesian point estimate of θ is the posterior mode, which if $\overline{\alpha} > 1$ and $\overline{\delta} > 1$ is found by differentiating the logarithm of (2.11) with respect to θ, equating the result to zero, and solving the resulting equation to yield

$$\hat{\theta} = \frac{\overline{\alpha} - 1}{\overline{\alpha} + \overline{\delta} - 2} = \frac{m + \underline{\alpha} - 1}{T + \underline{\alpha} + \underline{\delta} - 2}.$$

If $\overline{\alpha} = \overline{\delta} = 1$, then the posterior density is uniform and the posterior mode is not unique. If either $\overline{\alpha} < 1$ or $\overline{\delta} < 1$, then there is no posterior mode since the posterior density has an asymptote approaching infinity.

Exercise 3.7 (Point estimation for conjugate normal analysis) Consider the normal sampling problem in Exercise 2.3. Find the Bayesian point estimate $\hat{\theta}_1$ of θ_1 under loss functions (3.5)–(3.7). For loss function (3.7), consider the case as $d \rightarrow 0$.

Solution

Since the posterior distribution is normal, the posterior mean and mode are equal. Exercises 3.4 and 3.6 imply that this common value is the Bayesian point estimate under (3.5) and (3.7). Under loss function (3.6), Exercise 3.5 implies that the Bayesian point estimate $\hat{\theta}_1$ of θ_1 is given by the qth posterior quantile, $q = c_1/(c_1 + c_2)$, that is,

$$\hat{\theta}_1 = \overline{\mu} + \overline{\sigma}\Phi^{-1}\left(\frac{c_1}{c_1 + c_2}\right),$$

where $\overline{\mu}$ and $\overline{\sigma}$ are the posterior mean and standard deviation of θ_1 and $\Phi^{-1}(\cdot)$ is the inverse of the standard normal cdf. Note that when $c_1 = c_2$, $\Phi^{-1}(1/2) = 0$ and $\hat{\theta}_1$ reduces to simply the posterior mean/median/mode $\overline{\mu}$.

Exercise 3.8 (Point estimation under quadratic loss in a Pareto sampling model) Let y_t $(t = 1, 2, \ldots, T)$ be a random sample from a population with density

$$f(y_t|\theta) = \theta c^{\theta} y_t^{-(\theta+1)}, \quad y_t > c,$$

where $c > 0$ is known and θ is unknown. (a) Find the likelihood function and write it in terms of the logarithm of the geometric mean,

$$G = G(y) = \left[\Pi_{t=1}^{T} y_t\right]^{1/T}.$$

(b) Consider the gamma prior density function

$$p(\theta|\underline{a}, \underline{b}) = \frac{1}{\underline{b}^{\underline{a}}\Gamma(\underline{a})}\theta^{\underline{a}-1}\exp(-\theta/\underline{b}), \quad 0 < \theta < \infty,$$

with mean $E(\theta) = \underline{a}\underline{b}$, $\text{Var}(\theta) = \underline{a}\underline{b}^2$, and $\underline{a}$ and $\underline{b}$ known positive constants. Find the corresponding posterior density under this gamma prior. Is it a conjugate prior?
(c) Under quadratic loss, find the Bayesian point estimate of θ.

Solution
(a) The likelihood function is

$$\begin{aligned}L(\theta; y) &= \Pi_{t=1}^{T} f(y_t|\theta) = \Pi_{t=1}^{T}\theta c^{\theta} y_t^{-(\theta+1)} \\ &= \theta^T c^{T\theta}\left(\Pi_{t=1}^{T} y_t\right)^{-(\theta+1)} \\ &= \theta^T c^{T\theta} G^{-T(\theta+1)} \\ &= \theta^T c^{T\theta}\exp\left[-T(\theta+1)\ln(G)\right].\end{aligned}$$

(b) The posterior density is

$$\begin{aligned}p(\theta|y) &\propto p(\theta|\underline{a}, \underline{b})L(\theta; y) \\ &\propto \theta^{\underline{a}-1}\exp\left(-\theta/\underline{b}\right)\theta^T c^{T\theta}\exp\left[-T(\theta+1)\ln(G)\right] \\ &\propto \theta^{\overline{a}-1}\exp\left(-\theta/\overline{b}\right),\end{aligned}$$

where $\overline{a} = \underline{a} + T$ and $\overline{b} = \left[\underline{b}^{-1} + T\ln(G/c)\right]^{-1}$. This is again a gamma density, so the gamma prior is indeed conjugate for this Pareto sampling model.
(c) Under quadratic loss the Bayesian point estimate is the posterior mean. Hence,

$$\widehat{\theta} = E(\theta|y) = \overline{a}\overline{b}.$$

Exercise 3.9 (Point estimation under weighted squared error loss) Suppose $\theta \in \mathbb{R}^K$. Consider the weighted squared error loss function (3.8) and suppose that its posterior expected value exists. Show that the Bayesian point estimate $\hat{\theta}$ of θ is the posterior mean.

Solution
Proceeding as in Exercise 3.1, consider

$$\begin{aligned}C(\hat{\theta}, \theta) &= (\hat{\theta} - \theta)'Q(\hat{\theta} - \theta) \\ &= [\hat{\theta} - E(\theta|y) + E(\theta|y) - \theta]'Q[\hat{\theta} - E(\theta|y) + E(\theta|y) - \theta] \\ &= [\hat{\theta} - E(\theta|y)]'Q[\hat{\theta} - E(\theta|y)] + 2[\hat{\theta} - E(\theta|y)]'Q[E(\theta|y) - \theta] \\ &\quad + [E(\theta|y) - \theta]'Q[E(\theta|y) - \theta]. \qquad (3.15)\end{aligned}$$

Noting that only the last two terms of (3.15) involve θ, we see that the posterior expected loss of (3.15) is

$$E_{\theta|y}[C(\hat{\theta},\theta)] = [\hat{\theta} - E(\theta|y)]'Q[\hat{\theta} - E(\theta|y)] + [\hat{\theta} - E(\theta|y)]'QE_{\theta|y}[E(\theta|y) - \theta] \quad (3.16)$$
$$+ [E(\theta|y) - \theta]'Q[\hat{\theta} - E(\theta|y)] + E_{\theta|y}\left([E(\theta|y) - \theta]'Q[E(\theta|y) - \theta]\right)$$
$$= [\hat{\theta} - E(\theta|y)]'Q[\hat{\theta} - E(\theta|y)] + 0 + E_{\theta|y}\left([E(\theta|y) - \theta]'Q[E(\theta|y) - \theta]\right).$$

Picking $\hat{\theta} = E(\theta|y)$ minimizes (3.16). Note that $\hat{\theta}$ does *not* depend on Q.

Exercise 3.10 (Point estimation under alternative squared error loss) Consider the weighted squared error loss function $C(\hat{\theta},\theta) = w(\theta)(\theta - \hat{\theta})^2$, where $w(\theta) > 0$ and θ is a single unknown parameter. Show that the Bayesian point estimate corresponding to $C(\hat{\theta},\theta)$ is given by

$$\hat{\theta} = \frac{E_{\theta|y}[\theta w(\theta)]}{E_{\theta|y}[w(\theta)]}. \quad (3.17)$$

Compare the role of $w(\theta)$ to that of the prior for θ.

Solution
Minimizing expected posterior loss requires solving

$$\frac{\partial E_{\theta|y}[C(\hat{\theta},\theta)]}{\partial\hat{\theta}} = E_{\theta|y}\left(\frac{\partial[C(\hat{\theta},\theta)]}{\partial\hat{\theta}}\right)$$
$$= E_{\theta|y}[2w(\theta)(\hat{\theta} - \theta)]$$
$$= 2\left(\hat{\theta}E_{\theta|y}[w(\theta)] - E_{\theta|y}[\theta w(\theta)]\right) = 0,$$

provided one can differentiate under the integral sign. The solution to this equation follows immediately:

$$\hat{\theta} = \frac{E_{\theta|y}[\theta w(\theta)]}{E_{\theta|y}[w(\theta)]},$$

which is equivalent to (3.17).

It is also worth noting that

$$E_{\theta|y}[C(\hat{\theta},\theta)] = \int_{\Theta} w(\theta)(\hat{\theta} - \theta)^2\left[\frac{p(\theta)L(\theta)}{p(y)}\right]d\theta = \int_{\Theta}(\hat{\theta} - \theta)^2\left[\frac{w(\theta)p(\theta)L(\theta)}{p(y)}\right]d\theta,$$

and thus it is seen that minimizing the expected posterior loss $C(\hat{\theta},\theta) = w(\theta)(\hat{\theta} - \theta)^2$ using prior $p(\theta)$ is equivalent to minimizing expected quadratic loss using the prior

$$w(\theta)p(\theta)/\left[\int_{\Theta} w(\theta)p(\theta)d\theta\right].$$

Exercise 3.11 (Point estimation under non-conjugate normal analysis) Suppose $Y|\theta \sim N(\theta, 1)$ and $p(\theta) \propto \theta \exp(-\theta^2/2)$. Find the Bayesian point estimate of θ under quadratic loss.

Solution

Given $Y|\theta \sim N(\theta, 1)$ and $p(\theta) \propto \theta \exp(-\theta^2/2)$, the Bayesian point estimate of θ under quadratic loss is the posterior mean $E(\theta|y)$ corresponding to the posterior density

$$p(\theta|y) \propto \theta \exp\left(-\frac{\theta^2}{2}\right) \exp\left(-\frac{(y-\theta)^2}{2}\right) \propto \theta \exp\left(-\frac{(y-\theta)^2 + \theta^2}{2}\right).$$

Using identity (2.19) from Chapter 2 with $\underline{\mu} = 0$, $\theta_1 = \theta$, $\overline{y} = y$, $\underline{h} = 1$, and $h = 1$ implies

$$(y-\theta)^2 + \theta^2 = 2\left(\theta - \frac{y}{2}\right)^2 + \frac{y^2}{2},$$

and thus

$$p(\theta|y) \propto \theta \exp\left[-\frac{1}{2(1/2)}\left(\theta - \frac{y}{2}\right)^2\right]. \tag{3.18}$$

Using the results of Exercise 3.1, we know that the posterior mean of (3.18) is the minimizer of

$$\int (\hat{\theta} - \theta)^2 p(\theta|y)\, dy = \int \theta(\hat{\theta} - \theta)^2 \tilde{p}(\theta|y)\, dy,$$

where, from (3.18), $\tilde{p}(\theta|y)$ is the kernel of an $N(y/2, 1/2)$ density. In this alternate form, the results of Exercise 3.9 show

$$\hat{\theta} = \frac{E[\theta^2]}{E[\theta]},$$

where the expectation is taken with respect to θ following an $N(y/2, 1/2)$ density. This produces

$$\hat{\theta} = \frac{E(\theta^2)}{E(\theta)} = \frac{(1/2) + (y/2)^2}{y/2} = \frac{y^2 + 2}{2y}.$$

Exercise 3.12 (Point estimation under linex loss (Zellner 1986b)) Given a scalar parameter θ, consider the univariate *linex loss function*

$$C(\hat{\theta}, \theta) = \exp[a(\hat{\theta} - \theta)] - a(\hat{\theta} - \theta) - 1, \tag{3.19}$$

where $a \neq 0$. Its name arises from the fact that, if $a < 0$, $C(\hat{\theta}, \theta)$ rises almost linearly for $\hat{\theta} > \theta$ and almost exponentially for $\hat{\theta} < \theta$. For small values of $|a|$, the loss function is almost symmetric. For $a = 1$, the loss function is quite asymmetric with overestimation being more costly than underestimation. Find the Bayesian point estimate of θ.

Solution

Given the linex loss function (3.19), the posterior expected loss is

$$E_{\theta|y}[C(\hat{\theta},\theta)] = E_{\theta|y}\left(\exp[a(\hat{\theta}-\theta)] - a(\hat{\theta}-\theta) - 1\right)$$
$$= \exp(a\hat{\theta})M_{\theta|y}(-a) - a[\hat{\theta} - E(\theta|y)] - 1, \tag{3.20}$$

where $M_{\theta|y}(-a) = E_{\theta|y}[\exp(-a\theta)]$, the moment-generating function of the posterior distribution of θ, is assumed to exist.

Minimizing (3.20) with respect to $\hat{\theta}$ suggests equating

$$\frac{\partial E_{\theta|y}[C(\hat{\theta},\theta)]}{\partial\hat{\theta}} = a\exp(a\hat{\theta})M_{\theta|y}(-a) - a \tag{3.21}$$

to zero, yielding

$$\hat{\theta}_1 = -a^{-1}\ln\left(E_{\theta|y}[\exp(-a\theta)]\right)$$
$$= -a^{-1}\ln(M_{\theta|y}(-a)). \tag{3.22}$$

4

Frequentist Properties of Bayesian Estimators

As noted in Chapter 3, frequentists evaluate point estimators in terms of minimizing the *ex ante* risk function (3.1). In contrast, Bayesians focus on minimizing the *ex post* posterior loss (3.3). By construction, Bayesian point estimates are optimal from the *ex post* standpoint. In general they also have good risk properties. In this chapter we view the Bayesian point estimate $\hat{\theta} = \hat{\theta}(y)$ from an *ex ante* perspective, that is, we consider the Bayesian point estimator $\hat{\theta} = \hat{\theta}(Y)$.

Minimum risk estimators do not exist in general because (3.1) depends on θ and so any estimator that minimizes (3.1) will also depend on θ. Other conditions are often imposed (e.g., unbiasedness) to sidestep the problem. Some statisticians walk a fine line between Bayesian and classical point estimation by taking the risk function $R(\hat{\theta}|\theta)$ in (3.1) and "averaging" it over the permissible parameter space Θ to obtain a measure of the "average" performance of the estimator $\hat{\theta}(Y)$. The motivation is clear: To overcome the difficulty that risk functions of different estimators can cross each other at various points in Θ, it is natural to weight the performance of an estimator in a particular region of the parameter space by a weight function. The interpretation of such a function, however, is very close to a prior distribution for θ that weights heavily regions of the parameter space that the researcher feels are most likely to be relevant. Given a positive function $p(\theta)$, whatever its interpretation, consider the problem

$$\min_{\hat{\theta}} \overline{R}(\hat{\theta}), \tag{4.1}$$

where

$$\overline{R}(\hat{\theta}) = \int_{\Theta} R(\hat{\theta}|\theta)p(\theta)d\theta. \tag{4.2}$$

Substituting the risk function (3.1) into (4.2), where the sample space for Y is S_T, yields

$$\overline{R} = \int_{\Theta} \left[\int_{S_T} C[\hat{\theta}(Y), \theta] p(Y|\theta)\, dY \right] p(\theta)\, d\theta \tag{4.3}$$

$$= \int_{S_T} \int_{\Theta} C[\hat{\theta}(Y), \theta] p(Y|\theta) p(\theta)\, d\theta\, dY \tag{4.4}$$

$$= \int_{S_T} \left[\int_{\Theta} C[\hat{\theta}(Y), \theta] \left(\frac{p(Y|\theta)p(\theta)}{p(Y)} \right) d\theta \right] p(Y)\, dY, \tag{4.5}$$

provided it is permissible to switch the order of integration. From (4.5) it is clear that the $\hat{\theta}$ that minimizes $\overline{R}$ must also minimize the quantity enclosed in the square brackets in (4.5). This quantity, however, is exactly the expected posterior loss (3.3) corresponding to the prior distribution $p(\theta)$. Hence, a researcher minimizing $\overline{R}$ behaves *as if* solving (3.3) with prior distribution $p(\theta)$. Therefore, any estimator that minimizes weighted risk must be a Bayesian point estimator.

The preceding analysis shows that Bayesian point estimators have desirable frequentist properties. Any Bayesian estimator based on a *proper prior* (i.e., a prior pdf that integrates to unity) for which (4.2) is finite satisfies the minimal frequentist requirement of admissibility (i.e., there does not exist another estimator with lower risk function at all points in the parameter space) – the same cannot be said for maximum likelihood estimators. In this case (4.2) is often referred to as *Bayes risk*. Furthermore, Wald (1950) showed, in most interesting settings, that *all* admissible rules are either Bayes or limits thereof known as generalized Bayes estimators. A *generalized Bayes estimator* is a Bayes estimator based on an *improper prior* (i.e., a prior whose integral is unbounded).[1] In other words, preference for admissible decision rules implies a preference for Bayes rules. Also, if a Bayes estimator is unique, then it must be admissible. In short, Bayes estimators based on proper priors have desirable properties in terms of "final precision" (i.e., *ex post*) by construction, and also may have desirable "initial precision" (i.e., *ex ante*) properties. Bayes estimators corresponding to proper priors, however, are almost never unbiased (see Berger 1985, Chapter 8, for details).

Exercise 4.1 (Sampling properties under quadratic loss in conjugate normal analysis) Suppose Y_t $(t = 1, 2, \ldots, T)$ is a random sample from an $N(\mu, \sigma^2)$ distribution where σ^2 is known, and the prior distribution for μ is $N(\underline{\mu}, \sigma^2/\underline{T})$.
(a) Consider the quadratic loss function $C(\hat{\mu}, \mu) = (\hat{\mu} - \mu)^2$. Find the Bayesian *point estimate* $\hat{\mu}$ and compute its expected posterior loss.
(b) Find the expected posterior loss of the *estimate* $\tilde{\mu} = \overline{y}$.
(c) Compare $\hat{\mu}$ and $\tilde{\mu}$ according to expected posterior loss. Which is smaller?

[1] Examples of improper priors will be considered in Chapter 8.

(d) Find the mean squared error MSE$(\hat{\mu})$, where $\hat{\mu} = \hat{\mu}(Y)$ is the Bayesian point *estimator* found in (a).
(e) Find MSE$(\tilde{\mu})$, where $\tilde{\mu} = \tilde{\mu}(Y) = \overline{Y}$ is the maximum likelihood point *estimator* in (b).
(f) Under what conditions is MSE$(\hat{\mu}) <$ MSE$(\tilde{\mu})$?

Solution
(a) According to Exercise 3.1, the choice of $\hat{\mu}$ that minimizes expected posterior quadratic loss is $\hat{\mu} = E(\mu|y)$, which in this case is given by (2.39). Evaluated at $\hat{\mu} = E(\mu|y)$, the expected posterior quadratic loss is simply the posterior variance, Var$(\mu|y)$. An expression for this posterior variance is given in (2.23) and is denoted as $\overline{h}^{-1} = (\underline{h}+h)^{-1}$, as defined in (2.14). In terms of the parameterization of this exercise relative to the parameterization used in Exercise 2.3, we have, from (2.12), $\underline{h}^{-1} = \sigma^2/\underline{T}$, and from (2.13), $h = T\sigma^{-2}$. It follows that the minimized expected quadratic posterior loss (3.10) becomes

$$c(\hat{\mu}) = \text{Var}(\mu|y) = (\underline{T}\sigma^{-2} + T\sigma^{-2})^{-1} = \sigma^2(T+\underline{T})^{-1} = \frac{\sigma^2}{\overline{T}}, \tag{4.6}$$

where $\overline{T} = \underline{T} + T$.
(b) Upon adding and subtracting $E(\mu|y)$ in our quadratic loss function, much like Exercise 3.1, plugging $\tilde{\mu} = \overline{y}$ into (3.10) yields

$$c(\tilde{\mu}) = \frac{\sigma^2}{\overline{T}} + [E(\mu|y) - \overline{y}]^2 . \tag{4.7}$$

(c) Clearly (4.6) is less than (4.7), which follows by construction since $\hat{\mu}$ minimizes posterior expected loss.
(d) From the *ex ante* standpoint, (2.39) becomes

$$\hat{\mu} = \frac{\underline{T}\underline{\mu} + T\overline{Y}}{\overline{T}}. \tag{4.8}$$

To calculate MSE$(\hat{\mu})$, we need to determine its *sampling* mean and variance. From (4.8) the sampling mean and variance are

$$E(\hat{\mu}) = \frac{\underline{T}\underline{\mu} + TE(\overline{Y})}{\overline{T}^{-1}} = \frac{\underline{T}\underline{\mu} + T\mu}{\overline{T}} \tag{4.9}$$

and

$$\text{Var}(\hat{\mu}) = \frac{T^2\text{Var}(\overline{Y})}{\overline{T}^2} = \frac{T^2(\sigma^2/T)}{\overline{T}^2} = \frac{T\sigma^2}{\overline{T}^2}. \tag{4.10}$$

From (4.9) the bias of $\hat{\mu}$ is

$$\text{Bias}(\hat{\mu}) = E(\hat{\mu}) - \mu = \frac{\underline{T}\underline{\mu} + T\mu - \overline{T}\mu}{\overline{T}} = \frac{\underline{T}(\underline{\mu} - \mu)}{\overline{T}}.$$

Recall that the MSE of an estimator equals its sampling variance plus its squared bias. Therefore, MSE($\hat{\mu}$) is

$$\text{MSE}(\hat{\mu}) = \frac{T\sigma^2}{\overline{T}^2} + \left[\frac{\underline{T}(\underline{\mu} - \mu)}{\overline{T}}\right]^2 = \frac{T\sigma^2 + \underline{T}^2(\underline{\mu} - \mu)^2}{\overline{T}^2}. \tag{4.11}$$

(e) It is well known that $\tilde{\mu} = \overline{Y}$ is an unbiased estimator of μ with

$$\text{MSE}(\tilde{\mu}) = \text{Var}(\tilde{\mu}) = \frac{\sigma^2}{T}. \tag{4.12}$$

(f) From (4.11) and (4.12), MSE($\hat{\mu}$) < MSE($\tilde{\mu}$) iff

$$\frac{T\sigma^2 + \underline{T}^2(\underline{\mu} - \mu)^2}{\overline{T}^2} < \frac{\sigma^2}{T}, \tag{4.13}$$

or equivalently, iff

$$\left(\frac{\underline{\mu} - \mu}{\sigma/\sqrt{T}}\right)^2 < \underline{T}^{-1}(\underline{T} + 2T). \tag{4.14}$$

In other words, the Bayesian point estimator has a smaller MSE than the sample mean provided the prior mean $\underline{\mu}$ is "sufficiently close" to the unknown population mean μ, where closeness is measured relative to the sampling standard deviation $\sigma/\sqrt{T}$ in $\overline{Y}$. Therefore, the Bayes estimate wins expected posterior loss comparisons by definition, and sometimes wins MSE comparisons – even to the minimum variance unbiased estimator $\overline{Y}$.

Exercise 4.2 (Sampling properties under quadratic loss in conjugate exponential analysis) Consider a random sample Y_t $(t = 1, 2, \ldots, T)$ with exponential density

$$p(y_t|\theta) = \theta^{-1}[\exp(-y_t/\theta)], \quad 0 < y_t < \infty, \; 0 < \theta < \infty. \tag{4.15}$$

Note that $\overline{Y}$ is both the maximum likelihood and the method of moments estimator of θ.
(a) Find MSE($\overline{Y}$).
(b) Consider the estimator

$$\hat{\theta} = \frac{T\overline{Y}}{T+1}.$$

Find MSE($\hat{\theta}$).
(c) Compare the MSEs from (a) and (b). Which estimator has the lower MSE?
(d) Let $\delta = \theta^{-1}$ and rewrite (4.15) as

$$p(y_t|\delta) = \delta\exp(-\delta y_t), \quad 0 < y_t < \infty, \; 0 < \delta < \infty. \tag{4.16}$$

Suppose prior beliefs regarding δ have a gamma distribution with hyperparameters $\underline{\alpha}$ and $\underline{\beta}$ (i.e., $\delta \sim G(\underline{\alpha}, \underline{\beta})E(\delta) = \underline{\alpha}\underline{\beta}$, and $\text{Var}(\delta) = \underline{\alpha}\underline{\beta}^2$). Find the posterior distribution of δ.
(e) Find the posterior distribution of θ corresponding to the answer in part (d).

(f) Consider the loss function $C(\tilde{\theta},\theta) = (\tilde{\theta}-\theta)^2$. What is the Bayesian point estimate $\tilde{\theta}$ of θ? Be specific!
(g) Find MSE($\tilde{\theta}$). Compare it, in the case $\underline{\alpha} = 1$, to your answers in (a) and (b). Which estimator do you prefer?
(h) In the case $\underline{\alpha} = 1$, compare $\overline{Y}$, $\hat{\theta}$, and $\tilde{\theta}$ according to expected posterior quadratic loss.

Solution

(a) Since the mean and variance of the exponential pdf in (4.15) are θ and θ^2 (see Theorem A.2), respectively,

$$E(\overline{Y}) = \theta, \quad \text{Var}(\overline{Y}) = \theta^2/T,$$

and hence

$$\text{MSE}(\overline{Y}) = \theta^2/T.$$

(b) Because $E(\hat{\theta}) = T\theta/(T+1)$,

$$\text{Bias}(\hat{\theta}) = \frac{-\theta}{T+1},$$

and

$$\text{Var}(\hat{\theta}) = \frac{T^2\theta^2}{T(T+1)^2} = \frac{T\theta^2}{(T+1)^2},$$

it follows immediately that

$$\text{MSE}(\hat{\theta}) = \frac{T\theta^2+\theta^2}{(T+1)^2} = \frac{\theta^2}{T+1}.$$

(c) Clearly, $\text{MSE}(\hat{\theta}) < \text{MSE}(\overline{Y})$. Hence, the MLE $\overline{Y}$ is inadmissible under quadratic loss.
(d) The prior pdf for δ is

$$p(\delta) \propto \delta^{(\underline{\alpha}-1)} \exp(-\delta/\underline{\beta}), \tag{4.17}$$

and the likelihood function is

$$L(\delta) = \delta^T \exp\left(-\delta \sum_{t=1}^{T} y_t\right) = \delta^T \exp(-\delta T\overline{y}). \tag{4.18}$$

Thus,

$$p(\delta|y) \propto p(\delta)L(\delta) \propto \delta^{(\overline{\alpha}-1)} \exp(-\delta/\overline{\beta}), \tag{4.19}$$

where

$$\overline{\alpha} = \underline{\alpha} + T, \quad \overline{\beta} = \left[\underline{\beta}^{-1} + T\overline{y}\right]^{-1}.$$

Recognizing (4.19) as the kernel of a gamma density, it follows that

$$\delta|y \sim G(\overline{\alpha}, \overline{\beta}),$$

or

$$\delta|y \sim \gamma(\overline{\mu}, \overline{\nu}),$$

where $\overline{\mu} = \overline{\alpha}\overline{\beta}$ and $\overline{\nu} = 2\overline{\alpha}$. Remember that there are two different parameterizations of the gamma density and here we use both (see Definition A.2).
(e) Noting that $\partial\delta/\partial\theta = -\theta^{-2}$ and using a change-of-variables theorem (see, e.g., Poirier 1995, Chapter 4) gives the posterior pdf for θ:

$$p(\theta|y) \propto \left|\frac{\partial\delta}{\partial\theta}\right| p(\delta|y) \propto \theta^{-2}\theta^{1-\overline{\alpha}}\exp[-1/(\overline{\beta}\theta)] \propto \theta^{-(\overline{\alpha}+1)}\exp[-1/(\overline{\beta}\theta)]. \tag{4.20}$$

Recognizing (4.20) as the kernel of an inverted gamma density (see Theorem A.2), it follows that the posterior pdf of θ is inverted gamma, that is,

$$\theta|y \sim IG(\overline{\alpha}, \overline{\beta}).$$

(f) According to Exercise 3.1 the posterior mean minimizes expected posterior quadratic loss, which, in the case of (4.20), provided $\overline{\alpha} > 1$, is

$$\tilde{\theta} = [\overline{\beta}(\overline{\alpha} - 1)]^{-1} = \frac{\underline{\beta}^{-1} + T\overline{y}}{\underline{\alpha} + T - 1}. \tag{4.21}$$

(g) Viewed *ex ante*, the sampling mean and variance of (4.21) are

$$E_{Y|\theta}(\tilde{\theta}) = \frac{\underline{\beta}^{-1} + T\,\theta}{\underline{\alpha} + T - 1} \tag{4.22}$$

and

$$\mathrm{Var}_{Y|\theta}(\tilde{\theta}) = \frac{T^2(\theta^2/T)}{(\underline{\alpha} + T - 1)^2} = \frac{T\theta^2}{(\underline{\alpha} + T - 1)^2}. \tag{4.23}$$

From (4.22) the bias of $\tilde{\theta}$ is seen to be

$$\mathrm{Bias}(\tilde{\theta}) = \frac{\underline{\beta}^{-1} + (1 - \underline{\alpha})\theta}{\underline{\alpha} + T - 1}.$$

Therefore the MSE($\tilde{\theta}$) is

$$\mathrm{MSE}(\tilde{\theta}) = \frac{T\theta^2 + [\underline{\beta}^{-1} + (1 - \underline{\alpha})\theta]^2}{(\underline{\alpha} + T - 1)^2}. \tag{4.24}$$

When $\underline{\alpha} = 1$, (4.24) becomes

$$\mathrm{MSE}(\tilde{\theta}) = \frac{T\theta^2 + \underline{\beta}^{-2}}{T^2} = \frac{\theta^2}{T} + \frac{\underline{\beta}^{-2}}{T^2}.$$

Therefore,

$$\mathrm{MSE}(\hat{\theta}) < \mathrm{MSE}(\overline{Y}) < \mathrm{MSE}(\tilde{\theta}). \tag{4.25}$$

(h) Given $\underline{\alpha} = 1$, the respective posterior expected quadratic losses (3.10) are, provided $\overline{\alpha} > 2$,

$$\begin{aligned} c(\overline{y}) &= E_{\theta|y}(\overline{y} - \theta)^2 \\ &= \text{Var}(\theta|y) + [E(\theta|y) - \overline{y}]^2 \\ &= \text{Var}(\theta|y) + \left(\frac{\underline{\beta}^{-1} + T\overline{y}}{\underline{\alpha} + T - 1} - \overline{y} \right)^2 \\ &= \text{Var}(\theta|y) + \left[(\underline{\beta}T)^{-1} \right]^2 \end{aligned} \tag{4.26}$$

(where we have plugged in $\underline{\alpha} = 1$),

$$\begin{aligned} c(\hat{\theta}) &= E_{\theta|y}(\hat{\theta} - \theta)^2 \\ &= \text{Var}(\theta|y) + \left(\frac{\underline{\beta}^{-1} + T\overline{y}}{\underline{\alpha} + T - 1} - \frac{T\overline{y}}{T+1} \right)^2 \\ &= \text{Var}(\theta|y) + \left((\underline{\beta}T)^{-1} + \frac{\overline{y}}{T+1} \right)^2, \end{aligned} \tag{4.27}$$

and

$$\begin{aligned} c(\tilde{\theta}) &= E_{\theta|y}(\tilde{\theta} - \theta)^2 \\ &= \text{Var}(\theta|y). \end{aligned} \tag{4.28}$$

From (4.26)–(4.28) it is clear that $c(\tilde{\theta}) < c(\overline{y}) < c(\hat{\theta})$, reversing the MSE ranking in (4.25).

Exercise 4.3 (Expected bias of Bayesian point estimator) Let $\hat{\theta} = \hat{\theta}(Y)$ be the Bayesian estimator of a scalar parameter θ under quadratic loss based on a prior density $p(\theta)$ with finite prior mean. Let $b(\theta)$ be the bias of $\hat{\theta}$ as an estimator of θ. *A priori*, can you determine the expected sign of $b(\theta)$? If so, why? If not, why not?

Solution

According to Exercise 3.1, under quadratic loss, $\hat{\theta} = E(\theta|y)$. By definition,

$$b(\theta) = E_{Y|\theta}[E(\theta|y) - \theta].$$

Using iterated expectations,

$$\begin{aligned} E_\theta[b(\theta)] &= E_\theta \left(E_{Y|\theta}[E(\theta|y) - \theta] \right) \\ &= E_{\theta,Y}[E(\theta|y) - \theta] \\ &= E_Y \left(E_{\theta|y}[E(\theta|y) - \theta] \right) \\ &= E_Y \left(E(\theta|y) - E(\theta|y) \right) \\ &= 0. \end{aligned} \tag{4.29}$$

Therefore, the expected bias of $\hat{\theta}$ is zero.

Exercise 4.4 (Balanced loss in conjugate normal analysis (Zellner 1994)) Let Y_t $(t = 1, 2, \ldots, T)$ be a random sample from an $N(\theta, \sigma^2)$ distribution with σ^2 known. Consider the *balanced loss function*

$$C(\hat{\theta}, \theta) = w\left[\frac{1}{T}\sum_{t=1}^{T}(y_t - \hat{\theta})^2\right] + (1-w)(\hat{\theta} - \theta)^2$$
$$= w[\hat{\sigma}^2 + (\hat{\theta} - \overline{y})^2] + (1-w)(\hat{\theta} - \theta)^2, \tag{4.30}$$

where $\hat{\sigma}^2 = 1/T\sum_{t=1}^{T}(y_t - \overline{y})^2$. Suppose your prior distribution for θ is $N(\underline{\mu}, \sigma^2/\underline{T})$.
(a) Find the Bayesian point estimate of θ (and denote it as $\hat{\theta}$).
(b) Find the risk function for $\hat{\theta}$.

Solution
(a) The posterior for θ was reviewed in the solution to Exercise 4.1. Specifically, borrowing results from (4.6) and (4.8), we obtain

$$\theta|y \sim N(\overline{\mu}, \sigma^2/\overline{T}),$$

where

$$\overline{\mu} = (\underline{T}\underline{\mu} + T\overline{y})/\overline{T}, \quad \overline{T} = \underline{T} + T.$$

The posterior expectation of (4.30) is

$$E_{\theta|y}[C(\hat{\theta}, \theta)] = w[\hat{\sigma}^2 + (\hat{\theta} - \overline{y})^2] + (1-w)E_{\theta|y}[(\hat{\theta} - \theta)^2]$$
$$= w[\hat{\sigma}^2 + (\hat{\theta} - \overline{y})^2] + (1-w)\left(\text{Var}(\theta|y) + [\hat{\theta} - E(\theta|y)]^2\right), \tag{4.31}$$

which is quadratic in θ. Differentiating (4.31) with respect to $\hat{\theta}$, equating the result to zero, and solving for $\hat{\theta}$ yields

$$\hat{\theta} = w\overline{y} + (1-w)E(\theta|y)$$
$$= w\overline{y} + (1-w)\left(\frac{\underline{T}\underline{\mu} + T\overline{y}}{\underline{T} + T}\right)$$
$$= \tau\underline{\mu} + (1-\tau)\overline{y}, \tag{4.32}$$

where

$$\tau = \frac{(1-w)\underline{T}}{\underline{T} + T}.$$

(b) Viewing (4.30) *ex ante* and writing $\hat{\theta} - \overline{Y}$ as

$$\hat{\theta} - \overline{Y} = \tau\underline{\mu} + (1-\tau)\overline{Y} - \overline{Y} = \tau(\underline{\mu} - \overline{Y}),$$

it follows that

$$E_{Y|\theta}[(\hat{\theta} - \overline{Y})^2] = \tau^2\left[\frac{\sigma^2}{T} + (\theta - \underline{\mu})^2\right]. \tag{4.33}$$

Also, writing $\hat{\theta} - \theta$ as

$$\hat{\theta} - \theta = \tau\underline{\mu} + (1-\tau)\overline{Y} - \theta = (1-\tau)\left[\overline{Y} - \left(\frac{\theta - \tau\underline{\mu}}{1-\tau}\right)\right],$$

it follows, after some tedious algebra, that

$$E_{Y|\theta}(\hat{\theta} - \theta)^2 = (1-\tau)^2\left[\frac{\sigma^2}{T} + \frac{\tau^2(\theta - \underline{\mu})^2}{(1-\tau)^2}\right]. \tag{4.34}$$

From the definition of the loss function in (4.30) and the results in (4.33) and (4.34), we thus have

$$R(\hat{\theta}|\theta) = w\left(\frac{(T-1)\sigma^2}{T} + \tau^2\left[\frac{\sigma^2}{T} + (\theta - \underline{\mu})^2\right]\right)$$
$$+ (1-w)(1-\tau)^2\left[\frac{\sigma^2}{T} + \frac{\tau^2(\theta - \underline{\mu})^2}{(1-\tau)^2}\right].$$

Exercise 4.5 (Empirical Bayes estimation) Suppose $Y_t|\theta, \tau \ (t = 1, 2, \ldots, T) \overset{\text{iid}}{\sim} N(\theta, 1)$ and $\theta|\tau^2 \sim N(0, \tau^2)$.

(a) Find the marginal distribution of $y = [y_1 \ y_2 \ \cdots \ y_T]'$. (We revert to lowercase letters since this exercise is not concerned with describing sampling properties, but, instead, seeks to "optimally" choose the hyperparameter τ as a function of the realized data.)

(b) The idea of using the marginal distribution in (a) to estimate τ underlies the *empirical Bayes approach*. The related *type II maximum likelihood estimator* is defined to be the value of τ^2 that maximizes the marginal likelihood in (a). Find the type II maximum likelihood estimator of τ^2.

Solution

(a) Write

$$y = \theta\iota_T + \epsilon = \begin{bmatrix}\iota_T & I_T\end{bmatrix}\begin{bmatrix}\theta \\ \epsilon\end{bmatrix},$$

where

$$\begin{bmatrix}\theta \\ \epsilon\end{bmatrix} \sim N_{T+1}\left(0_{T+1}, \begin{bmatrix}\tau^2 & 0_T' \\ 0_T & I_T\end{bmatrix}\right).$$

Then $y|\tau^2 \sim N_T(0_T, \Sigma)$, where

$$\Sigma = \begin{bmatrix}\iota_T & I_T\end{bmatrix}\begin{bmatrix}\tau^2 & 0_T' \\ 0_T & I_T\end{bmatrix}\begin{bmatrix}\iota_T' \\ I_T\end{bmatrix} = I_T + \tau^2\iota_T\iota_T'.$$

(b) Consider

$$\ln[p(y|\tau^2)] = -\frac{T}{2}\ln(2\pi) - \frac{1}{2}\ln|\Sigma| - \frac{1}{2}y'\Sigma^{-1}y,$$

where

$$|\Sigma| = 1 + T\tau^2 \quad \text{and} \quad \Sigma^{-1} = I_T - \left(\frac{\tau^2}{1+T\tau^2}\right)\iota_T\iota_T'.$$

Let $\theta = \theta(\tau^2) \equiv \tau^2/(1+T\tau^2)$. Then, we note that

$$y'\Sigma^{-1}y = \sum_{t=1}^{T}(y_t - \theta T\overline{y})y_t = \sum_{t=1}^{T} y_t^2 - \theta T^2\overline{y}^2.$$

It follows that

$$\frac{\partial \ln[p(y|\tau^2)]}{\partial \tau^2} = -\frac{T}{2(1+T\tau^2)} + \frac{T^2\overline{y}^2}{2(1+T\tau^2)^2}. \tag{4.35}$$

Equating (4.35) to zero and solving for the empirical Bayes estimator of τ^2 yields

$$\hat{\tau}^2 = \begin{cases} \frac{T\overline{y}^2-1}{T} & \text{if } \overline{y}^2 > 1/T, \\ 0 & \text{if } \overline{y}^2 \le 1/T. \end{cases}$$

Exercise 4.6 (Point estimation under linex loss) Consider a random sample Y_t $(t = 1, 2, \ldots, T)$ from an $N(\mu, \sigma^2)$ population with σ^2 known. Suppose that prior beliefs for θ are represented by the normal distribution $\mu \sim N(\underline{\mu}, \sigma^2/\underline{T})$, where $\underline{\mu}$ and $\underline{T}$ are given. By Exercise 2.6(b), the corresponding posterior density for μ is $N(\overline{\mu}, \sigma^2/\overline{T})$, where $\overline{\mu} = (\underline{T}\underline{\mu} + T\overline{y})/\overline{T}$ and $\overline{T} = \underline{T} + T$. To simplify computations we consider the limiting case $\underline{T} \to 0$ (discussed further in Chapter 8) in which the prior information is weak compared to the sample information, and the posterior simplifies to $N(\overline{y}, \sigma^2/T)$. Finally, consider the linex loss function (3.19).
(a) Let $\hat{\mu}_1$ be the Bayesian point estimate (3.22) subject to expected posterior linex loss. Find its linex risk.
(b) Let $\hat{\mu}_2 = \overline{y}$. Find its linex risk.

Solution
(a) The posterior moment-generating function corresponding to posterior $N(\overline{y}, \sigma^2/T)$ is $M_{\theta|y}(v) = \exp(\overline{y}v + \sigma^2 v^2/2T)$. Hence, the Bayesian point estimate (3.22) becomes

$$\begin{aligned} \hat{\mu}_1 &= -a^{-1}\ln[M_{\theta|y}(-a)] \\ &= -a^{-1}\ln[\exp(-a\overline{y} + \sigma^2 a^2/2T)] \\ &= \overline{y} - \frac{a\sigma^2}{2T}. \end{aligned} \tag{4.36}$$

The sampling distribution of $\hat{\mu}_1$ is normal with mean $\mu - (a\sigma^2/2T)$ and variance σ^2/T. Therefore, viewed *ex ante*, the linex risk corresponding to the Bayesian estimate (4.36) is

$$\begin{aligned} R(\hat{\mu}_1|\mu) &= E_{Y|\mu}\left(\exp[a(\hat{\mu}_1 - \mu)] - a(\hat{\mu}_1 - \mu) - 1\right) \\ &= \exp(-a\mu)M_{\hat{\mu}_1|\mu}(a) - a[E_{Y|\mu}(\hat{\mu}_1) - \mu] - 1 \end{aligned}$$

$$= \exp(-a\mu)\exp\left(a\left[\mu - \frac{a\sigma^2}{2T}\right] + \frac{a^2\sigma^2}{2T}\right) - a\left(-\frac{a\sigma^2}{2T}\right) - 1$$
$$= \frac{a^2\sigma^2}{2T} - 1. \tag{4.37}$$

(b) The linex risk corresponding to $\hat{\mu}_2 = \overline{Y}$ is

$$R(\hat{\mu}_2|\mu) = E_{Y|\mu}\left(\exp[a(\overline{Y} - \mu)] - a(\overline{Y} - \mu) - 1\right) \tag{4.38}$$
$$= \exp(-a\mu)M_{\overline{Y}|\mu}(a) - a[E_{Y|\mu}(\overline{Y}) - \mu] - 1$$
$$= \exp(-a\mu)\exp\left(a\mu + \frac{a^2\sigma^2}{2T}\right) + 0 - 1$$
$$= \exp\left(\frac{a^2\sigma^2}{2T}\right) - 1.$$

Because (4.38) is greater than or equal to (4.37), this shows that $\hat{\mu}_2 = \overline{Y}$ is inadmissible with respect to linex loss.

Exercise 4.7 (Risk, Bayes risk, and admissibility (Berger 1985)) Consider a single data point generated from $Y|\theta \sim N(\theta, 1)$, a prior $\theta \sim N(0, 1)$, and the loss function

$$C(\hat{\theta}, \theta) = (\hat{\theta} - \theta)^2 \exp(3\theta^2/4). \tag{4.39}$$

(a) Find the Bayesian point estimate $\hat{\theta}$ of θ.
(b) Compare the risk of $\hat{\theta}$ to the risk of $\tilde{\theta} = Y$.
(c) Compute the Bayes risk of $\hat{\theta}$.

Solution

(a) Using Exercise 2.3, it follows that the posterior distribution of θ is $N(.5y, .5)$. Exercise 3.9 implies that the Bayesian point estimate that minimizes expected posterior loss is

$$\hat{\theta} = \frac{E_{\theta|y}[\theta w(\theta)]}{E_{\theta|y}[w(\theta)]}, \tag{4.40}$$

where $w(\theta) = \exp(3\theta^2/4)$. The denominator in (4.40) is

$$E_{\theta|y}[\exp(3\theta^2/4)] = \int_{-\infty}^{\infty} \exp(3\theta^2/4)\frac{1}{\sqrt{2(\pi/2)}}\exp\left[-\frac{1}{2}\frac{(\theta - .5y)^2}{.5}\right] d\theta$$
$$= \int_{-\infty}^{\infty} \frac{1}{\sqrt{2(\pi/2)}}\exp\left[\frac{3\theta^2}{4} - \theta^2 + y\theta - \frac{y^2}{4}\right] d\theta$$
$$= \int_{-\infty}^{\infty} \frac{1}{\sqrt{2(\pi/2)}}\exp\left[-\frac{1}{4}(\theta - 2y)^2 + \frac{3y^2}{4}\right] d\theta$$
$$= 2\exp\left(\frac{3y^2}{4}\right)\int_{-\infty}^{\infty} \frac{1}{\sqrt{2\pi(2)}}\exp\left[-\frac{1}{(2)(2)}(\theta - 2y)^2\right] d\theta$$
$$= 2\exp(3y^2/4), \tag{4.41}$$

where the integral in the second-to-last line in (4.41) is unity because the integrand corresponds to an $N(2y, 2)$ density. Repeating the procedure it follows that the numerator in (4.40) is

$$E_{\theta|y}[\theta \exp(3\theta^2/4)] = 4y \exp(3y^2/4). \tag{4.42}$$

Therefore, the ratio of (4.42) to (4.41) yields the Bayesian point estimate $\hat{\theta} = 2y$.
(b) The risk corresponding to $\hat{\theta}$ is

$$\begin{aligned} R(\hat{\theta}|\theta) &= E_{Y|\theta}[\exp(3\theta^2/4)(2Y - \theta)^2] \\ &= \exp(3\theta^2/4)E_{Y|\theta}\left[4(Y - (\theta/2))^2\right] \\ &= 4\exp(3\theta^2/4)\left[\text{Var}(Y|\theta) + ((\theta/2) - \theta)^2\right] \\ &= (4 + \theta^2)\exp(3\theta^2/4). \end{aligned} \tag{4.43}$$

Similarly, the risk corresponding to $\tilde{\theta}$ is

$$\begin{aligned} R(\tilde{\theta}|\theta) &= E_{Y|\theta}[\exp(3\theta^2/4)(Y - \theta)^2] \\ &= \exp(3\theta^2/4)\text{Var}(Y|\theta) \\ &= \exp(3\theta^2/4). \end{aligned} \tag{4.44}$$

Comparing (4.43) with (4.44), we see that the Bayesian point estimator is inadmissible under loss function (4.39) despite the fact that the prior $\theta \sim N(0, 1)$ is proper.
(c) The counterintuitive result in (b) can be explained by noting that the Bayes risk is

$$\begin{aligned} E_\theta[R(\hat{\theta}|\theta)] &= \int_{-\infty}^{\infty} (4 + \theta^2)\exp(3\theta^2/4)\frac{1}{\sqrt{2\pi}}\exp\left(-\frac{1}{2}\theta^2\right) d\theta \\ &= \int_{-\infty}^{\infty} (4 + \theta^2)\frac{1}{\sqrt{2\pi}}\exp\left(\frac{1}{4}\theta^2\right) d\theta \to \infty, \end{aligned} \tag{4.45}$$

which diverges since the integrand approaches ∞ as $|\theta| \to \infty$. Note that in this case it is not permissible to switch the order of integration in (4.3)–(4.5).

Exercise 4.8 (Likelihood principle) Consider two researchers, A and B. Each researcher must estimate the same unknown parameter $\theta < 0$ subject to the same prior $p(\theta)$ and the same loss function $C(\hat{\theta}, \theta)$. Researcher A observes a random variable X having the gamma distribution $G(3, \theta^{-1})$ with density

$$p(x|\theta) = \left(\frac{\theta^3}{\Gamma(3)}\right) x^2 \exp(-\theta x), \quad x > 0.$$

Researcher B observes a random variable Y having the Poisson distribution $Po(2\theta)$ with mass function

$$p(y|\theta) = \frac{(2\theta)^y \exp(-2\theta)}{y!}, \quad y = 0, 1, 2, 3, \ldots$$

In collecting one observation each, researcher A observes $X = 2$ and researcher B observes $Y = 3$. Compare and contrast Bayesian and maximum likelihood estimation for each researcher.

Solution
The respective likelihood functions are

$$L_A(\theta; x = 2) = \left(\frac{\theta^3}{\Gamma(3)}\right) 2^2 \exp(-2\theta) \propto \theta^3 \exp(-2\theta)$$

and

$$L_B(\theta; y = 3) = \frac{(2\theta)^3 \exp(-2\theta)}{3!} \propto \theta^3 \exp(-2\theta).$$

Since these likelihood functions are proportional, it follows from the likelihood principle (see Chapter 2) that the evidence in the data about θ is the same in both data sets. Because the priors and loss functions are the same, from the Bayesian standpoint the two researchers would obtain the same posterior distributions and the same point estimates. From the standpoint of maximum likelihood estimation, since the likelihoods are proportional, the maximum likelihood point *estimates* would be the same ($\theta = 1.5$). However, the maximum likelihood *estimators* would be very different. In the case of researcher A the sampling distribution would be continuous, whereas in the case of researcher B the sampling distribution would be discrete.

Exercise 4.9 (Inadmissibility under quadratic loss and improper prior: Case I)
Let $Y \sim N(\mu, 1)$ and consider the improper prior $p(\mu) = \exp(\mu)$.
(a) Find the posterior distribution of μ and identify it.
(b) Under quadratic loss, find the generalized Bayes estimate.
(c) Viewed *ex ante*, is the generalized Bayes estimator admissible under quadratic loss?

Solution
(a) The posterior pdf of μ is proportional to

$$\begin{aligned}
p(\mu|y) &\propto \exp(\mu) \exp\left[-\frac{1}{2}(y-\mu)^2\right] \\
&= \exp\left[\mu - \frac{1}{2}(y-\mu)^2\right] \\
&= \exp\left[-\frac{1}{2}\left(y^2 - 2\mu y + \mu^2 - 2\mu\right)\right] \\
&= \exp\left[-\frac{1}{2}\left(y^2 - 2\mu[y+1] + \mu^2\right)\right] \\
&\propto \exp\left[-\frac{1}{2}\left(y^2 - 2\mu[y+1] + \mu^2\right)\right] \exp\left[-\frac{1}{2}(2y+1)\right]
\end{aligned}$$

$$= \exp\left[-\frac{1}{2}\left(y^2 - 2\mu\left[y+1\right] + \mu^2 + 2y + 1\right)\right]$$
$$= \exp\left[-\frac{1}{2}\left(\left[y+1\right]^2 - 2\mu\left[y+1\right] + \mu^2\right)\right]$$
$$= \exp\left[-\frac{1}{2}\left(\mu - \left[y+1\right]\right)^2\right].$$

Hence, $\mu|y \sim N\left[(y+1), 1\right]$.
(b) $E(\mu|y) = y + 1$.
(c)

$$E_{Y|\mu}\left[(Y+1-\mu)^2\right] = E_{Y|\mu}\left[(Y-\mu+1)^2\right] = E_{Y|\mu}\left[(Y-\mu)^2 - 2(Y-\mu) + 1\right]$$
$$= E_{Y|\mu}\left[(Y-\mu)^2\right] - 0 + 1 \geq E_{Y|\mu}\left[(Y-\mu)^2\right].$$

Therefore, $Y+1$ is inadmissible because its *ex ante* expected quadratic loss is greater than that of Y. The culprit is the improper prior.

Exercise 4.10 (Inadmissibility under quadratic loss and improper prior: Case II) Suppose $Y|\theta \sim N(\theta, 1)$ and $p(\theta)$ is uniform over $\mathbb{R}$. Let $\alpha \equiv \theta^2$ be the quantity of interest.
(a) Find the posterior distribution of θ.
(b) Find the posterior distribution of α.
(c) Under quadratic loss, what is the optimal Bayesian point estimate $\hat{\alpha}$ of α? Be specific!
(d) Find the risk function $R(\hat{\alpha}|\alpha)$ for the corresponding Bayesian estimator in (c).
(e) Let $\tilde{\alpha} = y^2 - 1$. Find $R(\tilde{\alpha}|\alpha)$.
(f) What do you conclude from (d) and (e)?

Solution
(a) $\theta|y \sim N(y, 1)$.
(b) $\alpha|y \sim \chi^2\left(1, y^2/2\right)$, where $\chi^2(\nu, \lambda)$ denotes a non-central chi-square distribution with degrees of freedom parameter ν and non-centrality parameter λ. See the discussion following Definition A.2 for more on the non-central chi-square.
(c) The Bayesian point estimate is the posterior mean, i.e., $\hat{\alpha} = E(\alpha|y) = 1 + 2\left(y^2/2\right) = 1 + y^2$.
(d) $Y|\alpha \sim N(\sqrt{\alpha}, 1)$ implies $Y^2|\alpha \sim \chi^2\left(1, \frac{\alpha}{2}\right)$. Since loss is quadratic, the risk reduces to MSE $(\hat{\alpha})$. To that end, note that

$$E(\hat{\alpha}) = 1 + E\left(y^2\right) = 1 + \left[1 + 2(\alpha/2)\right] = 2 + \alpha$$

and

$$\text{Var}(\hat{\alpha}) = 2(1) + 8(\alpha/2) = 2 + 4\alpha.$$

Thus,

$$\begin{aligned}\text{MSE}(\hat{\alpha}) &= \text{Var}(\hat{\alpha}) + [\text{Bias}(\hat{\alpha})]^2 \\ &= 2 + 4\alpha + (2 + \alpha - \alpha)^2 \\ &= 6 + 4\alpha.\end{aligned}$$

(e) Noting that $\tilde{\alpha} = \hat{\alpha} - 2$ and proceeding as in (d),

$$\begin{aligned}E(\tilde{\alpha}) &= E(\hat{\alpha}) - 2 = (2 + \alpha) - 2 = \alpha, \\ \text{Var}(\tilde{\alpha}) &= \text{Var}(\hat{\alpha}) = 2 + 4\alpha.\end{aligned}$$

Hence, $\text{MSE}(\tilde{\alpha}) = \text{Var}(\tilde{\alpha}) = 2 + 4\alpha$.

(f) $\text{MSE}(\hat{\alpha}) - \text{MSE}(\tilde{\alpha}) = (6 + 4\alpha) - (2 + 4\alpha) = 4 > 0$. Therefore, the Bayesian point estimator is inadmissible under quadratic loss. Bayesian estimators based on proper priors are always admissible. Furthermore, all admissible estimators are Bayesian estimators based on proper priors or limits of Bayesian estimators based on improper priors. Because the prior here is improper, there is no guarantee that the Bayesian estimator will be admissible.

5

Interval Estimation

From the Bayesian standpoint, given a region $C \subset \Theta$ and the data y, it is meaningful to ask the following: What is the *probability* that θ lies in C? The answer is direct:

$$1 - \alpha \equiv \Pr(\theta \in C|y) = \int_C p(\theta|y)d\theta, \tag{5.1}$$

where $0 < \alpha < 1$ is defined implicitly in (5.1). The region C is known as a $1 - \alpha$ *Bayesian credible region*. There is no need to introduce the additional frequentist concept of "confidence."

This chapter focuses on the case in which the posterior probability content is first set at some preassigned α (say $\alpha = .10$, .05, or .01) and then the "smallest" credible region that attains posterior probability content of $1 - \alpha$ is sought. This leads to the following definition.

Definition 5.1 Let $p(\theta|y)$ be a posterior density function. Let $\Theta^* \subset \Theta$ satisfy:
(a) $\Pr(\theta \in \Theta^*|y) = 1 - \alpha$,
(b) for all $\theta_1 \in \Theta^*$ and $\theta_2 \notin \Theta^*$, $p(\theta_1|y) \geq p(\theta_2|y)$.
Then Θ^* is defined to be a *highest posterior density (HPD) region of content* $(1-\alpha)$ *for* θ.

Given a probability of content $1 - \alpha$, the HPD region Θ^* has the smallest possible volume in the parameter space Θ of any $1 - \alpha$ Bayesian credible region. If $p(\theta|y)$ is not uniform over Θ, then the HPD region of content $1 - \alpha$ is unique. Hereafter, we focus on the case in which there is a single parameter of interest and all other parameters have been integrated out of the posterior.

Constructing an HPD interval is conceptually straightforward. Part (b) of Definition 5.1 implies that, if $[a, b]$ is an HPD interval, then $p(a|y) = p(b|y)$. This suggests a graphical approach in which a horizontal line is gradually moved vertically downward across the posterior density; where it intersects the posterior density, the corresponding abscissa values are noted, and the posterior is integrated between these points. Once the desired posterior probability is reached, the process stops. If the posterior density is symmetric and unimodal with mode θ^m, then the resulting $1 - \alpha$ HPD interval is of the form $[\theta^m - \delta, \theta^m + \delta]$, for suitable δ, and it cuts off equal probability $\alpha/2$ in each tail.

In (5.1) we started with the region and then found its posterior probability content. In Definition 5.1 we started with the posterior probability content and then found the smallest region with that content. From a pure decision theoretic perspective, it is interesting to start with a cost function measuring the undesirability of large α and large region volume, and then to pick both α and C to minimize expected posterior cost (see Casella, Hwang, and Robert 1993). For a thorough discussion of both Bayesian and frequentist interval estimation, see Casella and Berger (2002).

Exercise 5.1 (Graphical determination of an HPD interval) Consider the posterior density in Figure 5.1. Use the graphical approach described earlier to obtain three sets of HPD intervals.

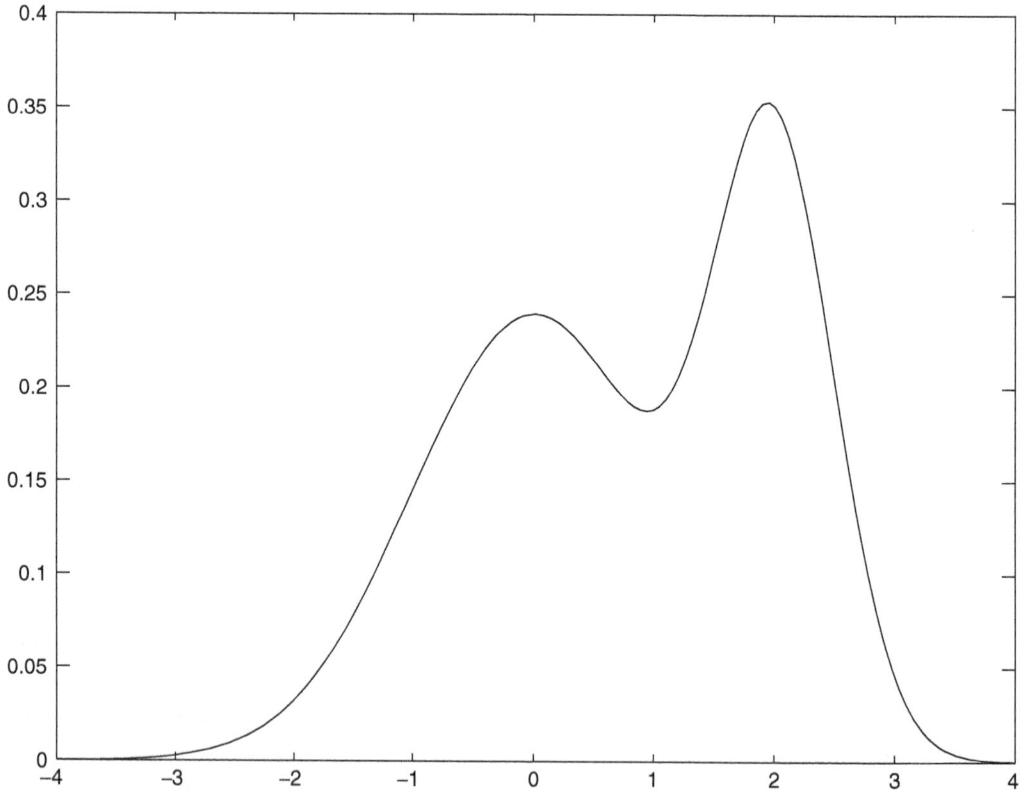

Figure 5.1. A hypothetical posterior density.

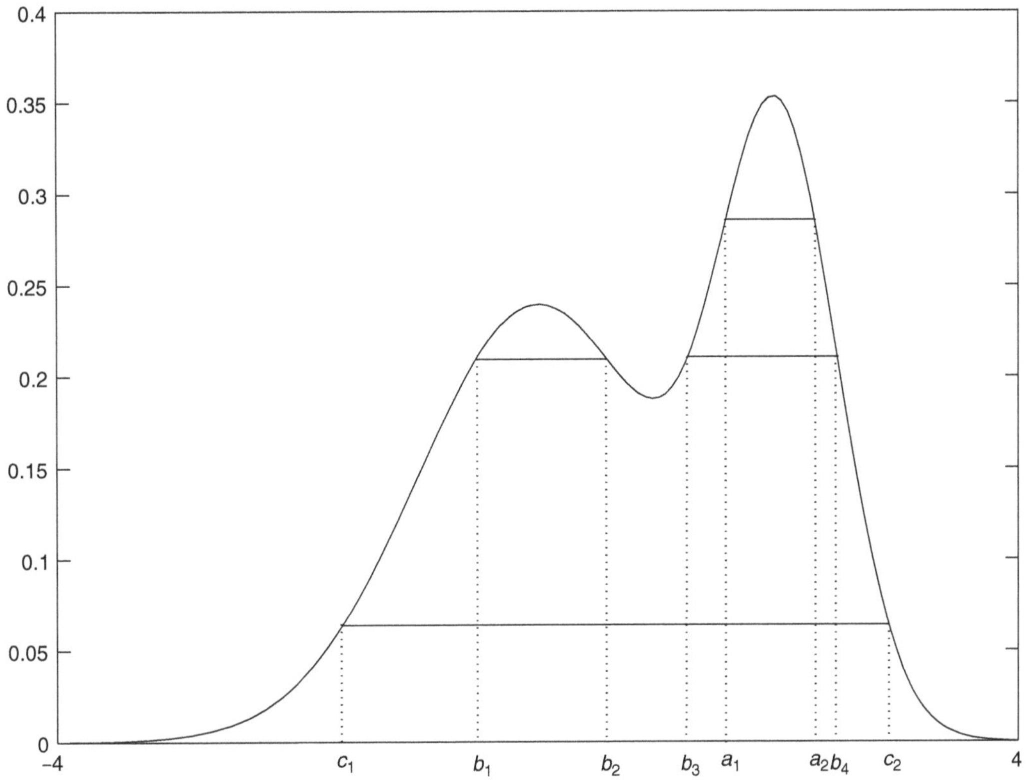

Figure 5.2. Three different HPD intervals.

Solution

In Figure 5.2, we present three different HPD intervals associated with the posterior in Figure 5.1. The highest line in the figure produces the interval $[a_1, a_2]$. This interval is narrow and contains a rather low posterior probability. If this process is repeated a second time the horizontal line produces the disjoint intervals $[b_1, b_2]$ and $[b_3, b_4]$, which contain more posterior probability, but still relatively little. If these two intervals, however, contain the desired posterior probability, then the process stops and the HPD region consists of the union of these two disjoint intervals. If a higher posterior content is desired, the process repeats again until, say, the third horizontal line that produces the interval $[c_1, c_2]$. If even more posterior content is desired, the process can be repeated again.

Exercise 5.2 (Calculating a posterior interval probability) Consider a random sample of size $T = 2$ from an exponential distribution with mean θ^{-1} and a gamma prior distribution $G(\underline{\alpha}, \underline{\beta})$ with $\underline{\alpha} = 2$ and $\underline{\beta} = 4$. Suppose the resulting sample mean is $\overline{y} = .125$. Find the posterior probability of the credible interval $[3.49, 15.5]$.

Solution

From Exercise 2.10 it follows that the posterior distribution of θ is $G(\overline{\alpha},\overline{\beta})$, where $\overline{\alpha} = 2+2 = 4$ and $\overline{\beta} = [4^{-1}+2(.125)]^{-1} = 2$. $\overline{\beta} = 2$ implies that the gamma distribution reduces to a chi-square distribution with eight degrees of freedom (see Poirier 1995, p. 100). Consulting a standard chi-square table (e.g., Poirier 1995, p. 662), we see that $\Pr(\chi^2(8) \leq 3.49) = .10$ and $\Pr(\chi^2(8) \leq 15.5) = .95$. Therefore, the posterior probability of $[3.49, 15.5]$ is $.95 - .10 = .85$.

Exercise 5.3 (HPD intervals under normal random sampling with known variance) Consider a random sample $Y_1, Y_2, \ldots, Y_T$ from an $N(\theta_1, \theta_2^{-1})$ distribution with *known* variance θ_2^{-1} and an $N(\underline{\mu}, \theta_2^{-1}/\underline{T})$ prior for the unknown mean θ_1.
(a) Find the $1-\alpha$ HPD interval for θ_1.
(b) Suppose $\alpha = .05$, $\theta_2 = .01$, $\underline{\mu} = 8$, $\underline{T} = 5$, $T = 25$, and $\overline{y} = 2$. Find the $1-\alpha$ HPD interval for θ_1.
(c) Consider the limiting prior as $\underline{T} \to 0$ in Exercise 4.6. Find the $1-\alpha$ HPD interval for θ_1.
(d) Suppose $\alpha = .05$, $\theta_2 = .01$, $T = 25$, and $\overline{y} = 2$. Find a 95% *confidence* interval and interpret your result.

Solution

(a) From Exercise 2.6(b) it follows that the posterior density for θ_1 is

$$p(\theta_1|y) = \phi(\theta_1; \overline{\mu}, \theta_2^{-1}/\overline{T}),$$

where $\overline{T}$ and $\overline{\mu}$ are given by (2.38) and (2.39), respectively. Since the posterior density is symmetric and unimodal with mode $\overline{\mu}$, the resulting HPD interval of content $1-\alpha$ cuts off equal probability $\alpha/2$ in each tail. Thus, a $1-\alpha$ HPD interval for θ_1 is

$$\overline{\mu} - z_{\alpha/2}(\theta_2^{-1}/\overline{T})^{1/2} < \theta_1 < \overline{\mu} + z_{\alpha/2}(\theta_2^{-1}/\overline{T})^{1/2}, \tag{5.2}$$

where $z_{\alpha/2}$ is the standard normal critical value that cuts off $\alpha/2$ probability in the right-hand tail. From the standpoint of subjective probability, (5.2) implies that the *posterior probability* of θ_1 lying between $\overline{\mu} \pm z_{\alpha/2}(\theta_2^{-1}/\overline{T})^{1/2}$ is .95.
(b) The given values correspond to an $N(8, 20)$ prior distribution for θ_1. Using a standard normal table, it follows that $z_{\alpha/2} = 1.96$. Plugging into (2.38) and (2.39) we obtain $\overline{T} = \underline{T} + T = 5 + 25 = 30$ and $\overline{\mu} = (\underline{T}\underline{\mu} + T\overline{y})/\overline{T} = [5(8) + 25(2)]/30 = 3$. Also note that $\theta_2^{-1}/\overline{T} = 100/30 = 10/3$. Hence, the posterior distribution for θ_1 is $N(3, 10/3)$ and (5.2) implies the .95 HPD interval $3 \pm 1.96(10/3)^{1/2}$ or $-.58 < \theta_1 < 6.58$.
(c) From Exercise 2.6 it is seen that the posterior hyperparameters simplify to $\overline{\mu} = \overline{y}$ and $\overline{T} = T$. Therefore, the HPD interval (5.2) reduces to

$$\overline{y} - z_{\alpha/2}(\theta_2^{-1}/T)^{1/2} < \theta_1 < \overline{y} + z_{\alpha/2}(\theta_2^{-1}/T)^{1/2}, \tag{5.3}$$

which is numerically identical to the standard non-Bayesian confidence interval. The interpretation of (5.3) is, however, in terms of "probability" and not "confidence": Given $\overline{Y} = \overline{y}$, the *ex post* probability of θ_1 falling in (5.3) is .95. The common misinterpretation of a classical confidence interval in terms of final precision is fortuitously correct in this special case.
(d) Plugging into (5.3) implies the .95 confidence interval

$$2 \pm 1.96(100/25)^{1/2} \quad \text{or} \quad -1.92 < \theta < 5.92.$$

The interpretation of this confidence interval is that it is a realization of a procedure that, upon repeated sampling, yields random intervals $[\overline{Y} - 3.92, \overline{Y} + 3.92]$ that have an *ex ante* sampling probability of .95 of capturing θ_1. The realized interval $-1.92 < \theta < 5.92$ either does or does not capture the unknown constant θ_1. The frequentist "confidence" lies in the procedure used to obtain the realized interval.

Exercise 5.4 (HPD intervals under normal random sampling with unknown variance) Consider Exercise 5.3 but with θ_2 *unknown*. Suppose the joint prior distribution for $\theta = [\theta_1\ \theta_2]'$ is the normal-gamma distribution, denoted $\theta \sim NG(\underline{\mu}, \underline{q}, \underline{s}^{-2}, \underline{\nu})$, with the density given in (2.26).
(a) Find the $1 - \alpha$ HPD interval for θ_1.
(b) Suppose $\underline{\mu} = 8$, $\underline{q} = .20$, $\underline{s}^{-2} = .25$, and $\underline{\nu} = 4$. Find the marginal prior density for θ_1.
(c) Suppose $\alpha = .05$, $T = 25$, $\overline{y} = 2$, and $s^2 = 102.5$. Find the $1 - \alpha$ HPD interval for θ_1.
(d) Using the values in (c), find the $1 - \alpha$ HPD interval for θ_2.

Solution
(a) The posterior distribution for θ is $NG(\overline{\mu}, \overline{q}, \overline{s}^{-2}, \overline{\nu})$, as given in the solution to Exercise 2.4. By using the solution to Exercise 2.8, it follows immediately that the marginal posterior distribution of θ_1 is $t(\theta_1; \overline{\mu}, \overline{s}^2\overline{q}, \overline{\nu})$. Hence, analogous to (5.2), a $1 - \alpha$ HPD interval for θ_1 is

$$\overline{\mu} - t_{\overline{\nu},\alpha/2}(\overline{s}^2\overline{q})^{1/2} < \theta_1 < \overline{\mu} + t_{\overline{\nu},\alpha/2}(\overline{s}^2\overline{q})^{1/2}, \tag{5.4}$$

where $t_{\overline{\nu},\alpha/2}$ cuts off $\alpha/2$ probability in the right-hand tail of a Student t distribution with $\overline{\nu}$ degrees of freedom. From the standpoint of subjective probability, (5.4) implies that the *posterior probability* of θ_1 lying between $\overline{\mu} \pm t_{\overline{\nu},\alpha/2}(\overline{s}^2\overline{q})^{1/2}$ is $1 - \alpha$.
(b) Again using the solution to Exercise 2.8, the given hyperparameter values imply that the marginal prior distribution for θ_1 is $t(\theta_1; 8, 0.8, 4)$.
(c) Plugging the given hyperparameter values into (2.28) and (2.30)–(2.32), we obtain

$$\begin{aligned}
\overline{\nu} &= 4 + 25 = 29, \\
\overline{q} &= [.20^{-1} + 25]^{-1} = 1/30, \\
\overline{\mu} &= [(.20)^{-1}(8) + (25)(2)]/30 = 3,
\end{aligned}$$

Table 5.1: Pdf and cdf values of a $\gamma(.011, 29)$ random variable.

θ_2	pdf	cdf
.00200	.0018	.0000
.00270	.0405	.0000
.00300	.1136	.0000
.00390	1.212	.0005
.00550	15.55	.0106
.005736	**20.15**	**.0148**
.00600	26.21	.0209
.00800	93.59	.1368
.00900	124.4	.2468
.01030	140.9	.4225
.01080	139.1	.4927
.01300	96.14	.7586
.01500	48.75	.9015
.01666	23.02	.9591
.01693	**20.15**	**.9648**
.01720	17.50	.9700
.02000	3.466	.9948
.02160	1.213	.9983
.02620	.0405	.9999

and

$$\overline{s}^2 = 29^{-1}[4(.25)^{-1} + 24(102.5) + (.20 + 25^{-1})^{-1}(2 - 8)^2] = 90.55.$$

Hence, the posterior distribution for θ_1 is $t(\theta_1; 3, 3.02, 29)$. Using a t table gives $t_{29}(.975) = 2.045$. Therefore, (5.4) implies the .95 HPD interval

$$3 \pm 2.045[3.02]^{1/2} \quad \text{or} \quad -.55 < \theta_1 < 6.55,$$

similar to the solution of Exercise 5.3(b).
(d) From the definition of the normal-gamma distribution, the marginal posterior distribution for the precision θ_2 is $\gamma(\overline{s}^{-2}, \overline{\nu}) = \gamma(.011, 29)$. Table 5.1 provides values of the pdf and cdf of a $\gamma(.011, 29)$ distribution. From inspection we see that the interval $[a, b]$ with equal pdf ordinates and that contains .95 posterior probability is $[.005736, .1693]$.

Exercise 5.5 (Berger and Wolpert 1988, pp. 5–6) To further clarify the difference between a Bayesian posterior interval and a confidence interval, consider the following. Given an unknown parameter θ, $-\infty < \theta < \infty$, suppose Y_i $(i = 1, 2)$ are iid binary random variables with probabilities of occurrence equally distributed over points of support $\theta - 1$ and $\theta + 1$. That is, $\Pr(Y_i = \theta - 1|\theta) = 1/2$ and $\Pr(Y_i = \theta + 1|\theta) = 1/2$.

Suppose the prior for θ is constant. Such an "improper" prior will be discussed in Chapter 8.

(a) Suppose we observe $y_1 \neq y_2$. Find the posterior distribution of θ.
(b) Suppose we observe $y_1 = y_2$. Find the posterior distribution of θ.
(c) Consider

$$\widehat{\theta} = \begin{cases} (1/2)(Y_1 + Y_2) & \text{if } Y_1 \neq Y_2, \\ Y_1 - 1 & \text{if } Y_1 = Y_2. \end{cases} \tag{5.5}$$

In repeated sampling, what is the *ex ante* probability that (5.5) contains θ? Note that the answer is the same if the second line of (5.5) is changed to $Y_1 + 1$ if $Y_1 = Y_2$.

Solution

(a) If $y_1 \neq y_2$, then one of the values must equal $\theta - 1$ and the other equals $\theta + 1$. *Ex post*, averaging these two values it is *absolutely certain* that $\theta = (1/2)(y_1 + y_2)$; that is, $\Pr[\theta = (1/2)(y_1 + y_2)|y_1, y_2] = 1$.
(b) If $y_1 = y_2 = y$, say, then the common value y is either $\theta - 1$ or $\theta + 1$. Since the prior does not distinguish among values of θ, *ex post*, it is *equally uncertain* whether $\theta = y - 1$ or $\theta = y + 1$; that is, $\Pr(\theta = y - 1|y_1, y_2) = \Pr(\theta = y + 1|y_1, y_2) = 1/2$.
(c) Parts (a) and (b) suggest the *ex post* (i.e., posterior) probability that (5.5) equals θ is either 1 or 1/2, depending on whether $y_1 \neq y_2$ or $y_1 = y_2$. Given the data, we can, of course, determine which posterior probability applies. From the *ex ante* perspective, however, $\Pr(Y_1 \neq Y_2) = \Pr(Y_1 = Y_2) = 1/2$. Therefore, *ex ante*, the probability that (5.5) contains θ is an equally weighted average of our two *ex post* coverage probabilities, and thus the *ex ante* sampling probability of (5.5) containing θ is $(1/2)(1)+(1/2)(1/2) = .75$. The embarrassing question for the pure frequentist is this: Why use the realized value of (5.5) to estimate θ and then report the *ex ante* confidence level 75% instead of the appropriate *ex post* measure of uncertainty?

Exercise 5.6 (Exercise 5.5 extended) Suppose Y is a Bernoulli random variable with pmf $\text{Prob}\,(Y = \theta - 1|\theta) = \text{Prob}\,(Y = \theta + 1|\theta) = .50$ and $\theta \in \mathbb{R}$. Suppose the prior distribution is $\theta \sim N\,(2, 1)$ with prior density $\phi\,(\cdot)$. Given one observation $Y = y$, find the posterior distribution of θ.

Solution

If $y = \theta - 1$, then $\theta = y + 1$ and

$$p\,(\theta|y) \propto p\,(\theta)\,L\,(\theta; y) \propto \phi\,(\theta|2, 1)\,\frac{1}{2} \propto \phi\,(y + 1|2, 1) \propto \phi\,(y - 1)\,.$$

If $y = \theta + 1$, then $\theta = y - 1$ and

$$p\,(\theta|y) \propto p\,(\theta)\,L\,(\theta; y) \propto \phi\,(\theta|2, 1)\,\frac{1}{2} \propto \phi\,(y - 1|2, 1) \propto \phi\,(y - 3)\,.$$

Therefore,

$$p(\theta|y) = \begin{cases} \dfrac{\phi(y-3)}{\phi(y-3)+\phi(y-1)} & \text{if } \theta = y-1, \\[2ex] \dfrac{\phi(y-1)}{\phi(y-3)+\phi(y-1)} & \text{if } \theta = y+1. \end{cases}$$

Exercise 5.7 (Conditional frequentist reasoning and ancillarity) The preceding exercise demonstrates the important difference between frequentist *ex ante* and Bayesian *ex post* reasoning. The latter is consistent with the likelihood principle (see Berger and Wolpert 1988), which, loosely speaking, states that two experiments involving the same unknown parameter θ that give rise to proportional likelihood functions contain the same evidence about θ. Likelihood principle proponents condition on all the data, whereas pure frequentist reasoning averages unconditionally over all the data that could have possibly been observed. *Conditional frequentists* lie somewhere between likelihood principle proponents and pure frequentists, arguing that inference should be conditional on ancillary statistics (statistics whose distribution does not depend on θ), but otherwise be unconditional. Conditional inference goes a long way toward eliminating some of the embarrassing problems in the pure frequentist approach. Demonstrate this observation using the design of Exercise 5.5 in terms of the statistic $Z = |Y_1 - Y_2|$.

Solution

First, note that Z is ancillary since its pmf is $\Pr(Z = 0) = \Pr(Z = 2) = 1/2$, which does not depend on θ. The coverage probabilities of (5.5), conditioned on Z, are the appealing *ex post* probabilities of .5 and 1, respectively, for $Z = 0$ and $Z = 2$. Therefore, the conditional frequentist inference in this case is identical to the Bayesian posterior probabilities.

Exercise 5.8 (HPD intervals and reparameterization) Given the likelihood $L(\theta)$ and the prior pdf $p(\theta)$, let $\gamma = g(\theta)$ be a one-to-one transformation of θ. Also, let A be a $1-\alpha$ HPD region for θ and define $B = \{\gamma : \gamma = g(\theta), \theta \in A\}$. Is B a $1-\alpha$ HPD region for γ?

Solution

No. Although condition (a) in Definition 5.1 holds, condition (b) does not. To see this consider the following. The fact that A is a $1-\alpha$ HPD interval for θ implies that if $\theta_1 \in A$ and $\theta_2 \notin A$, then $p(\theta_1|y) \geq p(\theta_2|y)$. By definition of B, $\gamma_1 \in B$ iff $\theta = g^{-1}(\gamma_1) \in A$. Suppose $\gamma_1 \in B$, and $\gamma_2 \notin B$. By a change of variables,

$$p(\gamma_1|y) = \left|\frac{\partial g^{-1}(\gamma_1)}{\partial \gamma}\right| p_{\theta|y}[g^{-1}(\gamma_1)],$$

$$p(\gamma_2|y) = \left|\frac{\partial g^{-1}(\gamma_2)}{\partial \gamma}\right| p_{\theta|y}[g^{-1}(\gamma_2)],$$

$\gamma_2 \notin B$ iff $\theta_2 = g^{-1}(\gamma_2) \notin A$. Therefore, although $p_{\theta|y}[g^{-1}(\gamma_1)] \geq p_{\theta|y}[g^{-1}(\gamma_2)]$, the Jacobian terms cannot be ordered. In other words, the posterior probability content is maintained under reparameterization, but the minimal length is not.

Exercise 5.9 (*Ex ante* versus *ex post* interpretation: Case I) Suppose X_1 and X_2 are two independent draws from a uniform distribution on the interval $\left(\theta - \frac{1}{2}, \theta + \frac{1}{2}\right)$. Let $Y_1 = \min\{X_1, X_2\}$ and $Y_2 = \max\{X_1, X_2\}$.
(a) Show that a 50% confidence interval for θ is given by $y_1 < \theta < y_2$.
(b) Suppose $y_2 - y_1 > \frac{1}{2}$. What further can you say about the confidence interval in (a)? Explain.

Solution
(a)

$$\begin{aligned}
\text{Prob}\,(Y_1 < \theta < Y_2) &= \text{Prob}\,(X_1 < \theta < X_2) + \text{Prob}\,(X_2 < \theta < X_1) \\
&= \text{Prob}\,(X_1 < \theta \text{ and } X_2 > \theta) + \text{Prob}\,(X_2 < \theta \text{ and } X_1 > \theta) \\
&= \text{Prob}\,(X_1 < \theta) \cdot \text{Prob}\,(X_2 > \theta) + \text{Prob}\,(X_2 < \theta) \cdot \text{Prob}\,(X_1 > \theta) \\
&= \left(\frac{1}{2}\right)\left(\frac{1}{2}\right) + \left(\frac{1}{2}\right)\left(\frac{1}{2}\right) = \frac{1}{2}.
\end{aligned}$$

Therefore, the interval $(y_1 < \theta < y_2)$ has 50% confidence.
(b) Clearly, $y_1 \geq \theta - \frac{1}{2}$ and $y_2 \leq \theta + \frac{1}{2}$. Therefore, we know with certainty that

$$y_2 - \frac{1}{2} \leq \theta \leq y_1 + \frac{1}{2}. \tag{5.6}$$

If $y_2 - y_1 \geq \frac{1}{2}$, then $y_1 \leq y_2 - \frac{1}{2}$ and (5.6) implies $y_1 < \theta$. Furthermore, because $y_1 + \frac{1}{2} \leq y_2$, this also implies $\theta < y_2$. Therefore, if $y_2 - y_1 > \frac{1}{2}$, then $y_1 < \theta < y_2$ with certainty, although we only assign it 50% confidence. "Confidence" is an *ex ante* concept which may not be a good indicator of what we know *ex post*.

Exercise 5.10 (*Ex ante* versus *ex post* interpretation: Case II) Let Y_t $(t = 1, 2, \ldots, T)$ be *iid* $N(\theta, \sigma^2)$, and let θ have an $N(\underline{\mu}, \underline{h}^{-1})$ prior where σ^2, $\underline{\mu}$, and $\underline{h}$ are all known. In particular, suppose $\underline{\mu} = 0$, $\underline{h} = .44h$, $h = T/\sigma^2 = 1$, and $\bar{y} = 1.44$.
(a) Give a 95% HPD interval for θ.
(b) Suppose $\theta = -3$. What is the *ex ante* coverage probability of the procedure you used to construct your interval in (a)?

Solution
(a) By Exercise 2.3, the posterior distribution is $\theta|y \sim N(\bar{\mu}, \bar{h}^{-1})$, where $\bar{\mu}$ and $\bar{h}$ are given by (2.14) and (2.15), respectively. Specifically, $\bar{\mu} = \bar{y}/1.44 = 1$ and $\bar{h} = 1.44$. A 95% HPD interval for θ is

$$P_{\theta|y}\left(\bar{\mu} - 1.96\bar{h}^{-\frac{1}{2}} < \theta < \bar{\mu} + 1.96\bar{h}^{-\frac{1}{2}}\right) = P_{\theta|y}\left(-.63 < \theta < 2.63\right) = .95.$$

(b) Remember, $h = 1$ and $\bar{h} = 1.44$. Viewed *ex ante*, $\bar{\mu} = \bar{Y}/1.44$. We know the sampling distributions $\bar{Y}|\theta \sim N(\theta, 1)$ and $\left(\bar{Y} - \theta\right)|\theta \sim N(0, 1)$. Thus,

$$\begin{aligned}
&\text{Prob}_{\bar{Y}|\theta}\left(\bar{\mu} - 1.96\bar{h}^{-\frac{1}{2}} < \theta < \bar{\mu} + 1.96\bar{h}^{-\frac{1}{2}}\right) \\
&= \text{Prob}_{\bar{Y}|\theta}\left(\frac{\bar{Y}}{1.44} - \frac{1.96}{1.2} < \theta < \frac{\bar{Y}}{1.44} + \frac{1.96}{1.2}\right) \\
&= \text{Prob}_{\bar{Y}|\theta}\left(\bar{Y} - (1.2)(1.96) < 1.44\theta < \bar{Y} + (1.2)(1.96)\right) \\
&= \text{Prob}_{\bar{Y}|\theta}\left(-1.44\theta - 2.352 < -\bar{Y} < -1.44\theta + 2.352\right) \\
&= \text{Prob}_{\bar{Y}|\theta}\left(1.44\theta - 2.352 < \bar{Y} < 1.44\theta + 2.352\right) \\
&= \text{Prob}_{\bar{Y}|\theta}\left(.44\theta - 2.352 < \bar{Y} - \theta < .44\theta + 2.352\right) \\
&= \Phi\left(.44\theta + 2.352\right) - \Phi\left(.44\theta - 2.352\right) \\
&= \Phi\left(1.035\right) - \Phi\left(-3.672\right) \\
&\approx .8485.
\end{aligned}$$

6

Hypothesis Testing

Suppose the relevant *decision space* is $D = \{d_1, d_2\}$, where d_j denotes choice of hypothesis H_j $(j = 1, 2)$. Let the unsubscripted "d" denote a generic decision (i.e., either d_1 or d_2). Extensions to cases involving more than two hypotheses are straightforward. Let $C(d; \theta) \geq 0$ denote the relevant loss function describing the consequences of decision d when the unknown state of nature is θ. From the subjectivist perspective, $C(d; \theta)$ is random because uncertainty regarding θ is expressed by a distribution function.

As in the case of estimation, the optimal decision d_* in the hypothesis-testing context minimizes expected cost. After observing data y yielding likelihood $L(\theta)$, the relevant expression of uncertainty is the posterior distribution. Therefore, d_* is defined by

$$d_* = \underset{d}{\operatorname{argmin}} \left[c(d|y) \right], \tag{6.1}$$

where $c(d|y)$, the *posterior expected cost (loss) of taking decision* d, is

$$c(d|y) = E_{\theta|y}[C(d; \theta)] = E[C(d; \theta)|y]. \tag{6.2}$$

From the Bayesian perspective, a hypothesis is of interest only if the prior distribution assigns it positive probability. Therefore, assume

$$\underline{\pi}_j = \Pr(H_j) = \Pr(\theta \in \Theta_j) > 0, \; j = 1, 2, \tag{6.3}$$

with $\underline{\pi}_1 + \underline{\pi}_2 = 1$. The prior probability function, density/(mass function), can be decomposed as

$$p(\theta) = \begin{cases} \underline{\pi}_1 p(\theta|H_1) & \text{if } \theta \in \Theta_1, \\ \underline{\pi}_2 p(\theta|H_2) & \text{if } \theta \in \Theta_2, \end{cases} \tag{6.4}$$

where $p(\theta|H_j)$ is the prior probability function under H_j $(j = 1, 2)$.

Under H_j, the probability function of the data, marginal of all parameters (known as the marginal likelihood), is

$$p(y|H_j) = \int_{\Theta_j} L(\theta) dP(\theta|H_j) = E_{\theta|H_j}[L(\theta)], \quad j = 1, 2. \tag{6.5}$$

From Bayes' theorem it follows immediately that the posterior probability of H_j is

$$\overline{\pi}_j = \Pr(H_j|y) = \frac{\underline{\pi}_j p(y|H_j)}{p(y)}, \quad j = 1, 2, \tag{6.6}$$

where the marginal probability function of the data (marginal of *both* parameters and hypotheses) is

$$p(y) = \underline{\pi}_1 p(y|H_1) + \underline{\pi}_2 p(y|H_2), \tag{6.7}$$

noting, of course, that $\overline{\pi}_1 + \overline{\pi}_2 = 1$.

With these preliminaries out of the way, we can now derive the posterior distribution for θ to be used in (6.2). Under H_j, the posterior probability function of θ is (according to Bayes' theorem)

$$p(\theta|y, H_j) = \frac{p(\theta|H_j) L(\theta)}{p(y|H_j)}, \quad \theta \in \Theta_j, \quad j = 1, 2. \tag{6.8}$$

Using the posterior probabilities (6.6), the marginal posterior probability function of θ is

$$p(\theta|y) = \begin{cases} \overline{\pi}_1 p(\theta|y, H_1) & \text{if } \theta \in \Theta_1, \\ \overline{\pi}_2 p(\theta|y, H_2) & \text{if } \theta \in \Theta_2. \end{cases} \tag{6.9}$$

Using (6.9) and defining the *expected posterior loss of decision* d *given* H_j as

$$c(\mathrm{d}|y, H_j) = E_{\theta|y,H_j}[C(\mathrm{d}; \theta)], \quad j = 1, 2, \tag{6.10}$$

we can write the posterior expected loss (6.2) as

$$c(\mathrm{d}|y) = \overline{\pi}_1 c(\mathrm{d}|y, H_1) + \overline{\pi}_2 c(\mathrm{d}|y, H_2). \tag{6.11}$$

Without loss of generality, assume that the correct decisions yield zero loss:

$$C(\mathrm{d}_1; \theta) = 0 \text{ if } \theta \in \Theta_1, \tag{6.12}$$
$$C(\mathrm{d}_2; \theta) = 0 \text{ if } \theta \in \Theta_2. \tag{6.13}$$

Under (6.12) and (6.13), it follows from (6.11) that

$$c(\mathrm{d}_1|y) = \overline{\pi}_2 c(\mathrm{d}_1|y, H_2), \tag{6.14}$$
$$c(\mathrm{d}_2|y) = \overline{\pi}_1 c(\mathrm{d}_2|y, H_1). \tag{6.15}$$

Therefore, it is optimal to choose H_2, i.e., $c(\mathrm{d}_2|y) < c(\mathrm{d}_1|y)$, denoted $\mathrm{d}_* = \mathrm{d}_2$, iff

$$\frac{\overline{\pi}_2}{\overline{\pi}_1} > \frac{c(\mathrm{d}_2|y, H_1)}{c(\mathrm{d}_1|y, H_2)}. \tag{6.16}$$

Because $\overline{\pi}_2 = 1 - \overline{\pi}_1$, (6.16) can also be written as

$$\mathrm{d}_* = \mathrm{d}_2 \text{ iff } \overline{\pi}_1 < \left[1 + \frac{c(\mathrm{d}_2|y, H_1)}{c(\mathrm{d}_1|y, H_2)}\right]^{-1}. \tag{6.17}$$

The quantities $\underline{\pi}_2/\underline{\pi}_1$ and $\overline{\pi}_2/\overline{\pi}_1$ are the *prior odds* and *posterior odds*, respectively, of H_2 versus H_1. From (6.6) it follows immediately that these two odds are related by

$$\frac{\overline{\pi}_2}{\overline{\pi}_1} = B_{21}\left(\frac{\underline{\pi}_2}{\underline{\pi}_1}\right), \tag{6.18}$$

where

$$B_{21} = \frac{p(y|H_2)}{p(y|H_1)} \tag{6.19}$$

is known as the *Bayes factor for* H_2 *versus* H_1. The Bayes factor (6.19) is a ratio of marginal likelihoods – see Equation (6.5). Also note that (6.18) implies that the posterior probabilities are related to prior odds by

$$\overline{\pi}_1 = \left[1 + B_{21}\left(\frac{\underline{\pi}_2}{\underline{\pi}_1}\right)\right]^{-1} \tag{6.20}$$

and

$$\overline{\pi}_2 = \left[1 + B_{12}\left(\frac{\underline{\pi}_1}{\underline{\pi}_2}\right)\right]^{-1}, \tag{6.21}$$

where $B_{12} = B_{21}^{-1}$. Finally, substituting (6.18) into (6.16) and rearranging yields

$$\mathrm{d}_* = \mathrm{d}_2 \text{ iff } B_{21} \geq \left[\frac{c(\mathrm{d}_2|y, H_1)}{c(\mathrm{d}_1|y, H_2)}\right]\left[\frac{\underline{\pi}_1}{\underline{\pi}_2}\right]. \tag{6.22}$$

In general, the expected posterior loss $c(\mathrm{d}|y, H_j)$ defined by (6.10) depends on the data y, and hence the Bayes factors (6.19) do not serve as complete data summaries. In other words, because the right-hand side of the inequality in (6.22) depends on the data, it cannot be interpreted as a "critical value" analogous to those that appear in frequentist testing. One exception is when both hypotheses are simple (see Exercise 6.1). The following shows another exception.

Suppose the loss resulting from decision d_i when $\theta \in \Theta_j$, $i \neq j$, is constant for all $\theta \in \Theta_j$:

$$C(\mathrm{d}_1; \theta) = \overline{C}_1 \text{ for all } \theta \in \Theta_2 \tag{6.23}$$

and

$$C(\mathrm{d}_2; \theta) = \overline{C}_2 \text{ for all } \theta \in \Theta_1, \tag{6.24}$$

where $\overline{C}_1$ and $\overline{C}_2$ are given constants. Under (6.23) and (6.24), the expected posterior losses (6.10) depend neither on the data nor on the prior for θ:

$$\begin{aligned} c(\mathrm{d}_i|y, H_j) &= E_{\theta|y,H_j}[C(\mathrm{d};\theta)] \\ &= \int_{\Theta_j} \overline{C}_i p(\theta|y, H_j) d\theta = \overline{C}_i \text{ for } i \neq j. \end{aligned} \tag{6.25}$$

Therefore, decision rule (6.22) reduces to

$$\mathrm{d}_* = \mathrm{d}_2 \text{ iff } B_{21} > \frac{\underline{\pi}_1 \overline{C}_2}{\underline{\pi}_2 \overline{C}_1}. \tag{6.26}$$

The right-hand side of the inequality in (6.26) is a known constant that serves as a *Bayesian critical value*.

How reasonable is the loss structure of (6.23) and (6.24)? Although it holds trivially when both hypotheses are simple, in the case of composite hypotheses its appropriateness is suspect. For example, when testing $H_1 : \theta = 0$ versus $H_2 : \theta > 0$, should not the loss associated with d_1 depend on how far θ under H_2 deviates from $\theta = 0$? Kadane and Dickey (1980) argue in the affirmative.

Exercise 6.1 (Two simple hypotheses and general likelihood) Suppose H_1 and H_2 are both simple hypotheses, with $\Theta_j = \{\theta_j\}$, $j = 1, 2$, so that the prior probability function (6.4) reduces to the simple two-point mass function

$$p(\theta) = \begin{cases} \underline{\pi}_1 & \text{if } \theta = \theta_1, \\ \underline{\pi}_2 & \text{if } \theta = \theta_2. \end{cases} \tag{6.27}$$

Consider data y yielding likelihood $L(\theta)$. Under what conditions is it optimal to reject H_1?

Solution

The posterior probability function (6.9) reduces to the two-point mass function

$$p(\theta|y) = \begin{cases} \overline{\pi}_1 & \text{if } \theta = \theta_1, \\ \overline{\pi}_2 & \text{if } \theta = \theta_2, \end{cases} \tag{6.28}$$

where the posterior probabilities of each hypothesis, see Equation (6.6), are simply

$$\overline{\pi}_j = \frac{\underline{\pi}_j L(\theta_j)}{p(y)}, \quad j = 1, 2, \tag{6.29}$$

and the marginal pdf (6.7) of the data is

$$p(y) = \underline{\pi}_1 L(\theta_1) + \underline{\pi}_2 L(\theta_2). \tag{6.30}$$

Also note that the Bayes factor (6.19) reduces to the simple likelihood ratio

$$B_{21} = \frac{L(\theta_2)}{L(\theta_1)}. \tag{6.31}$$

In the case of simple hypotheses,

$$c(\mathrm{d}_1|y, H_2) = C(\mathrm{d}_1; \theta_2), \tag{6.32}$$

$$c(\mathrm{d}_2|y, H_1) = C(\mathrm{d}_2; \theta_1). \tag{6.33}$$

Therefore, from (6.22) and (6.31)–(6.33) it follows that

$$\mathrm{d}_* = \mathrm{d}_2 \text{ iff } \frac{L(\theta_2)}{L(\theta_1)} > \left[\frac{C(\mathrm{d}_2; \theta_1)}{C(\mathrm{d}_1; \theta_2)}\right] \left[\frac{\underline{\pi}_1}{\underline{\pi}_2}\right]. \tag{6.34}$$

In other words, choose d_2 iff the likelihood ratio of H_2 versus H_1 is greater than the ratio of the prior expected loss from choosing d_2 relative to the prior expected loss from choosing d_1.

Exercise 6.2 (Two simple hypotheses and normal likelihoods) Suppose a random sample $Y_1, Y_2, \ldots, Y_T$ is available from an $N(\theta, \sigma^2)$ population in which θ is unknown and σ^2 is *known*. Consider Exercise 6.1 where it is desired to test the simple hypothesis $H_1 : \theta = \theta_1$ versus the simple hypothesis $H_2 : \theta = \theta_2$ with $\theta_1 < \theta_2$. Compute (6.34) and simplify your answer.

Solution

Analogous to (2.20) and (2.21), factor the likelihood as

$$L(\theta) = c_1 \phi(\overline{y}|\theta, h^{-1}), \tag{6.35}$$

where $c_1 = (2\pi\sigma^2)^{-(\nu/2)} T^{-(1/2)} \exp(-\nu s^2/[2\sigma^2])$, $h = T/\sigma^2$, and $\nu s^2 = \sum_{t=1}^{T}(y_t - \overline{y})^2$. Because c_1 does not depend on the unknown θ, (6.35) shows that the sample mean $\overline{y}$ is a sufficient statistic for θ. According to the likelihood principle (see Chapter 2), no information is lost by ignoring c_1 and merely considering the second factor. Similarly, we can work with $c(d|\overline{y}, H_j)$ instead of $c(d|y, H_j)$. The Bayes factor for H_2 versus H_1 is

$$\begin{aligned} B_{21} &= \frac{L(\theta_2)}{L(\theta_1)} \\ &= \frac{(2\pi\sigma^2/T)^{(-1/2)} \exp[-T(\overline{y} - \theta_2)^2/2\sigma^2]}{(2\pi\sigma^2/T)^{(-1/2)} \exp[-T(\overline{y} - \theta_1)^2/2\sigma^2]} \\ &= \exp\left(-\frac{1}{2} h[(\overline{y} - \theta_2)^2 - (\overline{y} - \theta_1)^2]\right) \\ &= \exp\left(\frac{1}{2} h[2\overline{y}(\theta_2 - \theta_1) + (\theta_1^2 - \theta_2^2)]\right). \end{aligned} \tag{6.36}$$

According to (6.34), H_1 should be rejected iff

$$\exp\left(\frac{1}{2} h[2\overline{y}(\theta_2 - \theta_1) + (\theta_1^2 - \theta_2^2)]\right) > \frac{\overline{C}_2 \underline{\pi}_1}{\overline{C}_1 \underline{\pi}_2},$$

or equivalently iff

$$\overline{y} > \frac{\theta_1 + \theta_2}{2} + [h(\theta_2 - \theta_1)]^{-1} \ln\left(\frac{\overline{C}_2 \underline{\pi}_1}{\overline{C}_1 \underline{\pi}_2}\right).$$

Exercise 6.3 (Two one-sided hypotheses and normal likelihoods) Consider $H_1 : \theta \leq \theta_*$ versus $H_2 : \theta > \theta_*$ with θ_* a given constant. In this situation, $\Theta_1 = \{\theta : \theta \leq \theta_*\}$ and $\Theta_2 = \{\theta : \theta > \theta_*\}$. A convenient prior distribution for θ is the split (or truncated) normal distribution

$$p(\theta|H_1) = [\Phi(\theta_*|\underline{\mu}_1, \underline{h}_1^{-1})]^{-1} \phi(\theta|\underline{\mu}_1, \underline{h}_1^{-1}), \quad \theta \in \Theta_1, \tag{6.37}$$

and

$$p(\theta|H_2) = [1 - \Phi(\theta_*|\underline{\mu}_2, \underline{h}_2^{-1})]^{-1} \phi(\theta|\underline{\mu}_2, \underline{h}_2^{-1}), \quad \theta \in \Theta_2. \tag{6.38}$$

Suppose a random sample $Y_1, Y_2, \ldots, Y_T$ is available from an $N(\theta, \sigma^2)$ population in which θ is unknown and σ^2 is *known*. Under what conditions is it optimal to reject H_1?

Solution

Analogous to (2.22), it is straightforward to show that

$$\phi(\theta|\underline{\mu}_j, \underline{h}_j^{-1}) L(\theta) = c_1 \phi(\theta|\overline{\mu}_j, \overline{h}_j^{-1}) \phi(\overline{y}|\underline{\mu}_j, \underline{h}_j^{-1} + h^{-1}), \quad j = 1, 2, \tag{6.39}$$

where

$$\overline{h}_j = \underline{h}_j + h, \quad h = T\sigma^{-2}, \tag{6.40}$$

and

$$\overline{\mu_j} = \frac{\underline{h}_j \underline{\mu}_j + h\overline{y}}{\overline{h}_j}. \tag{6.41}$$

From (6.37)–(6.39) it follows that

$$\begin{aligned} p(y|H_1) &= \int_{\Theta_1} p(\theta|H_1) L(\theta) d\theta \\ &= c_1 \left[\frac{\Phi(\theta_*|\overline{\mu}_1, \overline{h}_1^{-1})}{\Phi(\theta_*|\underline{\mu}_1, \underline{h}_1^{-1})}\right] \phi(\overline{y}|\underline{\mu}_1, \underline{h}_1^{-1} + h^{-1}) \end{aligned} \tag{6.42}$$

and

$$\begin{aligned} p(y|H_2) &= \int_{\Theta_2} p(\theta|H_2) L(\theta) d\theta \\ &= c_1 \left[\frac{1 - \Phi(\theta_*|\overline{\mu}_2, \overline{h}_2^{-1})}{1 - \Phi(\theta_*|\underline{\mu}_2, \underline{h}_2^{-1})}\right] \phi(\overline{y}|\underline{\mu}_2, \underline{h}_2^{-1} + h^{-1}). \end{aligned} \tag{6.43}$$

From (6.39) it also follows that the conditional posterior densities under each hypothesis are

$$p(\theta|y, H_1) = [\Phi(\theta_*|\overline{\mu}_1, \overline{h}_1^{-1})]^{-1}\phi(\theta|\overline{\mu}_1, \overline{h}_1^{-1}), \quad \theta \in \Theta_1, \tag{6.44}$$

and

$$p(\theta|y, H_2) = [1 - \Phi(\theta_*|\overline{\mu}_2, \overline{h}_2^{-1})]^{-1}\phi(\theta|\overline{\mu}_2, \overline{h}_2^{-1}), \quad \theta \in \Theta_2. \tag{6.45}$$

The hyperparameters $\overline{\mu}_j$ and $\overline{h}_j$ of conditional posterior densities (6.44) and (6.45) are updated – see Equations (6.40) and (6.41) – in the usual fashion from the prior hyperparameter values $\underline{\mu}_j$ and $\underline{h}_j$, $j = 1, 2$, because (6.37) and (6.38) form yet another conjugate prior for a random sample from an $N(\theta, \sigma^2)$ distribution with σ^2 known. The Bayes factor B_{21} for H_2 versus H_1 is simply the ratio of (6.43) to (6.42).

The unconstrained split-normal density implied by (6.37) and (6.38) is quite flexible but fairly "parameter-rich" – it requires specification of five hyperparameters: $\underline{\mu}_1$, $\underline{h}_1$, $\underline{\mu}_2$, $\underline{h}_2$, and $\underline{\pi}_1 = \Pr(H_1) = 1 - \underline{\pi}_2$. In the special case in which

$$\underline{\mu} = \underline{\mu}_1 = \underline{\mu}_2, \tag{6.46}$$

$$\underline{h} = \underline{h}_1 = \underline{h}_2, \tag{6.47}$$

$$\underline{\pi}_1 = \Phi\left(\theta_*|\underline{\mu}, \underline{h}^{-1}\right), \tag{6.48}$$

and

$$\underline{\pi}_2 = 1 - \Phi\left(\theta_*|\underline{\mu}, \underline{h}^{-1}\right), \tag{6.49}$$

$p(\theta) = \phi(\theta|\underline{\mu}, \underline{h}^{-1})$, as in the familiar normal estimation problem. The case in which (6.46) holds with

$$\underline{\mu} = \theta_* \tag{6.50}$$

is often attractive. Prior specification (6.37) and (6.38) with all of (6.46)–(6.49) holding, i.e., $p(\theta) = \phi(\theta|\theta_*, \underline{h}^{-1})$, is attractive in many settings and requires elicitation of only $\underline{h}$. Restrictions (6.46)–(6.49) impose continuity on the prior $p(\theta)$ and reduce the number of hyperparameters to be specified to two ($\underline{\mu}$ and $\underline{h}$). Under (6.46)–(6.49), the Bayes factor of H_2 versus H_1 simplifies to

$$B_{21} = \left[\frac{1 - \Phi(\theta_*|\overline{\mu}, \overline{h}^{-1})}{\Phi(\theta_*|\overline{\mu}, \overline{h}^{-1})}\right]\left[\frac{\underline{\pi}_1}{\underline{\pi}_2}\right], \tag{6.51}$$

where $\overline{\mu}$ and $\overline{h}$ are given by the common values across $j = 1, 2$ of (6.40) and (6.41). Bayes factor (6.51) implies – see Equation (6.20) – that the posterior probability $\overline{\pi}_1 = \Pr(H_1|y)$ equals simply

$$\overline{\pi}_1 = \Phi(\theta_*|\overline{\mu}, \overline{h}^{-1}).$$

Under "all-or-nothing" loss, (6.51) implies that the decision rule (6.26) reduces to reject H_1 iff

$$\overline{y} > \theta_* + (\underline{h}/h)\,(\theta_* - \underline{\mu}) + \gamma h^{-(1/2)}, \tag{6.52}$$

where

$$\gamma \equiv -\left[1 + (\underline{h}/h)\right]^{(1/2)} \Phi^{-1}\left[\left(1 + \frac{\overline{C}_2}{\overline{C}_1}\right)^{-1}\right]. \tag{6.53}$$

The second term in (6.52) serves as an additive adjustment to θ_*, requiring $\overline{y}$ to be larger to reject H_1 when the prior mean $\underline{\mu}$ lies to the left of θ_*. Under (6.50) this adjustment term vanishes.

The constant γ defined by (6.53) plays the role of the tabulated critical value used in frequentist testing. However, it is an explicit function of the relative cost of type I and type II errors. Usually, the problem is posed so that the ratio $\overline{C}_2/\overline{C}_1$ is greater than unity. Letting

$$\alpha = \left(1 + \frac{\overline{C}_2}{\overline{C}_1}\right)^{-1},$$

we see in this case that $\Phi^{-1}(\alpha) < 0$ and hence $\gamma > 0$. The quantity α is like the level of significance in a frequentist test. Provided the prior is informative (i.e., $0 < \underline{h} < \infty$), γ is a function of sample size T through $h = T/\sigma^2$ and the first factor in (6.53) is greater than unity. As prior information becomes diffuse (i.e., $\underline{h} \to 0$), the second term in (6.52) vanishes independently of (6.50) holding, and the first factor in (6.51) approaches unity. Therefore, if prior information is diffuse and $\overline{C}_2/\overline{C}_1 = 19$, then $\alpha = .05$, $\gamma = -\Phi^{-1}(.05) = 1.645$, and (6.52) is identical to the rejection region of a frequentist one-sided test at the .05 level of significance.

Exercise 6.4 (Simple null, two-sided alternative, and general likelihood) Consider $H_1 : \theta = \theta_*$ versus $H_2 : \theta \neq \theta_*$, where θ_* is a given constant. In this case $\Theta_1 = \{\theta_*\}$ and $\Theta_2 = \{\theta : \theta \in \Theta \text{ and } \theta \neq \theta_*\}$. Suppose the prior probability function (6.4) is of the mixed form

$$p(\theta) = \begin{cases} \underline{\pi}_1 & \text{if } \theta = \theta_*, \\ \underline{\pi}_2 p(\theta|H_2) & \text{if } \theta \in \Theta_2, \end{cases} \tag{6.54}$$

with a "spike" of height $\underline{\pi}_1$ at $\theta = \theta_*$. Consider data y yielding likelihood $L(\theta)$. Under what conditions is it optimal to reject H_1?

Solution

The posterior probability function is also of mixed form:

$$p(\theta|y) = \begin{cases} \overline{\pi}_1 & \text{if } \theta = \theta_*, \\ \overline{\pi}_2 p(\theta|y, H_2) & \text{if } \theta \in \Theta_2, \end{cases} \tag{6.55}$$

where

$$\overline{\pi}_1 = \Pr(H_1|y) = \frac{\underline{\pi}_1 L(\theta_*)}{p(y)}, \tag{6.56}$$

$$\overline{\pi}_2 = \Pr(H_2|y) = \frac{\underline{\pi}_2 p(y|H_2)}{p(y)}, \tag{6.57}$$

$$p(y) = \underline{\pi}_1 L(\theta_*) + \underline{\pi}_2 p(y|H_2), \tag{6.58}$$

and $p(y|H_2)$ is given by (6.5). Also note that the Bayes factor (6.19) yields

$$B_{21} = \frac{\int_{\Theta_2} p(\theta|H_2)L(\theta)\, d\theta}{L(\theta_*)}. \tag{6.59}$$

Compared to the numerator in (6.19), the numerator in (6.59) marginalizes the likelihood $L(\theta)$ using the prior density $p(\theta|H_2)$. Also, the right-hand side of the inequality in decision rule (6.22) depends on data, and so B_{21} does not fully summarize the effect of the data on the optimal decision.

Exercise 6.5 (Simple null hypothesis, two-sided alternative, and normal likelihoods) Consider Exercise 6.4. Suppose the prior density $p(\theta)$ is mixed prior density (6.54) with

$$p(\theta|H_2) = \phi(\theta|\underline{\mu}, \underline{h}^{-1}). \tag{6.60}$$

Also, suppose a random sample $Y_1, Y_2, \ldots, Y_T$ is available from an $N(\theta, \sigma^2)$ population in which θ is unknown and σ^2 is *known*. Under what conditions is it optimal to reject H_1?

Solution

From (6.43) and (2.23), and also noting that the integral over Θ_2 is equivalent to the integral over $-\infty$ to ∞, we have that

$$p(y|H_2) = c_1 \phi(\overline{y}|\underline{\mu}, \underline{h}^{-1} + h^{-1}) \tag{6.61}$$

and the Bayes factor for H_2 versus H_1 is

$$\begin{aligned} B_{21} &= \frac{\phi(\overline{y}|\underline{\mu}, \underline{h}^{-1} + h^{-1})}{\phi(\overline{y}|\theta_*, h^{-1})} \\ &= \left[\frac{h^{-1}}{\underline{h}^{-1} + h^{-1}}\right]^{(1/2)} \exp\left[-\frac{1}{2}\left((\underline{h}^{-1} + h^{-1})^{-1}(\overline{y} - \underline{\mu})^2 - h(\overline{y} - \theta_*)^2\right)\right]. \end{aligned} \tag{6.62}$$

By using identity (2.19) with $\theta_1 = \theta_*$, it follows from (6.62) that

$$B_{21} = \left(\underline{h}/\,\overline{h}\right)^{(1/2)} \exp\left(-\frac{1}{2}\left[\underline{h}(\theta_* - \underline{\mu})^2 - \overline{h}(\theta_* - \overline{\mu})^2\right]\right), \tag{6.63}$$

where $\overline{h} = \underline{h} + h$ is the posterior precision. Then (6.26) implies that $\mathrm{d}_* = \mathrm{d}_2$ iff

$$\ln(B_{21}) > \ln\left(\frac{\overline{C}_2 \underline{\pi}_1}{\overline{C}_1 \underline{\pi}_2}\right), \tag{6.64}$$

or equivalently, by using (6.63),

$$|\overline{h}^{(1/2)}(\overline{\mu}-\theta_*)| > \left(\underline{h}(\theta_*-\underline{\mu})^2 + 2\ln\left[\left(\frac{\overline{C}_2\underline{\pi}_1}{\overline{C}_1\underline{\pi}_2}\right)\left(\overline{h}/\,\underline{h}\right)^{(1/2)}\right]\right)^{1/2}, \tag{6.65}$$

with

$$\overline{\mu}-\theta_* = \frac{\underline{h}(\underline{\mu}-\theta_*) + h(\overline{y}-\theta_*)}{\overline{h}}. \tag{6.66}$$

Exercise 6.6 (Special cases of Exercise 6.5) Consider (6.65).
(a) What happens as $\underline{h} \to 0$?
(b) What happens when $\underline{\mu} = \theta_*$?
(c) Analyze $\overline{\pi}_1$ when $\underline{\mu} = \theta_*$.

Solution
(a) As $\underline{h} \to 0$, inequality (6.65) becomes $\sqrt{h}|\overline{y}-\theta_*| > \infty$, which cannot be satisfied. Hence, as the prior becomes less precise, H_1 is *never* rejected.
(b) When $p(\theta|H_2)$ is "centered" over H_1 (i.e., $\underline{\mu} = \theta_*$), then (6.65) reduces to reject H_1 iff

$$|h^{(1/2)}(\overline{y}-\theta_*)| > \left[\left(\frac{\overline{h}}{h}\right)2\ln\left[\left(\frac{\overline{C}_2\underline{\pi}_1}{\overline{C}_1\underline{\pi}_2}\right)(\overline{h}/\underline{h}^{1/2})\right]\right]^{1/2}, \tag{6.67}$$

where the left-hand side of (6.67) is the familiar frequentist test statistic. The right-hand side of (6.67) serves as a "critical value." Not only does this Bayesian "critical value" depend on the relative expected costs of type I and type II errors, but more importantly it is an increasing function of sample size T through $\overline{h} = \underline{h} + (T/\sigma^2)$. This is reminiscent of the common dictum shared by all good frequentist statisticians that the level of significance should be chosen to be a decreasing function of sample size. However, because the level of significance is usually chosen on the basis of "convention," this warning is seldom operationalized.
(c) Using (6.63) and (6.20) yields

$$\overline{\pi}_1 = \left[1 + \left(\frac{\underline{\pi}_1}{1-\underline{\pi}_1}\right)^{-1}\left(\frac{\underline{h}\sigma^2}{\underline{h}\sigma^2+T}\right)^{(1/2)}\exp\left[\frac{1}{2}\left(\frac{T}{\underline{h}\sigma^2+T}\right)z^2\right]\right]^{-1}, \tag{6.68}$$

where $z = |h^{(1/2)}(\overline{y}-\theta_*)|$. From (6.68) it is seen that the frequentist test statistic z can be large (suggesting to a frequentist with a fixed level of significance that H_1 should be rejected), while at the same time the posterior probability of H_1 is also close to unity. In fact, letting $T \to \infty$ in such a way that z (which also depends on T) is held fixed, it is easy to see that $\overline{\pi}_1 \to 1$. In other words, for any large finite value of the test statistic z, there is a sample size T for which the posterior probability $\overline{\pi}_1$ can be made arbitrarily close to unity.

Exercise 6.7 (Relationship among posterior probabilities under different prior probabilities) Consider J hypotheses $H_j : \theta_j \in \Theta_j$ $(j = 1, 2, \ldots, J)$. Define

$$m_j(y) = \frac{p_j(y|H_j)}{\sum_{i=1}^{J} p_i(y|H_i)}. \tag{6.69}$$

Show that $m_j(y)$ $(j = 1, 2, \ldots, J)$ are all that are required to summarize the data to compute posterior probabilities for *any* set of given prior probabilities.

Solution

In general,

$$\overline{\pi}_j = \frac{\underline{\pi}_j p_j(y|H_j)}{\sum_{i=1}^{J} \underline{\pi}_i p_i(y|H_i)} = \left[\sum_{i=1}^{J} \left(\frac{\underline{\pi}_i}{\underline{\pi}_j}\right) B_{ij}\right]^{-1}, \quad j = 1, 2, \ldots, J. \tag{6.70}$$

Because $B_{ij} = m_i(y)/m_j(y)$ $(j = 1, 2, \ldots, J)$, it follows from (6.70) that $\{m_j(y)\}_{j=1}^{J}$ are all that are required to summarize the data to compute posterior probabilities for *any* set of given prior probabilities $\underline{\pi}_j$ $(j = 1, 2, \ldots, J)$.

Exercise 6.8 (Savage–Dickey density ratio) Consider the likelihood $L(\theta)$ and the hypotheses $H_1 : \theta_2 = 0$ versus $H_2 : \theta_2 \neq 0$, where $\theta = [\theta_1', \theta_2']'$. Let $g(\theta_1, \theta_2) = g(\theta_1|\theta_2)g(\theta_2)$ be a continuous density defined over $\mathbb{R}^k$ and consider the prior densities $p(\theta_1|H_1) = g(\theta_1|\theta_2 = 0)$ and $p(\theta_1, \theta_2|H_2) = g(\theta_1, \theta_2)$. Show that the Bayes factor for H_1 versus H_2 can be written as the ratio (known as the *Savage–Dickey density ratio*) of the marginal *posterior* density of θ_2 to the marginal *prior* density of θ_2, each evaluated at $\theta_2 = 0$, and computed using $g(\theta_1, \theta_2)$ as the prior, that is,

$$B_{12} = \frac{p(\theta_2 = 0|H_2, y)}{p(\theta_2 = 0|H_2)}, \tag{6.71}$$

where

$$\begin{aligned} p(\theta_1, \theta_2|y, H_2) &= \frac{p(\theta_1, \theta_2|H_2)L(\theta_1, \theta_2)}{p(y|H_2)} \\ &= \frac{g(\theta_1, \theta_2)L(\theta_1, \theta_2)}{\int_\Theta g(\theta_1, \theta_2)L(\theta_1, \theta_2)\, d\theta_1\, d\theta_2}. \end{aligned} \tag{6.72}$$

Solution

Integrating (6.72) with respect to θ_1 yields

$$\begin{aligned} p(\theta_2|H_2, y) &= \int_{\Theta_1} p(\theta_1, \theta_2|H_2, y)\, d\theta_1 \\ &= \int_{\Theta_1} \left[\frac{g(\theta_1|\theta_2)g(\theta_2)L(\theta_1, \theta_2)}{\int_\Theta g(\theta_1, \theta_2)L(\theta_1, \theta_2)\, d\theta_1\, d\theta_2}\right] d\theta_1. \end{aligned} \tag{6.73}$$

Dividing (6.73) by $p(\theta_2|H_2)$ and evaluating both at $\theta_2 = 0$ implies

$$\begin{aligned}\frac{p(\theta_2 = 0|y, H_2)}{p(\theta_2 = 0|H_2)} &= \int_{\Theta_1} \left[\frac{g(\theta_1|\theta_2 = 0)g(\theta_2 = 0)L(\theta_1, \theta_2 = 0)}{g(\theta_2 = 0) \int_{\Theta} g(\theta_1, \theta_2)L(\theta_1, \theta_2)\, d\theta_1\, d\theta_2} \right] d\theta_1 \\ &= \int_{\Theta_1} \left[\frac{p(\theta_1|H_1)L(\theta_1, \theta_2 = 0)}{\int_{\Theta} g(\theta_1, \theta_2)L(\theta_1, \theta_2)\, d\theta_1\, d\theta_2} \right] d\theta_1 \\ &= \frac{p(y|H_1)}{p(y|H_2)} = B_{12}. \end{aligned} \tag{6.74}$$

Exercise 6.9 (Generalized Savage–Dickey density ratio) Consider Exercise 6.8. Without assuming any restriction on prior density $p(\theta|H_1)$ as done in Exercise 6.8, find a c such that

$$B_{12} = c \left(\frac{p(\theta_2 = 0|H_2, y)}{p(\theta_2 = 0|H_2)} \right).$$

Solution

Consider

$$\begin{aligned} B_{12} &= \frac{\int_{\Theta_1} L(\theta_1, \theta_2 = 0)p(\theta_1|H_1)\, d\theta_1}{p(y|H_2)} \\ &= p(\theta_2 = 0|y, H_2) \left[\int_{\Theta_1} \frac{L(\theta_1, \theta_2 = 0)p(\theta_1|H_1)}{p(\theta_2 = 0|y, H_2)p(y|H_2)}\, d\theta_1 \right] \\ &= p(\theta_2 = 0|y, H_2) \left[\int_{\Theta_1} \frac{L(\theta_1, \theta_2 = 0)p(\theta_1|H_1)}{\left(\frac{p(\theta_1, \theta_2 = 0|y, H_2)}{p(\theta_1|\theta_2 = 0, y, H_2)} \right) p(y|H_2)}\, d\theta_1 \right] \\ &= p(\theta_2 = 0|y, H_2) \left[\int_{\Theta_1} \frac{L(\theta_1, \theta_2 = 0)p(\theta_1|H_1)p(\theta_1|\theta_2 = 0, y, H_2)}{\left(\frac{L(\theta_1, \theta_2 = 0)p(\theta_1, \theta_2 = 0|H_2)}{p(y|H_2)} \right) p(y|H_2)}\, d\theta_1 \right] \\ &= \left(\frac{p(\theta_2 = 0|y, H_2)}{p(\theta_2 = 0|H_2)} \right) \left[\int_{\Theta_1} \left(\frac{p(\theta_1|H_1)}{p(\theta_1|\theta_2 = 0, H_2)} \right) p(\theta_1|\theta_2 = 0, y, H_2)\, d\theta_1 \right] \\ &= \left(\frac{p(\theta_2 = 0|y, H_2)}{p(\theta_2 = 0|H_2)} \right) E_{\theta_1|\theta_2 = 0, y, H_2} \left[\frac{p(\theta_1|H_1)}{p(\theta_1|\theta_2 = 0, H_2)} \right]. \end{aligned}$$

So,

$$c = E_{\theta_1|\theta_2 = 0, y, H_2} \left[\frac{p(\theta_1|H_1)}{p(\theta_1|\theta_2 = 0, H_2)} \right]$$

gives the desired result.

Exercise 6.10 (Composite null hypothesis) Consider a random sample Y_t $(t = 1, 2, \ldots, T)$ from an $N(\theta, 1)$ distribution yielding a likelihood function $L(\theta; y)$. Consider

two hypotheses: $H_1 : |\theta| \leq \epsilon$ and $|\theta| > \epsilon$, where ϵ is chosen to define what constitutes "small" (H_1). Assume $\epsilon = 1$ and the prior $\theta \sim N\left(0, \underline{h}^{-1}\right)$, where $\underline{h} > 0$ is chosen so that $\text{Prob}\left(H_1 : |\theta| \leq 1\right) = \frac{1}{2}$.
(a) Find $\underline{h}$ (approximately).
(b) Assume $\sigma^2 = 10$. Find the posterior distribution of θ based on a sample of size $T = 10$ that yields $\bar{y} = .7275$.
(c) Find the posterior probability that θ is "small."

Solution
(a) $\Phi^{-1}(.75) = .6745 = \sqrt{\underline{h}}$. So $\underline{h} = (.6745)^2 = .4550$.
(b) We calculate $h = T/\sigma^2 = 10/10 = 1$, $\bar{h} = \underline{h} + h = .4550 + 1 = 1.455$, and $\bar{\mu} = \bar{h}^{-1}\left(\underline{h} \cdot 0 + h\bar{y}\right) = .7275/1.4550 = \frac{1}{2}$. Therefore, $\theta|y \sim N\left(\frac{1}{2}, .6873\right)$.
(c) $\text{Prob}\left(H_2|y\right) = \Phi\left[\left(1 - \frac{1}{2}\right)/.8290\right] - \Phi\left[\left(-1 - \frac{1}{2}\right)/.8290\right] = \Phi(.6031) - \Phi(-1.809) = .7267 - .0352 = .6916$.

Exercise 6.11 (Expected Bayes factor) Consider an experiment with a countable number of possible outcomes $y_1, y_2, y_3, \ldots$ and two mutually exclusive and exhaustive statistical hypotheses H_1 and H_2. Is the statement "Given one observation Y, the expected Bayes factor in favor of a false hypothesis is unity" true or false? Explain your answer.

Solution
The statement is true. Suppose H_1 is true. The Bayes factor in favor of H_2, viewed *ex ante*, is $B_{21} = \text{Prob}\left(Y|H_2\right)/\text{Prob}\left(Y|H_1\right)$, and its expected value is

$$E\left[B_{21}\right] = \sum_{i=1}^{\infty}\left[\frac{\text{Prob}\left(Y = y_i|H_2\right)}{\text{Prob}\left(Y = y_i|H_1\right)}\right]\text{Prob}\left(Y = y_i|H_1\right) = \sum_{i=1}^{\infty}\text{Prob}\left(Y = y_i|H_2\right) = 1.$$

Exercise 6.12 (Simple null and alternative hypotheses) Suppose you have ten observations drawn randomly from a normal population with an unknown mean, θ, and known variance of unity.
(a) If the sample mean is 1.5, calculate the posterior odds relating to the hypotheses $H_1 : \theta = 1$ and $H_2 : \theta = 2$ when the prior probability for each hypothesis is $\frac{1}{2}$.
(b) Consider the following loss structure:

		State of the world	
		H_1	H_2
Action	Accept H_1	0	4
	Accept H_2	2	0

Which hypothesis would you choose?

Solution

(a) Since the prior odds are equal, the posterior odds are just the Bayes factor:

$$B_{21} = \frac{\prod_{t=1}^{10} \Phi\left(y_t|1,1\right)}{\prod_{t=1}^{10} \Phi\left(y_t|2,1\right)} = \frac{\exp\left[-\frac{1}{2}\sum_{t=1}^{10}\left(y_t-1\right)^2\right]}{\exp\left[-\frac{1}{2}\sum_{t=1}^{10}\left(y_t-2\right)^2\right]} = \frac{\exp\left[-\frac{1}{2}\left(9s^2+10\left(1.5-1\right)^2\right)\right]}{\exp\left[-\frac{1}{2}\left(9s^2+10\left(1.5-2\right)^2\right)\right]} = 1,$$

with s^2 defined in (2.18). Hence, the posterior odds are also 1.

(b) Pick H_1 because the expected loss is lower.

7

Prediction

Prediction provides discipline and pragmatic importance to empirical research. Suppose a deity told you the values of all unknown parameters in your model so that estimation and hypothesis testing became moot. What would you do with your model? The obvious answer is to use it for what it is intended to do: make *ex ante* probability statements about future observables.

Suppose the information set consists of the union of past data $Y = y$, yielding the parametric likelihood function $L(\theta)$, and other information in the form of a prior distribution $p(\theta)$. The sampling distribution of an out-of-sample Y_* (possibly a vector) given $Y = y$ and θ would be an acceptable predictive distribution if θ were known, but without knowledge of θ it cannot be used. Then the *Bayesian predictive probability distribution* $p(y_*|y)$ is

$$
\begin{aligned}
p(y_*|y) &= \frac{p(y_*, y)}{p(y)} \\
&= \int_\Theta \frac{p(y_*, y, \theta)}{p(y)} d\theta \\
&= \int_\Theta p(y_*|y, \theta) \left[\frac{p(\theta)p(y|\theta)}{p(y)}\right] d\theta \\
&= \int_\Theta p(y_*|y, \theta)p(\theta|y)d\theta \\
&= E_{\theta|y}[p(y_*|y, \theta)]. \qquad (7.1)
\end{aligned}
$$

In other words, the Bayesian predictive probability function is the posterior expectation of $p(y_*|y, \theta)$. If the past and future are independent, conditional on θ (as in random sampling), then $p(y_*|y, \theta) = p(y_*|\theta)$.

Given the predictive distribution, point prediction proceeds analogously to point estimation, as discussed in Chapter 3. Letting $C(\hat{Y}_*, Y_*)$ denote a *predictive cost (loss) function* measuring the performance of a predictor $\hat{Y}_*$ of Y_*, we define the optimal point predictor $\hat{Y}_{**}$ to be the solution

$$\hat{Y}_{**} = \underset{\hat{Y}_*}{\operatorname{argmin}} \left(E_{Y_*|Y}[C(\hat{Y}_*, Y_*)] \right). \tag{7.2}$$

For example, if Y_* is a scalar, and predictive loss is quadratic in *prediction (forecast) error* $\hat{Y}_* - Y_*$, i.e., $C(\hat{Y}_*, Y_*) = (\hat{Y}_* - Y_*)^2$, then the optimal point estimate according to (7.2) is

$$\hat{Y}_{**} = E(Y_*|Y). \tag{7.3}$$

Results for generating point predictions analogous to those for point estimates found in Chapter 3 can be derived for other familiar loss functions. Similarly, prediction (forecast) intervals for Y_* can be constructed from $p(y_*|y)$ similarly to the HPD intervals for θ from the posterior density $p(\theta|y)$ in Chapter 5.

In effect, the predictive density described in (7.1) treats all parameters as nuisance parameters and integrates them out of the predictive problem. A similar strategy is used when adding parametric hypotheses to the analysis. Suppose that the permissible parameter space Θ is partitioned into J mutually exclusive subsets Θ_j $(j = 1, 2, \ldots, J)$ such that $\Theta = \Theta_1 \cup \Theta_2 \cup \cdots \cup \Theta_J$. This partitioning gives rise to J hypotheses: $H_j : \theta \in \Theta_j$ $(j = 1, 2, \ldots, J)$. Also suppose that the likelihood $L(\theta)$, prior probabilities $\underline{\pi}_j = \Pr(H_j)$, and conditional prior pdfs $p(\theta|H_j)$ $(j = 1, 2, \ldots, J)$ are given. Conditional on hypothesis H_j and given data y leading to the posterior pdf $p(\theta|y, H_j)$, the jth conditional predictive density of Y_* is

$$p(y_*|y, H_j) = \int_{\Theta} p(y_*|\theta, y, H_j)p(\theta|y, H_j)d\theta. \tag{7.4}$$

Using the posterior probabilities $\overline{\pi}_j = \Pr(H_j|y)$ $(j = 1, 2, \ldots, J)$, the unconditional (marginal) predictive density of Y_* is the mixture

$$\begin{aligned} p(y_*|y) &= \sum_{j=1}^{J} p(y_*, H_j|y) \\ &= \sum_{j=1}^{J} \overline{\pi}_j p(y_*|y, H_j). \end{aligned} \tag{7.5}$$

The predictive probability function (7.5) is the basis for constructing prediction intervals and point forecasts unconditional on the competing hypotheses. For example, under quadratic loss the optimal Bayesian point estimate is the predictive mean

$$E(y_*|y) = \sum_{j=1}^{J} \overline{\pi}_j E(y_*|y, H_j). \tag{7.6}$$

Note that (7.6) is a weighted average of the optimal point forecasts $E(y_*|y, H_j)$ under each hypothesis. Furthermore, the weights in this case, the posterior probabilities $\overline{\pi}_j$ $(j = 1, 2, \ldots, J)$ of the respective hypotheses, have an intuitive appeal: the forecasts of more probable hypotheses *a posteriori* receive more weight. The "optimality" of these weights is self-evident to the Bayesian: Given the likelihood, hypotheses, and priors, (7.5) is the unique predictive distribution for future observables.

Exercise 7.1 (Predictive pmf for conjugate Bernoulli analysis) Consider the Bernoulli sampling problem in Exercise 2.1 with the beta prior $\theta \sim \beta(\underline{\alpha}, \underline{\delta})$. Find the predictive pmf for the out-of-sample value y_*.

Solution

According to Exercise 2.1 the posterior is $\theta|y \sim \beta(\overline{\alpha}, \overline{\delta})$, where $\overline{\alpha} = \underline{\alpha} + m$, $\overline{\delta} = \underline{\delta} + T - m$, and m is the number of successes in T observations. Hence the predictive pmf is

$$\begin{aligned}
p(y_*|y) &= \int_0^1 \theta^{y_*}(1-\theta)^{(1-y_*)}[\mathcal{B}(\overline{\alpha}, \overline{\delta})]^{-1}\theta^{\overline{\alpha}-1}(1-\theta)^{(\overline{\delta}-1)}d\theta \\
&= [\mathcal{B}(\overline{\alpha}, \overline{\delta})]^{-1}\int_0^1 \theta^{(y_*+\overline{\alpha}-1)}(1-\theta)^{(1-y_*+\overline{\delta}-1)}d\theta \\
&= \left[\frac{\mathcal{B}(\overline{\alpha}+y_*, \overline{\delta}+1-y_*)}{\mathcal{B}(\overline{\alpha}, \overline{\delta})}\right] \\
&\quad \times \int_0^1 [\mathcal{B}(\overline{\alpha}+y_*, \overline{\delta}+1-y_*)]^{-1}\theta^{(y_*+\overline{\alpha}-1)}(1-\theta)^{(1-y_*+\overline{\delta}-1)}d\theta \\
&= \left[\frac{\Gamma(\overline{\alpha}+y_*)\Gamma(\overline{\delta}+1-y_*)}{\Gamma(\overline{\alpha}+\overline{\delta}+1)}\right]\left[\frac{\Gamma(\overline{\alpha}+\overline{\delta})}{\Gamma(\overline{\alpha})\Gamma(\overline{\delta})}\right], \quad y_* = 0, 1, \qquad (7.7)
\end{aligned}$$

where the beta and gamma functions used in this question are discussed in Exercise 2.1 and the integral in the third line in (7.7) is unity because the integrand is the density of a $\beta(\overline{\alpha} + y_*, \overline{\delta} + 1 - y_*)$ distribution. The predictive pmf (7.7) is known as a *beta-binomial* pmf (see, e.g., Poirier 1995, p. 116). It has mean $\overline{\alpha}/(\overline{\alpha}+\overline{\delta})$ and variance $[\overline{\alpha}\overline{\delta}(\overline{\alpha}+\overline{\delta}+1)]/[(\overline{\alpha}+\overline{\delta})^2(\overline{\alpha}+\overline{\delta}+1)]$.

Exercise 7.2 (Predictive pmf for conjugate Poisson analysis) Suppose Y_t $(t = 1, 2, \ldots, T)$ is a random sample from a Poisson distribution with mean θ and that the prior distribution of θ is the gamma distribution $G(\underline{\alpha}, \underline{\beta})$, where $\underline{\alpha} > 0$ and $\underline{\beta} > 0$. Find the predictive density for an out-of-sample value y_*.

Solution

From Exercise 2.12 we know $\theta|y \sim G(\overline{\alpha}, \overline{\beta})$, where $\overline{\alpha} = \underline{\alpha} + T\overline{y}$ and $\overline{\beta} = (\underline{\beta}^{-1} + T)^{-1}$.

Therefore, the predictive pmf (7.1) becomes

$$
\begin{aligned}
p(y_*|y) &= \int_0^\infty p(y_*|\theta)p(\theta|y)d\theta \\
&= \int_0^\infty \left[\frac{\theta^{y_*}\exp(-\theta)}{y_*!}\right]\left[\left(\overline{\beta}^{\overline{\alpha}}\Gamma(\overline{\alpha})\right)^{-1}\theta^{\overline{\alpha}-1}\exp(-\theta/\overline{\beta})\right]d\theta \\
&= \left(y_*!\,\overline{\beta}^{\overline{\alpha}}\Gamma(\overline{\alpha})\right)^{-1}\int_0^\infty \theta^{(y_*+\overline{\alpha}-1)}\exp[-\theta/(\overline{\beta}^{-1}+1)^{-1}]\,d\theta \\
&= \left(\frac{(\overline{\beta}^{-1}+1)^{-(\overline{\alpha}+y_*)}\Gamma(\overline{\alpha}+y_*)}{y_*!\,\overline{\beta}^{\overline{\alpha}}\Gamma(\overline{\alpha})}\right) \\
&\quad\times \int_0^\infty \left((\overline{\beta}^{-1}+1)^{-(\overline{\alpha}+y_*)}\Gamma(\overline{\alpha}+y_*)\right)^{-1}\theta^{(\overline{\alpha}+y_*-1)}\exp[-\theta/(\overline{\beta}^{-1}+1)^{-1}]d\theta \\
&= \left(\frac{(\overline{\beta}^{-1}+1)^{-(\overline{\alpha}+y_*)}\Gamma(\overline{\alpha}+y_*)}{y_*!\,\overline{\beta}^{\overline{\alpha}}\Gamma(\overline{\alpha})}\right), \quad y_* = 0, 1, 2, \ldots,
\end{aligned} \tag{7.8}
$$

where the integral in the second-to-last line is unity because it is the density of a $G(\overline{\alpha} + y_*, [\overline{\beta}^{-1} + 1]^{-1})$ distribution. Predictive pmf (7.8) is known as the Poisson-gamma pmf.

Exercise 7.3 (Predictive density for conjugate normal analysis with known variance) Consider Exercise 2.6(b). Suppose σ^2 is known and that the prior distribution for μ is $N(\underline{\mu}, \sigma^2/\underline{T})$. Find the predictive density of an out-of-sample y_*.

Solution

Under this prior, the results of Exercise 2.6(b) in conjunction with (2.25) show that the posterior distribution for μ is $N(\overline{\mu}, \sigma^2/\overline{T})$, where $\overline{\mu} = \overline{T}^{-1}(\underline{T}\underline{\mu} + T\overline{y})$ and $\overline{T} = \underline{T} + T$. Noting that

$$
(y_* - \mu)^2 + \overline{T}(\mu - \overline{\mu})^2 = (1 + \overline{T})(\mu - c)^2 + \overline{T}(1 + \overline{T})^{-1}(y_* - \overline{\mu})^2, \tag{7.9}
$$

where $c = (1 + \overline{T})^{-1}(\overline{T}\overline{\mu} + y_*)$, we can obtain the predictive density (7.1) as

$$
\begin{aligned}
p(y_*|y) &= \int_{\mathbb{R}} p(y_*|y,\mu)p(\mu|y)d\mu \qquad (7.10)\\
&= \int_{\mathbb{R}} \phi(y_*|\mu,\sigma^2)\phi(\mu|\overline{\mu},\sigma^2/\overline{T})d\mu \\
&= \phi\left(y_*|\overline{\mu},\sigma^2[1+\overline{T}^{-1}]\right)\int_{\mathbb{R}} \phi\left(\mu|c,\sigma^2[1+\overline{T}]^{-1}\right)d\mu \\
&= \phi\left(y_*|\overline{\mu},\sigma^2[1+\overline{T}^{-1}]\right), \quad -\infty < y_* < \infty.
\end{aligned}
$$

Exercise 7.4 (Predictive point and interval estimation for conjugate normal analysis with known variance) Consider Exercise 7.3.
(a) Find the predictive point forecast of y_* under quadratic loss.
(b) Find a $1-\alpha$ forecast interval for y_*.

Solution
(a) Under quadratic loss, the Bayesian point forecast of y_* is the predictive mean $\overline{\mu}$.
(b) A $1-\alpha$ prediction (forecast) interval for y_* is given by

$$\overline{S}_* = \left\{ y_* : y_* \in \mathbb{R} \text{ and } \overline{\mu} - z_{\alpha/2}\sigma[1+\overline{T}^{-1}]^{(1/2)} < y_* < \overline{\mu} + z_{\alpha/2}\sigma[1+\overline{T}^{-1}]^{(1/2)} \right\}, \tag{7.11}$$

where $z_{\alpha/2}$ satisfies $\Phi(z_{\alpha/2}) - \Phi(-z_{\alpha/2}) = 1-\alpha$.

Exercise 7.5 (Predictive density for conjugate multivariate normal analysis with known covariance matrix) Consider the multivariate normal sampling distribution in Exercise 2.14. Suppose Σ is known and that the prior distribution for μ is $N_m(\underline{\mu}, \Sigma/\underline{T})$. Find the predictive density of an out-of-sample value y_*.

Solution
According to Exercise 2.14, the posterior distribution of μ is $N(\overline{\mu}, \overline{T}^{-1}\Sigma)$, where $\overline{\mu}$ and $\overline{T}$ are defined as in the solution to part (c). By using the identity

$$\begin{aligned}
&(y_* - \mu)'\Sigma^{-1}(y_* - \mu) + \overline{T}(\mu - \overline{\mu})'\Sigma^{-1}(\mu - \overline{\mu}) \\
&\quad = (1+\overline{T})(\mu - c)'\Sigma^{-1}(\mu - c) + \overline{T}(1+\overline{T})^{-1}(y_* - \overline{\mu})'\Sigma^{-1}(y_* - \overline{\mu}),
\end{aligned} \tag{7.12}$$

in the same manner as in Exercise 7.3, and with c defined accordingly, the predictive density is

$$\begin{aligned}
p(y_*|y) &= \int_{\mathbb{R}^m} p(y_*|y,\mu)p(\mu|y)d\mu \\
&= \int_{\mathbb{R}^m} \phi(y_*|\mu,\Sigma)\phi(\mu|\overline{\mu},\Sigma/\overline{T})d\mu \\
&= \phi(y_*|\overline{\mu},[1+\overline{T}^{-1}]\Sigma) \int_{\mathbb{R}^m} \phi(\mu|c,[1+\overline{T}]^{-1}\Sigma)d\mu \\
&= \phi(y_*|\overline{\mu},[1+\overline{T}^{-1}]\Sigma), \quad y_* \in \mathbb{R}^m.
\end{aligned} \tag{7.13}$$

Exercise 7.6 (Predictive estimation: Conjugate multivariate normal analysis with known covariance matrix) Consider Exercise 7.5.
(a) Find the predictive point forecast of y_* under quadratic loss.
(b) Find a $1-\alpha$ forecast region for y_*.

Solution

(a) Under quadratic loss, the Bayesian point forecast of y_* is the predictive mean $\overline{\mu}$.
(b) A $1-\alpha$ predictive (forecast) ellipsoid for y_* is given by

$$\overline{S}_{m*} = \left\{ y_* : y_* \in \mathbb{R}^m \text{ and } (y_* - \overline{\mu})'\Sigma^{-1}(y_* - \overline{\mu}) \leq c_\alpha[1 + \overline{T}^{-1}] \right\}, \tag{7.14}$$

where c_α cuts off α probability in the right-hand tail of the $\chi^2(m)$ distribution. Note that, in Exercises 7.3 through 7.6, frequentist results emerge as $\underline{T} \to 0$.

Exercise 7.7 (Predictive density for conjugate normal analysis with unknown mean and variance) Consider Exercise 7.3 with *both* μ and σ^2 unknown. Suppose the prior distribution for μ and σ^{-2} is the natural conjugate normal-gamma prior $NG(\underline{\mu}, \underline{T}^{-1}, \underline{s}^{-2}, \underline{\nu})$ introduced in Exercise 2.4. Find the predictive density of an out-of-sample y_*.

Solution

The posterior distribution for μ and σ^{-2} is $NG(\overline{\mu}, \overline{T}^{-1}, \overline{s}^{-2}, \overline{\nu})$, where $\overline{\mu}, \overline{T}, \overline{s}^{-2}$, and $\overline{\mu}$ are defined analogously to (2.31), (2.30), (2.32), and (2.28), respectively. From Exercise 7.3 we know that the predictive density given σ^{-2} is

$$\begin{aligned} p(y_*|y, \sigma^{-2}) &= \int_{\mathbb{R}} p(y_*|y, \mu, \sigma^{-2}) p(\mu|y, \sigma^{-2}) d\mu \\ &= \phi\left(y_*|\overline{\mu}, \sigma^2[1 + \overline{T}^{-1}]\right). \end{aligned} \tag{7.15}$$

Proceeding as in Exercise 2.8, we have that the predictive density *unconditional* of σ^{-2} is

$$\begin{aligned} p(y_*|y) &= \int_0^\infty \phi\left(y_*|\overline{\mu}, \sigma^2[1 + \overline{T}^{-1}]\right) f_\gamma(\sigma^{-2}|\overline{s}^{-2}, \overline{\nu}) d\sigma^{-2} \\ &= \int_0^\infty \left((2\pi\sigma^2[1 + \overline{T}^{-1}])^{-(1/2)} \exp\left[-\frac{(y_* - \overline{\mu})^2}{2\sigma^2[1 + \overline{T}^{-1}]} \right] \right) \\ &\quad \times \left(\left[\left(\frac{2}{\overline{\nu s}^2} \right)^{(\overline{\nu}/2)} \Gamma(\overline{\nu}/2) \right]^{-1} \sigma^{-2(\overline{\nu}-2)/2} \exp\left(-\frac{1}{2}\sigma^{-2}\overline{\nu s}^2 \right) \right) d\sigma^{-2} \\ &= f_t(y_*|\overline{\mu}, \overline{s}^2[1 + \overline{T}^{-1}], \overline{\nu}), \end{aligned} \tag{7.16}$$

a univariate Student t density with mean $\overline{\mu}$, scale parameter $\overline{s}^2[1 + \overline{T}^{-1}]$, and degrees of freedom parameter $\overline{\nu}$ (see Definition A.4).

Exercise 7.8 (Predictive estimation: Conjugate normal analysis with unknown mean and variance) Consider Exercise 7.7.
(a) Find the predictive point forecast of y_* under quadratic loss.
(b) Find a $1-\alpha$ forecast interval for y_*.

Solution
(a) Under squared error loss, the Bayesian point forecast of y_* is the predictive mean $\overline{\mu}$.
(b) A $1-\alpha$ predictive (forecast) interval for y_* is given by

$$\overline{S}_* = \left\{ y_* : \overline{\mu} - t_{[(\alpha/2),\overline{\nu}]}\overline{s}[1+\overline{T}^{-1}]^{1/2} < y_* < \overline{\mu} + t_{[(\alpha/2),\overline{\nu}]}\overline{s}[1+\overline{T}^{-1}]^{1/2} \right\}, \quad (7.17)$$

where $t_{[(\alpha/2),\overline{\nu}]}$ cuts off $(\alpha/2)$ probability in the right-hand tail of a Student t distribution with $\overline{\nu}$ degrees of freedom.

Exercise 7.9 (Conjugate multivariate normal analysis with unknown mean and covariance matrix) Consider Exercise 7.5 with both μ and Σ unknown. Suppose the prior distribution for μ and Σ^{-1} is the natural conjugate normal-Wishart prior $NW_m(\underline{\mu}, \underline{T}, \underline{S}, \underline{\omega})$ given in Exercise 2.14(c).
(a) Find the joint posterior distribution of μ and Σ^{-1}.
(b) Find the predictive point forecast for an out-of-sample y_* under quadratic loss.
(c) Find the posterior predictive density for y_* and calculate a $1-\alpha$ forecast interval for y_*.

Solution
(a) The prior specification implies $\mu|\Sigma^{-1} \sim N(\underline{\mu}, \underline{T}^{-1}\Sigma)$ and $\Sigma^{-1} \sim W_m(\underline{S}, \underline{\omega})$. Thus, from Exercise 2.14, the posterior distribution for μ and Σ^{-1} is $NW_m(\overline{\mu}, \overline{T}, \overline{S}, \overline{\omega})$, where $\overline{\mu} = \overline{T}^{-1}(\underline{T}\underline{\mu} + T\overline{y})$, $\overline{T} = \underline{T} + T$, and

$$\overline{S}^{-1} = \underline{S}^{-1} + S + \tfrac{\underline{T}T}{\underline{T}+T}(\underline{\mu} - \overline{y})(\underline{\mu} - \overline{y})', \quad (7.18)$$
$$\overline{\omega} = \underline{\omega} + T; \quad (7.19)$$

that is, $\mu|\Sigma^{-1}, y \sim N_m(\overline{\mu}, \overline{T}^{-1}\Sigma)$, and $\Sigma^{-1}|y \sim W_m(\overline{S}, \overline{\omega})$.
(b) Under quadratic loss, the optimal point predictor of Y_* is $\overline{\mu}$.
(c) By letting $\Sigma^{-1} > 0$ denote that Σ^{-1} is positive definite, the predictive density is

$$\begin{aligned} p(y_*|y) &= \int_{\Sigma^{-1}>0}\int_{\mathbb{R}^m} p(y_*|y, \Sigma^{-1}, \mu)p(\mu, \Sigma^{-1}|y)\, d\mu\, \mathrm{dvech}(\Sigma^{-1}) \\ &= \int_{\Sigma^{-1}>0}\left[\int_{\mathbb{R}^m} \phi(y_*|\mu, \Sigma)\phi_m(\mu|\overline{\mu}, \overline{T}^{-1}\Sigma)\, d\mu\right] f_W(\Sigma^{-1}|\overline{S}, \overline{\omega})\, \mathrm{dvech}(\Sigma^{-1}) \\ &= \int_{\Sigma^{-1}>0} \phi(y_*|\overline{\mu}, [1+\overline{T}^{-1}]\Sigma) f_W(\Sigma^{-1}|\overline{S}, \overline{\omega})\, \mathrm{dvech}(\Sigma^{-1}) \\ &= t(y_*|\overline{\mu}, [1+\overline{T}^{-1}]\overline{S}, \overline{\omega}). \end{aligned}$$

A $1-\alpha$ prediction (forecast) ellipsoid for y_* is given by

$$\overline{S}_* = \left\{ y_* : (y_* - \overline{\mu})'\overline{S}^{-1}(y_* - \overline{\mu}) \le c_\alpha[1+\overline{T}^{-1}] \right\},$$

where c_α cuts off α probability in the right-hand tail of the $F(m, \overline{\omega} - m)$ distribution.

Exercise 7.10 (Predictive density for conjugate exponential analysis) Suppose, as in Exercise 2.10, that Y_t $(t = 1, 2, \ldots, T)$ is a random sample from an exponential distribution with mean θ^{-1} and that the prior distribution of θ is the gamma distribution $G(\underline{\alpha}, \underline{\beta})$, where $\underline{\alpha} > 0$ and $\underline{\beta} > 0$. Find the predictive density for an out-of-sample value y_*.

Solution

From Exercise 2.10, we know $\theta|y \sim G(\overline{\alpha}, \overline{\beta})$, where $\overline{\alpha} = \underline{\alpha} + T$ and $\overline{\beta} = (\underline{\beta}^{-1} + T\overline{y})^{-1}$. Therefore, the predictive density (7.1) becomes

$$
\begin{aligned}
p(y_*|y) &= \int_0^\infty p(y_*|\theta)p(\theta|y)d\theta \qquad (7.20)\\
&= \int_0^\infty [\theta \exp(-\theta y_*)] \left[\left(\overline{\beta}^{\overline{\alpha}}\Gamma(\overline{\alpha})\right)^{-1} \theta^{\overline{\alpha}-1}\exp(-\theta/\overline{\beta})\right] d\theta\\
&= \left(\overline{\beta}^{\overline{\alpha}}\Gamma(\overline{\alpha})\right)^{-1} \int_0^\infty \left[\theta^{(\overline{\alpha}+1)-1}\exp[-\theta(y_* + \overline{\beta}^{-1})]\right] d\theta\\
&= \left(\frac{(\overline{\beta}^{-1} + y_*)^{-(\overline{\alpha}+1)}\Gamma(\overline{\alpha}+1)}{\overline{\beta}^{\overline{\alpha}}\Gamma(\overline{\alpha})}\right)\\
&\quad \times \int_0^\infty \left((\overline{\beta}^{-1} + y_*)^{-(\overline{\alpha}+1)}\Gamma(\overline{\alpha}+1)\right)^{-1} \theta^{(\overline{\alpha}+1)-1}\exp[-\theta/(y_* + \overline{\beta}^{-1})^{-1}]d\theta\\
&= \left(\frac{(\overline{\beta}^{-1} + y_*)^{-(\overline{\alpha}+1)}\Gamma(\overline{\alpha}+1)}{\overline{\beta}^{\overline{\alpha}}\Gamma(\overline{\alpha})}\right), \quad y_* > 0, \qquad (7.21)
\end{aligned}
$$

where the integral in the second-to-last line is unity because it is the density of a $G(\overline{\alpha} + 1, [\overline{\beta}^{-1} + y_*]^{-1})$ distribution. The density in the last line of (7.21) is known as the gamma-gamma pdf.

8

Choice of Prior

Most researchers find the logic of Bayesian analysis compelling, once a prior has been specified. The stage of the process where most frequentists can be found circling the wagons is when the prior is chosen.

The pure subjectivist engaged in personal research needs only to elicit the prior that reflects his or her subjective prior beliefs. Usually the likelihood is parameterized to facilitate thinking in terms of θ, and so subject matter considerations should suggest plausible values of θ. Elicitation techniques are nicely surveyed by Garthwaite, Kadane, and O'Hagan (2005). These techniques tend to advocate thinking in terms of beliefs concerning future observables and backing out the implied beliefs regarding the hyperparameters of a conjugate prior for the unobserved parameters. Unlike most researchers, economists seem equally adept at thinking in terms of observables or unobservable parameters. Perhaps this is because the econometrician is both the statistician and the substantive field expert.

But why should prior beliefs conform to the conjugate prior form? One reason is that natural conjugate priors have an interpretation in terms of a prior fictitious sample from the same process that gives rise to the likelihood function. This corresponds to organizing prior beliefs by viewing the observable world through the same parametric window used for viewing the data.

Public research, however, inevitably requires prior sensitivity analysis and the elicitation of a family of priors likely to interest a wide range of readers. This requires the researcher to wear various hats representing interesting professional positions in prior space. Objective Bayesians seek techniques that deliver a single compelling prior that warrants universal appeal to researchers as a reference standard. Because terms like "objective" and "subjective" are quite value loaded, we simply adopt Lindley's (2004) view that "objectivity is merely subjectivity when nearly everyone agrees."

Objective Bayesians evoke general rules or principles to determine priors in a wide variety of settings. Kass and Wasserman (1996) surveyed numerous formal rules that have been suggested for choosing a prior. Many of these rules reflect the desire to "let the data speak for themselves." These priors are intended to lead to proper posteriors dominated by the data. They also serve as benchmarks for posteriors derived from ideal subjective considerations. At first, many of these priors were also motivated on simplicity grounds. But as problems were discovered, and other issues were seen to be relevant, derivation of such priors became more complicated, possibly even more so than a legitimate attempt to elicit an actual subjective prior.

Technically, objective priors are only positive functions to be formally used in Bayes' theorem to obtain objective posteriors that, for a given model, describe whatever the data have to say about some particular quantity of interest, either a function of the model's parameters or a function of future observations. In other words, objective priors are those for which the contributions of the data are *posterior dominant* for the quantity of interest. The resulting objective posteriors are intended to describe the inferential content of the data for scientific communication.

Early interpretations of letting the data speak for themselves sought "non-informative" priors, but the inherent ambiguity of the term led to many candidates. Even in the simple Bernoulli case there were four legitimate candidates (see Geisser 1984). In nested hypothesis-testing situations, there arose questions such as: What does it mean to be "equally non-informative" in spaces of different dimensions? To sidestep such annoying questions, researchers have explored other interpretations of letting the data speak for themselves.

One interpretation is to use frequentist reasoning and require posterior probabilities to agree with sampling probabilities. For example, this led researchers to seek "matching" priors that result in credibility regions having approximately the same frequentist coverage (i.e., confidence level) as posterior coverage. But problems with multiparameter cases and nuisance parameters have plagued the approach. Another appeal to frequentist reasoning is to rationalize maximum likelihood estimates in a Bayesian framework by appropriate choice of prior distribution and loss function, specifically a uniform prior and an all-or-nothing loss function. But in what parameterization should one be uniform? This question can also be rephrased: In what parameterization should we wish to be "non-informative"?

To overcome parameterization problems, Jeffreys (1961) sought a general rule for choosing a prior so that the same posterior inferences were obtained regardless of the parameterization chosen. Jeffreys (1961) makes a general argument (but with numerous qualifications) in favor of choosing a prior proportional to the square root of the determinant of the information matrix, that is,

$$p(\theta) \propto |\mathcal{I}(\theta)|^{1/2},$$

where

$$\mathcal{I}(\theta) \equiv E_{Y|\theta}\left[-\frac{\partial^2 \ln L(\theta)}{\partial\theta\partial\theta'}\right]$$

is the *information matrix of the sample*. This prior has the desirable feature that if the model is reparameterized by a one-to-one transformation, say $\alpha = h(\theta)$, then choosing the prior

$$p(\alpha) \propto \left|E_{Y|\alpha}\left[-\frac{\partial^2 \ln L(\alpha)}{\partial\alpha\partial\alpha'}\right]\right|^{1/2}$$

leads to identical posterior inferences as using $p(\theta)$. Such priors are said to follow *Jeffreys' rule*. There is a fair amount of agreement that such priors may be reasonable in one-parameter problems, but substantially less agreement in multiple-parameter problems. For example, assuming the mean and variance are independent in the Neyman and Scott (1948) problem gives an inconsistent Bayesian estimator of the variance under Jeffreys' prior.

Kass and Wasserman (1996, p. 1343) argue that Jeffreys' viewpoint evolved toward seeking priors chosen by convention, rather than as unique representations of "ignorance." If the information matrix is difficult to compute (as is often the case with standard econometric models), then Jeffreys' prior is difficult to compute. Also, Jeffreys emphasized the distinction between estimation and testing problems and advocated different priors for each. This set the stage for a result that has plagued subsequent attempts to define "objective" priors where the intentions of the researcher matter.

Usually, Jeffreys' rule and other formal rules reviewed by Kass and Wasserman (1996) lead to *improper priors*, that is, priors that integrate to infinity rather than unity. When blindly plugged into Bayes' theorem as a prior they *can* lead to proper posterior densities, but not always. Furthermore, improper priors can dominate the data and lead to improper posteriors, inadmissible Bayesian point estimators, incoherent inferences, and *marginalization paradoxes*. See Kass and Wasserman (1996, pp. 1356–1359) for details.

Bernardo (1979) suggested a method for constructing *reference priors*, which was subsequently refined by Berger and Bernardo (1989, 1992). These priors are intended to serve as "defaults," that is, choices that can be made automatically without any contemplation of their suitability in a particular problem. Reference priors maximize the missing information in the experiment as measured by the Kullback–Leibler distance between the posterior and prior density as the sample size approaches infinity in a suitable fashion. In the one-dimensional case, the method leads to Jeffreys' prior. Reference priors deal with marginalization paradoxes. In regular continuous multiparameter problems, they usually lead to the solutions that Jeffreys suggested using ad hoc arguments rather than his general multivariate rule. Reference priors preserve desirable features of the Jeffreys' prior such as the invariance property, but they often avoid paradoxical results produced by Jeffreys' prior in multiparameter settings. For example, under the reference prior the Bayesian estimator of the variance in Neyman and Scott (1948) is consistent. Moreover, reference analysis can deal with non-regular cases that cause problems for other methods. A recent survey of reference analysis was done by Bernardo (2004). Kass and Wasserman (1996, p. 1362) describe reference priors as "the default among the defaults."

Objective priors often have properties that seem rather non-Bayesian. Most objective priors depend on some or all of the following: (a) the form of the likelihood, (b) the sample size, (c) an expectation with respect to the sampling distribution, (d) the parameters of interest, and (e) whether the researcher is engaging in estimating, testing, or predicting. The dependency in (c) of Jeffreys' prior on a sampling theory expectation makes it sensitive to a host of problems related to the likelihood principle. In light of (d), an objective prior can depend on *subjective* choices such as which are the parameters of interest and which are nuisance parameters. Different quantities of interest require different objective priors that cannot be combined in a coherent manner. Catalogues of objective prior distributions can be found in Kass and Wasserman (1996) and Yang and Berger (1996).

Improper priors cause more problems in hypothesis testing and model selection than in estimation or prediction. The reason is that improper priors involve arbitrary constants that are not restricted by the necessity of the prior to integrate to unity. Although these constants cancel when computing the posterior density, Bayes factors involve a ratio of arbitrary constants. One idea (Berger and Pericchi 1996) is to use enough data to update an improper prior into a proper posterior and to use the latter to compute a Bayes factor using the remaining data. Of course, there are many such potential training samples. So, try all possible ways and then somehow combine (via, e.g., arithmetic or geometric average) the different Bayes factors. Amazingly, sometimes this results in a legitimate Bayes factor corresponding to a proper prior called the intrinsic prior.

Particularly in high-dimensional problems, the effects of a prior can be subtle: it may have little posterior influence on some functions of the data and have an overwhelming influence on other functions. The message from this and similar examples is that improper priors must be used with care when the dimension of the parameter space is large. Of course, that does not imply that proper priors are necessarily better in these problems. The remarks by Efron (1973) emphasize the practical difficulties with diffuse proper priors that may accompany theoretical difficulties found with improper priors.

Choice of prior is as much an art as it is a science. In the exercises that follow we attempt to illustrate some of the analytical points just made. No exercises on formal elicitation are included, but in subsequent chapters the reader will see how we address the issue of prior choice in the context of specific empirical applications. Our advice is to *use objective priors only with great care, and never alone*. We recommend including objective priors in the class of priors over which a *sensitivity analysis* is performed.

Exercise 8.1 (Bernoulli sampling distribution) Consider a random sample from a Bernoulli distribution with the pmf given in (2.5). Find Jeffreys' prior.

Solution
The log likelihood is

$$\ln L(\theta) = \sum_{t=1}^{Y} [y_t \ln(\theta) + (1 - y_t) \ln(1 - \theta)]$$
$$= x \ln(\theta) + (T - x) \ln(1 - \theta),$$

where the number of successes, $x \equiv y_1 + y_2 + \cdots + y_T$, has a binomial distribution with pmf

$$p(x|T, \theta) = \frac{T!}{x!\,(T - x)!} \theta^x (1 - \theta)^{T-x}$$

and mean $T\theta$. Note that x is a sufficient statistic for θ. The Hessian is

$$\frac{\partial^2 \ln L(\theta)}{\partial \theta^2} = -\frac{x}{\theta^2} - \frac{T - x}{(1 - \theta)^2},$$

and the information matrix is

$$\mathcal{I}(\theta) = E_{X|\theta}\left[-\frac{\partial^2 \ln L(\theta)}{\partial \theta^2}\right] = \frac{T\theta}{\theta^2} + \frac{T - T\theta}{(1 - \theta)^2} = \frac{T}{\theta} + \frac{T}{(1 - \theta)} = \frac{T}{\theta(1 - \theta)}.$$

Therefore, Jeffreys' prior is

$$p(\theta) \propto \theta^{-1/2}(1 - \theta)^{-1/2}. \tag{8.1}$$

This is recognized as a $\beta(1/2, 1/2)$ distribution. This is a rare case in which the Jeffreys' prior is proper.

Exercise 8.2 (Negative binomial sampling distribution) In contrast to the random variable X in the preceding exercise, consider a random variable Z denoting the number of failures before the αth success. Then Z has a negative binomial distribution with pmf

$$p(z|\alpha, \theta) = \frac{\Gamma(\alpha + z)}{z!\,\Gamma(\alpha)} \theta^\alpha (1 - \theta)^z, \quad z = 0, 1, 2, \ldots, \tag{8.2}$$

where α is known, θ is unknown, and $E(Z|\alpha, \theta) = \alpha(1 - \theta)/\theta$. Suppose $\alpha = x$, the realized number of successes in Exercise 8.1. Find Jeffrey's prior for θ.

Solution
The log likelihood is

$$\ln L(\theta) = \ln(\Gamma[x + z]) - \ln(z!\,) - \ln(\Gamma[x]) + x \ln(\theta) + z \ln(1 - \theta).$$

The Hessian is

$$\frac{\partial^2 \ln L(\theta)}{\partial \theta^2} = -\frac{x}{\theta^2} - \frac{z}{(1 - \theta)^2},$$

and the information matrix is

$$\mathcal{I}(\theta) = E_{Z|\theta}\left[-\frac{\partial^2 \ln L(\theta)}{\partial \theta^2}\right] = \frac{x}{\theta^2} + \frac{x(1-\theta)/\theta}{(1-\theta)^2} = x\left[\frac{1}{\theta^2} + \frac{1}{\theta(1-\theta)}\right] = \frac{x}{\theta^2(1-\theta)}.$$

Therefore, Jeffreys' prior is

$$p(\theta) \propto \theta^{-1}(1-\theta)^{-1/2}, \tag{8.3}$$

which is improper. The Jeffreys' priors therefore differ in the binomial and negative binomial cases, even though their likelihood functions are proportional. Thus, use of the Jeffreys' prior can violate the likelihood principle. The sampling expectation in the definition is the culprit.

Exercise 8.3 (Kass and Wasserman 1996, Section 4.3) Aside from violating the likelihood principle, sample-space-dependent priors can lead to situations where the posterior depends on the order the data are received. Yet for a fixed prior, we get the same posterior no matter what order the data are processed, assuming independence.
(a) Suppose that y_1 is the number of successes (which in this example denotes the "heads" outcome) in n tosses of a coin with success probability θ. Find the posterior under Jeffreys' prior.
(b) Suppose that we flip the coin until another head appears, and suppose that this takes $Y_2 = y_2$ tosses. Using the posterior from (a) as a prior, find the corresponding posterior given y_1 and y_2.
(c) Now suppose the experiment is performed in reverse order. Beginning with Jeffreys' prior

$$p(\theta) \propto \theta^{-1}(1-\theta)^{-1/2}$$

for the negative binomial (Exercise 8.2), update sequentially on Y_2 then Y_1 to find the posterior.

Solution
(a) Using Bayes' theorem, (8.1), and the results of Exercise 8.1, we obtain the posterior

$$p_1(\theta|y_1) \propto \theta^{y_1-1/2}(1-\theta)^{n-y_1-1/2}.$$

(b) In terms of the negative binomial of Exercise 8.2, and (8.2) specifically, we have $\alpha = 1$ and $z = y_2 - 1$. Putting this together with the result in part (a), we obtain

$$p_2(\theta|y_1, y_2) \propto \theta^{y_1+1-1/2}(1-\theta)^{n-y_1+y_2-1-1/2}.$$

(c) Using Jeffreys' prior for the negative binomial together with the data y_2 yields a posterior of the form

$$p_3(\theta|y_2) \propto \theta^{-1+1}(1-\theta)^{y_2-1-1/2}.$$

Using this as a prior for θ and combining this prior with the binomial likelihood for the y_1 data gives

$$p_4(\theta|y_1, y_2) \propto \theta^{y_1-1+1}(1-\theta)^{n-y_1+y_2-1-1/2}.$$

So, the posterior in (c) is different from the posterior in (b).

Exercise 8.4 (Poisson sampling distribution) Suppose Y_t $(t = 1, 2, \ldots, T)$ is a random sample from a Poisson distribution with mean θ. Find Jeffreys' prior.

Solution

Using the likelihood function given in the solution to Exercise 2.12, the Hessian is

$$\frac{\partial^2 \ln L(\theta)}{\partial \theta^2} = -\frac{T\overline{y}}{\theta^2},$$

and the information matrix is

$$\mathcal{I}(\theta) = E_{\overline{Y}|\theta}\left[-\frac{\partial^2 \ln L(\theta)}{\partial \theta^2}\right] = \frac{T}{\theta}.$$

Therefore, Jeffreys' prior is

$$p(\theta) \propto \theta^{-1/2}.$$

Exercise 8.5 (Exponential sampling distribution and reparameterization) Suppose Y_t $(t = 1, 2, \ldots, T)$ are *iid* random variables from an exponential distribution with mean θ.

(a) Derive Jeffreys' prior for θ.
(b) Derive Jeffreys' prior for $\alpha = \theta^{-1}$.
(c) Find the posterior density of θ corresponding to the prior density in (a). Be specific in noting the family to which it belongs.
(d) Find the posterior density of α corresponding to the prior density in (b). Be specific in noting the family to which it belongs.

Solution

(a) The sampling density

$$p(y_t|\theta) = \theta^{-1}\exp(-y_t/\theta), \quad 0 < y_t < \infty,$$

implies the log likelihood

$$\ln L(\theta) = -T\ln(\theta) - T\overline{y}\theta^{-1}$$

and the derivatives

$$\frac{\partial \ln L(\theta)}{\partial \theta} = -\frac{T}{\theta} + \frac{T\overline{y}}{\theta^2},$$
$$\frac{\partial^2 \ln L(\theta)}{\partial \theta^2} = \frac{T}{\theta^2} - \frac{2T\overline{y}}{\theta^3}.$$

Hence, recalling that $E(\overline{Y}) = \theta$, we have the information matrix

$$\mathcal{I}(\theta) = E_{\overline{Y}|\theta}\left[-\frac{\partial^2 \ln L(\theta)}{\partial \theta^2}\right] = -\frac{T}{\theta^2} + \frac{2T}{\theta^2} = \frac{T}{\theta^2}.$$

Therefore, Jeffreys' prior is

$$p(\theta) \propto \theta^{-1}.$$

(b) Similarly,

$$\ln L(\alpha) = T\ln(\alpha) - T\overline{y}\alpha,$$

with derivatives

$$\frac{\partial \ln L(\alpha)}{\partial \alpha} = \frac{T}{\alpha} - T\overline{y},$$
$$\frac{\partial^2 \ln L(\alpha)}{\partial \alpha^2} = -\frac{T}{\alpha^2}.$$

Note that observed information is constant in this case. Therefore, Jeffreys' prior is

$$p(\alpha) \propto \alpha^{-1}.$$

(c) The posterior density of θ corresponding to the prior density in (a) is

$$p(\theta|y) \propto \theta^{-1}\theta^{-T}\exp(-T\overline{y}\theta^{-1})$$
$$= \theta^{-(T+1)}\exp(-T\overline{y}\theta^{-1}),$$

which is recognized to be the kernel of an inverted gamma density (see Theorem A.2), specifically $IG(T, [T\overline{y}]^{-1})$.

(d) The posterior density of α corresponding to the prior density in (b) is

$$p(\alpha|y) \propto \alpha^{-1}\alpha^{T}\exp(-T\overline{y}\alpha)$$
$$\propto \alpha^{T-1}\exp(-T\overline{y}\alpha),$$

which is recognized to be the kernel of a gamma density (see Theorem A.2), specifically $G(T, [T\overline{y}]^{-1})$. The invariance property of Jeffreys' prior refers to the fact that the posteriors in (c) and (d) are related by a simple change of variable.

Exercise 8.6 (Normal sampling distribution with unknown mean and variance) Consider a random sample from an $N(\mu, \sigma^2)$ distribution with $\theta = [\mu\ \sigma^2]'$ unknown. Find the prior that is proportional to the square root of the information matrix.

Solution

It is straightforward to show that the Hessian matrix is

$$\frac{\partial^2 \ln L(\theta)}{\partial\theta\partial\theta'} = \begin{bmatrix} -T/\sigma^2 & -(1/\sigma^4)\sum_{t=1}^{T}(y_t-\mu) \\ -(1/\sigma^4)\sum_{t=1}^{T}(y_t-\mu) & [T/(2\sigma^4)] - (1/\sigma^6)\sum_{t=1}^{T}(y_t-\mu)^2 \end{bmatrix},$$

and the information matrix is

$$\mathcal{I}(\theta) = E_{Y|\theta}\left[-\frac{\partial^2 \ln L(\theta)}{\partial\theta\partial\theta'}\right] = \begin{bmatrix} T/\sigma^2 & 0 \\ 0 & T/(2\sigma^4) \end{bmatrix}.$$

Therefore, $|\mathcal{I}(\theta)|^{1/2} = T/[\sqrt{2}\sigma^3]$, yielding the prior

$$p(\theta) \propto \sigma^{-3}.$$

This result led Jeffreys to modify his general rule. He argued that in this case the prior for each parameter should be treated separately and then multiplied. In the case of known σ^2, Jeffreys' prior for μ is $p(\mu) \propto c$, where c is an arbitrary constant. In the case of known μ, Jeffreys' prior for σ^2 is $p(\sigma^2) \propto \sigma^{-2}$. Therefore, in the case of unknown μ and σ^2, Jeffreys recommended the commonly used prior $p(\theta) \propto \sigma^{-2}$.

Exercise 8.7 (Hypothesis testing with improper priors) Problems arise in testing $H_1 : \theta_1 \in \Theta_1$ versus $H_2 : \theta_2 \in \Theta_2$ if improper priors such as $p(\theta_i|H_i) \propto c_i$, $i = 1, 2$, are used. Demonstrate this fact.

Solution

Consider the Bayes factor

$$B_{12} = \frac{\int_{\Theta_1} p(\theta_1|H_1)L(\theta_1)\, d\theta_1}{\int_{\Theta_2} p(\theta_2|H_2)L(\theta_2)\, d\theta_2} = \frac{c_1 \int_{\Theta_1} L(\theta_1)\, d\theta_1}{c_2 \int_{\Theta_2} L(\theta_2)\, d\theta_2}.$$

Even if the integrals converge, B_{12} remains indeterminate because c_1/c_2 is a ratio of arbitrary constants.

Exercise 8.8 (Bayes factor with a diffuse proper prior) We have noted earlier that Bayes factors are arbitrary when improper priors are used (e.g., Exercise 8.7) but that this difficulty does not occur with proper priors. This may lead the unwary reader to think that employing a proper prior with a very large variance overcomes the former problem, while at the same time serving to let the data speak for themselves. This exercise shows that such reasoning is incorrect.

Suppose Y_t $(t = 1, 2, \ldots, T)$, given θ, are *iid* $N(0, 1)$ under hypothesis H_1 and $N(\theta, 1)$ under hypothesis H_2. Assume the prior $\theta|H_2 \sim N(0, v)$, $v > 0$. Find the Bayes factor B_{21} and discuss its behavior for large v.

Solution
The problem can be embedded in Exercise 2.3 and its notation. Under H_1 there are no unknown parameters, and so the likelihood and marginal likelihood functions are the same. In particular,

$$p(y|H_1) = L(\theta) = (2\pi)^{-T/2} \exp\left[-(1/2)\sum_{t=1}^{T} y_t^2\right].$$

Under H_2, $p(y|H_2)$ can be obtained from (2.21) (with $\theta_2 = 1$) and (2.23) (with $\underline{\mu} = 0$):

$$p(y|H_2) = \left[(2\pi)^{-\nu/2}T^{-1/2}\exp(-\nu s^2/2)\right]\left[(2\pi[\upsilon + T^{-1}])^{-1/2}\exp\left(-\frac{\overline{y}^2}{2(\upsilon+T^{-1})}\right)\right]$$
$$= (2\pi)^{-T/2}T^{-1/2}(\upsilon + T^{-1})^{-1/2}\exp\left[-(1/2)\left(\sum_{t=1}^{T} y_t^2 - T\overline{y}^2 + \frac{\overline{y}^2}{\upsilon + T^{-1}}\right)\right].$$

The Bayes factor B_{21} is

$$B_{21} = \frac{p(y|H_2)}{p(y|H_1)}$$
$$= T^{-1/2}(\upsilon + T^{-1})^{-1/2}\exp\left[-(1/2)\left(\sum_{t=1}^{T} y_t^2 - T\overline{y}^2 + \frac{\overline{y}^2}{\upsilon + T^{-1}} - \sum_{t=1}^{T} y_t^2\right)\right]$$
$$= T^{-1/2}(\upsilon + T^{-1})^{-1/2}\exp\left[\left(\frac{\upsilon T}{1+\upsilon T}\right)\frac{T\overline{y}^2}{2}\right].$$

For moderate T and large υ,

$$B_{21} \approx \upsilon^{-1/2}T^{-1/2}\exp(T\overline{y}/2).$$

Therefore, B_{21} depends heavily on the arbitrarily chosen "large" value of υ.

Exercise 8.9 (Strong inconsistency of improper priors) Consider a random sample $Y_1, Y_2, \ldots, Y_T$ from an $N(\theta, 1)$ distribution. Let A be the event that $|\overline{Y}| \geq |\theta|$, where $\overline{Y}$ is the sample mean. Suppose the prior for θ is $p(\theta) \propto$ constant. Let $\Phi(c|\mu, \sigma^2)$ denote the normal cdf at c with mean μ and variance σ^2. That is, $\Phi(c|\mu,\sigma^2) \equiv \Pr(z \leq c)$, where $z \sim N(\mu, \sigma^2)$.

(a) From the standpoint of the sampling model, show that

$$\Pr(A|\theta) = (1/2) + \Phi(-2|\theta|\sqrt{T}|0,1).$$

(b) From the standpoint of the posterior distribution, show that

$$\Pr(A|y) = (1/2) - \Phi(-2|\overline{y}|\sqrt{T}|0,1).$$

(c) Are (a) and (b) consistent?

Solution

(a) We know that $\overline{Y}|\theta \sim N(\theta, T^{-1})$. Let $X = |\overline{Y}|$. Then the *sampling cdf* of X is

$$F_X(c) = \Pr(X \le c) = \Pr(|\overline{Y}| \le c) = \Pr(-c \le \overline{Y} \le c)$$
$$= \Phi(c|\theta, T^{-1}) - \Phi(-c|\theta, T^{-1}). \quad (8.4)$$

Therefore,

$$\begin{aligned}\Pr(A|\theta) &= \Pr(X \ge |\theta|)\\ &= 1 - F_X(|\theta|)\\ &= 1 - \Phi(|\theta| \mid \theta, T^{-1}) + \Phi(-|\theta| \mid \theta, T^{-1}). \quad (8.5)\end{aligned}$$

If $\theta > 0$ then $|\theta| = \theta$, $\Phi(|\theta| \mid \theta, T^{-1}) = (1/2)$, and $\Phi(-|\theta| \mid \theta, T^{-1}) = \Phi(-2\theta\sqrt{T}|0,1) = \Phi(-2|\theta|\sqrt{T}|0,1)$. Hence, (8.5) becomes

$$\Pr(A|\theta) = (1/2) + \Phi(-2|\theta|\sqrt{T}|0,1). \quad (8.6)$$

If $\theta \le 0$ then $|\theta| = -\theta$, $\Phi(|\theta| \mid \theta, T^{-1}) = \Phi(-2\theta\sqrt{T}|0,1) = \Phi(2|\theta|\sqrt{T}|0,1)$, and $\Phi(-|\theta| \mid \theta, T^{-1}) = (1/2)$. Hence, (8.5) becomes

$$\begin{aligned}\Pr(A|\theta) &= (3/2) - \Phi(2|\theta|\sqrt{T}|0,1)\\ &= (3/2) - [1 - \Phi(-2|\theta|\sqrt{T}|0,1)]\\ &= (1/2) + \Phi(-2|\theta|\sqrt{T}|0,1). \quad (8.7)\end{aligned}$$

Since (8.6) and (8.7) are the same, their common value holds for all θ.

(b) Under the uniform prior for θ, we know that $\theta|y \sim N(\overline{y}, T^{-1})$. Let $X = |\theta|$. Then, similar to (8.4), the *posterior cdf* of X is

$$F_{X|y}(c) = \Phi(c|\overline{y}, T^{-1}) - \Phi(-c|\overline{y}, T^{-1}). \quad (8.8)$$

Therefore,

$$\Pr(A|y) = \Pr(|\theta| \le |\overline{y}|\ |y) = F_X(|\overline{y}|) = \Phi(|\overline{y}| \mid \overline{y}, T^{-1}) - \Phi(-|\overline{y}| \mid \overline{y}, T^{-1}). \quad (8.9)$$

If $\overline{y} > 0$ then $|\overline{y}| = y$, $\Phi(|\overline{y}| \mid \overline{y}, T^{-1}) = (1/2)$, and $\Phi(-|\overline{y}| \mid \overline{y}, T^{-1}) = \Phi(-2\overline{y}\sqrt{T}|0,1) = \Phi(-2|\overline{y}|\sqrt{T}|0,1)$. Hence, (8.9) becomes

$$\Pr(A|y) = (1/2) - \Phi(-2|\overline{y}|\sqrt{T}|0,1). \quad (8.10)$$

If $\overline{y} \le 0$ then $|\overline{y}| = -\overline{y}$, $\Phi(|\overline{y}| \mid \overline{y}, T^{-1}) = \Phi(-2\overline{y}\sqrt{T}|0,1) = \Phi(2|\overline{y}|\sqrt{T}|0,1)$, and $\Phi(-|\overline{y}| \mid \overline{y}, T^{-1}) = (1/2)$. Hence, (8.9) becomes

$$\begin{aligned}\Pr(A|y) &= \Phi(2|\overline{y}|\sqrt{T}|0,1) - (1/2)\\ &= [1 - \Phi(-2|\overline{y}|\sqrt{T}|0,1)] - (1/2)\\ &= (1/2) - \Phi(-2|\overline{y}|\sqrt{T}|0,1). \quad (8.11)\end{aligned}$$

Since (8.10) and (8.11) are the same, their common value holds for all $\overline{y}$.

(c) No. According to (a), $\Pr(A|\theta) > 1/2$ for all θ and hence $\Pr(A) > 1/2$. However, according to (b), $\Pr(A|\overline{y}) < 1/2$ for all $\overline{y}$ and hence $\Pr(A) < 1/2$. Therefore, the two are inconsistent (known as *strong inconsistency* in the literature). This demonstrates one problem with improper priors and is related to incoherence. See Kass and Wasserman (1996, Section 4.2) for a discussion of further problems.

9

Asymptotic Bayes

As seen in previous chapters, the Bayesian approach typically involves the evaluation of multidimensional integrals such as those appearing in posterior expectations, marginal likelihoods, and predictive densities. In non-conjugate situations, these integrals cannot be calculated analytically. In future chapters we present questions relating to various methods for evaluating such integrals using posterior simulation. However, posterior simulation can be computationally demanding and, hence, Bayesians sometimes use asymptotic approximations. Such approximations are the focus of this chapter.

In most situations the prior pdf does not depend on the sample size T, and so in large samples, the likelihood eventually dominates the prior density over their common support. This suggests that consideration of the behavior of the posterior density as $T \to \infty$ may provide useful analytical approximations when T is in fact large. Such "Bayesian asymptotics" differ, however, from frequentist asymptotics in an important way. The thing being approximated in Bayesian asymptotics is conceptually well defined in finite samples, namely the posterior pdf. Nuisance parameters can be addressed in a straightforward manner by marginalizing them out of the posterior to obtain the exact marginal posterior pdf for the parameters of interest. In general, there is no frequentist classical sampling distribution of estimators in finite samples that is free of nuisance parameters.

In the same way that sampling distributions of maximum likelihood estimators (MLEs) in regular situations are asymptotically normal, posterior densities are also approximately normal. This result is stated informally in the following theorem. See Bernardo and Smith (1994, pp. 285–297) and the references cited therein for more details. Also see Kwan (1998) for discussion of cases in which Bayesian and frequentist asymptotic inferences differ because the asymptotic convergence is non-uniform (e.g., unit root models).

Theorem 9.1 Under suitable regularity conditions, the posterior density can be approximated as $T \to \infty$ by $\phi_k\left(\theta|\widehat{\theta}_{\text{ML}}, \left[\mathcal{I}\left(\widehat{\theta}_{\text{ML}}\right)\right]^{-1}\right)$, where $\widehat{\theta}_{\text{ML}}$ is the MLE and $\mathcal{I}(\cdot)$ is the information matrix.

While not providing a formal statement and proof of Theorem 9.1, we note that the prior, $p(\theta)$, must provide positive density to a neighborhood of the true θ_0 appearing in frequentist asymptotics, and the prior density should not depend on T. Also, the parameter vector needs to be identified. The approximation itself in Theorem 9.1 does not depend on the prior and is essentially numerically (but not conceptually) identical to the approximation offered by the asymptotic distribution theory for maximum likelihood. Berger (1985, p. 224) argues informally that the quality of the approximation in Theorem 9.1 can usually be improved in finite samples by the following approximations that reflect the observed data and the prior.

Corollary 9.1 The following approximations offer increasing improvements on the approximation in Theorem 9.1.

(a) $\phi_k\left(\theta|\widehat{\theta}_{\text{ML}}, \left[-\overline{\mathcal{H}}\left(\widehat{\theta}_{\text{ML}}\right)\right]^{-1}\right)$, where $\overline{\mathcal{H}}(\theta)$ is the Hessian of the log posterior,

$$\overline{\mathcal{H}}(\theta) = \frac{\partial^2 \ln[p(\theta)]}{\partial\theta\partial\theta'} + \frac{\partial^2 \ln L(\theta)}{\partial\theta\partial\theta'}; \tag{9.1}$$

(b) $\phi_k\left(\theta|\widehat{\theta}, \left[-\overline{\mathcal{H}}\left(\widehat{\theta}\right)\right]^{-1}\right)$, where $\widehat{\theta}$ is the posterior mode;

(c) $\phi_k(\theta|E[\theta|y], \text{Var}[\theta|y])$.

Any of these normal approximations can be used to provide approximations to, for example, posterior means and variances.

There are other, more accurate, approximations for posterior features of interest of which those based on *Laplace's approximation* are the most popular. To explain the use of Laplace's approximation, we begin at a high level of generality. The appearance of integrals is ubiquitous in Bayesian analysis, and often the integrals involved do not have closed-form expressions. Thus convenient approximations to such integrals are desirable. Consider the integral

$$J = \int_\Theta b(\theta)\exp[-Th(\theta)]\,d\theta, \tag{9.2}$$

where θ is $K \times 1$, $\Theta = \mathbb{R}^K$, $-h(\cdot)$ is a twice-differentiable function having a unique maximum at $\widehat{\theta}$, $\partial h(\theta)/\partial\theta|_{\theta=\widehat{\theta}} = 0$, $H(\theta) = \frac{\partial^2 h(\theta)}{\partial\theta\partial\theta'} > 0$, and $b(\cdot)$ is continuous in a neighborhood of $\widehat{\theta}$, with $b\left(\widehat{\theta}\right) \neq 0$. Expanding $h(\theta)$ as a second-order Taylor series around $\widehat{\theta}$ and dropping the remainder yields an approximation to $\exp[-Th(\theta)]$ proportional to a normal density. When integrated against this normal density, the $O\left(T^{-1/2}\right)$ terms of the expansion of $b(\theta)$ and $h(\theta)$ vanish and Laplace's approximation to (9.2) is

$$\widehat{J} = (2\pi)^{\frac{K}{2}} b\left(\widehat{\theta}\right) \left|TH\left(\widehat{\theta}\right)\right|^{-\frac{1}{2}} \exp\left[-Th\left(\widehat{\theta}\right)\right], \tag{9.3}$$

which satisfies $J = \widehat{J}\left[1 + O\left(T^{-1}\right)\right]$. The assumption $\Theta = \mathbb{R}^K$ can usually be satisfied by reparameterization.

Often, ratios of integrals such as (9.2) are encountered. Consider

$$r = \frac{J_N}{J_D} = \frac{\int_{\mathbb{R}^{K_N}} b_N(\theta_N) \exp\left[-Th_N(\theta_N)\right] d\theta_N}{\int_{\mathbb{R}^{K_D}} b_D(\theta_D) \exp\left[-Th_D(\theta_D)\right] d\theta_D}, \tag{9.4}$$

where for $i = N, D$, θ_i is $K_i \times 1$, $-h_i(\cdot)$ is a twice-differentiable function having a unique maximum at $\widehat{\theta}_i$, $\left.\frac{\partial h_i(\theta_i)}{\partial \theta_i}\right|_{\theta_i = \widehat{\theta}_i} = 0$, $H_i(\theta) = \frac{\partial^2 h_i(\theta_i)}{\partial \theta_i \partial \theta_i'} > 0$, and $b_i(\cdot)$ is continuous in a neighborhood of $\widehat{\theta}_i$, with $b_i\left(\widehat{\theta}_i\right) \neq 0$. If $h_D(\theta) = h_N(\theta)$, then (9.4) is said to be in *standard form*. Applying Laplace's method separately to the numerator and denominator in (9.4) yields

$$\widehat{r} = \frac{\widehat{J}_N}{\widehat{J}_D} = \frac{(2\pi)^{\frac{K_N}{2}} b_N\left(\widehat{\theta}_N\right) \left|TH_N\left(\widehat{\theta}_N\right)\right|^{-\frac{1}{2}} \exp\left[-Th_N\left(\widehat{\theta}_N\right)\right]}{(2\pi)^{\frac{K_D}{2}} b_D\left(\widehat{\theta}_D\right) \left|TH_D\left(\widehat{\theta}_D\right)\right|^{-\frac{1}{2}} \exp\left[-Th_D\left(\widehat{\theta}_D\right)\right]}. \tag{9.5}$$

Once again, $r = \widehat{r}\left[1 + O\left(T^{-1}\right)\right]$.

Posterior moments are an example of ratios such as (9.4). Suppose $g : \mathbb{R}^K \to \mathbb{R}$ and consider

$$\begin{aligned} G \equiv E\left[g(\theta)|y\right] &= \int_{\mathbb{R}^K} g(\theta) p(\theta|y)\, d\theta \\ &= \frac{\int_{\mathbb{R}^K} g(\theta) p(\theta) L(\theta)\, d\theta}{\int_{\mathbb{R}^K} p(\theta) L(\theta)\, d\theta}. \end{aligned} \tag{9.6}$$

A sufficient condition for the existence of G is that all integrals required are defined on bounded regions and have integrands of bounded variation. There are many ways of applying Laplace's method, yielding different estimates with relative error of $O\left(T^{-1}\right)$. The choice of $b_i(\cdot)$ and $h_i(\cdot)$ $(i = N, D)$ affects the Laplace estimate of G.

If $g(\theta) > 0$, then we can use the *fully exponential method* of Tierney and Kadane (1986) to get an easy approximation with an improved relative error of $O\left(T^{-2}\right)$. G in (9.6) is a special case of (9.4) where $\theta = \theta_N = \theta_D$, $K = K_N = K_D$, $b_N(\theta) = b_D(\theta) = 1$,

$$h_D(\theta) = -(1/T)\left(\ln[p(\theta)] + \ln[L(\theta)]\right),$$

$$h_N(\theta) = h_D(\theta) - (1/T)\ln[g(\theta)],$$

$\widehat{\theta}_N = \text{argmax}_\theta \{-h_N(\theta)\}$, and $\widehat{\theta}_D = \text{argmax}_\theta \{-h_D(\theta)\}$ is the posterior mode. Writing (9.6) as

$$G = \frac{\int_{\mathbb{R}^K} \exp[-Th_N(\theta)]\, d\theta}{\int_{\mathbb{R}^K} \exp[-Th_D(\theta)]\, d\theta}$$
$$= \frac{\int_{\mathbb{R}^K} \exp\left[-T\left(h_N\left(\widehat{\theta}_N\right) - \frac{1}{2}\left(\theta - \widehat{\theta}_N\right)'\left[-H_N\left(\widehat{\theta}_N\right)^{-1}\right]^{-1}\left(\theta - \widehat{\theta}_N\right) + R_N\right)\right] d\theta}{\int_{\mathbb{R}^K} \exp\left[-T\left(h_D\left(\widehat{\theta}_D\right) - \frac{1}{2}\left(\theta - \widehat{\theta}_D\right)'\left[-H_D\left(\widehat{\theta}_D\right)^{-1}\right]^{-1}\left(\theta - \widehat{\theta}_D\right) + R_D\right)\right] d\theta}, \tag{9.7}$$

where R_N and R_D denote Taylor series remainders, we obtain the Tierney–Kadane estimate

$$\widehat{G}_{\text{TK}} = \frac{\left|H_N\left(\widehat{\theta}_N\right)\right|^{-\frac{1}{2}} \exp\left[-Th_N\left(\widehat{\theta}_N\right)\right]}{\left|H_D\left(\widehat{\theta}_D\right)\right|^{-\frac{1}{2}} \exp\left[-Th_D\left(\widehat{\theta}_D\right)\right]}, \tag{9.8}$$

and $E[g(\theta)|y] = \widehat{G}_{\text{TK}}\left[1 + O\left(T^{-2}\right)\right]$.

In the full exponential parameterization the $O\left(T^{-1}\right)$ terms in the numerator and denominator cancel, resulting in the improved $O\left(T^{-2}\right)$ approximation. Note, however, that (9.8) is *not* invariant to reparameterizations. Illustrative examples suggest that the reparameterizations that lead to locally uniform non-informative prior representations typically improve the accuracy of approximations. Hence, we recommend reparameterizing so that the new Hessian matrices are constant over $\mathbb{R}^K$. If $g(\theta) \leq 0$, the fully exponential method cannot be applied directly. Tierney, Kass, and Kadane (1989) discuss two alternatives for this case.

In the following exercises we investigate these approximations in the context of simple problems in which analytical expressions for all steps are available and hence for which the quality of the approximations can be analytically studied.

Exercise 9.1 (Posterior means) Identify (9.6) in each of the following cases:
(a) $K = 1$ and $g(\theta) = \theta^r$.
(b) A is a subset of Θ and $g(\theta) = I_A(\theta)$ is an indicator function equal to unity when $\theta \in A$ and equal to zero when $\theta \notin A$.
(c) $g(\theta) = p(y_*|y, \theta)$ for some out-of-sample value y_*.
(d) $g(\theta) = \exp(v'\theta)$, where v is a given $K \times 1$ vector of constants.
(e) $\alpha = [\beta' \; \theta']'$ and $g(\theta) = p(\beta|\theta, y)$.

Solution
(a) G is the rth posterior moment of θ around the origin.
(b) $G = \Pr(A|y) = \Pr(\theta \in A|y)$.

(c) G is the predictive density $p(y_*|y)$.
(d) G is the posterior moment-generating function of θ evaluated at v.
(e) G is the marginal posterior density $p(\beta|y)$.

Exercise 9.2 (Laplace approximation of a gamma integrating constant I) Suppose $\theta|y \sim G(\overline{\alpha}, \overline{\beta})$ as in Exercise 2.10. The kernel of this distribution is $\theta^{\overline{\alpha}-1}\exp(-\theta/\overline{\beta})$. This exercise explores the use of the Laplace approximation to estimate the integrating constant $c = \overline{\beta}^{\overline{\alpha}}\Gamma(\overline{\alpha})$ of the gamma density. Discuss the Laplace approximation using (9.2) with $b(\theta) = \theta^{\overline{\alpha}-1}$ and $h(\theta) = \theta/[T\overline{\beta}]$.

Solution
Since $-h(\theta) = -\theta/[T\overline{\beta}]$ does not have an interior maximum over $\theta > 0$, the Laplace method cannot be used in this parameterization.

Exercise 9.3 (Laplace approximation of a gamma integrating constant II) Consider Exercise 9.2. Write the kernel in the full exponential form $\exp[-Th(\theta)]$ and find the Laplace approximation $\hat{c}_1$ of c.

Solution
Straightforwardly,

$$h(\theta) = -T^{-1}[(\overline{\alpha} - 1)\ln(\theta) - \theta/\overline{\beta}].$$

Equating

$$\frac{\partial h(\theta)}{\partial \theta} = -T^{-1}\left[\frac{\overline{\alpha} - 1}{\theta} - \overline{\beta}^{-1}\right]$$

to zero implies a mode at $\widehat{\theta} = \overline{\beta}(\overline{\alpha} - 1)$. Note that

$$\exp[-Th(\hat{\theta})] = \exp\left[(\overline{\alpha} - 1)\ln\hat{\theta} - \hat{\theta}/\overline{\beta}\right] = \left[\overline{\beta}(\overline{\alpha} - 1)\right]^{\overline{\alpha}-1}\exp[-(\overline{\alpha} - 1)].$$

Furthermore, the Hessian is

$$H(\theta) = \frac{\partial^2 h(\theta)}{\partial \theta^2} = \frac{\overline{\alpha} - 1}{T\theta^2}$$

and when evaluated at the mode equals

$$H(\theta) = \left[T\overline{\beta}^2(\overline{\alpha} - 1)\right]^{-1}.$$

Therefore, using (9.3) with $b(\theta) = 1$ yields the Laplace approximation

$$\begin{aligned}
\hat{c}_1 &= \sqrt{2\pi}|TH(\widehat{\theta})|^{-1/2}\exp[-Th(\hat{\theta})] \\
&= \sqrt{2\pi}\overline{\beta}(\overline{\alpha} - 1)^{1/2}[\overline{\beta}(\overline{\alpha} - 1)]^{\overline{\alpha}-1}\exp[-(\overline{\alpha} - 1)] \\
&= \overline{\beta}^{\overline{\alpha}}\left\{[2\pi(\overline{\alpha} - 1)]^{1/2}[\overline{\alpha} - 1]^{\overline{\alpha}-1}\exp[-(\overline{\alpha} - 1)]\right\}. \qquad (9.9)
\end{aligned}$$

It turns out that the term in curly braces in the last line of (9.9) is Stirling's approximation to $(\overline{\alpha}-1)! = \Gamma(\overline{\alpha})$. Therefore, $\hat{c}_1$ is a sensible estimate of $c = \overline{\beta}^{\overline{\alpha}}\Gamma(\overline{\alpha})$.

Exercise 9.4 (Laplace approximation of a gamma integrating constant III) Consider Exercise 9.3. Because $0 < \theta < \infty$, there is reason to believe the result in this case can be improved by transforming $\gamma \in \mathbb{R}$, where, say, $\gamma = \ln(\theta)$. Find the Laplace approximation $\hat{c}_2$ of c using the parameterization in terms of γ.

Solution

Noting that $d\gamma = \theta^{-1}d\theta$, we obtain the integral of the transformed kernel,

$$\begin{aligned}\int_0^\infty \theta^{\overline{\alpha}-1}\exp(-\theta/\overline{\beta})\,d\theta &= \int_{-\infty}^\infty \exp[\gamma(\overline{\alpha}-1)]\exp[-\exp(\gamma)/\overline{\beta}]\exp(\gamma)\,d\gamma \\ &= \int_{-\infty}^\infty \exp[\gamma\overline{\alpha}-\exp(\gamma)/\overline{\beta}]\,d\gamma \\ &= \int_{-\infty}^\infty \exp[-Th(\gamma)]\,d\gamma,\end{aligned}$$

where

$$h(\gamma) = -T^{-1}[\gamma\overline{\alpha} - \overline{\beta}^{-1}\exp(\gamma)].$$

Equating

$$\frac{\partial h(\gamma)}{\partial\gamma} = -T^{-1}[\overline{\alpha} - \overline{\beta}^{-1}\exp(\gamma)]$$

to zero implies a mode at

$$\widehat{\gamma} = \ln(\overline{\beta}\overline{\alpha}).$$

Note that this value of $\widehat{\gamma}$ implies $\hat{\theta} = \overline{\beta}\overline{\alpha}$, which is different than the mode in Exercise 9.3. Also note that

$$\exp[-Th(\widehat{\gamma})] = \exp[\overline{\alpha}\ln(\overline{\beta}\overline{\alpha}) - \overline{\alpha}] = \overline{\beta}^{\overline{\alpha}}\overline{\alpha}^{\overline{\alpha}}\exp(-\overline{\alpha}).$$

The Hessian is

$$H(\gamma) = \frac{\partial^2 h(\gamma)}{\partial\gamma^2} = T^{-1}\overline{\beta}^{-1}\exp(\gamma),$$

and when evaluated at the mode it equals

$$H(\widehat{\gamma}) = T^{-1}\overline{\alpha}.$$

Therefore, using (9.3) with $b(\cdot) = 1$ yields the Laplace approximation

$$\begin{aligned}\hat{c}_2 &= \sqrt{2\pi}|TH(\widehat{\theta})|^{-1/2}\exp[-Th(\widehat{\theta})] \qquad (9.10)\\ &= \sqrt{2\pi}\overline{\alpha}^{-1/2}[\overline{\beta}\overline{\alpha}]^{\overline{\alpha}}\exp[-\overline{\alpha}] \\ &= \overline{\beta}^{\overline{\alpha}}\left\{[2\pi\overline{\alpha}]^{1/2}\overline{\alpha}^{\overline{\alpha}}\exp[-\overline{\alpha}]\right\}\overline{\alpha}^{-1}.\end{aligned}$$

Table 9.1: Comparison of two Laplace approximations of a gamma integrating constant.

				Absolute percentage error	
$\overline{\alpha}$	$\Gamma(\overline{\alpha})$	$\hat{c}_1/[\overline{\beta}^{\overline{\alpha}}]$	$\hat{c}_1/[\overline{\beta}^{\overline{\alpha}}]$	$\hat{c}_1$	$\hat{c}_2$
2	1	.922	.960	7.8	4.0
3	2	1.919	1.945	4.0	2.7
4	6	5.836	5.877	2.7	2.1
5	24	23.506	23.604	2.1	1.7
6	120	118.019	118.346	1.7	1.4
7	720	710.078	711.485	1.4	1.2
8	5040	4 980.396	4 987.799	1.2	1.0
9	40 320	39 902.395	39 948.541	1.0	.9
10	362 880	359 536.870	359 869.560	.9	.8

Again, the term in curly braces in the final expression of (9.10) is Stirling's approximation to $\overline{\alpha}! = \Gamma(\overline{\alpha}+1)$. Hence, $\{\cdot\}\overline{\alpha}^{-1} = (\overline{\alpha}-1)\Gamma(\overline{\alpha})$. Therefore, $\hat{c}_2$ is also a sensible estimate of $c_2 = \overline{\beta}^{\overline{\alpha}}\Gamma(\overline{\alpha})$.

Exercise 9.5 (Comparison of Laplace approximations of a gamma integrating constant) Consider Exercises 9.3 and 9.4. Compare the relative approximation errors

$$|\hat{c}_i - c|/c, \quad i = 1, 2,$$

for $\overline{\alpha} = \underline{\alpha} + T = 2, 3, 4, \ldots, 10$.

Solution

In calculating the percentage errors the value of $\overline{\beta}$ drops out, and the comparison amounts to how well do $\hat{c}_i/[\overline{\beta}^{\overline{\alpha}}]$, $i = 1, 2$, approximate $\Gamma(\overline{\alpha})$. Straightforward computation yields the percentage errors in Table 9.1. Although the percentage errors are impressively small for both estimates, clearly the reparameterization to the form $\gamma = \ln(\theta)$ results in an improved Laplace approximation.

Exercise 9.6 (Laplace approximation of the posterior mean of an exponential random variable) Suppose $Y_t|\theta$, $t = 1, 2, \ldots, T$ are *iid* exponential random variables with mean θ. Consider Jeffreys' prior $p(\theta) = \theta^{-1}$. According to Exercise 8.5(c), the corresponding posterior distribution is the inverted gamma $IG(T, [T\overline{y}]^{-1})$ with posterior density

$$p(\theta|y) = c^{-1}\theta^{-(T+1)}\exp(-T\overline{y}\theta^{-1}),$$

$c = \Gamma(T)[T\overline{y}]^{-T}$, and posterior mean equaling $E(\theta|y) = T\overline{y}/(T-1)$. Write the integrand of the posterior mean in fully exponential form $\exp[-Th(\theta)]$ and find the

Laplace approximation to the posterior mean.

Solution

The posterior mean can be written

$$\begin{aligned} G = E(\theta|y) &= \int_0^\infty \theta c^{-1}\theta^{-(T+1)} \exp(-T\overline{y}\theta^{-1})\, d\theta \\ &= \int_0^\infty \exp[-T(T^{-1}\ln(c) + \ln\theta + \overline{y}\theta^{-1})]\, d\theta \\ &= \int_0^\infty \exp[-Th(\theta)]\, d\theta, \end{aligned}$$

where $h(\theta) = T^{-1}\ln(c) + \ln(\theta) + \overline{y}\theta^{-1}$. Equating the derivative

$$\frac{\partial h(\theta)}{\partial\theta} = \frac{1}{\theta} - \frac{\overline{y}}{\theta^2}$$

to zero and solving yields the mode $\hat{\theta} = \overline{y}$. The Hessian is

$$H(\theta) = -\frac{1}{\theta^2} + \frac{2\overline{y}}{\theta^3}.$$

The Laplace approximation to $G = E(\theta|y)$ requires

$$\begin{aligned} \exp[-Th(\widehat{\theta})] &= \exp[-\ln(c) - T\ln(\widehat{\theta}) - T\overline{y}/\widehat{\theta}] \\ &= [\Gamma(T)]^{-1}T^T\overline{y}^T\overline{y}^{-T}\exp(-T) \\ &= [\Gamma(T)]^{-1}T^T\exp(-T) \end{aligned}$$

and

$$TH(\widehat{\theta}) = -\frac{T}{\widehat{\theta}^2} + \frac{2T\overline{y}}{\widehat{\theta}^3} = \frac{T}{\overline{y}^2}.$$

Therefore, using (9.3) with $b(\cdot) = 1$ yields the Laplace approximation

$$\begin{aligned} \widehat{G}_{\mathrm{L}} &= (2\pi)^{1/2}|TH(\widehat{\theta})|^{-1/2}\exp[-Th(\widehat{\theta})] \\ &= (2\pi)^{1/2}T^{-1/2}\overline{y}[\Gamma(T)]^{-1}T^T\exp(-T) \\ &= \overline{y}[\Gamma(T)]^{-1}\left\{(2\pi T)^{1/2}T^T\exp(-T)\right\}T^{-1} \\ &= [\Gamma(T)]^{-1}\left\{(2\pi T)^{1/2}T^T\exp(-T)\right\}T^{-2}(T-1)\frac{T\overline{y}}{T-1}. \end{aligned} \tag{9.11}$$

Again, the term in curly braces is Stirling's approximation to $T! = \Gamma(T+1)$. Hence, $\{\cdot\}T^{-1} = \Gamma(T)$. Therefore, $\widehat{G}_{\mathrm{L}}$ is a sensible estimate of $E(\theta|y)$.

Exercise 9.7 (Tierney–Kadane approximation: Exponential posterior mean I (Achcar and Smith 1990)) Consider Exercise 9.6. Using the fully exponential method, find the Tierney–Kadane approximation to this posterior mean.

Solution

A random sample of size T from an exponential distribution with mean θ yields the log likelihood

$$\ln L(\theta) = -T \ln(\theta) - T\overline{y}\theta^{-1}.$$

The posterior mean is a ratio of integrals as in (9.6) with $g(\theta) = \theta$. To employ the fully exponential version of Tierney–Kadane, we need to express the integrands in the denominator and numerator of (9.6) in the forms $\exp[-Th_D(\theta)]$ and $\exp[-Th_N(\theta)]$, respectively. Thus we construct

$$\begin{aligned} h_D(\theta) &= -T^{-1}[\ln[p(\theta)] + \ln L(\theta)] \\ &= -T^{-1}[-(T+1)\ln(\theta) - T\overline{y}/\theta] \end{aligned} \tag{9.12}$$

and

$$h_N(\theta) = -T^{-1}[-T\ln(\theta) - T\overline{y}/\theta]. \tag{9.13}$$

Equating the derivatives

$$\frac{\partial h_D(\theta)}{\partial \theta} = -T^{-1}\left[-\frac{T+1}{\theta} + \frac{T\overline{y}}{\theta^2}\right] \tag{9.14}$$

and

$$\frac{\partial h_N(\theta)}{\partial \theta} = -T^{-1}\left[-\frac{T}{\theta} + \frac{T\overline{y}}{\theta^2}\right] \tag{9.15}$$

to zero and solving yields the modes $\hat{\theta}_D = T\overline{y}/(T+1)$ and $\hat{\theta}_N = \overline{y}$. The corresponding Hessians for the denominator and numerator are

$$H_D(\theta) = -T^{-1}\left[\frac{T+1}{\theta^2} - \frac{2T\overline{y}}{\theta^3}\right] \tag{9.16}$$

and

$$H_N(\theta) = -T^{-1}\left[\frac{T}{\theta^2} - \frac{2T\overline{y}}{\theta^3}\right], \tag{9.17}$$

respectively. The Tierney–Kadane approximation to $G = E(\theta|y)$ requires the evaluation of (9.12), (9.13), (9.16), and (9.17) at the posterior modes to obtain

$$\begin{aligned} \exp[-Th_D(\widehat{\theta}_D)] &= \exp[-(T+1)\ln(\widehat{\theta}_D) - T\overline{y}/\widehat{\theta}_D] \\ &= \left(\frac{T\overline{y}}{T+1}\right)^{-(T+1)} \exp[-(T+1)], \end{aligned} \tag{9.18}$$

$$\begin{aligned} \exp[-Th_N(\widehat{\theta}_N)] &= \exp[-T\ln(\widehat{\theta}_N) - T\overline{y}/\widehat{\theta}_N] \\ &= \overline{y}^{-T} \exp[-T], \end{aligned} \tag{9.19}$$

$$TH_D(\widehat{\theta}_D) = -\left[\frac{T+1}{\widehat{\theta}_D^2} - \frac{2T\overline{y}}{\widehat{\theta}_D^3}\right]$$
$$= \frac{(T+1)^3}{T^2\overline{y}^2}, \tag{9.20}$$

and

$$TH_N(\widehat{\theta}_N) = -\left[\frac{T}{\widehat{\theta}_N^2} - \frac{2T\overline{y}}{\widehat{\theta}_N^3}\right]$$
$$= \frac{T}{\overline{y}^2}. \tag{9.21}$$

Substituting (9.18)–(9.21) into (9.8) yields the Tierney–Kadane approximation

$$\hat{G}_{\text{TK}} = \frac{T^{T-(1/2)}\exp(1)\overline{y}}{(T+1)^{T-(1/2)}} = \left[\frac{T^{T-(1/2)}(T-1)\exp(1)}{(T+1)^{T-(1/2)}T}\right]\frac{T\overline{y}}{T-1}, \tag{9.22}$$

where the term outside the square brackets of (9.22) equals $E(\theta|y)$.

Exercise 9.8 (Tierney–Kadane approximation: Exponential posterior mean II (Achcar and Smith 1990)) Consider again Exercise 9.7. Because $0 < \theta < \infty$, there is reason to believe your result can be improved by transforming to $\gamma \in \mathcal{R}$, where, say, $\gamma = \ln(\theta)$. Proceeding as in Exercise 9.7, but parameterizing in terms of γ, we can show that the Laplace approximation of $E(\theta|y) = T\overline{y}/(T-1)$ is

$$\hat{G}_{\text{TK}} = \frac{(T-1)^{T-(3/2)}\exp(1)\overline{y}}{(T)^{T-(3/2)}} = \left[\frac{(T-1)^{T-(1/2)}\exp(1)}{T^{T-(1/2)}}\right]\frac{T\overline{y}}{T-1}, \tag{9.23}$$

where, again, the term appearing outside the square brackets of (9.23) equals $E(\theta|y)$. Note that the percentage errors $|\widehat{G}-G|/G$ of (9.11), (9.22), and (9.23) depend only on the sample size T and not the data. Compare these relative errors for $T = 2, 3, 4, \ldots, 10, 15, 20, 25$. Which estimator do you prefer?

Solution

Straightforward computation yields the percentage errors in Table 9.2. Two comments are worth noting. First, the simple Laplace approximation (9.11) is decidedly the worst of the three. At first this might be surprising since it uses the exact posterior density including its integrating constant – i.e., the denominator in (9.7) – and uses a Laplace approximation of the numerator. But this is precisely why the two Tierney–Kadane estimates (9.22) and (9.23), which use a Laplace approximation in *both* the numerator and denominator, dominate. As noted in the text, the $O(T^{-1})$ errors of the numerator and denominator cancel, leaving a multiplicative error of order $O(T^{-2})$ compared to the $O(T^{-1})$ error of (9.11). Second, as seen in the solution to Exercise 9.5, and specifically in Table 9.1, by

Table 9.2: Laplace and two Tierney–Kadane approximations for exponential mean.

	Absolute percentage errors		
T	(9.11)	(9.22)	(9.23)
2	52.0	26.0	3.9
3	35.2	11.7	1.4
4	26.5	6.6	.7
5	21.3	4.3	.4
6	17.8	3.0	.3
7	15.3	2.2	.2
8	13.4	1.7	.1
9	11.9	1.3	.1
10	10.7	1.1	.0
15	7.2	.0	.0
20	5.4	.0	.0
25	4.3	.0	.0

reparameterizing from $\theta \in \mathbb{R}^+$ to $\gamma \in \mathbb{R}$, the quality of the Tierney–Kadane approximation improves. Therefore, (9.23) is the clear winner.

Exercise 9.9 (Approximate Bayes factors) In Chapter 6 we considered Bayes factors that are ratios of marginal likelihoods. Approximation of these ratios differs importantly from the preceding discussion in that the integrals of the ratio are usually of different dimensions, i.e., $K_N \neq K_D$ in (9.7). In what follows we switch notation from K_N and K_D to K_1 and K_2, and similarly for other subscripted quantities. Given hypotheses H_i, $i = 1, 2$, and prior densities $p(\theta_i|H_i) = p_i(\theta_i)$, $i = 1, 2$, consider the marginal likelihoods

$$p(y|H_i) = \int_{\mathbb{R}^{K_i}} p_i(\theta_i) L(\theta_i) \, d\theta_i, \quad i = 1, 2. \tag{9.24}$$

(a) Using the fully exponential method, find the Laplace approximations $\hat{p}(y|H_i)$, $i = 1, 2$, to the marginal densities in (9.24).
(b) Find $-2\ln(\widehat{B}_{12})$, where

$$\widehat{B}_{12} = \frac{\hat{p}(y|H_1)}{\hat{p}(y|H_2)}$$

is an approximation of the Bayes factor

$$B_{12} = \frac{p(y|H_1)}{p(y|H_2)}.$$

Solution

(a) Using the fully exponential method, the Laplace approximations to (9.24) are

$$\widehat{p}(y|H_i) = (2\pi)^{\frac{K_i}{2}} \left|TH_i\left(\widehat{\theta}_i\right)\right|^{-\frac{1}{2}} \exp[-Th_i(\widehat{\theta}_i)], \tag{9.25}$$

where

$$h_i\left(\widehat{\theta}_i\right) = -\frac{1}{T}\ln\left[p_i\left(\widehat{\theta}_i\right)L\left(\widehat{\theta}_i\right)\right],$$

$$H_i\left(\widehat{\theta}_i\right) = \left.\frac{\partial^2 h_i(\theta_i)}{\partial\theta_i\partial\theta_i'}\right|_{\theta_i=\widehat{\theta}_i},$$

and

$$\widehat{\theta}_i = \underset{\theta_i}{\operatorname{argmax}}\left\{-h_i(\theta_i)\right\}$$

is the posterior mode under H_i.

(b) From (9.25) it follows that

$$\begin{aligned}-2\ln\left[\widehat{B}_{12}\right] &= -2\ln\left[(2\pi)^{\frac{K_1}{2}} p_1\left(\widehat{\theta}_1\right)\left|TH_1\left(\widehat{\theta}_1\right)\right|^{-\frac{1}{2}} L\left(\widehat{\theta}_1\right)\right] \\ &\quad -(-2)\ln\left[(2\pi)^{\frac{K_2}{2}} p_2\left(\widehat{\theta}_2\right)\left|TH_2\left(\widehat{\theta}_2\right)\right|^{-\frac{1}{2}} L\left(\widehat{\theta}_2\right)\right] \\ &= -2[\ln L(\widehat{\theta}_1) - \ln L(\widehat{\theta}_2)] + (K_1 - K_2)\ln(T) + c_{12},\end{aligned} \tag{9.26}$$

where

$$\begin{aligned}c_{12} &= -2\ln\left[(2\pi)^{\frac{K_1}{2}} p_1\left(\widehat{\theta}_1\right)\left|H_1\left(\widehat{\theta}_1\right)\right|^{-\frac{1}{2}}\right] \\ &\quad + 2\ln\left[(2\pi)^{\frac{K_2}{2}} p_2\left(\widehat{\theta}_2\right)\left|H_2\left(\widehat{\theta}_2\right)\right|^{-\frac{1}{2}}\right] + O\left(T^{-1}\right) \\ &= (K_2 - K_1)\ln(2\pi) + \ln\left[\frac{\left|H_1\left(\widehat{\theta}_1\right)\right|}{\left|H_2\left(\widehat{\theta}_2\right)\right|}\right] + 2\ln\left[\frac{p_2\left(\widehat{\theta}_2\right)}{p_1\left(\widehat{\theta}_1\right)}\right] + O\left(T^{-1}\right)\end{aligned} \tag{9.27}$$

is of $O(1)$. The posterior modes $\widehat{\theta}_1$ and $\widehat{\theta}_2$ can be replaced by their corresponding MLEs, $\widehat{\theta}_1^{ML}$ and $\widehat{\theta}_2^{ML}$, without any deterioration in the order of the approximation error.

Schwarz (1978) suggested a *consistent* model selection criterion with all quantities in (9.26) evaluated at $\widehat{\theta}_1^{ML}$ and $\widehat{\theta}_2^{ML}$, and $c_{12} = 0$. In general, however, setting $c_{12} = 0$ in (9.26) results in a relative error of size $O(1)$. Kass and Wasserman (1995) and Poirier (1996) noted choices of prior in which the relative error is only $O(T^{-1/2})$. Since c_{12} involves differences in prior densities at the respective posterior modes, priors have more effect on posterior odds analysis than on point estimates. In other words, the prior matters to $O(1)$ for testing, but it matters less for estimation since posterior modes and MLEs differ by only $O\left(T^{-1}\right)$.

Exercise 9.10 (Approximate marginal posteriors) Let $\theta = [\theta_1\ \theta_2]'$. Consider the normal-gamma posterior distribution

$$\begin{aligned} p(\theta|\overline{\mu}, \overline{q}, \overline{s}^{-2}, \overline{\nu}, y) &= \phi(\theta_1|\overline{\mu}, \theta_2^{-1}\overline{q})\gamma(\theta_2|\overline{s}^{-2}, \overline{\nu}) \\ &= \left((2\pi\theta_2^{-1}\overline{q})^{-1/2} \exp\left[-\frac{1}{2}\theta_2\overline{q}^{-1}(\theta_1 - \overline{\mu})^2\right]\right) \\ &\quad \times \left(\left[\left(\frac{2}{\overline{\nu}\overline{s}^2}\right)^{\overline{\nu}/2} \Gamma(\overline{\nu}/2)\right]^{-1} \theta_2^{(\overline{\nu}-2)/2} \exp[-(1/2)\theta_2\overline{\nu}\overline{s}^2]\right) \\ &\propto \theta_2^{(\overline{\nu}-1)/2} \exp\left(-\frac{1}{2}\theta_2[\overline{\nu}\overline{s}^2 + \overline{q}^{-1}(\theta_1 - \overline{\mu})^2]\right). \end{aligned}$$

Write the marginal posterior density of θ_1 as

$$\begin{aligned} p(\theta_1|y) &= \int_{-\infty}^{\infty} p(\theta_1, \theta_2|\overline{\mu}, \overline{q}, \overline{s}^2, \overline{\nu}, y)\, d\theta_2 \\ &= \frac{\int_{-\infty}^{\infty} p(\theta_1, \theta_2|\underline{\mu}, \underline{q}, \underline{s}^2, \underline{\nu})L(\theta_1, \theta_2)\, d\theta_2}{\int_{-\infty}^{\infty}\int_{-\infty}^{\infty} p(\theta_1, \theta_2|\underline{\mu}, \underline{q}, \underline{s}^2, \underline{\nu})L(\theta_1, \theta_2)\, d\theta_1\, d\theta_2}. \end{aligned} \tag{9.28}$$

Write both integrands appearing in (9.28) in fully exponential form and apply Laplace approximations to both the numerator (N) and denominator (D) to obtain an approximate marginal posterior density for θ_1. Tierney and Kadane (1986, p. 84) noted that this approximation results in a multiplicative error of $O(T^{-3/2})$ in $T^{-1/2}$ neighborhoods of $\hat{\theta}_{D1}$.

Solution

Define

$$h_D(\theta_1, \theta_2) = \frac{1}{2T}\left(\theta_2\left[\overline{q}^{-1}(\theta_1 - \overline{\mu})^2 + \overline{\nu}\overline{s}^2\right] - (\overline{\nu} - 1)\ln(\theta_2)\right),$$

and for given θ_1 define $h_N(\theta_2) = h_D(\theta_1, \theta_2)$. Then, canceling constants in (9.28), we can rewrite the kernels of the integrands so that (9.28) becomes

$$p(\theta_1|y) = \frac{\int_{-\infty}^{\infty} \exp[-Th_N(\theta_2)]\, d\theta_2}{\int_{-\infty}^{\infty}\int_{-\infty}^{\infty} \exp[-Th_D(\theta_1, \theta_2)]\, d\theta_1\, d\theta_2}. \tag{9.29}$$

The following derivatives are straightforward to obtain:

$$\begin{aligned} \frac{\partial h_D(\theta_1, \theta_2)}{\partial \theta_1} &= \frac{1}{T}\theta_2\overline{q}^{-1}(\theta_1 - \overline{\mu}), \\ \frac{\partial h_D(\theta_1, \theta_2)}{\partial \theta_2} &= \frac{1}{2T}\left(\overline{\nu}\overline{s}^2 + \overline{q}^{-1}(\theta_1 - \overline{\mu})^2 - (\overline{\nu} - 1)\theta_2^{-1}\right), \end{aligned}$$

$$\frac{\partial^2 h_D(\theta_1,\theta_2)}{\partial\theta_1^2} = \frac{\theta_2}{T\overline{q}},$$
$$\frac{\partial^2 h_D(\theta_1,\theta_2)}{\partial\theta_2^2} = \frac{\overline{\nu}-1}{2T\theta_2^2},$$
$$\frac{\partial^2 h_D(\theta_1,\theta_2)}{\partial\theta_1\partial\theta_2} = \frac{\theta_1-\overline{\mu}}{T\overline{q}},$$
$$\frac{\partial h_N(\theta_2)}{\partial\theta_2} = \frac{1}{2T}\left(\overline{\nu s}^2+\overline{q}^{-1}(\theta_1-\overline{\mu})^2-(\overline{\nu}-1)\theta_2^{-1}\right),$$
$$\frac{\partial^2 h_N(\theta_2)}{\partial\theta_2^2} = \frac{\overline{\nu}-1}{2T\theta_2^2}.$$

Equating first-order partial derivatives to zero and solving yields the denominator and numerator modes:

$$\hat{\theta}_{D1} = \overline{\mu},$$
$$\hat{\theta}_{D2} = \frac{\overline{\nu}-1}{\overline{\nu s}^2},$$
$$\hat{\theta}_{N2} = \frac{\overline{\nu}-1}{\overline{\nu s}^2+\overline{q}^{-1}(\theta_1-\overline{\mu})^2}.$$

The Laplace approximations require

$$\exp[-Th_D(\hat{\theta}_{D1},\hat{\theta}_{D2})] = \exp\left[-\frac{1}{2}(\overline{\nu}-1)\right](\overline{\nu}-1)^{(\overline{\nu}-1)/2}[\overline{\nu s}^2]^{-(\overline{\nu}-1)/2}, \tag{9.30}$$

$$\exp[-Th_N(\hat{\theta}_{N2})] = \exp\left[-\frac{1}{2}(\overline{\nu}-1)\right](\overline{\nu}-1)^{(\overline{\nu}-1)/2}[\overline{\nu s}^2+\overline{q}^{-1}(\theta_1-\overline{\mu})^2]^{-(\overline{\nu}-1)/2}, \tag{9.31}$$

$$|TH_D(\hat{\theta}_{D1},\hat{\theta}_{D2})| = \frac{\overline{\nu s}^2}{2\overline{q}T^2}, \tag{9.32}$$

$$|TH_N(\hat{\theta}_{N2})| = \frac{[\overline{\nu s}^2+\overline{q}^{-1}(\theta_1-\overline{\mu})^2]^2}{2T(\overline{\nu}-1)}. \tag{9.33}$$

Substituting (9.29)–(9.32) into (9.8) and simplifying yields the approximation

$$p(\theta_1|y) \propto (\overline{\nu s}^2\overline{q})^{-1/2}\left[1+\overline{\nu}^{-1}\left(\frac{\theta_1-\overline{\mu}}{\overline{s}^2\overline{q}}\right)^2\right]^{-(\overline{\nu}+1)/2}. \tag{9.34}$$

Since we know in this conjugate problem that the marginal posterior of θ_1 is a t distribution with location $\overline{\mu}$, scale $(\overline{s}^2\overline{q})^{1/2}$, and $\overline{\nu}$ degrees of freedom, it is seen from (9.34) that the method produces the exact kernel of the marginal posterior in this case! By varying θ_1 the marginal density can be traced out. However, it needs to be scaled to integrate to unity.

10

The Linear Regression Model

The linear regression model is the workhorse of econometrics. In addition to being important in its own right, this model is an important component of other, more complicated models. The linear regression model posits a linear relationship between the dependent variable y_i and a $1 \times k$ vector of explanatory variables, x_i, where $i = 1, \ldots, N$ indexes the relevant observational unit (e.g., individual, firm, time period, etc.). In matrix notation, the linear regression model can be written as

$$y = X\beta + \epsilon, \tag{10.1}$$

where $y = [y_1 \; y_2 \cdots y_N]'$ is an N vector,

$$X = \begin{bmatrix} x_1 \\ \vdots \\ x_N \end{bmatrix}$$

is an $N \times k$ matrix, and $\epsilon = [\epsilon_1 \; \epsilon_2 \; \cdots \; \epsilon_N]'$ is an N vector of errors. Assumptions about ϵ and X define the likelihood function. Unless explicitly noted otherwise, the questions in this chapter assume that ϵ and X satisfy what are often referred to as the classical assumptions. With regard to the explanatory variables, we assume that either they are not random or, if they are random variables, it is acceptable to proceed conditionally on them. That is, the distribution of interest is $y|X$ (for a more detailed discussion of the random explanatory variable case, see Poirier 1995, pp. 448–458). For simplicity of notation, we will not include X as a conditioning argument in most equations and leave this source of conditioning implicit. Finally, in this chapter and those that follow we typically reserve capital letters such as X to denote matrices and lowercase letters such as y and x_i to denote scalar or vector quantities. When the distinction between scalars and vectors is important, this will be made clear within the exercise. We also drop the convention of using capital letters to denote random variables, since our focus throughout the remainder of the book is almost exclusively *ex post*. This notation is primarily needed when considering *ex ante* properties and their contrast with those obtained from the *ex post* viewpoint (e.g., in Chapter 4). These issues are not taken up in the following chapters and thus this notational distinction is decidedly less critical.

With regard to the errors in the regression model, we assume they are independently normally distributed with mean zero and common variance σ^2. That is,

$$\epsilon \sim N\left(0_N, \sigma^2 I_N\right), \tag{10.2}$$

where 0_N is an N vector of zeros, I_N is the $N \times N$ identity matrix, and $N(\cdot, \cdot)$ denotes the multivariate normal distribution (see Definition A.3). In this chapter we choose to work with the error precision, $h \equiv \sigma^{-2}$, and thus the normal linear regression model depends on the parameter vector $[\beta' \; h]'$. By using the properties of the multivariate normal distribution, it follows that $p\left(y|\beta, h\right) = \phi\left(y; X\beta, h^{-1}I_N\right)$, and thus the likelihood function is given by

$$L\left(\beta, h\right) = \frac{h^{\frac{N}{2}}}{\left(2\pi\right)^{\frac{N}{2}}} \exp\left[-\frac{h}{2}\left(y - X\beta\right)'\left(y - X\beta\right)\right]. \tag{10.3}$$

In an analogous fashion to expressions given in Exercises 2.3 and 2.14, it is often convenient to write the likelihood function in terms of ordinary least squares (OLS) quantities,

$$\widehat{\beta} = \left(X'X\right)^{-1} X'y$$

and

$$SSE = \left(y - X\widehat{\beta}\right)'\left(y - X\widehat{\beta}\right).$$

This can be done by using the fact that

$$\left(y - X\beta\right)'\left(y - X\beta\right) = SSE + \left(\beta - \widehat{\beta}\right)' X'X \left(\beta - \widehat{\beta}\right)$$

and thus

$$L\left(\beta, h\right) = \frac{h^{\frac{N}{2}}}{\left(2\pi\right)^{\frac{N}{2}}} \exp\left[-\frac{h}{2}\left\{SSE + \left(\beta - \widehat{\beta}\right)' X'X \left(\beta - \widehat{\beta}\right)\right\}\right]. \tag{10.4}$$

Exercise 10.1 (Posterior distributions under a normal-gamma prior) For the normal linear regression model under the classical assumptions, use a normal-gamma prior – i.e., the prior for β and h is $NG\left(\underline{\beta}, \underline{Q}, \underline{s}^{-2}, \underline{\nu}\right)$; see Definition A.5. Derive the posterior for β and h and thus show that the normal-gamma prior is a conjugate prior for this model.

Solution

Using Bayes' theorem and the properties of the normal-gamma density, we have

$$\begin{aligned} p(\beta, h|y) &\propto p(\beta, h) L(\beta, h) \\ &= \phi\left(\beta; \underline{\beta}, h^{-1}\underline{Q}\right) f_{\gamma}\left(h|\underline{s}^{-2}, \underline{\nu}\right) \phi\left(y; X\beta, h^{-1}I_N\right), \end{aligned}$$

where $f_{\gamma}()$ denotes the gamma density (see Definition A.2) and $\phi()$ the multivariate normal pdf. This question can be solved by plugging in the forms for each of the densities in these expressions, rearranging them (using some theorems in matrix algebra), and recognizing that the result is the kernel of a normal-gamma density. Since the posterior and prior are both normal-gamma, conjugacy is established. The steps are elaborated in the remainder of this solution.

Begin by writing out each density (ignoring integrating constants not involving the parameters) and using the expression for the likelihood function in (10.4):

$$\begin{aligned} p(\beta, h|y) &\propto \left\{h^{\frac{k}{2}} \exp\left[-\frac{h}{2}\left(\beta - \underline{\beta}\right)' \underline{Q}^{-1}\left(\beta - \underline{\beta}\right)\right]\right\} \\ &\quad \times \left\{h^{\frac{\underline{\nu}-2}{2}} \exp\left[-\frac{h\underline{\nu}\underline{s}^2}{2}\right]\right\} \\ &\quad \times \left\{h^{\frac{N}{2}} \exp\left[-\frac{h}{2}\left\{SSE + \left(\beta - \widehat{\beta}\right)' X'X\left(\beta - \widehat{\beta}\right)\right\}\right]\right\} \\ &= h^{\frac{\overline{\nu}+k-2}{2}} \exp\left[-\frac{h}{2}\left(\underline{\nu}\underline{s}^2 + SSE + \left(\beta - \underline{\beta}\right)' \underline{Q}^{-1}\left(\beta - \underline{\beta}\right)\right.\right. \\ &\quad \left.\left. + \left(\beta - \widehat{\beta}\right)' X'X\left(\beta - \widehat{\beta}\right)\right)\right], \end{aligned}$$

where $\overline{\nu} = \underline{\nu} + N$. In this expression, β enters only in the terms in the exponent,

$$\left(\beta - \underline{\beta}\right)' \underline{Q}^{-1}\left(\beta - \underline{\beta}\right) + \left(\beta - \widehat{\beta}\right)' X'X\left(\beta - \widehat{\beta}\right).$$

Rewrite this term as

$$\begin{aligned} \left(\beta - \underline{\beta}\right)' \underline{Q}^{-1}\left(\beta - \underline{\beta}\right) + \left(\beta - \widehat{\beta}\right)' X'X\left(\beta - \widehat{\beta}\right) &= \left(\widehat{\beta} - \underline{\beta}\right)' X'X\overline{Q}\underline{Q}^{-1}\left(\widehat{\beta} - \underline{\beta}\right) \\ &\quad + \left(\beta - \overline{\beta}\right)' \overline{Q}^{-1}\left(\beta - \overline{\beta}\right), \end{aligned}$$

where

$$\overline{Q} = \left(\underline{Q}^{-1} + X'X\right)^{-1}$$

and

$$\overline{\beta} = \overline{Q}\left(\underline{Q}^{-1}\underline{\beta} + X'X\widehat{\beta}\right).$$

Thus, β enters only through the term $\left(\beta - \overline{\beta}\right)' \overline{Q}^{-1} \left(\beta - \overline{\beta}\right)$ and we can establish that the kernel of $\beta|y, h$ is given by

$$p\left(\beta|y, h\right) \propto \exp\left[-\frac{h}{2}\left(\beta - \overline{\beta}\right)' \overline{Q}^{-1} \left(\beta - \overline{\beta}\right)\right].$$

Since this is the kernel of a normal density, we have established that $\beta|y, h \sim N\left(\overline{\beta}, h^{-1}\overline{Q}^{-1}\right)$.

We can derive $p\left(h|y\right)$ by using the fact that

$$p\left(h|y\right) = \int p\left(\beta, h|y\right) d\beta = \int p\left(h|y\right) p\left(\beta|y, h\right) d\beta.$$

Since pdfs integrate to one, we can integrate out the component involving normal density for $p\left(\beta|y, h\right)$ and we are left with

$$\begin{aligned} p\left(h|y\right) &\propto h^{\frac{\overline{\nu}-2}{2}} \exp\left[-\frac{h}{2}\left\{\underline{\nu s}^2 + SSE + \left(\widehat{\beta} - \underline{\beta}\right)' X'X\overline{Q}\underline{Q}^{-1}\left(\widehat{\beta} - \underline{\beta}\right)\right\}\right] \\ &\equiv h^{\frac{\overline{\nu}-2}{2}} \exp\left[-\frac{h}{2}\overline{\nu s}^2\right], \end{aligned}$$

with

$$\overline{\nu s}^2 = \underline{\nu s}^2 + SSE + \left(\widehat{\beta} - \underline{\beta}\right)' X'X\overline{Q}\underline{Q}^{-1}\left(\widehat{\beta} - \underline{\beta}\right).$$

We recognize the final expression for $p(h|y)$ as the kernel of a gamma density, and thus we have established that $h|y \sim \gamma\left(\overline{s}^{-2}, \overline{\nu}\right)$.

Since $\beta|y, h$ is normal and $h|y$ is gamma, it follows immediately that the posterior for β and h is $NG\left(\overline{\beta}, \overline{Q}, \overline{s}^{-2}, \overline{\nu}\right)$. Since prior and posterior are both normal-gamma, conjugacy has been established.

Exercise 10.2 (A partially informative prior) Suppose you have a normal linear regression model with *partially informative* natural conjugate prior where prior information is available only on $J \leq k$ linear combinations of the regression coefficients and the prior for h is the standard non-informative one: $p\left(h\right) \propto 1/h$. Thus, $R\beta|h \sim N(r, h^{-1}\underline{V}_r)$, where R is a known $J \times k$ matrix with rank$(R) = J$, r is a known J vector, and $\underline{V}_r$ is a $J \times J$ positive definite matrix. Show that the posterior is given by

$$\beta, h|y \sim NG\left(\widetilde{\beta}, \widetilde{V}, \widetilde{s}^{-2}, \widetilde{\nu}\right),$$

where

$$\begin{aligned} \widetilde{V} &= \left(R'\underline{V}_r^{-1}R + X'X\right)^{-1}, \\ \widetilde{\beta} &= \widetilde{V}\left(R'\underline{V}_r^{-1}\underline{\beta} + X'X\widehat{\beta}\right), \\ \widetilde{\nu} &= N, \end{aligned}$$

and

$$\overline{\nu s}^2 = \underline{\nu s}^2 + \left(\widetilde{\beta} - \widehat{\beta}\right)' X'X \left(\widetilde{\beta} - \widehat{\beta}\right) + \left(R\widehat{\beta} - r\right)' \underline{V}_r^{-1} \left(R\widehat{\beta} - r\right).$$

Solution

Partition $X = [X_1 \; X_2]$ and $R = [R_1 \; R_2]$, where X_1 is $N \times (k - J)$, X_2 is $N \times J$, R_1 is $J \times (k - J)$, and R_2 is $J \times J$. Partition $\beta = [\beta_1' \; \beta_2']'$ conformably. The linear regression model in (10.1) can be written as

$$y = Z\gamma + \epsilon,$$

where $Z = XA^{-1}$ and $\gamma = A\beta$ for any $k \times k$ non-singular matrix A. If we take

$$A = \begin{bmatrix} I_{k-J} & 0_{(k-J)\times J} \\ R_1 & R_2 \end{bmatrix},$$

then

$$\begin{aligned} Z &= XA^{-1} = [Z_1, Z_2] \\ &= \left[X_1 - X_2 R_2^{-1} R_1, X_2 R_2^{-1}\right] \end{aligned}$$

and $\gamma = [\gamma_1' \; \gamma_2']' = \left[\beta_1' \; (R\beta)'\right]'$. In words, we have transformed the model so that an informative prior is employed for $\gamma_2 = R\beta$ whereas a non-informative prior is employed for γ_1. The remainder of the proof is essentially the same as for Exercise 10.1. Assuming a normal-gamma natural conjugate prior for γ and h leads to a normal-gamma posterior. Taking non-informative limiting cases for the priors for γ_1 and h and then transforming back to the original parameterization (e.g., using $\beta = A^{-1}\gamma$ and $X = ZA$) yields the expressions given in the question.

Exercise 10.3 (Ellipsoid bound theorem) Consider the normal linear regression model with natural conjugate prior, $\beta, h \sim NG\left(\underline{\beta}, \underline{Q}, \underline{s}^{-2}, \underline{\nu}\right)$. Show that if $\underline{\beta} = 0$ then, for any choice of $\underline{Q}$, the posterior mean $\overline{\beta}$ must lie in the ellipsoid

$$\left(\overline{\beta} - \frac{\widehat{\beta}}{2}\right)' X'X \left(\overline{\beta} - \frac{\widehat{\beta}}{2}\right) \leq \frac{\widehat{\beta}' X'X \widehat{\beta}}{4}.$$

Solution

When $\underline{\beta} = 0$, the formula for the posterior mean $\overline{\beta}$ is given in Exercise 10.1 as

$$\overline{\beta} = \overline{Q} X'X \widehat{\beta}, \tag{10.5}$$

where

$$\overline{Q} = \left(\underline{Q}^{-1} + X'X\right)^{-1}. \tag{10.6}$$

Multiplying (10.5) by $\overline{Q}^{-1}$, using the expression in Equation (10.6), we obtain

$$\left(\underline{Q}^{-1} + X'X\right)\overline{\beta} = X'X\widehat{\beta};$$

rearranging and multiplying both sides of the equation by $\overline{\beta}'$ yields

$$\overline{\beta}'\underline{Q}^{-1}\overline{\beta} = \overline{\beta}'X'X\left(\widehat{\beta} - \overline{\beta}\right),$$

and since $\underline{Q}^{-1}$ is positive semidefinite, it follows that $\overline{\beta}'\underline{Q}^{-1}\overline{\beta} \geq 0$ and hence

$$\overline{\beta}'X'X\left(\widehat{\beta} - \overline{\beta}\right) \geq 0. \tag{10.7}$$

But the ellipsoid bound equation given in the question can be rearranged to be identical to (10.7). In particular, expanding the quadratic form on the left-hand side of the ellipsoid bound equation yields

$$\overline{\beta}'X'X\overline{\beta} - \frac{\widehat{\beta}'}{2}X'X\overline{\beta} - \overline{\beta}'X'X\frac{\widehat{\beta}}{2} + \frac{\widehat{\beta}'}{2}X'X\frac{\widehat{\beta}}{2} \leq \frac{\widehat{\beta}'X'X\widehat{\beta}}{4},$$

which implies

$$\overline{\beta}'X'X\overline{\beta} - \overline{\beta}'X'X\widehat{\beta} \leq 0,$$

or

$$\overline{\beta}'X'X\left(\widehat{\beta} - \overline{\beta}\right) \geq 0.$$

Thus, (10.7) is equivalent to the ellipsoid bound theorem.

You may wish to read Leamer (1982) or Poirier (1995, pp. 526–537) for more details about ellipsoid bound theorems.

Exercise 10.4 (Problems with Bayes factors using non-informative priors: Leamer (1978, p. 111)) Suppose you have two normal linear regression models:

$$M_j : y = X_j\beta_j + \epsilon_j,$$

where $j = 1, 2$, X_j is an $N \times k_j$ matrix of explanatory variables, β_j is a k_j vector of regression coefficients, and ϵ_j is an N vector of errors distributed as $N\left(0_N, h_j^{-1}I_N\right)$. If natural conjugate priors are used for both models, i.e., $\beta_j, h_j|M_j \sim NG\left(\underline{\beta}_j, \underline{Q}_j, \underline{s}_j^{-2}, \underline{\nu}_j\right)$, then the posterior is $\beta_j, h_j|y, M_j \sim NG\left(\overline{\beta}_j, \overline{Q}_j, \overline{s}_j^{-2}, \overline{\nu}_j\right)$, where $\overline{\beta}_j$, $\overline{Q}_j$, $\overline{s}_j^{-2}$, and $\overline{\nu}_j$ are as given in the solution to Exercise 10.1, and the Bayes factor comparing M_2 to M_1 is given by

$$BF_{21} = \frac{c_2\left(\frac{|\overline{Q}_2|}{|\underline{Q}_2|}\right)^{\frac{1}{2}}\left(\overline{\nu}_2\overline{s}_2^2\right)^{-\frac{\overline{\nu}_2}{2}}}{c_1\left(\frac{|\overline{Q}_1|}{|\underline{Q}_1|}\right)^{\frac{1}{2}}\left(\overline{\nu}_1\overline{s}_1^2\right)^{-\frac{\overline{\nu}_1}{2}}},$$

where

$$c_j = \frac{\Gamma\left(\frac{\overline{\nu}_j}{2}\right)\left(\underline{\nu}_j \underline{s}_j^2\right)^{\frac{\underline{\nu}_j}{2}}}{\Gamma\left(\frac{\underline{\nu}_j}{2}\right)\pi^{\frac{N}{2}}}.$$

(a) Consider a non-informative prior created by letting $\underline{\nu}_j \to 0$, $\underline{Q}_j^{-1} = cI_{k_j}$, and letting $c \to 0$ for $j = 1, 2$. Show that the Bayes factor reduces to

$$\begin{cases} 0 & \text{if} \quad k_2 > k_1, \\ \left[\frac{|X_2'X_2|}{|X_1'X_1|}\right]^{-\frac{1}{2}} \left(\frac{SSE_2}{SSE_1}\right)^{-\frac{N}{2}} & \text{if} \quad k_2 = k_1, \\ \infty & \text{if} \quad k_2 < k_1. \end{cases}$$

The case $k_1 = k_2$ corresponds to two non-nested models with the same number of explanatory variables.

(b) Consider a non-informative prior created by setting $\underline{\nu}_j \to 0$, $\underline{Q}_j^{-1} = \left(c^{1/k_j}\right) I_{k_j}$, and letting $c \to 0$ for $j = 1, 2$. Show that the Bayes factor reduces to

$$\left[\frac{|X_2'X_2|}{|X_1'X_1|}\right]^{-\frac{1}{2}} \left(\frac{SSE_2}{SSE_1}\right)^{-\frac{N}{2}}.$$

(c) Consider a non-informative prior created by setting $\underline{\nu}_j \to 0$, $\underline{Q}_j^{-1} = \left(c^{1/k_j}\right) X_j'X_j$, and letting $c \to 0$ for $j = 1, 2$. Show that the Bayes factor reduces to

$$\left(\frac{SSE_2}{SSE_1}\right)^{-\frac{N}{2}}.$$

Solution

In all cases, if $\underline{\nu}_1 = \underline{\nu}_2 \to 0$ at the same rate then $c_1 = c_2$ and these integrating constants cancel out in the Bayes factor. Furthermore, under the various assumptions about $\underline{Q}_j^{-1}$ it can be seen that

$$\overline{\nu}_j \overline{s}_j^2 = SSE_j,$$

where $\overline{\nu}_j = N$ and $\overline{Q}_j = \left(X_j'X_j\right)^{-1}$ for $j = 1, 2$. Thus, in all cases, the Bayes factor reduces to

$$BF_{21} = \left(\frac{|\underline{Q}_2^{-1}|}{|\underline{Q}_1^{-1}|}\right)^{\frac{1}{2}} \left[\frac{|X_2'X_2|}{|X_1'X_1|}\right]^{-\frac{1}{2}} \left(\frac{SSE_2}{SSE_1}\right)^{-\frac{N}{2}}.$$

(a) Here, $|\underline{Q}_j^{-1}| = c^{k_j}$ and hence $\left(|\underline{Q}_2^{-1}|/|\underline{Q}_1^{-1}|\right) = c^{k_2-k_1}$. If $k_1 = k_2$ then $\left(|\underline{Q}_2^{-1}|/|\underline{Q}_1^{-1}|\right) = 1$ for all c. If $k_1 > k_2$ then $\left(|\underline{Q}_2^{-1}|/|\underline{Q}_1^{-1}|\right) \to \infty$ as $c \to 0$. If $k_1 < k_2$ then $\left(|\underline{Q}_2^{-1}|/|\underline{Q}_1^{-1}|\right) \to 0$ as $c \to 0$. Thus, the result in part (a) is established.

(b) Here, $|\underline{Q}_j^{-1}| = c$ and hence $\left(|\underline{Q}_2^{-1}|/|\underline{Q}_1^{-1}|\right) = 1$ for all c regardless of what k_j is. Thus, the result in part (b) is established.
(c) Here, $|\underline{Q}_j^{-1}| = c\,|X_j'X_j|$ and hence $\left(|\underline{Q}_2^{-1}|/|\underline{Q}_1^{-1}|\right) = |X_2'X_2|/|X_1'X_1|$ for all c regardless of what k_j is. Using this result simplifies the Bayes factor to the expression given in part (c).

Exercise 10.5 (Multicollinearity) Consider the normal linear regression model with natural conjugate prior: $NG\left(\underline{\beta}, \underline{Q}, \underline{s}^{-2}, \underline{\nu}\right)$. Assume in addition that $Xc = 0$ for some non-zero vector of constants c. Note that this is referred to as a case of *perfect multicollinearity*. It implies that the matrix X is not of full rank and $(X'X)^{-1}$ does not exist.
(a) Show that, despite this pathology, the posterior exists if $\underline{Q}$ is positive definite.
(b) Define

$$\alpha = c'\underline{Q}^{-1}\beta.$$

Show that, given h, the prior and posterior distributions of α are identical and equal to

$$N\left(c'\underline{Q}^{-1}\underline{\beta}, h^{-1}c'\underline{Q}^{-1}c\right).$$

Hence, although prior information can be used to surmount the problems caused by perfect multicollinearity, there are some combinations of the regression coefficients about which (conditional) learning does not occur.

Solution
(a) The solution to this question is essentially the same as to Exercise 10.1. The key thing to note is that, since $\underline{Q}$ is positive definite, $\underline{Q}^{-1}$ exists and, hence, $\overline{Q}^{-1}$ exists despite the fact that $X'X$ is rank deficient. In the same manner, it can be shown that the posterior for β and h is $NG\left(\overline{\beta}, \overline{Q}, \overline{s}^{-2}, \overline{\nu}\right)$ with

$$\begin{aligned}
\overline{Q} &= \left(\underline{Q}^{-1} + X'X\right)^{-1}, \\
\overline{\beta} &= \overline{Q}\left(\underline{Q}^{-1}\underline{\beta} + X'y\right), \\
\overline{\nu}\overline{s}^2 &= \underline{\nu}\underline{s}^2 + \left(y - X\overline{\beta}\right)'\left(y - X\overline{\beta}\right) + \left(\overline{\beta} - \underline{\beta}\right)'\underline{Q}^{-1}\left(\overline{\beta} - \underline{\beta}\right),
\end{aligned}$$

and $\overline{\nu} = N + \underline{\nu}$.
(b) The properties of the normal-gamma distribution imply that

$$\beta|h \sim N\left(\underline{\beta}, h^{-1}\underline{Q}\right).$$

The properties of the normal distribution imply that

$$\alpha|h \equiv c'\underline{Q}^{-1}\beta|h \sim N\left(c'\underline{Q}^{-1}\underline{\beta}, h^{-1}c'\underline{Q}^{-1}c\right),$$

which establishes that the prior has the required form.

Using the result from part (a) gives the relevant posterior of the form

$$\beta|y, h \sim N\left(\overline{\beta}, h^{-1}\overline{Q}\right),$$

which implies

$$\alpha|y, h \sim N\left(c'\underline{Q}^{-1}\overline{\beta}, h^{-1}c'\underline{Q}^{-1}\overline{Q}\underline{Q}^{-1}c\right).$$

The mean can be written as

$$\begin{aligned} c'\underline{Q}^{-1}\overline{\beta} &= c'\left(\overline{Q}^{-1} - X'X\right)\overline{Q}\left(\underline{Q}^{-1}\underline{\beta} + X'y\right) \\ &= c'\underline{Q}^{-1}\underline{\beta} + c'X'y - c'X'X\overline{Q}\left(\underline{Q}^{-1}\underline{\beta} + X'y\right) \\ &= c'\underline{Q}^{-1}\underline{\beta}, \end{aligned}$$

since $Xc = 0$.

The variance can be written as

$$\begin{aligned} h^{-1}c'\underline{Q}^{-1}\overline{Q}\underline{Q}^{-1}c &= h^{-1}c'\underline{Q}^{-1}\left[\left(\underline{Q}^{-1} + X'X\right)^{-1}\underline{Q}^{-1}\right]c \\ &= h^{-1}c'\underline{Q}^{-1}\left[I - \left(\underline{Q}^{-1} + X'X\right)^{-1}X'X\right]c \\ &= h^{-1}c'\underline{Q}^{-1}c, \end{aligned}$$

since $Xc = 0$. Note that this derivation uses a standard theorem in matrix algebra that says, if G and H are $k \times k$ matrices and $(G+H)^{-1}$ exists, then

$$(G+H)^{-1}H = I_k - (G+H)^{-1}G.$$

Combining these derivations, we see that the posterior is also

$$\alpha|y, h \sim N\left(c'\underline{Q}^{-1}\underline{\beta}, h^{-1}c'\underline{Q}^{-1}c\right),$$

as required.

Exercise 10.6 (Numerical multicollinearity exercise) Consider the standard normal linear regression model:

$$y_t = \beta_1 + \beta_2 x_{2t} + \beta_3 x_{3t} + u_t \quad (t = 1, 2, \ldots, T),$$

subject to perfect collinearity due to $x_{3t} = 2x_{2t}$ $(t = 1, 2, \ldots, T)$. For simplicity, assume $\sigma^2 = 1$. Based on $T = 10$ observations, suppose $\bar{y} = 15$, $\bar{x}_2 = 0$, $x_2'x_2 = 1$, and $x_2'y = 2$, where $x_2 = [x_{21}, x_{22}, \ldots, x_{2T}]'$ and $y = [y_1, y_2, \ldots, y_T]'$. Consider a researcher whose prior beliefs are $\beta \sim N_3(0_3, \underline{Q})$, where

$$\underline{Q}^{-1} = \begin{bmatrix} 5 & 0 & 0 \\ 0 & 1 & 0 \\ 0 & 0 & 1 \end{bmatrix}.$$

(a) Find the posterior distribution of β.
(b) Find a 95% HPD interval for β_3. Carefully interpret the interval you construct.
(c) Is multicollinearity a problem for this researcher?

Solution

(a) It follows that

$$X'X = \begin{bmatrix} 10 & 0 & 0 \\ 0 & 1 & 2 \\ 0 & 2 & 4 \end{bmatrix} \text{ and } X'y = \begin{bmatrix} 150 \\ 2 \\ 4 \end{bmatrix}.$$

Then $\beta|y \sim N_3\left(\bar{b}, \bar{Q}\right)$, where

$$\bar{Q} = \left[\mathrm{Q}^{-1} + X'X\right]^{-1} = \left(\begin{bmatrix} 5 & 0 & 0 \\ 0 & 1 & 0 \\ 0 & 0 & 1 \end{bmatrix} + \begin{bmatrix} 10 & 0 & 0 \\ 0 & 1 & 2 \\ 0 & 2 & 4 \end{bmatrix}\right)^{-1}$$

$$= \begin{bmatrix} 15 & 0 & 0 \\ 0 & 2 & 2 \\ 0 & 2 & 5 \end{bmatrix}^{-1} = \begin{bmatrix} \frac{1}{15} & 0 & 0 \\ 0 & \frac{5}{6} & -\frac{2}{6} \\ 0 & -\frac{2}{6} & \frac{2}{6} \end{bmatrix},$$

and

$$\bar{b} = \bar{Q}X'y = \begin{bmatrix} 15 & 0 & 0 \\ 0 & 2 & 2 \\ 0 & 2 & 5 \end{bmatrix}^{-1} \begin{bmatrix} 150 \\ 2 \\ 4 \end{bmatrix} = \begin{bmatrix} \frac{1}{15} & 0 & 0 \\ 0 & \frac{5}{6} & -\frac{2}{6} \\ 0 & -\frac{2}{6} & \frac{2}{6} \end{bmatrix} \begin{bmatrix} 150 \\ 2 \\ 4 \end{bmatrix} = \begin{bmatrix} 10 \\ \frac{1}{3} \\ \frac{2}{3} \end{bmatrix}.$$

(b) Because $\beta_3|y \sim N\left(\frac{2}{3}, \frac{1}{3}\right)$, a 95% HPD interval is

$$\frac{2}{3} - 1.96\left(\frac{1}{3}\right)^{\frac{1}{2}} < \beta_3 < \frac{2}{3} + 1.96\left(\frac{1}{3}\right)^{\frac{1}{2}}$$

or

$$-.4649 < \beta_3 < 1.798.$$

The interpretation of this interval is, given the prior, after seeing the data the *probability* that β_3 is between $-.4649$ and 1.798 is .95. There is no need to introduce the concept of *confidence*.

(c) From Exercise 10.5, the researcher will not learn about

$$\alpha = [0 \ -2 \ 1]\mathrm{Q}^{-1}\beta = [0 \ -2 \ 1] \begin{bmatrix} 5 & 0 & 0 \\ 0 & 1 & 0 \\ 0 & 0 & 1 \end{bmatrix} \beta = -2\beta_1 + \beta_2$$

in the sense that the prior and posterior for $-2\beta_1 + \beta_2$ is $N(0, 5)$.

11

Basics of Random Variate Generation and Posterior Simulation

In a variety of statistical/econometric problems of even moderate complexity, posterior distributions and their associated properties are not derivable analytically. Researchers who lack closed-form solutions yet still seek to conduct posterior inference may, however, find a path forward in these cases by applying one of a variety of different techniques to generate draws from the posterior distribution. Once such methods are applied, the draws obtained can be used to approximate posterior means (for example, as a sample average of the set of simulations), posterior variances, other posterior moments, or to simply plot histograms or kernel-smoothed marginal and joint posterior densities.

The purpose of this chapter is to discuss different techniques for generating draws from distributions of interest, and to discuss how to calculate moments of interest when analytic solutions are not available. Although our focus here is on the use of such methods for Bayesian computation, it is worth noting that the techniques described in this chapter also apply generally to problems of stochastic simulation.

The methods discussed in this chapter are distinct from the iterative approaches described in the next chapter in that the methods described here directly provide samples from the target distribution. Iterative techniques, and Markov chain Monte Carlo (MCMC) methods in particular, instead produce correlated draws from the target distribution, once the process has run for a sufficient amount of time and has converged to the stationary distribution. These iterative methods, which are widely used for Bayesian empirical work, are the subject of the next chapter.

This chapter is divided into three different sections. We begin with a few MATLAB examples illustrating Monte Carlo integration. The associated exercises in this first section review how researchers can use MATLAB to generate draws from common distributions, and how these draws can then be used to calculate statistics of interest. In the second section we move on to peek under the hood of some of these existing MATLAB routines, and describe and implement various algorithms and procedures that can be employed to generate draws from a given distribution. These methods reveal not only how the MATLAB built-in routines work, but also provide a recipe for what a researcher might do when faced with the problem of generating samples from a distribution that can be written down (at least up to proportionality) but is non-standard. We close the chapter by discussing a series of exercises related to importance sampling, which uses and reweights samples from an approximating distribution in order to calculate posterior statistics of interest.

11.1 Monte Carlo Integration with MATLAB

Exercise 11.1 (Numerical standard error of Monte Carlo estimate) Suppose a researcher can use MATLAB or some other statistical software package to generate draws from a posterior distribution $p(\theta|y)$. This researcher is primarily interested in the posterior mean $E(\theta|y)$, but does not know its analytic form.

The researcher decides to use Monte Carlo integration (so named given the use of random generation to evaluate integrals, and the similarity of such methods to games of chance) to estimate $E\left[\theta|y\right]$. Specifically, she considers the natural estimator

$$\widehat{\theta} \equiv \widehat{E(\theta|y)} = \frac{1}{R}\sum_{r=1}^{R} \theta^{(r)},$$

where $\theta^{(r)}$ represents the rth draw from $p(\theta|y)$. The researcher would like some guidance regarding the accuracy of this estimated posterior moment.

Use a central limit theorem to derive the standard error (known as the *numerical standard error*, or NSE) associated with the estimate that can be used to evaluate the accuracy of the estimate for any given R.

Solution

Since the draws are *iid*, with assumed finite variance, we can employ the Lindeberg–Lévy central limit theorem to obtain

$$\sqrt{R}\left(\widehat{\theta} - \theta\right) \xrightarrow{d} N\left(0, \sigma^2\right)$$

as $R \to \infty$. In the above, $\sigma^2 \equiv \text{Var}\left(\theta|y\right)$. This quantity can itself be estimated using Monte Carlo integration:

$$\widehat{\text{Var}}(\theta|y) \approx (1/R)\sum_{r}(\theta^{(r)} - \hat{\theta})^2,$$

and we shall denote this estimate by $\widehat{\sigma}^2$. The NSE can then be estimated as

$$\widehat{\text{NSE}} = \frac{\widehat{\sigma}}{\sqrt{R}},$$

which can be used to characterize the accuracy of the estimated posterior mean.

Exercise 11.2 (Drawing from standard distributions) In this exercise we discuss how MATLAB can be used to obtain draws from a variety of standard continuous distributions. Specifically, we obtain draws from the uniform, normal, Student t, beta, exponential, and chi-square distributions using MATLAB (see the appendix for definitions of these distributions). This exercise is designed to be illustrative – MATLAB is capable of generating variates from virtually any distribution that an applied researcher will encounter, and the same applies to other relevant computer languages.

Using MATLAB, obtain sets of 10, 100, and 100 000 draws from the uniform, standard normal, Student $t(3)$ (denoted $t(0,1,3)$ in the notation of the appendix), beta(3,2) (denoted $\beta(3,2)$ in the appendix), exponential with mean 5 (denoted exponential(5) in the following), and $\chi^2(3)$ distributions. For each sample size calculate the mean and standard deviation and compare these quantities to the known means and standard deviations from each distribution.

Solution

Our MATLAB program for implementing this exercise is provided on the website associated with this book. Table 11.1 gives a summary of these results.

For the largest sample size, $N = 100\,000$, our simulated means and standard deviations are virtually identical to the known means and standard deviations. It is also worth noting that the exponential(5) and $\chi^2(3)$ distributions are equivalent to the $G(1,5)$ and $G(3/2,2)$ distributions, respectively (see the appendix). The MATLAB routine for drawing from the flexible gamma distribution is `gamrnd`, thus providing an alternate way for obtaining draws from the exponential and chi-square distributions.

Exercise 11.3 (Monte Carlo integration in a regression problem)
(a) Generate an artificial data set of size $N = 100$ from the normal linear regression model, as described in Exercise 10.1, with an intercept and one other explanatory variable. Set the intercept (β_1) to 0, the slope coefficient (β_2) to 1.0, and h to 1.0. Generate the explanatory variable by taking random draws from the $U(0,1)$ distribution.
(b) Calculate the posterior mean and standard deviation for the slope coefficient β_2 for this data set using a normal-gamma prior with $\underline{\beta} = [0\ 1]'$, $\underline{V} = I_2$, $\underline{s}^{-2} = 1$, and $\underline{\nu} = 1$.
(c) Calculate the Bayes factor comparing the model $M_1 : \beta_2 = 0$ with $M_2 : \beta_2 \neq 0$.
(d) Carry out a prior sensitivity analysis by setting $\underline{V} = cI_2$ and repeating parts (b) and (c) for values of $c = 0.01$, 1.0, 100.0, and 1×10^6. How sensitive is the posterior to changes

Table 11.1: Simulation results.

	Uniform		Standard normal	
	Mean	Std.	Mean	Std.
True value	.500	$(1/\sqrt{12})$	0	1
$N = 10$	.482	.314	.204	.870
$N = 100$	.489	.303	.059	1.06
$N = 100\,000$	.500	.289	−.001	.999
	Student $t(3)$		Beta(3,2)	
	Mean	Std.	Mean	Std.
True value	0	$\sqrt{3}$	.6	.2
$N = 10$	.002	.920	.616	.181
$N = 100$	−.167	1.46	.585	.193
$N = 100\,000$	.003	1.70	.600	.199
	Exponential(5)		χ^2 (3)	
	Mean	Std.	Mean	Std.
True value	5	5	3	$\sqrt{6}$
$N = 10$	3.42	3.35	2.98	2.55
$N = 100$	4.61	4.75	2.85	2.43
$N = 100\,000$	5.01	5.02	3.00	2.45

in prior information? How sensitive is the Bayes factor? (See Exercises 6.7, 8.7, and 8.8 for related discussion.)
(e) Repeat part (b) using Monte Carlo integration for various values of R. How large does R have to be before you reproduce the results of the previous parts to two decimal places?
(f) Calculate the NSEs associated with the posterior mean of the slope coefficient for the models. Does the NSE seem to give a reliable guide to the accuracy of the approximation provided by Monte Carlo integration?

Solution

(a) A program to generate artificial data as described in this exercise has the following form:

Step 1: Set N, β_1, β_2, and h to the required values (i.e., 100, 0, 1, and 1 respectively).
Step 2: Take a draw of the explanatory variable x_i from the $U\,(0,1)$ distribution.
Step 3: Take a draw of the error ϵ_i from the $N\,(0,1)$ distribution.
Step 4: Set the dependent variable equal to $\beta_1 + \beta_2 x_i + \epsilon_i$.
Step 5: Repeat Steps 2 through 4 N times and save all the values of the dependent and explanatory variables.

(b and c) A program to calculate the posterior mean and standard deviation of the regression coefficients involves first setting the prior hyperparameters to their required values

Table 11.2: Results of prior sensitivity analysis for β_2.

	Posterior mean	Posterior std. dev.
$c = 0.01$	1.015	0.079
$c = 1.0$	1.066	0.289
$c = 100$	1.074	0.312
$c = 10^6$	1.074	0.312

Table 11.3: Bayes factors for $\beta_2 = 0$.

	Bayes factor
$c = 0.01$	4.7×10^{-7}
$c = 1.0$	0.008
$c = 100$	0.096
$c = 10^6$	9.251

and then evaluating the formulas in Chapter 10, Exercise 10.1. A program to calculate the marginal likelihood evaluates the formula from Chapter 10 (see, e.g., the formula for the Bayes factor in Exercise 10.4 and remember that the Bayes factor is the ratio of marginal likelihoods). A simple way to calculate the Bayes factor comparing the two models is simply to run the program with the artificial data set and then run it again with the only explanatory variable being an intercept. Again, the programs are provided on the website associated with this book.

The answer to part (d) provides empirical results.

(d) The prior sensitivity analysis can be done by running the program for $c = 0.01$, 1.0, 100.0, and 1×10^6. To calculate the Bayes factor the program can be run twice for each value of c, once with the entire artificial data set (i.e., $k = 2$) and once with X containing only an intercept (i.e., $k = 1$). Our results will differ from yours since you will generate a different artificial data set. Tables 11.2 and 11.3 present posterior means, standard deviations, and Bayes factors. The results for $c = 1$ complete the answer to part (b).

These tables show some interesting patterns. Note, first, that the posterior mean and standard deviation are more robust to changes in the prior than are the Bayes factors (a standard finding in empirical Bayesian work). In fact, except for the case where the prior is extremely informative (as in $c = 0.01$), the posterior means and standard deviations are virtually the same for all prior choices. The Bayes factors vary from strong evidence against $\beta_2 = 0$ through strong evidence in favor of $\beta_2 = 0$. This motivates the common belief that prior elicitation is more important when the researcher is interested in model comparison than when he or she is interested in estimating parameters in a single model. In general, as the prior for β_2 gets more non-informative (i.e., c gets larger), the Bayes factor indicates more support for the restricted model (i.e., $\beta_2 = 0$). It can be shown that a non-informative prior (i.e., $c \to \infty$) will yield an infinite Bayes factor and, thus, the restricted model will always be supported, regardless of the data evidence. This is referred to as *Bartlett's paradox* (see Poirier 1995, p. 390).

Second, our prior is centered over the value used to generate the artificial data. Thus, prior and likelihood information are not in conflict. In this case, having a more informative prior (i.e., setting c to a small value) will ensure more accurate estimation (i.e., the posterior standard deviation of β_2 decreases as c decreases). The reader interested in further investigation might want to experiment with different priors that are in conflict with the likelihood (e.g., what happens if $\underline{\beta} = [0\ 0]'$, or if $\underline{\beta} = [0\ -1]'$, etc.?).

(e and f) Monte Carlo integration for β can be done in two ways. The researcher can directly draw from the posterior for β using the multivariate t distribution (see Definition A.4). Alternatively, the researcher can draw from the posterior of h (which is gamma) and then draw from $p(\beta|y, h)$ (which is normal). This technique is referred to as the *method of composition*. Here we adopt the first approach. This requires computer code for randomly drawing from the t distribution, which can be done in MATLAB.

The structure of computer code that does Monte Carlo integration to carry out posterior inference on β is as follows:

Step 1: Do all the preliminary things to create all the variables used in the Monte Carlo procedure, i.e., load the data, specify prior hyperparameters, and evaluate the posterior mean, scale matrix, and degrees of freedom for the multivariate t posterior – see the code for part (c).

Step 2: Draw from the multivariate t posterior for β.

Step 3: Repeat Step 2 R times and average the draws of β_2 (which gives you the Monte Carlo estimate of the posterior mean), and average the draws of β_2^2, which gives you the Monte Carlo estimate of $E\left(\beta_2^2|y\right)$ – which, along with the posterior mean, can be used to calculate the posterior variance and standard deviation of the slope parameter.

MATLAB code for performing these calculations and those for part (f) are provided on the website associated with this book. The formula for the numerical standard error is derived in Exercise 11.1. As described there, this depends only on the Monte Carlo estimate of $\text{Var}(\beta_2|y)$, which was called $\widehat{\sigma}^2$ in Exercise 11.1, and R. These are readily available in the Monte Carlo integration procedure – see the code for part (e).

Table 11.4 presents the posterior mean and standard deviation for β_2 calculated analytically, see part (b), and using Monte Carlo integration with different numbers of replications. In addition, for Monte Carlo estimates we present the NSEs for $E(\beta_2|y)$.

The row labeled "Analytical" presents the correct posterior mean and standard deviation (with numbers taken from Table 11.2 with $c = 1$). Since Monte Carlo integration depends on random number generation, no two Monte Carlo procedures will yield exactly the same results. Hence, your numbers may be different from ours. However, the following patterns should be evident. First, as the number of replications increases, the approximation error associated with the Monte Carlo integration gets smaller. Second, it seems that roughly

Table 11.4: Posterior results for β_2.

	Posterior mean	Posterior std. dev.	NSE for $E(\beta_2\|y)$
Analytical	1.066	0.289	—
$R = 10$	1.121	0.341	0.108
$R = 100$	1.029	0.289	0.029
$R = 1\,000$	1.069	0.292	0.009
$R = 10\,000$	1.067	0.288	0.002
$R = 1\,000\,000$	1.066	0.289	3×10^{-3}

1000 replications are required to obtain results accurate to two decimal places. However, third, a better way of gauging the accuracy of the Monte Carlo approximation is through the numerical standard error, which does seem very reliable (in the sense that, for each value of R, the Monte Carlo estimate is within one or two numerical standard errors of the true posterior mean).

11.2 Inverse Transform, Acceptance/Rejection, and Weighted Bootstrap

In this section we discuss several different methods for generating samples from an arbitrary density function. When conducting a Bayesian analysis it is sometimes the case that the form of a marginal or conditional posterior distribution may be known, although that functional form does not correspond to any "standard" family of distributions. Here we review three methods that can be used for generating samples when a density function can be expressed mathematically, often only up to proportionality: the inverse transform, acceptance/rejection sampling, and the weighted bootstrap. We focus primarily on univariate cases throughout the derivations and examples.

Exercise 11.4 (The inverse transform) Suppose that X is a continuous random variable with distribution function F and density f. Further, assume that the distribution function F can be easily calculated. Let $U \sim U(0, 1)$, a uniform random variable on the unit interval, and define $Y = F^{-1}(U)$.

Derive the distribution of the random variable Y. How can this result help us to generate variates from the density f?

Solution

We describe two different approaches for deriving the distribution of Y. First, we consider the cdf method, and Figure 11.1 helps to illustrate this argument. Note that

$$\begin{aligned}\Pr[Y \leq a] &= \Pr[F^{-1}(U) \leq a] \\ &= \Pr[U \leq F(a)] \\ &= F(a),\end{aligned}$$

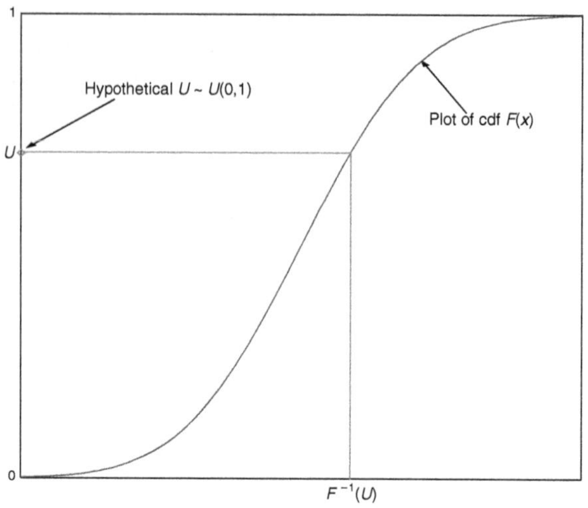

Figure 11.1. Graphical depiction of inverse transform method.

where the last line follows since $U \sim U(0,1)$, and the intuition behind the second line can be seen from Figure 11.1. This derivation shows that Y has distribution function F.

Another approach for establishing this result makes use of a change of variables. First note that $p(u) = I[0 \leq u \leq 1]$, with $I(\cdot)$ denoting an indicator function and $U = F(Y)$. Thus, $p(y) = f(y)I[0 \leq F(y) \leq 1] = f(y)$.

This result is extremely useful, because it provides a way to generate draws from f. If the cdf F and its inverse F^{-1} are easily calculated, we can first draw $U \sim U(0,1)$ and then calculate $Y = F^{-1}(U)$. It follows that Y is a draw from f. Although we have presented this in a univariate case, the technique can be extended to the multivariate case by decomposing the joint cdf into a product of marginal and conditional cdfs, and applying the inverse transform method to each component. The next exercise provides three applications of this method.

Exercise 11.5 (Applications of the inverse transform: Drawing exponential and truncated normal variates)
(a) Consider the exponential density (see Theorem A.2) with density function

$$p(x|\theta) = \theta^{-1}\exp(-x/\theta), \quad x > 0.$$

Show how the inverse transform method can be used to generate draws from the exponential density.
(b) Let $x \sim TN_{[a,b]}(\mu, \sigma^2)$ denote that x is a *truncated normal* random variable. Specifically, this notation defines that x is generated from a normal density with mean μ and variance σ^2, which is truncated to lie in the interval $[a, b]$. The density function for x in

this case is given as

$$p(x) = \frac{\phi(x;\mu,\sigma^2)}{\Phi\left(\frac{b-\mu}{\sigma}\right) - \Phi\left(\frac{a-\mu}{\sigma}\right)} I(a \leq x \leq b).$$

Show how the inverse transform method can be used to generate draws from the truncated normal density.
(c) The logistic density function is given by

$$p(x) = \frac{\exp(-[x-\mu]/\sigma)}{\sigma\left(1+\exp(-[x-\mu]/\sigma)\right)^2}, \quad -\infty < x < \infty, \; -\infty < \mu < \infty, \; \sigma > 0.$$

Describe how the inverse transform method can be used to generate draws from the logistic distribution.

Solution
(a) Note that

$$\begin{aligned} F(x) &= \int_0^x \frac{1}{\theta} \exp\left(-\frac{t}{\theta}\right) dt \\ &= 1 - \exp\left(-\frac{x}{\theta}\right). \end{aligned}$$

The results of Exercise 11.4 imply that if we solve for x in the equation

$$u = 1 - \exp\left(-\frac{x}{\theta}\right),$$

with u denoting a realized draw from a $U(0,1)$ distribution, then x has the desired exponential density. A little algebra provides

$$x = -\theta \ln(1-u)$$

as the solution.
(b) For $a \leq x \leq b$, the cdf of the truncated normal random variable is

$$\begin{aligned} F(x) &= \left[\Phi\left(\frac{b-\mu}{\sigma}\right) - \Phi\left(\frac{a-\mu}{\sigma}\right)\right]^{-1} \int_a^x \phi(t;\mu,\sigma^2)dt \\ &= \frac{\Phi\left(\frac{x-\mu}{\sigma}\right) - \Phi\left(\frac{a-\mu}{\sigma}\right)}{\Phi\left(\frac{b-\mu}{\sigma}\right) - \Phi\left(\frac{a-\mu}{\sigma}\right)}. \end{aligned}$$

The results of Exercise 11.4 reveal that if x is a solution to the equation

$$u = \frac{\Phi\left(\frac{x-\mu}{\sigma}\right) - \Phi\left(\frac{a-\mu}{\sigma}\right)}{\Phi\left(\frac{b-\mu}{\sigma}\right) - \Phi\left(\frac{a-\mu}{\sigma}\right)},$$

where u is realized draw from a $U(0,1)$ distribution, then $x \sim TN_{[a,b]}(\mu, \sigma^2)$. It follows that

$$x = \mu + \sigma\Phi^{-1}\left(\Phi\left(\frac{a-\mu}{\sigma}\right) + u\left[\Phi\left(\frac{b-\mu}{\sigma}\right) - \Phi\left(\frac{a-\mu}{\sigma}\right)\right]\right).$$

Our ability to draw from the truncated normal density will be quite important for the estimation of many models considered in Chapter 14.
(c) Letting $y = [x - \mu]/\sigma$, we note that

$$\begin{aligned} F(a) &= \int_{-\infty}^{[a-\mu]/\sigma} \left(\frac{\exp(-y)}{[1+\exp(-y)]^2}\right) dy \\ &= [1+\exp(-y)]^{-1}\Big|_{-\infty}^{[a-\mu]/\sigma} \\ &= [1+\exp(-[a-\mu]/\sigma)]^{-1}. \end{aligned}$$

Applying the inverse transform method, as reviewed in parts (a) and (b) above, if $u \sim U(0,1)$ we know that

$$x = \mu - \sigma \log\left(\frac{1-u}{u}\right)$$

provides a draw from the desired logistic distribution.

Exercise 11.6 (Acceptance/rejection sampling) Consider the following strategy for drawing from a density $f(x)$ defined over the compact support $a \leq x \leq b$:

1. Generate two independent uniform random variables U_1 and U_2 as follows:

$$U_i \overset{iid}{\sim} U(0,1), \quad i = 1, 2.$$

2. Let

$$M \equiv \max_{a \leq x \leq b} f(x).$$

If

$$MU_2 > f(a + [b-a]U_1),$$

start over. That is, go back to the first step and generate new values for U_1 and U_2, and again determine if $MU_2 > f(a + [b-a]U_1)$. When

$$MU_2 \leq f(a + [b-a]U_1)$$

set

$$x = a + (b-a)U_1$$

as a draw from $f(x)$.

(a) What is the probability that any particular application of this algorithm will produce a draw that is accepted?
(b) Sketch a proof as to why x, when it is accepted, has distribution function $F(x) = \int_a^x f(t)\, dt$.

Solution
(a) Note that

$$\begin{aligned}
\text{Pr(Acceptance)} &= \text{Pr}\left[MU_2 \leq f(a + [b-a]U_1)\right] \\
&= \text{Pr}\left[U_2 \leq M^{-1} f(a + [b-a]U_1)\right] \\
&= \int_0^1 \left[\int_0^{M^{-1}f(a+[b-a]U_1)} p(U_2)\, dU_2\right] p(U_1)\, dU_1 \\
&= \int_0^1 M^{-1} f(a + [b-a]U_1) p(U_1)\, dU_1 \\
&= \int_a^b M^{-1} f(t)(b-a)^{-1}\, dt \\
&= [M(b-a)]^{-1}.
\end{aligned}$$

The third line uses the fact that U_1 and U_2 are independent, the fourth and fifth lines follow from the fact that $U_i \sim U(0,1)$, $i = 1, 2$, and the fifth line also applies a change of variable, setting $t = a + (b-a)U_1$. Thus the probability of accepting a candidate draw in the algorithm is $[M(b-a)]^{-1}$. Note that, when using this method to sample from a uniform distribution on $[a, b]$, all candidates from the algorithm are accepted.
(b) Consider $\text{Pr}(x \leq c \mid x \text{ is accepted})$. We seek to show that this probability equals the cdf value $F(c) = \int_a^c f(t)\, dt$. We note that

$$\begin{aligned}
\text{Pr}(x \leq c \mid x \text{ is accepted}) &= \frac{\text{Pr}(x \leq c, x \text{ is accepted})}{\text{Pr}(x \text{ is accepted})} \\
&= M(b-a)\text{Pr}\left[a + (b-a)U_1 \leq c, U_2 \leq M^{-1} f(a + [b-a]U_1)\right] \\
&= M(b-a)\text{Pr}\left[U_1 \leq \frac{c-a}{b-a}, U_2 \leq M^{-1} f(a + [b-a]U_1)\right] \\
&= M(b-a) \int_0^{\frac{c-a}{b-a}} \int_0^{M^{-1}f(a+[b-a]U_1)} dU_2\, dU_1 \\
&= M(b-a) \int_0^{\frac{c-a}{b-a}} M^{-1} f(a + [b-a]U_1)\, dU_1 \\
&= M(b-a) \int_a^c M^{-1} f(t)(b-a)^{-1}\, dt \\
&= \int_a^c f(t)\, dt \\
&= F(c).
\end{aligned}$$

Therefore, a candidate draw that is accepted from the acceptance/rejection method has distribution function F, as desired.

Exercise 11.7 (Using acceptance/rejection sampling I)
(a) Consider the *triangular density* function, given as

$$p(x) = 1 - |x|, \quad x \in [-1, 1].$$

Use the acceptance/rejection sampling method of Exercise 11.6 to generate 25 000 draws from this distribution.
(b) Suppose it is desired to sample a random variable x from a $TN_{[0,4]}(1, 1)$ distribution, that is, a normal density with unit mean and variance, that has been truncated to the interval $[0, 4]$. Apply the acceptance/rejection method to generate 25 000 draws from this truncated normal distribution.
(c) Using the 25 000 draws obtained from (a) and (b), estimate the density functions of the accepted draws in each case. Evaluate the performance of the acceptance/rejection method by comparing the density estimates to the actual densities.

Solution
(a–c) The MATLAB code used to simulate draws from these distributions is provided on the website associated with this book. For (a), note that $M = 1$ and $b - a = 2$, so the overall acceptance rate is one-half. (That is, we would expect that 50 000 pairs of independent uniform variates in the acceptance/rejection algorithm are needed to produce a final sample of 25 000 draws.) For (b), $M \approx .475$ and $b - a = 4$, so the overall acceptance rate is approximately .53.

Graphs of the actual densities (dotted) and kernel density estimates based on the 25 000 draws (solid) are provided in Figure 11.2. For the triangular case, the estimated density is nearly indistinguishable from the actual density. For the truncated normal case, the two graphs are again very similar. The slight discrepancy at the lower limit of zero seems related to the performance of the kernel density estimator at the boundary.

Exercise 11.8 (A generalized acceptance/rejection algorithm) Suppose it is of interest to generate draws from a density $f(\theta)$ (henceforth referred to as the *target* density). Let Θ denote the support of $f(\theta)$, and suppose there exists some approximating density $s(\theta)$, called the *source density*, with support Θ^*, where $\Theta \subseteq \Theta^*$.

In many applications requiring posterior simulation, the normalizing constant of the target density is unknown, since the joint or conditional posteriors are only given up to proportionality. To this end, let us work with the kernels of both the source and target densities and write

$$f(\theta) = c_f \tilde{f}(\theta),$$
$$s(\theta) = c_s \tilde{s}(\theta),$$

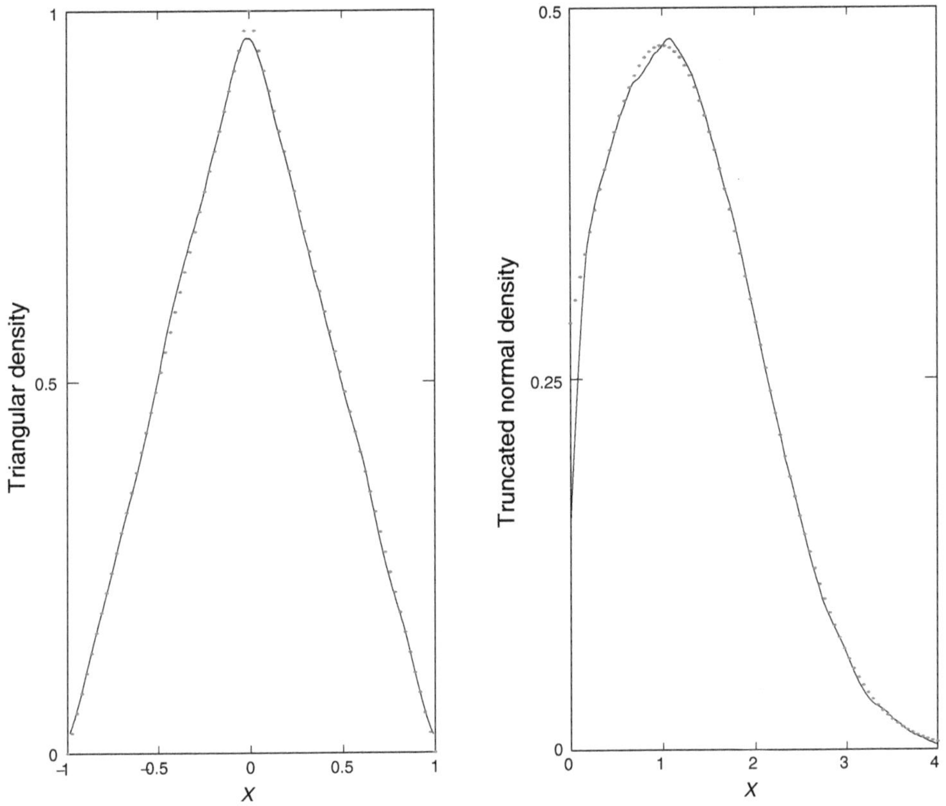

Figure 11.2. Analytical densities (dotted) and kernel density estimates (solid) obtained using 25 000 draws from acceptance/rejection sampler: triangular (left) and truncated normal (right).

so that $\tilde{f}$ and $\tilde{s}$ denote the target and source kernels, respectively, and c_f and c_s denote the associated normalizing constants. Finally, let

$$\tilde{M} \equiv \sup_{\theta \in \Theta} \left(\frac{\tilde{f}(\theta)}{\tilde{s}(\theta)} \right).$$

Consider the following algorithm:

1. Draw U uniformly on $[0, 1]$ – i.e., $U \sim U(0, 1)$.
2. Draw a candidate from the source density $s(\theta)$ – i.e., $\theta^{\text{cand}} \sim s(\theta)$.
3. If

$$U \leq \frac{\tilde{f}(\theta^{\text{cand}})}{\tilde{M}\tilde{s}(\theta^{\text{cand}})},$$

then set

$$\theta = \theta^{\text{cand}}$$

as a draw from $f(\theta)$. Otherwise, return to the first step and repeat the process until the condition in step 3 is satisfied.

(a) Show how this algorithm includes the one provided in Exercise 11.6 as a special case.
(b) What is the overall acceptance rate in this algorithm?
(c) Sketch a proof of why this algorithm provides a draw from $f(\theta)$.

Solution

(a) Consider using this algorithm to generate a draw from $f(\theta)$ with compact support $[a, b]$, as described in Exercise 11.6. In addition, employ a source density $s(\theta)$ that is uniform over the interval $[a, b]$.

In this case we can write

$$f(\theta) = c_f g(\theta) I(a \leq \theta \leq b) = c_f \tilde{f}(\theta),$$

where $\tilde{f}(\theta) = g(\theta) I(a \leq \theta \leq b)$, $\int_a^b g(\theta) = c_f^{-1}$, and

$$s(\theta) = [b - a]^{-1} I(a \leq \theta \leq b) = [b - a]^{-1} \tilde{s}(\theta).$$

It follows that

$$\tilde{M} = \max_{a \leq \theta \leq b} \left(\frac{\tilde{f}(\theta)}{\tilde{s}(\theta)} \right) = \max_{a \leq \theta \leq b} g(\theta) = c_f^{-1} \max_{a \leq \theta \leq b} f(\theta) = c_f^{-1} M,$$

where M is defined as the maximum of f in Exercise 11.6.

To implement the algorithm with the given uniform source density, we first generate $\theta^{\text{cand}} \sim U(a, b)$, which is equivalent to writing $\theta^{\text{cand}} = a + (b - a) U_1$, where $U_1 \sim U(0, 1)$. We then generate $U_2 \sim U(0, 1)$ and accept θ^{cand} provided

$$\begin{aligned} U_2 &\leq \frac{\tilde{f}(\theta^{\text{cand}})}{\tilde{M} \tilde{s}(\theta^{\text{cand}})} \\ &= \frac{c_f^{-1} f(a + [b - a] U_1)}{\tilde{M}} \\ &= \frac{c_f^{-1} f(a + [b - a] U_1)}{c_f^{-1} M} \\ &= \frac{f(a + [b - a] U_1)}{M}. \end{aligned}$$

This decision rule and the random variables U_1 and U_2 are identical to those described in Exercise 11.6. So the algorithm provided in this exercise reduces to that described in Exercise 11.6 when the target density has compact support and a source density that is uniform over that same support is employed.

(b) The overall acceptance rate is

$$\begin{aligned}\Pr\left(U \le [\tilde{f}(\theta)/\tilde{M}\tilde{s}(\theta)]\right) &= \int_\Theta \left[\int_0^{\tilde{f}(\theta)/\tilde{M}\tilde{s}(\theta)} dU\right] s(\theta)\, d\theta \\ &= \int_\Theta \frac{\tilde{f}(\theta)}{\tilde{M}\tilde{s}(\theta)} s(\theta)\, d\theta \\ &= \frac{c_s}{\tilde{M}c_f}.\end{aligned}$$

(c) Following Geweke (2005, Section 4.2.1), we note that for any subset A of Θ,

$$\begin{aligned}\Pr(\theta \text{ is accepted}, \theta \in A) &= \int_A \frac{\tilde{f}(\theta)}{\tilde{M}\tilde{s}(\theta)} s(\theta)\, d\theta \\ &= \frac{c_s}{\tilde{M}} \int_A \tilde{f}(\theta)\, d\theta.\end{aligned}$$

Since

$$\begin{aligned}\Pr(\theta \in A|\theta \text{ is accepted}) &= \frac{\Pr(\theta \text{ is accepted}, \theta \in A)}{\Pr(\theta \text{ is accepted})} \\ &= \frac{c_s\tilde{M}^{-1}\int_A \tilde{f}(\theta)\, d\theta}{c_s[\tilde{M}c_f]^{-1}} \\ &= c_f \int_A \tilde{f}(\theta)\, d\theta \\ &= \int_A f(\theta)\, d\theta,\end{aligned}$$

it follows that when θ is accepted from the algorithm, it is indeed a draw from $f(\theta)$.

Exercise 11.9 (Using acceptance/rejection sampling II)
(a) Using the algorithm of Exercise 11.8 and a $U(-1,1)$ source density, generate 25 000 draws from the triangular distribution $p(\theta) = 1 - |\theta|$, $\theta \in [-1,1]$. Comment on your results.
(b) Generate an equal number of draws from the triangular distribution using the same algorithm and a normal source density with mean zero and variance σ^2. First, consider a standard normal source with $\sigma^2 = 1$. Then, investigate the performance of the acceptance/rejection method with $\sigma^2 = 2$ and $\sigma^2 = 1/6$. Comment on your results.

Solution
(a–c). For the $U(-1,1)$ source density, note that the solution to part (a) of the previous exercise shows that the algorithm of Exercise 11.8 reduces to the algorithm of

Exercise 11.6. Thus, from part (a) of Exercise 11.6, it follows that the overall acceptance rate is .5. We regard this as a benchmark and seek to determine if an alternate choice of source density can lead to increased efficiency.

For the normal source density in part (b), when $\sigma^2 = 1$, the maximum of the target/source ratio occurs at $\theta = 0$, yielding a value of $\tilde{M} = 1$. Since the normalizing constant of the standard normal is $c_s = (2\pi)^{-1/2}$, it follows that the overall acceptance rate is $(2\pi)^{-1/2} \approx .40$. When comparing this algorithm to one with $\sigma^2 = 2$, it is clear that the standard normal source will be preferred. The maximum of the target/source ratio with $\sigma^2 = 2$ again occurs at $\theta = 0$, yielding $\tilde{M} = 1$. However, the overall acceptance probability reduces to $1/\sqrt{4\pi} \approx .28$.

The final choice of $\sigma^2 = 1/6$ is reasonably tailored to fit this application. One can easily show that the mean of the target is zero and the variance is $1/6$, so the $N(0, 1/6)$ source is chosen to match these two moments of the triangular density. With a little algebra, one can show that the maximum of the target/source ratio occurs at

$$\theta = \frac{1 + \sqrt{1/3}}{2} \approx .789.$$

(Note that another maximum also occurs at $-.789$ since both the target and source are symmetric about zero.) With this result in hand, the maximized value of the target/source ratio is $\tilde{M} \approx 1.37$, yielding a theoretical acceptance rate of $1/(1.37\sqrt{2\pi[1/6]}) \approx .72$. Thus, the $N(0, 1/6)$ source density is the most efficient of the candidates considered here.

In Figure 11.3 we plot the alternate source densities, scaled up by $\tilde{M}$, against the triangular density. The efficiency of the algorithm increases with the proximity of the scaled source density to the target. As the figure suggests, the $N(0, 1/6)$ source is the most efficient, as its selection results in the fewest number of discarded draws. Although it might seem that the figure suggests a preference for the $N(0, 1)$ source over the $U(-1, 1)$ alternative, note that this figure is only plotted over the support of the target density. When a candidate outside the $[-1, 1]$ range is drawn from the $N(0, 1)$ source, it must be discarded, resulting in increased inefficiency of the $N(0, 1)$ choice relative to the $U(-1, 1)$ source.

Exercise 11.10 (The weighted bootstrap) The *weighted bootstrap* of Smith and Gelfand (1992) and the highly related sampling-importance resampling (SIR) algorithm of Rubin (1987, 1988) circumvent the need to calculate the "blanketing constant" $\tilde{M}$ in acceptance sampling.

Consider the following procedure for obtaining a draw from a density of interest f:

1. Draw $\theta_1, \theta_2, \ldots, \theta_n$ from some approximating source density $s(\theta)$.

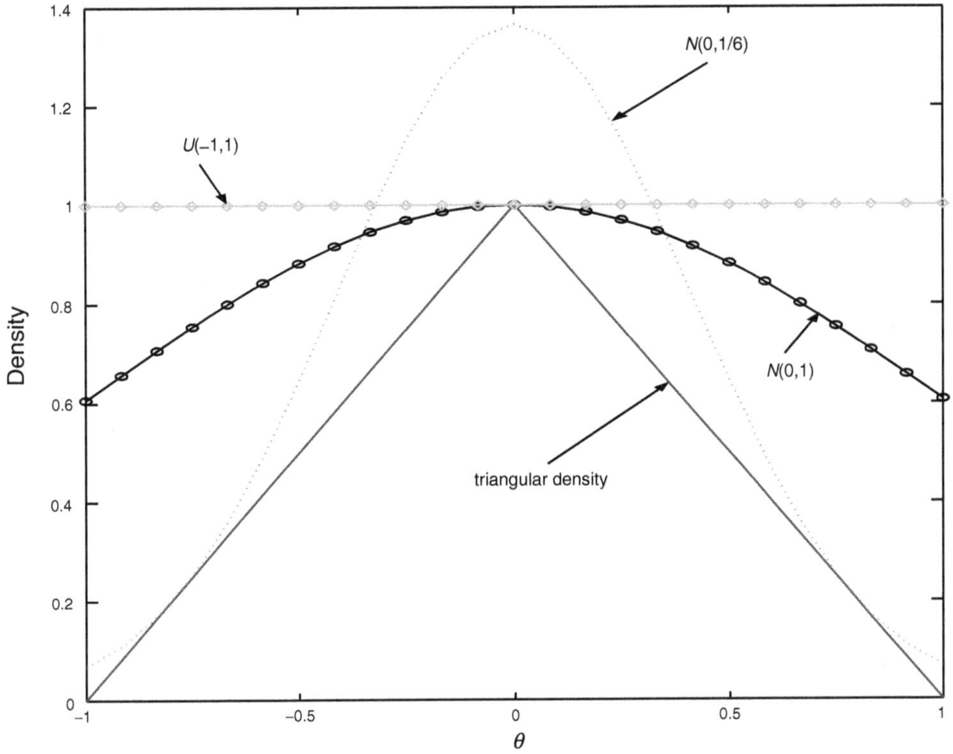

Figure 11.3. Triangular density together with three different scaled source densities.

2. Like Exercise 11.8, let us work with the kernels of the target and source densities and thus define

$$f(\theta) = c_f \tilde{f}(\theta),$$
$$s(\theta) = c_s \tilde{s}(\theta).$$

Set

$$w_i = w_i(\theta_i) = \frac{\tilde{f}(\theta_i)}{\tilde{s}(\theta_i)}$$

and define the normalized weights

$$\tilde{w}_i = \frac{w_i}{\sum_{i=1}^{n} w_i}.$$

3. Draw θ^* from the discrete set $\{\theta_1, \theta_2, \ldots, \theta_n\}$ with $\Pr(\theta^* = \theta_j) = \tilde{w}_j$, $j = 1, 2, \ldots, n$.

Show that θ^* provides an *approximate* draw from $f(\theta)$, with the accuracy of the approach improving with n, the simulated sample size from the source density.

Solution
Note that

$$
\begin{aligned}
\Pr(\theta^* \leq c) &= \sum_{j=1}^{n} \tilde{w}_j I(\theta_j \leq c) \\
&= \frac{\sum_{j=1}^{n} w_j I(\theta_j \leq c)}{\sum_{j=1}^{n} w_j} \\
&= \frac{[1/n]\sum_{j=1}^{n} w_j I(\theta_j \leq c)}{[1/n]\sum_{j=1}^{n} w_j} \\
&\to \frac{E[w(\theta) I(\theta \leq c)]}{E[w(\theta)]} \\
&= \frac{\int_{-\infty}^{\infty} w(\theta) I(\theta \leq c) s(\theta)\, d\theta}{\int_{-\infty}^{\infty} w(\theta) s(\theta)\, d\theta} \\
&= \frac{\int_{-\infty}^{c} [\tilde{f}(\theta)/\tilde{s}(\theta)] s(\theta)\, d\theta}{\int_{-\infty}^{\infty} [\tilde{f}(\theta)/\tilde{s}(\theta)] s(\theta)\, d\theta} \\
&= \frac{\int_{-\infty}^{c} \tilde{f}(\theta)\, d\theta}{\int_{-\infty}^{\infty} \tilde{f}(\theta)\, d\theta} \\
&= \int_{-\infty}^{c} f(\theta)\, d\theta \\
&\equiv F(c).
\end{aligned}
$$

In the fourth line, we consider the limit as the simulated sample size n approaches infinity. To proceed from line 6 to 7, we note that $s(\theta)/\tilde{s}(\theta) = c_s$, and similarly note that $f(\theta)/\tilde{f}(\theta) = c_f$ when moving from lines 7 to 8.

Again, this algorithm only provides an approximate draw from f, with its accuracy increasing with n. Of course, the performance of the algorithm depends on how accurately s approximates f. If, for example, the mass under s is concentrated in a region where f places little mass, then the algorithm will typically perform poorly.

11.3 Importance Sampling

Exercise 11.11 (Importance sampling I: Basics) Suppose our goal is to estimate a posterior moment of the form $E[f(\theta)|y]$. If we are able to generate draws from the posterior distribution $p(\theta|y)$, then the desired moment can be estimated directly from that set of simulations:

$$
\widehat{E[f(\theta)|y]} = \frac{1}{M} \sum_{m=1}^{M} f(\theta_m),
$$

where $\theta_m \overset{iid}{\sim} p(\theta|y),\ m = 1, 2, \ldots, M$. However, things are rarely this easy (apart from in contrived textbook questions!) and direct sampling from the posterior is typically not possible, rendering the estimator above infeasible in many cases.

Abstracting from the specific issue of posterior moment calculation, suppose, more generally, that we wish to estimate the expectation of a function of some possibly multivariate random variable X. We will denote this expectation of interest as $E_p[f(x)]$, where

$$\mu \equiv E_p[f(x)] = \int_{\mathcal{P}} f(x)p(x)dx,$$

with $\mathcal{P} \equiv \{x : p(x)f(x) \neq 0\}$. We assume that we are not able to sample from p directly.
(a) Suppose, however, that we can generate samples from some approximating density, say $I(x)$, which is known as an "importance function." Let us denote a collection of M simulations from I as $x_1, x_2, \ldots, x_M$. With these simulations in hand, provide a justification for the following estimator of the desired moment:

$$\hat{\mu}_{IS} \equiv \widehat{E_p[f(x)]} = \frac{1}{M}\sum_{m=1}^{M}\left(\frac{f(x_m)p(x_m)}{I(x_m)}\right),$$

and discuss conditions surrounding the choice of I. In the above, the subscript "IS" is used to denote the importance sampling estimator.
(b) Derive the variance of $\hat{\mu}_{IS}$ and describe how it can be estimated. Note that the "sample size" M in this context refers to the number of draws from $I(\cdot)$, which is completely under our control and can be made arbitrarily large.

Solution
(a) Let $\mathcal{I} \equiv \{x : I(x) > 0\}$, and furthermore require $I(x) > 0$ whenever $f(x)p(x) \neq 0$. (In practice, this can always be accomplished by choosing I such that $I(x) > 0$ whenever $p(x) > 0$.) We note that

$$\begin{aligned}
\mu \equiv E_p[f(x)] &= \int_{\mathcal{P}} p(x)f(x)dx \\
&= \int_{\mathcal{P}} \frac{p(x)f(x)}{I(x)} I(x)dx \\
&= \int_{\mathcal{I}} \frac{p(x)f(x)}{I(x)} I(x)dx \\
&= E_{\mathcal{I}}\left(\frac{p(x)f(x)}{I(x)}\right).
\end{aligned}$$

In the second step we never face the problem of dividing by zero since, by construction, $I(x) > 0\ \forall x \in \mathcal{P}$. Similarly, the third line is justified by the fact that $f(x)p(x) = 0$ for all x not in $\mathcal{P}$ but in $\mathcal{I}$.

The last line reveals that the initial moment (defined as an expectation in terms of p) has now been rewritten as an expectation of a different function, where that expectation is taken with respect to the computationally more convenient I. Since an iid sample of size M is available from I, we can apply direct Monte Carlo integration to the last line of the above and estimate μ as follows:

$$\hat{\mu}_{IS} = \widehat{E_p[f(x)]} = \frac{1}{M}\sum_{m=1}^{M}\left(\frac{f(x_m)p(x_m)}{I(x_m)}\right).$$

(b) Since the $\{x_m\}$ are iid, it follows that

$$\begin{aligned}
\sigma_{IS}^2 &\equiv \text{Var}_I\left[\frac{1}{M}\sum_{m=1}^{M}\left(\frac{f(x_m)p(x_m)}{I(x_m)}\right)\right] \\
&= \left(\frac{1}{M^2}\right)M\text{Var}_I\left(\frac{f(x)p(x)}{I(x)}\right) \\
&= \frac{1}{M}\left(E_I\left[\left(\frac{[f(x)p(x)]^2}{I^2(x)}\right)\right] - \mu^2\right) \quad \text{or} \\
&= \frac{1}{M}E_I\left[\left(\frac{f(x)p(x)}{I(x)} - \mu\right)^2\right],
\end{aligned}$$

since $E_I[f(x)p(x)/I(x)] = \int_\Theta f(x)p(x)dx = \mu$.

Assuming that the expectation above is finite, this final line suggests a way to estimate the variance via direct Monte Carlo integration:

$$\hat{\sigma}_{IS}^2 = \frac{1}{M^2}\sum_{m=1}^{M}\left(\frac{f(x_m)p(x_m)}{I(x_m)} - \hat{\mu}_{IS}\right)^2.$$

Exercise 11.12 (Importance sampling II: An example) Suppose you wish to determine the mean of the random variable X, where

$$p(x) = \mu^{-1}\exp(-\mu^{-1}x), \quad \mu > 0,\ x > 0.$$

Although this is recognized as an exponential density with mean μ, consider an importance-sampling-based solution (i.e., in the context of the previous question, employ importance sampling with $f(x) = x$).

For the class of importance functions in this exercise, consider those within the family of exponential distributions, indexed by the parameter α:

$$I(x|\alpha) = \alpha^{-1}\exp(-\alpha^{-1}x), \quad \alpha > 0, x > 0.$$

(a) To get a feel for how an importance sampling estimator is calculated and to see potential pitfalls associated with its use if sufficient care is not taken, conduct a numerical experiment. To fix ideas, set $\mu = 2$ and then proceed to use importance sampling to estimate μ, as if it were unknown. (That is, think about being handed a density function $p(x) = (1/2)\exp(-(1/2)x)$ and then being asked to use importance sampling to calculate its mean.) Numerically calculate an approximation to the sampling distribution of the importance sampling estimator under three different choices of α: $\alpha \in \{.5, 2, 4\}$. To do this, proceed as follows:

- Generate 1000 simulations from the $I(x|\alpha)$ distribution. Note that you will generate three different sets of 1000 simulations, one set for each value of $\alpha \in \{.5, 2, 4\}$.
- Following the previous exercise, compute the importance sampling estimate of μ, again for each value of α.
- Repeat the above process 1000 different times (that is, generate three different sets of 1000 simulations 1000 different times), storing the importance sampling estimate each time, for each value of α. When you have finished, you will have three different 1000×1 vectors of importance sampling estimates corresponding to the different values of α.
- Calculate the average of the three 1000×1 vectors of importance sampling estimates, along with their standard deviations. Note that these provide an approximation to the location and scale of the associated sampling distributions of the estimators.

Comment on the results you obtain.
(b) Rationalize the results you found numerically in part (a) by theoretically deriving the variance of the importance sampling estimator under the different choices of α. To make your answers as general as possible here, leave the results in terms of μ rather than impose $\mu = 2$.

Solution
(a) MATLAB code for this exercise is provided on the website associated with this book. In what follows we summarize the results obtained when running our MATLAB program. When $\alpha = .5$, we find that the importance sampling estimator exhibits a tremendous amount of sampling variability. Specifically, for $\alpha = .5$, the sample average of the collection of our $\hat{\mu}_{IS}$ values was 1.79 and the standard deviation equalled 3.8. Furthermore, the smallest importance sampling estimate among the set was .69, while the largest was 90.76. (Given the large amount of sampling variability in this case and the theoretical results that follow, you should expect results to change significantly when you run MATLAB on your own.) By contrast, for the $\alpha = 2$ and $\alpha = 4$ cases, the means are both very close to 2 (1.98 and 2.00, respectively) with much smaller sample standard deviations (which were equal to .063 and .027, respectively). It seems, then, that something is not quite right with the estimator's performance when $\alpha = .5$. Values of α equal to 2 and 4, on the other hand, appear to perform quite well, with $\alpha = 4$ producing the smallest sampling variability among this set. The solution to the next part of the exercise will provide an explanation for these observations.
(b) Let's theoretically derive the variance of the importance sampling estimator in this experiment. Using the third line of the solution of part (b) of the previous exercise, we can write

$$\text{Var}(\hat{\mu}_{IS}) = \frac{1}{M}\left[E_{I|\alpha}\left(\frac{[p(x)I(x|\alpha)]^2}{I^2(x|\alpha)}\right) - \mu^2\right].$$

It follows that the variance will be minimized by choosing an α that minimizes the expectation component of the expression above. To this end, we note that

$$\begin{aligned}
E_{I|\alpha}\left(\frac{[p(x)I(x|\alpha)]^2}{I^2(x|\alpha)}\right) &= \int_0^\infty \left(\frac{[x\mu^{-1}\exp(-\mu^{-1}x)]^2}{\alpha^{-1}\exp(-\alpha^{-1}x)}\right) dx \\
&= \left(\frac{\alpha}{\mu^2}\right)\int_0^\infty x^2 \exp\left(-\left(\frac{\mu\alpha}{2\alpha-\mu}\right)^{-1} x\right) dx \\
&= \frac{\alpha}{\mu^2}\left(\frac{\mu\alpha}{2\alpha-\mu}\right)\int_0^\infty x^2\left(\frac{\mu\alpha}{2\alpha-\mu}\right)^{-1}\exp\left(-\left(\frac{\mu\alpha}{2\alpha-\mu}\right)^{-1} x\right) dx \\
&= \left(\frac{\alpha}{\mu^2}\frac{\mu\alpha}{2\alpha-\mu}\right) E_{EXP(\mu\alpha/(2\alpha-\mu))}(X^2) \\
&= \left(\frac{2\alpha}{\mu^2}\frac{\mu\alpha}{2\alpha-\mu}\right)\left(\frac{\mu\alpha}{2\alpha-\mu}\right)^2 \\
&= \frac{2\alpha^4\mu}{(2\alpha-\mu)^3}.
\end{aligned}$$

The integral in the second equation converges provided $\alpha > \mu/2$; for α values smaller than this, the variance of the importance sampling estimator is infinite. This explains the erratic performance of the importance sampling estimator of part (a) when $\alpha = .5$; in this case, the variance does not exist. Furthermore, it can be shown that the expression $2\alpha^4\mu/(2\alpha-\mu)^3$ is minimized by choosing $\alpha^* = 2\mu$. This is consistent with the result of our numerical exercise in part (a), where we found that $\alpha = 4 = 2\mu$ yielded the smallest sampling standard deviation.

This exercise reveals a number of interesting results, including (i) emphasizing the need that the importance function have heavier tails than the target distribution, while also noting that σ_{IS}^2 can be infinite if the tails of the importance function are too thin (i.e., $\alpha \leq \mu/2$), and (ii) observing that the optimal choice in this case is *not* to set $\alpha = \mu$, which would correspond to the case of *iid* sampling from the target distribution. In this final case, note that the resulting estimator is an unbiased, but non-linear, estimator of μ.

Exercise 11.13 (Importance sampling III: Bayesian uses, asymptotics, and RNE)
In the previous questions on importance sampling, it was assumed that the density p was known. In Bayesian applications, however, the posterior distribution is usually only known up to a constant of proportionality.

(a) Show how the importance sampling estimator can be adapted to calculate a posterior moment of some scalar function of interest $f(\theta)$ when only the kernel of the posterior distribution is known.

(b) Derive the asymptotic distribution of the estimator in (a).

(c) Suggest a diagnostic that can be calculated that compares the efficiency of the importance sampling estimator to what would have been obtained under *iid* sampling from the posterior distribution.

Solution

(a) Suppose that a prior $p(\theta)$ is employed. Denote the likelihood as $L(\theta)$, and note that

$$E[f(\theta)|y] = \int_{\Theta} f(\theta)p(\theta|y)d\theta = \frac{\int_{\Theta} f(\theta)p(\theta)L(\theta)d\theta}{\int_{\Theta} p(\theta)L(\theta)d\theta}.$$

Using an importance function $I(\theta)$ whose support includes the support of the posterior distribution, we can write

$$E[f(\theta)|y] = \frac{E_I[f(\theta)p(\theta)L(\theta)/I(\theta)]}{E_I[p(\theta)L(\theta)/I(\theta)]},$$

yielding

$$\widehat{E[f(\theta)|y]}_{IS} = \left[\frac{1}{M}\sum_{m=1}^{M} f(\theta_m)p(\theta_m)L(\theta_m)/I(\theta_m)\right]\left[\frac{1}{M}\sum_{m=1}^{M} p(\theta_m)L(\theta_m)/I(\theta_m)\right]^{-1}.$$

This can be simplified to give

$$\begin{aligned}
[\widehat{E_{\theta|y}(f)}]_{IS} \equiv \widehat{E[f(\theta)|y]}_{IS} &= \frac{\sum_{m=1}^{M} f(\theta_m)p(\theta_m)L(\theta_m)/I(\theta_m)}{\sum_{m=1}^{M} p(\theta_m)L(\theta_m)/I(\theta_m)} \\
&= \frac{\sum_{m=1}^{M} f(\theta_m)w(\theta_m)}{\sum_{m=1}^{M} w(\theta_m)} \\
&= \sum_{m=1}^{M} f_m \tilde{w}_m,
\end{aligned}$$

with $f_m = f(\theta_m)$, $w_m = w(\theta_m) \equiv p(\theta_m)L(\theta_m)/I(\theta_m)$, $\tilde{w}_m = w_m / \sum_{m=1}^{M} w_m$, and $\theta_m \overset{iid}{\sim} I(\theta)$. In this final form we can interpret the importance sampling estimator as a weighted average of the $f(\theta_m)$ values, with larger weights assigned to draws with higher ordinates under $p(\theta|y)$. All that is required to implement this procedure is calculation of the likelihood as well as the prior and importance function (up to proportionality) at different values of θ.

(b) Begin by defining $c \equiv \int_{\Theta} p(\theta)L(\theta)d\theta$. In terms of asymptotics, let

$$z_m = \begin{bmatrix} f_m w_m \\ w_m \end{bmatrix},$$

which implies, $\forall m = 1, 2, \ldots, M$,

$$E_I(z_m) \equiv \mu_z = \begin{bmatrix} \int_{\Theta} f(\theta)p(\theta)L(\theta)d\theta \\ \int_{\Theta} p(\theta)L(\theta)d\theta \end{bmatrix} = \begin{bmatrix} cE_{\theta|y}(f) \\ c \end{bmatrix}.$$

A multivariate version of the Lindeberg–Levy central limit theorem establishes that

$$\sqrt{M}\left(\overline{z}_M - \mu_z\right) = \sqrt{M}\left[\begin{pmatrix}\frac{1}{M}\sum_{m=1}^{M} f_m w_m \\ \frac{1}{M}\sum_{m=1}^{M} w_m\end{pmatrix} - \begin{pmatrix} cE_{\theta|y}[f] \\ c\end{pmatrix}\right]$$

$$\xrightarrow{d} \mathcal{N}\left[\begin{pmatrix}0\\0\end{pmatrix}, \begin{pmatrix}\text{Var}_I(fw) & \text{Cov}_I(fw,w) \\ \text{Cov}_I(w,fw) & \text{Var}(w)\end{pmatrix}\right].$$

Note that the importance sampling estimator of the posterior mean is simply the ratio of the two elements in $\overline{z}_M$. We can apply the Delta method to characterize the asymptotic distribution of this ratio:

$$\sqrt{M}\left(\widehat{[E_{\theta|y}(f)]}_{IS} - E_{\theta|y}(f)\right) \xrightarrow{d} \mathcal{N}\left(0, \tau^2\right),$$

where

$$\tau^2 = \begin{bmatrix} c^{-1} \\ -c^{-1}E_{\theta|y}(f)\end{bmatrix}' \begin{bmatrix}\text{Var}_I(fw) & \text{Cov}_I(fw,w) \\ \text{Cov}_I(w,fw) & \text{Var}(w)\end{bmatrix}\begin{bmatrix} c^{-1} \\ -c^{-1}E_{\theta|y}(f)\end{bmatrix}.$$

Multiplying the expression above, we see that

$$\tau^2 = c^{-2}\left[\text{Var}_I(fw) - 2\left[E_{\theta|y}(f)\right]\text{Cov}_I(fw,w) + \left[E_{\theta|y}(f)\right]^2 \text{Var}_I(w)\right],$$

which can be rewritten as

$$\tau^2 = c^{-2}\text{Var}_I\left[\left(f - E_{\theta|y}(f)\right)w\right].$$

Since one can show that $E_I\left[\left(f - E_{\theta|y}(f)\right)w\right] = 0$, we can express τ^2 as

$$\tau^2 = c^{-2}E_I\left[\left(f - E_{\theta|y}(f)\right)^2 w^2\right].$$

Recalling that $c = \int_\Theta p(\theta)L(\theta)d\theta$ and using importance sampling to estimate both c and the squared moment above, we obtain:

$$\hat{\tau}^2_{IS} = \frac{\hat{E}_I\left[\left(f - E_{\theta|y}(f)\right)^2 w^2\right]}{\hat{c}^2} = \frac{(1/M)\sum_{m=1}^{M}[f_m - \widehat{[E_{\theta|y}(f)]}_{IS}]^2 w_m^2}{\left[(1/M)\sum_{m=1}^{M} w_m\right]^2}$$

$$= \frac{M\sum_{m=1}^{M}[f_m - \widehat{[E_{\theta|y}(f)]}_{IS}]^2 w_m^2}{\left[\sum_{m=1}^{M} w_m\right]^2}.$$

To assess the accuracy of an importance sampling estimator, we can define RNE (or *relative numerical efficiency*), as suggested by Geweke (1989) in his seminal work on the subject, as the ratio of the variance of an *iid* sampling-based estimate of $E_{\theta|y}(f)$ to the variance of the importance sampling estimator of the posterior mean:

$$RNE \equiv \frac{\text{Var}[f(\theta)|y]/M}{\tau^2/M} = \frac{\text{Var}[f(\theta)|y]}{\tau^2},$$

which can, again, be estimated using importance sampling as follows:

$$\widehat{RNE} = \frac{\sum_{m=1}^{M}[f_m - [\widehat{E_{\theta|y}(f)}]_{IS}]^2 w_m}{\sum_{m=1}^{M} w_m} \left(\frac{M\sum_{m=1}^{M}[f_m - [\widehat{E_{\theta|y}(f)}]_{IS}]^2 w_m^2}{\left[\sum_{m=1}^{M} w_m\right]^2} \right)^{-1}.$$

Since the numerical standard error of the importance sampling estimator is $\sqrt{\tau^2/M}$, this can be re-expressed as $\sqrt{\text{Var}[f(\theta)|y]/M \times RNE}$. Thus, $M \times RNE$ has the interpretation of an *effective sample size*. That is, when adopting the importance sampling estimator, the precision of the result is equivalent to what we would have obtained had $M \times RNE$ iid draws from the posterior been taken to calculate the desired moment. This diagnostic provides a useful interpretation of the degree of efficiency loss associated with the choice of importance function; values of RNE much smaller than one suggest that I may be a poor approximation of the target and significant improvement may be possible.

Exercise 11.14 (Importance sampling IV: Further experiments) Assume you have a model with a single parameter, θ, and its posterior is $N(0,1)$.
(a) Write a program that calculates the posterior mean and standard deviation of θ using Monte Carlo integration.
(b) Write a program that calculates the posterior mean and standard deviation of θ using importance sampling and calculates the mean and standard deviation of the importance sampling weights. Use the $t(0,1,\nu)$ distribution as the importance function.
(c) Carry out Monte Carlo integration and importance sampling with $\nu = 2$, 5, and 100 for a given number of replications (e.g., $R = 10$). Compare the accuracy of the estimates across different algorithms and choices for v. Discuss your results, paying attention to the issue of what happens to the importance sampling weights as v increases.
(d) Redo part (c) using the $t(3,1,\nu)$ as an importance function. Discuss the factors affecting the accuracy of importance sampling in light of the fact that this importance function is a poor approximation to the posterior.

Solution

(a and b) The structure of computer code that does Monte Carlo integration and importance sampling to carry out posterior inference on θ is as follows:

Step 1: Do all the preliminary things to create all the variables used in the Monte Carlo and importance sampling procedures (i.e., specify the parameters of the importance function and initialize all the Monte Carlo and importance sampling sums to zero).
Step 2: Draw θ from the normal posterior (for Monte Carlo integration).
Step 3: Draw θ from the importance function and calculate the importance sampling weight (and weight squared). Multiply the drawn θ by the importance sampling weight to obtain that draw's contribution to the numerator of the importance sampling estimator (see, e.g., the solution to part (a) of Exercise 11.13).

Step 4: Repeat Steps 2 and 3 R times.

Step 5: Average the Step 2 draws and draws squared (to produce the Monte Carlo estimate of the posterior mean and standard deviation). Divide the Step 3 draws and draws squared by the sum of the weights (to produce the importance sampling estimate of the posterior mean and standard deviation). Calculate the mean and standard deviation of the weights.

The MATLAB code used to perform these steps is provided on the website associated with this book.

(c and d) Table 11.4 presents Monte Carlo integration and importance sampling results for each of the different importance functions specified in the question using $R = 10$. Note that as $R \to \infty$ the posterior means and standard deviations will be the same for all approaches (i.e., they will equal their true values of 0 and 1). Hence, choosing a relatively small value of R is important to see the effect of the importance function on accuracy of estimation. In an empirical exercise you would choose R to be much larger.

Table 11.5 illustrates some of the issues relating to the selection of an importance function, as suggested by earlier exercises. First, note that as ν increases the t distribution approaches the normal; the $t(0, 1, 100)$ is virtually the same as the true $N(0, 1)$ posterior. Thus, importance sampling is virtually the same as Monte Carlo integration and the importance sampling weights are all virtually 1.0. Second, the $t(0, 1, 5)$ and $t(0, 1, 2)$ importance functions both approximate the posterior well, but have fatter tails. Thus, they yield results that are a bit less accurate than Monte Carlo integration and have importance sampling weights that vary widely across draws. That is, the standard deviation of the importance sampling weights indicates that some draws are receiving much more weight than others (in contrast to the more efficient Monte Carlo integration procedure, which weights all draws equally).

Third, the importance functions with mean 3.0 all approximate the $N(0, 1)$ posterior poorly. Results with these importance functions are way off, indicating that it is important

Table 11.5: Monte Carlo and importance sampling results for $N(0, 1)$ posterior.

	Post. mean	Post. std. dev.	Mean imp. samp. wt.	Std. dev. imp. samp. wt.
Monte Carlo	0.046	0.874	—	—
Importance sampling				
$t(0, 1, 2)$	−0.110	0.500	0.815	0.473
$t(0, 1, 5)$	0.055	0.721	0.948	0.106
$t(0, 1, 100)$	0.049	0.925	1.004	9.6×10^{-4}
$t(3, 1, 2)$	1.469	0.525	0.373	0.638
$t(3, 1, 5)$	1.576	0.426	0.186	0.439
$t(3, 1, 100)$	1.996	0.368	0.055	0.120

to choose an importance function that approximates the posterior well. Note that the posterior means are all too high. These importance functions are taking almost all of their draws in implausible regions of the parameter space (e.g., most of the importance sampling draws will be greater than 2.0, whereas the true posterior allocates very little probability to this region). Of course, importance sampling corrects for this by giving little weight to the draws greater than 2.0 and great weight to the (very few) draws less than 2.0 and, as $R \to \infty$, importance sampling estimates will converge to the true values. But with small R importance sampling results can be misleading and care should be taken (e.g., by looking at numerical standard errors) to make sure R is large enough to yield accurate results. You might wish to experiment to find out how large R has to be to obtain accurate results using the $t(3, 1, \nu)$ importance function. (We find setting $R = 10\,000$ yields reasonably accurate results.)

Fourth, of the $t(3, 1, 2)$, $t(3, 1, 5)$, and $t(3, 1, 100)$ importance functions, it is the one with $\nu = 2$ degrees of freedom that seems to be yielding the most accurate results. This is because, as stressed earlier, it has fatter tails and, thus, is taking more dispersed draws, which means more draws in regions where the $N(0, 1)$ posterior is appreciable.

Overall, these results suggest that it is important to get an importance function that approximates the posterior reasonably well. In empirical exercises, strategies such as setting the mean and variance of a t distribution importance function to maximum likelihood or posterior quantities are common. However, as an insurance policy it is common to choose a small degrees-of-freedom parameter to ensure that key regions of the parameter space are covered. A common rule of thumb is that importance functions should have fatter tails than the posterior.

Exercise 11.15 (Importance sampling V: Prior sensitivity) The purpose of this question is to see how importance sampling can be used to carry out a prior sensitivity analysis.

This question uses the normal linear regression model with natural conjugate prior and a data set. Definitions and notation for the model are given in the introduction to Chapter 10. Generate an artificial data set of size $N = 100$ from the normal linear regression model with an intercept and one other explanatory variable. Set the intercept (β_1) to 0, the slope coefficient (β_2) to 1.0, and h to 1.0. Generate the explanatory variable by taking random draws from the $U(0, 1)$ distribution (although you may wish to experiment with other data sets). Suppose your prior beliefs are reflected in your base prior, which has prior hyperparameter values of $\underline{\beta} = [0\ 1]'$, $\underline{V} = I_2$, $\underline{s}^{-2} = 1$, and $\underline{\nu} = 1$. However, you wish to carry out a prior sensitivity analysis with respect to the prior mean and standard deviation of the slope coefficient and, hence, also want to consider priors with $\underline{\beta} = [0\ c]'$ and $\underline{V} = \begin{bmatrix} 1 & 0 \\ 0 & d \end{bmatrix}$ for values of $c = 0$, 1, and 2 and $d = 0.01$, 1, and 100.

(a) Calculate the posterior mean and standard deviation for the slope coefficient β_2 for this data set for every one of these priors using analytical results.

(b) Write a program that does the same things as part (a) using Monte Carlo integration and use this program to produce $R = 100$ draws of β_2 using the base prior.
(c) Write a program that uses importance sampling to carry out the prior sensitivity analysis, *using only the draws produced in part (b)*. Compare the results obtained using this approach to those obtained in part (a). How do your results change when you set $R = 10\,000$?

Solution

(a and b) The solution to parts (a) and (b) is given as part of the solution to Exercise 11.3 earlier in this chapter. Empirical results for these parts are given below.

The answer to part (c) is based on the insight that the posterior for the normal linear regression model with the base prior can be treated as an importance function for the posteriors corresponding to the other priors used in the prior sensitivity analysis. Formally, let M_1 be the normal linear regression model with base prior, M_2 be the normal linear regression model with any other prior, and $\theta = [\beta_1\ \beta_2\ h]'$ be the parameter vector (common to both models). Monte Carlo integration using the program written for part (b) will provide draws from $p(\theta|y, M_1)$. If we treat this posterior as an importance function in a Bayesian analysis of M_2, then the importance sampling weights will be

$$w_r = \frac{p\left(\theta = \theta^{(r)}|y, M_2\right)}{p\left(\theta = \theta^{(r)}|y, M_1\right)},$$

where $\theta^{(r)}$ for $r = 1, \ldots, R$ are draws from $p(\theta|y, M_1)$. In a prior sensitivity analysis, the importance sampling weights simplify considerably since both models have the same likelihood function, which cancels out in the ratio, yielding

$$w_r = \frac{p\left(\theta = \theta^{(r)}|M_2\right)}{p\left(\theta = \theta^{(r)}|M_1\right)}.$$

In fact, for the particular prior structure in the question, the importance sampling weights simplify even further since the same prior is used for the error precision in each model and β_1 and β_2 are, *a priori*, uncorrelated with one another. Thus, we have

$$w_r = \frac{p\left(\beta_2 = \beta_2^{(r)}|M_2\right)}{p\left(\beta_2 = \beta_2^{(r)}|M_1\right)},$$

which is the ratio of two t densities.
(c) The sketch outline of the program is the same as for any Monte Carlo integration or importance sampling program (see, again, the solution to Exercise 11.3) and will not be repeated here. The MATLAB code used to answer parts (a), (b), and (c) is provided on the website associated with this book.

Table 11.6 presents the results using this program. A discussion of this table completes the answer to this question. It is worth noting that we are carrying out a sensitivity analysis

Table 11.6: Results from prior sensitivity analysis.

Hyperparameter values		Analytical results		Importance sampling results			
c	d	$E(\beta_2\|y)$	$\sqrt{\text{Var}(\beta_2\|y)}$	$R = 100$		$R = 10\,000$	
0.0	0.01	0.081	0.089	0.286	0.294	0.116	0.090
0.0	1.0	0.957	0.291	0.963	0.323	0.997	0.306
0.0	100.0	1.073	0.306	1.076	0.344	1.076	0.322
1.0	0.01	1.006	0.084	1.019	0.099	1.008	0.095
1.0	1.0	1.066	0.291	1.068	0.325	1.070	0.305
1.0	100.0	1.074	0.306	1.077	0.344	1.077	0.322
2.0	0.01	1.930	0.088	1.910	0.046	1.923	0.097
2.0	1.0	1.176	0.291	1.174	0.328	1.164	0.307
2.0	100.0	1.076	0.306	1.078	0.344	1.079	0.322

over a very wide range of priors for β_2. To give an idea about the information in the data, note that the OLS estimate of β_2 is 1.074 and its standard error is 0.311. The priors with large prior variances (i.e., $d = 100$) are very non-informative relative to the data, whereas priors with $d = 0.01$ are more informative than the data. Priors with $c = 1.0$ are centered over the true value used to generate the data, whereas priors with $c = 0.0$ and $c = 2.0$ are far away from the true value (at least for priors with informative values for the prior variance of β_2). In the columns of Table 11.6 labeled "Analytical results" we can see that the results are quite sensitive to the prior (especially when $d = 0.01$).

The posterior corresponding to the base prior (with $c = 1.0$ and $d = 1.0$) is used as an importance function for the posteriors corresponding to all the other priors. We expect importance sampling to work best when the former posterior is similar to the latter. Given the wide spread of priors, it might be the case that importance sampling works poorly, especially for the priors with $d = 0.01$. When $R = 100$ replications are used, then importance sampling results can, indeed, be a bit off, especially for the $d = 0.01$ cases. However, when $R = 10\,000$ replications are used, the importance sampling algorithm works much better, even for the extreme cases considered here. Thus, Table 11.6 indicates that importance sampling can be used to carry out prior sensitivity analyses, even when the sensitivity analysis is over a wide range of priors. Of course, for the normal linear regression model with a natural conjugate prior it is not necessary to use importance sampling since analytical results are available. However, for a model that does not allow for analytical posterior results, the strategy outlined in this question – of taking posterior draws from a model based on one prior and then reweighting them using importance sampling – may be a very efficient way of conducting a prior sensitivity analysis.

12

Posterior Simulation via Markov Chain Monte Carlo

Bayesian econometrics typically involves extensive use of *posterior simulation*. Posterior simulation is discussed in detail in, for example, Gelman, Carlin, Stern, and Rubin (1995), Geweke (1999), Carlin and Louis (2000), Chib (2001), Geweke and Keane (2001), Koop (2003), Lancaster (2004), Geweke (2005), and Greenberg (2013). The reader unfamiliar with the basic ideas and terminology of posterior computation is referred to these references for background reading.

Some of the most important methods of posterior simulation are Monte Carlo integration, importance sampling (as discussed in the previous chapter), Gibbs sampling, and the Metropolis–Hastings algorithm. The latter two of these are examples of *Markov chain Monte Carlo* (MCMC) algorithms. In this chapter we use simple distributions and commonly employed models to solve questions that illustrate how these and other algorithms are implemented.

Gibbs sampling is a popular algorithm commonly used when the conditional posterior distributions are easy to work with. We illustrate Gibbs sampling for the case where the parameter vector is broken into two blocks, $\theta' = [\theta_1' \ \theta_2']$, although the algorithm generalizes easily to the case of many blocks (including the case where some of the blocks contain latent data). Gibbs sampling produces a sequence of draws $\theta^{(r)}$ for $r = 1, \ldots, R$ with the property that

$$\widehat{g} = \frac{\sum_{r=1}^{R} g\left(\theta^{(r)}\right)}{R}$$

converges to $E\left[g\left(\theta\right)|y\right]$ as R goes to infinity (provided $E\left[g\left(\theta\right)|y\right]$ exists). Gibbs sampling produces this sequence by iteratively drawing from the posterior conditional distributions. That is, $\theta_2^{(r)}$ is drawn from $p\left(\theta_2|y, \theta_1^{(r-1)}\right)$ and $\theta_1^{(r)}$ is drawn from $p\left(\theta_1|y, \theta_2^{(r)}\right)$. It can be shown that, under weak conditions, this sequence of draws converges to a sequence of draws from the joint posterior. Note that the Gibbs sampler requires a choice of starting value $\theta_1^{(0)}$. To eliminate dependence on this starting value, it is common to discard the initial R_0 draws (referred to as burn-in draws) from the Gibbs sampler.

The *Metropolis–Hastings (M–H) algorithm* is really an entire class of algorithms. Like Monte Carlo integration and Gibbs sampling, it produces a sequence of draws $\theta^{(r)}$ for $r = 1, \ldots, R$ with the property that

$$\widehat{g} = \frac{\sum_{r=1}^{R} g\left(\theta^{(r)}\right)}{R}$$

converges to $E\left[g\left(\theta\right)|y\right]$ as R goes to infinity.

The Metropolis–Hastings algorithm involves drawing from a convenient density akin to the importance function of the previous chapter, referred to as the *candidate generating density*. We will denote this density as $q(\theta|\theta^{(r-1)})$, so that the potential dependence on the current value of the chain, $\theta^{(r-1)}$, is explicit. At each iteration of the algorithm a draw from q is obtained, say θ^*, and then is accepted with probability

$$\alpha(\theta^{(r-1)}, \theta^*) = \min\left\{\frac{p(\theta^*|y)}{q(\theta^*|\theta^{(r-1)})}\frac{q(\theta^{(r-1)}|\theta^*)}{p(\theta^{(r-1)}|y)}, 1\right\},$$

where $p(\cdot|y)$ denotes the joint or conditional posterior distribution from which samples are desired.

If the draw is accepted, then $\theta^{(r)} = \theta^*$, while if the draw is rejected, then $\theta^{(r)}$ is set to $\theta^{(r-1)}$. The acceptance probability above may be simplified depending on the precise form of the algorithm (see Chib 1995; Geweke 1999; Koop 2003). Two common variants are the *independence chain* and the *random walk chain* Metropolis–Hastings algorithms.

This chapter is divided into four sections. In the first section we review in further detail Gibbs sampling, slice sampling, and the M–H algorithm, and offer explanations surrounding why these methods work. The second section goes through three specific models in detail and walks the reader through the mathematical steps and coding required when implementing a Gibbs algorithm. The third section reviews Gibbs and MCMC sampling in a variety of linear regression models. The chapter concludes with exercises related to diagnostic checking of model assumptions, mistakes when coding a posterior simulator, and MCMC convergence.

12.1 Gibbs and Slice Sampling and the Metropolis–Hastings Algorithm

The algorithms presented in Chapter 11 fell under the heading of direct simulation methods. That is, no requirement was imposed that the algorithms needed to "converge" in order to generate draws from the posterior $p(\theta|y)$ or to accurately characterize posterior moments of the form $E[g(\theta)|y]$. In the following set of exercises, we describe three *iterative* Markov chain Monte Carlo algorithms: the Gibbs sampler, the Metropolis–Hastings algorithm, and the slice sampler. Since these methods are quite powerful and widely used, several exercises are designed to illustrate their use in fitting a selection of standard econometric models.

Exercise 12.1 (Gibbs sampling) The *Gibbs sampler* is an indispensable tool in the Bayesian's toolkit. As discussed in the introduction to this chapter, the Gibbs sampler is an iterative algorithm. Instead of drawing from the joint posterior distribution directly – which typically is not possible in problems of even moderate complexity – the researcher instead draws from the individual *posterior conditional distributions*. This essentially breaks the joint sampling problem into a series of smaller, more manageable problems. Under certain regularity conditions, iteratively sampling from the complete posterior conditional distributions (updating the conditioning to reflect the most recent values obtained from the algorithm) converges to drawing from the joint posterior distribution itself. Here, we do not discuss the theoretical properties of the sampler at length – we invite the reader to see Casella and George (1992) for an excellent introductory reference and Tierney (1994) for a more advanced reference. In this exercise we simply provide some suggestive evidence that the Gibbs sampler works; specifically, we show that, for the bivariate discrete case, the target distribution is an invariant distribution.

Suppose X and Y are discrete random variables with $X \in \{x_1, x_2, \ldots, x_J\}$ and $Y \in \{y_1, y_2, \ldots, y_K\}$. Let the joint distribution of X and Y be represented by p, with $p(x_j, y_k) = \Pr(X = x_j, Y = y_k)$.

Consider implementing the Gibbs sampler and suppose that the current value of the chain, denoted (x^t, y^t), was generated from the joint distribution p. Show that the next value of the chain, (x^{t+1}, y^{t+1}), obtained via the Gibbs sampler, must also be generated from p. That is, once we have converged to obtain a draw from p, then the subsequent draws in our parameter chain must also be drawn from p.

Solution

Without loss of generality, consider an arbitrary point in the support of the joint posterior distribution, (x_0, y_0). We note that

$$\begin{aligned}\Pr(x^{t+1} = x_0, y^{t+1} = y_0) = \sum_{j,k} \big[& \Pr(x^{t+1} = x_0, y^{t+1} = y_0 | x^t = x_j, y^t = y_k) \\ & \times \Pr(x^t = x_j, y^t = y_k) \big].\end{aligned}$$

Now, consider the first term in this summation. Again, without loss of generality, suppose that we first draw from $y|x$ and then, given the realized value of y, say y^*, we draw from $x|y = y^*$. In this case, we can write

$$\begin{aligned}\Pr(x^{t+1} = x_0, y^{t+1} = y_0 | x^t = x_j, y^t = y_k) = & \Pr(y^{t+1} = y_0 | x^t = x_j) \\ & \times \Pr(x^{t+1} = x_0 | y^{t+1} = y_0).\end{aligned}$$

Therefore, substituting this result into the summation, we obtain

$$\begin{aligned}\Pr(x^{t+1} = x_0, y^{t+1} = y_0) &= \Pr(x^{t+1} = x_0 | y^{t+1} = y_0) \\ &\times \sum_{j,k} \Pr(y^{t+1} = y_0 | x^t = x_j) \Pr(x^t = x_j, y^t = y_k).\end{aligned}$$

We are given that the current value of the chain is distributed according to p, and, of course, the complete conditionals are also based upon p. Thus, we can write

$$\begin{aligned}\Pr(x^{t+1} = x_0, y^{t+1} = y_0) &= \frac{p(x_0, y_0)}{p(y_0)} \sum_{j,k} \frac{p(x_j, y_0)}{p(x_j)} p(y_k | x_j) p(x_j) \\ &= \frac{p(x_0, y_0)}{p(y_0)} \sum_{j,k} p(x_j, y_0) p(y_k | x_j) \\ &= \frac{p(x_0, y_0)}{p(y_0)} \sum_j p(x_j, y_0) \sum_k p(y_k | x_j) \\ &= \frac{p(x_0, y_0)}{p(y_0)} \sum_j p(x_j, y_0) \\ &= \frac{p(x_0, y_0)}{p(y_0)} p(y_0) \\ &= p(x_0, y_0).\end{aligned}$$

Thus, the probability that the next value of the chain equals (x_0, y_0) is the actual joint probability of that event.

Exercise 12.2 (Metropolis–Hastings algorithm I: Gelman, Carlin, Stern, and Louis (1995)) Analogous to the results for the Gibbs sampler derived in Exercise 12.1, this exercise provides some suggestive evidence regarding why the Metropolis–Hastings algorithm works. Specifically, we show that, for the case of a discrete-valued random variable, the target distribution is an invariant distribution.

Suppose that θ is a discrete-valued random variable with probability mass function $p(\theta)$, and let θ^{t-1} be the current value of the M–H chain, where it is assumed that $\theta^{t-1} \sim p$. Show that $\theta^t \sim p$, when θ^t is obtained according to the M–H algorithm.

Solution

Without loss of generality, let us choose two distinct points in the support of θ, and call them θ^a and θ^b. As discussed at the outset of this chapter, we will define the M–H "acceptance ratio" as

$$r_t(\theta^a | \theta^b) = \frac{p(\theta^a)}{q(\theta^a | \theta^b)} \frac{q(\theta^b | \theta^a)}{p(\theta^b)}.$$

This ratio denotes the probability of accepting the candidate draw θ^a given that the chain is currently at θ^b; we note, of course, that the draw is automatically accepted if this ratio exceeds one. In this expression $q(\cdot|\cdot)$ denotes the *candidate-generating density* or *proposal density*. In a random walk chain, for example, candidate values might be generated from, say, an $N(\theta^{t-1}, \Sigma)$ distribution, and thus $q(\cdot|\cdot)$ would denote the normal density evaluated at the candidate point θ^a with mean equal to the current value of the chain, $\theta^{t-1} = \theta^b$.

Without loss of generality, let us label these points so that $r_t(\theta^a|\theta^b) > 1$, implying that $r_t(\theta^b|\theta^a) < 1$, since these terms are reciprocals. The case where $r_t(\theta^a|\theta^b) = 1$ follows similarly.

Now consider

$$\Pr(\theta^{t-1} = \theta^b, \theta^t = \theta^a) = \Pr(\theta^t = \theta^a|\theta^{t-1} = \theta^b)\Pr(\theta^{t-1} = \theta^b).$$

The first term on the right-hand side of the equation represents the probability that the next state of the chain is θ^a given that the chain is currently at θ^b.

To arrive at θ^a at the next iteration, two things must happen: (1) the candidate must be the value drawn from the proposal density, and (2) given that it is drawn, it must be accepted. Our labeling of the ratio r_t implies that θ^a will always be accepted once it is drawn. As a result,

$$\begin{aligned}\Pr(\theta^{t-1} = \theta^b, \theta^t = \theta^a) &= q(\theta^a|\theta^b)\Pr(\theta^{t-1} = \theta^b)\\ &= q(\theta^a|\theta^b)p(\theta^b),\end{aligned}$$

where the last line follows from our assumption that $\theta^{t-1} \sim p$. Now, consider another joint probability,

$$\Pr(\theta^{t-1} = \theta^a, \theta^t = \theta^b) = \Pr(\theta^t = \theta^b|\theta^{t-1} = \theta^a)\Pr(\theta^{t-1} = \theta^a).$$

For θ^b to be the next value of the chain, it must be both drawn from the proposal density and accepted once it has been drawn. Thus,

$$\begin{aligned}\Pr(\theta^{t-1} = \theta^a, \theta^t = \theta^b) &= q(\theta^b|\theta^a)r_t(\theta^b|\theta^a)\Pr(\theta^{t-1} = \theta^a)\\ &= q(\theta^b|\theta^a)\left(\frac{p(\theta^b)q(\theta^a|\theta^b)}{q(\theta^b|\theta^a)p(\theta^a)}\right)p(\theta^a)\\ &= q(\theta^a|\theta^b)p(\theta^b)\\ &= \Pr(\theta^{t-1} = \theta^b, \theta^t = \theta^a).\end{aligned}$$

Note that the equality of the joint probabilities implies that

$$\Pr(\theta^t = \theta^a|\theta^{t-1} = \theta^b)\Pr(\theta^{t-1} = \theta^b) = \Pr(\theta^{t-1} = \theta^a|\theta^t = \theta^b)\Pr(\theta^t = \theta^b).$$

Summing this equation over θ^a implies that

$$\Pr(\theta^{t-1} = \theta^b) = \Pr(\theta^t = \theta^b),$$

so that the marginals are indeed the same. Since $\theta^{t-1} \sim p$, it follows that $\theta^t \sim p$ as well.

Exercise 12.3 (Metropolis–Hastings algorithm II) The purpose of this question is to investigate the properties of two types of M–H algorithms.

Assume you wish to carry out Bayesian inference on a parameter θ with posterior given by

$$p(\theta|y) \propto \exp\left(-\frac{1}{2}|\theta|\right)$$

for $-\infty < \theta < \infty$. This is a special case of the Laplace distribution. For the purposes of this question you do not have to know the integrating constant. Readers who want to know what it is (or want to know more about the Laplace distribution) are referred to Poirier (1995, p. 110). This Laplace distribution has mean 0 and variance 8.

Suppose you cannot find a way of directly drawing from $p(\theta|y)$ and hence wish to use an M–H algorithm.

(a) Derive an independence chain M–H algorithm using an $N\left(0, d^2\right)$ candidate-generating density and write a program that implements this algorithm.

(b) Derive a random walk chain M–H algorithm using a normal increment and write a program that implements this algorithm.

(c) Compare the performance of the algorithms developed in parts (a) and (b).

Solution

The introduction to this chapter gives some references for the reader unfamiliar with the M–H algorithm.

(a) All M–H algorithms provide a sequence or "chain" of draws that are then averaged in the same way as Monte Carlo integration draws are to provide estimates of posterior functions of interest (e.g., posterior means). Denote this sequence of draws as $\theta^{(r)}$ for $r = 1, \ldots, R$. Metropolis–Hastings algorithms proceed by taking candidate draws from a convenient density. Denote a candidate for the rth draw in the sequence by θ^*. The candidate draw is either accepted (i.e., $\theta^{(r)} = \theta^*$) or rejected, in which case the chain remains where it is (i.e., $\theta^{(r)} = \theta^{(r-1)}$). The acceptance probability is chosen to ensure the chain can be treated as draws from the posterior.

The independence chain algorithm chooses a single candidate-generating density and simply takes random draws from it. In this case, the acceptance probability has the form (see, e.g., Koop 2003, p. 95)

$$\alpha\left(\theta^{(r-1)}, \theta^*\right) = \min\left[\frac{p\left(\theta = \theta^*|y\right) q\left(\theta = \theta^{(r-1)}\right)}{p\left(\theta = \theta^{(r-1)}|y\right) q\left(\theta = \theta^*\right)}, 1\right],$$

where $q(\cdot)$ is the candidate-generating density. If we substitute in the posterior given in the question and the suggested $N\left(0, d^2\right)$ candidate-generating density, we obtain

$$\alpha\left(\theta^{(r-1)}, \theta^*\right) = \min\left[\exp\left[\frac{1}{2}\left(\left|\theta^{(r-1)}\right| - |\theta^*| - \left\{\frac{\theta^{(r-1)}}{d}\right\}^2 + \left\{\frac{\theta^*}{d}\right\}^2\right)\right], 1\right]. \tag{12.1}$$

The parameter d should be chosen to optimize the performance of the M–H algorithm. Unfortunately, there is no hard and fast rule as to how this should be done. You may think you want to choose d so as to make the acceptance probability as high as possible. After all, if the candidate-generating density is exactly the same as the posterior, then the acceptance probability is one and the independence chain M–H algorithm is equivalent to Monte Carlo integration. However, a high acceptance probability can also be achieved if the candidate-generating density has too little dispersion. For instance, an extreme case would set d very close to zero. In this case, the acceptance probability is always near one. But this means all draws are virtually identical to one another and nonsensical results will be produced. In practice, it is always sensible to use convergence diagnostics (e.g., the ones developed for the Gibbs sampler also work for the M–H algorithm) to assess computational performance. Some diagnostics are reviewed in the final section of this chapter.

A computer program that carries out Bayesian inference using this independence chain M–H algorithm has the following form:

Step 1: Do all the preliminary things to create all the variables used in the M–H algorithm (i.e., initialize all the M–H sums to zero and specify an initial value, $\theta^{(0)}$).
Step 2: Draw θ^* from the $N\left(0, d^2\right)$ candidate-generating density.
Step 3: Calculate the acceptance probability $\alpha\left(\theta^{(r-1)}, \theta^*\right)$.
Step 4: Set $\theta^{(r)} = \theta^*$ with probability $\alpha\left(\theta^{(r-1)}, \theta^*\right)$, or else set $\theta^{(r)} = \theta^{(r-1)}$.
Step 5: Repeat Steps 2, 3, and 4 for $r = 1, \ldots, R$.
Step 6: Average the draws appropriately to produce M–H estimates of whatever posterior functions of interest (e.g., posterior means) are required.

Note that M–H algorithms, like Gibbs sampling algorithms, depend on an initial condition, $\theta^{(0)}$, which must be chosen by the researcher. It is common to discard an initial set of burn-in draws to remove the effects of this choice.

The MATLAB program that implements this algorithm is provided on the website associated with this book.

(b) The solution to part (b) is the same as part (a), except that the candidate-generating density is different and, as a result, the acceptance probability is different.

The random walk chain M–H algorithm generates candidate draws according to

$$\theta^* = \theta^{(r-1)} + z,$$

where z is called the *increment random variable*. In this question a normal increment is suggested, and thus θ^* is drawn from the $N\left(\theta^{(r-1)}, c^2\right)$ distribution, where c is calibrated to ensure a reasonable acceptance rate. In contrast to the independence chain M–H algorithm, a rule of thumb is available to provide guidance in choosing c. In particular, a common practice in scalar or very low dimension problems is to choose c so that about 50% of the candidate draws are accepted. As with any posterior simulation algorithm, though, it is always sensible to use appropriate convergence diagnostics.

For the random walk chain M–H algorithm, the acceptance probability is (see, e.g., Koop 2003, p. 97)

$$\alpha\left(\theta^{(r-1)}, \theta^*\right) = \min\left[\frac{p\left(\theta = \theta^*|y\right)}{p\left(\theta = \theta^{(r-1)}|y\right)}, 1\right].$$

Plugging in the form given for the posterior, we obtain

$$\alpha\left(\theta^{(r-1)}, \theta^*\right) = \min\left[\exp\left[\frac{1}{2}\left\{\left|\theta^{(r-1)}\right| - |\theta^*|\right\}\right], 1\right]. \tag{12.2}$$

The sketch of the computer program for the random walk chain M–H algorithm is the same as the one given in the solution to part (a), except that the candidate-generating density and acceptance probability are replaced as described here. A MATLAB program that has both independence and random walk chain M–H algorithms is provided on the website for this book.

(c) Table 12.1 gives the estimated posterior mean and variance of θ for various values of d (for the independence chain M–H algorithm) and c (for the random walk chain M–H algorithm) as well as the proportion of accepted draws. In all cases, we include 10 000 simulations (after discarding 100 burn-in simulations).

For the independence chain M–H algorithm, we can see that candidate-generating densities that are either too dispersed (e.g., $d = 100$) or not dispersed enough ($d = 1.0$) yield poor results. However, the problems associated with being not dispersed enough are worse since, if d is chosen to be too small, then some regions of the parameter space for θ may never be visited with a finite number of draws. Because we know the true variance of θ to be 8, it is likely that setting the variance of the candidate-generating density to be about 8 is sensible. This does seem to be the case.

For the random walk chain M–H algorithm we get a similar pattern of results. If the increment variable has too small a standard deviation, then the chain does not traverse the entire distribution (for finite R) and inaccurate estimates (especially of posterior variances) occur. In Table 12.1, this is revealed in the row for $c = 0.10$, which reveals serious underestimation of the posterior variance. If the standard deviation of the increment variable is too large, then poor results also occur. This is because too many extreme draws, in improbable regions of the posterior, are taken and these are not accepted (e.g., when $c = 100$, then only 3% of the candidate draws are accepted). This results in an inefficient computational algorithm.

Note that the commonly used rule of thumb that says you should choose c to yield approximately a 50% acceptance rate does seem to be working well in this case.

Exercise 12.4 (Slice sampling I) When fitting Bayesian models via MCMC methods, it is often the case that some of the complete posterior conditional distributions belong to recognized and easily sampled distributional families, while others can be derived but may not correspond to any "standard" distribution with well-known properties. The M–H

Table 12.1: Posterior results for θ for various M–H algorithms.

	Posterior mean	Posterior variance	Acceptance probability
True value	0.00	8.00	—
Independence chain M–H algorithm			
$d = 1.00$	0.16	3.48	0.65
$d = 2.00$	0.04	7.15	0.84
$d = 3.00$	0.01	7.68	0.79
$d = 6.00$	−0.05	8.03	0.49
$d = 20.00$	−0.07	7.87	0.16
$d = 100.00$	0.12	7.41	0.03
Random walk chain M–H algorithm			
$c = 0.10$	0.33	1.13	0.98
$c = 0.50$	0.20	6.87	0.91
$c = 1.00$	−0.08	7.01	0.83
$c = 4.00$	−0.03	7.93	0.52
$c = 10.00$	0.05	7.62	0.28
$c = 100.00$	0.23	6.25	0.03

algorithm, as outlined in previous exercises, offers a general-purpose method for sampling from such distributions, requiring only the calculation of the kernel of the conditional posterior. Slice sampling (e.g., Neal 2003), as outlined in this and the following question, offers yet another alternative.
(a) Consider the following sampling scheme:

- Suppose x is given as a draw from a distribution with bounded density function $f(x)$ and support $x \in \mathcal{X}$.
- Sample $y|x \sim U(0, f(x))$.
- Sample $x'|y \sim U\{x' : y \leq f(x')\}$.

Provide a graphical representation of what takes place in this sampling procedure and derive the distribution of x' (which we will denote below as $p(x')$). What does this suggest about a potential iterative procedure for generating samples from $f(x)$?
(b) Consider the density function $f(x) = 3x^2$, $0 \leq x \leq 1$. Describe how the procedure in part (a) can be used to generate samples from this distribution and write a MATLAB program to generate those samples.

Solution

(a) Begin by noting that the joint distribution of x and y is given as (using "p" to denote distributions induced by the sampling procedure)

$$\begin{aligned}
p(x, y) &= p(y|x)p(x) \\
&= \left[\frac{1}{f(x)} I\left(0 \le y \le f(x)\right)\right] f(x) I\left(x \in \mathcal{X}\right) \\
&= I\left(0 \le y \le f(x)\right) I\left(x \in \mathcal{X}\right),
\end{aligned}$$

so that the joint density of x and y is uniform over the area under $f(x)$.

Let us define

$$\mathcal{A}(y) \equiv \{x \in \mathcal{X} : y \le f(x)\} \text{ and } \overline{f} = \max_{x \in \mathcal{X}} f(x).$$

The marginal density for y is then:

$$\begin{aligned}
p(y) &= \int_{\mathcal{X}} p(x, y) dx \\
&= \int_{\mathcal{X}} I\left(0 \le y \le f(x)\right) I\left(x \in \mathcal{X}\right) dx \\
&= \left[\int_{\mathcal{A}(y)} dx\right] I(0 \le y \le \overline{f}),
\end{aligned}$$

where the indicator function $I(0 \le y \le \overline{f})$ denotes the marginal support of y. We then have

$$\begin{aligned}
p(x', y) &= p(x'|y)p(y) \\
&= \left[\frac{I\left(y \le f(x')\right)}{\left[\int_{\mathcal{A}(y)} dx\right]}\right] \left[\int_{\mathcal{A}(y)} dx\right] I(0 \le y \le \overline{f}) \\
&= I\left(y \le f(x')\right) I(0 \le y \le \overline{f}).
\end{aligned}$$

The marginal density for x' can then be obtained by integrating out y from the joint density above:

$$p(x') = \int_0^{f(x')} dy = f(x')$$

for all $x \in \mathcal{X}$. That is, x' is also a draw from f.

Figure 12.1 provides a graphical representation of the sampling procedure. In the first panel, an initial representative x value is presumed to be available as a draw from f. A value y is then sampled uniformly on $(0, f(x))$, and a representative realization of such a y is presented in the second panel. The set $\mathcal{A}(y)$ is then determined (in this graphical example of a unimodal distribution, this set is just an interval), and an x' is sampled uniformly from this set. As just shown, x' is also a sample from f.

Viewed as an iterative procedure this suggests first selecting some x_0 for which $f(x_0) > 0$, applying the steps of the algorithm, and iterating until convergence; by construction f is an invariant distribution of this process. The procedure above is called

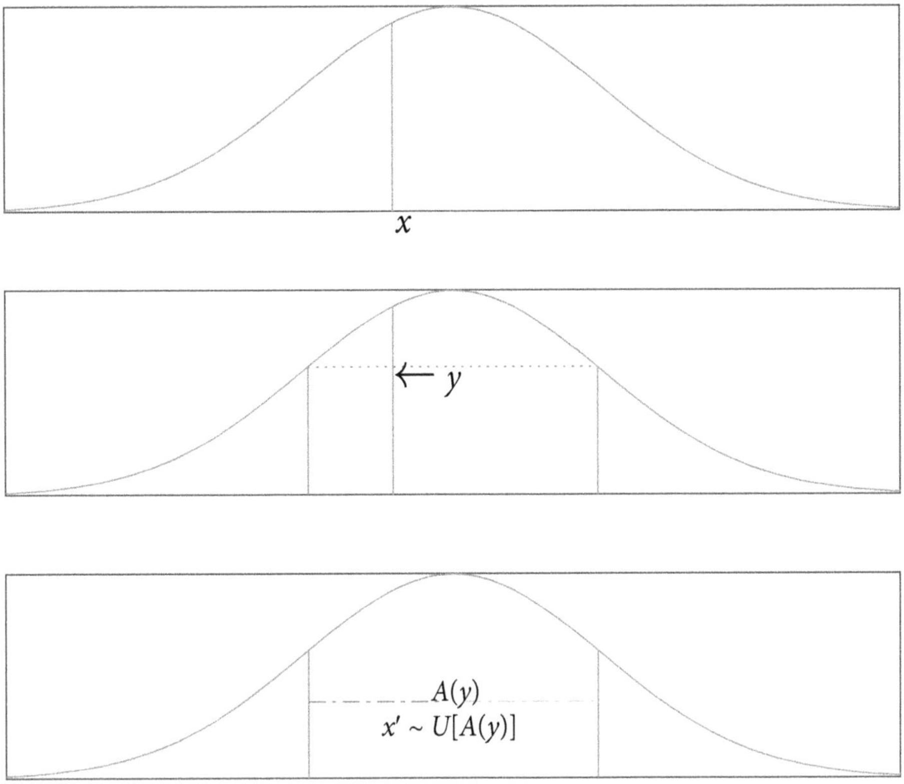

Figure 12.1. Graphical illustration of slice sampling.

slice sampling given the "cutting" of the density into horizontal slices at each step, and then sampling uniformly from those slices. (Note that samples of y can be discarded as they are merely introduced to facilitate the generation of samples from f.) Neal (2003) is a definitive reference on slice sampling; Damien, Wakefield, and Walker (1999) also employ a very similar technique in describing augmented posterior simulators for Bayesian inference problems.

(b) Following the results shown in part (a), the joint distribution of x and y in this example is

$$p(x, y) = I\,(0 \leq x \leq 1)\, I\left(0 \leq y \leq 3x^2\right).$$

This implies the following conditional distributions:

$$y|x \sim U(0, 3x^2),$$
$$x|y \sim U\left(\sqrt{\frac{y}{3}}, 1\right).$$

A small MATLAB program is provided on the website associated with this book that uses the slice sampling method to generate samples from $f(x) = 3x^2$, $0 \leq x \leq 1$.

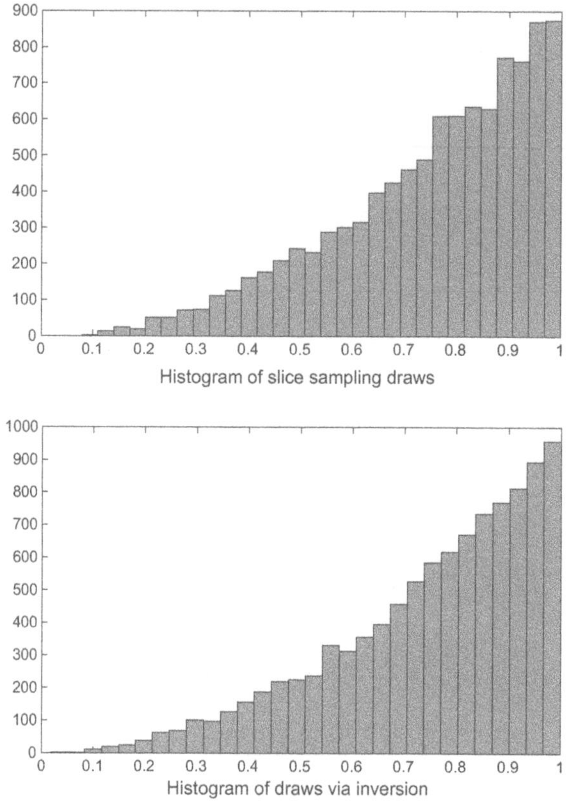

Figure 12.2. Comparison of slice sampling and inverse transform method.

The sampler is run for 11 000 iterations, and the first 1000 are discarded as the burn-in. We compare these results to those obtained using the inverse transform method (e.g., see Exercise 11.4), where one simply calculates $x_i = u_i^{1/3}, u_i \overset{iid}{\sim} U(0,1), i = 1, 2, \ldots, 10\,000$. Figure 12.2 shows that both approaches produce very similar results.

Exercise 12.5 (Slice sampling II) The previous example illustrated slice sampling in the case of a unimodal target distribution. Once one departs from such a case, $\mathcal{A}(y) \equiv \{x \in \mathcal{X} : y \leq f(x)\}$ may not be an interval and may, for example, be a union of disjoint intervals. For general problems, the set $\mathcal{A}(y)$ might be difficult to determine, creating difficulties when seeking to implement the slice sampler.

Neal (2003) provides two variants of the slice sampling algorithm of the previous exercise and terms them a "stepping out" procedure and a "doubling" procedure. Here, we describe the former and refer the reader to the article for details of the latter. The benefits of these methods are that, first, one does not need to obtain the normalizing constant of the target distribution in order to implement the stepping out method (or in order to implement slice sampling generally). This, of course, is a particularly attractive feature for Bayesian applications. Second, the set $\mathcal{A}(y)$ does not need to be determined exactly, but instead, an "approximate" interval from which sampling can be conducted is formed iteratively while leaving the uniform distribution over the entire slice invariant.

The stepping out procedure proceeds as follows: Suppose our simulation scheme currently has x_0 as a draw from the candidate density. Fix w as a reasonable interval width (although not required, w could perhaps be selected as a function of the standard deviation under $f(x)$, if that can be calculated). You then:

- Sample $y \sim U\left(0, f(x_0)\right)$.
- Randomly generate an interval around x_0 of length w as follows:

$$\text{Draw } u \sim U(0,1), \quad \text{set} \quad LL = x_0 - w * u, \quad UL = LL + w.$$

  Note that LL and UL can be thought of as the lower limit and upper limit of the interval around x_0 (which is guaranteed to be in the slice).
- Continue to expand the interval (LL, UL) by separately reducing the lower limit by w and/or increasing the upper limit by w until the (unnormalized) ordinates of the density at those two points, $f(LL)$ and $f(UL)$, are less than y. That is, the interval (LL, UL) continues to "step out" in both directions until it contains at least a local portion of the slice defining $\mathcal{A}(y)$.
- Once the stepping out procedure concludes, sample

$$x^* \sim U\left(LL, UL\right)$$

  and continue sampling until a value is obtained such that $f(x^*) > y$. Accept that x^* (i.e., set $x = x^*$) as a draw and repeat the process. *Note:* Since the sampling in this final step may be inefficient (i.e., it may take a long time to produce an x^* giving $f(x^*) > y$), one can adaptively reduce the size of the stepped out interval by shrinking it on the basis of unaccepted candidates. For example, when $f(x^*) < y$, then set LL to be x^* when $x^* < x_0$ and set $UL = x^*$ when $x^* > x_0$.

Listing 12.1 gives a sketch of a sample MATLAB program that implements the stepping out procedure. The sketch assumes that x and w are given, and $f(x)$, denoted fx, has been calculated. Given this structure, write a MATLAB program that uses the stepping out procedure to generate 100 000 samples from the following three-component normal mixture:

$$f(x) = .4\phi(x; -1, .1) + .2\phi(x; 0, .1) + .4\phi(x; 2, .2),$$

where $\phi(x, \mu, \sigma^2)$ denotes the normal density function for random variable x with mean μ and variance σ^2. Estimate the density function of your simulations and compare that density estimate to the true mixture density.

Listing 12.1: Structure for MATLAB program that implements the stepping out procedure.

```
y = fx * rand(1,1);
LL = x - w * rand(1,1);
UL = LL + w;
% Insert steps to calculate f(LL) and f(UL), denoted fLL and fUL below

**** Begin the stepping out procedure ****
while fLL > y;
  LL = LL - w;
  % Recalculate fLL
end;

while fUL > y;
  UL = UL + w;
  % Recalculate fUL
end;

**** Sample a candidate, determine if accepted, shrink interval ****
xstar = LL + (UL - LL) * rand(1,1);
% Insert step to calculate f(xstar), denoted fxstar

while fxstar < y;
  if xstar < x;
    LL = xstar;
  else;
    UL = xstar;
  end;
  xstar = LL + (UL - LL) * rand(1,1);
  % Insert step to calculate f(xstar), denoted fxstar
end;
x = xstar;
fx = fxstar;
```

Solution

MATLAB code is provided on the website associated with this book and follows the general scheme described in Listing 12.1. The sampler is run for 101 000 iterations and the first 1000 are discarded as the burn-in. Figure 12.3 provides a graph of both the actual three-component mixture density and a kernel-smoothed non-parametric density estimate of our 100 000 simulations. As one can see, the results are very close; small discrepancies are likely the result of a slightly oversmoothed kernel estimate.

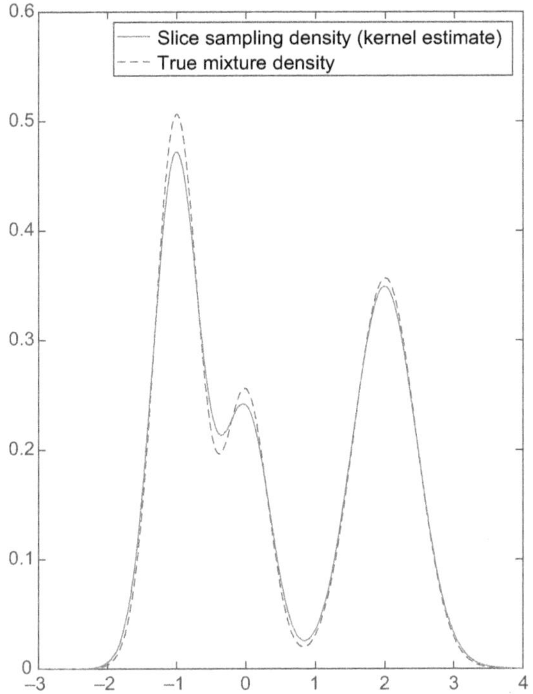

Figure 12.3. Slice sampling density estimate and true mixture density.

12.2 Three Introductory Examples of Gibbs Sampling

Exercise 12.6 (Gibbs sampling: A comprehensive introductory example) The purpose of this question is to introduce the reader to the process of implementing a Gibbs sampler. The goal here is to take the reader through all of the steps involved with deriving and programming a Gibbs algorithm, including using posterior simulations for practical out-of-sample purposes, in an application that is, hopefully, interesting and fairly representative of what may be encountered in some basic applied work.

Specifically, suppose for the purpose of this question that the lifetime of a lightbulb follows a lognormal distribution. (The authors have no idea if this is a reasonable assumption, although they ask that you maintain it for the purpose of this question.) The (generated) data provided on the website associated with this book contains lifetimes associated with two different types of bulbs: older-style incandescent bulbs and LED bulbs. You make 1000 observations in total, and the data provides information on lifespan y_i (in thousands of hours) and bulb type x_i, $i = 1, 2, \ldots, 1000$. Bulb type is binary and is coded as $x_i = 1$ if the ith bulb is LED style, while $x_i = 0$ if it is of the incandescent variety.

You wish to allow the location and scale parameters of the lognormal to potentially differ across bulb types, and to that end you specify as your sampling model:

$$p(y_i|\sigma_0^2, \sigma_1^2, \theta_0, \theta_1, x_i) = \frac{1}{\sqrt{2\pi\sigma_i^2}} y_i^{-1} \exp\left(-\frac{1}{2\sigma_i^2}[\ln y_i - (\theta_0 + \theta_1 x_i)]^2\right), \quad y_i > 0,$$

where $\sigma_i^2 = \sigma_0^2(1 - x_i) + \sigma_1^2 x_i$, so that σ_0^2 corresponds to the scale parameter of the incandescent type, and σ_1^2 the scale parameter for the LED type.

(a) Derive the likelihood function for this sampling model.

(b) Suppose you employ priors of the form

$$\sigma_j^2 \overset{ind}{\sim} IG(a_j, b_j), \quad j = 0, 1,$$
$$\theta_j \overset{ind}{\sim} EXP(\alpha_j), \quad j = 0, 1,$$

where IG and EXP refer to inverse gamma and exponential distributions, respectively (see the appendix for the parameterization of the inverse gamma and Exercise 2.10 for a description of the exponential). Derive the joint posterior distribution for the four parameters θ_0, θ_1, σ_0^2, and σ_1^2.

(c) Describe a Gibbs sampler for generating samples from this joint posterior. Given the description in the introduction and Exercise 12.1, this scheme will involve iteratively sampling from the complete posterior conditional distributions of this model. In this case there will be four such conditional distributions, and they can be derived from the expression obtained in part (b). The description of the Gibbs sampler here will be a characterization of these four conditional posterior distributions.

(d) Sketch the structure of a program for implementing a Gibbs sampler. Do not provide specific MATLAB syntax for this particular exercise just yet; simply describe the steps of what your code will need to accomplish. Note that this is useful for thinking, generally, about how MCMC coding will need to be structured.

(e) Using the simulated data set provided, the results in (c), and the code structure in (d), write a MATLAB program to fit your model. Recall, in the data set given, the responses y_i are bulb lifetimes in thousands of hours. Generate 51 000 simulations, discard the initial 1000, and retain the final 50 000 as samples from the joint posterior distribution. Calculate posterior means and posterior standard deviations for each of the four model parameters. What do your results suggest in terms of the lifespans of LED versus incandescent bulbs?

(f) To see how useful posterior simulations can be for purposes beyond model estimation, and to see how Bayesian methods can be applied to address useful practical questions, consider the following question. Suppose that a household demands 25 000 hours of lighting in a given period of time. Although this light surely comes from multiple bulbs at multiple sources, assume, just for the sake of simplicity, that this light comes from a single source. LED bulbs cost \$5 each and incandescent bulbs are \$1 each. LED bulbs are more efficient: they cost \$1.05 for 1000 hours of use while incandescent bulbs cost \$9 for each 1000 hours of use.

Describe how the posterior simulations in part (e) can be used to characterize the posterior predictive distributions of cost associated with LED and incandescent lighting. Note that your solution will take into account uncertainty over bulb lifetime.

Solution

(a) Given our model's assumptions, we have

$$L(\theta_0, \theta_1, \sigma_0^2, \sigma_1^2) = (2\pi)^{-n/2} \left(\prod_{i=1}^{n} y_i^{-1} (\sigma_i^2)^{-1/2} \right) \exp\left(-\frac{1}{2} \sum_{i=1}^{n} \left(\frac{\ln y_i - \theta_0 - \theta_1 x_i}{\sigma_i} \right)^2 \right).$$

This can also be written as

$$L(\theta_0, \theta_1, \sigma_0^2, \sigma_1^2) \propto (\sigma_0^2)^{n_0/2} (\sigma_1^2)^{n_1/2} \exp\left(-\frac{1}{2} \sum_{i:x_i=0} \left(\frac{\ln y_i - \theta_0}{\sigma_0} \right)^2 \right)$$
$$\times \left(\prod_{i=1}^{n} y_i^{-1} \right) \exp\left(-\frac{1}{2} \sum_{i:x_i=1} \left(\frac{\ln y_i - \theta_0 - \theta_1}{\sigma_1} \right)^2 \right), \quad (12.3)$$

where n_0 denotes the number of bulbs of type "0" (incandescent), n_1 denotes the number of bulbs of type "1" (LED), and $n = n_0 + n_1$.

(b) The joint posterior is given, up to proportionality, as the product of the priors described in part (b) of this question times the likelihood function in part (a). Thus,

$$p(\theta_0, \theta_1, \sigma_0^2, \sigma_1^2 | y) \propto p(\theta_0) p(\theta_1) p(\sigma_0^2) p(\sigma_1^2) (\sigma_0^2)^{n_0/2} (\sigma_1^2)^{n_1/2}$$
$$\times \exp\left(-\frac{1}{2} \sum_{i:x_i=0} \left(\frac{\ln y_i - \theta_0}{\sigma_0} \right)^2 \right)$$
$$\times \exp\left(-\frac{1}{2} \sum_{i:x_i=1} \left(\frac{\ln y_i - \theta_0 - \theta_1}{\sigma_1} \right)^2 \right). \quad (12.4)$$

(c) When deriving conditional posterior distributions generally, the starting point is the joint posterior itself. To see this consider, without loss of generality, the conditional posterior distribution for σ_1^2. We note that

$$p(\sigma_1^2 | \sigma_0^2, \theta_0, \theta_1, y) = \frac{p(\theta_0, \theta_1, \sigma_0^2, \sigma_1^2 | y)}{p(\theta_0, \theta_1, \sigma_0^2 | y)}.$$

The denominator of this expression does not involve σ_1^2 and acts as a normalizing constant for the density. Thus, we can write:

$$p(\sigma_1^2 | \sigma_0^2, \theta_0, \theta_1, y) \propto p(\theta_0, \theta_1, \sigma_0^2, \sigma_1^2 | y).$$

That is, the complete conditional posterior distribution we seek is proportional to the joint posterior distribution. The consequence of this result is, when deriving the conditionals of the model, we can simply look at the joint posterior – in this case, Equation (12.4) –

and keep track of all terms where σ_1^2 appears. Expressions in the joint posterior that enter multiplicatively and do not involve σ_1^2 can simply be ignored, as they remain part of the normalizing constant. Often, the kernel of the conditional posterior can be identified (as in conditionally conjugate cases), and thus the normalizing constants can be determined *ex post*, given the known forms of those distributional families.

Let's continue to work to derive the complete conditional posterior for σ_1^2. To do this, given the insight above, we look to the joint posterior in (12.4) and keep track of terms involving σ_1^2. This gives:

$$\begin{aligned}
&p(\sigma_1^2|\sigma_0^2, \theta_0, \theta_1, y) \\
&\quad \propto p(\sigma_1^2)(\sigma_1^2)^{-n_1/2} \exp\left(-\frac{1}{2}\sum_{i:x_i=1}\left(\frac{\ln y_i - \theta_0 - \theta_1}{\sigma_1}\right)^2\right) \\
&\quad \propto (\sigma_1^2)^{-(a_1+1)} \exp\left(-\frac{1}{b_1\sigma_1^2}\right)(\sigma_1^2)^{-\frac{n_1}{2}} \exp\left(-\frac{1}{2}\sum_{i:x_i=1}\left(\frac{\ln y_i - \theta_0 - \theta_1}{\sigma_1}\right)^2\right) \\
&\quad = (\sigma_1^2)^{-[(n_1/2)+a_1+1]} \exp\left(-\frac{1}{\sigma_1^2}\left[b_1^{-1} + \frac{1}{2}\sum_{i:x_i=1}(\ln y_i - \theta_0 - \theta_1)^2\right]\right).
\end{aligned}$$

The first line of the above accounts for all terms in (12.4) involving σ_1^2. The second line simply writes down the functional form of the inverse gamma prior, dropping the constant terms from that prior as they are absorbed in the normalizing constant. The third line simplifies the expression by grouping terms.

This final expression shows that we are left with the kernel of an inverse gamma distribution, with updated values of the parameters of that distribution. Specifically, we see that

$$\sigma_1^2|\sigma_0^2, \theta_0, \theta_1, y \sim IG\left(\frac{n_1}{2} + a_1, \left[b_1^{-1} + \frac{1}{2}\sum_{i:x_i=1}(\ln y_i - \theta_0 - \theta_1)^2\right]^{-1}\right). \tag{12.5}$$

Thus, we have derived one of the four complete posterior conditional distributions. To complete the requirements for implementing a Gibbs sampler, we must derive the remaining three. The complete posterior conditional distribution for the variance parameter σ_0^2 follows similarly. From (12.4), we obtain:

$$p(\sigma_0^2|\sigma_1^2, \theta_0, \theta_1, y) \propto p(\sigma_0^2)(\sigma_0^2)^{-n_0/2} \exp\left(-\frac{1}{2}\sum_{i:x_i=0}\left(\frac{\ln y_i - \theta_0}{\sigma_0}\right)^2\right).$$

Using steps identical to those in our previous derivation, we can combine prior and likelihood information again to obtain:

$$\sigma_0^2|\sigma_1^2, \theta_0, \theta_1, y \sim IG\left(\frac{n_0}{2} + a_0, \left[b_0^{-1} + \frac{1}{2}\sum_{i:x_i=0}(\ln y_i - \theta_0)^2\right]^{-1}\right). \tag{12.6}$$

Let's now move on to the conditional posterior distribution for θ_1. In the course of the derivation that follows, it will be useful to define:

$$S_1 = \sum_{i:x_i=1} (\ln y_i - \theta_0),$$
$$SS_1 = \sum_{i:x_i=1} (\ln y_i - \theta_0)^2,$$

noting that S_1 and SS_1 can be regarded as constants for the purpose of the posterior conditional for θ_1. We obtain:

$$\begin{aligned}
p(\theta_1|\theta_0, \sigma_0^2, \sigma_1^2, y) &\propto p(\theta_1) \exp\left(-\frac{1}{2\sigma_1^2} \sum_{i:x_i=1} (\ln y_i - \theta_0 - \theta_1)^2\right) \\
&\propto \exp(-\alpha_1\theta_1) \exp\left(-\frac{1}{2\sigma_1^2}\left[SS_1 - 2\theta_1 S_1 + n_1\theta_1^2\right]\right) \\
&= \exp\left(-\frac{1}{2n_1^{-1}\sigma_1^2}\left[\theta_1^2 - 2\theta_1 n_1^{-1}[S_1 - \alpha_1\sigma_1^2] + n_1^{-1}SS_1\right]\right) \\
&= \exp\left(-\frac{1}{2n_1^{-1}\sigma_1^2}\left[\left[\theta_1 - n_1^{-1}(S_1 - \alpha_1\sigma_1^2)\right]^2 - \right.\right. \\
&\qquad \left.\left.\left[n_1^{-1}(S_1 - \alpha_1\sigma_1^2)\right]^2 + n_1^{-1}SS_1\right]\right) \\
&\propto \exp\left(-\frac{1}{2n_1^{-1}\sigma_1^2}\left(\left[\theta_1 - n_1^{-1}(S_1 - \alpha_1\sigma_1^2)\right]^2\right)\right).
\end{aligned}$$

The first line of the above captures all terms in the joint posterior involving θ_1. The second line writes out the kernel of the exponential prior, expands the quadratic in the Gaussian kernel, and uses our definitions of S_1 and SS_1. The fourth line completes the square in θ_1, and the final line notes that the additive terms within the exponential kernel not involving θ_1 can be pulled out and are thus absorbed in the normalizing constant.

Since the final expression above is recognized as a Gaussian distribution up to proportionality, we determine that

$$\theta_1|\theta_0, \sigma_0^2, \sigma_1^2, y \sim N\left(n_1^{-1}[S_1 - \alpha_1\sigma_1^2], n_1^{-1}\sigma_1^2\right). \tag{12.7}$$

Our fourth and final posterior conditional distribution follows similarly to the previous step. In an analogous way, we again define

$$S_0 = \sum_{i=1}^{n} \frac{\ln y_i - \theta_1 x_i}{\sigma_i^2},$$
$$SS_0 = \sum_{i=1}^{n} \left(\frac{\ln y_i - \theta_1 x_i}{\sigma_i}\right)^2,$$
$$A_0 = \frac{n_1\sigma_0^2 + n_0\sigma_1^2}{\sigma_0^2\sigma_1^2},$$

noting that these quantities do not involve θ_0 and thus can be regarded as constants when deriving its posterior conditional distribution. Examining the joint posterior in (12.4) and finding the terms where θ_0 appears, we obtain:

$$p(\theta_0|\theta_1, \sigma_0^2, \sigma_1^2, y) \propto \exp(-\alpha_0\theta_0) \exp\left(-\frac{1}{2}\sum_{i=1}^{n}\left[\frac{\ln y_i - \theta_0 - \theta_1 x_i}{\sigma_i}\right]^2\right).$$

Let's outline some preliminary steps toward simplifying this expression. We first group the exponential terms together and expand the quadratic within the exponential as follows:

$$\exp\left(-\frac{1}{2}\left[\sum_{i=1}^{n}\left(\frac{\ln y_i - \theta_1 x_i}{\sigma_i}\right)^2 - 2\theta_0\sum_{i=1}^{n}\left(\frac{\ln y_i - \theta_1 x_i}{\sigma_i^2}\right) + \theta_0^2\sum_{i=1}^{n}\sigma_i^{-2}\right] - \alpha_0\theta_0\right),$$

which, given our previous definitions of S_0 and SS_0, can be expressed as

$$\exp\left(-\frac{1}{2}\left[SS_0 - 2\theta_0 S_0 + A_0\theta_0^2\right] - \alpha\theta_0\right).$$

Working to complete the square in θ_0, we can express our conditional posterior distribution as follows:

$$\begin{aligned} p(\theta_0|\theta_1, \sigma_0^2, \sigma_1^2, y) &\propto \exp\left(-\frac{1}{2A_0^{-1}}\left[\theta_0^2 - 2\theta_0 A_0^{-1}S_0 + 2\theta_0 A_0^{-1}\alpha_0 + A_0^{-1}SS_0\right]\right) \\ &= \exp\left(-\frac{1}{2A_0^{-1}}\left[\theta_0^2 - 2\theta_0[A_0^{-1}(S_0 - \alpha_0)] + A_0^{-1}SS_0\right]\right). \end{aligned}$$

In this last form, we can again complete the square in θ_0 and then group resulting terms not involving θ_0 into the normalizing constant. This will show, like the derivation of the θ_1 conditional posterior above, that

$$\theta_0|\theta_1, \sigma_0^2, \sigma_1^2, y \sim N\left(A_0^{-1}(S_0 - \alpha_0), A_0^{-1}\right). \tag{12.8}$$

A Gibbs sampler involves cycling through the conditionals in (12.5), (12.6), (12.7), and (12.8). Which conditional is sampled first, second, etc. does not matter; a sample from the Gibbs algorithm simply denotes a complete pass through all four conditional densities, where conditioning information is updated at each step to reflect the most recent parameter values available from the sampler.

(d) The flowchart in Figure 12.4 describes a general structure for implementing a Gibbs sampling routine. The first four steps need not follow the order listed in the flowchart; for example, one can declare the number of iterations ($Iter$) and burn-in period ($Burn$) prior to setting values for the prior hyperparameters. These items simply need to be completed prior to beginning the Gibbs loop. By "Define storage objects" we mean initializing the vectors/matrices that will store our posterior simulations. Within the Gibbs loop we will generate a draw at each iteration and will store or save all such draws after the burn-in period is reached. It is generally more computationally efficient to define and declare

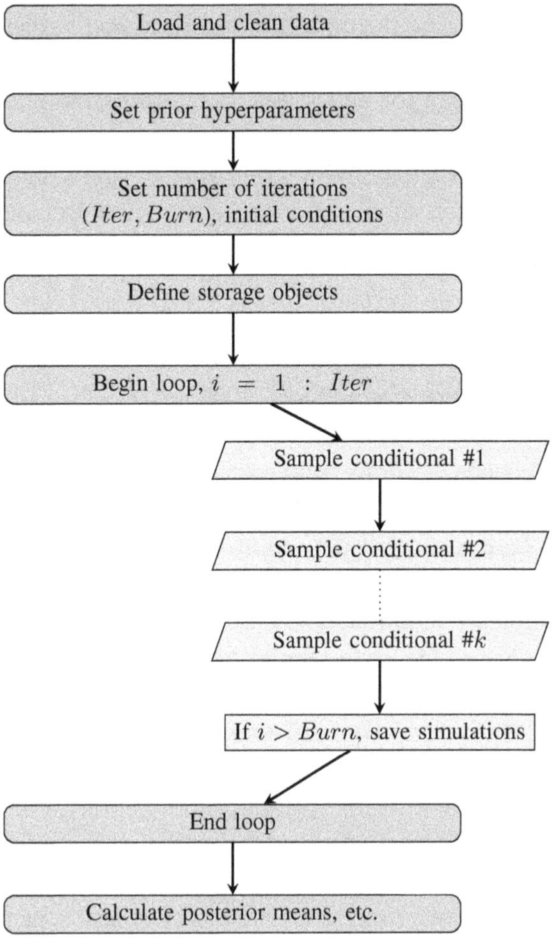

Figure 12.4. Flowchart for a Gibbs sampling routine.

the size of the matrices outside of the loop rather than have these objects be redefined and increase in size with each passing loop iteration. Once the loop has concluded, the posterior simulations can be used for whatever purpose is needed.
(e) MATLAB code is provided for this exercise. In order to better understand what each portion of the code does, we have commented each part of the code with the same headings as in Figure 12.4. For our priors, we set $\alpha_0 = \alpha_1 = 5$. We also set $a_0 = a_1 = 3$ and $b_0 = b_1 = .5$, which sets the prior mean and prior standard deviation of σ_1^2 and σ_2^2 to one.

In terms of interpreting the results, note that the mean of the lognormal distribution is known to be $\exp[(\theta_0 + \theta_1 x_i) + \sigma_i^2/2]$ and the variance is $[\exp(\sigma_i^2) - 1][\exp(2(\theta_0 + \theta_1 x_i) + \sigma_i^2)]$. We can use our posterior simulations to calculate these quantities: for each post-convergence sample, we calculate the mean and variance above for each bulb type (for LED bulbs when $x_i = 1$ and $\sigma_i^2 = \sigma_1^2$, and for incandescent bulbs when $x_i = 0$

and $\sigma_i^2 = \sigma_0^2$). We then average the collection of mean and variance values to obtain a point estimate of each quantity. Doing so, we find that the mean lifespan of incandescent bulbs was 7.95 while the mean for LEDs was 24.5. Furthermore, the variances for each were 7.24 and 71.48. This is consistent with how the data were generated, where LED lifetimes were sampled from a lognormal with mean 25 and standard deviation of 25/3, while incandescent bulbs were sampled from a lognormal with a mean of 8 and standard deviation of 8/3. Mean lifespans were taken to match publicly available reports of bulb longevity.
(f) Note that the total cost for LED use is $\$5 \times$ nLED $+ \$(1.05) \times 25$ and the cost for incandescent use is $\$(1) \times$ nINCAND $+ \$9 \times (25)$, where nLED and nINCAND represent the number of bulbs of each type required for 25 000 hours of use. To trace out the posterior predictive distribution of cost for each type of bulb, given a $(\theta_0, \theta_0, \sigma_0^2, \sigma_1^2)$ sample from the joint posterior, we independently draw from each of the LED and incandescent lognormal lifetime densities until a cumulative sum of such draws exceeds 25. This induces a discrete distribution on cost, where cost varies depending on the number of bulbs required to reach 25 000 hours of use. For the incandescent type, cost ranges from \$226 to \$231, the latter achieved when six bulbs are required. The posterior predicted probability that cost will equal \$228 or \$229 is .88, as the vast majority of simulations were associated with three or four such bulbs. For LED lighting, cost ranged from \$31.25 (requiring only one bulb) to \$41.25 (where three bulbs were required). Only one bulb was required 41% of the time, while two bulbs were required approximately 58% of the time.

Exercise 12.7 (Gibbs sampling in a count data model with an unknown changepoint) We continue to show how Gibbs sampling can be applied in practice in a second example. Suppose that $y_1, y_2, \ldots, y_T$ are a time series of *count* responses, generated as follows:

$$y_t|\gamma, \delta, \lambda \sim \begin{cases} Po(\gamma) & \text{if } t \leq \lambda, \\ Po(\delta) & \text{if } t > \lambda, \end{cases}$$

where $Po(\mu)$ denotes the Poisson distribution with mean μ (see Definition A.8). The parameter λ is a *changepoint*; for periods up to and including λ, the counts are generated with mean γ, and for periods after λ, the counts are generated with mean equal to δ.

Suppose you employ priors of the form

$$\begin{aligned} \gamma &\sim G(a_1, a_2), \\ \delta &\sim G(d_1, d_2), \\ \lambda &\sim \text{uniform}\{1, 2, \ldots, T-1\}. \end{aligned}$$

(a) Derive the likelihood function for this model.
(b) Describe how the Gibbs sampler can be employed to estimate the parameters of this model.
(c) On the website associated with this book, we provide data on the number of British coal mine disasters over the period 1851–1962 (for further analysis, see Carlin, Gelfand,

and Smith 1992; Gill 2002). Based on a quick inspection of these data, it appears as if the number of coal mine accidents has decreased over time, perhaps owing to increased safety concerns or technological innovations. Consistent with this idea, use the coal mine data and fit the Poisson model with an unknown changepoint. When does the change occur? What are the expected number of disasters before and after this change?

Solution

(a) The likelihood function for the model is as follows:

$$L(\gamma, \delta, \lambda) = \prod_{t=1851}^{\lambda} \frac{\gamma^{y_t} \exp(-\gamma)}{y_t!} \prod_{t=\lambda+1}^{1962} \frac{\delta^{y_t} \exp(-\delta)}{y_t!}.$$

Given the priors described, the joint posterior distribution can be expressed as

$$p(\gamma, \delta, \lambda | y) \propto \left[\gamma^{a_1 - 1} \exp\left(-\frac{\gamma}{a_2}\right) \delta^{d_1 - 1} \exp\left(-\frac{\delta}{d_2}\right)\right] \times \prod_{t=1851}^{\lambda} \frac{\gamma^{y_t} \exp(-\gamma)}{y_t!} \prod_{t=\lambda+1}^{1962} \frac{\delta^{y_t} \exp(-\delta)}{y_t!}.$$

(b) Collecting all the terms in the posterior involving γ, we obtain

$$p(\gamma | \delta, \lambda, y) \propto \gamma^{a_1 + [\sum_{t=1851}^{\lambda} y_t] - 1} \exp[-\gamma(a_2^{-1} + n_\lambda)],$$

where $n_\lambda \equiv \lambda - 1851 + 1$. We recognize this as the kernel of a

$$G\left(a_1 + \sum_{t=1851}^{\lambda} y_t, [a_2^{-1} + n_\lambda]^{-1}\right)$$

density. Similarly, we obtain

$$\delta | \gamma, \lambda, y \sim G\left(d_1 + \sum_{t=\lambda+1}^{1962} y_t, [d_2^{-1} + \tilde{n}_\lambda]^{-1}\right),$$

where $\tilde{n}_\lambda = 1962 - (\lambda + 1) + 1 = 1962 - \lambda$.

For the posterior conditional for the changepoint λ, we have

$$p(\lambda | \gamma, \delta, y) \propto \prod_{t=1851}^{\lambda} \frac{\gamma^{y_t} \exp(-\gamma)}{y_t!} \prod_{t=\lambda+1}^{1962} \frac{\delta^{y_t} \exp(-\delta)}{y_t!}, \quad \lambda = 1851, 1852, \ldots, 1961.$$

This conditional posterior distribution is discrete valued. We can sample from this distribution by first calculating the (unnormalized) density ordinates across all different years from 1851 to 1962. The resulting mass function can then be made proper by dividing each ordinate by the sum of all ordinate values. Draws from this discrete distribution can be easily obtained.

(c) Applying the algorithm described in part (b) to our coal mine data, we obtain a posterior mean (and standard deviation) of the changepoint λ equal to 1890 (2.4). Looking quickly at the raw data, we see that this seems to be a reasonable division. The frequency of no disasters appears to increase significantly after 1890, whereas disasters consistently and frequently took place prior to 1890. Similarly, γ, the expected number of disasters prior to the changepoint, had a posterior mean of 3.07 and a posterior standard deviation equal to .303. The expected number of disasters after the changepoint, δ, had a posterior mean of .924 and a standard deviation equal to .117. These results appear consistent with the raw data and suggest a significant reduction in major coal mine accidents after 1890.

Exercise 12.8 (Gibbs sampling from the bivariate normal) The purpose of this question is to further explore the properties of the Gibbs sampler, and to document some potential issues with its use. We do so in a very simple case.

Assume that you have a model that yields a bivariate normal posterior,

$$\begin{pmatrix} \theta_1 \\ \theta_2 \end{pmatrix} \sim N\left(\begin{bmatrix} 0 \\ 0 \end{bmatrix}, \begin{bmatrix} 1 & \rho \\ \rho & 1 \end{bmatrix} \right),$$

where $|\rho| < 1$ is the (known) posterior correlation between θ_1 and θ_2.

(a) Write a program that uses Monte Carlo integration to calculate the posterior means and standard deviations of θ_1 and θ_2.

(b) Write a program that uses Gibbs sampling to calculate the posterior means and standard deviations of θ_1 and θ_2.

(c) Set $\rho = 0$ and compare the programs from parts (a) and (b) for a given number of replications (e.g., $R = 100$) and compare the accuracy of the two algorithms.

(d) Repeat part (c) of this question for $\rho = .5, .9, .99$, and .999. Discuss how the degree of correlation between θ_1 and θ_2 affects the performance of the Gibbs sampler. Make graphs of the Monte Carlo and Gibbs sampler replications of θ_1 (i.e., make a graph with the x axis being replication number and the y axis being θ_1). What can the graphs you have made tell you about the properties of Monte Carlo and Gibbs sampling algorithms?

(e) Repeat parts (c) and (d) using more replications (e.g., $R = 10\,000$) and discuss how Gibbs sampling accuracy improves with the number of replications.

Solution

(a and b) A MATLAB program for this question is provided on the website associated with this book. Monte Carlo and Gibbs sampling algorithms have the same general structure: an introductory part where quantities are initialized (in this question, this means a value for ρ is set and all the sums used to calculate Monte Carlo and Gibbs estimates are initialized at zero), then a loop (in MATLAB this is a "for loop"; in other languages it is often called a "do loop"), which repeatedly draws from the posterior (in the case of Monte Carlo integration) or the posterior conditionals (in the case of Gibbs sampling) and sums the draws. Finally, the program ends with the final calculations (e.g., dividing sums by number of replications to get Monte Carlo or Gibbs estimates) and printing out and/or graphing of results.

The Monte Carlo integration algorithm requires the program to take random draws from the bivariate normal posterior given in the question. The Gibbs sampling algorithm requires the posterior conditionals. Using the properties of the multivariate normal distribution (see Theorem A.3) it follows immediately that

$$\theta_1|\theta_2, y \sim N\left(\rho\theta_2, 1-\rho^2\right)$$

and

$$\theta_2|\theta_1, y \sim N\left(\rho\theta_1, 1-\rho^2\right).$$

Of course, in practice there would be no need to do either Gibbs sampling or Monte Carlo integration since the true mean and standard deviation of θ_1 and θ_2 are given in the question. However, the purpose of this question is to compare posterior simulation algorithms and it is useful to know what the true answer should be when making such comparisons.

(c and d) Table 12.2 provides Monte Carlo integration and Gibbs sampler results for θ_1 and θ_2 for all the posteriors specified in the question. With the Gibbs sampler we discard an initial 100 burn-in replications to remove the effect of the initial conditions. We stress that since posterior simulation depends on random number generation, you may get results different from those presented in Table 12.2. That is, a posterior simulation algorithm run twice will not yield the same answer, especially with a small number of replications such as $R = 100$. With these qualifications in mind, the patterns in Table 12.2 are clear: For

Table 12.2: Posterior means and standard deviations of θ_1 and θ_2 with $R = 100$.

	$E(\theta_1\|y)$	$\sqrt{\text{Var}(\theta_1\|y)}$	$E(\theta_2\|y)$	$\sqrt{\text{Var}(\theta_2\|y)}$
True value	0.00	1.00	0.00	1.00
Monte Carlo integration				
$\rho = 0.00$	0.07	1.02	0.16	1.13
$\rho = 0.50$	0.02	0.89	0.06	0.94
$\rho = 0.90$	0.03	0.95	−0.06	0.97
$\rho = 0.99$	−0.07	1.09	0.06	1.08
$\rho = 0.999$	0.02	1.00	0.02	1.02
Gibbs sampling				
$\rho = 0.00$	0.14	1.16	0.06	1.09
$\rho = 0.50$	0.19	1.03	0.24	0.99
$\rho = 0.90$	0.42	0.78	0.29	0.83
$\rho = 0.99$	−0.42	0.64	−0.40	0.63
$\rho = 0.999$	0.61	0.17	0.62	0.16

Monte Carlo integration the degree of accuracy does not depend upon ρ, but for Gibbs sampling it does.

When $\rho = 0$, Gibbs sampling is equivalent to Monte Carlo integration since, in this case, θ_1 and θ_2 are independent of one another, and drawing from the posterior conditionals is equivalent to drawing from the two marginal distributions, which is equivalent to drawing from the joint distribution (owing to independence). Table 12.2 indicates that, for $\rho = 0$, Gibbs sampling is as accurate as Monte Carlo integration. However, as ρ becomes bigger and bigger, Gibbs sampling becomes less and less accurate. Note, in particular, that the posterior standard deviations become much smaller than their true values when ρ is large.

The reason for the poor performance of Gibbs sampling when θ_1 and θ_2 are highly correlated is that the sequence of Gibbs draws becomes highly correlated as well. This can be seen in Figure 12.5 (or inferred from the equations for the conditional posteriors just given), which plots the draws of θ_1 for $\rho = 0.999$. The Monte Carlo integration sequence is constructed from purely random draws from the posterior, but the Gibbs sampling draws are highly correlated with one another, resulting in the smooth, trendlike behavior of the Gibbs sequence. Intuitively, R random draws from a distribution are typically going to contain more information than R correlated draws (i.e., if two draws are highly correlated with one another, the second draw will mostly contain the same information as the first),

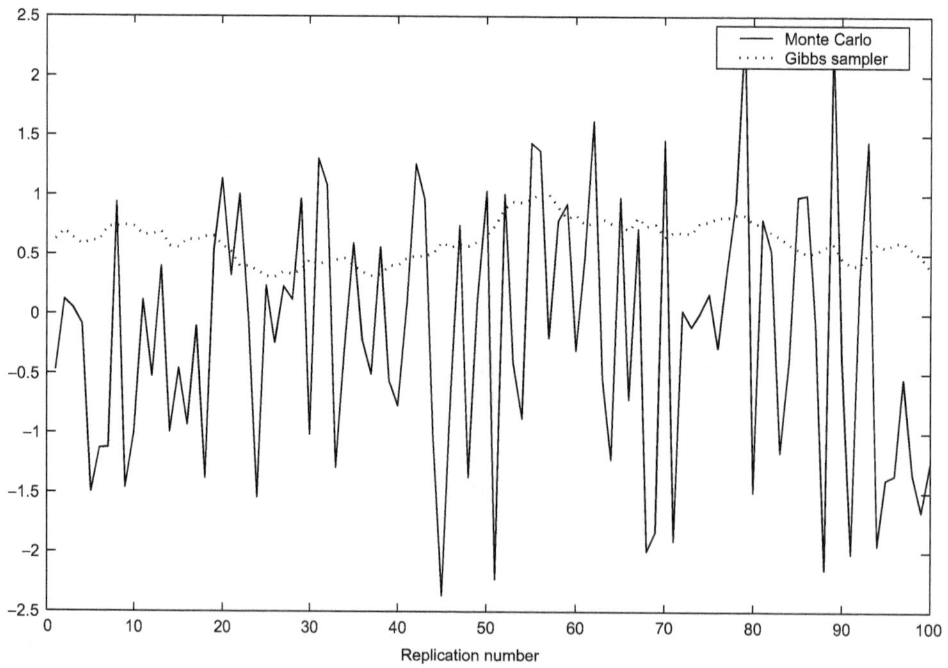

Figure 12.5. Path of Monte Carlo and Gibbs sampling draws for θ_1 with $\rho = .999$.

Table 12.3: Posterior means and standard deviations of θ_1 and θ_2 with $R = 10\,000$.

	$E(\theta_1 \vert y)$	$\sqrt{\text{Var}(\theta_1 \vert y)}$	$E(\theta_2 \vert y)$	$\sqrt{\text{Var}(\theta_2 \vert y)}$
True value	0.00	1.00	0.00	1.00
Monte Carlo integration				
$\rho = 0.00$	0.01	0.99	−0.01	1.00
$\rho = 0.50$	0.01	1.00	0.02	1.00
$\rho = 0.90$	0.00	1.00	0.00	0.99
$\rho = 0.99$	−0.01	1.00	0.00	1.00
$\rho = 0.999$	−0.02	0.99	−0.02	0.99
Gibbs sampling				
$\rho = 0.00$	0.00	0.99	0.01	1.00
$\rho = 0.50$	−0.03	0.99	−0.02	1.00
$\rho = 0.90$	0.04	0.99	0.05	1.00
$\rho = 0.99$	−0.07	0.95	−0.07	0.95
$\rho = 0.999$	−0.32	0.87	−0.32	0.87

and thus Monte Carlo integration is to be preferred to Gibbs sampling in this special case where the researcher has the choice between approaches.

Graphs of the Gibbs sampler and Monte Carlo integration draws (not presented here) for other values of ρ exhibit the expected patterns. When $\rho = 0$, the graphs of the Gibbs and Monte Carlo draws have the same erratic random pattern. However, as ρ increases, the graphs of Monte Carlo draws remain random, but the Gibbs draws become smoother and smoother (exhibiting greater serial correlation) until we reach the extreme case presented in Figure 12.5.

(e) Table 12.3 is the same as Table 12.2, except that the program was run using $R = 10\,000$ draws. With this larger number of draws, Monte Carlo integration is now quite accurate for all posteriors. The performance of the Gibbs sampler is much improved as well. However, for high values of ρ, the accuracy of the Gibbs sampler is still reasonably poor. We ran the program with $R = 100\,000$ for the posterior with $\rho = 0.999$, and even with this many draws we found the posterior mean of θ_1 to be 0.09 and the posterior standard deviation of θ_1 to equal 0.93, which are still reasonably far from the true values.

These findings highlight the importance of choosing a sufficient number of draws for the Gibbs sampler. For Monte Carlo integration, a reliable rule of thumb is that $R = 10\,000$ will yield an estimate of a parameter's posterior mean with error that is 1% of its posterior standard deviation. This is usually accurate enough for empirical work. For Gibbs sampling, no such rule of thumb exists (as is demonstrated by this question) and careful use of Gibbs sampling convergence diagnostics is required (see, e.g., Koop 2003, pp. 64–68; see also the exercises in the final section of this chapter).

12.3 MCMC Sampling in Linear Models and their Variants

Exercise 12.9 (Gibbs sampling in a regression problem) Consider the regression model

$$y_i = x_i\beta + \epsilon_i, \quad \epsilon_i \stackrel{iid}{\sim} N(0, \sigma^2), \quad i = 1, 2, \ldots, n.$$

In this exercise, unlike many of the others appearing to this point, we choose to work with the error variance σ^2 rather than the error precision σ^{-2}. We employ proper priors for these parameters of the form

$$\beta \sim N(\mu_\beta, V_\beta),$$
$$\sigma^2 \sim IG(a, b),$$

with μ_β, V_β, a, and b given, where $IG(\cdot,\cdot)$ denotes the inverted gamma density. Show how the Gibbs sampler can be used to fit this linear regression model.

Solution

The likelihood function for this regression model is

$$L(\beta, \sigma^2) = (2\pi)^{(-n/2)}(\sigma^2)^{(-n/2)} \exp\left(-\frac{1}{2\sigma^2}(y - X\beta)'(y - X\beta)\right),$$

with

$$y = \begin{bmatrix} y_1 \\ y_2 \\ \vdots \\ y_n \end{bmatrix} \quad \text{and} \quad X = \begin{bmatrix} x_1 \\ x_2 \\ \vdots \\ x_n \end{bmatrix}.$$

By Bayes' theorem, it follows that

$$p(\beta, \sigma^2|y) \propto L(\beta, \sigma^2) \exp\left(-\frac{1}{2}(\beta - \mu_\beta)'V_\beta^{-1}(\beta - \mu_\beta)\right)(\sigma^2)^{-[a+1]} \exp\left(-\frac{1}{b\sigma^2}\right).$$

To implement the Gibbs sampler we first need to derive the complete posterior distributions for all the parameters of our model. The complete posterior conditional for β follows immediately from an application of standard results (see, e.g., Exercise 10.1), since we are conditioning on the value of σ^2:

$$\beta|\sigma^2, y \sim N(D_\beta d_\beta, D_\beta),$$

where

$$D_\beta = \left(X'X/\sigma^2 + V_\beta^{-1}\right)^{-1}$$

and

$$d_\beta = X'y/\sigma^2 + V_\beta^{-1}\mu_\beta.$$

For the complete conditional for σ^2, we have

$$\begin{aligned} p(\sigma^2|\beta, y) &\propto p(\beta, \sigma^2|y) \\ &\propto (\sigma^2)^{-[(n/2)+a+1]} \exp\left(-\frac{1}{\sigma^2}\left[b^{-1} + \frac{1}{2}(y - X\beta)'(y - X\beta)\right]\right), \end{aligned}$$

so that, using the parameterization described in Theorem A.2,

$$\sigma^2|\beta, y \sim IG\left(\frac{n}{2} + a, \left[b^{-1} + \frac{1}{2}(y - X\beta)'(y - X\beta)\right]^{-1}\right).$$

To implement the Gibbs sampler, we would start with an initial value for σ^2, and then sample from the posterior conditional $\beta|\sigma^2, y$ described here. Given a draw from this conditional, say β^*, we would then draw a new value of σ^2 from $\sigma^2|\beta = \beta^*, y$. Repeating in this fashion, we will converge to drawing from the joint posterior density.

Exercise 12.10 (Gibbs sampling in a regression model with an unknown changepoint) Suppose that the density for a time series y_t, $t = 1, 2, \ldots, T$, conditioned on its lags, the model parameters, and other covariates, can be expressed as

$$y_t|\theta_1, \theta_2, \beta_1, \beta_2, \sigma^2, \tau^2, \lambda, x_t \sim \begin{cases} N(\theta_1 + \theta_2 x_t, \sigma^2) & \text{if } t \leq \lambda, \\ N(\beta_1 + \beta_2 x_t, \tau^2) & \text{if } t > \lambda. \end{cases}$$

In this model, like Exercise 12.7, λ is a *changepoint*: for periods until λ, one regression is assumed to generate y; following λ, a new regression is assumed to generate y.

Suppose you employ priors of the form

$$\begin{aligned} \theta = [\theta_1\ \theta_2]' &\sim N(\mu_\theta, V_\theta), \\ \beta = [\beta_1\ \beta_2]' &\sim N(\mu_\beta, V_\beta), \\ \sigma^2 &\sim IG(a_1, a_2), \\ \tau^2 &\sim IG(b_1, b_2), \\ \lambda &\sim \text{uniform}\{1, 2, \ldots, T-1\}. \end{aligned}$$

Note that λ is treated as a parameter of the model, and by placing a uniform prior over the elements $1, 2, \ldots, T-1$ a changepoint is assumed to exist.

(a) Derive the likelihood function for this model.

(b) Describe how the Gibbs sampler can be employed to estimate the parameters of this model, given these priors.

(c) Generate 500 observations from the changepoint model

$$y_t|\theta_1, \theta_2, \beta_1, \beta_2, \sigma^2, \tau^2, \lambda, x_t \sim \begin{cases} N(2 + x_t, .2) & \text{if } t \leq 85, \\ N(1.5 + .8x_t, .5) & \text{if } t > 85, \end{cases}$$

where $x_t \overset{iid}{\sim} N(0, 1)$ for simplicity. Select prior hyperparameters as follows: $\mu_\theta = \mu_\beta = 0_2$, $V_\theta = V_\beta = 100I_2$, $a_1 = b_1 = 3$, and $a_2 = b_2 = (1/2)$. Using the generated data and the algorithm from part (b), fit the model and compare point estimates with the parameter values used to generate the data.

Solution

(a) The likelihood function for this model is

$$L(\theta_1, \theta_2, \beta_1, \beta_2, \sigma^2, \tau^2, \lambda) = \prod_{t \leq \lambda} \phi(y_t; \theta_1 + \theta_2 x_t, \sigma^2) \prod_{t > \lambda} \phi(y_t; \beta_1 + \beta_2 x_t, \tau^2).$$

The joint posterior is proportional to this likelihood times the given priors for the model parameters.

(b) Conveniently, and much like a Gaussian mixture model (see Chapter 15 for exercises related to mixtures), the data divide into two parts given the changepoint λ. As such, standard results can be used for the linear regression model (see Exercise 12.9) to simulate the regression and variance parameters within each of the two regimes. Specifically, we obtain

$$\theta | \beta, \sigma^2, \tau^2, \lambda, y \sim N(D_\theta d_\theta, D_\theta),$$

where

$$D_\theta = \left(X_\theta' X_\theta / \sigma^2 + V_\theta^{-1} \right)^{-1} \quad \text{and} \quad d_\theta = X_\theta' y_\theta / \sigma^2 + V_\theta^{-1} \mu_\theta.$$

In these expressions, we have defined

$$X_\theta = X_\theta(\lambda) = \begin{bmatrix} 1 & x_1 \\ 1 & x_2 \\ \vdots & \vdots \\ 1 & x_\lambda \end{bmatrix} \quad \text{and} \quad y_\theta = y_\theta(\lambda) = \begin{bmatrix} y_1 \\ y_2 \\ \vdots \\ y_\lambda \end{bmatrix}.$$

Similarly, we obtain the posterior conditional for β:

$$\beta | \theta, \sigma^2, \tau^2, \lambda, y \sim N(D_\beta d_\beta, D_\beta),$$

where

$$D_\beta = \left(X_\beta' X_\beta / \tau^2 + V_\beta^{-1} \right)^{-1} \quad \text{and} \quad d_\beta = X_\beta' y_\beta / \tau^2 + V_\beta^{-1} \mu_\beta.$$

Again, we define

$$X_\beta = X_\beta(\lambda) = \begin{bmatrix} 1 & x_{\lambda+1} \\ 1 & x_{\lambda+2} \\ \vdots & \vdots \\ 1 & x_T \end{bmatrix} \quad \text{and} \quad y_\beta = y_\beta(\lambda) = \begin{bmatrix} y_{\lambda+1} \\ y_{\lambda+2} \\ \vdots \\ y_T \end{bmatrix}.$$

For the conditionals for the variance parameters, we have

$$\sigma^2 | \beta, \theta, \tau^2, \lambda, y \sim IG\left(\frac{\lambda}{2} + a_1, \left[a_2^{-1} + (1/2) \sum_{t=1}^{\lambda} (y_t - \theta_1 - \theta_2 x_t)^2 \right]^{-1} \right)$$

and

$$\tau^2|\beta,\theta,\sigma^2,\lambda,y \sim IG\left(\frac{T-\lambda}{2}+b_1, \left[b_2^{-1}+(1/2)\sum_{t=\lambda+1}^{T}(y_t-\beta_1-\beta_2 x_t)^2\right]^{-1}\right).$$

Finally, for the changepoint λ, we obtain

$$p(\lambda|\beta,\theta,\sigma^2,\tau^2,y) \propto \prod_{t\leq\lambda}\phi(y_t;\theta_1+\theta_2 x_t,\sigma^2)\prod_{t>\lambda}\phi(y_t;\beta_1+\beta_2 x_t,\tau^2),\ \ \lambda=1,2,\ldots,T-1.$$

This distribution is discrete valued and can be sampled as described in the solution to Exercise 12.7.

(c) The MATLAB code used is available on the website associated with this book. We run the Gibbs sampler for 1000 iterations and discard the first 200 of these as the burn-in. In terms of the regression coefficients θ and β, respectively, we obtain posterior means (and their true values) equal to 1.94 (2), .977 (1), 1.51 (1.5), and .803 (.8). For the variance parameters σ^2 and τ^2, respectively, we obtain posterior means (and true values) equal to .190 (.2) and .487 (.5). Finally, for the changepoint λ, we obtain a posterior mean of 82.87 and standard deviation equal to 9.09. Thus, all point estimates were quite close to the values used to generate the data.

Exercise 12.11 (Gibbs sampling in a model of groupwise heteroscedasticity) Suppose we generalize the regression model in the previous exercise so that

$$y = X\beta + \epsilon,$$

where

$$E(\epsilon\epsilon'|X) \equiv \Sigma = \begin{bmatrix} \sigma_1^2 & 0 & 0 & 0 & 0 & 0 & 0 & 0 & 0 & 0 \\ \vdots & \ddots & \vdots & \vdots & \vdots & \vdots & \vdots & \vdots & \vdots & \vdots \\ 0 & 0 & \sigma_1^2 & 0 & 0 & 0 & 0 & 0 & 0 & 0 \\ 0 & 0 & 0 & \sigma_2^2 & 0 & 0 & 0 & 0 & 0 & 0 \\ \vdots & \vdots & \vdots & \vdots & \ddots & \vdots & \vdots & \vdots & \vdots & \vdots \\ 0 & 0 & 0 & 0 & 0 & \sigma_2^2 & 0 & 0 & 0 & 0 \\ \vdots & \vdots & \vdots & \vdots & \vdots & \vdots & \ddots & \vdots & \vdots & \vdots \\ 0 & 0 & 0 & 0 & 0 & 0 & 0 & \sigma_J^2 & 0 & 0 \\ \vdots & \vdots & \vdots & \vdots & \vdots & \vdots & \vdots & \vdots & \ddots & \vdots \\ 0 & 0 & 0 & 0 & 0 & 0 & 0 & 0 & 0 & \sigma_J^2 \end{bmatrix}.$$

That is, we relax the homoscedasticity assumption with one of *groupwise heteroscedasticity*, where we presume there are J different groups with identical variance parameters within each group, but different parameters across groups. Let n_j represent the number of observations belonging to group j.

Given priors of the form

$$\beta \sim N(\mu_\beta, V_\beta),$$
$$\sigma_j^2 \overset{ind}{\sim} IG(a_j, b_j), \quad j = 1, 2, \ldots J,$$

show how the Gibbs sampler can be used to estimate this model.

Solution

We obtain the following complete posterior conditional for β (since conditioned on all the variance parameters, Σ is known):

$$\beta | \{\sigma_j^2\}_{j=1}^J, y \sim N(D_\beta d_\beta, D_\beta),$$

where

$$D_\beta = \left(X'\Sigma^{-1}X + V_\beta^{-1} \right)^{-1}$$

and

$$d_\beta = X'\Sigma^{-1}y + V_\beta^{-1}\mu_\beta.$$

For the complete posterior for each σ_j^2, first note that the likelihood function for this problem can be written as

$$L(\beta, \{\sigma_j^2\}) = \prod_{j=1}^J (2\pi)^{-(n_j/2)} (\sigma_j^2)^{-(n_j/2)} \exp\left(-\frac{1}{2\sigma_j^2}(y_j - X_j\beta)'(y_j - X_j\beta) \right),$$

with y_j and X_j being the $n_j \times 1$ outcome vector and $n_j \times k$ design matrix, respectively, for group j. Given this form of the likelihood together with the independent inverse gamma priors for $\{\sigma_j^2\}_{j=1}^J$, similar arguments to those given in Exercise 12.9 show that

$$\sigma_j^2 | \Gamma_{-\sigma_j^2}, y \overset{ind}{\sim} IG\left(\frac{n_j}{2} + a_j, \left[b_j^{-1} + \frac{1}{2}(y_j - X_j\beta)'(y_j - X_j\beta) \right]^{-1} \right), \quad j = 1, 2, \ldots, J,$$

with Γ denoting all the parameters in our model and Γ_{-x} denoting all parameters other than x.

Thus, to implement the sampler, one can start with an initial condition for Σ, sample β from $\beta | \{\sigma_j^2\}, y$, and then, given the value of β just drawn, sample independently from the posterior conditionals for the σ_j^2. Iterating over this process will produce a set of draws from the joint posterior density.

Exercise 12.12 (Theoretical results for a regression model with general covariance matrix) Chapter 10 contained many questions relating to the normal linear regression model under classical assumptions. This model assumed the error covariance matrix to be $h^{-1}I$. Econometricians are often interested in relaxing this assumption to allow for factors such as heteroscedasticity and autocorrelation; an example of a type of the former was given in the previous exercise. Other specifications such as the seemingly unrelated regressions model (covered later in this chapter) and some panel data models (see Chapter 13) also require relaxation of this assumption. This exercise contains theoretical results relating to a regression model with a general covariance structure.

Begin by writing

$$y = X\beta + \epsilon, \tag{12.9}$$

where we now assume $\epsilon|X \sim N\left(0, h^{-1}\Omega\right)$, where Ω is an $N \times N$ positive definite matrix.

Assume a prior of the form

$$p\left(\beta, h, \Omega\right) = p\left(\beta\right) p\left(h\right) p\left(\Omega\right), \tag{12.10}$$

where

$$p\left(\beta\right) = \phi\left(\beta; \underline{\beta}, \underline{V}\right), \tag{12.11}$$
$$p\left(h\right) = f_\gamma\left(h|\underline{s}^{-2}, \underline{\nu}\right), \tag{12.12}$$

and $p\left(\Omega\right)$ is left unspecified.

(a) Derive the full posterior conditionals for this model: $p\left(\beta|y, h, \Omega\right)$, $p\left(h|y, \beta, \Omega\right)$, and $p\left(\Omega|y, \beta, h\right)$.

(b) Using your results for part (a), discuss how a Gibbs sampler could be set up for the case where Ω is known.

Solution

(a) A standard theorem in matrix algebra (see, e.g., Koop 2003, p. 316) says that, since Ω is positive definite, an $N \times N$ matrix P exists with the property that $P\Omega P' = I_N$. If we multiply both sides of (12.9) by P, we obtain a transformed model

$$y^* = X^*\beta + \epsilon^*, \tag{12.13}$$

where $y^* = Py$, $X^* = PX$, $\epsilon^* = P\epsilon$, and ϵ^* is $N(0_N, h^{-1}I_N)$. If we work with this transformed model, the derivation of the posterior is very similar to Exercise 10.1. The only difference arises since Exercise 10.1 used a natural conjugate normal-gamma prior, whereas here we are using an independent normal-gamma prior. The following material provides details.

Using properties of the multivariate normal distribution gives us the likelihood function:

$$L(\beta, h, \Omega) = \frac{h^{\frac{N}{2}}}{(2\pi)^{\frac{N}{2}}} \left\{ \exp\left[-\frac{h}{2} \left(y^* - X^*\beta\right)' \left(y^* - X^*\beta\right) \right] \right\}. \tag{12.14}$$

Multiplying prior times the likelihood gives us the posterior:

$$
\begin{aligned}
p(\beta, h, \Omega | y) \propto\, & p(\Omega) \\
& \times \left\{ \exp\left[-\frac{1}{2} \left\{ h (y^* - X^* \beta)' (y^* - X^* \beta) + (\beta - \underline{\beta})' \underline{V}^{-1} (\beta - \underline{\beta}) \right\} \right] \right\} \\
& \times h^{\frac{N+\underline{\nu}-2}{2}} \exp\left[-\frac{h\underline{\nu}}{2\underline{s}^{-2}} \right].
\end{aligned}
\tag{12.15}
$$

It can be verified that this posterior is not of the form of any common density. However, we can collect terms involving β to figure out the conditional posterior $p(\beta|y, h, \Omega)$. If we do this, using the same derivations as in the solution to Exercise 10.1, we obtain

$$
\beta | y, h, \Omega \sim N\left(\overline{\beta}, \overline{V}\right), \tag{12.16}
$$

where

$$
\overline{V} = \left(\underline{V}^{-1} + hX'\Omega^{-1}X\right)^{-1} \tag{12.17}
$$

and

$$
\overline{\beta} = \overline{V}\left(\underline{V}^{-1}\underline{\beta} + hX'\Omega^{-1}X\widehat{\beta}(\Omega)\right), \tag{12.18}
$$

where

$$
\widehat{\beta}(\Omega) = \left(X^{*\prime}X^*\right)^{-1} X^{*\prime}y^* = \left(X'\Omega^{-1}X\right)^{-1} X'\Omega^{-1}y. \tag{12.19}
$$

Similarly, if we collect terms involving h to figure out the conditional posterior $p(h|y, \beta, \Omega)$, we obtain

$$
h | y, \beta, \Omega \sim \gamma(\overline{s}^{-2}, \overline{\nu}), \tag{12.20}
$$

where

$$
\overline{\nu} = N + \underline{\nu} \tag{12.21}
$$

and

$$
\overline{s}^2 = \frac{(y - X\beta)' \Omega^{-1} (y - X\beta) + \underline{\nu}\underline{s}^2}{\overline{\nu}}. \tag{12.22}
$$

The posterior for Ω conditional on β and h has a kernel of the form

$$
p(\Omega | y, \beta, h) \propto p(\Omega) |\Omega|^{-\frac{1}{2}} \left\{ \exp\left[-\frac{h}{2} (y - X\beta)' \Omega^{-1} (y - X\beta) \right] \right\}. \tag{12.23}
$$

(b) If we knew Ω, then we could simply plug its value into the posterior conditionals $p(\beta|y, h, \Omega)$ and $p(h|y, \beta, \Omega)$. Thus a Gibbs sampler involving (12.16) and (12.20) involves only the normal and gamma distributions. When Ω is unknown, as we shall see in the following, Gibbs samplers for a wide variety of models with general error covariance structure involve blocks of this form for $p(\beta|y, h, \Omega)$ and $p(h|y, \beta, \Omega)$, and only differ in the form for $p(\Omega|y, \beta, h)$.

Exercise 12.13 (Metropolis-within-Gibbs in a model of parametric heteroscedasticity) Heteroscedasticity occurs if

$$\Omega = \begin{bmatrix} \omega_1 & 0 & \cdots & 0 \\ 0 & \omega_2 & 0 & \cdots \\ \vdots & 0 & \cdots & \vdots \\ \vdots & \cdots & \cdots & 0 \\ 0 & \cdots & 0 & \omega_N \end{bmatrix}. \tag{12.24}$$

In this exercise, assume that

$$\omega_i = \left(1 + \alpha_1 z_{i1} + \alpha_2 z_{i2} + \cdots + \alpha_p z_{ip}\right)^2, \tag{12.25}$$

where z_i is a $1 \times p$ vector of data that may include some or all of the explanatory variables in (12.9). Let $\alpha = [\alpha_1\ \alpha_2\ \cdots\ \alpha_p]'$.
(a) Assuming a prior of the form given in (12.10)–(12.12), derive the full posterior conditionals for this model.
(b) Assuming a non-informative prior for the parameters that define Ω,

$$p(\alpha) \propto 1,$$

describe how a Metropolis-within-Gibbs algorithm can be developed to carry out Bayesian inference in this model.
(c) Program the algorithm described in part (b) and carry out a Bayesian investigation of heteroscedasticity using a suitable data set and choices for the prior hyperparameters $\underline{\beta}$, $\underline{V}$, $\underline{\nu}$, and $\underline{s}^{-2}$. A possible application, and one taken up in our solution, involves analyzing determinants of house prices. This data set, provided on the website associated with this book, contains the sales price of $N = 546$ houses sold in Windsor, Canada in 1987. Interest centers on finding out which factors affect house prices, and hence sales price is our dependent variable. We use four explanatory variables: the size of the lot the house is on, the number of bedrooms, number of bathrooms, and number of storeys. Thus, in our application, we will have:

- y_i = sales price of the ith house measured in Canadian dollars
- x_{i2} = lot size of the ith house measured in square feet
- x_{i3} = number of bedrooms in the ith house
- x_{i4} = number of bathrooms in the ith house
- x_{i5} = number of storeys in the ith house.

Solution
(a) The theoretical derivations are exactly the same as in Exercise 12.12. The conditional posterior for Ω has the form given in (12.23). There are a few ways of simplifying this expression a little bit (e.g., using $|\Omega| = \prod \omega_i$), but none are that instructive.

(b) The results for part (a) suggest that a Metropolis-within-Gibbs algorithm can be developed since $p(\beta|y,h,\alpha)$ is normal and $p(h|y,\beta,\alpha)$ is gamma, and we require only a method for taking draws from $p(\alpha|y,\beta,h)$. The latter density does not have a convenient form, and thus we employ an M–H step to conduct the sampling. In this solution, we will use a random walk chain M–H algorithm, although other algorithms could be used. Equation (12.23) evaluated at old and candidate draws is used to calculate the acceptance probability.

(c) The necessary MATLAB code is provided on the website associated with this book. In this solution, we provide our empirical results using the house price data set. The variance of the proposal density, which we will call Σ, is chosen by first setting $\Sigma = cI$ and experimenting with different values of the scalar c until a value is found that yields reasonable acceptance probabilities. The posterior simulator is then run using this value to yield an estimate of the posterior variance of α, $\widehat{\text{Var}(\alpha|y)}$. We then set $\Sigma = c\widehat{\text{Var}(\alpha|y)}$ and experiment with different values of c until we find one that yields an average acceptance probability of roughly .50. Then a final long run of 30 000 replications, with 5000 burn-in replications discarded, is taken. For the prior hyperparameters we choose $\underline{\nu} = 5$, $\underline{s}^{-2} = 4.0 \times 10^{-8}$,

$$\underline{\beta} = \begin{bmatrix} 0.0 \\ 10 \\ 5000 \\ 10\,000 \\ 10\,000 \end{bmatrix},$$

and

$$\underline{V} = \begin{bmatrix} 10\,000^2 & 0 & 0 & 0 & 0 \\ 0 & 5^2 & 0 & 0 & 0 \\ 0 & 0 & 2500^2 & 0 & 0 \\ 0 & 0 & 0 & 5000^2 & 0 \\ 0 & 0 & 0 & 0 & 5000^2 \end{bmatrix}.$$

It can be confirmed that the resulting prior is located in a sensible region of the parameter space but is relatively non-informative.

Table 12.4 contains posterior means, standard deviations, and 95% HPDIs for all parameters in the model. The results indicate that heteroscedasticity does seem to exist for this data set. That is, the 95% HPD intervals do not include zero for α_1, α_2, α_3, and α_4.

Exercise 12.14 (Heteroscedasticity of an unknown form: Student t errors) Building from the previous exercise, let us now assume that you have heteroscedasticity as in (12.24), but you do not know its exact form – i.e., you do not know Equation (12.25) – but are willing to assume all of the error variances are drawn from a common distribution, the gamma. If we work with error precisions rather than variances, and hence define

Table 12.4: Posterior results for β, h, and α.

	Mean	Standard deviation	95% HPDI
β_1	-5455.66	2941.55	$[-10\,281, -626]$
β_2	6.27	0.42	$[5.59, 6.97]$
β_3	3034.73	999.93	$[1392, 4678]$
β_4	$14\,207.85$	1602.56	$[11\,597, 16\,901]$
β_5	7814.81	922.64	$[6290, 9327]$
h	7.90×10^{-8}	2.55×10^{-8}	$[4 \times 10^{-8}, 1 \times 10^{-7}]$
α_1	5.02×10^{-4}	1.29×10^{-4}	$[3 \times 10^{-4}, 8 \times 10^{-4}]$
α_2	0.39	0.13	$[0.16, 0.56]$
α_3	0.32	0.07	$[0.20, 0.41]$
α_4	-0.22	0.08	$[-0.33, -0.09]$

$\lambda \equiv [\lambda_1 \; \lambda_2 \; \cdots \; \lambda_N]' \equiv \left[\omega_1^{-1} \; \omega_2^{-1} \; \cdots \; \omega_N^{-1}\right]'$, we assume the following hierarchical prior for λ:

$$p(\lambda|\nu_\lambda) = \prod_{i=1}^{N} f_\gamma(\lambda_i|1, \nu_\lambda). \tag{12.26}$$

This prior is hierarchical because λ depends on a parameter, ν_λ, which in turn has its own prior, $p(\nu_\lambda)$. We will assume the latter to be exponential:

$$p(\nu_\lambda) = f_\gamma(\nu_\lambda|\underline{\nu}_\lambda, 2). \tag{12.27}$$

As an aside, we note that this specification is a popular one since it can be shown (if we integrate out λ) that we obtain a linear regression model with Student t errors. That is,

$$p(\epsilon_i) = f_t\left(\epsilon_i|0, h^{-1}, \nu_\lambda\right).$$

The interested reader is referred to Exercise 15.1 or Geweke (1993) for proof and further details. Geweke (1993) also shows that if you use a common non-informative prior for β – i.e., $p(\beta) \propto 1$ on the interval $(-\infty, \infty)$ – then the posterior mean does not exist, unless $p(\nu_\lambda)$ is zero on the interval $(0, 2]$. The posterior standard deviation does not exist unless $p(\nu_\lambda)$ is zero on the interval $(0, 4]$. Hence, the researcher who wants to use a non-informative prior for β should either use a prior that excludes small values for ν_λ or present posterior medians and interquartile ranges (which will exist for any valid pdf). With an informative normal prior for β, the posterior mean and standard deviation of β will exist.
(a) Assume a prior given by (12.10), (12.11), (12.12), (12.26), and (12.27). Derive the full posterior conditionals for this model and, using these, discuss how posterior simulation can be done.
(b) Program the algorithm described in part (a) and carry out an empirical Bayesian analysis using a suitable data set (e.g., the house price data set described earlier in this chapter) and suitable choices for prior hyperparameters.

Solution

(a) The posterior conditionals $p(\beta|y,h,\lambda)$ and $p(h|y,\beta,\lambda)$ will be exactly as in (12.16) and (12.24), with the precise form for Ω given in (12.24) plugged in. Thus we need only derive $p(\lambda|y,\beta,h,\nu_\lambda)$ and $p(\nu_\lambda|y,\beta,h,\lambda)$. The former can be derived by plugging the prior given in (12.26) into the general form for the conditional posterior given in (12.23). An examination of the resulting density shows that the λ_i are independent of one another (conditional on the other parameters of the model) and each of the conditional posteriors for λ_i has the form of a gamma density. Thus, we have

$$p(\lambda|y,\beta,h,\nu_\lambda) = \prod_{i=1}^{N} p(\lambda_i|y,\beta,h,\nu_\lambda) \tag{12.28}$$

and

$$p(\lambda_i|y,\beta,h,\nu_\lambda) = f_\gamma\left(\lambda_i|\frac{\nu_\lambda+1}{h\epsilon_i^2+\nu_\lambda},\nu_\lambda+1\right). \tag{12.29}$$

Note that, conditional on knowing β, ϵ_i can be calculated, and hence the parameters of the gamma density in (12.29) can be calculated in the posterior simulator.

The density $p(\nu_\lambda|y,\beta,h,\lambda)$ is relatively easy to derive since ν_λ does not enter the likelihood and $p(\nu_\lambda|y,\beta,h,\lambda) = p(\nu_\lambda|\lambda)$. It follows from Bayes' theorem that

$$p(\nu_\lambda|\lambda) \propto p(\lambda|\nu_\lambda)\,p(\nu_\lambda),$$

and thus the kernel of the posterior conditional of ν_λ is (12.26) times (12.27). Thus, we obtain

$$p(\nu_\lambda|y,\beta,h,\lambda) \propto \left(\frac{\nu_\lambda}{2}\right)^{\frac{N\nu_\lambda}{2}} \Gamma\left(\frac{\nu_\lambda}{2}\right)^{-N} \exp(-\eta\nu_\lambda), \tag{12.30}$$

where

$$\eta = \frac{1}{\underline{\nu}_\lambda} + \frac{1}{2}\sum_{i=1}^{N}\left[\ln\left(\lambda_i^{-1}\right)+\lambda_i\right].$$

This density is a non-standard one. Hence, an M–H step will be required in our posterior simulation algorithm.

Thus, a Metropolis-within-Gibbs algorithm that sequentially draws from (12.16), (12.20), (12.28), and (12.30) can be used to carry out Bayesian inference in this model.

(b) We will use the house price data set and prior as described in Exercise 12.13. The prior for ν_λ depends on the hyperparameter $\underline{\nu}_\lambda$, its prior mean. We set $\underline{\nu}_\lambda = 25$, a value that allocates substantial prior weight to both very fat tailed error distributions (e.g., $\nu_\lambda < 10$) and error distributions that are roughly normal (e.g., $\nu_\lambda > 40$).

All posterior conditionals except for $p(\nu_\lambda|y,\beta,h,\lambda)$ are standard densities (i.e., normal or gamma). There are many ways of drawing from $p(\nu_\lambda|y,\beta,h,\lambda)$. For instance, Geweke (1993) uses acceptance sampling. The MATLAB code on the website associated with this book uses a random walk chain M–H algorithm with a normal increment random

Table 12.5: Posterior results for β and ν_λ.

	Mean	Standard deviation	95% HPDI
β_1	−413.15	2898.24	$[-5153, 4329]$
β_2	5.24	0.36	$[4.65, 5.83]$
β_3	2118.02	972.84	$[501, 3709]$
β_4	14 910.41	1665.83	$[12\,188, 17\,631]$
β_5	8108.53	955.74	$[6706, 9516]$
ν_λ	4.31	0.85	$[3.18, 5.97]$

variable. Equation (12.23), evaluated at old and candidate draws, is used to calculate the acceptance probability. Candidate draws of ν_λ that are less than or equal to zero have the acceptance probability set to zero. The variance of the proposal density, Σ, is chosen by first setting $\Sigma = c$ and experimenting with different values of the scalar c until a value is found that yields reasonable acceptance probabilities. The posterior simulator is then run using this value to yield an estimate of the posterior variance of ν_λ, $\widehat{\text{Var}\left(\nu_\lambda|y\right)}$. We then set $\Sigma = c\widehat{\text{Var}\left(\nu_\lambda|y\right)}$ and experiment with different values of c until we find one that yields an average acceptance probability of roughly .50. Then a final long run of 30 000 replications, with 5000 burn-in replications discarded, is taken.

Table 12.5 contains posterior results for the key parameters. It can be seen that, although posteriors for the elements of β are qualitatively similar to those presented in Table 12.4, the posterior for ν_λ indicates that the errors exhibit substantial deviations from normality. Because this crucial parameter is univariate, you may also want to plot a histogram approximation of its posterior. For this data set, such a histogram will indicate that $p\left(\nu_\lambda|y\right)$ has a shape that is quite skewed and confirms the finding that virtually all of the posterior probability is allocated to small values for the degrees of freedom parameter. Note, however, that there is virtually no support for extremely small values, which would imply extremely fat tails. Remember that the Cauchy distribution is the Student t with $\nu_\lambda = 1$. It has such fat tails that its mean does not exist. There is no evidence for this sort of extreme behavior in the errors for the present data set.

Exercise 12.15 (Autocorrelated errors) In this exercise, assume that you have time series data. We will use a subscript t to indicate time. That is, y_t for $t = 1, \ldots, T$ indicates observations on the dependent variable from period 1 through T. We consider the regression model

$$y_t = x_t\beta + \epsilon_t$$

and assume that the errors follow an autoregressive process of order 1 or AR(1) process:

$$\epsilon_t = \rho\epsilon_{t-1} + u_t. \tag{12.31}$$

We also assume that $u_t \overset{iid}{\sim} N\left(0, h^{-1}\right)$ and that the error process is stationary: $|\rho| < 1$.

It can be shown that the covariance matrix of ϵ is $h^{-1}\Omega$, where

$$\Omega = \frac{1}{1-\rho^2} \begin{bmatrix} 1 & \rho & \rho^2 & \cdots & \rho^{T-1} \\ \rho & 1 & \rho & \cdots & \rho^{T-2} \\ \rho^2 & \rho & 1 & \cdots & \rho^{T-3} \\ \vdots & \vdots & \vdots & \ddots & \vdots \\ \rho^{T-1} & \rho^{T-2} & \rho^{T-3} & \cdots & 1 \end{bmatrix}, \tag{12.32}$$

and thus the regression model with AR(1) errors falls in the class of models being studied in this chapter.

For the new parameter in this model, assume a prior of the form

$$p(\rho) \propto \phi\left(\rho; \underline{\rho}, \underline{V}_\rho\right) I\left(|\rho| < 1\right), \tag{12.33}$$

where $I\left(|\rho| < 1\right)$ is the indicator function that equals one for the stationary region and zero otherwise.

(a) Given the priors in (12.10), (12.11), (12.12), and (12.33), derive the full posterior conditionals for this model and, using these, discuss how posterior simulation can be carried out.

(b) Show how the Savage–Dickey density ratio (see Chapter 6, Exercise 6.8) can be used to find the Bayes factor in favor of $\rho = 0$.

(c) Using the results from parts (a) and (b), carry out a Bayesian analysis using a suitable time series data set. You may use the baseball data set described in the following (available on the website associated with this book as YANKEES.TXT). Conduct a prior sensitivity analysis with respect to the prior variance of ρ by trying different values for $\underline{V}_\rho$ between 0.01 and 100. Discuss the sensitivity of the Bayes factor of part (b) to changes in this prior.

Solution

(a) As noted in Exercise 12.12, a suitably transformed regression can be found where the errors satisfy the classical assumptions. First, take the regression model

$$y_t = x_t\beta + \epsilon_t, \tag{12.34}$$

where $x_t = [1\ x_{t2}\ \cdots\ x_{tk}]$, and multiply both sides of (12.34) by $(1 - \rho L)$, where L is the lag operator. Define $y_t^* = (1 - \rho L)\, y_t$ and $x_t^* = (1 - \rho L)\, x_t$. We obtain

$$y_t^* = x_t^{*\prime}\beta + u_t. \tag{12.35}$$

We have assumed that u_t is $iid\ N\left(0, h^{-1}\right)$, and thus the transformed model given in (12.35), which has $T - 1$ observations, is simply a normal linear regression model with iid errors. To simplify things, you may work with data from $T = 2, \ldots, T$ and ignore the (minor) complications relating to the treatment of initial conditions. Thus, if we define $y^* = [y_2^*\ y_3^*\ \cdots\ y_T^*]'$ and X^* conformably, we can use the results from Exercise 12.12 to obtain

$$\beta|y, h, \rho \sim N\left(\overline{\beta}, \overline{V}\right), \tag{12.36}$$

where

$$\overline{V} = \left(\underline{V}^{-1} + hX^{*\prime}X^{*}\right)^{-1} \tag{12.37}$$

and

$$\overline{\beta} = \overline{V}\left(\underline{V}^{-1}\underline{\beta} + hX^{*\prime}y^{*}\right). \tag{12.38}$$

The posterior for h conditional on the other parameters in the model is gamma:

$$h|y, \beta, \rho \sim \gamma(\overline{s}^{-2}, \overline{\nu}), \tag{12.39}$$

where

$$\overline{\nu} = T - 1 + \underline{\nu} \tag{12.40}$$

and

$$\overline{s}^2 = \frac{(y^* - X^*\beta)'(y^* - X^*\beta) + \underline{\nu}\underline{s}^2}{\overline{\nu}}. \tag{12.41}$$

Conditional on β and h, it follows that (12.31) defines a regression model for ϵ_t (with known error variance). By using standard results that we have derived in earlier exercises for the normal linear regression model (e.g., Chapter 10, Exercise 10.1; Chapter 2, Exercise 2.3) it follows immediately that

$$p(\rho|y, \beta, h) \propto \phi\left(\rho; \overline{\rho}, \overline{V}_\rho\right) I\left(|\rho| < 1\right), \tag{12.42}$$

where

$$\overline{V}_\rho = \left(\underline{V}_\rho^{-1} + h\epsilon_{-1}'\epsilon_{-1}\right)^{-1}, \tag{12.43}$$

$$\overline{\rho} = \overline{V}\rho\left(\underline{V}_\rho^{-1}\underline{\rho} + h\epsilon_{-1}'\epsilon\right), \tag{12.44}$$

$\epsilon_{-1} = [\epsilon_1\ \epsilon_2\ \cdots\ \epsilon_{T-1}]'$, and $\epsilon = [\epsilon_2\ \epsilon_3\ \cdots\ \epsilon_T]'$.

Posterior simulation can be done by using an MCMC algorithm that sequentially draws from (12.36), (12.39), and (12.43), which are normal, gamma, and truncated normal, respectively. The fact that the last is truncated normal could be dealt with by drawing from the corresponding untruncated normal part, $\phi\left(\rho; \overline{\rho}, \overline{V}_\rho\right)$, discarding any draws outside the interval $|\rho| < 1$, and redrawing until a draw in the interval is obtained. This is equivalent to doing importance sampling using $\phi\left(\rho; \overline{\rho}, \overline{V}_\rho\right)$ as an importance function (i.e., importance sampling weights are zero for draws outside the interval $|\rho| < 1$, which is equivalent to simply discarding such draws). Alternatively, if the number of discarded draws proves to be quite high, one could draw from the truncated normal directly. (See the solution of Exercise 11.5 for an algorithm to draw from a univariate truncated normal.)

(b) The Savage–Dickey density ratio produces the Bayes factor in favor of the hypothesis that $\rho = 0$ and is given by (see Chapter 6, Exercise 6.8)

$$B_{12} = \frac{p(\rho = 0|y)}{p(\rho = 0)},$$

where the numerator and denominator are both evaluated in the unrestricted model. For the numerator, we require the *marginal posterior ordinate* at $\rho = 0$. Given the simulated output, this could be calculated using a kernel density estimator, or, more efficiently, using "Rao–Blackwellization":

$$\widehat{p(\rho = 0|y)} = \frac{\sum_{r=1}^{R} p\left(\rho = 0|y, \beta^{(r)}, h^{(r)}\right)}{R},$$

an average of the *conditional posterior ordinates* at $\rho = 0$. This approaches $p(\rho = 0|y)$ as $R \to \infty$ by the law of large numbers. Calculation of the ordinate in this way is feasible in this example, since implementation of the Gibbs sampler assumes that the conditional distribution $\rho|\beta, h, y$ is known, at least up to proportionality. However, the Savage–Dickey density ratio calculation requires you to know the complete density and not just its posterior kernel. Specifically, to implement this procedure we need to know the full density

$$p\left(\rho|y, \beta, h\right) = \frac{\phi\left(\rho|\overline{\rho}, \overline{V}_{\rho}\right) 1\left(\rho \in \Phi\right)}{\int_{-1}^{1} \phi\left(\rho|\overline{\rho}, \overline{V}_{\rho}\right) d\rho},$$

which requires evaluation of the integrating constant in the denominator. This, however, can be easily calculated since $p\left(\rho|y, \beta, h\right)$ is a univariate truncated normal and the properties of this density are easily evaluated in any relevant software program. To calculate the denominator in our expression for the Bayes factor, one needs to obtain the *prior ordinate* at zero, which, again, can be easily calculated from the univariate truncated normal density.
(c) To illustrate Bayesian inference in the normal regression model with autocorrelated errors, we use a data set pertaining to baseball. (You can use this data set, YANKEES.TXT, or one of your own, or artificially generate data.) The dependent variable is the winning percentage of the New York Yankees baseball team every year between 1903 and 1999. Interest centers on explaining the Yankees performance using various measures of team offensive and defensive performance. Thus,

$$\begin{aligned}
y_t &= \text{winning percentage (PCT) in year } t = \text{wins}/(\text{wins} + \text{losses}) \\
x_{t2} &= \text{team on-base percentage (OBP) in year } t \\
x_{t3} &= \text{team slugging average (SLG) in year } t \\
x_{t4} &= \text{team earned run average (ERA) in year } t.
\end{aligned}$$

We will use a non-informative prior for β and set $\underline{V}^{-1} = 0_{k \times k}$. We will also use a non-informative prior for the error precision and set $\underline{\nu} = 0$. With these choices, the values of $\underline{\beta}$ and $\underline{s}^{-2}$ are irrelevant. The informative prior for ρ we use sets $\underline{\rho} = 0$ and $\underline{V}_{\rho} = cI_p$.

Table 12.6: Posterior results for β.

	Mean	Standard deviation	95% HPDI
β_1	0.01	0.07	$[-0.11, 0.12]$
β_2	1.09	0.35	$[0.52, 1.66]$
β_3	1.54	0.18	$[1.24, 1.83]$
β_4	-0.12	0.01	$[-0.13, -0.10]$

Table 12.7: Posterior results for ρ.

	Mean	Standard deviation	95% HPDI	Bayes factor for $\rho_1 = 0$
$c = 0.01$	0.10	0.07	$[-0.02, 0.23]$	0.49
$c = 0.09$	0.20	0.10	$[0.03, 0.36]$	0.43
$c = 0.25$	0.21	0.11	$[0.04, 0.39]$	0.56
$c = 1.0$	0.22	0.11	$[0.05, 0.40]$	0.74
$c = 100$	0.22	0.11	$[0.05, 0.40]$	0.84

The posterior simulator is described in part (a) of this exercise and MATLAB code is provided on the website associated with this book. All results are based on 30 000 replications, with 5000 burn-in replications discarded and 25 000 replications retained.

Table 12.6 presents posterior results for β with $c = 0.09$, a reasonably small value reflecting a prior belief that autocorrelation in the errors is fairly small (i.e., the prior standard deviation of ρ is 0.3). It can be seen that OBP and SLG are positively associated and ERA is negatively associated with winning.

Table 12.7 contains results from the prior sensitivity analysis where various values of c are used. This table reveals that prior information has little effect on the posterior, unless prior information is extremely strong as in the $c = 0.01$ case. This can be seen by noting that posterior means, standard deviations, and HPDIs are almost the same for all values of c between 0.09 and 100. The latter is a very large value, which, to all intents and purposes, implies that the prior is flat and non-informative over the stationary region. The Bayes factors are also fairly robust to changes in the prior. It is worth noting that this robustness of the Bayes factor in part has to do with the fact that the prior is truncated to a bounded interval – the stationary region. We remind the reader of problems associated with Bayes factors when non-informative improper priors are used on parameters whose support is unbounded (see, e.g., Chapter 10, Exercise 10.4).

Exercise 12.16 (Moving average errors) In Exercise 12.15 we studied a time series model in which the errors follow an AR(1) process. A popular alternative is the following moving average process of order 1 or MA(1):

$$\epsilon_t = \psi\epsilon_{t-1} + u_t.$$

We assume $u_t \stackrel{iid}{\sim} N(0, h^{-1})$ and that the error process is invertible: $|\psi| < 1$. For simplicity we assume $\epsilon_0 = 0$. This MA(1) process implies a very different autocovariance structure compared to the AR(1) process. Specifically, only the covariance between consecutive errors is non-zero: $\text{cov}(\epsilon_t, \epsilon_{t-1}) = \psi h^{-1}$ and $\text{cov}(\epsilon_t, \epsilon_{t-s}) = 0$ for $s \geq 2$.

For the new MA(1) parameter in this model assume a prior of the form

$$p(\psi) \propto \phi(\psi; \underline{\psi}, \underline{V}_\psi)I(|\psi| < 1), \tag{12.45}$$

where $I(|\psi| < 1)$ is the indicator function that equals one if $|\psi| < 1$ and zero otherwise.
(a) Given the priors in (12.10), (12.11), (12.12), and (12.45), derive the full posterior conditionals for this model.
(b) The full conditional of ψ is not a standard distribution. Describe how one can use the griddy Gibbs sampler of Ritter and Tanner (1992) to approximately draw from this distribution.
(c) Using the results from parts (a) and (b), carry out a Bayesian analysis using a suitable time series data set. You may use the same baseball data set in Exercise 12.15 (available on the website associated with this book as YANKEES.TXT). Find the Bayes factor in favor of $\psi = 0$ using the Savage–Dickey density ratio.

Solution

(a) Following the approach in Exercise 12.15, we first transform the regression so that the transformed errors satisfy the classical assumptions (see also Chib and Greenberg 1994). To that end, write the regression model in matrix form as follows:

$$y = X\beta + \epsilon, \tag{12.46}$$

$$\epsilon = H_\psi u, \tag{12.47}$$

where $\epsilon = (\epsilon_1, \ldots, \epsilon_T)'$, $u = (u_1, \ldots, u_T)'$, and

$$H_\psi = \begin{pmatrix} 1 & 0 & 0 & \cdots & 0 \\ \psi & 1 & 0 & \cdots & 0 \\ 0 & \psi & 1 & \cdots & 0 \\ \vdots & & & \ddots & \vdots \\ 0 & 0 & \cdots & \psi & 1 \end{pmatrix}.$$

Since H_ψ is a square matrix with unit determinant (hence non-zero), it is invertible. Multiply both sides of (12.46) by H_ψ^{-1} and define $y^* = H_\psi^{-1}y$ and $X^* = H_\psi^{-1}X$. We therefore obtain

$$y^* = X^*\beta + u, \tag{12.48}$$

where $u \sim N(0, h^{-1}I_T)$ with I_T being the T-dimensional identity matrix. One can compute y^* and X^* efficiently without obtaining the inverse H_ψ^{-1}. See, e.g., Chan (2013) and the discussions in Chapter 18 for computational details.

The transformed regression in (12.48) has exactly the same form as that in Exercise 12.15; the only difference is the construction of X^* and y^*. Therefore, the full conditionals of β and h have exactly the same form as before. Lastly, given the prior $p(\psi)$ in (12.45), the full conditional of ψ is

$$p(\psi|y, \beta, h) \propto p(y|\beta, h, \psi)p(\psi). \tag{12.49}$$

The Kalman filter is typically used to evaluate the likelihood $p(y|\beta, h, \psi)$. However, this can be done more efficiently by using the transformed system (12.48). More specifically, given ψ, y, and X, we first compute $y^* = H_\psi^{-1}y$ and $X^* = H_\psi^{-1}X$. Then we use (12.48) to obtain the density

$$p(y|\beta, h, \psi) = (2\pi h^{-1})^{-T/2} e^{-\frac{h}{2}(y^* - X^*\beta)'(y^* - X^*\beta)}.$$

(b) The density $p(\psi|y, \beta, h)$ is non-standard, but it has bounded support in $(-1, 1)$ and can be evaluated efficiently as discussed in part (a). Hence, we can apply the griddy Gibbs sampler – which is simply a finite approximation of the inverse transform method discussed in Exercise 11.4 – to approximately draw from this distribution. To apply the griddy Gibbs sampler, we first evaluate the (unnormalized) density $p(\psi|y, \beta, h)$ on a fine grid from -1 to 1. Then we normalize the density and construct the associated cdf, denoted as $F(\psi|y, \beta, h)$, on the grid. Finally, we draw U uniformly from 0 to 1, and return the smallest grid point ψ_U such that $F(\psi_U|y, \beta, h) > U$.

(c) We now fit the normal regression model with moving average errors using the baseball data set. The dependent variable is the winning percentage of the New York Yankees baseball team every year between 1903 and 1999. For the descriptions of the independent variables, see Exercise 12.15.

For hyperparameter values, we set $\underline{\beta} = 0$, $\underline{V}^{-1} = 100I_{k\times k}$, $\underline{\nu} = 0$, $\underline{s}^{-2} = 0.001$, $\underline{\psi} = 0$, and $\underline{V}_\psi = 0.3^2$. The posterior simulator is described in parts (a) and (b) of this exercise, and MATLAB code is provided on the website associated with this book. All results are based on 30 000 replications, with 5000 burn-in replications discarded and 25 000 replications retained.

Table 12.8 presents posterior results for β and ψ. Compared to the results in Exercise 12.15 under the regression with autocorrelated errors, the point estimates of β are almost identical. Moreover, the estimate of the MA(1) coefficient, ψ, is also very close to the estimate of ρ, the AR(1) coefficient.

Finally, we use the Savage–Dickey density ratio to produce the Bayes factor in favor of the hypothesis that $\psi = 0$:

$$B_{12} = \frac{p(\psi = 0|y)}{p(\psi = 0)}.$$

Table 12.8: Posterior results for β and ψ.

	Mean	Standard deviation	95% credible intervals
β_1	0.02	0.07	$[-0.11, 0.15]$
β_2	1.01	0.33	$[0.37, 1.66]$
β_3	1.56	0.17	$[1.22, 1.89]$
β_4	−0.12	0.01	$[-0.13, -0.10]$
ψ	0.17	0.09	$[-0.01, 0.35]$

The Bayes factor is estimated to be 0.54, indicating that the data slightly prefers the MA model compared to the standard regression with independent errors, although the evidence is not strong.

Exercise 12.17 (Gibbs sampling in a regression model with inequality constraints: Geweke (1996b)) Consider the regression model

$$y_i = \beta_0 + \beta_1 x_{i1} + \beta_2 x_{i2} + \cdots + \beta_k x_{ik} + \epsilon_i, \quad i = 1, 2, \ldots, n,$$

where $\epsilon_i \stackrel{iid}{\sim} N(0, \sigma^2)$.

Let $\beta = [\beta_0 \ \beta_1 \ \cdots \ \beta_k]'$. Suppose that the regression coefficients are known to satisfy constraints of the form

$$a < H\beta < b,$$

where a and b are known $(k+1) \times 1$ vectors of lower and upper limits, respectively, and H is a non-singular matrix that selects elements of β to incorporate the known constraints. The vectors a and b may also contain elements equal to $-\infty$ or ∞, respectively, if a particular linear combination of β is not to be bounded from above or below (or both). Thus, in this formulation of the model, we are capable of imposing up to $k + 1$ inequality restrictions, but no more.

(a) Reparameterize the model in terms of $\gamma = H\beta$, introduce a prior for γ, and provide a posterior simulator for the reparameterized model.

(b) Consider, as a special case of the regression model in part (a), the Cobb–Douglas production function where

$$\ln y_i = \beta_0 + \beta_1 \ln L_i + \beta_2 \ln K_i + \epsilon_i,$$

with y_i denoting output, L_i denoting labor, and K_i denoting capital. How would you impose that the production function satisfies diminishing returns to scale?

(c) Using the output, capital, and labor data presented on the website associated with this book (with 39 annual observations for the cigarette industry from 1958 to 1996), fit the Cobb–Douglas production function without imposing any inequality constraints. To do

this, employ a diffuse prior on σ^2 of the form $p(\sigma^2) \propto \sigma^{-2}$ and a normal prior for β of the form $\beta \sim N(0, 10I_3)$. Do the data provide evidence of diminishing returns to scale?
(d) Now, reparameterize the model, as in (b), to restrict the production function to satisfy diminishing returns to scale. Fit the model using the algorithm in part (a) under $p(\sigma^2) \propto \sigma^{-2}$. For the regression coefficients, employ independent, truncated $N(0, 10I_3)$ priors, where the regions of truncation for each element of γ are defined as in part (b). How do your results compare to those of part (c)?

Solution

(a) First, write the regression model as

$$y = X\beta + \epsilon,$$

where

$$y = \begin{bmatrix} y_1 \\ y_2 \\ \vdots \\ y_n \end{bmatrix}, \quad X = \begin{bmatrix} 1 & x_{11} & \cdots & x_{1k} \\ 1 & x_{21} & \cdots & x_{2k} \\ \vdots & \vdots & \ddots & \vdots \\ 1 & x_{n1} & \cdots & x_{nk} \end{bmatrix}, \quad \text{and} \quad \epsilon = \begin{bmatrix} \epsilon_1 \\ \epsilon_2 \\ \vdots \\ \epsilon_n \end{bmatrix}.$$

Since $\gamma = H\beta$ and H is non-singular, write $\beta = H^{-1}\gamma$. The reparameterized regression model thus becomes

$$\begin{aligned} y &= XH^{-1}\gamma + \epsilon_i \\ &= \tilde{X}\gamma + \epsilon_i, \end{aligned}$$

with

$$\tilde{X} \equiv XH^{-1} \quad \text{and} \quad a < \gamma < b.$$

In the γ parameterization, note that independent priors can be employed that satisfy the stated inequality restrictions. To this end, we specify independent truncated normal priors for elements of γ of the form

$$p(\gamma_j) \propto \phi(\gamma_j; 0, V_j) I(a_j < \gamma_j < b_j), \quad j = 0, 1, \ldots, k,$$

with $I(\cdot)$ denoting the standard indicator function. The posterior distribution is proportional to the product of the prior and likelihood:

$$p(\gamma, \sigma^2|y) \propto \sigma^{-2} \left[\prod_{j=0}^{k} p(\gamma_j) \right] \phi(y; \tilde{X}\gamma, \sigma^2 I_n).$$

By using the results of Exercise 12.9 (and appropriately accounting for the region of truncation), it follows that the posterior conditional for $\gamma|\sigma^2, y$ takes the following form:

$$p(\gamma|\sigma^2, y) \propto \phi(\gamma; \overline{\gamma}, \overline{H}) I(a < \gamma < b), \tag{12.50}$$

where

$$\overline{H} = (\tilde{X}'\tilde{X}/\sigma_\epsilon^2 + V^{-1})^{-1}, \quad \overline{\gamma} = \overline{H}(\tilde{X}'y/\sigma_\epsilon^2),$$

and V is the $(k+1) \times (k+1)$ diagonal matrix with jth diagonal element equal to V_j.

The density in (12.50) is a multivariate normal density truncated to the regions defined by a and b. Drawing directly from this multivariate truncated normal is non-trivial in general, but as Geweke (1991, 1996b) points out, the posterior conditional distributions $\gamma_j|\gamma_{-j}, \sigma^2, y$ (with γ_{-j} denoting all elements of γ other than γ_j) are univariate truncated normal. Thus, one can change the algorithm of Exercise 12.9 to sample *individually* from each coefficient's conditional posterior (rather than sampling γ in a single step), where each draw is obtained from a univariate truncated normal distribution. Fortunately, such draws can be easily obtained. (See Exercise 11.5 for an efficient procedure for sampling from the univariate truncated normal.)

Let $\Omega = [\overline{H}]^{-1} = \tilde{X}'\tilde{X}/\sigma_\epsilon^2 + V^{-1}$, ω_{ij} denote the (i,j) element of Ω, and $\overline{\gamma}_j$ denote the jth element of $\overline{\gamma}$. Using properties of the conditional normal distribution (see Theorem A.3) and the formula for a partitioned inverse (see Abadir, Heijmans, and Magnus 2006, p. 106), we obtain

$$\gamma_j|\gamma_{-j}, \sigma^2, y \overset{ind}{\sim} TN_{(a_j,b_j)}\left(\overline{\gamma}_j - \omega_{jj}^{-1}\sum_{i \neq j}\omega_{ji}(\gamma_i - \overline{\gamma}_i), \omega_{jj}^{-1}\right), \quad j = 0, 1, \ldots, k, \tag{12.51}$$

where $TN_{(a,b)}(\mu, \sigma^2)$ denotes a normal density with mean μ and variance σ^2 truncated to the interval (a, b).

The derivation of the posterior conditional for the variance parameter utilizes steps similar to those in Exercise 12.9, though in this case an improper prior for σ^2 has been employed. It follows that

$$\sigma^2|\gamma, y \sim IG\left(\frac{n}{2}, \left[\frac{1}{2}(y - \tilde{X}\gamma)'(y - \tilde{X}\gamma)\right]^{-1}\right). \tag{12.52}$$

A Gibbs sampling algorithm for the regression model with linear inequality constraints thus follows by independently sampling from (12.51) for each j and then sampling from (12.52).

(b) It is well known that $\beta_1 + \beta_2$ determines returns to scale. In particular, our production function is characterized by diminishing returns to scale provided $\beta_1 + \beta_2 < 1$.

To impose diminishing returns to scale, yet leave other parameters unrestricted, we can therefore specify

$$\begin{bmatrix} -\infty \\ -\infty \\ -\infty \end{bmatrix} < \begin{bmatrix} 1 & 0 & 0 \\ 0 & 1 & 0 \\ 0 & 1 & 1 \end{bmatrix} \begin{bmatrix} \beta_0 \\ \beta_1 \\ \beta_2 \end{bmatrix} < \begin{bmatrix} \infty \\ \infty \\ 1 \end{bmatrix},$$

and thus a, b, and H are defined accordingly. With these definitions, H^{-1} is simply

$$H^{-1} = \begin{bmatrix} 1 & 0 & 0 \\ 0 & 1 & 0 \\ 0 & -1 & 1 \end{bmatrix},$$

and $\tilde{X}$, the transformed X matrix, has columns equal to a constant, $\ln[L/K]$ and $\ln K$. Similarly,

$$\gamma = \begin{bmatrix} \gamma_0 \\ \gamma_1 \\ \gamma_2 \end{bmatrix} = H\beta = \begin{bmatrix} \beta_0 \\ \beta_1 \\ \beta_1 + \beta_2 \end{bmatrix},$$

and thus γ_2 represents the return to scale in the reparameterized model.
(c and d) On the website associated with this book we provide MATLAB code for fitting the production function model without inequality constraints, as in part (c), and also when imposing that the production function exhibits diminishing returns to scale. In both cases, we make use of the Gibbs sampler to fit the model. When no constraints are imposed, we run the simulator for 3000 iterations, discarding the first 1000 as the burn-in. When constraints are imposed, as in part (d), we run the sampler for 105 000 iterations and discard the first 5000 as the burn-in. In the latter case, our posterior simulations suffer from high degrees of autocorrelation. We retain every 50th draw from this algorithm and thus obtain a final posterior sample of 2000 simulations. (Note in this case that γ_0 and γ_1 could be drawn jointly in our posterior simulator to gain efficiency.) For the constrained simulator, OLS estimates are used as starting values.

Presented in Figure 12.6 are posterior frequencies associated with the return-to-scale parameter in the unconstrained and constrained models. For the model in part (c), which does not require a reparameterization, the figure plots a histogram of $\beta_1 + \beta_2$, and for the model in part (d), an analogous histogram for γ_2 is provided. In the unconstrained case, which is presented in the lower half of the figure, the return-to-scale posterior places only very small mass on values exceeding one. Thus, our data lend support to the hypothesis of decreasing returns to scale. In the top portion of the figure, which formally imposes decreasing returns to scale through our prior, no mass is placed to the right of one. The fact that both figures possess similar shapes should not be regarded as surprising, since the data appear to support the hypothesis of decreasing returns to scale.

Exercise 12.18 (Gibbs sampling in the SUR model) Consider a two-equation version of the seemingly unrelated regression (SUR) model (Zellner 1962):

$$y_{i1} = x_{i1}\beta_1 + \epsilon_{i1},$$
$$y_{i2} = x_{i2}\beta_2 + \epsilon_{i2},$$

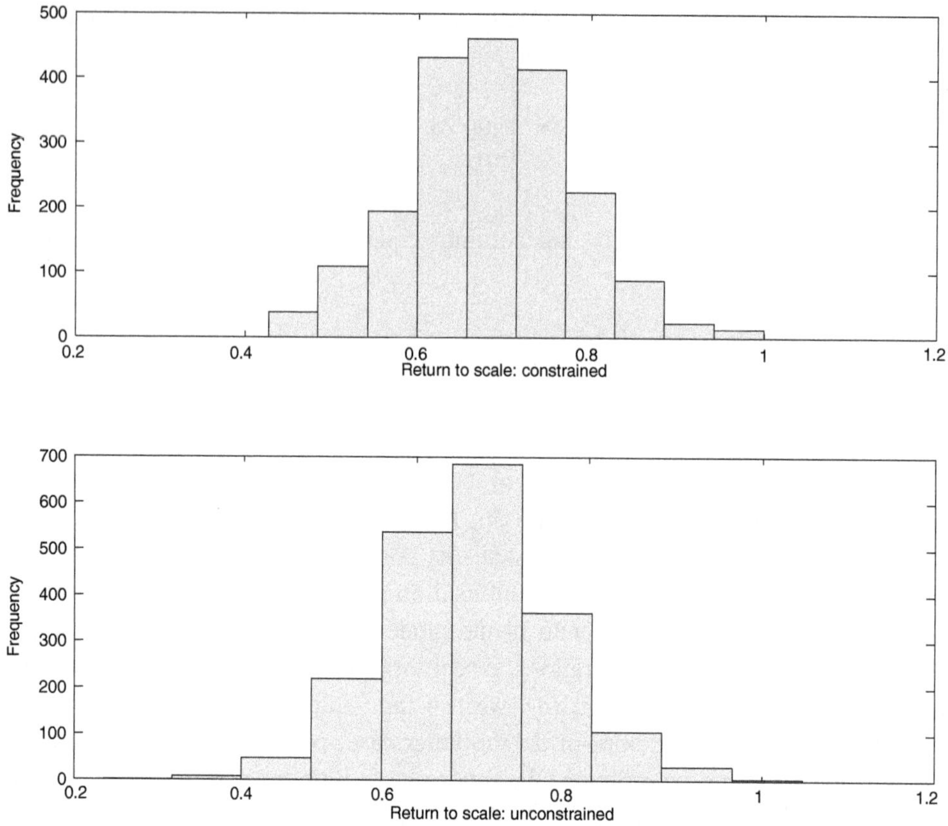

Figure 12.6. Posterior histograms for return-to-scale parameter in constrained (upper) and unconstrained (lower) models.

where

$$\epsilon_i = [\epsilon_{i1}\ \epsilon_{i2}]'|X \overset{iid}{\sim} N(0, \Sigma), \quad i = 1, 2, \ldots, n,$$

x_{i1} and x_{i2} are $1 \times k_1$ and $1 \times k_2$, respectively, and

$$\Sigma \equiv \begin{bmatrix} \sigma_1^2 & \sigma_{12} \\ \sigma_{12} & \sigma_2^2 \end{bmatrix}.$$

Suppose you employ priors of the form

$$\beta = [\beta_1'\ \beta_2']' \sim N(\mu_\beta, V_\beta)$$

and

$$\Sigma^{-1} \sim W(\Omega, \nu),$$

where W denotes a Wishart distribution (see Definition A.6 for a more detailed description of the Wishart).

(a) Derive a posterior simulator for fitting this two-equation SUR model.
(b) Conduct an experiment by first generating $n = 2500$ draws from the model

$$y_{i1} = 1 + .3x_{i1} + \epsilon_{i1},$$
$$y_{i2} = 2 - .7x_{i2} + \epsilon_{i2},$$

with

$$\Sigma = \begin{bmatrix} .5 & -.45\sqrt{.5}\sqrt{.3} \\ -.45\sqrt{.5}\sqrt{.3} & .3 \end{bmatrix}$$

and $x_{ij} \stackrel{iid}{\sim} N(0,1)$. Written in this way, the correlation between ϵ_1 and ϵ_2 is $-.45$.

Using the hyperparameters $\mu_\beta = 0_4$, $V_\beta = 1000I_4$, $\Omega = I_4$, and $\nu = 4$, fit the generated data using the results in part (a). Compare parameter posterior means to the parameter values used to generate the data.

Solution

(a) First, note that the likelihood function can be expressed as

$$L(\beta, \Sigma) = \prod_{i=1}^{n} (2\pi)^{-1} |\Sigma|^{-1/2} \exp\left(-\frac{1}{2} \sum_{i=1}^{n} (\tilde{y}_i - \tilde{X}_i\beta)'\Sigma^{-1}(\tilde{y}_i - \tilde{X}_i\beta) \right),$$

where

$$\tilde{y}_i = [y_{i1} \; y_{i2}],' \quad \tilde{X}_i = \begin{bmatrix} x_{i1} & 0 \\ 0 & x_{i2} \end{bmatrix},$$

and $\tilde{X}_i$ is $2 \times (k_1 + k_2)$. Combining this likelihood function with the Wishart prior for Σ^{-1}, we obtain the following posterior conditional distribution (Exercise 13.3 will provide full details of the steps involved with this derivation):

$$\Sigma^{-1}|\beta, y \sim W\left[\left(\Omega^{-1} + \sum_{i=1}^{n} (\tilde{y}_i - \tilde{X}_i\beta)(\tilde{y}_i - \tilde{X}_i\beta)' \right)^{-1}, n + \nu \right].$$

Alternatively, stacking the SUR model as

$$y = X\beta + \epsilon,$$

where

$$y = [y_1' \; y_2']', \quad X = \begin{bmatrix} X_1 & 0 \\ 0 & X_2 \end{bmatrix}, \quad \epsilon = [\epsilon_1' \; \epsilon_2'],'$$

and y_j, X_j, and ϵ_j have been stacked over i for $j = 1, 2$, we obtain the following complete posterior conditional for β:

$$\beta|\Sigma, y \sim N(D_\beta d_\beta, D_\beta),$$

where

$$D_\beta = \left(X'(\Sigma^{-1} \otimes I_N)X + V_\beta^{-1}\right)^{-1}$$

and

$$d_\beta = X'(\Sigma^{-1} \otimes I_N)y + V_\beta^{-1}\mu_\beta.$$

We implement our posterior simulator by first sampling from the posterior conditional for β and then sampling from the conditional for Σ^{-1}. We also note that similar derivations would apply for a SUR model with more than two equations.
(b) We fit the model by cycling though the posterior conditionals derived in part (a). For the elements of the parameter vector β, we obtain posterior means equal to 1.00, .294, 1.99, and $-.706$, and the values used to generate the data were 1, .3, 2, and $-.7$, respectively. The true values of σ_1^2, σ_2^2, and ρ_{12} were .5, .3, and $-.45$, and we obtain posterior means for these quantities equal to .502, .300, and $-.432$, respectively. Thus, our posterior simulator performs well at recovering the parameters used to generate these data.

12.4 Diagnostic Checking with MCMC

Exercise 12.19 (Error diagnostics with Gibbs sampling) Consider the simple regression model

$$y_i = \beta_0 + \beta_1 x_i + \epsilon_i, \quad \epsilon_i \overset{iid}{\sim} N(0, \sigma^2).$$

As an applied researcher, you are concerned that the assumption of normal errors may not be appropriate for your given application.
(a) Suggest some possible diagnostics that one could use (given simulated output from the posterior) to investigate whether the data are at odds with the normality assumption.
(b) Now generate 2000 observations from this simple regression model with $\beta_0 = 1$, $\beta_1 = .5$, and $x_i \overset{iid}{\sim} N(0,1)$. Do this for three different cases. In the first case, generate the errors from a normal density with $\sigma^2 = .4$. In the second case, generate the errors from a uniform density over the interval $[-5, 5]$. In the final case, generate the errors from a $\chi^2(5)$ density. (In this final case, you may want to subtract 5 from each simulated error so that the resulting errors are centered over zero.) Fit each model using the Gibbs sampler (see Exercise 12.9) and perform the diagnostics suggested in part (a) to investigate whether normality is appropriate for each data set.

Solution
(a) There are numerous ways one could examine whether the normality assumption is appropriate. An intuitive idea is to compare known features of the normal density to the

posterior distribution of those features that are implied by the model. For example, if the errors are truly normal, then the error *skewness*

$$\frac{E(\epsilon^3)}{[E(\epsilon^2)]^{(3/2)}}$$

is equal to zero (i.e., the distribution is symmetric about zero), and the error *kurtosis*

$$\frac{E(\epsilon^4)}{[E(\epsilon^2)]^2}$$

equals 3. In terms of our model, we might approximate the first of these quantities as

$$\text{skewness} \approx \frac{(1/n)\sum_{i=1}^{n}(y_i - \beta_0 - \beta_1 x_i)^3}{(\sigma^2)^{(3/2)}},$$

and, similarly,

$$\text{kurtosis} \approx \frac{(1/n)\sum_{i=1}^{n}(y_i - \beta_0 - \beta_1 x_i)^4}{(\sigma^2)^{(2)}}.$$

Both of these expressions are functions of the model parameters (and data), and thus we can summarize the posterior distributions associated with these quantities. (For each draw from the posterior, we calculate skewness and kurtosis as shown here. We collect these draws for each iteration of the posterior simulator and then use this collection of values to calculate posterior means, posterior standard deviations, etc.) If we were to find that the posterior distribution of skewness, for example, was centered away from zero, or that the kurtosis posterior placed little mass near 3, we would find evidence against the normality assumption.

Other possibilities for diagnostic checking include the QQ plot (e.g., Lancaster 2004, p. 148) or calculating posterior predictive p-values. The posterior predictive p-value essentially quantifies how reliably actual features of the data density y can be replicated by generating artificial data from the predictive density of the model, and then calculating those same features using simulated output from the posterior predictive. See, for example, Koop (2003, pp. 100–104) for more discussion of posterior predictive p-values.

(b) Data are generated as stated in part (b) of this exercise. For each model, we run the Gibbs sampler for 2000 iterations, discarding the first 200 as the burn-in period. For each of the 1800 post-convergence draws for each model under consideration, we calculate skewness and kurtosis as in the solution to part (a). We plot the posterior densities of these quantities in Figure 12.7.

As you can see from the figure, when the errors are generated from a normal density, the skewness posterior is approximately centered over zero and the kurtosis posterior is concentrated over values near 3. Based on this evidence, we would not be able to conclude that normality was inappropriate, and thus we would likely proceed with the normal model. When the errors are generated from a uniform density, the skewness posterior is again centered near zero (since the errors remain symmetric), but the kurtosis value is clearly

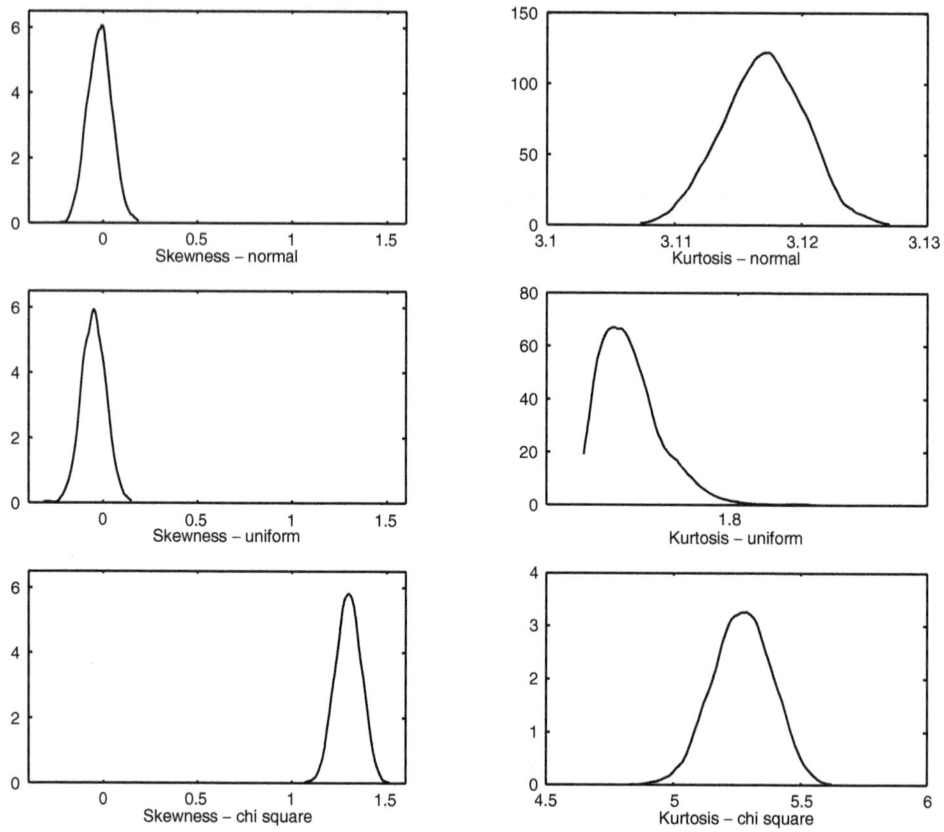

Figure 12.7. Posterior densities of skewness and kurtosis for three different experimental designs.

bounded away from 3. For the χ^2 case, we see that the skewness posterior is concentrated over positive values, which is sensible given that the $\chi^2(5)$ has a pronounced right tail, with a kurtosis clearly larger than 3. These results suggest that normality is not an appropriate assumption for these data sets. In cases such as these, the researcher may wish to expand the model to include more flexible classes of error distributions. We discuss alternatives for doing this in the exercises of Chapter 15.

Exercise 12.20 (Calculating numerical standard errors with Gibbs sampling) Consider a set of m *correlated* draws from the posterior of a scalar parameter θ, and denote these draws as $\{\theta_i\}_{i=1}^m$. Suppose that $\text{Var}(\theta_i) = \sigma^2 \; \forall i$ and $\text{Cov}(\theta_j, \theta_{j-k}) = \sigma_k \; \forall j, k$. In Gibbs sampling, we typically report a point estimate (posterior mean) of θ of the form

$$\overline{\theta} = \frac{1}{m}\sum_{i=1}^{m} \theta_i.$$

What is the *numerical standard error* associated with $\overline{\theta}$?

Solution

We note that

$$\begin{aligned}
\text{Var}\left(\overline{\theta}\right) &= \frac{1}{m^2}\text{Var}\left(\sum_i \theta_i\right) \\
&= \frac{1}{m^2}\text{Var}\left(\theta_1 + [\theta_2 + \theta_3 + \cdots + \theta_m]\right) \\
&= \frac{1}{m^2}\left[\text{Var}(\theta_1) + 2\text{Cov}(\theta_1, \theta_2 + \cdots + \theta_m) + \text{Var}(\theta_2 + \cdots + \theta_m)\right] \\
&= \frac{1}{m^2}\left[\sigma^2 + 2\left(\sigma_1 + \sigma_2 + \cdots + \sigma_{m-1}\right) + \text{Var}(\theta_2 + \cdots + \theta_m)\right].
\end{aligned}$$

Applying the same type of argument to the sum $\theta_2 + \cdots + \theta_m$ in the last part of this final equality, we obtain

$$\text{Var}(\theta_2 + \cdots + \theta_m) = \sigma^2 + 2\left(\sigma_1 + \sigma_2 + \cdots + \sigma_{m-2}\right) + \text{Var}(\theta_3 + \cdots + \theta_m).$$

Continuing in this fashion, and grouping together the resulting terms, we obtain

$$\text{Var}(\overline{\theta}) = \frac{1}{m^2}\left(m\sigma^2 + 2\left[(m-1)\sigma_1 + (m-2)\sigma_2 + \cdots + \sigma_{m-1}\right]\right).$$

Factoring out an $m\sigma^2$ from this expression, we obtain

$$\begin{aligned}
\text{Var}(\overline{\theta}) &= \frac{1}{m^2}m\sigma^2\left(1 + 2\left[\frac{(m-1)\sigma_1}{m\sigma^2} + \frac{(m-2)\sigma_2}{m\sigma^2} + \cdots + \frac{\sigma_{m-1}}{m\sigma^2}\right]\right) \\
&= \frac{\sigma^2}{m}\left[1 + 2\sum_{j=1}^{m-1}\left(\frac{m-j}{m}\right)\frac{\sigma_j}{\sigma^2}\right] \\
&= \frac{\sigma^2}{m}\left[1 + 2\sum_{j=1}^{m-1}\left(1 - \frac{j}{m}\right)\rho_j\right],
\end{aligned}$$

where $\rho_j \equiv \sigma_j/\sigma^2$ is a measure of the correlation (i.e., the *lag correlation*) between θ_i and θ_{i-j}.

This expression provides a way for researchers to calculate *numerical standard errors*, or NSEs, associated with a Gibbs sampling estimate of a posterior moment of interest. Given the derivation here, we have

$$\text{NSE}(\overline{\theta}) = \sqrt{\frac{\sigma^2}{m}\left[1 + 2\sum_{j=1}^{m-1}\left(1 - \frac{j}{m}\right)\rho_j\right]}. \tag{12.53}$$

Note that ρ_j can be calculated from the draws themselves by simply computing the correlation coefficient between the vectors $[\theta_1\ \theta_2\ \cdots\ \theta_{m-j}]$ and $[\theta_{j+1}\ \theta_{j+2}\ \cdots\ \theta_m]$. In practice, the summation in the NSE calculation is usually "cut off" when the lag correlations fall below a certain threshold, such as .05 or .01. Also note that if the $\rho_j > 0$, as is typically the case in Gibbs sampling, then $\text{Var}(\overline{\theta}) > \sigma^2/m$, the variance obtained under *iid* sampling.

Note that the term in square brackets in (12.53), $\left[1 + 2\sum_{j=1}^{m-1}\left(1 - \frac{j}{m}\right)\rho_j\right]$, represents an *inefficiency factor*. Since $\sqrt{\sigma^2/m}$ would represent the standard error of the mean estimator under an *iid* sample of size m, the inefficiency factor serves as a diagnostic tool to quantify how much is lost relative to this standard. Alternatively,

$$m\left[1 + 2\sum_{j=1}^{m-1}\left(1 - \frac{j}{m}\right)\rho_j\right]^{-1}$$

can be thought of as an *effective sample size* since it equates the precision of the MCMC-based estimate to the precision that would have been obtained under that number of *iid* simulations from the target distribution.

Finally, it is worth mentioning that, unlike frequentist standard errors, the numerical standard errors here can be made arbitrarily small by choosing m sufficiently large (i.e., taking enough draws from the posterior). The degree of precision with which the (finite-sample) posterior mean is estimated is not a function of the size of the data set, but rather is a function of the number of simulations taken from the posterior.

Exercise 12.21 (Diagnosing MCMC convergence I) Many of the exercises of this chapter have described Gibbs sampling routines for estimating the parameters of various linear models. These questions typically walked the reader through the steps of deriving conditional posterior distributions in a variety of different situations, yet left the reader with a somewhat incomplete sense of how to take those results to the data. While we know that the derived conditional distributions are to be sampled sequentially, and this process is to be repeated over and over again, what is specifically meant by "over and over" remains unclear, and the length of the burn-in period may seem similarly elusive.

In our experience, practitioners sometimes (perhaps often) proceed by generating what would seem to be a very large number of simulations, and discard a large number of those (say, 10 000 to 50 000) as the burn-in. When many simulations are generated in this way, it would seem likely that the influence of the initial conditions has effectively been eliminated, and the chain should have had sufficient time to converge. While this "seems-to-be-a-big-enough-number" approach may placate referees and work reasonably well in many cases (particularly in standard models), it is certainly possible that errors remain when following this strategy. Specifically, (i) the code may contain a mistake, or several mistakes: when running the posterior simulator, everything can appear to "work," but the chain may have converged to something other than the target distribution; and (ii) there may be an identification problem or near-identification problem resulting in the sampler's failure to converge, even with a very large number of simulations. As an example, Chan and Tobias (2015) consider a treatment–response model with an imperfect instrument, where *billions* of simulations would be required in order to achieve a desired numerical standard error for the estimated posterior mean.

What we describe in this exercise is a suggested first pass at checking the accuracy of one's code and diagnosing when the sampler appears to have converged. The exercises that follow this one provide additional checks, culminating in a formal test provided by Geweke (2004) for the accuracy of a posterior simulator. The procedure described here is not a formal test, but we believe it represents good practice and a useful first step in that direction. The recommended procedure is as follows:

1. Generate a "reasonably large" data set from the model you seek to estimate. Note that when doing so, you will assign "true" values to the parameters of that model.
2. Apply your Gibbs sampling / MCMC code to this generated data set. Obtain parameter posterior means and standard deviations. Do this several different times, each time starting from a different set of beginning parameter values. Choose these initial parameter values to be quite different from one another and "overdispersed" with respect to where you expect the marginal posteriors might concentrate.
3. To assess the speed of convergence, plot the paths of the different MCMC chains on a single graph. Do this for a selection of different parameters of the model. When these *trace plots* for each chain settle down and explore the same region of the parameter space, you might interpret that as evidence of convergence, thus providing you with a sense of a reasonable burn-in period when you take your code to actual (i.e., non-generated) data.
4. Compare the results of the trace plots, parameter posterior means, and standard deviations to the true values used to generate the data. If posterior means and true values are "close" (and the priors are reasonably non-informative), this provides suggestive evidence that the code is error free and the algorithm appears to perform well.
5. Repeat the process a few different times, each time changing the true parameter values, data set, and initial conditions. If results consistently point toward agreement between posterior means and true values, and a consistent pattern of convergence, proceed to the formal tests described in the next exercises. We also note that Cowles and Carlin (1996) surveyed a variety of different convergence critera beyond those discussed here, and the reader is referred to that reference for additional suggestions.

Generate data from a simple regression model, as in Exercise 12.9. Your model will contain three different parameters: an intercept, a slope coefficient, and a variance parameter. Apply the Gibbs sampler to this generated data three different times (corresponding to three different overdispersed starting values). Provide trace plots of all three chains on a single graph, and do this for each of the three parameters of the model. Summarize the results you obtain.

Solution

MATLAB code for this exercise is provided on the website associated with this book. In our code, we set the variance parameter equal to .5, the intercept equal to -1, and the slope

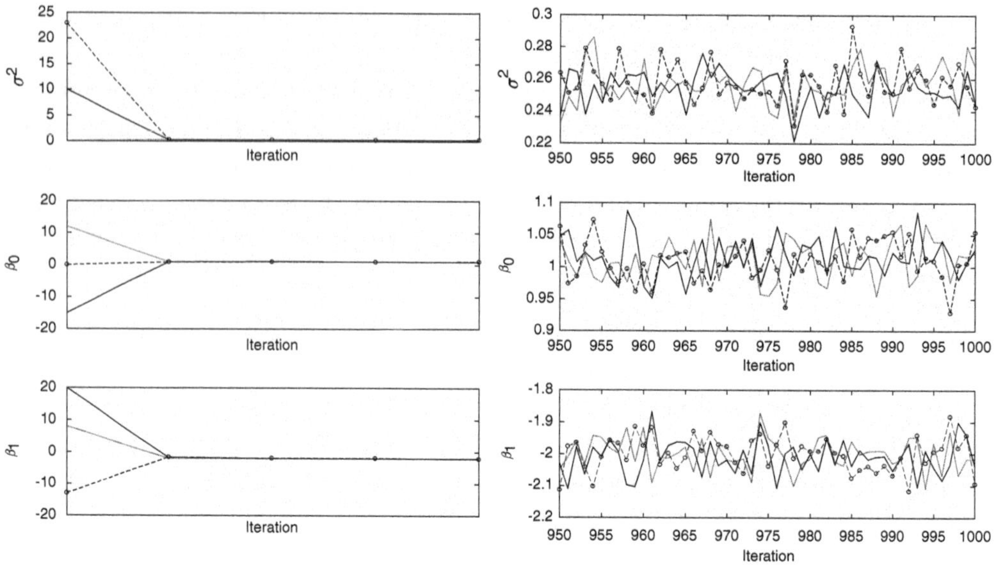

Figure 12.8. Trace plots of three regression parameters.

equal to 2 when generating the data. We generate 1000 observations and run the sampler for 1000 iterations, using the priors $\beta \sim N(0, 100I_2)$ and $\sigma^2 \sim IG(3, .5)$. For the initial conditions we started one chain with $\sigma^2 = 10$, a second chain with $\sigma^2 = .01$, and a final chain with $\sigma^2 = 23$. We also selected dispersed starting values for the intercept and slope coefficients; these choices are largely irrelevant, however, as the first step in our sampler is to draw the vector β, and thus only the σ^2 initial condition informs the progression of our chains.

Trace plots are provided in Figure 12.8. The left column of the figure plots the simulated values of the three parameters across the three different chains. This is done for the first five iterations of the sampler. What you can see from this left column is that the three chains start out at very different places but then converge quickly and explore the same area; given that the starting values are quite dispersed, and the left columns have a "zoomed out" perspective as a consequence, the three chains appear to form a common straight line after the second iteration. This suggests very rapid convergence. The right-hand column of the graph again plots the paths of the three chains for each of the three parameters, but this time for the final 50 of our 1000 simulations. Here you can see that the chains have settled down to explore the same area and appear to fluctuate around the values of the parameters that were used to generate the data. In summary, convergence in this application appears to happen very quickly – within just a few iterations – and we find no obvious evidence of an error in our code, given that our marginal posteriors are seen to concentrate around the "true" parameter values. (We did not repeat the process here by changing the true values and regenerating our data set, although doing so produces similar evidence of good performance.) The more formal procedures described in the following two exercises can also be used to diagnose convergence and to help uncover bugs in one's code.

Exercise 12.22 (Diagnosing MCMC convergence II: Zellner and Min (1995)) Zellner and Min (1995) describe a simple test for the convergence of a two-block Gibbs sampler, such as the regression model in Exercise 12.9, when the normalizing constants of the conditional posterior distributions are known.

To understand their approach, first suppose that the parameter vector can be decomposed into two potentially multivariate blocks, and denote these as α and β. Furthermore, pick two pairs of points in the parameter space, and call these pairs $(\alpha^{(j)}, \beta^{(j)})$, $j = 1, 2$. Since

$$p(\alpha, \beta|y) \propto p(\alpha, \beta)L(\alpha, \beta),$$

it follows that

$$\theta_{12} \equiv \frac{p(\alpha^{(1)}, \beta^{(1)}|y)}{p(\alpha^{(2)}, \beta^{(2)}|y)} = \frac{p(\alpha^{(1)}, \beta^{(1)})L(\alpha^{(1)}, \beta^{(1)})}{p(\alpha^{(2)}, \beta^{(2)})L(\alpha^{(2)}, \beta^{(2)})}.$$

That is, the (likely unknown) normalizing constant of the joint posterior cancels in the ratio. Thus, θ_{12} can be calculated exactly.

Describe how θ_{12} can also be estimated via the MCMC output, and describe how this can be used to test for the convergence of the posterior simulator.

Solution

Begin by noting that θ_{12} can also be calculated via a marginal/conditional factorization:

$$\theta_{12} = \frac{p(\alpha^{(1)}|\beta^{(1)}, y)p(\beta^{(1)}|y)}{p(\alpha^{(2)}|\beta^{(2)}, y)p(\beta^{(2)}|y)}.$$

(The choice to work with the conditional for α and marginal for β is arbitrary, and the order could be reversed.) By assumption, the conditional posterior distribution $\alpha|\beta, y$ is known, including its normalizing constant, and thus can be calculated exactly. The ordinates of the marginal posterior, however, must be estimated. This can be done as follows:

$$\widehat{p(\beta^{(j)}|y)} = \frac{1}{N}\sum_{i=1}^{N} p\left(\beta^{(j)}|\alpha = \alpha_i, y\right), \quad j = 1, 2,$$

where N represents the number of post-convergence simulations, and α_i is the ith such simulation. It follows that

$$\hat{\theta}_{12} = \frac{p(\alpha^{(1)}|\beta^{(1)}, y)\sum_{i=1}^{N} p\left(\beta^{(1)}|\alpha = \alpha_i, y\right)}{p(\alpha^{(2)}|\beta^{(2)}, y)\sum_{i=1}^{N} p\left(\beta^{(2)}|\alpha = \alpha_i, y\right)}.$$

If the MCMC algorithm has converged and is coded correctly, then $\hat{\theta}_{12}$ should be close to θ_{12} for all pairs of points selected. When these differ, either the code may be incorrect or the sampler has not yet converged.

Exercise 12.23 (Checking for errors in a posterior simulator: Geweke (2004)) Even the most careful researcher can make mistakes when programming a posterior simulator. A reasonably comprehensive way to avoid (or at least significantly limit) such problems is to apply the posterior simulator to a large artificial data set that is generated from the model under consideration. In such a case, the parameters of the data-generating process are known and point estimates (e.g., posterior means) can be compared to the "true" parameter values used to generate the data. If the point estimates are far from the "true" parameters, even under reasonably diffuse priors and with a large data set, this suggests that a programming error may have occurred (or, potentially, this reveals a type of identification problem). Conversely, when agreement is reached between estimates and actual values under a variety of different experimental designs (i.e., upon changing the "true" parameters' values), this provides support, though not proof, that the code is error free.

Geweke (2004) provides a more formal procedure for testing a posterior simulator, and the intent of this exercise is to review and apply this technique. We stress that the method that follows can be used to check the accuracy of *any* posterior simulator and is not limited only to those models that make use of Gibbs sampling. We have chosen to include this exercise in the Gibbs sampling section simply because we employ the Gibbs sampler in our generated-data experiment of part (b).

Let $p(y, \theta)$ be a joint density of observables y and unobservables θ, and consider two alternate strategies for simulating from this joint density.

The first approach, termed the *marginal-conditional simulator*, follows from the method of composition. That is, obtain draws $\theta^{(m)}$ and $y^{(m)}$ from the joint distribution $p(y, \theta)$ by drawing

$$\theta^{(m)} \sim p(\theta), \tag{12.54}$$

$$y^{(m)} \sim p(y|\theta = \theta^{(m)}), \tag{12.55}$$

where $p(\theta)$ denotes the prior and $p(y|\theta)$ the data density.

As an alternative, consider the *successive-conditional simulator*, defined as follows:

$$\tilde{y}^{(m)} \sim p(y|\theta = \tilde{\theta}^{(m-1)}), \tag{12.56}$$

$$\tilde{\theta}^{(m)} \sim q(\theta|\tilde{\theta}^{(m-1)}, \tilde{y}^{(m)}). \tag{12.57}$$

Here, q generically represents the *transition kernel* of a posterior simulator. For example, if a Gibbs sampler is employed, then q represents the conditional distributions corresponding to each element of the (potentially blocked) parameter vector. Thus, in the successive-conditional simulator, the spirit is to apply the Gibbs sampler to aid in sampling from $p(y, \theta)$ – first drawing from $y|\theta$, and then drawing from $\theta|y$ (as a posterior simulator is designed to do). Importantly, the successive-conditional simulator requires a starting value $\tilde{\theta}^{(0)}$, which is obtained from the prior – i.e., $\tilde{\theta}^{(0)} \sim p(\theta)$.

(a) Show how these two distinct simulation approaches can be used to check for errors in a posterior simulator.

(b) Consider the following regression model:

$$y_i = \beta_0 + \beta_1 x_i + \epsilon_i, \;\; x_i \overset{iid}{\sim} N(0,1), \;\; \epsilon_i \overset{iid}{\sim} N(0,\sigma^2), \;\; i = 1, 2, \ldots, 10.$$

Suppose priors of the form $\sigma^2 \sim IG(a, b)$ and $\beta \sim N(\mu_\beta, V_\beta)$ are employed. Following Exercise 12.9, we have the posterior conditional distributions associated with this regression model given as

$$\beta|\sigma^2, y \sim N(D_\beta d_\beta, D_\beta), \tag{12.58}$$

where

$$D_\beta = (X'X/\sigma^2 + V_\beta^{-1})^{-1}, \qquad d_\beta = X'y/\sigma^2 + V_\beta^{-1}\mu_\beta,$$

and

$$\sigma^2|\beta, y \sim IG\left([10/2] + a, [b^{-1} + .5(y - X\beta)'(y - X\beta)]^{-1}\right). \tag{12.59}$$

Using the hyperparameters $a = 3$, $b = 1/2$, $\mu_\beta = [1\ 1]'$, and $V_\beta = .25I_2$, generate 100 000 draws from $p(y, \theta)$ using both the marginal-conditional and successive-conditional simulators. For the latter, use the Gibbs sampler, as described by (12.58) and (12.59), to generate draws from (12.57). Given your solution in part (a), provide a test for the correctness of the Gibbs sampler that was used for fitting the regression model.
(c) Now, deliberately include some mistakes in your Gibbs sampling algorithm. Specifically, (i) replace V_β^{-1} with V_β in the expression for D_β in the posterior conditional for β; (ii) assume that the prior mean for β is $[0\ 0]'$, even though a prior mean of $[1\ 1]'$ was used; and (iii) replace $b^{-1} = (1/2)^{-1}$ with $b = (1/2)$ in the conditional posterior for σ^2 in (12.59). Do the tests derived in part (b) diagnose these mistakes?

Solution
(a) First, note that the marginal-conditional simulator only requires drawing from the prior and data densities. Typically, this is easy to do and easy to program.

Let $g^{(m)} = g(\theta^{(m)}, y^{(m)})$ be the mth value of some function g mapping $\Theta \times Y$ into the real line, which is evaluated using output from the marginal-conditional simulator. Define $\tilde{g}^{(m)} = g(\tilde{\theta}^{(m)}, \tilde{y}^{(m)})$ analogously, noting that $\tilde{g}$ uses output from the successive-conditional simulator.

We can think of g as being a *test function* in the following sense: If both simulators are programmed correctly, both will provide draws from the joint distribution $p(y, \theta)$, and thus moments and other functions of interest should be similar when evaluated using the outputs of both simulators. This suggests that, for a given g, averages of the form $\overline{g} = [1/M_1]\sum_{m=1}^{M_1} g^{(m)}$ and $\overline{\tilde{g}} = [1/M_2]\sum_{m=1}^{M_2} \tilde{g}^{(m)}$ (where M_1 and M_2 denote the number of simulations in the marginal-conditional and successive-conditional simulators) should be similar. To the extent that $\overline{g}$ and $\overline{\tilde{g}}$ differ significantly, this provides evidence that a mistake has occurred in the programming of *at least one of* the simulators. In general, the error is more likely to take place in the successive-conditional simulator since the posterior simulator is most difficult to program and the marginal-conditional simulator is comparably easy to implement.

Different choices of g define different test functions. For concreteness here, we can think about comparing moments of θ across our two simulators, and thus choose, for example, $g(\theta, y) = \theta_j$ (for some element θ_j of θ) or $g(\theta, y) = \theta_j^2$. In practice, a variety of moments could be used.

Geweke shows that, provided no programming errors are present in both simulators,

$$\frac{\overline{g} - \tilde{\overline{g}}}{(M_1^{-1}\hat{\sigma}_g^2 + M_2^{-1}\hat{\tau}_g^2)^{1/2}} \to N(0, 1), \tag{12.60}$$

where $\hat{\sigma}_g^2 = M_1^{-1} \sum_{m=1}^{M_1} [g^{(m)}]^2 - \overline{g}^2$ and $M_1^{-1}\hat{\sigma}_g^2$ is the variance of $\overline{g}$. Similarly, $M_2^{-1}\hat{\tau}_g^2$ is the variance of $\tilde{\overline{g}}$. For the case of the successive-conditional simulator, the draws are not independent, and thus $M_2^{-1}\hat{\tau}_g^2$ must be calculated using the formula provided in Exercise 12.20.

(b) Code for the marginal-conditional and successive-conditional simulators is available on the website associated with this book. For our test functions, we individually compare the means of β_0, β_1, and σ^2 across both simulators. When doing so, we calculate test statistics according to (12.60) equal to 1.03, .25, and .75 for the respective means. Thus, our tests do not offer conclusive evidence that errors are present in our code.

(c) When replacing V_β^{-1} with V_β in the definition of D_β, we obtain test statistics equal to -260.3, -292.5, and $-.6$ for equality of means associated with β_0, β_1, and σ^2, respectively. When assuming that $\mu_\beta = [0\ 0]'$, we obtain test statistics equal to 224.67, 206.49, and $-.158$, respectively. Finally, when replacing b^{-1} with b in the posterior conditional for σ^2, we obtain test statistics equal to $-.30$, $-.275$, and 181, respectively. Thus, when programming errors are present, the tests clearly reveal evidence of an error. Moreover, the pattern of rejection also seems to suggest the posterior conditional where the error was made.

13

Hierarchical Models

In this chapter we take up issues relating to estimation in hierarchical models. Many models belong in this class, and indeed, several exercises appearing in later chapters (e.g., mixture models and panel probit models) involve specifications with hierarchical structures that could be included as exercises here. In this chapter, however, we confine our attention to linear specifications and pay particular attention to normal hierarchical linear regression models. In econometrics, these are commonly used with panel (also called longitudinal) data, and several of the questions in this chapter use such data. Exercises in this chapter emphasize estimation using Gibbs sampling; introductory exercises illustrating the use of the Gibbs sampler were provided in Chapter 12. MATLAB code for all the empirical work is also provided on the website associated with this book.

Exercise 13.1 (General results for normal hierarchical linear models) Let y be an N vector and θ_1, θ_2, and θ_3 be parameter vectors of length k_1, k_2, and k_3, respectively. Let X, W, and Z be known $N \times k_1$, $k_1 \times k_2$, and $k_2 \times k_3$ matrices, and C_1, C_2, and C_3 be $N \times N$, $k_1 \times k_1$, and $k_2 \times k_2$ known positive definite matrices. Assume that

$$y|\theta_1 \sim N\left(X\theta_1, C_1\right), \tag{13.1}$$

$$\theta_1|\theta_2 \sim N\left(W\theta_2, C_2\right), \tag{13.2}$$

and

$$\theta_2|\theta_3 \sim N\left(Z\theta_3, C_3\right). \tag{13.3}$$

We make conditional independence assumptions such that $p\left(y|\theta_1, \theta_2\right) = p\left(y|\theta_1\right)$ and $p\left(\theta_1|\theta_2, \theta_3\right) = p\left(\theta_1|\theta_2\right)$.

(a) Show that

$$y|\theta_2 \sim N\left(XW\theta_2, C_1 + XC_2X'\right), \tag{13.4}$$

and thus that this normal linear regression model with hierarchical prior can be written as a different normal linear regression model with non-hierarchical prior.
(b) Derive $p\left(\theta_2|y,\theta_3\right)$.
(c) Show that

$$\theta_1|y,\theta_3 \sim N\left(Dd, D\right),$$

where

$$D^{-1} = X'C_1^{-1}X + \left(C_2 + WC_3W'\right)^{-1}$$

and

$$d = X'C_1^{-1}y + \left(C_2 + WC_3W'\right)^{-1}WZ\theta_3.$$

Solution
(a) Equation (13.1) is equivalent to

$$y = X\theta_1 + \epsilon,$$

where $\epsilon \sim N\left(0, C_1\right)$. Similarly, (13.2) can be written as

$$\theta_1 = W\theta_2 + v,$$

where $v \sim N\left(0, C_2\right)$. Substituting, we obtain

$$y = XW\theta_2 + Xv + \epsilon.$$

Using the properties of the normal distribution leads immediately to: (i) $y|\theta_2$ is normal, (ii) its mean is $XW\theta_2$, and (iii) its covariance is $E\left[\left(Xv+\epsilon\right)\left(Xv+\epsilon\right)'\right] = C_1 + XC_2X'$ (since the question assumptions imply ϵ and v are independent of one another). Hence, the required result is proven.
(b) By Bayes' theorem,

$$p\left(\theta_2|y,\theta_3\right) \propto p\left(\theta_2|\theta_3\right)p\left(y|\theta_2,\theta_3\right).$$

The first term on the right-hand side is simply the normal prior in (13.3) and the second term is the normal likelihood in (13.4). The derivation of the resulting posterior is standard (see Exercises 10.1 and 12.12 for related derivations). It can be verified that

$$\theta_2|y,\theta_3 \sim N(Hh, H),$$

where

$$H = \left(W'X'\left(C_1 + XC_2X'\right)^{-1}XW + C_3^{-1}\right)^{-1}$$

and

$$h = W'X'\left(C_1 + XC_2X'\right)^{-1} y + C_3^{-1} Z\theta_3.$$

(c) Again, Bayes' theorem implies $p(\theta_1|y, \theta_3) \propto p(\theta_1|\theta_3)\, p(y|\theta_1, \theta_3)$. The assumptions of the question imply that $p(y|\theta_1, \theta_3)$ is given in (13.1). A proof the same as that for part (a), except that (13.2) and (13.3) are used, establishes that the prior for θ_1 with θ_2 integrated out takes the form

$$\theta_1|\theta_3 \sim N\left(WZ\theta_3, C_2 + WC_3W'\right). \tag{13.5}$$

Hence, just as in part (b), we have a normal likelihood (13.1) times a normal prior (13.5). The derivation of the resulting posterior is standard (see Exercises 2.3 and 10.1 for closely related derivations). It can be verified that the mean and covariance of the normal posterior, $p(\theta_1|y, \theta_3)$, are as given in the question.

Exercise 13.2 (Hierarchical modeling with longitudinal data) Consider the following longitudinal data model:

$$y_{it} = \alpha_i + \epsilon_{it}, \quad \epsilon_{it} \stackrel{iid}{\sim} N(0, \sigma_\epsilon^2), \tag{13.6}$$

$$\alpha_i \stackrel{iid}{\sim} N(\alpha, \sigma_\alpha^2), \tag{13.7}$$

where y_{it} refers to the outcomes for individual (or more generally, group) i at time t, and α_i is a person-specific random effect. We assume $i = 1, 2, \ldots, N$ and $t = 1, 2, \ldots, T$ (i.e., a balanced panel).

(a) Comment on how the presence of the random effects accounts for correlation patterns within individuals over time.

(b) Derive the conditional posterior distribution $p(\alpha_i|\alpha, \sigma_\epsilon^2, \sigma_\alpha^2, y)$.

(c) Obtain the mean of the conditional posterior distribution in part (b). Comment on its relationship to a shrinkage estimator (see, e.g., Poirier 1995, Chapter 6). How does the mean change as T and $\sigma_\epsilon^2/\sigma_\alpha^2$ change?

Solution

(a) Conditional on the random effects $\{\alpha_i\}_{i=1}^N$, the y_{it} are independent. However, marginalized over the random effects, outcomes are correlated within individuals over time. To see this, note that we can write (13.6) equivalently as

$$y_{it} = \alpha + u_i + \epsilon_{it},$$

where we have rewritten (13.7) as

$$\alpha_i = \alpha + u_i, \quad u_i \stackrel{iid}{\sim} N(0, \sigma_\alpha^2),$$

and substituted this result into (13.6). Thus, for $t \neq s$,

$$\text{Cov}(y_{it}, y_{is}|\alpha, \sigma_\epsilon^2, \sigma_\alpha^2) = \text{Cov}(u_i + \epsilon_{it}, u_i + \epsilon_{is}) = \text{Cov}(u_i, u_i) = \text{Var}(u_i) = \sigma_\alpha^2,$$

so that outcomes are correlated over time within individuals. However, the random effects have not permitted any degree of correlation between the outcomes of different individuals.
(b) From Exercise 12.9,

$$\alpha_i|\alpha, \sigma_\epsilon^2, \sigma_\alpha^2, y \sim N(Dd, D),$$

where

$$D = \left(\iota_T'\iota_T/\sigma_\epsilon^2 + 1/\sigma_\alpha^2\right)^{-1} = \frac{\sigma_\alpha^2\sigma_\epsilon^2}{T\sigma_\alpha^2 + \sigma_\epsilon^2}$$

and

$$d = \frac{\iota_T' y_i}{\sigma_\epsilon^2} + \frac{\alpha}{\sigma_\alpha^2} = \frac{\sigma_\alpha^2 \sum_t y_{it} + \alpha\sigma_\epsilon^2}{\sigma_\alpha^2\sigma_\epsilon^2}.$$

In these expressions, we have let ι_T denote a $T \times 1$ vector of ones and $y_i = [y_{i1}\ y_{i2}\ \cdots\ y_{iT}]'$.
(c) The mean of this conditional posterior distribution is easily obtained from our solution in part (b):

$$\begin{aligned}
E(\alpha_i|\beta, \sigma_\epsilon^2, \sigma_\alpha^2, y) &= \frac{\sigma_\alpha^2 \sum_t y_{it} + \alpha\sigma_\epsilon^2}{T\sigma_\alpha^2 + \sigma_\epsilon^2} \\
&= \left(\frac{T\sigma_\alpha^2}{T\sigma_\alpha^2 + \sigma_\epsilon^2}\right)\overline{y}_i + \left(\frac{\sigma_\epsilon^2}{T\sigma_\alpha^2 + \sigma_\epsilon^2}\right)\alpha \\
&= \left(\frac{T}{T + (\sigma_\epsilon^2/\sigma_\alpha^2)}\right)\overline{y}_i + \left(\frac{(\sigma_\epsilon^2/\sigma_\alpha^2)}{T + (\sigma_\epsilon^2/\sigma_\alpha^2)}\right)\alpha.
\end{aligned}$$

Let

$$w = w(T, [\sigma_\epsilon^2/\sigma_\alpha^2]) \equiv \frac{T}{T + (\sigma_\epsilon^2/\sigma_\alpha^2)}.$$

Then we can write

$$E(\alpha_i|\beta, \sigma_\epsilon^2, \sigma_\alpha^2, y) = w\overline{y}_i + (1 - w)\alpha.$$

This is in the form of a shrinkage estimator, where the conditional posterior mean of α_i is a weighted average (with w serving as the weight) of the averaged outcomes for individual i, $\overline{y}_i$, and the common mean for all individuals, α. As $T \to \infty$ (and holding all else constant) we see that $w \to 1$, so the conditional posterior mean approaches the average of the individual outcomes. Intuitively this makes sense, since as $T \to \infty$, we acquire more and more information on individual i, and thus data information from individual i dominates any information provided by the outcomes of other individuals in the sample. As $(\sigma_\epsilon^2/\sigma_\alpha^2) \to \infty$, $w \to 0$, so our posterior mean collapses to the common mean α. In this case the error variability in the outcome equation continues to grow relative to the variability in the random effects equation, and thus our posterior mean reduces the common effect for all individuals, α.

Table 13.1: Rat growth data from Gelfand et al. (1990).

Rat	Weight measurements					Rat	Weight measurements				
i	y_{i1}	y_{i2}	y_{i3}	y_{i4}	y_{i5}	i	y_{i1}	y_{i2}	y_{i3}	y_{i4}	y_{i5}
1	151	199	246	283	320	16	160	207	248	288	324
2	145	199	249	293	354	17	142	187	234	280	316
3	147	214	263	312	328	18	156	203	243	283	317
4	155	200	237	272	297	19	157	212	259	307	336
5	135	188	230	280	323	20	152	203	246	286	321
6	159	210	252	298	331	21	154	205	253	298	334
7	141	189	231	275	305	22	139	190	225	267	302
8	159	201	248	297	338	23	146	191	229	272	302
9	177	236	285	340	376	24	157	211	250	285	323
10	134	182	220	260	296	25	132	185	237	286	331
11	160	208	261	313	352	26	160	207	257	303	345
12	143	188	220	273	314	27	169	216	261	295	333
13	154	200	244	289	325	28	157	205	248	289	316
14	171	221	270	326	358	29	137	180	219	258	291
15	163	216	242	281	312	30	153	200	244	286	324

Exercise 13.3 (A posterior simulator for a linear hierarchical model: Gelfand et al. (1990)) We illustrate Bayesian procedures for estimating hierarchical linear models using a data set that has become something of a "classic" in the MCMC literature. These data come from the study of Gelfand, Hills, Racine-Poon, and Smith (1990). In this exercise we derive in full detail the complete posterior conditionals. In the following exercise we fit this model and provide some diagnostic checks for convergence. In subsequent examples, complete derivations of the conditionals will not typically be provided, as these derivations will often follow similarly to those described in this exercise.

In the rat growth model of Gelfand et al. (1990), 30 different rats were weighed at five different points in time. We denote the weight of rat i at measurement j as y_{ij} and let x_{ij} denote the age of the ith rat at the jth measurement. Since each of the rats was weighed at exactly the same number of days since birth, we have

$$x_{i1} = 8, \; x_{i2} = 15, \; x_{i3} = 22, \; x_{i4} = 29, \; x_{i5} = 36 \; \forall i.$$

The data used in the analysis are provided in Table 13.1.

In our model, we want to permit unit-specific variation in initial birth weight and growth rates. This leads us to specify the following model:

$$y_{ij}|\alpha_i, \beta_i, \sigma^2, x_{ij} \overset{ind}{\sim} N(\alpha_i + \beta_i x_{ij}, \sigma^2), \quad i = 1, 2, \ldots, 30, \; j = 1, 2, \ldots, 5,$$

so that each rat possesses its own intercept α_i and growth rate β_i.

We also assume that the rats share some degree of "commonality" in their weight at birth and rates of growth, and thus we assume that the intercept and slope parameters are drawn from the same normal population:

$$\theta_i = \begin{bmatrix} \alpha_i \\ \beta_i \end{bmatrix} \sim N(\theta_0, \Sigma),$$

where $\theta_0 = [\alpha_0 \; \beta_0]'$ and Σ is a 2×2 positive definite symmetric covariance matrix.

We complete our Bayesian analysis by specifying the following priors:

$$\sigma^2 | a, b \sim IG(a, b),$$
$$\theta_0 | \eta, C \sim N(\eta, C),$$
$$\Sigma^{-1} | \rho, R \sim W([\rho R]^{-1}, \rho),$$

with W denoting the Wishart distribution (see Definition A.6 for details).

Derive the complete conditionals for this model and comment on any intuition behind the forms of these conditionals.

Solution

Given the assumed conditional independence across observations, the joint posterior distribution for all the parameters of this model can be written as

$$p(\Gamma|y) \propto \left[\prod_{i=1}^{30} p(y_i|x_i, \theta_i, \sigma^2) p(\theta_i|\theta_0, \Sigma^{-1})\right] p(\theta_0|\eta, C) p(\sigma^2|a, b) p(\Sigma^{-1}|\rho, R),$$

where $\Gamma \equiv [\{\theta_i\}, \theta_0, \Sigma^{-1}, \sigma^2]$ denotes all the parameters of the model. We will also use the notation Γ_{-x} to denote all parameters other than x. We have stacked the observations over time for each individual rat so that

$$y_i = \begin{bmatrix} y_{i1} \\ y_{i2} \\ \vdots \\ y_{i5} \end{bmatrix}, \qquad X_i = \begin{bmatrix} 1 & x_{i1} \\ 1 & x_{i2} \\ \vdots & \vdots \\ 1 & x_{i5} \end{bmatrix}.$$

Complete posterior conditional for θ_i:

We first note that this complete conditional is proportional to the aforementioned joint posterior. Thus, all of the terms in the product that do not involve θ_i are absorbed into the normalizing constant of this conditional. Hence,

$$p(\theta_i|\Gamma_{-\theta_i}, y) \propto p(y_i|X_i, \theta_i, \sigma^2) p(\theta_i|\theta_0, \Sigma).$$

This fits directly into the framework of Exercise 12.12 (see also Lindley and Smith 1972), and thus we find

$$\theta_i|\Gamma_{-\theta_i}, y \sim N(D_{\theta_i} d_{\theta_i}, D_{\theta_i}), \quad i = 1, 2, \ldots, 30,$$

where

$$D_{\theta_i} = \left(X_i'X_i/\sigma^2 + \Sigma^{-1}\right)^{-1}, \quad d_{\theta_i} = X_i'y_i/\sigma^2 + \Sigma^{-1}\theta_0.$$

Because of the conditional independence, we can draw each of the θ_i in turn by sampling from the corresponding complete conditional.

Complete posterior conditional for θ_0:

For θ_0, a similar argument shows that

$$p(\theta_0|\Gamma_{-\theta_0}, y) \propto \left(\prod_{i=1}^{30} p(\theta_i|\theta_0, \Sigma^{-1}) \right) p(\theta_0|\eta, C).$$

Since the second stage of our model specifies $p(\theta_i|\theta_0, \Sigma^{-1})$ as *iid*, we can write

$$\begin{bmatrix} \theta_1 \\ \theta_2 \\ \vdots \\ \theta_{30} \end{bmatrix} = \begin{bmatrix} I_2 \\ I_2 \\ \vdots \\ I_2 \end{bmatrix} \theta_0 + \begin{bmatrix} u_1 \\ u_2 \\ \vdots \\ u_{30} \end{bmatrix},$$

or equivalently,

$$\tilde{\theta} = \tilde{I}\theta_0 + \tilde{u},$$

with $\tilde{\theta} = [\theta_1' \; \theta_2' \cdots \theta_{30}']'$, $\tilde{I} = [I_2 \; I_2 \cdots I_2]'$, $\tilde{u} = [u_1' \; u_2' \cdots u_{30}']'$, and $E(\tilde{u}\tilde{u}') = I_{30} \otimes \Sigma$.

In this form, the results of Exercise 12.12 again apply with

$$\theta_0|\Gamma_{-\theta_0}, y \sim N(D_{\theta_0} d_{\theta_0}, D_{\theta_0}),$$

where

$$D_{\theta_0} = \left(\tilde{I}'(I_{30} \otimes \Sigma^{-1})\tilde{I} + C^{-1}\right)^{-1} = \left(30\Sigma^{-1} + C^{-1}\right)^{-1}$$

and

$$d_{\theta_0} = (\tilde{I}'(I_{30} \otimes \Sigma^{-1})\tilde{\theta} + C^{-1}\eta) = (30\Sigma^{-1}\overline{\theta} + C^{-1}\eta),$$

and where $\overline{\theta} = (1/30) \sum_{i=1}^{30} \theta_i$.

Complete posterior conditional for σ^2:

For σ^2, we find that

$$\begin{aligned} p(\sigma^2|\Gamma_{-\sigma^2}, y) &\propto \left(\prod_{i=1}^{30} p(y_i|X_i\theta_i, \sigma^2) \right) p(\sigma^2|a, b) \\ &\propto \frac{1}{[\sigma^2]^{N/2}} \exp\left(-\frac{1}{2\sigma^2} \sum_{i=1}^{30} (y_i - X_i\theta_i)'(y_i - X_i\theta_i) \right) \\ &\quad \times \frac{1}{[\sigma^2]^{a+1}} \exp\left(-\frac{1}{b\sigma^2} \right) \\ &= \frac{1}{[\sigma^2]^{N/2+a+1}} \exp\left(-\frac{1}{\sigma^2} \left[1/2 \sum_{i=1}^{30} (y_i - X_i\theta_i)'(y_i - X_i\theta_i) + b^{-1} \right] \right). \end{aligned}$$

Thus,

$$\sigma^2|\Gamma_{-\sigma^2}, y \sim IG\left(N/2 + a, \left[1/2\sum_{i=1}^{30}(y_i - X_i\theta_i)'(y_i - X_i\theta_i) + b^{-1}\right]^{-1}\right),$$

where $N = 5(30) = 150$.
Complete posterior conditional for Σ^{-1}*:*
We find that

$$\begin{aligned}
p(\Sigma^{-1}|\Gamma_{-\Sigma^{-1}}, y) &\propto \left[\prod_{i=1}^{30} p(\theta_i|\theta_0, \Sigma^{-1})\right] p(\Sigma^{-1}|\rho, R) \\
&\propto |\Sigma^{-1}|^{30/2} \exp\left(-1/2\sum_{i=1}^{30}(\theta_i - \theta_0)'\Sigma^{-1}(\theta_i - \theta_0)\right) \\
&\quad \times |\Sigma^{-1}|^{(\rho-3)/2} \exp\left(-[1/2]\text{tr}[\rho R\Sigma^{-1}]\right) \\
&= |\Sigma^{-1}|^{(30+\rho-3)/2} \\
&\quad \times \exp\left(-1/2\left(\left[\sum_{i=1}^{30} \text{tr}(\theta_i - \theta_0)(\theta_i - \theta_0)'\Sigma^{-1}\right] + \text{tr}[\rho R\Sigma^{-1}]\right)\right) \\
&= |\Sigma^{-1}|^{(30+\rho-3)/2} \\
&\quad \times \exp\left[-(1/2)\text{tr}\left(\left[\sum_{i=1}^{30}(\theta_i - \theta_0)(\theta_i - \theta_0)' + \rho R\right]\Sigma^{-1}\right)\right].
\end{aligned}$$

Therefore,

$$\Sigma^{-1}|\Gamma_{-\Sigma^{-1}}, y \sim W\left(\left[\sum_{i=1}^{30}(\theta_i - \theta_0)(\theta_i - \theta_0)' + \rho R\right]^{-1}, 30 + \rho\right).$$

We can gather some intuition regarding the forms of these conditionals. First, note from the complete conditional for θ_i that the conditional posterior mean can be regarded as a weighted average of the OLS estimate using data from that individual: $(X_i'X_i)^{-1}X_i'y_i$ and the common or "pooled" mean across all individuals θ_0. In this sense, the conditional mean is similar to a "shrinkage" estimator as it combines information from the outcomes on the individual rat with cross-section information from the outcomes of all the rats. Further, as $\Sigma^{-1} \to 0$, holding all else constant, the conditional posterior mean approaches the OLS estimate. This is seemingly reasonable since $\Sigma^{-1} \approx 0$ implies a large amount of second-stage variability, and thus most of the weight will be given to the OLS estimate from the outcomes of the individual rat.

For the complete conditional for θ_0, note that for very flat priors (choosing C large and thus C^{-1} "small"), the conditional posterior mean reduces to the sample averages of all of the θ_i. Thus, in this case, the individual-level parameter estimates are "shrunk" toward the average of all parameter estimates for all the rats.

Finally, for the complete conditional posterior mean of Σ^{-1}, note that for relatively vague priors corresponding to small values of ρ, the conditional posterior mean of Σ^{-1} is approximately $k[\sum_{i=1}^{k}(\theta_i - \theta_0)(\theta_i - \theta_0)']^{-1}$, so that $E(\Sigma) \approx 1/k \sum_{i=1}^{k}(\theta_i - \theta_0)(\theta_i - \theta_0)'$. Thus, when the prior information is not informative relative to the data information, the conditional posterior mean of the covariance matrix Σ is approximately equal to the sample variability of the individual-level parameters around the common mean θ_0.

Exercise 13.4 (The linear hierarchical model II: Estimation and convergence diagnostics) Use the data and algorithm provided in the previous exercise.
(a) Fit the rat growth model using the following priors:

$$\eta = \begin{bmatrix} 100 \\ 15 \end{bmatrix}, \; C = \begin{bmatrix} 40^2 & 0 \\ 0 & 10^2 \end{bmatrix}, \; \rho = 5, \;\; R = \begin{bmatrix} 10^2 & 0 \\ 0 & .5^2 \end{bmatrix}, \;\; a = 3, \;\; b = 1/40.$$

(b) Perform some diagnostic checking to detect convergence of the sampler (see, e.g., Exercises 12.20–12.23). For a related discussion of MCMC convergence diagnostics, see, e.g., Cowles and Carlin (1996).
(c) How do the Bayesian estimation results differ from OLS estimates? Can you explain the differences in the results?

Solution
(a) The priors employed specify that the expected weight at birth is 100 g, and the growth per day is 15 g. The prior covariance matrix C is chosen to be quite diffuse around these mean values. For the Wishart prior, we set $\rho = 5$ and choose the prior to reflect some degree of variability in the initial weights and growth rates across rats. Finally, for the variance parameter σ^2, we have selected the hyperparameters so that the prior mean and prior standard deviation are equal to 20, a reasonably diffuse choice.

Estimation results for a selection of parameters are provided in Table 13.2. The results are obtained after running the Gibbs sampler for 10 000 iterations and discarding the first 500 of them as the burn-in period. MATLAB code for this exercise is provided on the website associated with this book.

In Table 13.2, we present results for the common intercept α_0, common slope β_0, variance parameters of the second-stage covariance matrix Σ (denoted σ_α^2 and σ_β^2), the correlation between the intercept and slope, denoted $\rho_{\alpha,\beta}$, and the slope and intercept results for the 10th and 25th rats in the sample. For the covariance matrix, we report the variance parameters as well as the correlation between the intercept and slope.

Our results suggest that the birth weight of an "average" rat is about 106.6 g, and the average weight gained per day is about 6.2 g. For the covariance matrix results, we do see evidence of individual heterogeneity across rats as both σ_α^2 and σ_β^2 are reasonably large, and the correlation between the intercept and growth rate is mostly negative, though it is rather imprecisely estimated. This suggests that smaller rats at birth may tend to have higher growth rates, as they tend to "catch up" to the weights of the other rats.

Table 13.2: Posterior quantities for a selection of parameters.

Parameter	Post. mean	Post. std.	10th percentile	90th percentile
α_0	106.6	2.34	103.7	109.5
β_0	6.18	.106	6.05	6.31
σ^2_α	124.5	42.41	77.03	179.52
σ^2_β	.275	.088	.179	.389
$\rho_{\alpha,\beta}$	$-.120$	.211	$-.390$	.161
α_{10}	93.76	5.24	87.09	100.59
α_{25}	86.91	5.81	79.51	94.45
β_{10}	5.70	.217	5.43	5.98
β_{25}	6.75	.243	6.44	7.05

(b) For our estimation results, we ran the Gibbs sampler for 10 000 iterations and discarded the first 500 of those draws. We now provide some suggestive evidence that these choices were adequate for convergence.

In Figure 13.1 we present trace plots for the common intercepts and slope (α_0 and β_0), the $(1,1)$ element of Σ (σ^2_α), and the intercept for the 20th rat in the sample (α_0). We obtain two different trace plots from two different chains that were run with different and overdispersed starting values. As shown in the table, it appears as if the simulated draws from both chains settle down and explore the same region remarkably quickly. In fact, after the first ten iterations or so, the progression of both chains seems very similar. This provides suggestive evidence that the use of 500 iterations as a burn-in period is more than sufficient for this application.

We can also gauge the number of draws required by examining the degree of autocorrelation in our parameter chains. In Table 13.3 we present the within-parameter autocorrelations at different lags. As shown in the table, even the first-order autocorrelations are not excessively large, and the lag 5 correlations are virtually zero. As such, we do not expect autocorrelation in our parameter chains to substantially slow our convergence, so the number of iterations used here appears to be sufficient.

(c) One might think that there is a much easier way to obtain the same results. Specifically, one might be able to obtain the same results by taking the five observations corresponding to each rat and using those five observations to obtain intercept and slope estimates via a linear regression model.

Although this OLS method is indeed computationally more attractive, this approach ignores the fact that the individual-level parameters are also involved in the second stage. That is, you can think about obtaining an estimate of α_i from the first-stage OLS regression as well as from the second-stage common mean α. In our hierarchical model, the conditional posterior distribution of the individual-level intercept and slope parameters balance information from the OLS regression using outcomes for the given rat with information obtained from the intercept and slope estimates from all other rats. This suggests that

Table 13.3: Autocorrelations in parameter chains at various lag orders.

Parameter	Lag 1	Lag 5	Lag 10
α_0	.24	.010	.007
β_0	.22	$-.004$	$-.009$
σ^2_α	.36	.020	$-.010$
$\rho_{\alpha,\beta}$	.37	.036	.003
α_{15}	.18	.025	.018

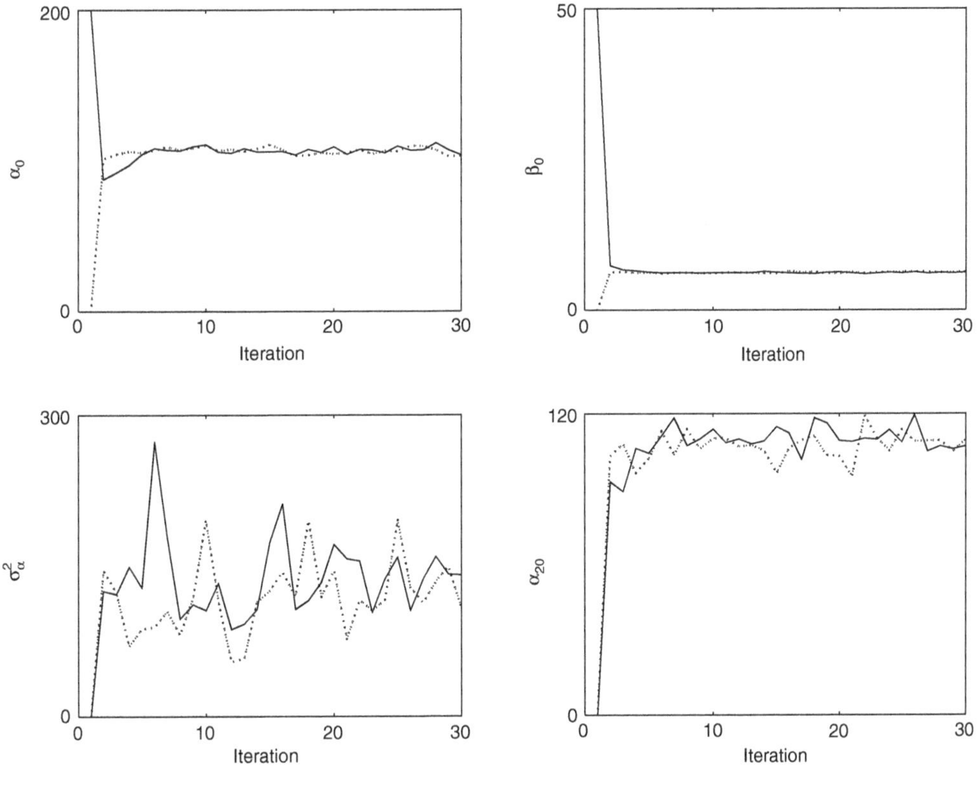

Figure 13.1. Trace plots of selected parameters from two different chains.

models like these should not be fit "sequentially," where point estimates of parameters from a given stage of the hierarchy are then used as a dependent variable in subsequent stages of the hierarchy.

To show how these approaches can yield different results in our example, we provide in Figure 13.2 OLS estimates of the intercepts and slopes as well as posterior means of the same intercepts and slopes from our hierarchical model. As shown in the figures, the

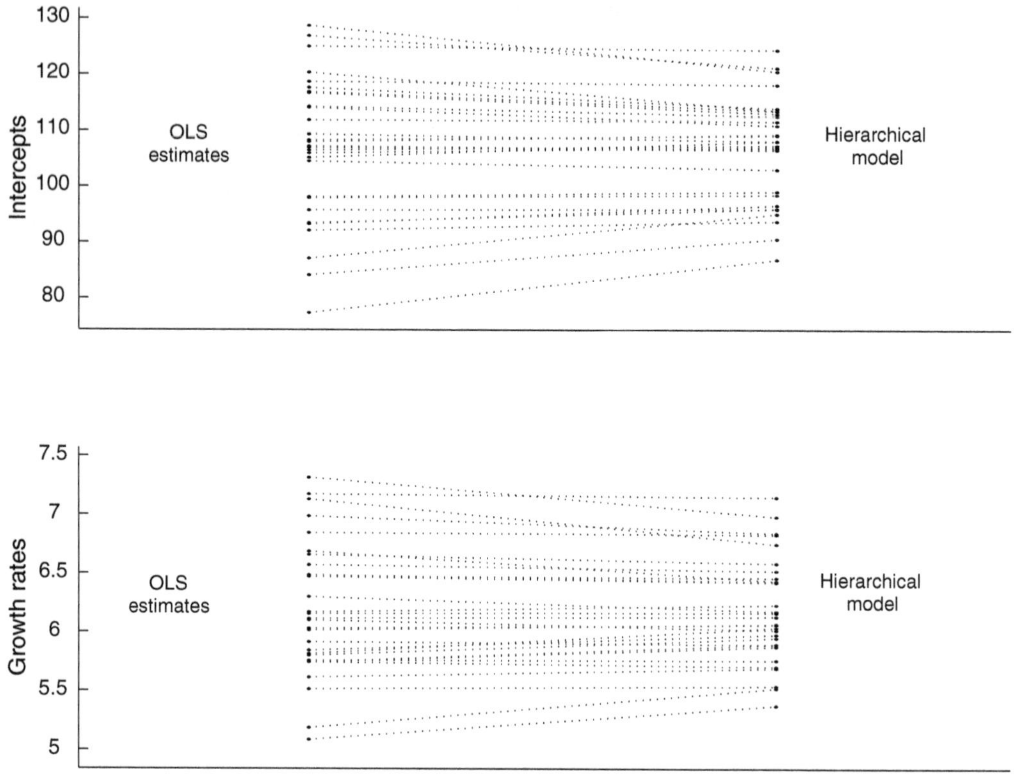

Figure 13.2. Ordinary least squares and hierarchical model point estimates of intercepts and growth rates.

hierarchical model estimates tend to be less variable and are "shrunk" toward the common mean α. The sequential OLS procedure, in general, exhibits a tendency to "overfit" the model.

Exercise 13.5 (Blocking steps in random effects models) In the rat growth model in the previous exercise, both the intercept and slope were permitted to vary across the units. Consider, instead, a model that combines some elements of the random coefficients model and some elements of the pooled model. In particular, we will permit the intercept to vary across individuals but restrict the other regression coefficients to be constant across individuals. That is, we consider the *mixed model*

$$y_{it} = \alpha_i + x_{it}\beta + \epsilon_{it}, \quad \epsilon_{it} \stackrel{iid}{\sim} N(0, \sigma_\epsilon^2),$$
$$\alpha_i \stackrel{iid}{\sim} N(\alpha, \sigma_\alpha^2).$$

For this model we employ independent priors of the form

$$\begin{aligned}\beta &\sim N(\beta_0, V_\beta),\\ \alpha &\sim N(\alpha_0, V_\alpha),\\ \sigma_\epsilon^2 &\sim IG(e_1, e_2),\\ \sigma_\alpha^2 &\sim IG(a_1, a_2).\end{aligned}$$

The model is sometimes termed a "mixed" model because the random effects α_i are permitted to vary across i, while we impose the restriction that the slope parameters β are constant across individuals. In the beginning of this exercise, we continue to assume a balanced panel ($i = 1, 2, \dots, N, t{=}1, 2, \dots, T$), though we relax this condition in part (d).
(a) Derive the complete posterior conditionals

$$p(\alpha_i|\beta, \alpha, \sigma_\epsilon^2, \sigma_\alpha^2, y) \quad \text{and} \quad p(\beta|\{\alpha_i\}, \alpha, \sigma_\epsilon^2, \sigma_\alpha^2, y),$$

where $\{\alpha_i\}$ simply denotes the collection of the N individual random effects, $\{\alpha_i\}_{i=1}^N$.
(b) Describe how one could use a *blocking* or *grouping* step (e.g., Chib and Carlin 1999) to obtain draws directly from the *joint posterior conditional* $p(\{\alpha_i\}, \beta|\alpha, \sigma_\epsilon^2, \sigma_\alpha^2, y)$.
(c) Describe how the Gibbs sampler can be used to fit the model, given your result in part (b). Would you expect any improvements in this blocked algorithm relative to the standard Gibbs algorithm in part (a)?
(d) How does your answer in part (c) change for the case of an *unbalanced panel* where $T = T_i$?

Solution

(a) The complete posterior conditionals can be obtained in the same manner as in previous exercises in this chapter. Specifically, we obtain

$$p(\alpha_i|\beta, \alpha, \sigma_\epsilon^2, \sigma_\alpha^2, y) \sim N(Dd, D), \tag{13.8}$$

where

$$D = \left(T/\sigma_\epsilon^2 + 1/\sigma_\alpha^2\right)^{-1}, \quad d = \sum_{t=1}^{T}(y_{it} - x_{it}\beta)/\sigma_\epsilon^2 + \alpha/\sigma_\alpha^2.$$

The complete posterior conditional for β follows similarly:

$$\beta|\{\alpha_i\}, \alpha, \sigma_\epsilon^2, \sigma_\alpha^2, y \sim N(Hh, H),$$

where

$$H = \left(X'X/\sigma_\epsilon^2 + V_\beta^{-1}\right)^{-1}, \quad h = X'(y - \overline{\alpha})/\sigma_\epsilon^2 + V_\beta^{-1}\beta_0,$$

and X, y, and α are the $NT \times k$, $NT \times 1$, and $NT \times 1$ design matrix, outcome vector, and random effect vector, respectively, stacked appropriately. Specifically,

$$\overline{\alpha} = [(\iota_T\alpha_1)' \; (\iota_T\alpha_2)' \; \cdots \; (\iota_T\alpha_N)']'.$$

(b) Instead of the strategy described in part (a), we seek to draw the random effects $\{\alpha_i\}$ and "fixed effects" β in a single block. (The notation "fixed effects" is somewhat common in statistics and is used to denote the set of parameters that do not vary across i.) This strategy of grouping together correlated parameters will generally facilitate the mixing of the chain and thereby reduce numerical standard errors associated with the Gibbs sampling estimates.

We break this joint posterior conditional into the following two pieces:

$$p(\{\alpha_i\}, \beta|\alpha, \sigma_\epsilon^2, \sigma_\alpha^2, y) = p(\{\alpha_i\}|\beta, \alpha, \sigma_\epsilon^2, \sigma_\alpha^2, y)p(\beta|\alpha, \sigma_\epsilon^2, \sigma_\alpha^2, y).$$

Because of the assumed structure of the problem, the random effects $\{\alpha_i\}$ are conditionally independent, so that

$$p(\{\alpha_i\}, \beta|\alpha, \sigma_\epsilon^2, \sigma_\alpha^2, y) = \left[\prod_{i=1}^{N} p(\alpha_i|\beta, \alpha, \sigma_\epsilon^2, \sigma_\alpha^2, y)\right] p(\beta|\alpha, \sigma_\epsilon^2, \sigma_\alpha^2, y).$$

This suggests that one can draw from this joint posterior conditional via the method of composition by first drawing from $p(\beta|\alpha, \sigma_\epsilon^2, \sigma_\alpha^2, y)$ and then drawing each α_i independently from its complete posterior conditional distribution in (13.8).

We now derive the conditional posterior distribution for β, marginalized over the random effects. Note that our model can be rewritten as follows:

$$\begin{aligned} y_{it} &= \alpha + x_{it}\beta + u_i + \epsilon_{it}, \\ \beta &\sim N(\beta_0, V_\beta), \end{aligned}$$

where $u_i \overset{iid}{\sim} N(0, \sigma_\alpha^2)$. Let $v_{it} = u_i + \epsilon_{it}$. If we stack this equation over t within i we obtain

$$y_i = \iota_T \alpha + x_i \beta + v_i,$$

where

$$E(v_i v_i') \equiv \Sigma = \sigma_\epsilon^2 I_T + \sigma_\alpha^2 \iota_T \iota_T'$$

and $y_i = [y_{i1}\ y_{i2}\ \cdots\ y_{iT}]'$, $x_i = [x_{i1}'\ x_{i2}'\ \cdots\ x_{iT}']'$, and $v_i = [v_{i1}\ v_{i2}\ \cdots\ v_{iT}]'$. Stacking again over i we obtain

$$y = i_{NT}\alpha + X\beta + v,$$

where

$$E(vv') = I_N \otimes \Sigma$$

and $y = [y_1'\ y_2'\ \cdots\ y_N']'$, $X = [x_1'\ x_2'\ \cdots\ x_N']'$, and $v = [v_1'\ v_2'\ \cdots\ v_N']'$. In this form, we can now appeal to our standard results for the regression model to obtain

$$\beta|\alpha, \sigma_\epsilon^2, \sigma_\alpha^2, y \sim N(Gg, G),$$

where

$$G = \left(X'(I_N \otimes \Sigma^{-1})X + V_\beta^{-1}\right)^{-1} = \left(\sum_{i=1}^{N} x_i'\Sigma^{-1}x_i + V_\beta^{-1}\right)^{-1}$$

and

$$g = X'(I_N \otimes \Sigma^{-1})(y - \iota_{NT}\alpha) + V_\beta^{-1}\beta_0 = \sum_{i=1}^{N} x_i'\Sigma^{-1}(y_i - \iota_T\alpha) + V_\beta^{-1}\beta_0.$$

Thus, to sample from the desired joint conditional, you first sample β from the distribution given here and then sample the random effects independently from their complete conditional posterior distributions.

Finally, it is also worth noting that β and α could be drawn together in the first step of this process. That is, one could draw from the joint posterior conditional

$$p(\{\alpha_i\}, \alpha, \beta|\sigma_\epsilon^2, \sigma_\alpha^2, y) = \left[\prod_{i=1}^{N} p(\{\alpha_i\}|\beta, \alpha, \sigma_\alpha^2, \sigma_\epsilon^2, y)\right] p(\beta, \alpha|\sigma_\epsilon^2, \sigma_\alpha^2, y)$$

in a similar way to that described here.

(c) Given the result in part (b), we now need to obtain the remaining complete conditionals. These are

$$\alpha|\{\alpha_i\}, \beta, \sigma_\epsilon^2, \sigma_\alpha^2, y \sim N(Rr, R),$$

where

$$R = \left(N/\sigma_\alpha^2 + V_\alpha^{-1}\right)^{-1}, \quad r = \sum_{i=1}^{N} \alpha_i/\sigma_\alpha^2 + V_\alpha^{-1}\alpha_0,$$

$$\sigma_\alpha^2|\{\alpha_i\}, \beta, \sigma_\epsilon^2, y \sim IG\left((N/2) + a_1, \left[a_2^{-1} + .5\sum_{i=1}^{N}(\alpha_i - \alpha)^2\right]^{-1}\right),$$

$$\sigma_\epsilon^2|\{\alpha_i\}, \beta, \sigma_\alpha^2, y$$
$$\sim IG\Big((NT/2) + e_1, \left[e_2^{-1} + .5(y - \iota_{NT}\alpha - X\beta)'(y - \iota_{NT}\alpha - X\beta)\right]^{-1}\Big).$$

(d) Only slight changes are required in the case of unbalanced panels. Let NT continue to denote the total number of observations (i.e., $NT \equiv \sum_{i=1}^{N} T_i$). In addition, let $\Sigma_i \equiv \sigma_\epsilon^2 I_{T_i} + \sigma_\alpha^2 \iota_{T_i}\iota_{T_i}'$. Then, for the unbalanced panel model, we will obtain the same complete conditionals as described in part (c), upon replacing Σ^{-1} with Σ_i^{-1} and T with T_i in the complete conditional for α_i and stacking x_i, y_i, X, and y appropriately in the unbalanced model.

Exercise 13.6 (Hierarchical recentering: Gelfand, Sahu, and Carlin (1995)) Consider the following hierarchical model:

$$y_i = \iota_T \eta_i + \epsilon_i, \quad i = 1, 2, \ldots, n, \tag{13.9}$$

where $y_i = [y_{i1}\ y_{i2}\ \cdots\ y_{iT}]'$, $\epsilon_i = [\epsilon_{i1}\ \epsilon_{i2}\ \cdots\ \epsilon_{iT}]' \stackrel{iid}{\sim} N(0, \sigma_\epsilon^2 I_T)$, η_i is a scalar, and ι_T is a $T \times 1$ vector of ones. Suppose further that the following prior (sometimes referred to as a *population model*) for the η_i is employed:

$$\eta_i | \mu \stackrel{iid}{\sim} N(\mu, \sigma_\eta^2). \tag{13.10}$$

Finally, assume that the variance parameters σ_η^2 and σ_ϵ^2 are *known* and that a flat prior $p(\mu) \propto c$, for some constant c, is adopted.

(a) Find the marginal and conditional posterior distributions $\mu|y$, $\eta_i|\mu, y$, and $\eta_i|y$, where $y = [y_1'\ y_2'\ \cdots\ y_n']'$.

(b) Calculate $\text{Cov}(\eta_i, \mu|y)$ and $\text{Corr}(\eta_i, \mu|y)$.

(c) Consider an equivalent formulation of the model:

$$y_i = \iota_T \mu + \iota_T(\eta_i - \mu) + \epsilon_i, \tag{13.11}$$

$$\eta_i - \mu \stackrel{iid}{\sim} N(0, \sigma_\eta^2), \tag{13.12}$$

or, by letting $\alpha_i \equiv \eta_i - \mu$,

$$y_i = \iota_T \mu + \iota_T \alpha_i + \epsilon_i, \tag{13.13}$$

$$\alpha_i \stackrel{iid}{\sim} N(0, \sigma_\eta^2). \tag{13.14}$$

As in Gelfand, Sahu, and Carlin (1995), call the model in (μ, η) space, i.e., (13.9) and (13.10), the *centered* parameterization, and call the model in the (μ, α) space, i.e., (13.13) and (13.14), the *uncentered* parameterization.

Derive $\mu|y$ and $\alpha_i|y$ for the uncentered model.

(d) Use the results in parts (a) through (c) to calculate $\text{Cov}(\alpha_i, \mu|y)$ and $\text{Corr}(\alpha_i, \mu|y)$. Can you establish any ordering between the correlations in the (μ, α) space and the (μ, η) space? What might this imply for the performance of a posterior simulator under each parameterization?

(e) For the particular values $N = 10$, $T = 2$, $\sigma_\epsilon^2 = 1$, and $\sigma_\eta^2 = 10$, calculate $\text{Corr}(\eta_i, \mu|y)$ and $\text{Corr}(\alpha_i, \mu|y)$.

(f) Generate data consistent with the sample sizes and parameter values in part (e). Using these data, fit both the centered and uncentered models using the Gibbs sampler. Calculate the first-order autocorrelation coefficients for a represented set of simulated parameters in each case and comment on your results.

Solution

(a) Given that the variance parameters are known, it follows that the joint posteriors are multivariate normal under each parameterization. In terms of the specific quantities required in part (a), we first note, upon marginalizing over η_i, that

$$y_i|\mu \sim N(\iota_T\mu, \sigma_\epsilon^2 I_T + \sigma_\eta^2 \iota_T\iota_T'). \tag{13.15}$$

Let $\Sigma_T \equiv \sigma_\epsilon^2 I_T + \sigma_\eta^2\iota_T\iota_T'$. Under the flat prior for μ, it follows that

$$\mu|y \sim N(\hat{\mu}, V_\mu), \tag{13.16}$$

where

$$V_\mu = (n\iota_T'\Sigma_T^{-1}\iota_T)^{-1} \quad \text{and} \quad \hat{\mu} = V_\mu\left[\sum_{i=1}^{n}\iota_T'\Sigma_T^{-1}y_i\right].$$

Using derivations like those of Exercise 12.12, we find

$$\eta_i|u, y \sim N(Bb_i, B), \tag{13.17}$$

where

$$B = \frac{\sigma_\epsilon^2\sigma_\eta^2}{T\sigma_\eta^2 + \sigma_\epsilon^2} \quad \text{and} \quad b_i = \left[\sum_{t=1}^{T} y_{it}/\sigma_\epsilon^2\right] + (\mu/\sigma_\eta^2).$$

Note that the marginal posterior for η_i will also be normal, and thus it remains to calculate its mean and variance. For the mean,

$$E(\eta_i|y) = E_{\mu|y}[E(\eta_i|\mu, y)] = BE_{\mu|y}(b_i) = B\hat{b}_i, \tag{13.18}$$

where $\hat{b}_i \equiv [\sum_t y_{it}/\sigma_\epsilon^2] + \hat{\mu}/\sigma_\eta^2$. To calculate the variance, we make use of a well-known identity:

$$\begin{aligned}
\text{Var}(\eta_i|y) &= E_{\mu|y}[\text{Var}(\eta_i|\mu, y)] + \text{Var}_{u|y}[E(\eta_i|\mu, y)] \\
&= B + \text{Var}_{\mu|y}(Bb_i) \\
&= B + B^2\text{Var}_{\mu|y}(b_i) \\
&= B + [B/\sigma_\eta^2]^2 V_\mu.
\end{aligned} \tag{13.19}$$

Thus, the marginal posterior $\eta_i|y$ is normal with mean (13.18) and variance (13.19).
(b) Consider $\text{Cov}(\eta_i, \mu|y)$. The densities $\eta_i|\mu, y$ and $\mu|y$ derived in part (a) define the joint (normal) density $\eta_i, \mu|y$. Using well-known properties of the conditional normal distribution (see Theorem A.3), we can obtain the desired covariance by carefully examining the conditional mean $E(\eta_i|\mu, y)$. Specifically, from (13.17), we can write

$$\begin{aligned}
E(\eta_i|\mu, y) &= B\sum_t y_{it}/\sigma_\epsilon^2 + (B/\sigma_\eta^2)\mu \\
&= \left[B\sum_t y_{it}/\sigma_\epsilon^2 + (B/\sigma_\eta^2)\hat{\mu}\right] + (B/\sigma_\eta^2)(\mu - \hat{\mu}) \\
&= \left[B\sum_t y_{it}/\sigma_\epsilon^2 + (B/\sigma_\eta^2)\hat{\mu}\right] (BV_\mu/\sigma_\eta^2)(1/V_\mu)(\mu - \hat{\mu}).
\end{aligned}$$

In this last form it becomes clear (again using properties of the conditional normal distribution) that

$$\text{Cov}(\eta_i, \mu|y) = BV_\mu/\sigma_\eta^2. \tag{13.20}$$

The correlation coefficient $\text{Corr}(\eta_i, \mu|y)$ simply takes the covariance in (13.20) and divides it by the posterior standard deviations for η_i and μ implied from (13.19) and (13.16), respectively.

(c) Upon marginalizing (13.13) over the prior for α_i in (13.14), a density $y_i|\mu$ is obtained that is identical to (13.15). Since we continue to employ a flat prior for μ, it follows that $\mu|y$ is identical to the posterior in (13.16).

The marginal posterior $\alpha_i|y$, like all of the posteriors here with known variance parameters, will also be normal. It thus remains to characterize its mean and variance. For its mean, we have

$$E(\alpha_i|y) = E(\eta_i - \mu|y) = E(Bb_i - \mu|y) = B\hat{b}_i - \hat{\mu}, \tag{13.21}$$

and for its variance, we have

$$\begin{aligned}\text{Var}(\alpha_i|y) &= \text{Var}(\eta_i - \mu|y) = \text{Var}(\eta_i|y) + \text{Var}(\mu|y) - 2\text{Cov}(\eta_i, \mu|y) \\ &= B + [B/\sigma_\eta^2]^2 V_\mu + V_\mu - 2[BV_\mu/\sigma_\eta^2],\end{aligned} \tag{13.22}$$

using previous results in parts (a) and (b). Thus, $\alpha_i|y$ is normal with mean (13.21) and variance (13.22).

(d) Using the results of the previous parts of this exercise, we obtain

$$\text{Cov}(\alpha_i, \mu|y) = \text{Cov}(\eta_i - \mu, \mu|y) = \text{Cov}(\eta_i, \mu|y) - \text{Var}(\mu|y) = [BV_\mu/\sigma_\eta^2] - V_\mu. \tag{13.23}$$

Gelfand, Sahu, and Carlin (1995) argued that the choice of parameterization depends critically on the value of B/σ_η^2. Specifically, when $0 \leq B/\sigma_\eta^2 \leq 1$ is near zero, $\text{Corr}(\eta_i, \mu) < \text{Corr}(\alpha_i, \mu)$, and thus the centered parameterization is to be preferred. Conversely, when B/σ_η^2 is near one, $\text{Corr}(\eta_i, \mu) > \text{Corr}(\alpha_i, \mu)$, and thus the uncentered parameterization will be preferred. The idea behind this reasoning is that, all else being equal, it is better to have little correlation among the parameters of our posterior distribution, as highly correlated parameters will negatively affect the performance and convergence behavior of a posterior simulator (see, e.g., Exercise 12.8). In this particular context, if the researcher has strong prior information about the magnitude of the fraction $B/\sigma_\eta^2 = \sigma_\epsilon^2/(\sigma_\epsilon^2 + T\sigma_\eta^2)$, such information would suggest the best parameterization to employ. In the following two parts of this exercise, we quantify how the posterior correlation structure changes with the parameterization employed, and using generated data we document how a posterior simulator can be affected by this change in correlation structure.

(e) By using the given parameter values and substituting into the expressions in (13.16), (13.17), (13.19), and (13.20), it follows that $V_\mu = 1.05$, $B = .476$, $\text{Var}(\eta_i|y) = .478$, $\text{Cov}(\eta_i, \mu|y) = .05$, and thus $\text{Corr}(\eta_i, \mu|y) = .0706$.

When performing the same calculations for the (μ, α) space, we obtain $\text{Var}(\alpha_i|y) = 1.43$, $\text{Cov}(\alpha_i, \mu|y) = -1$, and thus $\text{Corr}(\alpha_i, \mu|y) = -.816$.

In this particular example, $B/\sigma_\eta^2 = .0476$ is small, and thus the results of Gelfand, Sahu, and Carlin (1995) suggest working with the centered parameterization. Our calculations do indeed show that, with this experimental design, the centered parameterization yields a posterior with less correlation among these elements.

(f) On the website associated with this book, we provide MATLAB code for four posterior simulators and apply each of these simulators to data generated according to the design described in part (e). For both the centered and uncentered parameterizations, we fit the model using both the Gibbs sampler and Monte Carlo integration. For the case of Monte Carlo integration, we first draw from the marginal posterior of μ in (13.16) and then draw independently from the posterior conditionals for η_i or α_i.

The results of these experiments echoed the conclusions of part (e) – the calculated correlations using both the Monte Carlo and Gibbs output were close to the analytical values derived in (e). For the case of the Gibbs algorithm, we also note a tremendous increase in the first-order autocorrelation coefficients associated with our simulated parameter draws when using the uncentered parameterization. The lag-1 correlation between the μ posterior simulations, for example, in the (μ, α) space exceeded .9, whereas the same correlation in the (μ, η) space was less than .05. This example suggests that parameterization issues can be quite important and can substantially impact the performance of a posterior simulator. Such a conclusion may seem surprising, since the difference between parameterizations in this simple example seems innocuous, yet leads to posterior simulators with substantially different performance.

Exercise 13.7 (A hierarchical/smoothness prior approach to non-parametric regression) Consider the non-parametric regression model

$$y_i = f(x_i) + \epsilon_i, \quad i = 1, 2, \dots, n, \tag{13.24}$$

where $\epsilon_i \overset{iid}{\sim} N(0, \sigma^2)$ and x_i is a scalar, and suppose that the data have been sorted so that $x_1 < x_2 < \cdots < x_n$. (For simplicity, consider the case where x is continuous so that, within sample, $x_j \neq x_{j-1}$. When different observations share the same x values, the framework presented here can be modified in a straightforward fashion to accommodate this feature of the data.)

Let $\theta_i = f(x_i)$ and write $y_i = \theta_i + \epsilon_i$, so that every point on the non-parametric regression line is treated as a new parameter.

Define $\Delta_j = x_j - x_{j-1}$, $j = 2, 3, \dots, n$, and construct an $n \times n$ matrix H as follows:

$$H = \begin{bmatrix} 1 & 0 & 0 & 0 & \cdots & 0 & 0 & 0 \\ 0 & 1 & 0 & 0 & \cdots & 0 & 0 & 0 \\ \Delta_2^{-1} & -(\Delta_2^{-1} + \Delta_3^{-1}) & \Delta_3^{-1} & 0 & \cdots & 0 & 0 & 0 \\ 0 & \Delta_3^{-1} & -(\Delta_3^{-1} + \Delta_4^{-1}) & \Delta_4^{-1} & \cdots & 0 & 0 & 0 \\ \vdots & \vdots & \vdots & \vdots & \ddots & \vdots & \vdots & \vdots \\ 0 & 0 & 0 & 0 & \cdots & \Delta_{n-1}^{-1} & -(\Delta_{n-1}^{-1} + \Delta_n^{-1}) & \Delta_n^{-1} \end{bmatrix}.$$

Let $\theta = [\theta_1\ \theta_2\ \cdots\ \theta_n]'$, and suppose a prior of the following form is employed:

$$H\theta|\eta \sim N\left(\begin{bmatrix} \mu_1 \\ 0 \end{bmatrix}, \begin{bmatrix} V_1 & 0 \\ 0 & \eta I_{n-2} \end{bmatrix}\right) \equiv N(\mu, V), \tag{13.25}$$

where μ_1 is 2×1 and V_1 is 2×2.
(a) Interpret this prior, paying particular attention to the role of η. Using a prior for σ^2 of the form $\sigma^2 \sim IG(a, b)$, reparameterize the model in terms of $\gamma = H\theta$ and derive a Gibbs sampling algorithm for fitting the reparameterized non-parametric regression model.
(b) Generate $n = 200$ observations from the following regression model:

$$y_i = .15x_i + .3\exp[-4(x_i + 1)^2] + .7\exp[-16(x_i - 1)^2] + \epsilon_i,$$

where $x_i \overset{iid}{\sim} U(-2, 2)$ (with U denoting a uniform distribution; see Definition A.1) and $\epsilon_i \overset{iid}{\sim} N(0, .01)$. Using the algorithm in part (a), fit the model for three different values of η: .00001, .15, and 100. Plot the posterior mean of θ in each case and comment on the results.

Solution

(a) First, note that $H\theta$ serves to transform the coefficient vector into a vector of "initial conditions" (i.e., the first two points on the regression curve) and first differences in pointwise slopes of the curve. That is,

$$\gamma = H\theta = \begin{bmatrix} \theta_1 \\ \theta_2 \\ \frac{\theta_3 - \theta_2}{\Delta_3} - \frac{\theta_2 - \theta_1}{\Delta_2} \\ \frac{\theta_4 - \theta_3}{\Delta_4} - \frac{\theta_3 - \theta_2}{\Delta_3} \\ \vdots \\ \frac{\theta_n - \theta_{n-1}}{\Delta_n} - \frac{\theta_{n-1} - \theta_{n-2}}{\Delta_{n-1}} \end{bmatrix},$$

where terms of the form $(\theta_j - \theta_{j-1})/\Delta_j$ can be interpreted as pointwise derivatives of f at x_{j-1}.

The parameter η controls how "tightly" these first differences are centered around zero. When η is very small, the prior restricts these differences to be approximately equal. As a result, the prior will essentially restrict the regression function to be linear, with the initial conditions serving to define the intercept and slope of the line. When η is quite large, little prior information is imposed in the analysis; as a result, the posterior mean of $\theta = H^{-1}\gamma$ will be excessively "jumpy." For intermediate η, the prior is designed to embed a degree of smoothness into the regression function.

For a posterior simulator, the prior for γ is given in (13.25). The non-parametric regression model can also be rewritten as follows:

$$\begin{aligned} y &= I_n\theta + \epsilon \\ &= H^{-1}\gamma + \epsilon, \end{aligned} \tag{13.26}$$

where $y = [y_1\ y_2\ \cdots\ y_n]'$ and $\epsilon = [\epsilon_1\ \epsilon_2\ \cdots\ \epsilon_n]'$, and thus we are in the framework of a normal linear regression model with normal and inverted gamma priors, as in Exercise 12.9.

A Gibbs sampler for the model in (13.26) under the given priors thus follows immediately:

$$\gamma|\sigma^2, y \sim N(D_\gamma d_\gamma, D_\gamma), \tag{13.27}$$

where

$$D_\gamma = (H^{-1\prime}H^{-1}/\sigma^2 + V^{-1})^{-1}, \quad d_\gamma = H^{-1\prime}y/\sigma^2 + V^{-1}\mu.$$

Similarly,

$$\sigma^2|y \sim IG\left(\frac{n}{2} + a, \left[b^{-1} + (1/2)(y - H^{-1}\gamma)'(y - H^{-1}\gamma)\right]^{-1}\right). \tag{13.28}$$

The posterior simulator involves sampling from (13.27) and (13.28). To recover the original parameter vector θ, which represents $f(x)$ at each data point, simply calculate $\theta = H^{-1}\gamma$ at each iteration.

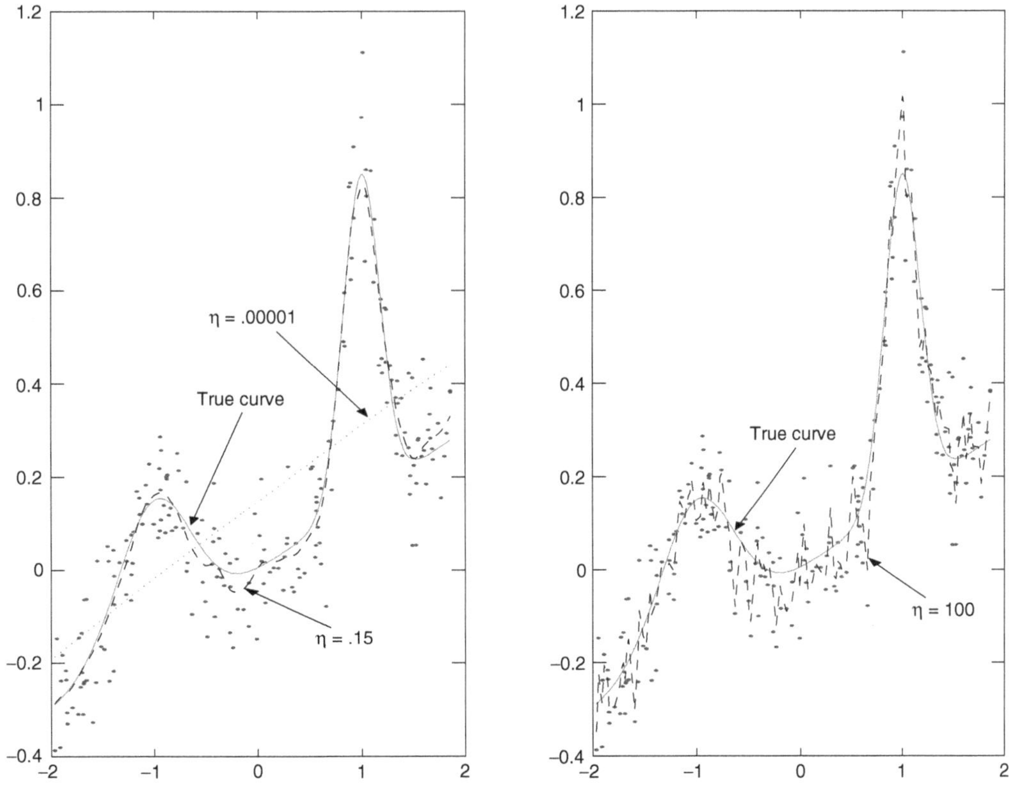

Figure 13.3. True curve and posterior means of regression function under different values of η.

(b) Using data generated as specified, we run the Gibbs sampler for 250 iterations for each of the three values of η. The first 50 of these are discarded as the burn-in period. In Figure 13.3 we present posterior means of θ for this exercise. The graph on the left presents the scatter plot, true curve, and posterior means when $\eta = .0001$ and $\eta = .15$. As you can see, when η is very small, the regression curve is constrained to be linear. When $\eta = .15$, the posterior mean matches the true curve reasonably well. The graph on the right presents the posterior mean when $\eta = 100$. With weak prior information with this value of η, we obtain an undersmoothed, erratic point estimate of the regression function.

14

Latent Variable Models

Many microeconometric applications (including binary, discrete choice, tobit, and generalized tobit analyses) involve the use of latent data. These latent data are unobserved by the econometrician, but the observed choices economic agents make typically impose some type of truncation or ordering among the latent variables.

In this chapter we show how the Gibbs sampler can be used to fit a variety of common microeconomic models involving the use of latent data. In particular, we review how *data augmentation* (see, e.g., Tanner and Wong 1987; Chib 1992; Albert and Chib 1993) can be used to simplify the computations in these models. Importantly, we recognize that many popular models in econometrics are essentially linear regression models on suitably defined latent data. Thus, conditioned on the latent data's values, we can apply all of the known techniques discussed in previous chapters (especially Chapter 10) for inference in the linear regression model. The idea behind data augmentation is to add (or augment) the joint posterior distribution with the latent data itself. In the Gibbs sampler, then, we can typically apply standard techniques to draw from the model parameters given the latent data, and then add an additional step to draw values of the latent data given the model parameters.

To review the idea behind data augmentation in general terms, suppose that we are primarily interested in characterizing the joint posterior $p(\theta|y)$ of a k-dimensional parameter vector θ. An alternative to analyzing this posterior directly involves working with a seemingly more completed posterior $p(\theta, z|y)$ for some *latent data* z. The desired marginal posterior for θ is then obtained by integrating out z.

Although the addition of the variables z might seem to needlessly complicate the estimation exercise, it often proves to be computationally convenient. To implement the Gibbs sampler here, we need to obtain the posterior conditionals $p(\theta|z, y)$ and $p(z|\theta, y)$. Often, the posterior conditional $p(\theta|z, y)$ will take a convenient form, thus making it possible to fit the model using the Gibbs sampler. Upon convergence, the set of draws for θ can be used to characterize its marginal posterior. We begin illustrating these methods with perhaps the most celebrated latent variable model: the probit. We remind the reader that MATLAB code for carrying out the empirical parts of the questions is provided on the website associated with this book. In addition to our previously used notation of y/X for the vector/matrix of observations on the dependent/explanatory variables, in this chapter we will also let $z = [z_1 \ \cdots \ z_n]'$, $z^* = [z_1^* \ \cdots \ z_n^*]'$, and $x_{-\theta}$ denote all quantities in x other than θ.

Exercise 14.1 (Posterior simulation in the probit model) Consider the following latent variable representation of the probit model:

$$z_i = x_i\beta + \epsilon_i, \quad \epsilon_i \stackrel{iid}{\sim} N(0,1), \tag{14.1}$$

$$y_i = \begin{cases} 1 & \text{if } z_i > 0, \\ 0 & \text{if } z_i \leq 0. \end{cases}$$

The value of the binary variable y_i is observed, as are the values of the explanatory variables x_i. The latent data z_i, however, are unobserved.
(a) Derive the likelihood function for this model.
(b) Using a prior for β of the form $\beta \sim N(\mu_\beta, V_\beta)$, derive the *augmented* joint posterior $p(\beta, z|y)$.
(c) Verify that, marginalized over z, the joint posterior for the parameters β is exactly the same as the posterior you would obtain without introducing any latent variables to the model. For an interesting comparison, see Zellner and Rossi (1984) for a discussion of Bayesian analysis of binary choice models prior to the use of MCMC methods.
(d) Given your result in part (b), derive the complete posterior conditionals and discuss how the Gibbs sampler can be employed to fit the model.

Solution
(a) Note that

$$\Pr(y_i = 1|x_i, \beta) = \Pr(x_i\beta + \epsilon_i > 0) = \Pr(\epsilon_i > -x_i\beta) = 1 - \Phi(-x_i\beta) = \Phi(x_i\beta).$$

Similarly,

$$\Pr(y_i = 0|x_i, \beta) = 1 - \Phi(x_i\beta).$$

Because of the assumed independence across observations, the likelihood function is obtained as

$$L(\beta) = \prod_{i=1}^{n} \Phi(x_i\beta)^{y_i}[1 - \Phi(x_i\beta)]^{1-y_i}.$$

(b) To derive the *augmented* joint posterior, note that

$$p(\beta, z|y) = \frac{p(y, z|\beta)p(\beta)}{p(y)},$$

implying that

$$p(\beta, z|y) \propto p(y, z|\beta)p(\beta).$$

The term $p(\beta)$ is simply our prior, whereas $p(y, z|\beta)$ represents the *complete* or *augmented* data density. To characterize this density in more detail, note that

$$p(y, z|\beta) = p(y|z, \beta)p(z|\beta).$$

Immediately, from our latent variable representation, we know that

$$p(z|\beta) = \prod_{i=1}^{n} \phi(z_i; x_i\beta, 1). \tag{14.2}$$

For the conditional for y given z and β, note that when $z_i > 0$ then y_i must equal one, whereas when $z_i \leq 0$ then y_i must equal zero. In other words, the sign of z_i perfectly predicts the value of y. Hence, we can write

$$p(y|z, \beta) = \prod_{i=1}^{n} \left[I(z_i > 0)I(y_i = 1) + I(z_i \leq 0)I(y_i = 0)\right], \tag{14.3}$$

with I denoting the indicator function, which takes on the value one if the statement in the parentheses is true and is otherwise zero. This expression simply states that when z_i is positive, then y_i is one with probability one, and conversely, when z_i is negative, then y_i is zero with probability one.

Putting the pieces in (14.2) and (14.3) together, we obtain the augmented data density $p(y, z|\beta)$. We combine this with our prior to obtain

$$p(\beta, z|y) \propto p(\beta) \prod_{i=1}^{n} \left[I(z_i > 0)I(y_i = 1) + I(z_i \leq 0)I(y_i = 0)\right] \phi(z_i, x_i\beta, 1). \tag{14.4}$$

(c) To show the equality of these quantities, we integrate (14.4) over z to obtain

$$\begin{aligned}
p(\beta|y) &= \int_z p(\beta, z|y)dz \\
&\propto p(\beta) \int_z \prod_{i=1}^{n} \left[I(z_i > 0)I(y_i = 1) + I(z_i \leq 0)I(y_i = 0)\right] \phi(z_i, x_i\beta, 1)dz_1 \cdots dz_n \\
&= p(\beta) \prod_{i=1}^{n} \left[\int_{-\infty}^{\infty} \left[I(z_i > 0)I(y_i = 1) + I(z_i \leq 0)I(y_i = 0)\right] \phi(z_i, x_i\beta, 1)dz_i\right]
\end{aligned}$$

$$= p(\beta) \prod_{i=1}^{n} \left[\int_{-\infty}^{0} I(y_i = 0)\phi(z_i; x_i\beta, 1)dz_i + \int_{0}^{\infty} I(y_i = 1)\phi(z_i; x_i\beta, 1)dz_i \right]$$
$$= p(\beta) \prod_{i=1}^{n} [I(y_i = 0)[1 - \Phi(x_i\beta)] + I(y_i = 1)\Phi(x_i\beta)]$$
$$= p(\beta) \prod_{i=1}^{n} \Phi(x_i\beta)^{y_i}[1 - \Phi(x_i\beta)]^{1-y_i}.$$

Note that this is exactly the prior times the likelihood obtained from part (a), which can be obtained without explicitly introducing any latent variables. What is important to note is that the posterior of β is unchanged by the addition of the latent variables. So, augmenting the posterior with z will not change any inference regarding β, though it does make the problem computationally easier, as described in the solution to the next question.

(d) With the addition of the latent data, the complete conditionals are easily obtained. In particular, the complete conditional for β *given* z and the data y follows directly from (14.4) and standard results from the linear regression model (details of which are provided in Exercise 12.9):

$$\beta|z, y \sim N(D_\beta d_\beta, D_\beta), \tag{14.5}$$

where

$$D_\beta = (X'X + V_\beta^{-1})^{-1}, \qquad d_\beta = X'z + V_\beta^{-1}\mu_\beta.$$

For the complete conditional for z, first note that the conditional independence across observations implies that each z_i can be drawn independently. We also note from (14.4) that

$$z_i|\beta, y \propto I(z_i > 0)\phi(z_i; x_i\beta, 1) \quad \text{if } y_i = 1,$$
$$z_i|\beta, y \propto I(z_i \leq 0)\phi(z_i; x_i\beta, 1) \quad \text{if } y_i = 0.$$

Thus,

$$z_i|\beta, y \overset{ind}{\sim} \begin{cases} TN_{(-\infty,0]}(x_i\beta, 1) & \text{if } y_i = 0, \\ TN_{(0,\infty)}(x_i\beta, 1) & \text{if } y_i = 1, \end{cases} \tag{14.6}$$

where the notation $TN_{[a,b]}(\mu, \sigma^2)$ denotes a normal distribution with mean μ and variance σ^2 truncated to the interval $[a, b]$.

Implementation of the Gibbs sampler involves iteratively sampling from (14.5) and (14.6). To generate draws from the truncated normal in (14.6), one can use the inverse transform method as described in the solution to Exercise 11.5.

Exercise 14.2 (Parameter identification in the probit model) Generate data from a probit model, as described in Exercise 14.1, and consider what happens when you relax the normalization that the variance parameter is unity. Instead, specify $\epsilon_i \overset{iid}{\sim} N(0, \sigma^2)$.

Derive the complete conditionals for this model. Implement the Gibbs sampler and plot the posterior simulations of β, σ, and β/σ obtained from your generated-data experiment.

Solution

For this exercise, we employed priors of the form

$$\beta \sim N(\mu_\beta, V_\beta)$$

and

$$\sigma^2 \sim IG(a, b).$$

Let us first derive the complete posterior conditionals when σ^2 is not normalized to unity:

$$\beta|z, \sigma^2, y \sim N(D_\beta d_\beta, D_\beta), \tag{14.7}$$

where

$$D_\beta = (X'X/\sigma^2 + V_\beta^{-1})^{-1}, \qquad d_\beta = X'z/\sigma^2 + V_\beta^{-1}\mu_\beta,$$

$$z_i|\sigma^2, \beta, y_i \overset{\text{ind}}{\sim} \begin{cases} TN_{(-\infty,0]}(x_i\beta, \sigma^2) & \text{if } y_i = 0, \\ TN_{(0,\infty)}(x_i\beta, \sigma^2) & \text{if } y_i = 1, \end{cases} \tag{14.8}$$

and

$$\sigma^2|z, \beta, y \sim IG\left[\frac{n}{2} + a, \left(b^{-1} + (1/2)\sum_i (z_i - x_i\beta)^2\right)^{-1}\right]. \tag{14.9}$$

It is important to recognize that the complete conditionals in (14.7)–(14.9) do not necessarily alert us of the problem that the regression parameters are only identified up to scale. The densities in this algorithm are well defined, easily sampled, and offer no direct evidence of an identification problem. We will see, however, that the output from the posterior simulator will suggest a problem and reveal that the regression coefficients and scale parameter are not jointly identifiable.

We generate 2000 observations from a probit model containing an intercept β_0 and one slope coefficient β_1. Specifically, we generate $x_i \overset{iid}{\sim} N(0, 1)$and $\beta = [\beta_0\ \beta_1]' = [.2\ .6]'$, and fix $\sigma^2 = 1$. For our hyperparameters we set $\mu_\beta = 0$, $V_\beta = 100I_2$, $a = 3$, and $b = .5$. We run the Gibbs sampler by cycling through (14.7), (14.8), and (14.9). The first 500 simulations are discarded as the burn-in and the final 2000 are retained and used for our posterior analysis. Since the β parameters are only identified up to scale, we expect that the actual draws of β_0, σ, and β_1 will not converge to anything, whereas the quantities β_0/σ and β_1/σ should converge to their generated-data values of .2 and .6, respectively.

Presented in Figure 14.1 are plots of the β_1, σ, β_0/σ, and β_1/σ draws from our posterior simulator. As seen from the figure, the draws from the marginal posteriors of β_1 and σ wander throughout the parameter space and do not settle down around their generated-data values. However, they do move together, and as shown in the bottom row of the figure, the

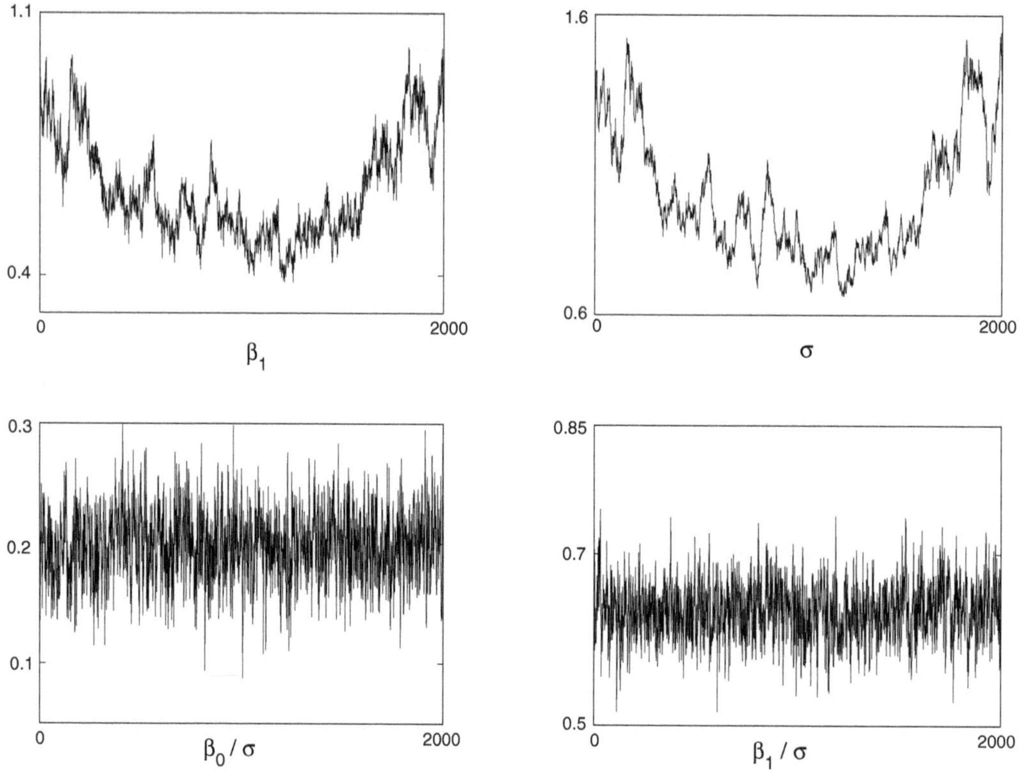

Figure 14.1. Plots of parameter values for 2000 Gibbs iterations using generated probit data.

identified quantities β_0/σ and β_1/σ do approximately converge to .2 and .6, the values used to generate these data.

Exercise 14.3 (Probit model: Application using Fair's (1978) data) In an interesting paper that has been used to illustrate the binary choice model in econometrics texts (e.g., Gujarati 2003, pp. 618–620), Fair (1978) analyzed the decision to have an extramarital affair. We have made a version of these data available on the website associated with this book. Take these data and perform a binary choice analysis. Fit the model using the Gibbs sampler and interpret your results.

Solution

Fair (1978) used the results of surveys conducted by *Psychology Today* and *Redbook* magazines to model extramarital affairs. In this application we take 601 responses from the *Psychology Today* survey, noting that the variables constructed and used here are slightly different than the ones used in his original study. All observations are taken from individuals currently married and married for the first time.

Table 14.1: Coefficient and marginal effect posterior means and standard deviations from the probit model using Fair's (1978) data.

	Coefficient		Marginal effect	
	Mean	Std. dev.	Mean	Std. dev.
CONS	−.726	(.417)	—	—
MALE	.154	(.131)	.047	(.040)
YS-MARRIED	.029	(.013)	.009	(.004)
KIDS	.256	(.159)	.073	(.045)
RELIGIOUS	−.514	(.124)	−.150	(.034)
ED	.005	(.026)	.001	(.008)
HAPPY	−.514	(.125)	−.167	(.042)

We specify a probit model where the decision to have an extramarital affair depends on an intercept (CONS), a male dummy (MALE), number of years married (YS-MARRIED), a dummy variable if the respondent has children from the marriage (KIDS), a dummy for classifying one's self as "religious" (RELIGIOUS), years of schooling completed (ED), and a final dummy variable denoting whether the person views the marriage as happier than an average marriage (HAPPY).

For our prior for the 7×1 parameter vector β, we specify

$$\beta \sim N(0, 10^2 I_7),$$

so that the prior is quite non-informative and centered at zero. We run the Gibbs sampler for 2000 iterations and discard the first 500 as the burn-in.

Shown in Table 14.1 are coefficient posterior means and standard deviations from the binary choice model. To illustrate how quantities of interest other than regression coefficients can also be calculated, we report posterior means and standard deviations associated with *marginal effects* from the probit model. For a continuous explanatory variable we note that

$$\frac{\partial E(y|x, \beta)}{\partial x_j} = \beta_j \phi(x\beta).$$

For given x, this is a function of the regression parameters β. Thus, the *posterior distribution of the marginal effect* can be obtained by calculating and collecting the values $\{\beta_j^{(i)} \phi(x\beta^{(i)})\}_{i=1}^{1500}$, where $\beta^{(i)}$ represents the ith post-convergence draw obtained from the Gibbs sampler. When x_j is binary, we calculate the marginal effect as the difference between the normal cdfs when the binary indicator is set to 1 and then 0. In all cases, we choose to evaluate the marginal effects at the sample means of the x's. (If desired, one can instead set the binary variables to specific integer values rather than sample means, though we do not pursue this in our calculations.)

From the table, we see that people reporting themselves as religious are 15% less likely to have affairs (holding the x's at mean values), and those reporting to be in happy marriages are 17% less likely. The posterior standard deviations for these quantities are small relative to their means, indicating that virtually all of the posterior masses associated with these marginal effects are placed over negative values.

Exercise 14.4 (Posterior simulation in the panel probit model) Consider a panel probit model of the form

$$z_{it} = \alpha_i + x_{it}\beta + \epsilon_{it}, \quad \epsilon_{it} \overset{iid}{\sim} N(0,1), \; i = 1, 2, \dots, n, \; t = 1, 2, \dots, T. \tag{14.10}$$

The observed binary responses y_{it} are generated according to

$$y_{it} = \begin{cases} 1 & \text{if } z_{it} > 0, \\ 0 & \text{if } z_{it} \leq 0, \end{cases}$$

and the random effects $\{\alpha_i\}$ are drawn from a common distribution:

$$\alpha_i \overset{iid}{\sim} N(\alpha, \sigma_\alpha^2).$$

Suppose that you employ priors of the following forms:

$$\begin{aligned} \beta &\sim N(\mu_\beta, V_\beta), \\ \alpha &\sim N(\mu_\alpha, V_\alpha), \\ \sigma_\alpha^2 &\sim IG(a, b). \end{aligned}$$

Show how a Gibbs sampler can be employed to fit the panel probit model.

Solution

Just like the probit without a panel structure (e.g., Exercise 14.1), we will use data augmentation to fit the model. Specifically, we will work with an augmented posterior distribution of the form $p(z, \{\alpha_i\}, \alpha, \sigma_\alpha^2, \beta | y)$. Derivation of the complete posterior conditionals follows similarly to those derived in Exercise 14.1 for the probit and Exercises 13.2 and 13.5 for linear hierarchical models. Specifically, we obtain

$$z_{it} | \alpha, \{\alpha_i\}, \sigma_\alpha^2, \beta, y \overset{ind}{\sim} \begin{cases} TN_{(-\infty,0]}(\alpha_i + x_{it}\beta, 1) & \text{if } y_{it} = 0, \\ TN_{(0,\infty)}(\alpha_i + x_{it}\beta, 1) & \text{if } y_{it} = 1, \end{cases} \tag{14.11}$$

$$\alpha_i | \alpha, \sigma_\alpha^2, \beta, z, y \overset{\text{ind}}{\sim} N(D_{\alpha_i} d_{\alpha_i}, D_{\alpha_i}), \quad i = 1, 2, \dots, n, \tag{14.12}$$

where

$$D_{\alpha_i} = (T + \sigma_\alpha^{-2})^{-1}, \quad d_{\alpha_i} = \sum_t (z_{it} - x_{it}\beta) + \sigma_\alpha^{-2}\alpha,$$

$$\beta | \alpha, \{\alpha_i\}, \sigma_\alpha^2, z, y \sim N(D_\beta d_\beta, D_\beta), \tag{14.13}$$

$$D_\beta = (X'X + V_\beta^{-1})^{-1}, \quad d_\beta = X'(z - \overline{\overline{\alpha}}) + V_\beta^{-1}\mu_\beta,$$

X and z have been stacked appropriately, and $\overline{\overline{\alpha}} \equiv [\alpha_1 \iota_T' \ \cdots \ \alpha_n \iota_T']'$, with ι_T denoting a $T \times 1$ vector of ones, and

$$\alpha|\beta, \{\alpha_i\}, \sigma_\alpha^2, z, y \sim N(D_\alpha d_\alpha, D_\alpha), \tag{14.14}$$

where

$$D_\alpha = (n/\sigma_\alpha^2 + V_\alpha^{-1})^{-1}, \quad d_\alpha = \sum_i \alpha_i/\sigma_\alpha^2 + V_\alpha^{-1}\mu_\alpha.$$

Finally,

$$\sigma_\alpha^2|\alpha, \{\alpha_i\}, \beta, z, y \sim IG\left(\frac{n}{2} + a, \left[b^{-1} + .5\sum_i (\alpha_i - \alpha)^2\right]^{-1}\right). \tag{14.15}$$

Fitting the model involves cycling through (14.11) through (14.15). Of course, blocking steps can and should be used to improve the mixing of the posterior simulator (see, e.g., Exercise 13.5).

Exercise 14.5 (Posterior simulation in the ordered probit I) Consider the latent variable representation of the *ordered probit model*:

$$z_i = x_i\beta + \epsilon_i, \quad \epsilon_i \stackrel{iid}{\sim} N(0, 1), \tag{14.16}$$

and

$$y_i = \begin{cases} 1 & \text{if } \alpha_0 < z_i \leq \alpha_1, \\ 2 & \text{if } \alpha_1 < z_i \leq \alpha_2, \\ \vdots & \qquad \vdots \\ M & \text{if } \alpha_{M-1} < z_i \leq \alpha_M. \end{cases}$$

We do not observe the latent variable z, but instead, we observe the ordered response $y_i \in \{1, 2, \ldots, M\}$, where y is generated in terms of z. For identification purposes, we set $\alpha_0 = -\infty$, $\alpha_1 = 0$, and $\alpha_M = \infty$. The α_i are often called *cutpoints*.
(a) Write down the likelihood function for this model.
(b) How would you calculate marginal effects in the ordered probit?
(c) Show how the Gibbs sampler can be used to fit this model (e.g., Albert and Chib 1993) under flat priors for α and β – i.e., $p(\alpha, \beta) \propto c$].
(d) Consider an ordered probit model where $y_i \in \{1, 2, 3\}$. Generate 500 observations from this ordered probit where $z_i = .5 + .3x_i + \epsilon_i$, $x_i \stackrel{iid}{\sim} N(0, 1)$, and $\alpha_2 = 1$. Present a table of posterior means and standard deviations of the model parameters, and also present a plot of the lagged autocorrelations for the cutpoint α_2.

Solution

(a) For each i, the contribution to the likelihood function is

$$\begin{aligned}\Pr(y_i = k|\beta, \{\alpha_m\}) &= \Pr(\alpha_{k-1} < z_i \leq \alpha_k) \\ &= \Pr(\alpha_{k-1} - x_i\beta < z_i - x_i\beta \leq \alpha_k - x_i\beta) \\ &= \Phi(\alpha_k - x_i\beta) - \Phi(\alpha_{k-1} - x_i\beta).\end{aligned}$$

Thus, the likelihood function can be written as

$$L(\beta, \{\alpha_m\}) = \prod_{i=1}^{n} \Phi\left(\alpha_{y_i} - x_i\beta\right) - \Phi\left(\alpha_{y_i-1} - x_i\beta\right). \tag{14.17}$$

(b) For this model we have

$$\begin{aligned}\Pr(y = 1|x, \beta, \{\alpha_m\}) &= 1 - \Phi(x\beta), \\ \Pr(y = k|x, \beta, \{\alpha_m\}) &= \Phi(\alpha_k - x\beta) - \Phi(\alpha_{k-1} - x\beta), \quad 1 < k < M, \\ \Pr(y = M|x, \beta, \{\alpha_m\}) &= 1 - \Phi(\alpha_{M-1} - x\beta).\end{aligned}$$

Thus, we obtain the following marginal effects:

$$\begin{aligned}\frac{\partial \Pr(y = 1|x, \beta, \{\alpha_m\})}{\partial x_j} &= -\phi(x\beta)\beta_j, \\ \frac{\partial \Pr(y = k|x, \beta, \{\alpha_m\})}{\partial x_j} &= \left[\phi(\alpha_{k-1} - x\beta) - \phi(\alpha_k - x\beta)\right]\beta_j, \quad 1 < k < M, \\ \frac{\partial \Pr(y = M|x, \beta, \{\alpha_m\})}{\partial x_j} &= \phi(\alpha_{M-1} - x\beta)\beta_j.\end{aligned}$$

Hence, we can calculate how a change in a covariate changes the probabilities of y equaling each ordered value. Interestingly, note that the signs of the marginal effects for the "interior" values of y cannot be determined just given the sign of β_j. This was not the case in the linear regression and probit models.

(c) We again pursue a data augmentation approach in our Gibbs sampling algorithm. Let $\alpha = [\alpha_2 \; \alpha_3 \; \cdots \; \alpha_{M-1}]$ denote the vector of cutpoints and note that

$$p(\beta, \alpha, z|y) \propto p(y, z|\beta, \alpha)p(\beta, \alpha), \tag{14.18}$$

where

$$p(y, z|\beta, \alpha) = p(y|z, \beta, \alpha)p(z|\beta, \alpha)$$

is the complete or augmented likelihood function. Conditioned on z and α, the value of y is known with certainty. Specifically, we can write

$$\Pr(y_i = k|z_i, \alpha, \beta) = I\left(\alpha_{k-1} < z_i \leq \alpha_k\right), \tag{14.19}$$

or equivalently,

$$p(y_i|z_i, \alpha, \beta) = I\left(\alpha_{y_i-1} < z_i \leq \alpha_{y_i}\right), \quad y_i \in \{1, 2, \ldots, M\}. \tag{14.20}$$

Under flat priors for α and β, it follows that the joint posterior distribution can be written as

$$p(\alpha, \beta, z|y) \propto \prod_{i=1}^{n} \phi(z_i; x_i\beta, 1) I\left(\alpha_{y_i-1} < z_i \leq \alpha_{y_i}\right). \tag{14.21}$$

Given this joint posterior distribution, we obtain the following complete posterior conditionals:

$$\beta|\alpha, z, y \sim N\left((X'X)^{-1}X'z, (X'X)^{-1}\right), \tag{14.22}$$

with X and z stacked appropriately and

$$z_i|\alpha, \beta, z_{-i}, y \stackrel{ind}{\sim} TN_{(\alpha_{y_i-1}, \alpha_{y_i}]}(x_i\beta, 1), \quad i = 1, 2, \ldots, n. \tag{14.23}$$

For the complete posterior conditional for the cutpoints, note that

$$\alpha_k|\alpha_{-k}, \beta, z, y \propto \prod_{i:y_i=k} I\left(\alpha_{k-1} < z_i \leq \alpha_k\right) \prod_{i:y_i=k+1} I\left(\alpha_k < z_i \leq \alpha_{k+1}\right).$$

It follows that

$$\alpha_k|\alpha_{-k}, \beta, z, y \stackrel{ind}{\sim} U[a_k, b_k], \tag{14.24}$$

where

$$a_k = \max\left\{\alpha_{k-1}, \max_{i:y_i=k} z_i\right\}$$

and

$$b_k = \min\left\{\alpha_{k+1}, \min_{i:y_i=k+1} z_i\right\}.$$

Implementing the Gibbs sampler involves successively sampling from (14.22), (14.23), and (14.24).

(d) Starting with the initial conditions $\alpha_2 = .5$ and $\beta = [\beta_0\ \beta_1]' = [0\ 0]'$, we cycle through these complete posterior conditionals (starting with the latent data). We run the sampler for 2500 iterations and discard the first 500 as the burn-in period. The posterior means and standard deviations are presented in Table 14.2. We see that our posterior means with 500 observations are close to the values used to generate the data. To get a feeling of the

Table 14.2: Posterior means and standard deviations from the ordered probit model.

Parameter	True value	Post. mean	Post. std.
β_0	.5	.479	.057
β_1	.3	.569	.051
α_2	1	.972	.053

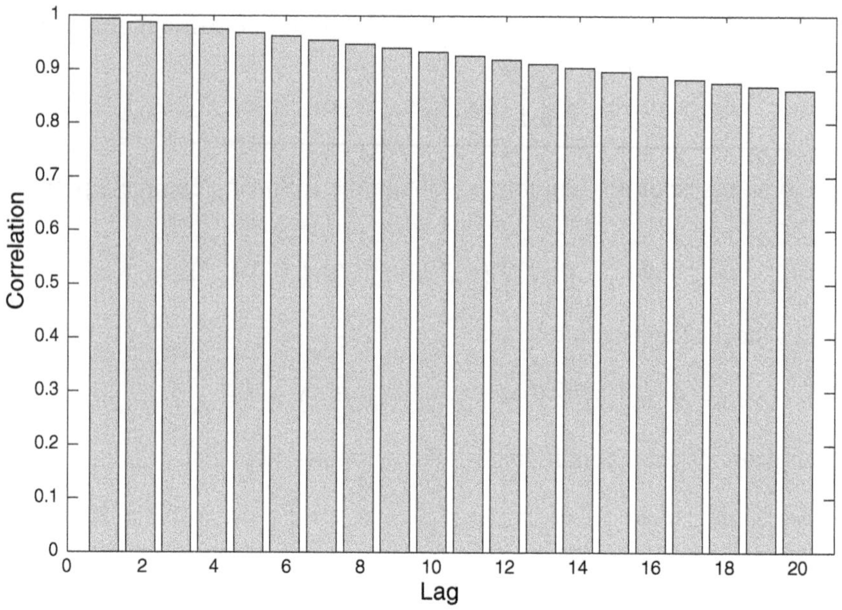

Figure 14.2. Plots of lagged autocorrelations for α_2.

mixing of the chain, we plot in Figure 14.2 the lagged correlations up to order 20 for the cutpoint α_2.

As one can see from Figure 14.2, the autocorrelations among the Gibbs draws are quite high and diminish very slowly. The correlation between simulated α_2 values that are 20 iterations away from one another is almost .9. This suggests very slow mixing of the chain, and, as a result, high numerical standard errors (see, e.g., Exercise 12.20). The following exercise suggests a reparameterization that may help facilitate mixing in the ordered probit model.

Exercise 14.6 (Posterior simulation in the ordered probit II: Nandram and Chen (1996)) Consider the ordered probit model with $M = 3$ discussed in Exercise 14.5 and make the following reparameterization as suggested in Nandram and Chen (1996):

$$\delta = 1/\alpha_2, \quad \alpha^* = \delta\alpha, \quad \beta^* = \delta\beta, \quad z^* = \delta z.$$

(a) Derive the joint posterior distribution $p(\delta, \beta^*, z^*|y)$. Note that, for the case of $M = 3$ with this parameterization, there are no unknown cutpoints, since $\alpha_0^* = -\infty$, $\alpha_1^* = 0$, $\alpha_2^* = 1$, and $\alpha_3^* = \infty$.
(b) Describe how the Gibbs sampler can be used to fit this reparameterized model.
(c) Using the same data that were employed in part (d) of Exercise 14.5, estimate the reparameterized model and present a similar plot of the lagged autocorrelations for α_2.

Solution
(a) For the case of $M = 3$, under flat priors, we showed in the previous exercise that

$$p(\alpha_2, \beta, z|y) \propto \prod_{i=1}^{n} \phi(z_i; x_i\beta, 1) I\left(\alpha_{y_i-1} < z_i \leq \alpha_{y_i}\right). \tag{14.25}$$

We seek to determine the joint posterior distribution $p(\delta, \beta^*, z^*|y)$.

The joint posterior $p(\delta, \beta^*, z^*|y)$ follows from a change of variables from $p(\alpha_2, \beta, z|y)$. With a bit of work, one can show that the Jacobian of this transformation is $\delta^{-[n+r+2]}$, where β is an $r \times 1$ vector. Thus, we have

$$p(\delta, \beta^*, z^*|y) \propto \delta^{-[n+r+2]} \prod_{i=1}^{n} \exp\left(-\frac{1}{2}\left[\frac{z_i^*}{\delta} - \frac{1}{\delta}x_i\beta^*\right]^2\right) I\left(\frac{\alpha_{y_i-1}^*}{\delta} < \frac{z_i^*}{\delta} \leq \frac{\alpha_{y_i}^*}{\delta}\right)$$

$$= \delta^{-[n+r+2]} \prod_{i=1}^{n} \exp\left(-\frac{1}{2\delta^2}(z_i^* - x_i\beta^*)^2\right) I\left(\alpha_{y_i-1}^* < z_i^* \leq \alpha_{y_i}^*\right),$$

where, again, all $\alpha_{y_i}^*$ are known.
(b) For this parameterization, we obtain the following complete conditional posterior distributions:

$$\beta^*|z^*, \delta, y \sim N\left((X'X)^{-1}X'z^*, \delta^2(X'X)^{-1}\right), \tag{14.26}$$

$$z_i^*|\beta^*, \delta, y \overset{ind}{\sim} TN_{(\alpha_{y_i-1}^*, \alpha_{y_i}^*]}(x_i\beta, \delta^2), \tag{14.27}$$

where the α_i^* are known. Finally,

$$\delta^2|\beta^*, z^*, y \sim IG\left(\frac{n+r}{2}, \left[\frac{1}{2}(z^* - X\beta^*)'(z^* - X\beta^*)\right]^{-1}\right). \tag{14.28}$$

We fit the model by cycling through the complete conditionals in (14.26) through (14.28). To recover the original coefficient vector β and cutpoint α_2, we simply use the inverse transformations $\beta = (1/\delta)\beta^*$ and $\alpha_2 = (1/\delta)$.
(c) Table 14.3 presents posterior means and standard deviations, using the same data that were employed in Exercise 14.5(d). Figure 14.3 presents the lagged autocorrelations for

Table 14.3: Posterior means and standard deviations from the ordered probit model.

Parameter	True value	Post. mean	Post. std.
β_0	.5	.476	.057
β_1	.3	.324	.053
α_2	1	.957	.061

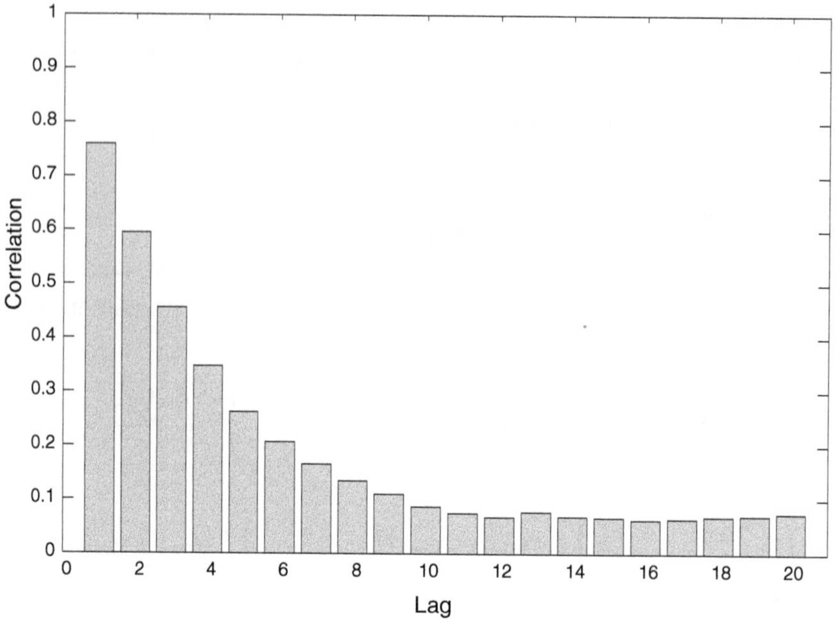

Figure 14.3. Plots of lagged autocorrelations for α_2 using the reparameterized model.

α_2 using the reparameterized model. As you can see, the mixing of the chain in this reparameterized model improves dramatically relative to that reported in the previous exercise. This rescaling transformation can also be used in a similar manner (also adding α^* to the sampler) when $M > 3$.

Exercise 14.7 (Posterior simulation in the multinomial probit) Suppose that an agent has a choice among J alternatives, with no natural ordering among the alternatives. Let y_i denote the observed choice of the agent, with $y_i \in \{0, 1, \ldots, J-1\}$.

Let U_{ij} represent the latent utility received by agent i from making choice j. We assume

$$U_{ij} = x_{ij}\beta_j + \epsilon_{ij}, \quad i = 1, 2, \ldots, n, \; j = 0, 1, \ldots, J-1.$$

We treat choice 0 as the base alternative and choose to work with utility differences between the choices:

$$U_{ij} - U_{i0} = (x_{ij} - x_{i0})\beta_j + \epsilon_{ij} - \epsilon_{i0},$$

or equivalently,

$$U_{ij}^* = z_{ij}\beta_j + \epsilon_{ij}^*, \quad i = 1, 2, \ldots, n, \; j = 1, 2, \ldots, J-1, \tag{14.29}$$

with $U_{ij}^* \equiv U_{ij} - U_{i0}$, $z_{ij} \equiv x_{ij} - x_{i0}$, and $\epsilon_{ij}^* \equiv \epsilon_{ij} - \epsilon_{i0}$. We assume that

$$\epsilon_i^* = \begin{bmatrix} \epsilon_{i1}^* \\ \epsilon_{i2}^* \\ \vdots \\ \epsilon_{iJ-1}^* \end{bmatrix} \stackrel{iid}{\sim} N(0, \Sigma), \quad i = 1, 2, \ldots, n,$$

where Σ is a $(J-1) \times (J-1)$ positive definite matrix with off-diagonal element (i, j) denoted σ_{ij} and the jth diagonal element denoted σ_j^2. Since we only observe the choice yielding maximal utility, there is an indeterminacy problem; the likelihood $L(\beta, \Sigma)$ is identical to $L(c\beta, c^2\Sigma)$. There are a variety of strategies one can use to impose identification, the most common of which is to restrict one of the diagonal elements of Σ to unity. We follow this identification strategy in the discussion that follows.

The observed choice made by the agent, y_i, is related to the latent U_{ij}^* as follows:

$$y_i = \begin{cases} 0 & \text{if } \max\{U_{ij}^*\}_{j=1}^{J-1} \leq 0, \\ k & \text{if } \max\left\{0, \{U_{ij}^*\}_{j=1}^{J-1}\right\} = U_{ik}^*. \end{cases} \tag{14.30}$$

That is, the agent chooses the base alternative if all utility differences are negative and chooses k if k yields more utility than the base choice and all other alternatives.

Finally, suppose priors of the following forms are specified:

$$\beta \sim N(\mu_\beta, V_\beta),$$
$$\Sigma^{-1} \sim W([\rho R]^{-1}, \rho) I(\sigma_{J-1}^2 = 1),$$

where the indicator function on the Wishart prior serves to enforce the identification restriction that the $(J-1, J-1)$ element of Σ is unity.

(a) Using data augmentation, describe how the Gibbs sampler can be employed to fit this model.

(b) Perform a generated-data experiment by simulating data from a multinomial probit model with three alternatives and one covariate. Specifically, generate 500 observations from the following model:

$$U_{ij}^* = \beta_0 + \beta_1 z_{ij} + \epsilon_{ij}^*, \quad j = 1, 2,$$

where $\beta_0 = -.5$, $\beta_1 = 1$, $z_{ij} \stackrel{iid}{\sim} N(0, 1)$, and $\epsilon_i^* = [\epsilon_{i1}^* \; \epsilon_{i2}^*]' \stackrel{iid}{\sim} N(0, \Sigma)$, where

$$\Sigma = \begin{bmatrix} \sigma_1^2 & \rho_{12}\sigma_1 \\ \rho_{12}\sigma_1 & 1 \end{bmatrix}.$$

Note that we have restricted the regression coefficients to be constant across alternatives for simplicity (i.e., $\beta_j = \beta$), though such a restriction need not be imposed in the analysis – see part (a) of this exercise. Finally, set $\sigma_1^2 = .5$ and $\rho_{12} = .4$.

Fit the model using the generated data and algorithm presented in part (a). Present posterior means and compare them to the parameter values used to generate the data.

Solution

(a) First, note that we can stack the observations over j for each i as follows:

$$\begin{bmatrix} U_{i1}^* \\ U_{i2}^* \\ \vdots \\ U_{iJ-1}^* \end{bmatrix} = \begin{bmatrix} z_{i1} & 0 & \cdots & 0 \\ 0 & z_{i2} & \cdots & 0 \\ \vdots & \vdots & \ddots & \vdots \\ 0 & 0 & \cdots & z_{iJ-1} \end{bmatrix} \begin{bmatrix} \beta_1 \\ \beta_2 \\ \vdots \\ \beta_{J-1} \end{bmatrix} + \begin{bmatrix} \epsilon_{i1}^* \\ \epsilon_{i2}^* \\ \vdots \\ \epsilon_{iJ-1}^* \end{bmatrix},$$

or equivalently,

$$U_i^* = Z_i\beta + \epsilon_i^*, \quad \epsilon_i^* \overset{iid}{\sim} N(0, \Sigma), \quad i = 1, 2, \ldots, n, \tag{14.31}$$

where

$$U_i^* \equiv \begin{bmatrix} U_{i1}^* \\ U_{i2}^* \\ \vdots \\ U_{iJ-1}^* \end{bmatrix}, \quad Z_i \equiv \begin{bmatrix} z_{i1} & 0 & \cdots & 0 \\ 0 & z_{i2} & \cdots & 0 \\ \vdots & \vdots & \ddots & \vdots \\ 0 & 0 & \cdots & z_{iJ-1} \end{bmatrix}, \quad \beta \equiv \begin{bmatrix} \beta_1 \\ \beta_2 \\ \vdots \\ \beta_{J-1}, \end{bmatrix},$$

and ϵ_i^* was defined previously.

We work with the augmented joint posterior of the form $p(U^*, \beta, \Sigma^{-1}|y)$, where

$$U^* = \begin{bmatrix} U_1^* \\ U_2^* \\ \vdots \\ U_n^* \end{bmatrix}.$$

This posterior distribution can be expressed as follows:

$$p(U^*, \beta, \Sigma^{-1}|y) \propto p(\beta)p(\Sigma^{-1}) \left[\prod_{i=1}^{n} \phi(U_i^*; Z_i\beta, \Sigma) \Bigg(I(y_i = 0) I(\max\{U_{ij}^*\} \le 0) + \sum_{k=1}^{J-1} I(y_i = k) I[U_{ik}^* > \max\{0, U_{i-k}^*\}] \Bigg) \right],$$

with U_{i-k}^* denoting the collection of utility differences for agent i other than the kth difference.

In this form, derivation of the complete posterior conditionals is relatively straightforward. In particular, one can show that

$$\beta|\Sigma^{-1}, U^*, y \sim N(D_\beta d_\beta, D_\beta), \tag{14.32}$$

where

$$D_\beta = \left(\sum_i Z_i' \Sigma^{-1} Z_i + V_\beta^{-1} \right)^{-1}, \quad d_\beta = \sum_i Z_i' \Sigma^{-1} U_i^* + V_\beta^{-1} \mu_\beta,$$

$$\Sigma^{-1} | U^*, \beta, y \sim W \left(\left[\rho R + \sum_i \epsilon_i^* \epsilon_i^{*\prime} \right]^{-1}, n + \rho \right) I(\sigma_{J-1}^2 = 1). \tag{14.33}$$

The algorithm of Nobile (2000) can be employed to generate draws from this Wishart, conditioned on the $(J-1, J-1)$ element. For more on this issue (and multinomial probit models generally), see, for example, Keane (1992), McCulloch and Rossi (1994), Geweke, Keane, and Runkle (1997), and McCulloch, Polson, and Rossi (2000).

Finally,

$$U_i^* | \beta, \Sigma^{-1}, y \overset{ind}{\sim} MTN_{R_i(y_i)}(Z_i \beta, \Sigma), \quad i = 1, 2, \ldots, n, \tag{14.34}$$

where $MTN_R(\mu, \Omega)$ denotes a multivariate normal distribution with mean μ and covariance matrix Ω that is truncated to the region R. In this case, if $y_i = 0$, R_i consists of the region where each component of U_i^* is negative. Similarly, when $y_i = k$, R_i restricts U_{ik}^* to be positive and greater than all other U_{ij}^*. Procedures for drawing from the multivariate truncated normal (and Student *t*) are provided in Geweke (1991), and MATLAB code is provided on the website associated with this book.

(b) We fit the model by sampling from (14.32) through (14.34), discarding the first 200 of 1000 simulations as the burn-in period. For our priors, we specify $\beta \sim N(0, 400 I_2)$, and for the hyperparameters in the inverse Wishart prior we select $\rho = 3$ and $R = I_2$. For the regression parameters β_0 and β_1, we obtain posterior means (and standard deviations) of $-.522$ (.070) and 1.05 (.079), respectively, which are close to the intercept and slope values used to generate the data. For the variance parameter σ_2^2 and correlation parameter ρ_{12}, we obtain .549 (.102) and .418 (.154), respectively. These posterior means are, again, close to the values used to generate the data.

Exercise 14.8 (Posterior simulation in the tobit model) The tobit model (e.g., Tobin 1958) specifies a mixed discrete–continuous distribution for a censored outcome variable y. In most applications of tobit models, values of y are assumed to follow a normal distribution provided y is positive, whereas we simultaneously see a clustering of y values at zero. Formally, we can write the tobit specification in terms of a latent variable model:

$$z_i = x_i \beta + \epsilon_i, \qquad \epsilon_i \overset{iid}{\sim} N(0, \sigma^2), \quad i = 1, 2, \ldots, n, \tag{14.35}$$

and

$$y_i = \max\{0, z_i\}. \tag{14.36}$$

For every observation, we observe the $(y_i,\ x_i)$ pair.
(a) Write down the likelihood function for the tobit model.
(b) What is the expression for the marginal effect $\partial E(y|x)/\partial x_j$?
(c) Describe how data augmentation can be used in conjunction with the Gibbs sampler to carry out a Bayesian analysis of this model.

Solution
(a) The likelihood function breaks into two parts. For the set of observations censored at zero, the contribution to the likelihood is:

$$\Pr(y_i = 0|x_i, \beta, \sigma^2) = \Pr(\epsilon_i \leq -x_i\beta) = 1 - \Phi(x_i\beta/\sigma).$$

Similarly, when $y_i > 0$, the likelihood is identical to that from a standard linear regression model, and thus the contribution of the ith uncensored observation to the likelihood is

$$\phi(y_i; x_i\beta, \sigma^2) = \frac{1}{\sigma}\phi\left[\left(\frac{y_i - x_i\beta}{\sigma}\right)\right],$$

with $\phi(\cdot)$ denoting the *standard* normal density function. Hence, the likelihood function can be expressed as

$$L(\beta, \sigma^2) = \prod_{i:y_i=0}\left[1 - \Phi\left(\frac{x_i\beta}{\sigma}\right)\right]\prod_{i:y_i>0}\frac{1}{\sigma}\phi\left[\left(\frac{y_i - x_i\beta}{\sigma}\right)\right]. \tag{14.37}$$

(b) Unlike the linear regression model, the marginal effect for the tobit or censored regression model is not simply the regression coefficient β_j. This was pointed out by Poirier and Melino (1978) and McDonald and Moffitt (1980), and we review the derivations here.

Note that

$$\begin{aligned} E(y|x, \beta, \sigma^2) &= E(y|x, \beta, \sigma^2, z > 0)\Pr(z > 0|x, \beta, \sigma^2) \\ &\quad + E(y|x, \beta, \sigma^2, z \leq 0)\Pr(z \leq 0|x, \beta, \sigma^2) \\ &= E(y|x, \beta, \sigma^2, z > 0)\Pr(z > 0|x, \beta, \sigma^2). \end{aligned}$$

For convenience in notation, simply let $\Phi \equiv \Phi(x\beta/\sigma)$ and $\phi \equiv \phi(x\beta/\sigma)$. For the two pieces in our expression for $\mathrm{E}(y|x, \beta, \sigma^2)$, we know that $\Pr(z > 0|x, \beta, \sigma^2) = \Phi$ and that

$$\begin{aligned} E(y|x, \beta, \sigma^2, z > 0) &= x\beta + E(\epsilon|\epsilon > -x\beta) \\ &= x\beta + \sigma\frac{\phi}{\Phi}, \end{aligned}$$

using known properties of the truncated normal distribution. Since

$$\begin{aligned} \frac{\partial E(y|x, \beta, \sigma^2)}{\partial x_j} &= \frac{\partial E(y|x, \beta, \sigma^2, z > 0)}{\partial x_j}\Pr(z > 0|x, \beta, \sigma^2) \\ &\quad + E(y|x, \beta, \sigma^2, z > 0)\frac{\partial \Pr(z > 0|x, \beta, \sigma^2)}{\partial x_j}, \end{aligned}$$

we obtain

$$\frac{\partial E(y|x,\beta,\sigma^2)}{\partial x_j} = \left[\beta_j + \sigma\left(\frac{-\phi\Phi(x\beta/\sigma)(\beta_j/\sigma) - \phi^2(\beta_j/\sigma)}{\Phi^2}\right)\right]\Phi + \left(x\beta + \sigma\frac{\phi}{\Phi}\right)\phi(\beta_j/\sigma).$$

Canceling terms gives

$$\frac{\partial E(y|x,\beta,\sigma^2)}{\partial x_j} = \Phi\beta_j. \tag{14.38}$$

Thus, the marginal effect in the tobit model does not equal β_j in general and only equals β_j as $\Phi \to 1$. We might interpret this extreme case as the linear regression model in the limit, since $\Phi \to 1$ implies that no probability is placed over the discrete mass point at zero.

(c) Chib (1992) was the original Bayesian tobit paper. Before discussing how the model can be fit using the Gibbs sampler, we note that the following prior specifications are employed:

$$\beta \sim N(\mu_\beta, V_\beta),$$
$$\sigma^2 \sim IG(a, b).$$

Following Chib (1992), we augment the joint posterior with the latent data z_i and thus will work with $p(z, \beta, \sigma^2|y)$. It is also important to recognize that when $y_i > 0$, z_i is observed (and equals y_i), whereas when $y_i = 0$, we know that z_i is truncated from above at zero.

To this end, let D_i be a binary variable that equals one if the observation is censored ($y_i = 0$) and equals zero otherwise. We define

$$y_z = Dz + (1 - D)y,$$

so that y_z just takes the value y for the uncensored observations, and for the censored observations y_z will take the value of the latent data z. Conditioned on z, this makes it easy to draw from the β conditional. We thus obtain the complete posterior conditionals:

$$\beta|z, \sigma^2, y \sim N(D_\beta d_\beta, D_\beta), \tag{14.39}$$

where

$$D_\beta = \left(X'X/\sigma^2 + V_\beta^{-1}\right)^{-1}, \qquad d_\beta = X'y_z/\sigma^2 + V_\beta^{-1}\mu_\beta,$$

$$\sigma^2|\beta, z, y \sim IG\left(\frac{n}{2} + a, \left(b^{-1} + (1/2)\sum_{i=1}^{n}(y_{z_i} - x_i\beta)^2\right)^{-1}\right), \tag{14.40}$$

and

$$z_i|\beta, \sigma^2, y \overset{ind}{\sim} TN_{(-\infty,0]}(x_i\beta, \sigma^2), \quad \forall i : y_i = 0. \tag{14.41}$$

A Gibbs sampler involves drawing from (14.39) through (14.41).

Exercise 14.9 (A tobit model with two-sided censoring: A female labor supply application) On our website we have provided data describing the number of weeks worked in 1990 by a sample of 2477 married women. The data are taken from the National Longitudinal Survey of Youth (NLSY).

Write down a tobit model appropriate for these data. Importantly, note that number of weeks worked in this sample is clustered both at 0 and at 52 (full-time employment). Account for this two-sided censoring in your model specification.
(a) Describe an algorithm for fitting this model.
(b) How can you calculate marginal effects given the two-sided censoring problem?
(c) Using the NLSY data, estimate the model using all the covariates provided and comment on your results.

Solution
(a) We use the same notation as used in Exercise 14.8. For our prior hyperparameters we set

$$\mu_\beta = 0, \quad V_\beta = 10^2 I_5, \quad a = 3, \quad b = (1/40).$$

As described in this exercise, we have a pronounced two-sided censoring problem, where there are discrete masses placed at 0 weeks worked (out of the labor force) and 52 weeks worked (full-time employment). Approximately 45% of the sample reports working 52 hours per week and 17% of the sample reports working 0 weeks per year. To account for this feature of our data, we specify a slightly generalized form of the tobit model:

$$z_i = x_i\beta + \epsilon_i, \qquad \epsilon_i \overset{iid}{\sim} N(0, \sigma^2), \tag{14.42}$$

and

$$y_i = \begin{cases} 0 & \text{if } z_i \leq 0, \\ z_i & \text{if } 0 < z_i \leq 52, \\ 52 & \text{if } z_i > 52. \end{cases} \tag{14.43}$$

Equivalently,

$$y_i = \min\{52, \max\{0, z_i\}\}. \tag{14.44}$$

In terms of the Gibbs sampler, the only difference between the algorithm required for this model and the one described in Exercise 14.8(c) is that the value of z_i must be truncated from below at 52 for all of those observations with $y_i = 52$.

One possible programming expedient (though certainly not computationally efficient) is to sample a latent variable truncated from above at 0 (say z_i^1) and one truncated from below at 52 (say z_i^2) for *every* observation in the sample. Let D_i^1 be a dummy variable if $y_i = 0$ and D_i^2 be a dummy if $y_i = 52$. We can then construct our complete data vector y_z as

$$y_z = D^1 z^1 + D^2 z^2 + (1 - D^1 - D^2)y. \tag{14.45}$$

With this construction, the Gibbs sampler then proceeds as in Exercise 14.8(c).

Table 14.4: Coefficient and marginal effect posterior means and standard deviations from tobit model of weeks worked by married women.

	Coefficient		Marginal effect	
	Mean	Std. dev.	Mean	Std. dev.
CONST	29.65	(6.06)	—	—
AFQT	.107	(.047)	.043	(.019)
SPOUSE-INC	−.245	(.053)	−.098	(.021)
KIDS	−26.65	(2.44)	−10.61	.971
ED	2.94	(.513)	1.17	(.202)
σ	44.35	(1.20)	—	—

(b and c) We use the data provided to model the number of hours worked by a sample of 2477 married women. We seek to determine how a measure of cognitive ability (denoted AFQT for Armed Forces Qualifying Test, which was administered to the NLSY participants), years of schooling completed (ED), husband's income in the previous year (1989 – denoted SPOUSE-INC), and an indicator for having children (KIDS) affect the decision regarding number of weeks worked.

We report in the following posterior means and standard deviations of parameters and marginal effects based on the final 5000 of 5500 total iterations. For the marginal effects with two-sided censoring, one can use a similar derivation to that used to derive the marginal effect in Exercise 14.8(b) for one-sided censoring. For this case we can show that

$$\frac{\partial E(y|x,\beta)}{\partial x_j} = \beta_j \left[\Phi\left(\frac{52 - x\beta}{\sigma}\right) - \Phi\left(\frac{-x\beta}{\sigma}\right)\right].$$

A general result is provided in Greene (1999). Table 14.4 reveals that the parameters generally possess the signs that we expect *a priori*. Married women with low test scores, few years of education, and children in the home are likely to work fewer weeks during the year. Apparently, the largest factor governing female labor supply behavior is whether or not children are present in the home. The presence of children in the home reduces the expected number of weeks of work by approximately 11 weeks, and the posterior standard deviation associated with this effect is quite small relative to the mean. The acquisition of one more year of education also increases the expected number of weeks of work by approximately one week.

Exercise 14.10 (Posterior simulation in a treatment–effect model) In economics and social sciences generally, it is often of interest to estimate the *causal* impact of a binary treatment on a continuous outcome. For example, one might wish to quantify the impact of a job training program on earnings, the effect of smoking on health outcomes, or the impact of dropping out of high school on wages. The primary problem when trying to extract such a "causal" effect is one of *unobserved confounding*, whereby unobservable characteristics of the agent not captured in the model are correlated with both the treatment decision (denoted D) and the outcome of interest (denoted y). A useful model to investigate such problems is given by the following two-equation system:

$$y_i = \alpha_0 + \alpha_1 D_i + \epsilon_i, \tag{14.46}$$
$$D_i^* = z_i\theta + u_i, \tag{14.47}$$

where

$$\begin{pmatrix} \epsilon_i \\ u_i \end{pmatrix} \overset{iid}{\sim} N\left[\begin{pmatrix} 0 \\ 0 \end{pmatrix}, \begin{pmatrix} \sigma_\epsilon^2 & \sigma_{u\epsilon} \\ \sigma_{u\epsilon} & 1 \end{pmatrix}\right] \equiv N(0, \Sigma). \tag{14.48}$$

The covariance term $\sigma_{u\epsilon}$ in (14.48) is added to account for the potential of confounding on unobservables. The binary decision D is included in the mean function of y in (14.46), and α_1 might be referred to as the "causal" impact of the treatment on y. The second equation of the system in (14.47) is a latent variable equation that generates D, i.e., $D = I(D^* > 0)$, like the probit model discussed in Exercise 14.1.

Describe a Gibbs sampling algorithm for fitting this two-equation system and the priors employed in your analysis.

Solution

First, note that we can stack the model into the form

$$\tilde{y}_i = X_i\beta + \tilde{u}_i, \tag{14.49}$$

where

$$\tilde{y}_i = \begin{bmatrix} y_i \\ D_i^* \end{bmatrix}, \quad X_i = \begin{bmatrix} 1 & D_i & 0 \\ 0 & 0 & z_i \end{bmatrix}, \quad \beta = \begin{bmatrix} \alpha_0 \\ \alpha_1 \\ \theta \end{bmatrix}, \quad \tilde{u}_i = \begin{bmatrix} \epsilon_i \\ u_i \end{bmatrix}.$$

To simplify drawing parameters of the covariance matrix Σ, which is complicated by the restriction that $\text{Var}(u_i) = 1$, it is desirable to work with the population expectation of ϵ given u:

$$\epsilon_i = \sigma_{u\epsilon} u_i + v_i, \tag{14.50}$$

where $v_i \sim N(0, \sigma_v^2)$ and $\sigma_v^2 \equiv \sigma_\epsilon^2 - \sigma_{u\epsilon}^2$. This representation of the error structure suggests that we can choose to work with an *equivalent* representation of the model instead:

$$y_i = \alpha_0 + \alpha_1 D_i + \sigma_{u\epsilon} u_i + v_i, \tag{14.51}$$
$$D_i^* = z_i\theta + u_i, \tag{14.52}$$

where u and v are independently distributed, as implied by (14.50). With this definition of σ_v^2, we choose to parameterize the model in terms of σ_v^2 and $\sigma_{u\epsilon}$ (instead of σ_ϵ^2 and $\sigma_{u\epsilon}$). The covariance matrix Σ in (14.48) then takes the form

$$\Sigma = \begin{bmatrix} \sigma_v^2 + \sigma_{u\epsilon}^2 & \sigma_{u\epsilon} \\ \sigma_{u\epsilon} & 1 \end{bmatrix}.$$

Rewriting the model in this way, and parameterizing in terms of σ_v^2 and $\sigma_{u\epsilon}$, will help us avoid computational difficulties that arise when diagonal restrictions are imposed on Σ, as in (14.48). We choose priors of the following forms:

$$\begin{aligned}\beta &\sim N(\mu_\beta, V_\beta),\\ \sigma_{u\epsilon} &\sim N(\mu_0, V_0),\\ \sigma_v^2 &\sim IG(a, b),\end{aligned}$$

and we note that Σ is positive definite for $\sigma_v^2 > 0$, which is enforced through our prior.

We work with an augmented posterior distribution of the form $p(\beta, D^*, \sigma_v^2, \sigma_{u\epsilon}|y, D)$. One can show that the complete posterior conditionals are as follows:

$$\beta|D^*, \Sigma, y, D \sim N(D_\beta d_\beta, D_\beta) \tag{14.53}$$

where

$$D_\beta = \left(\sum_i X_i'\Sigma^{-1}X_i + V_\beta^{-1}\right)^{-1}, \quad d_\beta = \sum_i X_i'\Sigma^{-1}\tilde{y}_i + V_\beta^{-1}\mu_\beta,$$

$$D_i^*|\beta, \Sigma, y, D \overset{ind}{\sim} \begin{cases} TN_{(0,\infty)}[z_i\theta + [\sigma_{u\epsilon}/(\sigma_v^2 + \sigma_{u\epsilon}^2)](y_i - \alpha_0 - \alpha_1), (1 - \rho_{u\epsilon}^2)] & \text{if } D_i = 1,\\ TN_{(-\infty,0]}[z_i\theta + [\sigma_{u\epsilon}/(\sigma_v^2 + \sigma_{u\epsilon}^2)](y_i - \alpha_0), (1 - \rho_{u\epsilon}^2)] & \text{if } D_i = 0,\end{cases} \tag{14.54}$$

where $\rho_{u\epsilon}^2 = \sigma_{u\epsilon}^2/(\sigma_v^2 + \sigma_{u\epsilon}^2)$ and

$$\sigma_{u\epsilon}|\beta, D^*, \sigma_v^2, y, D \sim N(Dd, D), \tag{14.55}$$

with

$$D = (u'u/\sigma_v^2 + V_0^{-1})^{-1}, \quad d = u'(y - \alpha_0 - \alpha_1 D)/\sigma_v^2 + V_0^{-1}\mu_0.$$

(In (14.55), note that the error vector $u = D^* - z_i\theta$ is "known" given D^* and θ.) Finally,

$$\sigma_v^2|\sigma_{u\epsilon}, \beta, D^*, y, D \sim IG\left(\frac{n}{2} + a, \left[b^{-1} + .5\sum_i (y_i - \alpha_0 - \alpha_1 D_i - \sigma_{u\epsilon}u_i)^2\right]^{-1}\right). \tag{14.56}$$

The sampler proceeds by drawing from (14.53) through (14.56). Given $\sigma_{u\epsilon}$ and σ_v^2 from the final two steps of the sampler, one can construct Σ. See Li (1998) for a discussion of a related model.

Exercise 14.11 (Posterior simulation in a generalized tobit: A model of potential outcomes I) There have been many generalizations of the tobit model described in Exercise 14.8. For example, Amemiya (1985) outlines five different types of tobit models, discusses estimation via two-step methods (e.g., Heckman 1976) and maximum likelihood, and provides numerous references to applications of these different models. In these generalized tobit models, there is often the problem of *incidental truncation*, where the value of an outcome variable y is only observed in magnitude depending on the sign of some other variable, say z (and not y itself).

In this question, we take up Bayesian estimation of the most general type 5 tobit model (using Amemiya's enumeration system), often referred to as a model of *potential outcomes*. Inference in the remaining generalized models follows similarly. This particular model, much like the model discussed in Exercise 14.10, has seen considerable use in the "program evaluation" literature, where the goal is to determine the effectiveness of a program or treatment when individuals are not randomly assigned into the treated or untreated states. Formally, the model we consider here can be written as

$$D_i^* = z_i\theta + U_{Di}, \tag{14.57}$$

$$y_{1i} = x_i\beta_1 + U_{1i}, \tag{14.58}$$

$$y_{0i} = x_i\beta_0 + U_{0i}. \tag{14.59}$$

In these expressions, y_1 and y_0 are continuous *outcome* variables, with y_1 denoting the *treated* outcome and y_0 denoting the *untreated* outcome. The variable D^* is a latent variable that generates an *observed binary treatment decision* D according to

$$D_i = I(D_i^* > 0) = I(z_i\theta + U_{Di}) > 0. \tag{14.60}$$

We also assume the availability of some *exclusion restriction* or instrument in z that does not appear in x.

One interesting feature of this model is that only one outcome is observed for each observation in the sample. That is, if we let y denote the observed vector of outcomes in the data, we can write

$$y = Dy_1 + (1 - D)y_0. \tag{14.61}$$

In other words, if an individual takes the treatment ($D_i = 1$), then we only observe his or her treated outcome y_{1i}, and conversely, if $D_i = 0$, we only observe y_{0i}.

We make the following joint normality assumption:

$$U_i \overset{iid}{\sim} N(0, \Sigma), \tag{14.62}$$

where

$$U_i = [U_{Di}\; U_{1i}\; U_{0i}]' \quad \text{and} \quad \Sigma \equiv \begin{bmatrix} 1 & \rho_{1D}\sigma_1 & \rho_{0D}\sigma_0 \\ \rho_{1D}\sigma_1 & \sigma_1^2 & \rho_{10}\sigma_1\sigma_0 \\ \rho_{0D}\sigma_0 & \rho_{10}\sigma_1\sigma_0 & \sigma_0^2 \end{bmatrix}.$$

The variance parameter in the latent variable equation for the binary treatment indicator D has been normalized to unity for identification purposes. In the following, we write this restriction in an alternate, though equivalent, form as $\sigma_{D^*}^2 = 1$ and impose this condition through our prior.

(a) Write down the likelihood function for this model. Comment on the role of the correlation parameter ρ_{10} in the likelihood function.

(b) Derive the complete posterior conditionals for this model using priors of the form

$$\beta \equiv \begin{bmatrix} \theta \\ \beta_1 \\ \beta_0 \end{bmatrix} \sim N(\mu_\beta, V_\beta)$$

and

$$\Sigma^{-1} \sim W([\rho R]^{-1}, \rho) I(\sigma^2_{D^*} = 1).$$

Note, again, that the indicator function is added to the standard Wishart prior so that the variance parameter in the latent data D^* equation is normalized to unity.

Solution

(a) When $D_i = 1$, we observe y_{1i} and the event that $D_i = 1$. Conversely, when $D_i = 0$, we observe y_{0i} and the event that $D_i = 0$. We thus obtain

$$\begin{aligned} L(\beta, \Sigma) &= \prod_{\{i:D_i=1\}} p(y_{1i}, D_i^* > 0) \prod_{\{i:D_i=0\}} p(y_{0i}, D_i^* \le 0) \\ &= \prod_{\{i:D_i=1\}} \int_0^\infty p(y_{1i}, D_i^*) dD_i^* \prod_{\{i:D_i=0\}} \int_{-\infty}^0 p(y_{0i}, D_i^*) dD_i^* \\ &= \prod_{\{i:D_i=1\}} \int_0^\infty p(D_i^* | y_{1i}) p(y_{1i}) dD_i^* \prod_{\{i:D_i=0\}} \int_{-\infty}^0 p(D_i^* | y_{0i}) p(y_{0i}) dD_i^*. \end{aligned}$$

The conditional and marginal densities in these expressions can be determined from the assumed joint normality of the error vector. Performing the required calculations (which involves applying Theorem A.3 to derive the conditional normal distributions, and then performing the necessary integration), we obtain

$$\begin{aligned} L(\beta, \Sigma) = &\prod_{\{i:D_i=1\}} \Phi\left(\frac{\tilde{U}_{Di} + \rho_{1D}\tilde{U}_{1i}}{(1-\rho_{1D}^2)^{-1/2}} \right) \frac{1}{\sigma_1} \phi(\tilde{U}_{1i}) \\ &\times \prod_{\{i:D_i=0\}} \left[1 - \Phi\left(\frac{\tilde{U}_{Di} + \rho_{0D}\tilde{U}_{0i}}{(1-\rho_{0D}^2)^{-1/2}} \right) \right] \frac{1}{\sigma_0} \phi(\tilde{U}_{0i}), \end{aligned} \qquad (14.63)$$

where

$$\begin{aligned} \tilde{U}_{Di} &= z_i \theta, \\ \tilde{U}_{1i} &= (y_{1i} - x_i \beta_1)/\sigma_1, \\ \tilde{U}_{0i} &= (y_{0i} - x_i \beta_0)/\sigma_0, \end{aligned}$$

and $\phi(\cdot)$ denotes the standard normal density.

Note that the correlation parameter ρ_{10} does not enter this likelihood function, and thus it is *not identified*. The reason is that the pair of outcomes (y_1, y_0) are never observed for any individual, and thus the correlation between these two outcomes will not enter the density function for the observed data.

(b) To implement the Gibbs sampler, we will augment the posterior with the latent desire for the receipt of treatment (D^*) and the missing potential outcome, which we will denote y^{Miss}. We therefore work with the augmented joint posterior $p(y^{\text{Miss}}, D^*, \beta, \Sigma^{-1}|y, D)$. Conditional on the unobserved latent quantities D^* and y^{Miss}, the regression parameters and inverse covariance matrix can be sampled in a straightforward manner. We now turn to a discussion of the complete posterior conditionals for each of these quantities:

Missing outcome data y^{Miss}

Since the Jacobian of the transformation from the error vector to the outcome quantities is unity, the trivariate normal distribution for $[D_i^* \; y_{1i} \; y_{0i}]$ is easily derived. The missing outcome data are then sampled by drawing from the conditional posterior:

$$y_i^{\text{Miss}}|\Gamma_{-y_i^{\text{Miss}}}, y, D \stackrel{\text{ind}}{\sim} N((1-D_i)\mu_{1i} + (D_i)\mu_{0i}, (1-D_i)\omega_{1i} + (D_i)\omega_{0i}), \quad (14.64)$$

where

$$\mu_{1i} = x_i\beta_1 + (D_i^* - z_i\theta)\left[\frac{\sigma_0^2\sigma_{1D} - \sigma_{10}\sigma_{0D}}{\sigma_0^2 - \sigma_{0D}^2}\right] + (y_i - x_i\beta_0)\left[\frac{\sigma_{10} - \sigma_{0D}\sigma_{1D}}{\sigma_0^2 - \sigma_{0D}^2}\right],$$

$$\mu_{0i} = x_i\beta_0 + (D_i^* - z_i\theta)\left[\frac{\sigma_1^2\sigma_{0D} - \sigma_{10}\sigma_{1D}}{\sigma_1^2 - \sigma_{1D}^2}\right] + (y_i - x_i\beta_1)\left[\frac{\sigma_{10} - \sigma_{0D}\sigma_{1D}}{\sigma_1^2 - \sigma_{1D}^2}\right],$$

$$\omega_{1i} = \sigma_1^2 - \frac{\sigma_{1D}^2\sigma_0^2 - 2\sigma_{10}\sigma_{0D}\sigma_{1D} + \sigma_{10}^2}{\sigma_0^2 - \sigma_{0D}^2},$$

$$\omega_{0i} = \sigma_0^2 - \frac{\sigma_{0D}^2\sigma_1^2 - 2\sigma_{10}\sigma_{0D}\sigma_{1D} + \sigma_{10}^2}{\sigma_1^2 - \sigma_{1D}^2},$$

and σ_{10}, σ_{1D}, and σ_{0D} refer to the covariance parameters between the treated and untreated outcome errors (i.e., $\sigma_{10} \equiv \rho_{10}\sigma_1\sigma_0$) and outcome and selection equation errors (i.e., $\sigma_{1D} \equiv \rho_{1D}\sigma_1$ and $\sigma_{0D} \equiv \rho_{0D}\sigma_0$). Note that this construction automatically samples from the posterior conditional for y_1 if $D = 0$ and samples from the posterior conditional for y_0 if $D = 1$.

Missing latent data D^*

The latent data D_i^* are also drawn from a conditional normal, which is truncated by the observed value of D_i:

$$D_i^*|\Gamma_{-D_i^*}, y, D \stackrel{ind}{\sim} \begin{cases} TN_{(0,\infty)}(\mu_{Di}, \omega_{Di}) & \text{if } D_i = 1, \\ TN_{(-\infty,0]}(\mu_{Di}, \omega_{Di}) & \text{if } D_i = 0, \quad i = 1, 2, \ldots, n, \end{cases} \quad (14.65)$$

where

$$\mu_{Di} = z_i\theta + \left(D_i y_i + (1 - D_i)y_i^{\text{Miss}} - x_i\beta_1\right)\left[\frac{\sigma_0^2\sigma_{1D} - \sigma_{10}\sigma_{0D}}{\sigma_1^2\sigma_0^2 - \sigma_{10}^2}\right]$$
$$+ \left(D_i y_i^{\text{Miss}} + (1 - D_i)y_i - x_i\beta_0\right)\left[\frac{\sigma_1^2\sigma_{0D} - \sigma_{10}\sigma_{1D}}{\sigma_1^2\sigma_0^2 - \sigma_{10}^2}\right],$$
$$\omega_{Di} = 1 - \frac{\sigma_{1D}^2\sigma_0^2 - 2\sigma_{10}\sigma_{0D}\sigma_{1D} + \sigma_1^2\sigma_{0D}^2}{\sigma_1^2\sigma_0^2 - \sigma_{10}^2},$$

and $TN_{(a,b)}(\mu, \sigma^2)$ denotes a univariate normal density with mean μ and variance σ^2, truncated to the interval (a, b).

Given these drawn quantities, we then compute the *complete data* vector

$$r_i^* = \begin{bmatrix} D_i^* \\ D_i y_i + (1 - D_i)y_i^{\text{Miss}} \\ D_i y_i^{\text{Miss}} + (1 - D_i)y_i \end{bmatrix}.$$

Regression parameters β

Conditioned on the values of the missing and latent data, it is straightforward to sample from the complete conditional for the $k \times 1$ vector $\beta \equiv [\theta' \ \beta_1' \ \beta_0']'$:

$$\beta|\Gamma_{-\beta}, y, D \sim N(\mu_\beta, \omega_\beta), \tag{14.66}$$

where

$$\mu_\beta = [W'(\Sigma^{-1} \otimes I_n)W + V_\beta^{-1}]^{-1}[W'(\Sigma^{-1} \otimes I_n)\overline{y} + V_\beta^{-1}\mu_\beta]$$
$$\omega_\beta = [W'(\Sigma^{-1} \otimes I_n)W + V_\beta^{-1}]^{-1},$$

$$W_{3n\times k} \equiv \begin{bmatrix} Z & 0 & 0 \\ 0 & X & 0 \\ 0 & 0 & X \end{bmatrix}, \quad \text{and} \quad \overline{y}_{3n\times 1} \equiv \begin{bmatrix} D^* \\ Dy + (1 - D)y^{\text{Miss}} \\ Dy^{\text{Miss}} + (1 - D)y \end{bmatrix}.$$

Inverse covariance matrix Σ^{-1}

For the inverse covariance matrix, Σ^{-1}, a slight complication is again introduced as the complete conditional is no longer Wishart, given that the $(1, 1)$ element must be normalized to unity. However, as described in Exercise 14.7, Nobile (2000) provides an algorithm for drawing from such a Wishart, conditional on a diagonal restriction. (MATLAB code for this algorithm is available on the website associated with this book.) We express this conditional as

$$\Sigma^{-1}|\Gamma_{-\Sigma}, y, D \sim W\left(\left[\sum_{i=1}^{n}(r_i^* - \tilde{W}_i\beta)(r_i^* - \tilde{W}_i\beta)' + \rho R\right]^{-1}, n + \rho\right) I(\sigma_{D^*}^2 = 1), \tag{14.67}$$

where

$$\tilde{W}_i \equiv \begin{bmatrix} z_i & 0 & 0 \\ 0 & x_i & 0 \\ 0 & 0 & x_i \end{bmatrix}.$$

A Gibbs sampler involves cycling through the conditionals in (14.64) through (14.67). Finally, this exercise has assumed that the x variables are the same across the treated and untreated states. This assumption is not necessary, though it is arguably appropriate for most empirical work.

Exercise 14.12 (A model of potential outcomes II)
(a) Using the notation in Exercise 14.11, generate 5000 observations from the following selection model:

$$\begin{aligned} D_i^* &= \theta_0 + z_i\theta_1 + U_{Di}, \\ y_{1i} &= \beta_1 + U_{1i}, \\ y_{0i} &= \beta_0 + U_{0i}, \end{aligned}$$

with

$$\theta_0 = 0, \quad \theta_1 = .5, \quad \beta_1 = 2, \quad \beta_0 = 1, \quad z_i \overset{iid}{\sim} N(0,1)$$

and

$$\sigma_1^2 = \sigma_0^2 = 1, \quad \rho_{1D} = .9, \quad \rho_{0D} = .7, \quad \rho_{10} = .6.$$

(b) Using the data generated in part (a), estimate β_1 and β_0 from single-equation analyses using OLS. How do the OLS estimates perform?
(c) Fit the model via the Gibbs sampler using the data generated in part (a). (See Exercise 14.11 for the Gibbs algorithm.) How do your estimation results compare to those obtained from OLS in part (b)?
(d) Compare and contrast the prior and posterior for the correlation parameter ρ_{10}. Comment on this result.

Solution
(a and b) We generate 5000 observations according to the model described. Running separate OLS regressions for the set of observations with $D_i = 1$ and $D_i = 0$, we found that $\hat{\beta}_1 = 2.63$ and $\hat{\beta}_0 = .501$ with these data. The OLS point estimates do not perform well because of the strong correlation between unobservables in the selection and outcome equations. Specifically,

$$E(U_{1i}|D_i = 1) = E(U_{1i}|U_{Di} < -z_i\theta) = \rho_{1D}\sigma_1 \left[\frac{\phi(z_i\theta)}{\Phi(z_i\theta)}\right] \neq 0.$$

Thus, mean independence between the regressor and error is violated unless $\rho_{1D} = 0$; as a result, OLS estimates will be biased and inconsistent in general.

Table 14.5: Posterior means and standard deviations from a generalized tobit-generated data experiment.

Parameter	True value	Post. mean	Post. std. dev.
β_1	2	2.07	.04
β_0	1	1.02	.04
θ_0	0	$-.001$	.03
θ_1	.5	.535	.02
σ_1	1	.950	.03
σ_0	1	1.02	.03
ρ_{1D}	.9	.837	.02
ρ_{0D}	.7	.722	.03
ρ_{10}	.6	.675	.07

(c) The Gibbs sampler is run for 5500 iterations, and the first 500 simulations are discarded as the burn-in. For our prior hyperparameters, we specified

$$\mu_\beta = 0, \quad V_\beta = 10^2 I_4, \quad \rho = 4, \quad R = I_3.$$

Posterior means and standard deviations of the parameters are presented in Table 14.5. From the table, we see that the posterior means are quite close to the true values of the parameters used to generate the data.

(d) We simulate 5500 draws from our (restricted) Wishart prior and use these draws to plot the prior density for the non-identified correlation parameter ρ_{10}. We also use the 5000 post-convergence draws to plot the posterior density for this parameter. These plots are provided in Figure 14.4 and are obtained by non-parametrically smoothing the simulated prior and posterior draws (for an introduction to non-parametric density estimation, see, e.g., Silverman 1986; DiNardo and Tobias 2001).

As seen in the figure, the priors and posteriors differ dramatically. But how is this possible, since ρ_{10} does not enter the likelihood function? How can the data update our beliefs about the values of this parameter?

As shown in Vijverberg (1993), Koop and Poirier (1997), Poirier and Tobias (2003), and Li, Poirier, and Tobias (2003), the positive definiteness of the 3×3 covariance matrix serves to place bounds on ρ_{10}. Specifically, these bounds imply that, conditionally,

$$\underline{\rho}_{10} \leq \rho_{10} \leq \overline{\rho}_{10},$$

where

$$\underline{\rho}_{10} = \rho_{1D}\rho_{0D} - \left[(1 - \rho_{1D}^2)(1 - \rho_{0D}^2)\right]^{1/2} \tag{14.68}$$

and

$$\overline{\rho}_{10} = \rho_{1D}\rho_{0D} + \left[(1 - \rho_{1D}^2)(1 - \rho_{0D}^2)\right]^{1/2}. \tag{14.69}$$

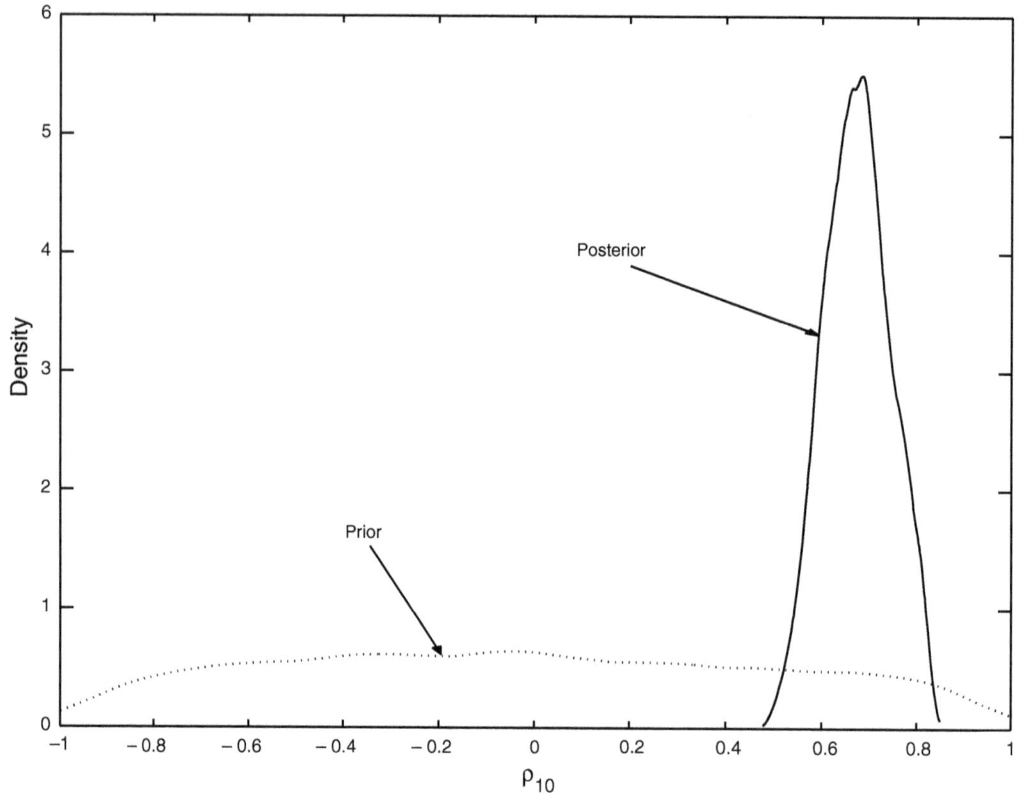

Figure 14.4. Plots of priors and posteriors of ρ_{10} using generated data from a generalized tobit model.

These bounds are only functions of the *identified* correlation parameters ρ_{1D} and ρ_{0D}. The values of the identified correlation parameters used to generate these data imply a lower bound of $\underline{\rho}_{10} \approx .32$ and an upper bound of $\overline{\rho}_{10} \approx .94$.

As seen from Table 14.5, the posteriors for the identified correlations ρ_{1D} and ρ_{0D} are quite tight around their generated-data values. As a result, the data provide substantial information about the lower and upper conditional support bounds $\underline{\rho}_{10}$ and $\overline{\rho}_{10}$. Hence, as the figure suggests, virtually all of the mass of the posterior for ρ_{10} is placed within the interval $[.3\ .93]$. In short, information learned about ρ_{1D} and ρ_{0D} "spills over" and serves to update our beliefs about the non-identified correlation parameter ρ_{10} via the enforced positive definiteness of Σ. See Poirier (1998) for more examples of such learning.

Exercise 14.13 (Posterior simulation in an ordered-treatment, ordered-outcome model) Like Exercise 14.10, consider the general problem of estimating the effect of treatment on an outcome of interest. In this exercise, however, suppose that y, the outcome of interest, and r, the treatment, can take only three distinct values: $y_i \in \{1, 2, 3\}$ and

$r_i \in \{1, 2, 3\}$, $i = 1, 2, \ldots, n$. We additionally assume that each variable is *ordered* in nature so that one could reasonably adopt, say, an ordered probit (see, e.g., Exercise 14.5) to model each random variable.

To formally account for the discrete, ordered nature of our variables y and r within the treatment–response framework of Exercise 14.10, we consider a latent variable model,

$$z_{yi} = x_{yi}\beta_y + d_{ri}\theta + \epsilon_{yi}, \tag{14.70}$$

$$z_{ri} = x_{ri}\beta_r + \epsilon_{ri}, \tag{14.71}$$

where an intercept has been excluded from x_y and d_{ri} is the 1×3 dummy variable vector for r_i that contains a one in the r_ith column and zeros elsewhere. We interpret the parameter vector θ as quantifying the *treatment effect* of levels of r on y. In our triangular system, we model the endogeneity of r_i by permitting correlation between ϵ_y and ϵ_r. Throughout this exercise, we therefore assume that

$$\begin{bmatrix} \epsilon_{yi} \\ \epsilon_{ri} \end{bmatrix} \stackrel{iid}{\sim} N\left[\begin{pmatrix} 0 \\ 0 \end{pmatrix}, \begin{pmatrix} 1 & \sigma_{yr} \\ \sigma_{yr} & 1 \end{pmatrix}\right], \tag{14.72}$$

where the error variances in each of the latent variable equations have been normalized to unity for identification purposes.

Like the single-equation ordered probit of Exercise 14.5, we relate the observed ordered y and r variables to the latent z_y in (14.70) and z_r in (14.71) through the restrictions

$$y_i = j \text{ iff } \gamma_j < z_{yi} \leq \gamma_{j+1}, \quad j = 1, 2, 3, \tag{14.73}$$

and

$$r_i = k \text{ iff } \tilde{\gamma}_k < z_{ri} \leq \tilde{\gamma}_{k+1}, \quad k = 1, 2, 3. \tag{14.74}$$

For identification purposes, we impose standard restrictions on certain values of the *cutpoints* γ_j and $\tilde{\gamma}_k$, namely $\gamma_1 = \tilde{\gamma}_1 = -\infty$, $\gamma_2 = \tilde{\gamma}_2 = 0$, and $\gamma_4 = \tilde{\gamma}_4 = \infty$. Thus, with three possible values for each random variable y and r, γ_3 and $\tilde{\gamma}_3$ are the only cutpoints whose values are unknown.

(a) Describe a posterior simulator for fitting this treatment effect model. When doing so, consider, as in Li and Tobias (2007), making use of a reparameterization of the following form:

$$\sigma_y = 1/[\gamma_3^2], \quad \beta_y^* = \sqrt{\sigma_y}\beta_y, \quad z_y^* = \sqrt{\sigma_y}z_y, \tag{14.75}$$

and

$$\sigma_r = 1/[\tilde{\gamma}_3^2], \quad \beta_r^* = \sqrt{\sigma_r}\beta_r, \quad z_r^* = \sqrt{\sigma_r}z_r, \quad \tilde{\sigma}_{yr} = \sqrt{\sigma_y}\sqrt{\sigma_r}\sigma_{yr}. \tag{14.76}$$

How does this reparameterization facilitate posterior computation in the ordered-treatment, ordered-response model?

(b) The data provided on the website associated with this book can be used to investigate the impact of maternal alcohol consumption during pregnancy on subsequent infant health. For our purposes here, we create alcohol consumption and health status variables that are ordered and take three possible values. Specifically, infant health is constructed from a variable describing the number of doctor visits made by the infant during his or her first year of life for reasons related to illness or injury. Our constructed measure of infant health takes the value 1 if the child had no such doctor visits, 2 if the child had one or two such visits, and 3 if the child had at least three visits. Maternal alcohol consumption while pregnant takes the value of 1 if the mother never consumed alcohol while pregnant, 2 if the mother drank about once per month (or less), and 3 if the mother drank at least once a month.

Using these data and the algorithm described in part (a), fit the ordered-treatment, ordered-outcome model and interpret your results.

Solution

(a) To motivate the suggested reparameterization, consider taking Equations (14.70) and (14.71) and multiplying them by $\sqrt{\sigma_y}$ and $\sqrt{\sigma_r}$, respectively. With the notation of Equations (14.75) and (14.76), such a multiplication produces a model of the form

$$z^*_{yi} = \overline{x}_{yi}\beta^*_y + \epsilon^*_{yi}, \tag{14.77}$$

$$z^*_{ri} = x_{ri}\beta^*_r + \epsilon^*_{ri}, \tag{14.78}$$

where

$$\begin{bmatrix} \epsilon^*_{yi} \\ \epsilon^*_{ri} \end{bmatrix} \overset{iid}{\sim} N\left[\begin{pmatrix} 0 \\ 0 \end{pmatrix}\begin{pmatrix} \sigma_y & \tilde{\sigma}_{yr} \\ \tilde{\sigma}_{yr} & \sigma_r \end{pmatrix}\right] \equiv N(0, \Sigma^*), \tag{14.79}$$

and $\tilde{\sigma}_{yr} = \sqrt{\sigma}_y\sqrt{\sigma}_r\sigma_{yr}$. To simplify notation, we have included d_{ri} as an element of $\overline{x}_{yi}$ (i.e., $\overline{x}_{yi} = [x_{ri}\ d_{ri}]$), and we have similarly absorbed $\theta^* = \sqrt{\sigma_y}\theta$ in β^*_y.

In terms of the latent data z^*_y and z^*_r, note that the restrictions in (14.73) and (14.74) imply that

$$y_i = j \text{ iff } \gamma^*_j < z^*_{yi} \leq \gamma^*_{j+1}, \quad j = 1, 2, 3, \tag{14.80}$$

and

$$r_i = k \text{ iff } \tilde{\gamma}^*_k < z^*_{ri} \leq \tilde{\gamma}^*_{k+1}, \quad k = 1, 2, 3, \tag{14.81}$$

where $\gamma^* \equiv \sqrt{\sigma_y}\gamma$ and $\tilde{\gamma}^* \equiv \sqrt{\sigma}_y\tilde{\gamma}$. Note that all elements of γ^* and $\tilde{\gamma}^*$ are *known*, since our reparameterization implies γ^*_3 and $\tilde{\gamma}^*_3 = 1$.

The primary benefits afforded by this parameterization are twofold. First, as already noted, there are no unknown cutpoints in this reparameterized model, and thus the researcher does not need to address the issue of how to best simulate the cutpoint values. Next, note that our reparameterization essentially eliminates the diagonal restrictions on the covariance matrix in (14.72) and thus "restores" our ability to apply standard simulation-based posterior analysis, where the requisite posterior conditionals will have convenient forms (as shown in the following).

To this end, we employ the following priors:

$$\beta_y^* \sim N(0, V_y), \tag{14.82}$$

$$\beta_r^* \sim N(0, V_r), \tag{14.83}$$

$$\Sigma^{*-1} \sim W(H, a). \tag{14.84}$$

Let $\beta^* = [\beta_y^{*\prime} \; \beta_r^{*\prime}]'$. These priors combined with the augmented likelihood for the observed data yield the following posterior:

$$p(\beta^*, \Sigma^{*-1}, z_y^*, z_r^* | y, r) \propto p(\beta^*)p(\Sigma^{*-1}) \left\{ \prod_{i=1}^{n} \phi_2 \left[\begin{pmatrix} z_{yi}^* \\ z_{ri}^* \end{pmatrix}; \begin{pmatrix} \overline{x}_{yi}\beta_y^* \\ x_{ri}\beta_r^* \end{pmatrix}, \begin{pmatrix} \sigma_y & \tilde{\sigma}_{yr} \\ \tilde{\sigma}_{yr} & \sigma_r \end{pmatrix} \right] \right.$$

$$\left. \times I(\gamma_{y_i}^* < z_{yi}^* \leq \gamma_{y_i+1}^*) I(\tilde{\gamma}_{r_i}^* < z_{ri}^* \leq \tilde{\gamma}_{r_i+1}^*) \right\}, \tag{14.85}$$

where $\beta^* \sim N(0, V_\beta)$ and V_β is block diagonal with V_y and V_r along the upper and lower blocks, respectively.

The posterior simulator for this model involves sampling from the posterior conditionals for β^*, the latent variables, and inverse covariance matrix Σ^{*-1}. For the first of these,

$$\beta^* | \Xi_{-\beta^*}, y, r \sim N(D_\beta d_\beta, D_\beta), \tag{14.86}$$

where $\Xi_{-\theta}$ denotes all quantities in the posterior other than θ,

$$D_\beta = \left[X'(\Sigma^{*-1} \otimes I_n)X + V_\beta^{-1} \right]^{-1}, \quad d_\beta = X'(\Sigma^{*-1} \otimes I_n)z^*,$$

$$X = \begin{pmatrix} \overline{X}_y & 0_{n \times k_r} \\ 0_{n \times k_y} & X_r \end{pmatrix}, \quad V_\beta = \begin{pmatrix} V_y & 0_{k_y \times k_r} \\ 0_{k_r \times k_y} & V_r \end{pmatrix},$$

$$z^* = \begin{bmatrix} z_{y1}^* \\ \vdots \\ z_{yn}^* \\ z_{r1}^* \\ \vdots \\ z_{rn}^* \end{bmatrix}, \quad \overline{X}_y = \begin{bmatrix} \overline{x}_{y1} \\ \vdots \\ \overline{x}_{yn} \end{bmatrix}, \quad \text{and} \quad X_r = \begin{bmatrix} x_{r1} \\ \vdots \\ x_{rn} \end{bmatrix}.$$

Here, k_y and k_r denote the dimensions of β_y^* and β_r^*, respectively.

The latent data in the outcome equation, z_{yi}^*, are sampled independently from conditionals of the form

$$z_{yi}^* | \Xi_{-z_{yi}^*}, y, r \overset{ind}{\sim} TN_{(\gamma_{y_i}^*, \gamma_{y_i+1}^*]}(\mu_{i,y|r}, \sigma_{y|r}), \quad i = 1, 2, \ldots, n, \tag{14.87}$$

where $\mu_{i,y|r} \equiv \overline{x}_{yi}\beta_y^* + \tilde{\sigma}_{yr}\sigma_r^{-1}(z_{ri}^* - x_{ri}\beta_r^*)$, $\sigma_{y|r} \equiv \sigma_y - \tilde{\sigma}_{yr}^2\sigma_r^{-1}$, and $TN_{(a,b]}(\mu, \sigma)$ denotes a normal distribution with mean μ and variance σ truncated to the interval between a and b.

The latent data in the treatment equation, z_{ri}^*, are sampled similarly:

$$z_{ri}^*|\Xi_{-z_{ri}^*}, y, r \stackrel{ind}{\sim} TN_{(\tilde{\gamma}_{r_i}^*, \tilde{\gamma}_{r_i+1}^*]}(\mu_{i,r|y}, \sigma_{r|y}), \quad i = 1, 2, \ldots, n, \tag{14.88}$$

where $\mu_{i,r|y} \equiv x_{ri}\beta_r^* + \tilde{\sigma}_{yr}\sigma_y^{-1}(z_{yi}^* - \overline{x}_{yi}\beta_y^*)$ and $\sigma_{r|y} \equiv \sigma_r - \tilde{\sigma}_{yr}^2\sigma_y^{-1}$.

Finally, the inverse covariance matrix Σ^{*-1} is sampled from its posterior conditional:

$$\Sigma^{*-1}|\Xi_{-\Sigma^{*-1}}, y, r \sim W\left(\left(H^{-1} + \sum_{i=1}^{n}[\epsilon_{yi}^*\ \epsilon_{ri}^*]'[\epsilon_{yi}^*\ \epsilon_{ri}^*]\right)^{-1}, n + a\right), \tag{14.89}$$

where ϵ_y^* and ϵ_r^* are effectively known given z_y^*, z_r^*, and β^*. The posterior simulator involves successively sampling from (14.86) through (14.89). To recover the original parameters of interest in (14.70) through (14.73), simply invert the identities given in (14.75) and (14.76) at each iteration of the sampler. In cases where y and r take on more than three values, an additional step must be added to the posterior simulator to sample the added cutpoint values. For such cases, Nandram and Chen (1996) and Li and Tobias (2007) recommend sampling *differences* between cutpoint values using a Dirichlet proposal density.

(b) For this analysis, we employ priors with hyperparameters given as follows: $a = 2$, $H = I_2$, $V_y = 10I_{k_y}$, and $V_r = 10I_{k_r}$. The Gibbs sampler is run for 500 iterations, the first 100 of which are discarded as the burn-in.

In our analysis we include controls for education and family income in both the drinking and doctor visit equations. In the drinking equation, we additionally include an indicator denoting whether the mother had a parent who had a drinking problem or was an alcoholic (Parent Drink). In the doctor visit equation, we also include an indicator denoting whether the mother has had children before and an indicator denoting whether the mother has a health problem that limits her ability to work (Health Problem). Table 14.6 presents posterior means and standard deviations associated with parameters of this model.

From an examination of the posterior means in Table 14.6, we see that higher levels of alcohol consumption while pregnant generally resulted in the infant experiencing more doctor visits during his or her first year of life. Note, of course, that coefficients in this case are not directly interpretable as marginal effects of interest, though such effects can be calculated using the simulated draws from the posterior. We have not done any formal model comparison tests here, but an informal examination of posterior standard deviations suggests that versions of this model with some coefficients restricted to zero may be preferred. Interestingly, the posterior mean of the covariance parameter σ_{yr} (which in this case is also the correlation) is negative, and most of the mass of this posterior is placed over negative values. A potential explanation for this result is that "indifferent" mothers – who are more likely to drink while pregnant – may also be less likely to take their children to the doctor at the onset of illness, leading to fewer observed visits, on average.

Table 14.6: Coefficient posterior means and standard deviations from an ordered-treatment, ordered-outcome model.

	Drinking frequency equation	
Variable/parameter	Post. mean	Post. std. dev.
Constant	−1.10	.233
Education	.050	.020
Family Income ($10 000)	.024	.029
Parent Drink	.255	.083
$\tilde{\gamma}_3$	.852	.045
	Doctor visit equation	
Variable/parameter	Post. mean	Post. std. dev.
Never Drink	−.286	.213
Drink once/month or less	.286	.305
Drink more than once/month	.483	.406
Education	.022	.020
Havekids Before	.002	.063
Family Income ($10 000)	.023	.029
Health Problem	.130	.066
γ_3	1.16	.064
σ_{yr}	−.328	.149

Exercise 14.14 (Posterior simulation in the stochastic frontier model) Consider a model of production where output of firm i at time t, Y_{it}, is produced using a vector of inputs, X_{it}^*, $(i = 1, \ldots, N, t = 1, \ldots, T)$. Firms have access to a common best-practice technology for turning inputs into output characterized by a production frontier $f(X_{it}^*; \beta)$. Since actual output can fall short of the maximum possible, we write

$$Y_{it} = f(X_{it}^*; \beta)\tau_i, \tag{14.90}$$

where $0 < \tau_i \leq 1$ is a measure of firm-specific efficiency and $\tau_i = 1$ indicates firm i is fully efficient. Following standard econometric practice, we allow for a random error to the model, ζ_{it}, to capture measurement (or specification) error, resulting in

$$Y_{it} = f(X_{it}^*; \beta)\tau_i\zeta_{it}. \tag{14.91}$$

The inclusion of measurement error makes the frontier stochastic, and hence the model is named the *stochastic frontier* model. If the production frontier $f()$ is log-linear we can take logs and obtain

$$y_{it} = X_{it}\beta + \epsilon_{it} - z_i, \tag{14.92}$$

where $\beta = [\beta_1\ \beta_2\ \cdots\ \beta_k]'$, $y_{it} = \ln(Y_{it})$, $\epsilon_{it} = \ln(\zeta_{it})$, $z_i = -\ln(\tau_i)$, and X_{it} is the counterpart of X_{it}^* with the inputs transformed to logarithms. The variable z_i is referred to as *inefficiency* and, since $0 < \tau_i \leq 1$, it is a non-negative random variable. We assume ϵ_{it} to be iid $N\left(0, h^{-1}\right)$ and independent of z_i. This is a latent variable model since the inefficiencies z_i are unobserved.

Equation (14.92) can be written

$$y_i = X_i\beta + \epsilon_i - z_i\iota_T, \tag{14.93}$$

if we stack all variables into matrices in the obvious fashion.

In this exercise, assume $p(\beta, h) = p(\beta)\,p(h)$, with

$$\beta \sim N\left(\underline{\beta}, \underline{V}\right) \tag{14.94}$$

and

$$h \sim \gamma\left(\underline{s}^{-2}, \underline{\nu}\right). \tag{14.95}$$

For the inefficiencies, assume an exponential hierarchical prior, with z_i and z_j being *a priori* independent for $i \neq j$. Thus, for all i,

$$z_i \sim \gamma\left(\mu_z, 2\right). \tag{14.96}$$

For μ_z, use a prior of the form

$$\mu_z^{-1} \sim \gamma\left(\underline{\mu}_z^{-1}, \underline{\nu}_z\right). \tag{14.97}$$

(a) Derive the full posterior conditionals for this model.
(b) Using the results from part (a) carry out an empirical Bayesian analysis using a suitable data set. Note that the answer in the following uses an artificial data set that was generated from

$$y_{it} = 1.0 + 0.75x_{2,it} + 0.25x_{3,it} - z_i + \epsilon_{it}$$

for $i = 1, \ldots, 100$ and $t = 1, \ldots, 5$. We assume $\epsilon_{it} \sim N(0, 0.04)$, $z_i \sim \gamma\left(-\ln[.85], 2\right)$, $x_{2,it} \sim U(0,1)$, and $x_{3,it} \sim U(0,1)$, where all the random variables are independent of one another and independent over all i and t.

Solution

(a) From the properties of the normal distribution, we have

$$p(y|\beta, h, z) = \prod_{i=1}^{N} \frac{h^{\frac{T}{2}}}{(2\pi)^{\frac{T}{2}}} \left\{\exp\left[-\frac{h}{2}\left(y_i - X_i\beta + z_i\iota_T\right)'\left(y_i - X_i\beta_i + z_i\iota_T\right)\right]\right\}. \tag{14.98}$$

However, conditional on z, this is simply a standard normal likelihood function. So derivations very similar to those in previous exercises can be used (e.g., Chapter 10, Exercise 10.1, or Chapter 13, Exercise 13.1). In particular, if we multiply (14.94) by (14.98) it can be seen that the resulting posterior conditional is

$$\beta|y, h, z, \mu_z \sim N\left(\overline{\beta}, \overline{V}\right), \tag{14.99}$$

where

$$\overline{V} = \left(\underline{V}^{-1} + h \sum_{i=1}^{N} X_i' X_i \right)^{-1}$$

and

$$\overline{\beta} = \overline{V} \left(\underline{V}^{-1} \underline{\beta} + h \sum_{i=1}^{N} X_i' \left[y_i + z_i \iota_T \right] \right).$$

Multiplying (14.95) by (14.98), we obtain

$$h | y, \beta, z, \mu_z \sim \gamma(\overline{s}^{-2}, \overline{\nu}), \tag{14.100}$$

$$\overline{\nu} = TN + \underline{\nu},$$

and

$$\overline{s}^2 = \frac{\sum_{i-1}^{N} (y_i + z_i \iota_T - X_i \beta)' (y_i + z_i \iota_T - X_i \beta) + \underline{\nu} \underline{s}^2}{\overline{\nu}}.$$

Using Bayes' theorem, we have

$$p(z | y, \beta, h, \mu_z) \propto p(y | z, \beta, h, \mu_z) \, p(z | \beta, h, \mu_z),$$

which is simply (14.96) times (14.98). Doing this multiplication and noting that the posterior conditionals for the inefficiencies are independent of one another (i.e., z_i and z_j are independent for $i \neq j$), it follows immediately that

$$p(z_i | y_i, X_i, \beta, h, \mu_z) \propto \phi(z_i | \overline{X}_i \beta - \overline{y}_i - (Th\mu_z)^{-1}, (Th)^{-1}) I(z_i \geq 0), \tag{14.101}$$

where $\overline{y}_i = \left(\sum_{t=1}^{T} y_{it} \right) / T$ and $\overline{X}_i$ is a $(1 \times k)$ matrix containing the average value of each explanatory variable for individual i. Recall that $I(z_i \geq 0)$ is the indicator function, which equals one if $z_i \geq 0$ and is otherwise equal to zero.

An examination of (14.97) times (14.98) yields the posterior conditional for μ_z^{-1}, which can be seen to be

$$\mu_z^{-1} | y, \beta, h, z \sim \gamma(\overline{\mu}_z, \overline{\nu}_z), \tag{14.102}$$

$$\overline{\nu} = 2N + \underline{\nu}_z,$$

and

$$\overline{\mu}_z = \frac{2N + \underline{\nu}_z}{2 \sum_{i=1}^{N} z_i + \underline{\nu}_z \underline{\mu}_z}.$$

(b) A Gibbs sampler with data augmentation involves sequentially drawing from (14.99), (14.100), (14.101), and (14.102). All of these posterior conditionals involve standard distributions. (See Exercise 11.5 for a discussion of drawing from the truncated normal.) MATLAB code that does this is available on the website associated with this book.

Table 14.7: Posterior results for an artificial data set from the stochastic frontier model.

	Mean	Standard deviation
β_1	0.98	0.03
β_2	0.74	0.03
β_3	0.27	0.03
h	26.69	1.86
μ_z	0.15	0.02
τ_{min}	0.56	0.05
τ_{med}	0.89	0.06
τ_{max}	0.97	0.03

With regard to prior hyperparameters we choose

$$\underline{\beta} = \begin{bmatrix} 0.0 \\ 0.5 \\ 0.5 \end{bmatrix}$$

and

$$\underline{V} = \begin{bmatrix} 100.0 & 0.0 & 0.0 \\ 0.0 & 0.25^2 & 0.0 \\ 0.0 & 0.0 & 0.25^2 \end{bmatrix}.$$

These values are chosen to be relatively non-informative about the intercept, but they are slightly more informative about the slope coefficients. In particular, they reflect a belief that large deviations from constant returns to scale are unlikely. For the error precision, we make the non-informative choice of $\underline{\nu} = 0$, which makes the choice of $\underline{s}^2$ irrelevant. For μ_z, we make the relatively non-informative choice of $\underline{\nu}_z = 2$ with $\underline{\mu}_z = -\ln(0.85)$, which implies that the median of the prior efficiency distribution is 0.85. Posterior results are based on 30 000 replications, with 5000 burn-in replications discarded and 25 000 replications retained.

Table 14.7 contains posterior means and standard deviations for the parameters of the stochastic frontier model. With stochastic frontier models, interest often centers on the firm-specific efficiencies, τ_i for $i = 1, \ldots, N$. Since $\tau_i = \exp(-z_i)$, and the Gibbs sampler yields draws of z_i, we can simply transform them and average to obtain estimates of $E(\tau_i|y)$. For the sake of brevity, we do not present results for all $N = 100$ efficiencies. Rather, we select the firms that have the minimum, median, and maximum values for $E(\tau_i|y)$. These are labeled τ_{min}, τ_{med}, and τ_{max} in Table 14.7.

It can be seen that the posterior means of all parameters are quite close to the true values used to generate the data set – note that $-\ln(0.85) = 0.16$ – and they are all accurately estimated. The posterior means of the efficiencies are reasonable, although their posterior standard deviations are relatively large.

Exercise 14.15 (Posterior simulation in the two-part (hurdle) model) A variant of the tobit model (see Exercise 14.8) for analyzing a censored outcome is the *two-part model* (e.g., Cragg 1971). Like the tobit, the two-part specification provides a framework for modeling a mixed discrete–continuous variable that is characterized by a discrete mass over zero and a continuous distribution over strictly positive values. As the name suggests, the two-part model is composed of two equations: one equation determining whether the outcome is positive or zero (i.e., a "decision-to-use" equation) and a second equation specifying a continuous distribution over strictly positive values (i.e., a "level-of-use" equation). In contrast to the tobit model, which introduces only one equation, the two-part model can allow different covariates to enter the decision-to-use and level-of-use equations and does not impose restrictions on parameters across equations. This added flexibility is often argued to be beneficial for capturing key features of the censored variable, particularly in situations where the model is characterized by a large fraction of zero responses.

The two-part model has seen considerable use in empirical work and was championed by researchers at RAND for use in health economics and the modeling of medical expenditure data (e.g., Manning, Morris, and Newhouse 1981; Manning, Duan, and Rogers 1987). These works predate the MCMC revolution in econometrics, though recent Bayesian treatments of the model can be found in van Hasselt (2005) and Deb, Munkin, and Trivedi (2006).

In what follows, we consider the following representation of the two-part model:

$$D_i^* = x_{1i}\beta_1 + \epsilon_{1i}, \tag{14.103}$$

$$\ln y_i | D_i^* > 0 = x_{2i}\beta_2 + \epsilon_{2i}. \tag{14.104}$$

Equation (14.103) for the latent variable D_i^* denotes the "first" part of the model and describes whether the outcome y_i is positive or zero. Specifically,

$$D_i \equiv I(D_i^* > 0) = I(y_i > 0).$$

The quantities $(D_i, y_i, x_{1i}, x_{2i})$ denote the data observed for i. Finally, in most applications, the level-of-use equation is specified in logarithmic form, which explains the appearance of $\ln y$ on the left-hand side of (14.104).

The two-part model typically assumes $\epsilon_{1i} \stackrel{iid}{\sim} N(0,1)$ and $\epsilon_{2i} \stackrel{iid}{\sim} N(0,\sigma_\epsilon^2)$. Thus, the model assumes that the level of the outcome is independent of the decision to use, conditioned on the event that some level of use has taken place. That is, the errors of (14.103) and (14.104) are assumed independent, conditioned on $\epsilon_1 > -x_1\beta_1$.

(a) Using priors of the form

$$\beta_j \sim N(\mu_{\beta_j}, V_{\beta_j}), \;\; j = 1, 2, \tag{14.105}$$

$$\sigma_\epsilon^2 \sim IG(a, b), \tag{14.106}$$

describe a posterior simulator for fitting the two-part model.
(b) Consider the two-part specification with only an intercept in Equations (14.103) and (14.104). Generate 1000 observations from this two-part model by setting $\beta_1 = .5$, $\beta_2 = 1$, and $\sigma_\epsilon^2 = 4$. For the prior hyperparameters, set $\mu_j = 0$, $V_{\beta_j} = 10$ $(j = 1, 2)$, $a = 3$, and $b = 1$. Write a program to implement the algorithm derived in part (a), and apply this program to your generated data.
(c) On the website associated with this book, we provide data on the volumes of bilateral trade (in thousands of U.S. dollars) among 79 pairs of countries. Specifically, the data set quantifies the amount of trade occurring between 79 different countries in a product type called "differentiated goods." Each country is observed to trade (or not trade) with all other countries, producing a grand total of 3081 observations. Using only an intercept in Equations (14.103) and (14.104), fit the two-part model to these data and comment on your results.

Solution
(a) To fit this model, we make use of data augmentation and work with a joint posterior of the form $p(D^*, \beta_1, \beta_2, \sigma_\epsilon^2 | D, y)$, where

$$D^* = \begin{bmatrix} D_1^* \\ D_2^* \\ \vdots \\ D_n^* \end{bmatrix}, \quad D = \begin{bmatrix} D_1 \\ D_2 \\ \vdots \\ D_n \end{bmatrix}, \quad \text{and} \quad y = \begin{bmatrix} y_1 \\ y_2 \\ \vdots \\ y_n \end{bmatrix}.$$

Though the conditioning on D in the posterior is essentially redundant given y, we maintain this notation and conditioning for the sake of clarity.

Note that

$$\begin{aligned} p(D^*, \beta_1, \beta_2, \sigma_\epsilon^2 | D, y) &\propto p(\beta_1)p(\beta_2)p(\sigma_\epsilon^2)p(D^*, y|\beta_1, \beta_2, \sigma_\epsilon^2) \\ &\quad \times p(D|D^*, y, \beta_1, \beta_2, \sigma_\epsilon^2) \\ &= p(\beta_1)p(\beta_2)p(\sigma_\epsilon^2)\left[p(D|D^*, y, \beta_1, \beta_2, \sigma_\epsilon^2)\right. \\ &\quad \left.\times\, p(y|D^*, \beta_1, \beta_2, \sigma_\epsilon^2)p(D^*|\beta_1, \beta_2, \sigma_\epsilon^2)\right] \\ &= p(\beta_1)p(\beta_2)p(\sigma_\epsilon^2) \\ &\quad \times \prod_{i=1}^n \Bigg([I(D_i = 1)I(D_i^* > 0) + I(D_i = 0)I(D_i^* \le 0)] \\ &\quad \times \left[\frac{1}{y_i}\phi(\ln y_i; x_{2i}\beta_2, \sigma_\epsilon^2)I(D_i^* > 0) + I(y_i = 0)I(D_i^* \le 0)\right] \\ &\quad \times \phi(D_i^*; x_{1i}\beta_1, 1)\Bigg). \end{aligned} \tag{14.107}$$

A Gibbs sampler involves cycling through conditionals of the form $D^*|\cdot, y, D$, $\beta_1|\cdot, y, D$, $\beta_2|\cdot, y, D$, and $\sigma_\epsilon^2|\cdot, y, D$, where "·" is simplifying notation serving to denote the remaining parameters of the model. When sampling β_2 and σ_ϵ^2 from their posterior conditionals, the augmented posterior in (14.107) reveals that only the x_2 and y data arising from the subsample for which $y_i > 0$ are used. Let X_2^+ and y^+ denote this subsample of data (arranged conformably) and also define

$$X_1 = \begin{bmatrix} x_{11} \\ x_{12} \\ \vdots \\ x_{1n} \end{bmatrix}.$$

With this notation in hand, we obtain posterior conditionals of the following forms:

$$D_i^*|\beta_1, \beta_2, \sigma_\epsilon^2, y, D \overset{ind}{\sim} \begin{cases} TN_{(-\infty,0]}(x_{1i}\beta_1, 1) & \text{if } D_i = 0, \\ TN_{(0,\infty)}(x_{1i}\beta_1, 1) & \text{if } D_i = 1, \end{cases} \tag{14.108}$$

and

$$\beta_1|D^*, \beta_2, \sigma_\epsilon^2, y, D \sim N(D_{\beta_1}d_{\beta_1}, D_{\beta_1}), \tag{14.109}$$

where

$$D_{\beta_1} = \left(X_1'X_1 + V_{\beta_1}^{-1}\right)^{-1}, \quad d_{\beta_1} = X_1'D^* + V_{\beta_1}^{-1}\mu_{\beta_1}.$$

For the remaining two posterior conditionals, we obtain

$$\beta_2|D^*, \beta_1, \sigma_\epsilon^2, y, D \sim N(D_{\beta_2}d_{\beta_2}, D_{\beta_2}), \tag{14.110}$$

where

$$D_{\beta_2} = \left(X_2^{+\prime}X_2^+/\sigma_\epsilon^2 + V_{\beta_2}^{-1}\right)^{-1}, \qquad d_{\beta_2} = X_2^{+\prime}\ln y^+/\sigma_\epsilon^2 + V_{\beta_2}^{-1}\mu_{\beta_2},$$

and

$$\sigma_\epsilon^2|D^*, \beta_1, \beta_2, y, D \sim IG\left(\frac{n^+}{2} + a, \left[b^{-1} + .5(\ln y^+ - X_2^+\beta_2)'(\ln y^+ - X_2^+\beta)\right]^{-1}\right), \tag{14.111}$$

where n^+ is defined as the number of elements in $\ln y^+$. A posterior simulator proceeds by sampling from (14.108) through (14.111).

(b) MATLAB code for generating the data and fitting the two-part model are provided on the website associated with this book. In our code, the Gibbs sampler is run for 3000 iterations, and the first 1000 of these are discarded as the burn-in. In Table 14.8 we provide posterior means and the actual parameters used to generate the data. The results show that the algorithm fares well in recovering the parameters of the data-generating process.

(c) We apply the same code used in part (b) to fit the trade data, setting the prior variances of β_1 and β_2 to 1000. Posterior means of β_1, β_2, and σ^2 were equal to .790, .935, and 11.63, respectively. These results imply the probability that no trade occurs is equal to

Table 14.8: Posterior means and true values of the parameters.

	β_1	β_2	σ_ϵ^2
Post. mean	.489	.976	3.94
True value	.500	1.00	4.00

$\Pr(\epsilon_i \leq -\beta_1) = 1 - \Phi(\beta_1) \approx .215$, which matches the fraction of observations with zero trade in the sample. The posterior means of β_2 and σ^2 also match the sample mean and sample variance of log trade values for those observations associated with positive trade. Finally, given our lognormality assumption, the mean of trade, given that trade occurs, is $\exp(\beta_2 + \sigma_\epsilon^2/2)$. Evaluated at posterior means, this quantity equals \$3.8 billion (where we recall that trade has been measured in thousands of dollars).

Exercise 14.16 (Posterior simulation in the sample-selection model) Closely related to the two-part model of Exercise 14.15 is the *sample-selection model.* Unlike the two-part model, the sample-selection model allows for correlation between unobservables in the decision-to-use and level-of-use equations, and also provides an explicit role for the *counterfactual* or *potential outcome* – the amount of expenditure that could have been observed but was not. The merits of and assumptions made by the sample-selection and two-part models have received considerable attention in the literature (e.g., Manning, Duan, and Rogers 1987; Hay and Olsen 1984; Leung and Yu 1996). We do not review these issues here; instead, we seek to introduce a Bayesian posterior simulator for the sample-selection model, along the lines of the analysis of van Hasselt (2005).

We consider the following representation of the sample-selection model:

$$D_i^* = x_{1i}\beta_1 + \epsilon_{1i}, \tag{14.112}$$

$$y_i^* = x_{2i}\beta_2 + \epsilon_{2i}, \tag{14.113}$$

where

$$\begin{aligned}\begin{bmatrix}\epsilon_{1i}\\ \epsilon_{2i}\end{bmatrix} &\overset{iid}{\sim} N\left[\begin{pmatrix}0\\0\end{pmatrix}, \begin{pmatrix}1 & \sigma_{12}\\ \sigma_{12} & \sigma_2^2\end{pmatrix}\right], \quad i = 1, 2, \ldots, n\\ &\equiv N(0, \Sigma).\end{aligned}$$

Like Equation (14.103), (14.112) is the latent variable decision-to-use equation. If $D_i \equiv I(D_i^* > 0)$ is zero, then observed expenditure is zero, whereas if $D_i = 1$, then a positive amount of expenditure is observed. The latent variable y_i^* in (14.113), like (14.104), describes the *logarithm* of observed or *potential* expenditure. Formally, observed expenditure y_i is linked to the latent D_i^* and y_i^* as follows:

$$y_i = \begin{cases} 0 & \text{if } D_i^* \leq 0, \\ \exp(y_i^*) & \text{if } D_i^* > 0. \end{cases} \tag{14.114}$$

The observed data for individual i consist of y_i, D_i, x_{1i}, and x_{2i}. Derive a posterior simulator for fitting the sample-selection model and the priors employed in your analysis.

Solution

Let

$$D^* = \begin{bmatrix} D_1^* \\ \vdots \\ D_n^* \end{bmatrix}, \quad y^* = \begin{bmatrix} y_1^* \\ \vdots \\ y_n^* \end{bmatrix}, \quad D = \begin{bmatrix} D_1 \\ \vdots \\ D_n \end{bmatrix}, \quad \text{and} \quad y = \begin{bmatrix} y_1 \\ \vdots \\ y_n \end{bmatrix}.$$

To facilitate posterior computations, we will work with an augmented posterior distribution of the form $p(D^*, y^*, \beta, \Sigma | y, D)$. Note that, under independent priors for β and Σ, denoted $p(\beta)$ and $p(\Sigma)$, we obtain

$$\begin{aligned} p(D^*, y^*, \beta, \Sigma | y, D) &\propto p(D^*, y^*, D, y | \beta, \Sigma) p(\beta) p(\Sigma) \\ &= p(y, D | y^*, D^*, \beta, \Sigma) p(y^*, D^* | \beta, \Sigma) p(\beta) p(\Sigma) \\ &= p(y | D, y^*) p(D | D^*) p(y^*, D^* | \beta, \Sigma) p(\beta) p(\Sigma) \\ &= p(\beta) p(\Sigma) \prod_{i=1}^{n} p(y_i | D_i, y_i^*) p(D_i | D_i^*) \phi\left(\begin{bmatrix} D_i^* \\ y_i^* \end{bmatrix}; \begin{bmatrix} x_{1i}\beta_1 \\ x_{2i}\beta_2 \end{bmatrix}, \Sigma \right). \end{aligned}$$

In the third line of this expression, we write the joint distribution of y and D given the parameters of the augmented posterior as the conditional $y|D$ times the marginal for D, and we have dropped extraneous variables from the conditioning set. These two densities can be shown to equal

$$p(D_i | D_i^*) = I(D_i = 1) I(D_i^* > 0) + I(D_i = 0) I(D_i^* \leq 0)$$

and

$$p(y_i | D_i, y_i^*) = D_i I[y_i = \exp(y_i^*)] + (1 - D_i) I(y_i = 0).$$

Before describing the posterior conditionals of this model, let

$$r_i \equiv \begin{bmatrix} D_i^* \\ y_i^* \end{bmatrix}, \quad X_i \equiv \begin{bmatrix} x_{1i} & 0 \\ 0 & x_{2i} \end{bmatrix}, \quad \text{and} \quad \beta = \begin{bmatrix} \beta_1 \\ \beta_2 \end{bmatrix}.$$

Then, under a prior for β of the form $\beta \sim N(\mu_\beta, V_\beta)$,

$$\beta | D^*, y^*, \Sigma, y, D \sim N(D_\beta d_\beta, D_\beta), \tag{14.115}$$

where

$$D_\beta = \left(\sum_{i=1}^{n} X_i' \Sigma^{-1} X_i + V_\beta^{-1} \right)^{-1}, \quad d_\beta = \sum_{i=1}^{n} X_i' \Sigma^{-1} r_i + V_\beta^{-1} \mu_\beta.$$

To sample from the joint posterior conditional distribution of D^* and y^*, we need to consider two distinct cases. When $D_i = 1$, the conditional posterior distribution of y_i^* is degenerate, i.e., $y_i^* = \ln(y_i)$, and

$$D_i^* | \beta, \Sigma, y^*, y, D \stackrel{ind}{\sim} TN_{(0,\infty)} \left[x_{1i}\beta_1 + \frac{\sigma_{12}}{\sigma_2^2}[y_i^* - x_{2i}\beta_2], \left(1 - \frac{\sigma_{12}^2}{\sigma_2^2}\right)\right]. \tag{14.116}$$

When $D_i = 0$ we obtain

$$p(D_i^*, y_i^* | \beta, \Sigma, y, D) \propto I(D_i^* \leq 0) \phi\left(\begin{bmatrix} D_i^* \\ y_i^* \end{bmatrix}, \begin{bmatrix} x_{1i}\beta_1 \\ x_{2i}\beta_2 \end{bmatrix}, \Sigma \right).$$

We can employ a blocking step to sample D_i^*, y_i^* jointly from this conditional. Specifically, marginalized over y_i^*, it follows that

$$D_i^* | \beta, \Sigma, y, D \stackrel{ind}{\sim} TN_{(-\infty,0]}(x_{1i}\beta, 1), \tag{14.117}$$

and the complete conditional for y_i^* is given as

$$y_i^* | D_i^*, \beta, \Sigma, y, D \stackrel{ind}{\sim} N\left(x_{2i}\beta_2 + \sigma_{12}(D_i^* - x_{1i}\beta_1), \sigma_2^2 \left[1 - \frac{\sigma_{12}^2}{\sigma_2^2}\right]\right). \tag{14.118}$$

To sample the parameters of the covariance matrix Σ, we follow the reparameterization strategy described in Exercise 14.10, Equations (14.50)–(14.52). Specifically, we write $\epsilon_{2i} = \sigma_{12}\epsilon_{1i} + \nu_i$, $\nu_i \sim N(0, \sigma_v^2)$ with $\sigma_\nu^2 = \sigma_2^2 - \sigma_{12}^2$. Under this parameterization, we can write Σ as

$$\Sigma = \begin{bmatrix} 1 & \sigma_{12} \\ \sigma_{12} & \sigma_\nu^2 + \sigma_{12}^2 \end{bmatrix}$$

and employ priors of the form $\sigma_\nu^2 \sim IG(a, b)$ and $\sigma_{12} \sim N(\mu_0, V_0)$. Our two-equation system in (14.112) and (14.113) can then be rewritten as

$$\begin{aligned} D_i^* &= x_{1i}\beta_1 + \epsilon_{1i}, \\ y_i^* &= x_{2i}\beta_2 + \sigma_{12}\epsilon_{1i} + \nu_i, \end{aligned}$$

whence it follows that

$$\sigma_{12} | \sigma_\nu^2, \beta, D^*, y^*, y, D \sim N(D_\sigma d_\sigma, D_\sigma), \tag{14.119}$$

where

$$D_\sigma = \left(\epsilon_1'\epsilon_1/\sigma_\nu^2 + V_0^{-1}\right)^{-1}, \quad d_\sigma = \epsilon_1'(y^* - X_2\beta_2)/\sigma_\nu^2 + V_0^{-1}\mu_0,$$

and

$$\sigma_\nu^2 | \sigma_{12}, \beta, D^*, y^*, y, D \sim IG\left(\frac{n}{2} + a, \left[b^{-1} + \frac{1}{2}\nu'\nu\right]^{-1}\right). \tag{14.120}$$

In (14.119), note that $\epsilon_1 = [\epsilon_{1i}\ \epsilon_{2i}\ \cdots\ \epsilon_{ni}]'$ is known given D^* and β; in (14.120), note that $\nu \equiv [\nu_1\ \cdots\ \nu_n]'$ is known given y^*, D^*, β, and σ_{12}, and

$$X_2 = \begin{bmatrix} x_{21} \\ x_{22} \\ \vdots \\ x_{2n} \end{bmatrix}.$$

The Gibbs sampler involves drawing from (14.115) through (14.120). Note that when drawing from the posterior conditional for the latent data D^* and y^*, either (14.116) or (14.117)–(14.118) is applied for a given i, depending on the observed value of D_i.

Exercise 14.17 (Missing data I) Consider the regression model

$$y_i^* = \beta_0 + \beta_1 x_i + \epsilon_i, \quad \epsilon_i \overset{iid}{\sim} N(0, \sigma^2).$$

Assume that x_i is observed for all $i = 1, 2, \ldots, n$, and that y_i^* is observed (and equal to y_i) for $i = 1, 2, \ldots, m$, $m < n$. For $i = m+1, m+2, \ldots, n$, the dependent variable is missing, and is presumed to be generated by the equation given here. Note that this question and those that follow do not deal with issues related to data being missing completely at random, at random, or not at random. Here, the "missing" indicator is presumed to be generated by a process unrelated to the regression parameters and y^* (i.e., the data are missing completely at random). See, e.g., Gelman, Carlin, Stern, and Rubin (2004, Chapter 21) for further discussion and references.
(a) Let $\beta = [\beta_0 \ \beta_1]'$ and employ priors of the form $\beta \sim N(\mu_\beta, V_\beta)$ and $\sigma^2 \sim IG(a, b)$. Describe a data augmentation approach for "filling in" the missing data and fitting the regression model.
(b) Is posterior inference regarding β_0, β_1, and σ^2 sharpened by including the latent missing data into the joint posterior?

Solution
(a) First, stack the regression equation into vector and matrix form as follows:

$$\begin{bmatrix} y_1 \\ \vdots \\ y_m \\ y_{m+1}^* \\ \vdots \\ y_n^* \end{bmatrix} = \begin{bmatrix} 1 & x_1 \\ \vdots & \vdots \\ 1 & x_m \\ 1 & x_{m+1} \\ \vdots & \vdots \\ 1 & x_n \end{bmatrix} \begin{bmatrix} \beta_0 \\ \beta_1 \end{bmatrix} + \begin{bmatrix} \epsilon_1 \\ \vdots \\ \epsilon_m \\ \epsilon_{m+1} \\ \vdots \\ \epsilon_n \end{bmatrix},$$

or compactly as

$$y^* = X\beta + \epsilon,$$

with y^*, X, β, and ϵ defined in the obvious ways.

Let y_{obs} denote the first m entries of y^* and let $y_{\text{miss}} = [y^*_{m+1} \ \cdots \ y^*_n]'$. Including y_{miss} as an element of the joint posterior, we can write

$$\begin{aligned} p(y_{\text{miss}}, \beta, \sigma^2 | y_{\text{obs}}) &\propto p(y_{\text{obs}}, y_{\text{miss}} | \beta, \sigma^2) p(\beta) p(\sigma^2) \\ &= \phi(y^*; X\beta, \sigma^2 I_n) p(\beta) p(\sigma^2). \end{aligned}$$

Given this result, it follows that the posterior conditionals $\beta | y_{\text{miss}}, \sigma^2, y_{\text{obs}}$ and $\sigma^2 | y_{\text{miss}}, \beta, y_{\text{obs}}$ are of the following forms:

$$\beta | y_{\text{miss}}, \sigma^2, y_{\text{obs}} \sim N(D_\beta d_\beta, D_\beta), \tag{14.121}$$

where

$$D_\beta = (X'X/\sigma^2 + V_\beta^{-1})^{-1}, \quad d_\beta = X'y^*/\sigma^2 + V_\beta^{-1}\mu_\beta,$$

and

$$\sigma^2 | y_{\text{miss}}, \beta, y_{\text{obs}} \sim IG\left\{\frac{n}{2} + a, \left[b^{-1} + (1/2)(y^* - X\beta)'(y^* - X\beta)\right]^{-1}\right\}. \tag{14.122}$$

Similarly, since

$$p(y_{\text{miss}}, \beta, \sigma^2 | y_{\text{obs}}) \propto p(y_{\text{obs}} | \beta, \sigma^2) p(y_{\text{miss}} | \beta, \sigma^2) p(\beta) p(\sigma^2), \tag{14.123}$$

it follows that the missing data y_{miss} can be drawn independently as follows:

$$y_i^* | \beta, \sigma^2, y_{\text{obs}} \overset{ind}{\sim} N(\beta_0 + \beta_1 x_i, \sigma^2), \quad i = m+1, m+2, \ldots, n. \tag{14.124}$$

A posterior simulator proceeds by sampling from (14.121), (14.122), and (14.124).
(b) Though somewhat obvious, we note that

$$p(\beta, \sigma^2 | y_{\text{obs}}) = \int_{R_{y_{\text{miss}}}} p(y_{\text{miss}}, \beta, \sigma^2 | y_{\text{obs}}) dy_{\text{miss}} \propto p(y_{\text{obs}} | \beta, \sigma^2) p(\beta) p(\sigma^2).$$

Thus, the addition of the latent, missing data does nothing to "sharpen" inference regarding β and σ^2. We obtain the same marginal posterior for β and σ^2 that we would have obtained had we worked directly with the density for y_{obs} and ignored the contribution of all observations with missing y data. Since the addition of the missing variables will likely slow down the mixing of the posterior simulator, it really does not pay to work with the augmented likelihood in this case.

Exercise 14.18 (Missing data II) Similar to the SUR model of Exercise 12.18, suppose

$$\begin{bmatrix} y_{1i} \\ y_{2i} \end{bmatrix} \overset{ind}{\sim} N\left(\begin{bmatrix} x_{1i}\beta_1 \\ x_{2i}\beta_2 \end{bmatrix}, \begin{bmatrix} \sigma_1^2 & \sigma_{12} \\ \sigma_{12} & \sigma_2^2 \end{bmatrix}\right), \quad i = 1, 2, \ldots, n, \tag{14.125}$$

or equivalently,

$$\tilde{y}_i \overset{ind}{\sim} N(\tilde{X}_i \beta, \Sigma), \quad i = 1, 2, \ldots, n,$$

where

$$\tilde{y}_i \equiv \begin{bmatrix} y_{1i} \\ y_{2i} \end{bmatrix}, \quad \tilde{X}_i \equiv \begin{bmatrix} x_{1i} & 0 \\ 0 & x_{2i} \end{bmatrix}, \quad \text{and} \quad \beta = \begin{bmatrix} \beta_1 \\ \beta_2 \end{bmatrix}.$$

In addition to this structure, suppose that $[y_{2m+1}\ y_{2m+2}\ \cdots\ y_n]'$ are missing, but data on all other variables (i.e., y_1, x_1, and x_2) are available. Denote the first m observed elements of y_2 as $y_{2,\text{obs}}$ and the final $n-m$ elements as $y_{2,\text{miss}}$ so that $y_2 = [y_{2,\text{obs}}'\ y_{2,\text{miss}}']'$.
(a) Employing priors of the forms

$$\beta \sim N(\mu_\beta, V_\beta), \quad \Sigma^{-1} \sim W(\Omega, \nu),$$

augment the posterior with $y_{2,\text{miss}}$ and describe a posterior simulator for fitting the model.
(b) Comment on how the incorporation of the missing data into the posterior simulator facilitates computation in this model.

Solution
(a) Let $y_{\text{obs}} = [y_1'\ y_{2,\text{obs}}']'$ denote the observed outcome data, where y_1 denotes the $n \times 1$ vector of y_{1i} outcomes stacked over i, and y_2 is defined similarly. The augmented posterior distribution can be expressed as

$$\begin{aligned} p(y_{2,\text{miss}}, \beta, \Sigma^{-1}|y_{\text{obs}}) &\propto p(y_1, y_2|\beta, \Sigma)p(\beta)p(\Sigma^{-1}) \\ &= p(\beta)p(\Sigma^{-1})\prod_{i=1}^{n} \phi(\tilde{y}_i; \tilde{X}_i\beta, \Sigma). \end{aligned}$$

A Gibbs sampler applied to this model involves drawing from the complete posterior conditionals for β, Σ^{-1}, and $y_{2,\text{miss}}$. Since, conditioned on the missing outcome data, this model has the same structure as the SUR model of Exercise 12.18, the posterior conditionals for β and Σ^{-1} are the same as those reported in that exercise and thus are not repeated here.

For the posterior conditional for $y_{2,\text{miss}}$, note that the assumptions of our model imply

$$y_{2i}|\beta, \Sigma^{-1}, y_{\text{obs}} \overset{ind}{\sim} N\left(x_{2i}\beta_2 + \frac{\sigma_{12}}{\sigma_1^2}(y_{1i} - x_{1i}\beta_1), \sigma_2^2(1-\rho_{12}^2)\right), \quad i = m+1, \ldots, n, \tag{14.126}$$

where $\rho_{12}^2 \equiv \sigma_{12}^2/\sigma_1^2\sigma_2^2$. The Gibbs sampler involves drawing from the posterior conditionals for β and Σ^{-1}, as described in the SUR analysis of Exercise 12.18, and then drawing independently from (14.126) for $i = m+1, \ldots, n$.
(b) Note that when marginalizing the joint posterior in part (a) over the latent data, we obtain

$$p(\beta, \Sigma^{-1}|y_{\text{obs}}) \propto p(\beta)p(\Sigma^{-1})\prod_{i=1}^{m} \phi(\tilde{y}_i; \tilde{X}_i\beta, \Sigma) \prod_{i=m+1}^{n} \phi(y_{1i}; x_{1i}\beta_1, \sigma_1^2). \tag{14.127}$$

This is a quite natural and expected result – when the y_2 data are missing, the appropriate contribution to the likelihood is simply the marginal density for the observed y_{1i}.

When working with the observed data only, posterior computation becomes somewhat more cumbersome, given the form of the posterior in (14.127). The appeal of the augmentation approach presented in part (a) is that, by conditioning on the latent data, we essentially restore the problem to the standard SUR analysis of Exercise 11.10. This contrasts with Exercise 14.17, where the addition of the missing data to the posterior simulator offered no real computational benefit and needlessly complicated the estimation exercise.

Exercise 14.19 (Missing data III) Consider a two-equation model of the form

$$y_i = \beta_0 + \beta_1 x_i + u_i, \tag{14.128}$$

$$x_i = \theta_0 + \theta_1 z_i + \epsilon_i. \tag{14.129}$$

We assume that $u_i \stackrel{iid}{\sim} N(0, \sigma_u^2)$, $\epsilon_i \stackrel{iid}{\sim} N(0, \sigma_\epsilon^2)$, u and ϵ are independent, and $z_i \stackrel{iid}{\sim} N(0, 1)$. In addition to this structure, suppose that $x_i = [x_1 \; \cdots \; x_m \; x_{m+1} \; \cdots \; x_n]'$, where $x_{\text{obs}} \equiv [x_1 \; \cdots \; x_m]'$ are observed in the data set, whereas $x_{\text{miss}} \equiv [x_{m+1} \; \cdots \; x_n]'$ are not observed. Data on y and z are available for every observation.

Finally, let

$$\beta = [\beta_0 \; \beta_1]', \quad \theta = [\theta_0 \; \theta_1]', \quad \pi = [\beta' \; \theta' \; \sigma_u^2 \; \sigma_\epsilon^2]',$$

and employ priors of the form $\beta \sim N(\mu_\beta, V_\beta)$, $\theta \sim N(\mu_\theta, V_\theta)$, $\sigma_u^2 \sim IG(a_1, b_1)$, and $\sigma_\epsilon^2 \sim IG(a_2, b_2)$.

(a) Augment the posterior with the missing data x_{miss} and describe a posterior simulator for fitting this model.

(b) Derive an expression for the marginal posterior $p(\pi|y, x_{\text{obs}})$. Is the posterior for β_0 and β_1 affected only by those observations with observed x values?

(c) Generate 2000 observations from the model in part (a) with $\beta_0 = 2$, $\beta_1 = -.7$, $\theta_0 = 1$, $\theta_1 = .35$, $\sigma_u^2 = .4$, and $\sigma_\epsilon^2 = .01$. Once the complete data set has been generated, treat the first 500 x values as observed, and discard the remaining 1500 as missing.

Consider two different approaches in this situation. For the first case, consider only the equation $y_i = \beta_0 + \beta_1 x_i + u_i$ for the first 500 observations with non-missing data. Fit the model and comment on your results. Next, estimate the complete model, as given in (14.128) and (14.129) using the algorithm described in part (a). Comment on your results. For the priors, center β and θ around a prior mean of zero with $V_\beta = V_\theta = 10I_2$, and choose $a_1 = a_2 = 3$ and $b_1 = b_2 = 1/(2 \times .25)$ (so that the prior means and standard deviations of σ_u^2 and σ_ϵ^2 are all .25).

Solution

(a) Given the assumptions of our model, it follows that

$$p(x_{\text{miss}}, \pi|y, x_{\text{obs}}) \propto p(\pi) \prod_{i=1}^{n} p(y_i, x_i|\pi).$$

Given the distributional assumptions made in this problem, we obtain

$$y_i|x_i, \pi \stackrel{ind}{\sim} N(\beta_0 + \beta_1 x_i, \sigma_u^2), \tag{14.130}$$

$$y_i|\pi \stackrel{ind}{\sim} N\left(\beta_0 + \beta_1[\theta_0 + \theta_1 z_i], \sigma_u^2 + \beta_1^2\sigma_\epsilon^2\right), \tag{14.131}$$

$$x_i|\pi \stackrel{ind}{\sim} N(\theta_0 + \theta_1 z_i, \sigma_\epsilon^2), \tag{14.132}$$

$$x_i|y_i, \pi \stackrel{ind}{\sim} N\Bigg(\theta_0 + \theta_1 z_i + \frac{\beta_1\sigma_\epsilon^2}{\sigma_u^2 + \beta_1^2\sigma_\epsilon^2}[y_i - \beta_0 - \beta_1(\theta_0 + \theta_1 z_i)], \sigma_\epsilon^2\left[1 - \frac{\beta_1^2\sigma_\epsilon^4}{\sigma_\epsilon^2(\sigma_u^2 + \beta_1^2\sigma_\epsilon^2)}\right]\Bigg). \tag{14.133}$$

A posterior simulator can be implemented by first sampling x_{miss} from $x_i|y_i, \pi$ in (14.133), for $i = m+1, m+2, \ldots, n$. The remaining posterior conditionals are as follows:

$$\theta|x_{\text{miss}}, \pi_{-\theta}, y, x_{\text{obs}} \sim N(D_\theta d_\theta, D_\theta), \tag{14.134}$$

where

$$D_\theta = (Z'Z/\sigma_\epsilon^2 + V_\theta^{-1})^{-1}, \quad d_\theta = Z'x/\sigma_\epsilon^2 + V_\theta^{-1}\mu_\theta,$$

$$Z \equiv \begin{bmatrix} 1 & z_1 \\ 1 & z_2 \\ \vdots & \vdots \\ 1 & z_n \end{bmatrix},$$

and $x = [x'_{\text{obs}}\ x'_{\text{miss}}]'$ has been updated with the most recent values of x_{miss} from the previous step,

$$\sigma_\epsilon^2|x_{\text{miss}}, \pi_{-\sigma_\epsilon^2}, y, x_{\text{obs}} \sim IG\left(\frac{n}{2} + a_2, [b_2^{-1} + (1/2)(x - Z\theta)'(x - Z\theta)]^{-1}\right), \tag{14.135}$$

$$\beta|x_{\text{miss}}, \pi_{-\beta}, y, x_{\text{obs}} \sim N(D_\beta d_\beta, D_\beta), \tag{14.136}$$

where

$$D_\beta = (X'X/\sigma_u^2 + V_\beta^{-1})^{-1}, \quad d_\beta = X'y/\sigma_u^2 + V_\beta^{-1}\mu_\beta,$$

and

$$X \equiv \begin{bmatrix} 1 & x_1 \\ 1 & x_2 \\ \vdots & \vdots \\ 1 & x_n \end{bmatrix}.$$

(Alternatively, θ and β could be sampled jointly.) Finally,

$$\sigma_u^2|x_{\text{miss}}, \pi_{-\sigma_u^2}, y, x_{\text{obs}} \sim IG\left(\frac{n}{2} + a_1, [b_1^{-1} + (1/2)(y - X\beta)'(y - X\beta)]^{-1}\right). \tag{14.137}$$

A posterior simulator proceeds by sampling from (14.133) (for the missing x data) through (14.137).

(b) From our general expression for the joint posterior in part (a), it follows that

$$p(\pi|y, x_{\text{obs}}) \propto p(\pi) \prod_{i=1}^{m} p(y_i|x_i, \pi)p(x_i|\pi) \prod_{i=m+1}^{n} p(y_i|\pi).$$

Each of the densities on the right-hand side of this expression is represented in (14.130)–(14.133). From the expression for $p(y_i|\pi)$ in (14.131), it is clear that even the observations with missing x values play a role in the posterior for β_0, β_1, and σ_u^2. The observed x data aid us in learning about θ_0, θ_1, and σ_ϵ^2, which, in turn, help us to "impute" x when it is missing. In the limiting case where $\sigma_\epsilon^2 \approx 0$ and θ_0 and θ_1 are known, the missing data feature of the problem essentially vanishes, as the imputation equation in (14.129) perfectly predicts x.

(c) MATLAB code for implementing this exercise is provided on the website associated with this book. For each of the two procedures, we ran the sampler for 5000 iterations, discarding the first 1000 of those as the burn-in. Generally speaking (and as one should expect), both procedures provided reasonably accurate point estimates (e.g., posterior means) of β and σ_u^2. The posterior standard deviations, however, revealed a different story. For the approach using only the first 500 observations, the posterior standard deviations of β_0 and β_1 were .083 and .078, respectively. When estimating the full model, the standard deviations were nearly cut in half, equaling .043 and .041, respectively. This suggests the potential for some efficiency gains, particularly when an accurate imputation equation is available.

15

Mixture Models

The reader has undoubtedly noted that the majority of exercises in previous chapters have included normality assumptions. These assumptions should not be taken as necessarily "correct," and indeed, such assumptions will not be appropriate in all situations (see, e.g., Exercise 12.19 for an example related to error-term diagnostic checking). In this chapter, we review a variety of computational strategies for extending analyses beyond the textbook normality assumption. The strategies we describe, perhaps ironically, begin with the normal model and proceed to augment it in some way. In the first section, we describe *scale mixtures of normals* models, which enable the researcher to generalize error distributions to the Student t and double exponential classes (among others). Exercises 15.5 and 15.6 then describe *finite normal mixture models*, which can accommodate, among other features, skewness and multimodality in error distributions. Importantly, these models are *conditionally normal* (given values of certain mixing or component indicator variables), and thus standard computational techniques for the normal linear regression model can be directly applied (see, e.g., Exercises 10.1 and 12.9). The techniques described here are thus computationally tractable, flexible, and generalizable. That is, the basic methods provided in this chapter can often be adapted in a straightforward manner to add flexibility to many of the models introduced in previous and future exercises. Some exercises related to mixture models beyond those involving conditional normal sampling distributions are also provided within this chapter.

For the case of finite mixtures, we do not discuss issues of identifiability of the model's parameters up to relabeling of the mixture components, and we invite the reader to consult, for example, Richardson and Green (1997), McLachlan and Peel (2000), Celeux, Hurn, and Robert (2000), and Geweke (2006) for further discussion of this and related issues.

Instead, we focus on algorithms for fitting mixture models, and providing generated-data experiments and illustrative applications. We remind the reader that MATLAB code for carrying out the empirical parts of the questions is on the website associated with this book.

15.1 Some Scale Mixture of Normals Models

Exercise 15.1 (The Student t distribution as a scale mixture of normals) Suppose you specify the density

$$y|\beta, \lambda, \sigma^2 \sim N(x\beta, \lambda\sigma^2) \tag{15.1}$$

and specify the following prior for λ (treating ν as given):

$$\lambda|\nu \sim IG\left(\frac{\nu}{2}, \frac{2}{\nu}\right) \Rightarrow p(\lambda) = \left[\Gamma\left(\frac{\nu}{2}\right)\left(\frac{2}{\nu}\right)^{\nu/2}\right]^{-1} \lambda^{-[(\nu/2)+1]} \exp\left(-\frac{\nu}{2\lambda}\right). \tag{15.2}$$

(a) Derive the density

$$p(y|\beta, \sigma^2) = \int_0^\infty p(y|\beta, \lambda, \sigma^2)p(\lambda)\, d\lambda.$$

(b) Given the result in part (a), comment on how the addition of λ to the error variance can be a useful computational device for an applied Bayesian researcher.

Solution

(a) It follows that

$$\begin{aligned} p(y|\beta, \sigma^2) &= \int_0^\infty \left(\left[\sqrt{2\pi}\sigma\right]^{-1} \lambda^{-(1/2)} \exp\left[-\frac{1}{2\lambda}\left(\frac{y - x\beta}{\sigma}\right)^2\right]\right) \\ &\quad \times \left(\left[\Gamma\left(\frac{\nu}{2}\right)\left(\frac{2}{\nu}\right)^{\nu/2}\right]^{-1} \lambda^{-[(\nu/2)+1]} \exp\left(-\frac{\nu}{2\lambda}\right)\right) d\lambda \\ &= \left[\sqrt{2\pi}\sigma\right]^{-1} \left[\Gamma\left(\frac{\nu}{2}\right)\left(\frac{2}{\nu}\right)^{\nu/2}\right]^{-1} \\ &\quad \times \int_0^\infty \lambda^{-[(\nu+3)/2]} \exp\left[-\frac{1}{\lambda}\left(\frac{1}{2}\left[\frac{y - x\beta}{\sigma}\right]^2 + \frac{\nu}{2}\right)\right] d\lambda. \end{aligned}$$

The expression within this integral is the kernel of an

$$IG\left(\frac{\nu+1}{2}, \left(\frac{1}{2}\left[\left(\frac{y - x\beta}{\sigma}\right)^2 + \nu\right]\right)^{-1}\right)$$

density. Thus,

$$p(y|\beta,\sigma^2) = \left[\sqrt{2\pi}\sigma\right]^{-1}\left[\Gamma\left(\frac{\nu}{2}\right)\left(\frac{2}{\nu}\right)^{\nu/2}\right]^{-1}$$
$$\times\,\Gamma\left(\frac{\nu+1}{2}\right)\left(\frac{1}{2}\left[\left(\frac{y-x\beta}{\sigma}\right)^2+\nu\right]\right)^{-[(\nu+1)/2]}.$$

Rearranging and canceling terms, we obtain

$$p(y|\beta,\sigma^2) = \frac{\Gamma\left(\frac{\nu+1}{2}\right)}{\sqrt{\nu\pi}\sigma\Gamma\left(\frac{\nu}{2}\right)}\left[1+\frac{1}{\nu}\left(\frac{y-x\beta}{\sigma}\right)^2\right]^{-[(\nu+1)/2]}, \tag{15.3}$$

which is in the form of a Student t density, i.e., $y|\beta,\sigma^2 \sim t(x\beta,\sigma,\nu)$.
(b) This result is useful to the applied Bayesian researcher as it, in conjunction with the Gibbs sampler, allows the estimation of models with Student t errors, thus relaxing the normality assumption. To see this, regard the conditional density in part (a) as one observation's contribution to the likelihood function and note (adding i subscripts to denote the individual observations) that

$$p(\beta,\sigma^2,\{\lambda_i\}|y) \propto \left[\prod_{i=1}^{n}\phi(y_i;x_i\beta,\lambda_i\sigma^2)p(\lambda_i)\right]p(\beta,\sigma^2), \tag{15.4}$$

which implies that

$$p(\beta,\sigma^2|y) = \int_0^\infty\cdots\int_0^\infty p(\beta,\sigma^2,\{\lambda_i\}|y)\,d\lambda_1\cdots d\lambda_n \tag{15.5}$$
$$\propto \left[\prod_{i=1}^{n}\int_0^\infty \phi(y_i;x_i\beta,\lambda_i\sigma^2)p(\lambda_i)\,d\lambda_i\right]p(\beta,\sigma^2) \tag{15.6}$$
$$= \prod_{i=1}^{n} f_t(y_i|x_i\beta,\sigma,\nu)p(\beta,\sigma^2). \tag{15.7}$$

Thus, working with the seemingly more complicated joint posterior in (15.4), which contains the inverted-gamma mixing variables λ_i, yields the same inference for β and σ^2 that would be obtained by directly working with a regression model with Student t errors in (15.7). By working with the joint posterior in (15.4), we can work in terms of conditional normal distributions, and thus we can exploit well-known results associated with those distributions. Indeed, this feature will provide a computationally more attractive approach to modeling Student t errors, as revealed in the next exercise.

Exercise 15.2 (Student t errors in regression and binary choice models) Consider the regression model

$$y_i = x_i\beta + \epsilon_i, \quad \epsilon_i|\lambda_i, \sigma^2 \overset{ind}{\sim} N(0, \lambda_i\sigma^2), \tag{15.8}$$

$$\lambda_i \overset{iid}{\sim} IG\left(\frac{\nu}{2}, \frac{2}{\nu}\right), \quad i = 1, 2, \ldots, n, \tag{15.9}$$

$$\beta \sim N(\mu_\beta, V_\beta), \tag{15.10}$$

$$\sigma^2 \sim IG(a, b). \tag{15.11}$$

(a) Show how the Gibbs sampler can be used to fit this model.
(b) Describe how the degrees-of-freedom parameter ν can also be estimated within the model.
(c) Describe how the addition of the inverted gamma mixing variables λ_i can be used to generalize the probit model discussed in Exercise 14.1.

Solution

(a) Exercises 12.12 and 12.13 describe a closely related solution within the framework of the linear regression model. We review many of those derivations here to facilitate answering parts (b) and (c) of this exercise.

To implement the Gibbs sampler we need to obtain the complete posterior conditionals for the parameters β, σ^2, and $\{\lambda_i\}$. The joint posterior distribution is given as

$$p(\beta, \{\lambda_i\}, \sigma^2|y) \propto \left[\prod_{i=1}^{n} \phi(y_i; x_i\beta, \lambda_i\sigma^2)p(\lambda_i)\right] p(\beta)p(\sigma^2).$$

From this joint posterior, the following complete conditional posterior distributions are obtained:

$$\beta|\{\lambda_i\}, \sigma^2|y \sim N\Big[\left(X'\Lambda^{-1}X/\sigma^2 + V_\beta^{-1}\right)^{-1}\left(X'\Lambda^{-1}y + V_\beta^{-1}\mu_\beta\right), \left(X'\Lambda^{-1}X/\sigma^2 + V_\beta^{-1}\right)^{-1}\Big], \tag{15.12}$$

where $\Lambda \equiv \text{diag}\{\lambda_i\}$ and thus $\Lambda^{-1} = \text{diag}\{\lambda_i^{-1}\}$, and X and y are stacked appropriately,

$$\sigma^2|\beta, \{\lambda_i\}, y \sim IG\left[\frac{n}{2} + a, \left(b^{-1} + \frac{1}{2}(y - X\beta)'\Lambda^{-1}(y - X\beta)\right)^{-1}\right], \tag{15.13}$$

and

$$\lambda_i|\beta, \sigma^2, y \overset{ind}{\sim} IG\left[\frac{\nu+1}{2}, \left(\frac{1}{2}\left[\frac{y_i - x_i\beta}{\sigma}\right]^2 + \frac{\nu}{2}\right)^{-1}\right], \quad i = 1, 2, \ldots, n. \tag{15.14}$$

A Gibbs sampler involves drawing from (15.12), (15.13), and (15.14).

(b) To allow ν to be determined within the model (e.g., Albert and Chib 1993), one can specify the following hierarchical prior:

$$\lambda_i|\nu \stackrel{iid}{\sim} IG\left(\frac{\nu}{2}, \frac{2}{\nu}\right),$$
$$\nu \sim \pi,$$

with π denoting a prior over the degrees-of-freedom parameter.

With this formulation, the complete posterior conditionals for the parameters β, σ^2, and $\{\lambda_i\}$ remain the same. (Of course, noting that ν is now a parameter of our model, one must condition on its most recent draw when sampling from these conditionals.) The complete posterior conditional for ν is obtained as

$$\nu|\sigma^2, \beta, \{\lambda_i\} \propto \pi(v)\left[\Gamma\left(\frac{\nu}{2}\right)\left(\frac{2}{\nu}\right)^{(\nu/2)}\right]^{-n}\prod_{i=1}^{n}\lambda_i^{-[(\nu/2)+1]}\exp\left(-\frac{\nu}{2\lambda_i}\right). \quad (15.15)$$

This distribution is not of standard form. One approach to simulation is to discretize this distribution and draw from the discrete approximation (e.g., Albert and Chib 1993). Another approach is to use an M–H step (sometimes called a Metropolis-within-Gibbs step) to sample from this conditional.

(c) Consider the probit model as described in Exercise 14.1. To generalize the assumption of normal errors to the Student t errors, we would write

$$z_i = x_i\beta + \epsilon_i, \quad \epsilon_i \stackrel{ind}{\sim} N(0, \lambda_i), \quad (15.16)$$

where

$$y_i = \begin{cases} 1 & \text{if } z_i > 0, \\ 0 & \text{if } z_i \leq 0, \end{cases} \quad (15.17)$$

and $\{y_i, x_i\}$ constitutes the observed data. As was the case in parts (a) and (b) of this exercise, we specify the priors

$$\lambda_i \stackrel{ind}{\sim} IG\left(\frac{\nu}{2}, \frac{2}{\nu}\right), \quad i = 1, 2, \ldots, n, \quad (15.18)$$

so that, marginalized over the mixing variables λ_i, $\epsilon_i \sim t(0, 1, \nu)$. We also specify the prior

$$\beta \sim N(\mu_\beta, V_\beta).$$

With this in hand, we obtain the *augmented* joint posterior distribution

$$p(\beta, \lambda, z|y) \propto p(y, z|\lambda, \beta)p(\lambda)p(\beta)$$
$$= \left[\prod_{i=1}^{n}\phi(z_i; x_i\beta, \lambda_i)\left[I(y_i = 1)I(z_i > 0) + I(y_i = 0)I(z_i \leq 0)\right]p(\lambda_i)\right]p(\beta),$$

where $z = [z_1\ z_2\ \cdots\ z_n]'$, $y = [y_1\ y_2\ \cdots\ y_n]'$, and $\lambda = [\lambda_1\ \lambda_2\ \cdots\ \lambda_n]'$. Using standard arguments, it follows that the complete posterior conditionals are given by

$$\beta|\{\lambda_i\}, \{z_i\}, y \sim N\Big[\left(X'\Lambda^{-1}X + V_\beta^{-1}\right)^{-1}\left(X'\Lambda^{-1}z + V_\beta^{-1}\mu_\beta\right), \\ \left(X'\Lambda^{-1}X + V_\beta^{-1}\right)^{-1}\Big], \tag{15.19}$$

$$\lambda_i|\beta, \{z_i\}, y \overset{ind}{\sim} IG\left[\frac{\nu+1}{2}, \left(\frac{1}{2}[z_i - x_i\beta]^2 + \frac{\nu}{2}\right)^{-1}\right], \quad i = 1, 2, \ldots, n, \tag{15.20}$$

and

$$z_i \overset{ind}{\sim} \begin{cases} TN_{(0,\infty)}(x_i\beta, \lambda_i) & \text{if } y_1 = 1, \\ TN_{(-\infty,0]}(x_i\beta, \lambda_i) & \text{if } y_1 = 0. \end{cases} \tag{15.21}$$

A Gibbs sampler involves drawing from (15.19) through (15.21).

Exercise 15.3 (Posterior simulation in a regression model with double exponential errors) Consider the regression model

$$y_i = x_i\beta + \epsilon_i, \quad \epsilon_i|\lambda_i, \sigma^2 \overset{ind}{\sim} N(0, \lambda_i\sigma^2).$$

Suppose that the following hierarchical prior for the scale-mixing variables λ_i is employed:

$$\lambda_i \overset{iid}{\sim} Exp(2),$$

an exponential density with mean 2 (see Definition A.2 and Theorem A.2).
(a) Derive $p(\epsilon_i|\sigma^2)$.
(b) Describe a posterior simulator for fitting this model, using priors of the form $\beta \sim N(\mu_\beta, V_\beta)$ and $\sigma^2 \sim IG(a, b)$.

Solution
(a) We note that

$$\begin{aligned} p(\epsilon_i|\sigma^2) &= \int_0^\infty p(\epsilon_i|\lambda_i, \sigma^2)p(\lambda_i)\, d\lambda_i \\ &= \int_0^\infty (2\pi\lambda_i\sigma^2)^{-1/2} \exp\Big[-\epsilon_i^2/(2\lambda_i\sigma^2)\Big](1/2)\exp\Big(-\lambda_i/2\Big)\, d\lambda_i \\ &= (1/2)(2\pi\sigma^2)^{-1/2}\int_0^\infty \lambda_i^{-1/2}\exp\Big[-(1/2)(\lambda_i + [\epsilon_i/\sigma]^2\lambda_i^{-1})\Big]\, d\lambda_i. \end{aligned}$$

Now, make a change of variable and let $\psi_i = \lambda_i^{1/2}$. We can then express this integral as

$$p(\epsilon_i|\sigma^2) = (2\pi\sigma^2)^{-1/2}\int_0^\infty \exp\Big(-[1/2](\psi_i^2 + [\epsilon_i/\sigma]^2\psi_i^{-2})\Big)\, d\psi_i. \tag{15.22}$$

The integral in (15.22) can be evaluated analytically. For example, Andrews and Mallows (1974) observed that

$$\int_0^\infty \exp\left[- (1/2)(a^2u^2 + b^2u^{-2})\right] du = \left(\frac{\pi}{2a^2}\right)^{1/2} \exp\left(-|ab|\right).$$

Applying this to Equation (15.22), we obtain

$$\begin{aligned} p(\epsilon_i|\sigma^2) &= (2\pi\sigma^2)^{-1/2}\left(\frac{\pi}{2}\right)^{1/2} \exp\left(-\frac{|\epsilon_i|}{\sigma}\right) \\ &= \frac{1}{2\sigma}\exp\left(-\frac{|\epsilon_i|}{\sigma}\right), \end{aligned}$$

a *double exponential* or *Laplace* distribution with scale parameter σ (see, e.g., Poirier 1995, p. 110). So, the addition of the exponential mixing variables to the disturbance variance allows for the possibility of double exponential errors in our regression model.

(b) A posterior simulator via the Gibbs sampler will draw from the complete conditionals for β, σ^2, and $\lambda = [\lambda_1\ \lambda_2\ \cdots\ \lambda_n]'$. Apart from the distribution associated with the mixing variables λ_i, this exercise is identical to Exercise 15.2, and as a consequence, the posterior conditionals for β and σ^2 are the same as those in Equations (15.12) and (15.13), respectively.

The kernel of the λ_i posterior conditional is given as

$$\lambda_i|\beta, \sigma^2, y \propto \lambda_i^{-1/2}\exp\left[-\frac{1}{2}\left(\lambda_i + \left(\frac{y_i - x_i\beta}{\sigma}\right)^2 \lambda_i^{-1}\right)\right]. \tag{15.23}$$

This distribution is of the *generalized inverse Gaussian* (GIG) form. Following Shuster (1968), Michael, Schucany, and Haas (1976), and Carlin and Polson (1991), we outline a strategy for obtaining a draw from this GIG density. To this end we first consider a cousin of the GIG density, the *inverse Gaussian density* (see, e.g., Poirier 1995, p. 100). In the discussion that follows, we say that x follows an inverse Gaussian distribution (which we denote as $x \sim invGauss(\psi, \mu)$; see Definition A.14) if

$$p(x|\psi, \mu) \propto x^{-3/2}\exp\left(-\frac{\psi(x-\mu)^2}{2x\mu^2}\right), \quad x > 0. \tag{15.24}$$

Now, let $z = x^{-1}$. It follows by a change of variables that

$$\begin{aligned} p(z|\psi, \mu) &\propto z^{-2}z^{3/2}\exp\left(-\frac{\psi(z^{-1}-\mu)^2}{2z^{-1}\mu^2}\right) \\ &\propto z^{-1/2}\exp\left(-\frac{\psi}{2}\left[z + \mu^{-2}z^{-1}\right]\right). \end{aligned}$$

In terms of the posterior conditional for λ_i, it follows that the reciprocal of an

$$invGauss(1, |\sigma/(y_i - x_i\beta)|)$$

random variable has the density in (15.23).

It remains to discuss how to draw from the inverse Gaussian distribution. Shuster (1968) notes that if x has the inverse Gaussian density in (15.24), then $\psi(x-\mu)^2/x\mu^2 \sim \chi^2(1)$, a chi-square distribution with one degree of freedom. Let ν_0 denote a draw from the $\chi^2(1)$ density. The roots of $\nu_0 = \psi(x-\mu)^2/\mu^2 x$ are given as x_1 and x_2, where

$$x_1 = \mu + \frac{\mu^2\nu_0}{2\psi} - \frac{\mu}{2\psi}\sqrt{4\mu\psi\nu_0 + \mu^2\nu_0^2},$$
$$x_2 = \mu^2/x_1.$$

Michael et al. (1976) used this idea to show that one can obtain a draw from the inv-$Gauss(\psi, \mu)$ density by first drawing $\nu_0 \sim \chi^2(1)$, calculating the roots x_1 and x_2 from the preceding equations, and then setting x equal to the smaller root x_1 with probability $\mu/(\mu + x_1)$ and equal to the larger root x_2 with probability $x_1/(\mu + x_1)$. In terms of sampling from (15.23), we first use this strategy to draw from the inverse Gaussian distribution with $\psi = 1$ and $\mu = |\sigma/(y_i - x_i\beta)|$. This draw is then inverted, producing a draw from (15.23). This process is repeated (independently) for $i = 1, 2, \ldots, n$ in order to sample each scale-mixing variable λ_i from its posterior conditional.

15.2 Other Continuous and Finite-Mixture Models

Exercise 15.4 (The negative binomial as a continuous mixture of the Poisson) We say a (count) random variable $x = 0, 1, 2, \ldots$ has a *negative binomial* distribution, denoted $NB(a, p)$ with $a > 0, 0 < p < 1$, if

$$p(x|a,p) = \frac{\Gamma(a+x)}{x!\,\Gamma(a)} p^a (1-p)^x. \tag{15.25}$$

Now, consider the *Poisson* density for a count variable y_i:

$$p(y_i|\lambda_i) = \frac{\exp(-\lambda_i)\lambda_i^{y_i}}{y_i!}, \quad y_i = 0, 1, 2, \ldots, \quad \lambda_i > 0. \tag{15.26}$$

It is common practice in empirical work to incorporate covariates in the analysis by specifying the mean function λ_i as follows:

$$\ln \lambda_i = x_i\beta.$$

Suppose, instead, that you seek to capture a greater degree of heterogeneity across individuals i and thus include a random error in the specification of $\ln \lambda_i$:

$$\begin{aligned} \ln \lambda_i &= x_i\beta + \epsilon_i \qquad (15.27) \\ &= \ln \mu_i + \ln v_i, \end{aligned}$$

with $\mu_i = \exp(x_i\beta)$ and $v_i = \exp(\epsilon_i)$. For the heterogeneity distribution, you assume

$$v_i \sim G(\theta, \theta^{-1}), \tag{15.28}$$

with G denoting the gamma density (see Definition A.2). Under these assumptions, derive $p(y_i|\mu_i, \theta)$.

Solution

First, note that

$$p(y_i|\mu_i, \theta) = \int_0^\infty p(y_i|\mu_i, v_i, \theta)p(v_i|\theta)\, dv_i.$$

This follows since v_i is assumed independent of μ_i. Substituting the Poisson density in (15.26) [with λ_i defined in (15.27)] and the gamma density for v_i in (15.28), we obtain

$$\begin{aligned}
p(y_i|\mu_i, \theta) &= \int_0^\infty \left(\frac{\exp[-\mu_i v_i](\mu_i v_i)^{y_i}}{(y_i!)}\right) \frac{\theta^\theta v_i^{\theta-1}\exp[-\theta v_i]}{\Gamma(\theta)}\, dv_i \\
&= \frac{\theta^\theta \mu_i^{y_i}}{(y_i!)\Gamma(\theta)} \int_0^\infty \exp[-(\theta+\mu_i)v_i]v_i^{(\theta+y_i-1)}\, dv_i.
\end{aligned}$$

Let us now make a change of variables. Let $\tilde{v}_i = (\theta + \mu_i)v_i$. Then

$$\begin{aligned}
\int_0^\infty \exp[-(\theta+\mu_i)v_i]v_i^{(\theta+y_i-1)}\, dv_i &= \int_0^\infty \Big(\exp[-\tilde{v}_i]\tilde{v}_i^{(\theta+y_i-1)} \\
&\qquad \times (\theta+\mu_i)^{-(\theta+y_i-1)}(\theta+\mu_i)^{-1}\, d\tilde{v}_i\Big) \\
&= (\theta+\mu_i)^{-(\theta+y_i)} \int_0^\infty \exp[-\tilde{v}_i]\tilde{v}_i^{(\theta+y_i-1)}\, d\tilde{v}_i \\
&= (\theta+\mu_i)^{-(\theta+y_i)}\Gamma(\theta+y_i).
\end{aligned}$$

Therefore,

$$p(y_i|\mu_i, \theta) = \frac{\theta^\theta \mu_i^{y_i}\Gamma(\theta+y_i)(\theta+\mu_i)^{-(\theta+y_i)}}{(y_i!)\Gamma(\theta)}. \tag{15.29}$$

Let $p_i = \theta/[\mu_i + \theta]$. This implies

$$\mu_i^{y_i} = [(1-p_i)(\mu_i+\theta)]^{y_i} = [(1-p_i)(\theta/p_i)]^{y_i}.$$

Similarly,

$$(\theta+\mu_i)^{-(\theta+y_i)} = [\theta/p_i]^{-(\theta+y_i)}.$$

Substituting these results back into (15.29) gives

$$p(y_i|\mu_i, \theta) = \frac{\Gamma(\theta + y_i)}{(y_i!)\Gamma(\theta)}(\theta^\theta)[(1 - p_i)(\theta/p_i)]^{y_i}[\theta/p_i]^{-(\theta+y_i)}$$
$$= \frac{\Gamma(\theta + y_i)}{(y_i!)\Gamma(\theta)}p_i^\theta(1 - p_i)^{y_i},$$

which is indeed an $NB(\theta, p_i)$ density.

Exercise 15.5 (Experiments with two-component normal mixtures) Consider the two-component normal mixture model

$$y_i|P, \mu_1, \mu_2, \sigma_1^2, \sigma_2^2 \overset{iid}{\sim} PN(\mu_1, \sigma_1^2) + (1 - P)N(\mu_2, \sigma_2^2), \quad 0 \leq P \leq 1. \tag{15.30}$$

To generate values y from this model, note that one can first draw from a two-point distribution with probabilities P and $1 - P$. Given a draw from this two-point distribution, one can then draw from the associated *component* of the mixture – either $N(\mu_1, \sigma_1^2)$ or $N(\mu_2, \sigma_2^2)$ – to obtain a draw y. Repeating this process a number of times will produce a set of draws from the desired mixture density.

(a) Using this intuition, *augment* the mixture model with a set of *component indicator variables*, say $\{\tau_i\}_{i=1}^n$, where τ_i is either zero or one, and $\tau_i = 1$ implies that the ith observation is drawn from the first component of the mixture. (When $\tau_i = 0$, the implication is that the ith observation is drawn from the second component.) Assign a hierarchical prior to τ_i so that the probability associated with the first component is P, and then place a beta prior on P. Use this augmented structure to describe how a Gibbs sampler can be employed to fit the mixture model.

(b–d) Now, illustrate the flexibility of the two-component mixture model by first generating data from some non-normal distributions. Write a program to implement the Gibbs sampler for this two-component model, given your answer to part (a), and compare your estimated results to the actual densities. To fix ideas, generate the following:

(b) 2000 observations from a lognormal distribution with parameters $\mu = \ln 10$ and $\sigma^2 = .04$. In this case, the lognormal random variable has density function

$$p(x) = \frac{1}{x\sqrt{2\pi\sigma^2}} \exp\left(-\frac{1}{2\sigma^2}[\ln x - \mu]^2\right), \quad x > 0.$$

(c) 5000 observations from a chi-square distribution with ten degrees of freedom.

(d) 3000 observations from a two-component mixture model with $P = .4$, $\mu_1 = 0$, $\mu_2 = 2$, $\sigma_1^2 = 1$, and $\sigma_2^2 = .5$. For this last case, compare the parameter estimates with the actual values used to generate the data.

Solution

(a) Before describing the augmented representation, let θ denote all the model's parameters and θ_{-x} denote all parameters other than x. The model can be written as

$$p(y|\theta, \{\tau_i\}) = \prod_{i=1}^{n} \left[\phi(y_i; \mu_1, \sigma_1^2)\right]^{\tau_i} \left[\phi(y_i; \mu_2, \sigma_2^2)\right]^{1-\tau_i}, \tag{15.31}$$

$$\tau_i \overset{iid}{\sim} B(1, P), \quad i = 1, 2, \ldots, n, \tag{15.32}$$

$$P \sim \beta(\underline{p}_1, \underline{p}_2), \tag{15.33}$$

$$\mu_i \overset{ind}{\sim} N(\underline{\mu}_i, \underline{v}_i), \quad i = 1, 2, \tag{15.34}$$

$$\sigma_i^2 \overset{ind}{\sim} IG(\underline{a}_i, \underline{b}_i), \quad i = 1, 2. \tag{15.35}$$

Here, $B(1, P)$ denotes a binomial density on one trial with "success" probability P, or equivalently, a Bernoulli density with success probability P. Similarly, $\beta(a, b)$ denotes the beta density with parameters a and b; properties of these densities and their respective parameterizations are described in Definitions A.7 and A.10.

Note that when marginalizing the conditional likelihood $p(y|\theta, \{\tau_i\})$ over τ_i, we are left with the two-component mixture model described at the outset of this section. To see this, note that the assumed conditional independence across observations, together with the fact that τ_i is binary, implies

$$\begin{aligned} p(y|\theta) &= \prod_{i=1}^{n} \sum_{j=0}^{1} p(y_i|\theta, \tau_i = j) \Pr(\tau_i = j|\theta) \\ &= \prod_{i=1}^{n} \left[P\phi(y_i; \mu_1, \sigma_1^2) + (1 - P)\phi(y_i; \mu_2, \sigma_2^2)\right]. \end{aligned}$$

Thus, the component indicators serve the practical purpose of facilitating computation, but their presence does not affect the joint posterior distribution of our parameters of interest, θ. Our complete posterior distribution consists of $p(\theta, \{\tau_i\}|y) = p(\mu_1, \mu_2, \sigma_1^2, \sigma_2^2, P, \{\tau_i\}|y)$.

The following complete posterior conditionals are obtained:

$$\mu_1|\theta_{-\mu_1}, \tau, y \sim N(D\mu_1 d\mu_1, D\mu_1), \tag{15.36}$$

where

$$D\mu_1 = \left(n_1/\sigma_1^2 + \underline{v}_1^{-1}\right)^{-1}, \quad d\mu_1 = \sum_i \tau_i y_i + \underline{v}_1^{-1}\underline{\mu}_1,$$

$n_1 \equiv \sum_i \tau_i$ denotes the number of observations "in" the first component of the mixture, and n_2 will be defined as $n_2 \equiv \sum_i (1 - \tau_i) = n - n_1$. The complete conditional for μ_2 follows similarly. The conditional posterior distribution for the variance parameter σ_2^2 is

$$\sigma_2^2|\theta_{-\sigma_2^2}, \{\tau\}, y \sim IG\left(\frac{n_2}{2} + \underline{a}_2, \left[\underline{b}_2^{-1} + .5\sum_{i=1}^{n}(1 - \tau_i)(y_i - \mu_2)^2\right]^{-1}\right), \tag{15.37}$$

and the complete conditional for σ_1^2 follows similarly. Finally, for the component indicator variables $\{\tau_i\}$ and component probability P,

$$\tau_i|\theta, \tau_{-i}, y \overset{ind}{\sim} B\left[1, \frac{P\phi(y_i;\mu_1,\sigma_1^2)}{P\phi(y_i;\mu_1,\sigma_1^2)+(1-P)\phi(y_i;\mu_2,\sigma_2^2)}\right], \tag{15.38}$$

$$P|\theta_{-P}, \{\tau_i\}, y \sim \beta(n_1 + \underline{p}_1, n_2 + \underline{p}_2). \tag{15.39}$$

With these conditionals in hand, we can implement the Gibbs sampler by drawing from (15.36) through (15.39), noting, of course, that similar conditionals need to be obtained for μ_2 and σ_1^2.

(b–d) The preceding algorithm is coded in MATLAB (and made available on the website associated with this book), and the Gibbs sampler is run in cases where the data are generated from lognormal, chi-square, and mixture densities. Hyperparameters for all cases were chosen so that the priors were non-informative relative to the data. The results of these three experiments are presented in Figure 15.1.

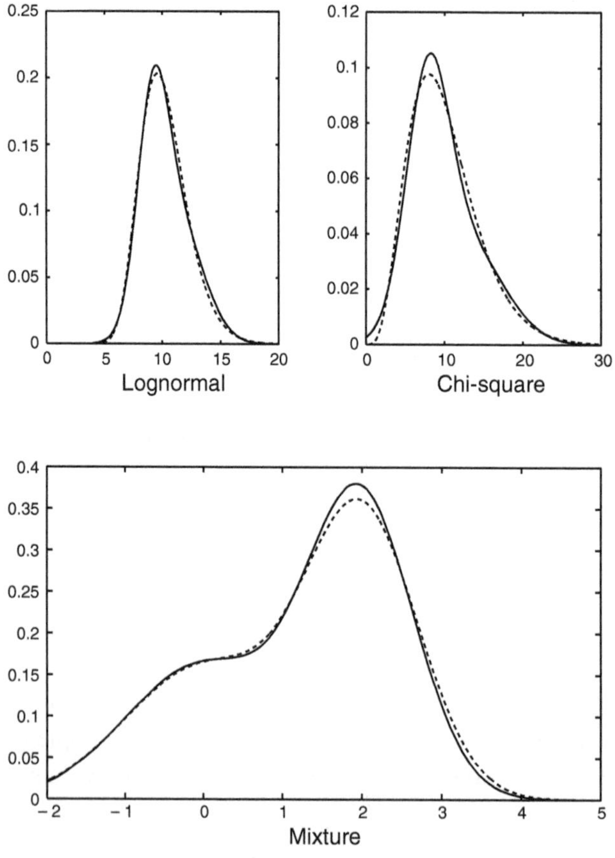

Figure 15.1. Actual densities and two-component normal mixture estimates.

Table 15.1: Results of generated-data experiment.

	P	μ_1	σ_1^2	μ_2	σ_2^2
Actual	.400	.000	1.00	2.00	.500
Post. mean	.400	−.007	.961	1.98	.445

As shown in the figure, the mixture estimates tend to do a good job at recovering the shape of the "true" density for all the examples. In the first two cases, we see that the mixtures can accommodate the right skew associated with the lognormal and chi-square distributions. In the last example – an example of correct specification – the mixture estimate performs quite well. Table 15.1 shows the actual parameter values used, as well as the posterior means obtained from our simulations.

Exercise 15.6 (Using finite normal mixtures in a regression model) Consider the general setup for a regression model using G normal mixture components:

$$y_i|x_i, \{\beta_g, \sigma_g^2, \pi_g\}_{g=1}^G \overset{ind}{\sim} \sum_{g=1}^G \pi_g N(x_i\beta_g, \sigma_g^2), \quad \sum_{g=1}^G \pi_g = 1. \tag{15.40}$$

In this model we allow each mixture component to possess its own variance parameter, σ_g, and set of regression parameters, β_g. This level of generality is not required – if desired, we could restrict some of these parameters to be constant across the mixture components.
(a) Consider, for the purposes of computation, augmenting this model with a set of *component label vectors*, $\{z_i\}_{i=1}^n$, where

$$z_i = [z_{1i} \; z_{2i} \; \cdots \; z_{Gi}], \tag{15.41}$$

and $z_{gi} = 1$ implies that the ith individual is "drawn from" the gth component of the mixture.

To complete the augmentation step, add a multinomial prior (see Definition A.9) for the component label vector z_i that depends on a vector of component probabilities π, and then specify a Dirichlet prior (see Definition A.10) for π. Given this setup, write down the augmented likelihood and the above priors.
(b) Add the following prior specifications to complete the model:

$$\beta_g \overset{ind}{\sim} N(\beta_{0g}, V_{\beta_g}), \quad g = 1, 2, \ldots, G,$$
$$\sigma_g^2 \overset{ind}{\sim} IG(a_g, b_g), \quad g = 1, 2, \ldots, G,$$

and derive the complete posterior conditionals for use with the Gibbs sampler.

Solution
(a) Let θ denote all parameters and component indicator variables in the model, and let θ_{-x} denote all quantities other than x. If we condition on the values of the component indicator variables, the conditional likelihood function can be expressed as

$$L(\theta) = \prod_{i=1}^{n} \left[\phi(y_i; x_i\beta_1, \sigma_1^2)\right]^{z_{1i}} \left[\phi(y_i; x_i\beta_2, \sigma_2^2)\right]^{z_{2i}} \cdots \left[\phi(y_i; x_i\beta_G, \sigma_G^2)\right]^{z_{Gi}}. \quad (15.42)$$

As stated, we add the following priors for the component indicators and component probabilities:

$$z_i|\pi \overset{iid}{\sim} M(1, \pi) \Rightarrow p(z_i|\pi) = \prod_{g=1}^{G} \pi_g^{z_{gi}}, \quad \pi = [\pi_1 \; \pi_2 \; \cdots \; \pi_G]', \quad (15.43)$$

$$\pi \sim D(\alpha_1, \alpha_2, \cdots \alpha_G) \Rightarrow p(\pi) \propto \pi_1^{\alpha_1 - 1}\pi_2^{\alpha_2 - 1} \cdots \pi_G^{\alpha_G - 1}. \quad (15.44)$$

The multinomial prior (M) is a multivariate generalization of the binomial, and the Dirichlet prior (D) is a multivariate generalization of the beta. Note that, analogous to the derivation of the previous exercise, if we take the likelihood function conditional on the component indicators in (15.42) and integrate out the component indicators using (15.43), we obtain an unconditional likelihood that is equivalent to the one implied by (15.40).

(b) The *augmented posterior density* $p(\{\beta_g, \sigma_g^2, \pi_g\}_{g=1}^G, \{z_i\}_{i=1}^n|y)$ is proportional to the product of the augmented likelihood, the multinomial and beta priors, and the given priors for the regression and variance parameters.

The following complete posterior conditionals can be obtained:

$$\beta_g|\theta_{-\beta_g}, y \overset{ind}{\sim} N(D_{\beta_g} d_{\beta_g}, D_{\beta_g}), \quad g = 1, 2, \ldots, G, \quad (15.45)$$

where, again, θ_{-x} denotes all parameters in our posterior other than x, and

$$D_{\beta_g} = \left[\left(\sum_i z_{gi} x_i x_i'\right) / \sigma_g^2 + V_{\beta_g}^{-1}\right]^{-1}, \; d_{\beta_g} = \left(\sum_i z_{gi} x_i' y_i\right) / \sigma_g^2 + V_{\beta_g}^{-1} \beta_{0g},$$

$$\sigma_g^2|\theta_{-\sigma_g^2}, y \overset{ind}{\sim} IG\left(\frac{n_g}{2} + a_g, \left[b_g^{-1} + (1/2)\sum_i z_{gi}(y_i - x_i\beta_g)^2\right]^{-1}\right), \quad g = 1, 2, \ldots, G, \quad (15.46)$$

where $n_g \equiv \sum_{i=1}^N z_{gi}$ denotes the number of observations in the gth component of the mixture.

$$z_i|\theta_{-z_i}, y \overset{ind}{\sim} M\left(1, \left[\frac{\pi_1\phi(y_i; x_i\beta_1, \sigma_1^2)}{\sum_{g=1}^G \pi_g\phi(y_i; x_i\beta_g, \sigma_g^2)} \; \frac{\pi_2\phi(y_i; x_i\beta_2, \sigma_2^2)}{\sum_{g=1}^G \pi_g\phi(y_i; x_i\beta_g, \sigma_g^2)} \right.\right.$$
$$\left.\left. \cdots \frac{\pi_G\phi(y_i; x_i\beta_G, \sigma_G^2)}{\sum_{g=1}^G \pi_g\phi(y_i; x_i\beta_g, \sigma_g^2)}\right]'\right), \quad (15.47)$$

and

$$\pi \mid \theta_{-\pi}, y \sim D(n_1 + \alpha_1, n_2 + \alpha_2, \ldots, n_G + \alpha_G). \quad (15.48)$$

Algorithms for drawing from the multinomial and Dirichlet distributions are provided on the website associated with this book, and also, for example, in Gelman, Carlin, Stern, and Rubin (1995, pp. 481–483). The Gibbs sampler is implemented by drawing from (15.45) through (15.48).

Exercise 15.7 (A normal mixture with covariates affecting the mixture assignment: Response delays) This question uses data from an experiment in psychology that measures the (log) reaction times of 17 different subjects. Each of the 17 subjects had his or her reaction times measured at 30 different trials, and we focus our attention on modeling the average of those 30 response times. The data and application presented here are simplified versions of those discussed by Gelman et al. (1995, Section 16.4). The data are provided in Table 15.2 (and are available on the website associated with this book).

What is interesting to note is that the last six subjects presented in the final three rows of Table 15.2 were diagnosed schizophrenics, whereas the first 11 were not schizophrenics. Psychological theory suggests that, for a variety of reasons, schizophrenic individuals are likely to suffer from response delays relative to those who are not schizophrenic. For this reason, we adopt a model that supposes that the data in the table arise from two separate component populations. We also recognize that the observed schizophrenia indicator should play a strong role in allocating individuals to the delayed or non-delayed component of the mixture.

In Figure 15.2 we take a quick pass at the data and smooth these 17 observations non-parametrically. We do indeed see that the data appear bimodal, and given the entries from Table 15.2, schizophrenics appear to be far more likely to be drawn from the delayed component of the mixture.

Write down a normal mixture model for analyzing these data. In this model, determine the additional delay received by the high response-time component, and introduce the schizophrenia indicator variable to help allocate individuals to the mixture components.

Solution

Let T_i denote the average response time of individual i, $T = [T_1 \; T_2 \; \cdots \; T_{17}]'$ denote the vector of all average response times, and S_i, $i = 1, 2, \ldots, 17$, be the observed schizophrenia indicator, taking the value of 1 if individual i is schizophrenic.

Table 15.2: Average natural log of response times for 17 subjects.

5.73	5.89	5.71
5.71	5.57	5.80
5.87	5.58	5.54
5.78	5.72	5.71
6.03	6.27	6.32
6.34	6.14	

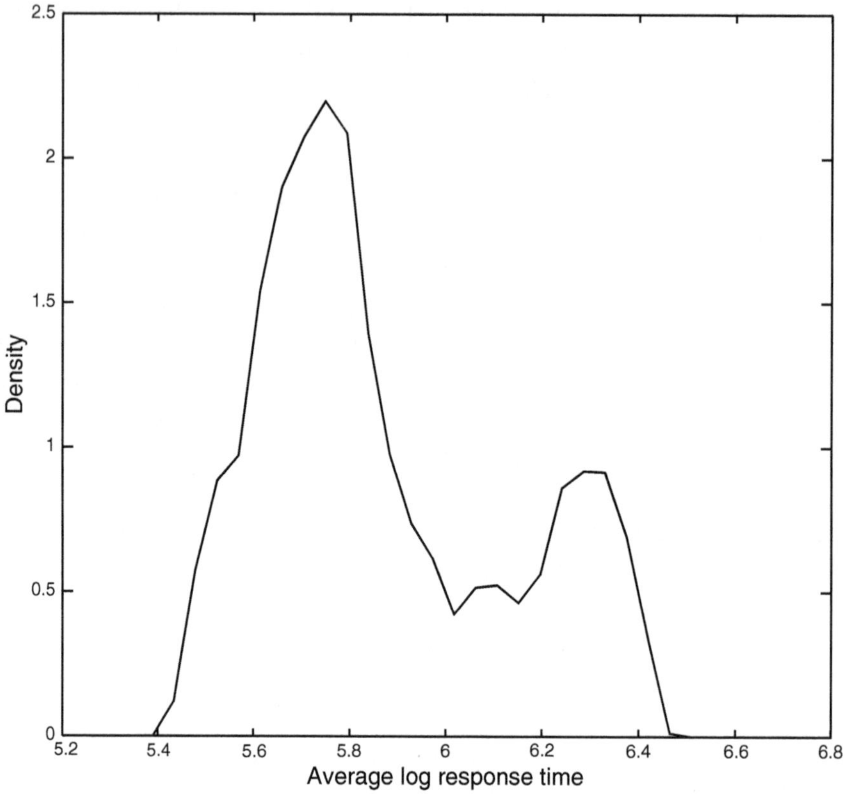

Figure 15.2. Non-parametric estimate of response-time density.

We assume independence across observations and specify our response-time density as follows:

$$p(T_i|S_i, \theta) = [1-\Phi(\beta_0+\beta_1 S_i)]\phi(T_i; \mu_1, \sigma_1^2)+\Phi(\beta_0+\beta_1 S_i)\phi(T_i; \mu_1+\alpha, \sigma_2^2). \quad (15.49)$$

We wish to restrict $\alpha > 0$ so that the second component of the mixture corresponds to our delayed component. The probability of being in the first component of the mixture is $1 - \Phi(\beta_0 + \beta_1 S_i)$. We expect that schizophrenics are more likely to be in the delayed component, and thus expect $\beta_1 > 0$.

As with the other mixture models, it will prove to be computationally advantageous to augment our model with component indicator variables. Thus, we consider an equivalent model:

$$p(T_i|S_i, \theta, z_i^*) = \phi(T_i; \mu_1, \sigma_1^2)^{I(z_i^* \leq 0)}\phi(T_i; \mu_1 + \alpha, \sigma_2^2)^{I(z_i^* > 0)}, \quad (15.50)$$

$$z_i^* = \beta_0 + \beta_1 S_i + \epsilon_i, \quad \epsilon_i \overset{iid}{\sim} N(0, 1). \quad (15.51)$$

Note, again, that when marginalized over the component indicators, we are back to our original specification of the data density. We add the following priors to our model:

$$\begin{aligned}\mu_1 &\sim N(\underline{\mu}, V_\mu),\\ \alpha &\sim TN_{(0,\infty)}(\mu_\alpha, V_\alpha),\\ \sigma_i^2 &\sim IG(a_i, b_i), \quad i = 1, 2,\\ [\beta_0\ \beta_1]' &\sim N(\mu_\beta, V_\beta),\end{aligned}$$

where a truncated normal prior for α has been employed for component identification purposes so that the second component will represent the delayed component. Thus, our joint posterior $p(\mu_1, \alpha, \sigma_1^2, \sigma_2^2, \beta_0, \beta_1, \{z_i^*\}|y)$ is proportional to

$$\left(\prod_{i=1}^{N}\left[\phi(T_i; \mu_1, \sigma_1^2)^{I(z_i^* \leq 0)}\phi(T_i; \mu_1+\alpha, \sigma_2^2)^{I(z_i^*>0)}\right]\phi(z_i^*; \beta_0+\beta_1 S_i, 1)\right)$$
$$\times\, p(\beta_0, \beta_1)p(\mu_1)p(\alpha)p(\sigma_1^2)p(\sigma_2^2),$$

where the priors for the parameters listed in the second row have been specified explicitly above.

Fitting the model
The following complete posterior conditionals are obtained:

$$\mu_1|\theta_{-\mu_1}, y \sim N(D_{\mu_1}d_{\mu_1}, D_{\mu_1}), \tag{15.52}$$

where

$$D_{\mu_1} = (\iota'\Sigma^{-1}\iota + V_\mu^{-1})^{-1}, \quad d_{\mu_1} = \iota'\Sigma^{-1}(T - z\alpha) + V_\mu^{-1}\underline{\mu},$$

ι is a 17×1 vector of ones, $z_i \equiv I(z_i^* > 0)$, $z = [z_1 z_2 \cdots z_n]$, $\Sigma \equiv \text{Diag}\{(1-z_i)\sigma_1^2 + z_i\sigma_2^2\}$,

$$\alpha|\theta_{-\alpha}, y \sim TN_{(0,\infty)}(D_\alpha d_\alpha, D_\alpha), \tag{15.53}$$

with

$$D_\alpha = (n_2/\sigma_2^2 + V_\alpha^{-1})^{-1}, \quad d_\alpha = \sum_{i=1}^{17} z_i(T_i - \mu_1)/\sigma_2^2 + V_\alpha^{-1}\mu_\alpha,$$

and $n_2 \equiv \sum_i z_i$ [and, as before, we will also define $n_1 = 17 - n_2 = \sum_i(1-z_i)$],

$$\beta_0, \beta_1|\theta_{-\beta_0,\beta_1}, y \sim N(D_\beta d_\beta, D_\beta), \tag{15.54}$$

where

$$D_\beta = (X'X + V_\beta^{-1})^{-1}, \quad d_\beta = X'z^* + V_\beta^{-1}\mu_\beta,$$

where $z^* = [z_1^*\ z_2^*\ \cdots\ z_{17}^*]'$, $S = [S_1\ S_2\ \cdots S_{17}]'$, and $X = [\iota\ S]$,

$$\sigma_1^2|\theta_{-\sigma_1^2}, y \sim IG\left(\frac{n_1}{2} + a_1, \left[b_1^{-1} + .5\sum_{i=1}^{17}(1-z_i)(T_i - \mu_1)^2\right]^{-1}\right), \tag{15.55}$$

and

$$\sigma_2^2|\theta_{-\sigma_2^2}, y \sim IG\left(\frac{n_2}{2} + a_2, \left[b_2^{-1} + .5\sum_{i=1}^{17} z_i(T_i - \mu_1 - \alpha)^2\right]^{-1}\right). \quad (15.56)$$

For the complete posterior conditional for z^*, note that each z_i^* can be drawn independently and that

$$p(z_i^*|\theta_{-z_i^*}, y) \propto \left[\phi(T_i; \mu_1, \sigma_1^2)^{I(z_i^* \leq 0)} \phi(T_i; \mu_1 + \alpha, \sigma_2^2)^{I(z_i^* > 0)}\right] \phi(z_i^*; \beta_0 + \beta_1 S_i, 1). \quad (15.57)$$

Though seemingly non-standard, one can obtain draws from this distribution by first drawing a binary U from a two-point distribution $U \in \{0, 1\}$, where

$$\Pr(U = 1) = \frac{[1 - \Phi(\beta_0 + \beta_1 S_i)]\phi(T_i; \mu_1, \sigma_1^2)}{[1 - \Phi(\beta_0 + \beta_1 S_i)]\phi(T_i; \mu_1, \sigma_1^2) + \Phi(\beta_0 + \beta_1 S_i)\phi(T_i; \mu_1 + \alpha, \sigma_2^2)}.$$

We then draw z_i^* from its posterior conditional as follows:

$$z_i^*|U, \theta_{-z_i^*}, y \begin{cases} TN_{(-\infty,0]}(\beta_0 + \beta_1 S_i, 1) & \text{if } U = 1, \\ TN_{(0,\infty)}(\beta_0 + \beta_1 S_i, 1) & \text{if } U = 0. \end{cases}$$

The conditionals in (15.52) through (15.57) define the Gibbs sampler.

Estimation results

We ran the Gibbs sampler for 50 000 iterations, discarding the first 1000 simulations as the burn-in period. To obtain the results in Tables 15.3 and 15.4 we employed relatively informative priors and selected the following hyperparameter values: $\underline{\mu} = 5.5$, $\underline{v}_\mu = .2^2$, $\underline{\alpha} = .4$, $\underline{v}_\alpha = .2^2$, $a_1 = a_2 = 2$, $b_1 = b_2 = (.01)^{-1}$, $\underline{\beta} = [0\ 0]'$, and $\underline{V}_\beta = 4I_2$.

From the results in Table 15.3, we see that the first component is centered around a log response time of 5.7, and the second component is centered at about 6.2, given our estimated value of α. These results are consistent with the descriptive non-parametric density estimate in Figure 15.2.

The last four entries of the table describe probabilities of assignment to the delayed or non-delayed component of the model according to the value of the schizophrenia indicator. For example, the probability of belonging to the non-delayed component of the mixture given that a person is not a schizophrenic is $1 - \Phi(\beta_0)$, and the posterior mean of this

Table 15.3: Posterior means of quantities of interest.

				Prob. non-delay		Prob. delay	
μ_1	σ_1	α	σ_2	$S = 1$	$S = 0$	$S = 1$	$S = 0$
5.72	.11	.50	.12	.26	.94	.74	.06

Table 15.4: Probabilities of belonging to delayed component, observed average natural log of response time (T_i), and schizophrenia indicator (S_i) for 17 subjects.

$\Pr(z_i = 1\|y)$	T_i	S_i
.00	5.73	0
.02	5.90	0
.00	5.71	0
.00	5.71	0
.00	5.57	0
.00	5.80	0
.01	5.87	0
.00	5.58	0
.00	5.54	0
.00	5.78	0
.00	5.72	0
.03	5.71	1
.87	6.03	1
.99	6.27	1
.99	6.32	1
.99	6.34	1
.98	6.14	1

quantity was found to be .94. To summarize these results, it is very unlikely that non-schizophrenics will suffer any delays, and schizophrenics are most likely to belong to the delayed component. However, there is a modest probability that schizophrenics will not suffer any additional delays, as the posterior mean of the probability that schizophrenics will come from the non-delayed component of the mixture is .26.

Additionally, we can look at the component assignment mechanism at the individual level. At each iteration in our sampler we obtain a value of the component indicator variable z_i for every individual. We can thus compute individual-level probabilities of belonging to the delayed component of the mixture. These results are presented in Table 15.4.

With the exception of one of the schizophrenic subjects, the mapping of individuals to components can be completely divided along values of the schizophrenia indicator. That is, all of the 11 non-schizophrenic individuals are allocated to the non-delayed component with very high probability, whereas five of the six schizophrenic individuals are allocated to the delayed component with very high probability. The schizophrenic individual with an average response time of 5.71 does not apparently suffer any response delays and is assigned to the non-delayed component with high probability.

Exercise 15.8 (Are my students randomly guessing?) Those of us who have had the opportunity to teach a large introductory class in statistics or econometrics have probably held the suspicion that a subset of the class has simply randomly guessed at the answers

Table 15.5: Hypothetical test scores for 200 students.

22	20	21	20	23	21	20	17	21	20
21	19	21	21	20	20	20	17	19	19
19	21	19	22	24	19	6	17	21	24
20	20	21	22	19	20	19	20	19	18
23	21	19	19	21	19	21	17	19	20
23	21	21	8	19	21	21	20	18	16
18	21	17	22	21	22	19	19	19	22
23	23	18	7	21	21	19	18	19	5
21	20	17	20	20	19	20	19	24	18
20	5	5	19	18	19	20	20	22	22
21	19	22	23	21	16	21	20	21	20
23	4	18	16	23	20	21	22	22	21
22	17	21	6	23	20	18	19	20	23
22	3	21	23	19	21	21	19	23	18
19	21	21	19	17	20	21	24	14	17
20	17	19	21	20	22	21	18	22	4
19	16	18	17	24	21	22	3	16	21
19	22	22	20	20	20	20	16	18	19
20	21	22	18	21	19	16	22	18	18
23	18	20	24	19	16	18	5	23	23

on a multiple-choice exam. We create a similar scenario in this exercise using artificial data and illustrate how mixture analysis can be used in non-normal models. Specifically, let us suppose that you administer a multiple choice exam with $Q = 25$ questions with five possible answers to each question. All questions are assumed to have an equal level of difficulty. You obtain the (hypothetical) data set giving the test scores of 200 students, as shown in Table 15.5. You assume that scores are independent across individuals.
(a) Consistent with your prior suspicions about the nature of the students in the class, write down a two-component mixture model appropriate for analyzing these test score data.
(b) Discuss how the Gibbs sampler can be employed to fit this model and then fit it using the data given in Table 15.5. Interpret your results.
(c) Now, suppose that three students miss the exam, and thus they retake the same exam at a later date. After grading the three exams, you find that the scores are 8, 12, and 22. Based on the estimation results you obtained for the 200 students in the class, what would be your (predictive) probability that each of these three students were randomizing? Specifically, what are the probabilities that they belong to the low-scoring component of the mixture?

Solution

(a) Let y_i denote the number of correct answers on test i, $i = 1, 2, \ldots, 200$, and suppose the test scores are drawn from two distinct subpopulations, which we might think of conceptually as randomizers and non-randomizers. Let p_1 denote the probability of success (correctly answering each question) associated with the first component, p_2 denote the probability of success associated with the second component, and π denote the probability that people are drawn from the first component. To fix ideas, we will regard the first component as the component of "randomizers." Within each component, the distribution of test scores is assumed to follow a binomial distribution, where the number of questions (trials) is denoted by Q (here $Q = 25$), the number of successes on test i is denoted as y_i, and the probability of success in each component is p_g, $g = 1, 2$.

With this notation in hand our model can be written as

$$p(y|p_1, p_2, \{\tau_i\}) = \prod_{i=1}^{n} \left[\binom{Q}{y_i} p_1^{y_i}(1-p_1)^{Q-y_i} \right]^{\tau_i} \left[\binom{Q}{y_i} p_2^{y_i}(1-p_2)^{Q-y_i} \right]^{1-\tau_i}, \tag{15.58}$$

$$\begin{aligned} \tau_i|\pi &\overset{ind}{\sim} B(1, \pi), \\ \pi &\sim \beta(a_1, b_1), \\ p_1 &\sim \beta(a_2, b_2), \\ p_2 &\sim \beta(a_3, b_3), \end{aligned}$$

where B and β denote the binomial and beta densities, respectively (see Definitions A.7 and A.10).

(b) The complete posterior conditionals for this model are as follows:

$$p_1|\theta_{-p_1}, y \sim \beta \left[\sum_i \tau_i y_i + a_2, \sum_i \tau_i(Q - y_i) + b_2 \right], \tag{15.59}$$

$$p_2|\theta_{-p_2}, y \sim \beta \left[\sum_i (1-\tau_i) y_i + a_3, \sum_i (1-\tau_i)(Q - y_i) + b_3 \right], \tag{15.60}$$

$$\pi|\theta_{-\pi}, y \sim \beta \left[\sum_i \tau_i + a_1, \sum_i (1-\tau_i) + b_1 \right], \tag{15.61}$$

$$\tau_i|\theta_{-\tau_i}, y \overset{ind}{\sim} B \left[1, \frac{\pi \left(p_1^{y_i}(1-p_1)^{Q-y_i}\right)}{\pi \left(p_1^{y_i}(1-p_1)^{Q-y_i}\right) + (1-\pi)\left(p_2^{y_i}(1-p_2)^{Q-y_i}\right)} \right]. \tag{15.62}$$

Estimation

Using the 200 observations presented in Table 15.5, we implement the Gibbs sampler, iteratively drawing from (15.59) through (15.62). We run the sampler for 1000 iterations, discarding the first 200 as the burn-in. For the prior hyperparameters, we set $a_i = b_i = 2$, $i = 1, 2, 3$.

In Table 15.6 we present posterior means of parameters in this model. In addition, we also present the actual values of the parameters that were used to generate the 200 observations in Table 15.5. Specifically, we generated these data so that the randomized component had a probability of success equal to $(1/5) = .2$, the non-randomizing

Table 15.6: Posterior means and actual parameter values.

	p_1	p_2	π
Posterior mean	.21	.80	.07
Actual values	.20	.80	.05

component had a probability of success equal to .8, and 5% of the class pursued the randomization strategy. As you can see from Table 15.6, the first component is associated with the group of randomizers, where the estimated probability of success, .21, is quite close to the actual value used. In the second component, the average probability of success for each question is significantly higher, and the estimated value of .80 equals the actual value to the first two decimal places. Based on our estimation results, approximately 7% of the class pursues the strategy of randomization, and the data were actually generated so that 5% of the sample were randomly guessing. Thus, we see that our estimates tend to approximate the actual values used to generate the data very well. Also note that, as a by-product of the algorithm, individual-level component indicators are produced, and thus it is possible to compute probabilities that each individual is randomizing.

To illustrate the performance of our mixture model in a slightly different way, Figure 15.3 presents the estimated distribution of test scores from our mixture model as well as the probability of each score based on our sample of $n = 200$ outcomes. As seen from the figure, the mixture model fits these data quite well.

(c) To address this question, let τ_f denote the as-yet unobserved component indicator for each of the three "future" students and let y_f denote the future test score outcome. We seek to obtain

$$\Pr(\tau_f = 1|y_f, y), \tag{15.63}$$

the predicted probability of being in the randomizing (or low-scoring) component given the future test score y_f and past data. Note that

$$\Pr(\tau_f = 1|y_f, y) = \int_\Theta \Pr(\tau_f = 1|y_f, \theta, y)p(\theta|y_f, y)d\theta, \tag{15.64}$$

where θ denotes all the parameters in the model. Taking each of these terms in the integral of (15.64) separately, we note that

$$\begin{aligned}\Pr(\tau_f = 1|y_f, \theta, y) &= \frac{p(y_f|\tau_f = 1, \theta, y)\Pr(\tau_f = 1, \theta, y)}{p(y_f, \theta, y)} \\ &= \frac{p(y_f|\tau_f = 1, \theta, y)\Pr(\tau_f = 1|\theta, y)}{p(y_f|\theta, y)}.\end{aligned} \tag{15.65}$$

The second term in the integral of (15.64) is

$$p(\theta|y_f, y) = \frac{p(y_f|\theta, y)p(\theta|y)p(y)}{p(y_f, y)} = \frac{p(y_f|\theta, y)p(\theta|y)}{p(y_f|y)}. \tag{15.66}$$

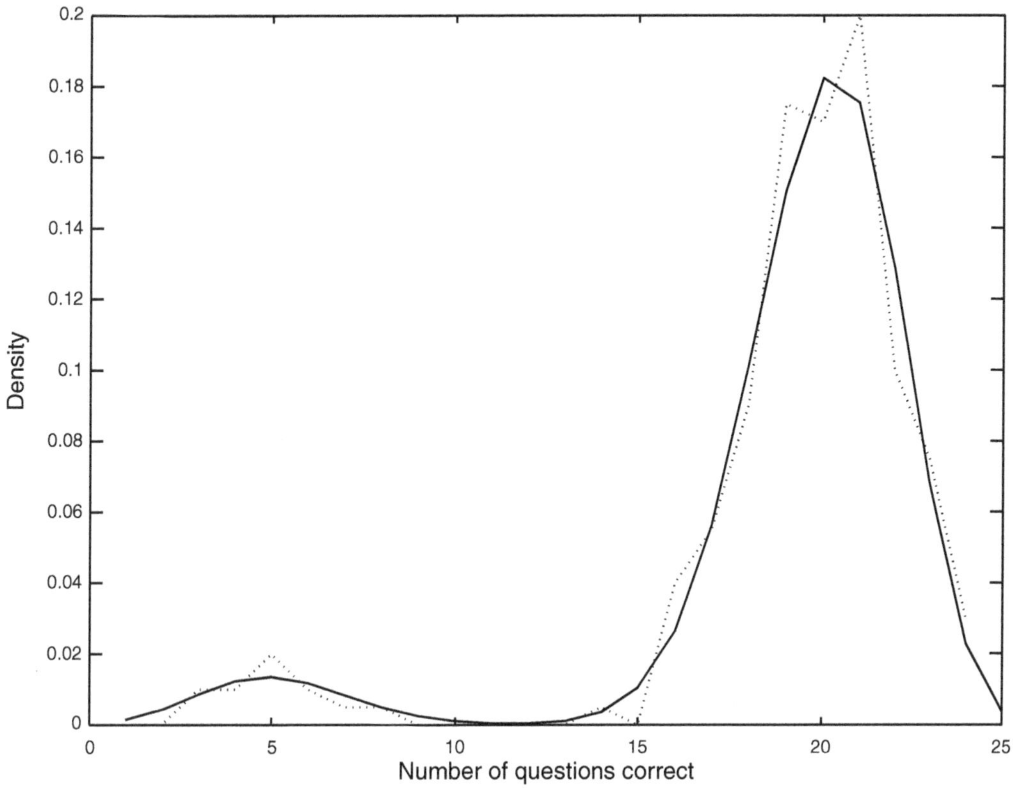

Figure 15.3. Two-component mixture of binomials estimate (solid) and observed test score probabilities (dashed).

In terms of the components of (15.66), $p(y_f|\theta, y)$ is seen as a mixture of binomials, upon marginalizing over τ_f:

$$p(y_f|\theta, y) = \pi \begin{pmatrix} Q \\ y_f \end{pmatrix} p_1^{y_f}(1-p_1)^{Q-y_f} + (1-\pi) \begin{pmatrix} Q \\ y_f \end{pmatrix} p_2^{y_f}(1-p_2)^{Q-y_f}$$

and

$$\begin{aligned} p(y_f|y) &= \int_{\Theta} p(y_f|\theta, y)p(\theta|y)d\theta \\ &\approx \frac{1}{R}\Bigg[\sum_{i=1}^{R} \pi(i) \begin{pmatrix} Q \\ y_f \end{pmatrix} p_1(i)^{y_f}[1-p_1(i)]^{Q-y_f} \\ &\quad + [1-\pi(i)] \begin{pmatrix} Q \\ y_f \end{pmatrix} p_2(i)^{y_f}[1-p_2(i)]^{Q-y_f}\Bigg], \end{aligned} \tag{15.67}$$

with $x(i)$ denoting the ith post-convergence draw for the parameter x and R denoting the number of post-convergence Gibbs sampler simulations.

Substituting (15.65) and (15.66) into (15.64), canceling terms, and noting that $\Pr(\tau_f = 1|\theta, y) = \pi$, we obtain

$$\Pr(\tau_f = 1|y_f, y) = \frac{1}{p(y_f|y)} \int_\Theta \pi p(y_f|\tau_f = 1, \theta, y) p(\theta|y) d\theta. \tag{15.68}$$

Substituting for $p(y_f|y)$ in (15.67) and noting that $y_f|\tau_f = 1, \theta, y$ is just the density of the first mixture component, we obtain

$$\Pr(\tau_f = 1|y_f, y)$$
$$\approx \frac{\frac{1}{R}\sum_{i=1}^R \pi(i) p_1(i)^{y_f}[1 - p_1(i)]^{Q-y_f}}{\frac{1}{R}\sum_{i=1}^R \left[\pi(i)p_1(i)^{y_f}[1-p_1(i)]^{Q-y_f} + [1-\pi(i)]p_2(i)^{y_f}[1-p_2(i)]^{Q-y_f}\right]}.$$

Using all our post-convergence draws, we apply this estimator and evaluate the probabilities of coming from the first component given that the test scores were 8, 12, or 22. Our point predictions for each of these quantities are 1.00, .37 and .00 for the test scores 8, 12, and 22, respectively. Thus, we see that a person with a score of 8 is very likely to arise from the group of randomizers (or, more specifically, the low-scoring component), whereas a person scoring 22 is almost certainly a non-randomizer. The person scoring 12 is somewhat ambiguous: Either he or she is a fortunate guesser or an unfortunate non-randomizer.

Exercise 15.9 (A skewed regression model) Consider the following regression model:

$$y_i = x_i\beta + \delta z_i + \epsilon_i, \quad \epsilon_i \overset{iid}{\sim} N(0, \sigma^2), \quad z_i \overset{iid}{\sim} TN_{(0,\infty)}(0, 1), \quad i = 1, 2, \dots, n, \tag{15.69}$$

with $TN_{(a,b)}(\mu, \sigma^2)$ denoting a normal distribution with mean μ and variance σ^2 truncated to the interval (a, b). Thus, z has a *half-normal* distribution. We observe (x_i, y_i), yet z_i is unobserved.

(a) For y, a scalar generated from the model in (15.69), derive the mixture density $p(y|x, \beta, \delta, \sigma^2)$. Comment on the role of δ in this conditional distribution.

(b) Let $\beta^* = [\beta' \ \delta]'$. Employing priors of the form $\sigma^2 \sim IG(a, b)$ and $\beta^* \sim N(0, V_\beta)$, derive a posterior simulator for fitting this regression model.

(c) Using the wage data available on the website associated with this book, fit the regression model in (15.69) and comment on your results. In this application, $x_i = 1 \ \forall i$; that is, the model only contains an intercept.

Solution

(a) For ease of exposition, let us drop the conditioning on β, σ^2, and δ in our notation and leave this implicit. That is, simply write $p(y|x, \beta, \delta, \sigma^2)$ as $p(y|x)$. We note that

$$
\begin{aligned}
p(y|x) &= \int_0^\infty p(y|x,z)p(z)\,dz \\
&= \int_0^\infty \frac{1}{\sqrt{2\pi\sigma^2}} \exp\left(-\frac{1}{2\sigma^2}(y - x\beta - \delta z)^2\right) \frac{2}{\sqrt{2\pi}} \exp\left(-\frac{1}{2}z^2\right) dz \\
&= \frac{1}{\pi\sqrt{\sigma^2}} \exp\left(-\frac{(y-x\beta)^2}{2(\sigma^2+\delta^2)}\right) \int_0^\infty \exp\left(-\frac{\sigma^2+\delta^2}{2\sigma^2}\left[z - \frac{\delta}{\sigma^2+\delta^2}(y-x\beta)\right]^2\right) dz \\
&= 2\phi(y; x\beta, \sigma^2+\delta^2)\Phi\left(\frac{\delta(y-x\beta)}{\sigma\sqrt{\sigma^2+\delta^2}}\right).
\end{aligned}
$$

This density is known as a *skew-normal* distribution (e.g., Azzalini and Dalla Valle 1996; Branco and Dey 2002) and is sometimes written as $y \sim SN(x\beta, \sigma^2 + \delta^2, \delta/\sigma)$.

The parameter δ acts as a skewness parameter; specifically, the density is right-skewed when $\delta > 0$ and left-skewed when $\delta < 0$. When $\delta = 0$, the density is symmetric and we obtain $y \sim N(x\beta, \sigma^2)$. We provide in Figure 15.4 plots of the skew-normal density across different values of δ when $\sigma^2 = 1$ and $x\beta = 0$.

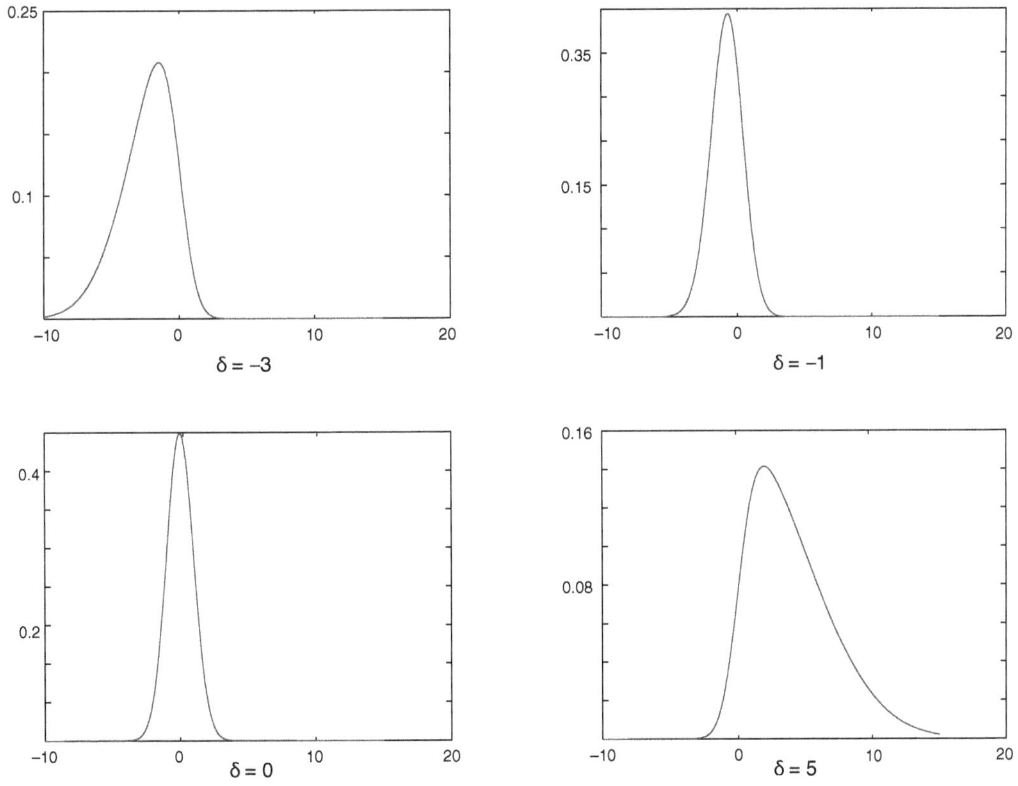

Figure 15.4. Skew-normal densities for various values of δ.

(b) For our posterior simulator, we make use of data augmentation and include $z = [z_1 \ z_2 \ \cdots \ z_n]'$ in the posterior distribution. When doing so, sampling from the posterior conditional for β^* and σ^2 is straightforward and will proceed similarly to Exercise 12.9. Before describing how one can sample from the posterior conditional for z, we first note that

$$p(z, \beta^*, \sigma^2|y) \propto p(\beta^*)p(\sigma^2)p(y, z|\beta^*, \sigma^2)$$
$$\propto p(\beta^*)p(\sigma^2)\prod_{i=1}^{n}\phi(y_i; x_i\beta + z_i\delta, \sigma^2)\exp\left(-\frac{1}{2}z_i^2\right)I(z_i > 0).$$

Let θ denote all the quantities in our joint posterior, and let θ_{-x} denote all quantities other than x. It follows that

$$z_i|\theta_{-z_i}, y \propto \exp\left(-\frac{1}{2\sigma^2}(y_i - x_i\beta - z_i\delta)^2\right)\exp\left(-\frac{1}{2}z_i^2\right)I(z_i > 0).$$

Completing the square on z_i, and noting that z_i is truncated at zero, we obtain

$$z_i|\theta_{-z_i}, y \overset{ind}{\sim} TN_{(0,\infty)}\left(\frac{\delta(y_i - x_i\beta)}{\sigma^2 + \delta^2}, \frac{\sigma^2}{\sigma^2 + \delta^2}\right), \ i = 1, 2, \ldots, n. \tag{15.70}$$

Let

$$X = \begin{bmatrix} x_1 \\ x_2 \\ \vdots \\ x_n \end{bmatrix}$$

and $W = [X \ z]$. With this notation, the posterior conditional for β^* is of the form

$$\beta^*|\theta_{-\beta^*}, y \sim N(D_\beta d_\beta, D_\beta), \tag{15.71}$$

where

$$D_\beta = (W'W/\sigma^2 + V_\beta^{-1})^{-1}, \quad d_\beta = W'y/\sigma^2.$$

Finally,

$$\sigma^2|\theta_{-\sigma^2}, y \sim IG\left(\frac{n}{2} + a, \left[b^{-1} + \left(\frac{1}{2}\right)(y - W\beta^*)'(y - W\beta^*)\right]^{-1}\right). \tag{15.72}$$

The posterior simulator proceeds by sampling independently from (15.70), for $i = 1, 2, \ldots, n$, and then from (15.71) and (15.72).

(c) For our prior hyperparameters, we set $a = 3$, $b = 1/2$, and $V_\beta = 10I_2$. The Gibbs sampler is run for 5000 iterations, and the first 2000 are discarded as the burn-in. Based on the final 3000 simulations, we calculate posterior means of β, δ, and σ^2 equal to 4.12, 10.3, and 1.80, respectively. These results suggest a strong right skew associated with the wage density, which is well documented in the empirical literature.

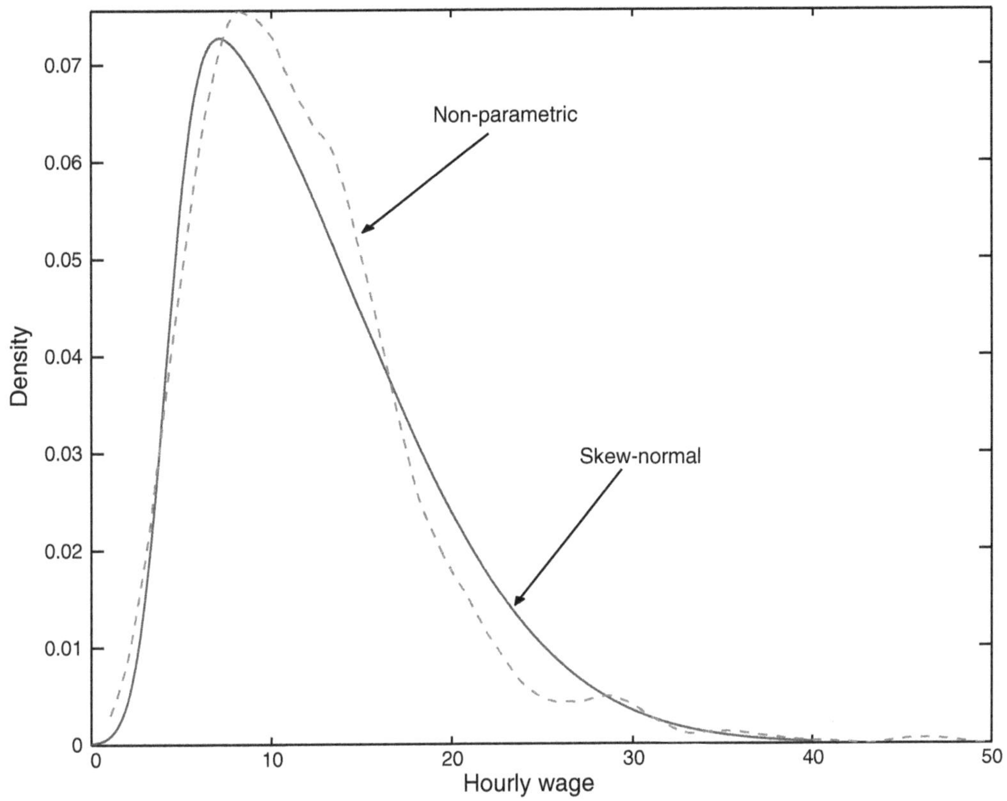

Figure 15.5. Non-parametric and skew-normal wage densities.

To investigate the skew-normal density's ability to capture key features of these wage data, we first calculate a non-parametric density estimate and then compare it to the density in (a) evaluated at posterior mean values of β, σ^2, and δ (which, admittedly, is a crude comparison). We present these results in Figure 15.5. As you can see, the densities are rather similar and both have clearly accounted for the right skew of the wage data.

Exercise 15.10 (Quantile regression I) Quantile regression, as described by Koenker and Bassett (1978), for example, offers a useful way for applied researchers to examine how covariate effects vary across different parts of the conditional outcome distribution. Instead of minimizing a sum of squared residuals as OLS does, quantile regression minimizes absolute deviations that are potentially asymmetric about zero. (See Exercise 3.2 for a related question.) This is done through the so-called "check function,"

$$\rho_p(x) \equiv x\left[p - I(x < 0)\right], \quad p \in (0, 1),$$

yielding a linear specification / loss structure with slope p for $x > 0$ and slope $p - 1$ for $x < 0$. Note that the function is not differentiable at $x = 0$.

Let us define the quantile regression objective function as follows:

$$\mathcal{Q}_p(\beta_p) \equiv \sum_{i=1}^{n} \rho_p(y_i - x_i\beta_p),$$

and define the quantile regression estimator, say β_p^*, as the minimizer of $\mathcal{Q}_p(\beta_p)$.

Consider a version of the quantile regression problem with just an intercept parameter (i.e., $x_i = 1\ \forall i$) and suppose a sample of data $\{y_i\}_{i=1}^n$ are available. You may assume there are no ties among the y_i for the sake of simplicity. Show that the optimal solution is to set the intercept parameter, α_p^*, equal to the pth quantile of the sample of data.

Solution

First, order the data and write $y_{(1)} < y_{(2)} < \cdots < y_{(n)}$. Next, consider possible solutions of the form $\alpha_p^* = y_{(j)}$ for different values of $j = 1, 2, \ldots, n$. Our objective function at such a point can be expressed as

$$\mathcal{Q}_p\left(y_{(j)}\right) = p\sum_i y_i - [npy_{(j)}] - \sum_{i=1}^{j-1}[y_{(i)} - y_{(j)}],$$

where it is understood that the rightmost summation in the equation above is simply zero when $\alpha_p = y_{(1)}$. Now, consider the value of the objective function when $\alpha_p = y_{(j+1)}$:

$$\mathcal{Q}_p\left(y_{(j+1)}\right) = p\sum_i y_i - [npy_{(j+1)}] - \sum_{i=1}^{j}[y_{(i)} - y_{(j+1)}].$$

It follows that the difference between objective functions at these points is

$$\begin{aligned}\mathcal{Q}_p\left(y_{(j+1)}\right) - \mathcal{Q}_p\left(y_{(j)}\right) &= -np(y_{(j+1)} - y_{(j)}) + jy_{(j+1)} - \sum_{i=1}^{j} y_{(i)} + \sum_{i=1}^{j-1} y_{(i)} - (j-1)y_{(j)} \\ &= [j - np](y_{(j+1)} - y_{(j)}).\end{aligned}$$

Since the term $y_{(j+1)} - y_{(j)}$ is always positive, this suggests that the objective function will continue to fall while $j < np$. So, in terms of solutions restricted to order statistics, it is optimal to choose $\alpha_p^* = y_{(j^*+1)}$, where j^* is the largest integer such that $j^* < np$. Note that $y_{(j^*+1)}$ is then the smallest sample value whose empirical cdf, $F(y_{(j^*+1)})$, is greater than or equal to p. In other words, the optimal choice among the order statistics is to set $\alpha_p^* = y_{(j^*+1)}$, the pth sample quantile of the $\{y_i\}$.

Now suppose we were to increase α_p^* slightly by, say, $0 < \delta < y_{(j^*+2)} - y_{(j^*+1)}$. Some algebra shows that, in such a case,

$$\mathcal{Q}_p\left(y_{(j^*+1)} + \delta\right) - \mathcal{Q}_p\left(y_{(j^*+1)}\right) = -\delta[np - (j^* + 1)] > 0.$$

Similarly, consider subtracting a small $\delta > 0$ so that $y_{(j^*+1)} - \delta > y_{(j^*)}$. In this case we have

$$\mathcal{Q}_p\left(y_{(j^*+1)} - \delta\right) - \mathcal{Q}_p\left(y_{(j^*+1)}\right) = \delta[np - (j^*)] > 0.$$

This shows that it is optimal, at least locally, to select $\alpha^* = y_{(j^*+1)}$ and that $y_{(j^*+1)}$ is optimal among the set of order statistics. The argument, however, generalizes and shows that this is optimal globally; the objective function decreases for all positive increments to α_p until one reaches $y_{(j^*+1)}$ and then increases for all subsequent positive increments.

Exercise 15.11 (Quantile regression II) Yu and Moyeed (2001) provide a likelihood-based rationale for quantile regression. Specifically, they consider the model

$$y_i = x_i\beta_p + \epsilon_i$$

where $\epsilon_i = \epsilon_i(p)$ follows an asymmetric Laplace distribution:

$$f_p(\epsilon) = p(1-p)\exp\left[-\epsilon_i(p - I(\epsilon_i < 0))\right]. \tag{15.73}$$

This yields a likelihood function of the form

$$L(\beta_p) = p^n(1-p)^n \exp\left(-\sum_{i=1}^{n} \rho_p(y_i - x_i\beta_p)\right).$$

Thus, under an improper flat prior, which Yu and Moyeed show yields a proper posterior, the posterior mode coincides with the traditional quantile regression estimate, as discussed in the previous question. This gives rise to a Bayesian approach to quantile regression.

Yu and Moyeed (2001) fit this model using a M–H algorithm. Kozumi and Kobayashi (2011) exploit a mixture representation that permits estimation via the Gibbs sampler and discuss a location-scale extension of the asymmetric Laplace. Specifically, they make use of the result that the asymmetric Laplace density, as given in (17.53), can be expressed as the following mixture:

$$\epsilon = \theta z + \tau\sqrt{z}u,$$

where

$$\theta = \frac{1-2p}{p(1-p)}, \quad \tau^2 = \frac{2}{p(1-p)}, \quad z \sim Exp(1), \text{ and } u \sim N(0,1).$$

A scale-adjusted asymmetric Laplace distribution can be obtained by multiplying the left- and right-hand sides of the above by σ, or

$$\sigma\epsilon_i = \sigma\theta z_i + \sigma\tau\sqrt{z_i}u_i = \theta\nu_i + \tau\sqrt{\sigma\nu_i}u_i,$$

where $\nu_i \equiv \sigma z_i$. We use this result to provide an alternate representation of the errors in our quantile regression equation:

$$\begin{aligned} y_i &= x_i\beta_p + \sigma\epsilon_i \\ &= x_i\beta_p + \theta\nu_i + \tau\sqrt{\sigma\nu_i}u_i. \end{aligned}$$

(a) Under a normal prior for β_p and an inverse gamma prior for σ, use data augmentation to discuss how a Gibbs algorithm can be employed to fit this model.
(b) The data on the website associated with this book provides wage and education outcomes for a random sample of 888 individuals. Using the algorithm derived in part (a), fit this model to the data at the following quantiles: $p = .1, .25, .5, .75$, and .90. Briefly discuss the results.

Solution

(a) The results discussed here follow those presented in Section 3 of Kozumi and Kobayashi (2011). A few observations are worth noting prior to discussing details of the posterior simulator. First, both θ and τ are known – they are only functions of the quantile p, which is specified at the outset. As the researcher examines behaviors at different quantiles, she changes the value of p, but this value is given when a posterior simulator is executed. Second, the mixture representation of the asymmetric Laplace is very useful in conjunction with MCMC: when using data augmentation, we condition on the values of ν, which enables us to apply standard conditionally conjugate results for the posterior simulation of β_p. In what follows, we make use of the priors

$$\beta_p \sim N(\mu_p, V_p) \quad \text{and} \quad \sigma \sim IG(a, b).$$

We obtain the augmented posterior:

$$\begin{aligned} p(\beta_p, \nu, \sigma|y) &\propto p(y|\beta, \nu, \sigma)p(\beta)p(\nu|\sigma)p(\sigma) \\ &= \sigma^{-n/2}\left(\prod_{i=1}^{n} \nu_i^{-1/2}\right) \exp\left(-\sum_{i=1}^{n} \frac{(y_i - x_i\beta_p - \theta\nu_i)^2}{2\sigma\tau^2\nu_i}\right) \\ &\quad \times \left(\prod_{i=1}^{n} \sigma^{-1}\exp(-\sigma^{-1}\nu_i)\right) p(\beta_p)p(\sigma). \end{aligned}$$

In terms of the complete posterior conditional distribution for β_p, the standard results of Lindley and Smith (1972) imply that

$$\beta_p|\nu, \sigma, y, \sim N(D_p d_p, D_p), \tag{15.74}$$

where

$$D_p = \left(\sum_i x_i' x_i/(\tau^2\sigma\nu_i) + V_p^{-1}\right)^{-1}, \quad d_p = \sum_i x_i'(y_i - \theta\nu_i)/(\tau^2\sigma\nu_i) + V_p^{-1}\mu_p.$$

For the scale parameter σ, we obtain

$$\sigma|\beta_p, \nu, y \sim IG\left(a + (3/2)n, \left[b^{-1} + \sum_i \nu_i + \sum_{i=1}^{n} \frac{(y_i - x_i\beta_p - \theta\nu_i)^2}{2\tau^2\nu_i}\right]^{-1}\right). \tag{15.75}$$

Table 15.7: Parameter posterior means in quantile regression model.

p	Intercept	Education
.10	.853	.104
.25	1.07	.114
.50	1.42	.118
.75	1.70	.126
.90	2.03	.125

As for the sampling of ν, our expression for the augmented joint posterior implies that they can be sampled independently, $i = 1, 2, \ldots, n$. We obtain

$$p(\nu_i|\beta_p, \sigma, y) \propto \nu_i^{-1/2} \exp\left(-\sigma^{-1}\nu_i - \frac{1}{2\tau^2\sigma\nu_i}(y_i - x_i\beta_p - \theta\nu_i)^2\right),$$

which can be simplified to

$$p(\nu_i|\beta_p, \sigma, y) \propto \nu_i^{-1/2} \exp\left[-\frac{1}{2}\left(\left[\frac{2}{\sigma} + \frac{\theta^2}{\sigma\tau^2}\right]\nu_i + \frac{(y_i - x_i\beta_p)^2}{\sigma\tau^2}\nu_i^{-1}\right)\right]. \quad (15.76)$$

Although this density function appears non-standard, the above is recognized as the kernel of a *generalized inverse Gaussian* (GIG) distribution. For a generic GIG random variable, we can write

$$y \sim GIG(\nu, a, b) \Rightarrow p(y|\nu, a, b) \propto y^{\nu-1} \exp\left(-\frac{1}{2}[ax^{-1} + bx]\right).$$

It follows that

$$\nu_i|\beta_p, \sigma, y \overset{ind}{\sim} GIG(1/2, (y_i - x_i\beta_p)^2/\sigma\tau^2, 2/\sigma + \theta^2/\sigma\tau^2).$$

Posterior simulation in the quantile regression model thus involves successively sampling from (15.74), (15.75), and (15.76). To sample from the GIG distribution, we first sample from an inverse Gaussian distribution, using the method of Michael, Schucany, and Haas (1976). This simulation can then be inverted to produce the desired GIG draw. (See Exercise 15.3 for a related discussion.)

(b) We use the algorithm described in part (a) to obtain results for $p \in \{.1, .25, .50, .75, .9\}$. In each case, the sampler is run for 25 000 iterations and the first 1000 are discarded as the burn-in. For each quantile analysis, we employ an improper prior for β_p of the form $p(\beta_p) \propto c$ and specify $\sigma \sim IG(3, 1/2)$. Posterior results are provided in Table 15.7. These results suggest that returns to schooling generally increase as one moves further into the right-tail of the conditional earnings distribution.

16

Bayesian Methods for Model Comparison, Selection, and Big Data

In Chapter 6 on hypothesis testing, exercises relating to model selection were provided. The concepts and approaches introduced there, such as marginal likelihoods, Bayes factors, and posterior odds ratios, can be used to select a model.

As an alternative to model *selection*, many Bayesians prefer to *average across models* rather than select a single model. The motivation for Bayesian model averaging (BMA) follows immediately from the laws of probability. That is, if we let M_r for $r = 1, \ldots, R$ denote the R different models under consideration and ϕ be a vector of parameters that has a common interpretation in all models, then the rules of probability say

$$p(\phi|y) = \sum_{r=1}^{R} p(\phi|y, M_r)\, p(M_r|y).$$

Alternatively, if $g(\phi)$ is a function of ϕ, the rules of conditional expectation imply that

$$E[g(\phi)|y] = \sum_{r=1}^{R} E[g(\phi)|y, M_r]\, p(M_r|y).$$

The logic of Bayesian inference says that one should obtain results for every model under consideration and average them, with weights given by the posterior model probabilities, $p(M_r|y)$.

Given that hypothesis testing was covered in Chapter 6, the reader may be wondering why we devote a separate chapter to exercises on Bayesian model selection and averaging. One reason is that marginal likelihoods, though conceptually straightforward, can be difficult to calculate in many models and it is therefore of value to review a few general methods of marginal likelihood calculation. Another reason is that, in many empirical examples, the number of models under consideration is simply too large for evaluation of a marginal likelihood for every model. For instance, in the regression model (which we will focus on in most of this chapter), one has K potential explanatory variables. If models are defined by the inclusion/exclusion of every potential explanatory variable then $R = 2^K$. If K is moderate or large (e.g., $K > 20$), then it is computationally difficult or impossible to evaluate every model. Accordingly, a large Bayesian literature has emerged for developing computational methods (closely related to posterior simulation methods) for doing BMA and Bayesian model selection in the regression model when the number of potential explanatory variables is large. For further reading on BMA see Raftery, Madigan, and Hoeting (1997), Hoeting, Madigan, Raftery, and Volinsky (1999), and the Bayesian Model Averaging website (http://stats.research.att.com/volinsky/bma.html). George and McCulloch (1993, 1997) are important references for Bayesian model selection.

This chapter is divided into two sections. The first set of exercises discuss several different techniques for the general calculation of marginal likelihoods. The second and final section of the chapter discusses procedures for model averaging as well as covariate selection in a "big data" context, including an application of the Bayesian LASSO.

16.1 Procedures for Calculating Marginal Likelihoods

Exercise 16.1 (Calculating the marginal likelihood with simulated output: Gelfand and Dey (1994))

(a) Show that, for any proper density function $f(\theta)$,

$$E_{\theta|y}\left[\frac{f(\theta)}{p(\theta)p(y|\theta)}\right] = p(y)^{-1}.$$

(b) How is this result useful when trying to calculate the marginal likelihood for a particular model?

Solution

(a) Note that

$$\begin{aligned}
E_{\theta|y}\left[\frac{f(\theta)}{p(\theta)p(y|\theta)}\right] &= \int_\Theta \frac{f(\theta)}{p(\theta)p(y|\theta)} p(\theta|y)\, d\theta \\
&= \int_\Theta \frac{f(\theta)}{p(\theta)p(y|\theta)} \frac{p(\theta)p(y|\theta)}{p(y)}\, d\theta \\
&= p(y)^{-1} \int_\theta f(\theta)\, d\theta \\
&= p(y)^{-1}.
\end{aligned}$$

(b) This is a very useful result as it shows how one can use *posterior* simulations from a sampler to calculate the marginal likelihood $p(y)$. The "direct" way to calculate the marginal likelihood $p(y) = \int_\Theta p(y|\theta)p(\theta)\, d\theta$ by Monte Carlo integration would require draws from the *prior* $p(\theta)$. Since the prior is typically flat relative to the likelihood, the resulting estimate of the marginal likelihood is quite inaccurate and unstable under this approach. The Gelfand–Dey algorithm instead makes use of posterior simulations to calculate the marginal likelihood; one simply calculates $f(\theta)/[p(\theta)p(y|\theta)]$ for each θ value simulated from the posterior and averages this collection of values to estimate the (inverse) marginal likelihood.

Geweke (1999) points out that for the asymptotics of the Gelfand–Dey method to go through, the expression $f(\theta)/[p(\theta)p(y|\theta)]$ must be bounded from above. (One might worry that, in the tails, the denominator will be quite small, potentially leading this expression to explode.) Geweke's suggestion is to alleviate this problem by choosing $f(\theta)$ to be a normal approximation to the posterior $p(\theta|y)$ with a tail truncation. See Exercise 16.3, Geweke (1999), and Koop (2003, pp. 105–106) for more on this issue.

Exercise 16.2 (Calculating the marginal likelihood with simulated output: Chib (1995)) Chib (1995) notes that, for any model M, data y, and parameter vector θ,

$$p(y, \theta|M) = p(y|\theta, M)p(\theta|M) = p(\theta|y, M)p(y|M),$$

and thus

$$p(y|M) = \frac{p(y|\theta, M)p(\theta|M)}{p(\theta|y, M)}.$$

Taking logs of both sides, we obtain

$$\ln p(y|M) = \ln p(y|\theta, M) + \ln p(\theta|M) - \ln p(\theta|y, M).$$

This expression provides an identity in θ: The log marginal likelihood on the left-hand side does not involve θ, and so the equation must hold for any value of θ. Thus, for purposes of computational reliability, let us choose a $\hat{\theta}$ of high posterior density (e.g., a posterior mean or mode) and note that

$$\ln p(y|M) = \ln p(y|\hat{\theta}, M) + \ln p(\hat{\theta}|M) - \ln p(\hat{\theta}|y, M).$$

Some quick accounting suggests that for most problems, the first two terms on the right-hand side of the equality are readily available. That is, $\ln p(y|\hat{\theta}, M)$ is the log likelihood evaluated at $\hat{\theta}$ and $\ln p(\hat{\theta}|M)$ is the log prior ordinate at $\hat{\theta}$. In general, these two quantities can be computed. The last term, $\ln p(\hat{\theta}|y, M)$, requires more care, since the normalizing constant of the posterior is typically unknown.

(a) Suppose that the parameter vector θ can be broken into two blocks (i.e., $\theta = [\theta_1' \ \theta_2']'$) and that a Gibbs sampler can be applied to fit this model, cycling through the two posterior conditionals $\theta_1|\theta_2, y, M$ and $\theta_2|\theta_1, y, M$. Show how the Gibbs output can be used to estimate $p(\hat{\theta}|y, M)$, the posterior ordinate needed to calculate the log marginal likelihood. You may assume that the normalizing constants of the complete conditional distributions are known.

(b) Repeat the exercise in part (a) when the Gibbs sampler cycles through three blocks ($\theta = [\theta_1' \; \theta_2' \; \theta_3']'$).

Solution
(a) First, write

$$p(\hat{\theta}|y, M) = p(\hat{\theta}_1, \hat{\theta}_2|y, M) = p(\hat{\theta}_1|\hat{\theta}_2, y, M)p(\hat{\theta}_2|y, M). \tag{16.1}$$

Note that the first term following the last equality, $p(\hat{\theta}_1|\hat{\theta}_2, y, M)$, can be evaluated as it is an ordinate of the complete conditional $\theta_1|\theta_2, y, M$, which is assumed to be known. For the term $p(\hat{\theta}_2|y, M)$, note that

$$p(\theta_2|y, M) = \int_{\Theta_1} p(\theta_2|\theta_1, y, M)p(\theta_1|y, M)\, d\theta_1.$$

This representation suggests that one can estimate the desired ordinate via "Rao–Blackwellization." That is,

$$p(\hat{\theta}_2|y, M) \approx \frac{1}{R}\sum_{r=1}^{R} p(\hat{\theta}_2|\theta_1^{(r)}, y, M), \tag{16.2}$$

and $\theta_1^{(r)} \sim \theta_1|y, M$, which are provided from the post-convergence output from the Gibbs sampler. Again, note that the conditional distribution $\theta_2|\theta_1, y, M$ (including its normalizing constant) is assumed known. Equation (16.2) plus the conditional ordinate $p(\hat{\theta}_1|\hat{\theta}_2, y, M)$ provide what are needed to calculate (16.1) and thus the log marginal likelihood.
(b) Much like part (a), to calculate the marginal likelihood we need to obtain

$$p(\hat{\theta}_1, \hat{\theta}_2, \hat{\theta}_3|y, M) = p(\hat{\theta}_1|\hat{\theta}_2, \hat{\theta}_3, y, M)p(\hat{\theta}_2|\hat{\theta}_3, y, M)p(\hat{\theta}_3|y, M). \tag{16.3}$$

The first and last of these three pieces can be calculated in a manner similar to that described in the solution to part (a). That is, $p(\hat{\theta}_1|\hat{\theta}_2, \hat{\theta}_3, y, M)$ is known, as it is simply an ordinate of the complete conditional for θ_1. Similarly,

$$p(\hat{\theta}_3|y, M) \approx \frac{1}{R}\sum_{r=1}^{R} p(\hat{\theta}_3|\theta_1^{(r)}, \theta_2^{(r)}, y, M),$$

where $(\theta_1^{(r)}, \; \theta_2^{(r)})$ denote the rth set of $(\theta_1, \; \theta_2)$ values simulated from the posterior.

The middle term of (16.3) introduces a new complication. However, one can estimate this ordinate using some additional *reduced runs* of our posterior simulator. That is, suppose that we ran the Gibbs sampler again, and specifically, suppose we iterate through the posterior conditionals $\theta_2|\hat{\theta}_3, \theta_1, y, M$ and $\theta_1|\hat{\theta}_3, \theta_2, y, M$. Then, after a suitable pre-convergence period, we would expect these draws to converge to $\theta_1, \theta_2|\hat{\theta}_3, y, M$ (and thus, individually, the θ_1 and θ_2 draws would converge to their corresponding marginal distributions). Since

$$p(\theta_2|\theta_3, y, M) = \int_{\Theta_1} p(\theta_2|\theta_1, \theta_3, y, M)p(\theta_1|\theta_3, y, M)\, d\theta_1,$$

it follows that

$$p(\hat{\theta}_2|\hat{\theta}_3, y, M) \approx \frac{1}{R}\sum_{r=1}^{R} p(\hat{\theta}_2|\theta_1^{(r)}, \hat{\theta}_3, y, M),$$

where

$$\theta_1^{(r)} \sim \theta_1|\hat{\theta}_3, y, M,$$

and these draws are obtained from the reduced runs by cycling through the conditionals $\theta_2|\hat{\theta}_3, \theta_1, y, M$ and $\theta_1|\hat{\theta}_3, \theta_2, y, M$. With this ordinate in hand, we have the three pieces needed to calculate the posterior ordinate in (16.3) and thus the log marginal likelihood. A similar procedure can be applied to calculate the marginal likelihood in cases of more than three blocks.

Exercise 16.3 (Calculating marginal likelihoods with generated data) Generate 100 observations from the simple regression model

$$y_i = \beta_0 + \beta_1 x_i + \epsilon_i, \quad \epsilon_i \stackrel{iid}{\sim} N(0, \sigma^2),$$

with $\beta_0 = 1$, $\beta_1 = .5$, $\sigma^2 = .2$, and $x_i \stackrel{iid}{\sim} N(0,1)$. Employ a normal-gamma prior of the form

$$\beta|\sigma^2 \sim N(0, 4\sigma^2 I_2),$$

$$\sigma^2 \sim IG(3, 2.5).$$

Analytically determine the log marginal likelihood (see Exercise 10.4 for a related discussion) and calculate it given your generated data. Next, use the Gibbs sampler to fit the linear regression model (see, e.g., Exercise 12.9). Given the Gibbs draws, calculate the log marginal likelihood using the methods of Gelfand and Dey (1994) – see Exercise 16.1 – and Chib (1995) – see Exercise 16.2 – and compare these results to those you obtained analytically.

Solution

MATLAB code for this exercise is provided on the website associated with this book. The analytical expression of the marginal likelihood was covered in Exercise 10.4, and we do not repeat those derivations here. For the Gelfand–Dey and Chib approaches, we fit the model using the Gibbs sampler, running it for 20 000 iterations and discarding the first 100 as the burn-in. In the Gelfand–Dey approach (Exercise 16.1), we choose $f(\theta)$ as the following truncated normal density:

$$f(\theta) \propto (2\pi)^{-k/2}|\hat{\Omega}|^{-1/2}\exp\left[-.5(\theta - \hat{\theta})'\hat{\Omega}^{-1}(\theta - \hat{\theta})\right] I(\theta \in \Theta),$$

where $\theta = [\beta_0 \; \beta_1 \; \sigma^2]'$, $\hat{\theta}$ is the posterior mean of the Gibbs draws, $\hat{\Omega} = \frac{1}{R}\sum_{r=1}^{R}(\theta^{(r)} - \hat{\theta})(\theta^{(r)} - \hat{\theta})'$ is an approximation of the posterior covariance matrix, and $k = 3$. The support of the density, Θ, is constructed as

$$\Theta = \{\theta : (\theta - \hat{\theta})'\hat{\Omega}^{-1}(\theta - \hat{\theta}) \leq 11.34\},$$

where 11.34 is the 99th percentile of the $\chi^2(3)$ distribution. With Θ defined in this way, the normalizing constant of f is (1/.99).

Given the generated data, our analytical calculation of the log marginal likelihood was -74.0951, whereas the methods of Gelfand–Dey and Chib produced numerical estimates of -74.0952 and -74.1118, respectively.

16.2 Bayesian Model Averaging and Variable Selection

Exercise 16.4 (Basic g-prior results commonly used with BMA) When performing Bayesian model averaging, or BMA, it is common to use reference, or *benchmark*, priors that yield analytical results for quantities such as $p(M_r|y)$ and $E(\beta_r|y)$. Such priors ease the job of prior elicitation for huge numbers of models and lessen the computational burden. A common benchmark prior (see, e.g., Fernandez, Ley, and Steel 2001a,b) sets

$$p(h) \propto \frac{1}{h}, \tag{16.4}$$

and for the intercept

$$p(\alpha) \propto 1. \tag{16.5}$$

To make absolutely certain that the non-informative prior for the intercept has the same implications for every model, Fernandez et al. (2001b) recommend standardizing all the explanatory variables by subtracting off their means. This will have no effect on the slope coefficients β_r, but it ensures that the intercept can be interpreted in the same manner in every model as measuring the mean of y.

For the regression coefficients the prior is of the form

$$\beta_r|h \sim N(\underline{\beta}_r, h^{-1}\underline{V}_r), \tag{16.6}$$

with

$$\underline{\beta}_r = 0_{k_r}$$

and

$$\underline{V}_r = \left[g_r X_r' X_r\right]^{-1}. \tag{16.7}$$

With this choice of $\underline{V}_r$, the prior in (16.6) is termed a *g-prior*, as introduced by Zellner (1986a).

Derive $p(\beta_r|y, M_r)$ and $p(M_r|y)$.

Solution

The g-prior is simply a special case of the natural conjugate prior. Thus, the derivations of Exercise 10.1 of Chapter 10 apply directly. Using these results and properties of the normal-gamma distribution, it follows immediately that the posterior for β_r follows a multivariate t distribution with mean

$$E(\beta_r|y, M_r) \equiv \overline{\beta}_r = \overline{V}_r X_r' y, \tag{16.8}$$

covariance matrix

$$\text{Var}(\beta_r|y, M_r) = \frac{\overline{\nu}\overline{s}_r^2}{\overline{\nu}-2}\overline{V}_r, \tag{16.9}$$

and $\overline{\nu} = N$ degrees of freedom. Plugging (16.7) into the general form for $\overline{V}_r$, we obtain

$$\overline{V}_r = \left[(1+g_r) X_r' X_r\right]^{-1} \tag{16.10}$$

and

$$\overline{s}_r^2 = \frac{\frac{1}{g_r+1} y' P_{X_r} y + \frac{g_r}{g_r+1}(y - \overline{y}\iota_N)'(y - \overline{y}\iota_N)}{\overline{\nu}}, \tag{16.11}$$

where

$$P_{X_r} = I_N - X_r \left(X_r' X_r\right)^{-1} X_r'.$$

Plugging the g-prior form for $\overline{V}_r$ into the formula for the marginal likelihood for the normal linear regression model with natural conjugate prior yields

$$p(y|M_r) \propto \left(\frac{g_r}{g_r+1}\right)^{\frac{k_r}{2}} \left[\frac{1}{g_r+1} y' P_{X_r} y + \frac{g_r}{g_r+1}(y - \overline{y}\iota_T)'(y - \overline{y}\iota_T)\right]^{-\frac{N-1}{2}}. \tag{16.12}$$

The posterior model probabilities can be calculated using

$$p(M_r|y) = cp(y|M_r)p(M_r), \tag{16.13}$$

where c is a constant, which is the same for all models. This constant will cancel out in all relevant formulas in the following and can be ignored. Alternatively, the fact that $\sum_{r=1}^{R} p(M_r|y) = 1$ can be used to determine c.

Exercise 16.5 (Markov chain Monte Carlo model composition (MC^3)) The exercise asks you to derive the MC^3 algorithm of Madigan and York (1995). The model space used in this chapter, defined by M_r for $r = 1, \ldots, R$, can be expressed in terms of a $K \times 1$ vector $\gamma = (\gamma_1, \ldots, \gamma_K)'$, where all elements are either 0 or 1. Models defined by $\gamma_j = 1$ indicate that the jth explanatory variable enters the model (or else $\gamma_j = 0$). There are 2^K possible configurations of γ and the space of this parameter is equivalent to the model space. Construct an M–H algorithm for γ and discuss how this can be used to carry out BMA using the setup of Exercise 16.4.

Solution

In the case of continuous random variables, the random walk chain M–H algorithm employs a candidate density in which a candidate draw equals the current draw plus an increment. We can modify this intuition involving the discrete random vector γ. That is, a candidate value, γ^*, is drawn with equal probability from the set containing the current draw, $\gamma^{(s-1)}$, and all configurations that change *one* element of $\gamma^{(s-1)}$. In terms of the model space, this means a candidate model, M^*, is proposed that is drawn randomly (with equal probability) from the set of models including (i) the current model, $M^{(s-1)}$, (ii) all models that delete one explanatory variable from $M^{(s-1)}$, and (iii) all models that add one explanatory variable to $M^{(s-1)}$. If candidate models are generated in this way, we can use the standard acceptance probability formula for the random walk chain M–H algorithm (see Exercise 12.3, or Koop 2003, p. 97):

$$\alpha\left(M^{(s-1)}, M^*\right) = \min\left[\frac{p(y|\gamma^*)p(\gamma^*)}{p(y|\gamma^{(s-1)})p(\gamma^{(s-1)})}, 1\right]. \tag{16.14}$$

The quantities $p(y|\gamma^{(s-1)})$ and $p(y|\gamma^*)$ can be calculated using (16.12). In the common case where equal prior weight is allocated to each model, $p\left(\gamma^*\right) = p\left(\gamma^{(s-1)}\right)$, and these terms cancel out of (16.14).

Posterior results based on the sequence of models generated from the MC^3 algorithm can be calculated by averaging over draws in the standard MCMC manner. So, for instance, (16.2) can be approximated by $\widehat{g}_{S_1}$, where

$$\widehat{g}_{S_1} = \frac{1}{S_1}\sum_{s=S_0+1}^{S} E\left[g\left(\phi\right)|y, \gamma^{(s)}\right]. \tag{16.15}$$

As with other MCMC algorithms, $\widehat{g}_{S_1}$ converges to $E\left[g(\phi)|y\right]$ as S_1 goes to infinity, where $S_1 = S - (S_0 + 1)$. Note that a starting value for the chain, $\gamma^{(0)}$, must be chosen and hence S_0 burn-in replications should be discarded to eliminate the effects of this choice. Note also that the frequencies with which models are drawn can be used to calculate Bayes factors. For instance, if the MC^3 algorithm draws the model M_r A times and the model M_s B times, then the ratio A/B will converge to the Bayes factor comparing M_r to M_s.

Exercise 16.6 (BMA: An application in economic growth) Using the solutions to Exercises 16.4 and 16.5, carry out a BMA exercise with a data set from the economic growth literature and the g-prior value $g = 1/N$. This choice of g is recommended by Fernandez et al. (2001b). The data set used in this exercise is taken from Fernandez et al. (2001a) and is available on the website associated with this book. This data set covers $N = 72$ countries and contains $K = 41$ potential explanatory variables. The dependent variable is average per capita GDP growth for the period 1960–1992. For the sake of brevity, we will not list all of the explanatory variables here (see the original paper for a detailed description of all the data). Furthermore, Table 16.1 in the solution provides a list of short-form names for all explanatory variables, which should be enough to provide a rough idea of what each explanatory variable is measuring.

Solution

The computer code implementing the MC^3 algorithm described in Exercise 16.5 is available on the website associated with this book. The following results are based on taking 1 100 000 draws and discarding the first 100 000 as burn-in replications (i.e., $S_0 = 100\,000$ and $S_1 = 1\,000\,000$).

Elements in the column of Table 16.1 labeled "BMA post. prob." can be interpreted as the probability that the corresponding explanatory variable should be included. It is calculated as the proportion of models drawn by the MC^3 algorithm that contain the corresponding explanatory variable. Informally, this is a useful diagnostic for deciding whether an individual explanatory variable has an important role in explaining economic growth. It can be seen that several variables (i.e., Life expectancy, GDP level in 1960, Equipment investment, and Fraction Confucian) do have an important role in explaining economic growth. Regardless of which other explanatory variables are included, these variables almost always exhibit strong explanatory power. However, for the remainder of the explanatory variables there is some uncertainty as to whether they have important roles to play in explaining economic growth. And, for many of the explanatory variables, there is strong evidence that they should not be included.

The other two columns of Table 16.1 contain posterior means and standard deviations for each regression coefficient, averaged across models. Remember that models where a particular explanatory variable is excluded are interpreted as implying a zero value for its coefficient. Hence, the average in (16.15) involves some terms where $E\left[g\left(\phi\right)|y, M^{(s)}\right]$ is calculated and others where the value of zero is used. With the exception of the few variables with high BMA posterior probability, most of the posterior means are small relative to their standard deviations. Thus, BMA is indicating a high degree of uncertainty about which factors explain economic growth. Undoubtedly, this is an honest representation of the fact that the data are not informative enough to send a clear story.

The MC^3 algorithm allows for the calculation of posterior model probabilities by simply counting the proportion of draws taken from each model. For the top ten models, the column of Table 16.2 labeled "$p\left(M_r|y\right)$ MC^3 estimate" contains posterior model probabilities calculated in this way. The column labeled "$p\left(M_r|y\right)$ analytical" contains the exact values calculated using (16.12) and (16.13). It can be seen that the posterior model probability is widely scattered across models, with no single model dominating. In fact, the top ten models account for only a little more than 4% of the total posterior model probability.

The numbers in tables such as this (perhaps with many more models) allow for an assessment of the convergence of the MC^3 algorithm. The numbers in the last three rows of Table 16.2 are slightly different from one another. These differences are small enough for present purposes and we can be confident that the numbers in Table 16.1 are approximately correct. However, for a research paper a higher degree of accuracy is typically called

Table 16.1: Bayesian model averaging results.

Explanatory variable	BMA post. prob.	Posterior mean	Posterior std. dev.
Primary school enrollment	0.207	0.004	0.010
Life expectancy	0.935	0.001	3.4×10^{-4}
GDP level in 1960	0.998	−0.016	0.003
Fraction GDP in mining	0.460	0.019	0.023
Degree of capitalism	0.452	0.001	0.001
No. years open economy	0.515	0.007	0.008
% of pop. speaking English	0.068	-4.3×10^{-4}	0.002
% of pop. speaking foreign lang.	0.067	2.9×10^{-4}	0.001
Exchange rate distortions	0.081	-4.0×10^{-6}	1.7×10^{-5}
Equipment investment	0.927	0.161	0.068
Non-equipment investment	0.427	0.024	0.032
Std. dev. of black market premium	0.049	-6.3×10^{-7}	3.9×10^{-6}
Outward orientation	0.039	-7.1×10^{-5}	5.9×10^{-4}
Black market premium	0.181	−0.001	0.003
Area	0.031	-5.0×10^{-9}	1.1×10^{-7}
Latin America	0.207	−0.002	0.004
Sub-Saharan Africa	0.736	−0.011	0.008
Higher education enrollment	0.043	−0.001	0.010
Public education share	0.032	0.001	0.025
Revolutions and coups	0.030	-3.7×10^{-6}	0.001
War	0.076	-2.8×10^{-4}	0.001
Political rights	0.094	-1.5×10^{-4}	0.001
Civil liberties	0.127	-2.9×10^{-4}	0.001
Latitude	0.041	9.1×10^{-7}	3.1×10^{-5}
Age	0.083	-3.9×10^{-6}	1.6×10^{-5}
British colony	0.037	-6.6×10^{-5}	0.001
Fraction Buddhist	0.201	0.003	0.006
Fraction Catholic	0.126	-2.9×10^{-4}	0.003
Fraction Confucian	0.989	0.056	0.014
Ethnolinguistic fractionalization	0.056	3.2×10^{-4}	0.002
French colony	0.050	2.0×10^{-4}	0.001
Fraction Hindu	0.120	−0.003	0.011
Fraction Jewish	0.035	-2.3×10^{-4}	0.003
Fraction Muslim	0.651	0.009	0.008
Primary exports	0.098	-9.6×10^{-4}	0.004
Fraction Protestant	0.451	−0.006	0.007
Rule of law	0.489	0.007	0.008
Spanish colony	0.057	2.2×10^{-4}	1.5×10^{-3}
Population growth	0.036	0.005	0.046
Ratio workers to population	0.046	-3.0×10^{-4}	0.002
Size of labor force	0.072	6.7×10^{-9}	3.7×10^{-8}

Table 16.2: Posterior model probabilities for top ten models.

	$p(M_r\|y)$ analytical	$p(M_r\|y)$ MC^3 estimate
1	0.0089	0.0088
2	0.0078	0.0080
3	0.0052	0.0052
4	0.0035	0.0035
5	0.0032	0.0035
6	0.0029	0.0029
7	0.0028	0.0028
8	0.0028	0.0025
9	0.0028	0.0025
10	0.0024	0.0023

for and the number of replications should be increased. Here, we have used 1 000 000 replications, which sounds like a large number. However, the number of possible models is 2^{41} and, with 1 000 000 replications, we have visited only a tiny fraction of them.

Exercise 16.7 (Stochastic search variable selection) Another popular method that addresses issues similar to Bayesian model averaging, described in George and McCulloch (1993), is known as *stochastic search variable selection* (SSVS). This approach involves using the normal linear regression model with an independent normal-gamma prior (see Exercise 12.9) with one minor alteration. This alteration is in the prior for the regression coefficients and is useful for the case where a large number of explanatory variables exist, but the researcher does not know which ones are likely to be important. To capture this, the prior for each regression coefficient is specified as a mixture of two normals, both with mean zero. One of the terms in the mixture has very small variance (i.e., it says the coefficient is virtually zero and thus the variable can be effectively excluded from the model) and the other has a large variance (i.e., it is most likely different from zero and thus the variable should be retained in the model). To be precise, for each coefficient β_j for $j = 1, \ldots, K$, the prior is

$$\beta_j|\gamma_j \sim (1-\gamma_j)\, N\left(0, \tau_j^2\right) + \gamma_j N\left(0, c_j^2\tau_j^2\right), \tag{16.16}$$

where c_j and τ_j are known prior hyperparameters with τ_j^2 being small and $c_j^2\tau_j^2$ large. In addition, the γ_j are binary variables that equal 1 with prior probability $\Pr(\gamma_j = 1) = p_j$, $0 \le p_j \le 1$. If $\gamma_j = 0$, the coefficient β_j "belongs to" the first component of the mixture, which is tightly centered around zero. We interpret this as evidence that variable x_j (the jth column of the stacked regressor matrix) can be excluded from the model. Conversely, if $\gamma_j = 1$, we interpret this as evidence that x_j should be retained in the model.

(a) Suppose you use the prior $\Pr(\gamma_j = 1) = p \; \forall j$, so that the prior probability that each variable is included is p. Derive a Gibbs sampler for fitting a linear regression model with the SSVS hierarchical prior described here.
(b) Using the results and prior specification from part (a), perform a generated-data experiment to illustrate the performance of the SSVS approach. Specifically, generate

$$\begin{bmatrix} x_{1i} \\ x_{2i} \\ \vdots \\ x_{5i} \end{bmatrix} \stackrel{iid}{\sim} N\left[\begin{pmatrix} 0 \\ 0 \\ \vdots \\ 0 \end{pmatrix}, \begin{pmatrix} 1 & .4 & .4 & 0 & .6 \\ .4 & 1 & .7 & 0 & .3 \\ .4 & .7 & 1 & 0 & .3 \\ 0 & 0 & 0 & 1 & 0 \\ .6 & .3 & .3 & 0 & 1 \end{pmatrix}\right], \quad i = 1, 2, \ldots, 1000. \tag{16.17}$$

Then, set

$$y_i = 2 + .25x_{1i} - .4x_{2i} + .6x_{3i} + .2\epsilon_i, \tag{16.18}$$

where

$$\epsilon_i \stackrel{iid}{\sim} N(0, 1).$$

In this design, note that we are generating five potential explanatory variables (some of which are correlated with one another), and y is generated using only the first three of these. Apply the SSVS algorithm using all five explanatory variables, and determine the posterior probabilities that each variable should be retained in the model. For the intercept, simply employ a normal prior, and fix attention on the issue of excluding or retaining the x's from the model.

Solution
(a) First, let us write the linear regression model as

$$y_i = \beta_0 + \sum_{j=1}^{K} x_{ji}\beta_j + \epsilon_i, \quad \epsilon_i \stackrel{iid}{\sim} N(0, \sigma^2). \tag{16.19}$$

Place an inverted gamma prior on σ^2 of the form

$$\sigma^2 \sim IG(a, b),$$

use an independent normal prior for the intercept β_0 of the form

$$\beta_0 \sim N(0, \underline{V}_0),$$

and specify conditionally independent priors for the slope coefficients using (16.16). The augmented joint posterior (which contains the component indicators γ) is $p(\beta, \sigma^2, \gamma|y)$, where $\beta = [\beta_0 \; \beta_1 \; \cdots \; \beta_K]'$ and $\gamma = [\gamma_1 \; \gamma_2 \; \cdots \; \gamma_k]'$. We obtain the following posterior conditionals for this model:

$$\beta|\gamma, \sigma^2, y \sim N(D_\beta d_\beta, D_\beta), \tag{16.20}$$

where

$$D_\beta = \left(X'X/\sigma^2 + V_\beta^{-1}(\gamma)\right)^{-1}, \quad d_\beta = X'y/\sigma^2.$$

In these definitions of D_β and d_β, X and y have been stacked over i and j in the obvious way and $V_\beta(\gamma)$ is a $(K+1) \times (K+1)$ diagonal matrix with $\underline{V}_0$ as the $(1,1)$ element and $\gamma_i c_i^2 \tau_i^2 + (1-\gamma_i)\tau_i^2$ as the (i,i) element, $i = 2, 3, \ldots, K+1$. We also have

$$\sigma^2|\beta, \gamma, y \sim IG\left(\frac{N}{2} + a, \left[b^{-1} + .5(y - X\beta)'(y - X\beta)\right]^{-1}\right), \tag{16.21}$$

and finally,

$$\alpha_j|\alpha_{-j}, \beta, \sigma^2, y \overset{ind}{\sim} B\left(1, \frac{p\phi(\beta_j; 0, c_j^2\tau_j^2)}{p\phi(\beta_j; 0, c_j^2\tau_j^2) + (1-p)\phi(\beta_j; 0, \tau_j^2)}\right), \quad j = 1, 2, \ldots, K, \tag{16.22}$$

with B denoting the binomial distribution (see Definition A.7).

(b) We generate 1000 observations from the stated model and choose prior hyperparameters of the form $\tau_j^2 = .000\,0001$, $c_j^2 = 9/\tau_j^2$, and $p = 1/2$. With these hyperparameters, our prior probability that each variable should be included in the model is 1/2, the prior standard deviation for the "slab" component (for which the variable is to be retained in the model) is 3, and the prior standard deviation for the "spike" component (for which the variable is to be excluded from the model) is .0003. The sampler is run for 10 000 iterations, drawing from (16.20) through (16.22), and the first 200 simulations are discarded as the burn-in.

Posterior means for the β parameters were found to be 2.01, .258, $-.395$, .595, $-.0001$, and .002, which are close to the values actually used to generate the data. The values of γ_1, γ_2, and γ_3 at each iteration of the sampler were equal to unity, providing clear evidence that these variables belong in the model. This, of course, is consistent with the true data-generating process. Finally, the posterior means of γ_4 and γ_5 were .003 and .008, respectively, indicating rather strongly that these variables can be excluded from the model.

Exercise 16.8 (The least absolute shrinkage and selection operator (LASSO)) Consider the regression model

$$y = X\beta + \varepsilon \tag{16.23}$$

where y is an N-vector of dependent variables, X is an $N \times K$ matrix of explanatory variables, $\beta = (\beta_1, \ldots, \beta_K)'$ is a vector of regression coefficients and ε is an N-vector of errors. ε is $N\left(0, h^{-1}I\right)$ where $h = \sigma^{-2}$ is the precision of the error. In many cases, K can be large relative to N and it is even possible that $K > N$. The LASSO was developed as a frequentist shrinkage and variable selection method to deal with such cases in Tibshirani (1996). Whereas OLS estimates minimize the sum of squared residuals, the LASSO adds a penalty term which depends on the magnitude of the regression coefficients. Thus, LASSO estimates are chosen to minimize

$$(y - X\beta)'(y - X\beta) + \lambda \sum_{i=1}^{K} |\beta_i|,$$

where λ is a shrinkage parameter.

It turns out that LASSO estimates of regression coefficients can be given a Bayesian interpretation: they are equivalent to Bayesian posterior modes if independent Laplace priors are placed on the regression coefficients.

(a) Using the fact that the Laplace distribution can be written as a scale mixture of normals (see Exercise 15.3), derive a Gibbs sampler for carrying out Bayesian inference in this model. In particular, assume each regression coefficient has a prior (independent from the prior for the other regression coefficients) which can be written as

$$\beta_i | h, \tau_i^2 \sim N\left(0, h^{-1}\tau_i^2\right), \tag{16.24}$$

$$p(\tau_i^2|\lambda) \propto \exp\left(-\frac{\lambda\tau_i^2}{2}\right), \tag{16.25}$$

for $i = 1, \ldots, K$, so that τ_i^2 has an exponential prior distribution. It can be shown that this prior specification is equivalent to assuming a Laplace prior for the regression coefficients and λ has the same shrinkage interpretation as in the frequentist LASSO. To complete the model, assume that h has a non-informative prior, $p(h) \propto \frac{1}{h}$, and λ^2 has a gamma prior: $\lambda^2 \sim \gamma\left(\underline{\mu}_\lambda, \underline{\nu}_\lambda\right)$.

(b) Exercise 16.6 introduced and employed a cross-country growth data set. That data set contains information on GDP growth for $N = 72$ different countries and contains 41 explanatory variables as possible determinants of economic growth. Using your results from part (a), carry out an empirical exercise using this data set and produce estimates of all the parameters in the model.

Solution

(a) A Gibbs sampler can be constructed based on the following four posterior conditionals:

$$p\left(\beta|y, h, \tau^2, \lambda^2\right),$$
$$p\left(h|y, \beta, \tau^2, \lambda^2\right),$$
$$p\left(\tau^2|y, \beta, h, \lambda^2\right),$$
$$p\left(\lambda^2|y, \beta, h, \tau^2\right),$$

where $\tau^2 = \left(\tau_1^2, \ldots, \tau_K^2\right)'$. For the first two of these, standard results for the normal linear regression model with independent normal-gamma prior can be used (e.g., Koop 2003, pp. 60–62). That is, conditional on τ^2, (16.24) defines a normal prior for the regression coefficients with mean zero and prior covariance matrix

$$\underline{V} = h^{-1}D,$$

where D is a diagonal matrix with diagonal elements $d_i = \tau_i^2$ for $i = 1,\ldots,K$. Thus, $\beta|y,h,\tau,\lambda$ is $N\left(\overline{\beta},\overline{V}\right)$, where

$$\overline{\beta} = \left(X'X + D^{-1}\right)^{-1} X'y$$

and

$$\overline{V} = h^{-1}\left(X'X + D^{-1}\right)^{-1}.$$

Next we have $h|y,\beta,\tau,\lambda$ being $\gamma(\overline{s}^{-2},\overline{\nu})$, where

$$\overline{\nu} = N + K$$

and

$$\overline{s}^2 = \frac{(y - X\beta)'(y - X\beta) + \beta' D^{-1}\beta}{\overline{\nu}}.$$

To obtain $p\left(\tau^2|y,\beta,h,\lambda\right)$, let us return to the unconditional posterior:

$$p\left(\beta,h,\tau^2,\lambda^2|y\right) \propto L\left(\beta,h\right) p\left(\beta|h,\tau^2\right) p\left(h\right) p\left(\tau^2|\lambda^2\right) p\left(\lambda^2\right). \tag{16.26}$$

Note that the likelihood function, $L\left(\beta,h\right)$, does not depend on τ. The only places τ enters are in $p\left(\beta|h,\tau^2\right)$ and $p\left(\tau^2|\lambda^2\right)$. If we combine this fact with the prior independence assumptions in (16.24) and (16.25), it follows that the conditional posterior for the elements of τ are independent of one another with forms given by

$$p\left(\tau_i^2|y,\beta_i,h,\lambda^2\right) \propto p\left(\beta_i|h,\tau_i^2\right) p\left(\tau_i^2|\lambda^2\right).$$

Multiplying the normal pdf of $p\left(\beta_i|h,\tau_i^2\right)$ and the exponential pdf of $p\left(\tau_i^2|\lambda\right)$ yields a conditional posterior for τ_i^2 up to proportionality:

$$p\left(\tau_i^2|y,\beta_i,h,\lambda^2\right) \propto \frac{\exp\left\{-\frac{1}{2}\left(\frac{\beta_i^2 h}{\tau_i^2}\right) + \lambda^2\tau_i^2\right\}}{\left(\tau_i^2\right)^{\frac{1}{2}}}.$$

This density may look unfamiliar, but $\frac{1}{\tau_i^2}$ can be seen to have an inverse Gaussian distribution. The latter distribution, which we denote by $invGauss(a,b)$, is defined in Definition A.14. Standard algorithms exist for taking random draws from the inverse Gaussian (see, e.g., Exercise 15.3) and so it is straightforward to include it in a Gibbs sampling algorithm. In the present context, $p\left(\frac{1}{\tau_i^2}|y,\beta,h,\lambda\right)$ is $invGauss(\overline{c},\overline{d}_i)$ with

$$\overline{c} = \lambda^2$$

and

$$\overline{d}_i = \sqrt{\frac{\lambda^2}{h\beta_i^2}}.$$

Finally, (16.26) implies that the conditional posterior for λ^2 depends only on τ, and thus we can write

$$p\left(\lambda^2|y,\tau\right) \propto p\left(\tau^2|\lambda^2\right)p\left(\lambda^2\right).$$

Deriving this conditional posterior is straightforward since $p\left(\lambda^2\right)$ is a gamma pdf and $p\left(\tau^2|\lambda^2\right)$ is a product of exponential pdfs (and the exponential is a special case of a gamma distribution). Multiplying this product together, we have $p\left(\lambda^2|y,\tau\right)$ being a $\gamma(\overline{\mu}_\lambda, \overline{\nu}_\lambda)$ distribution with

$$\overline{\nu}_\lambda = \underline{\nu}_\lambda + 2K$$

and

$$\overline{\mu}_\lambda = \frac{\underline{\nu}_\lambda + 2K}{2\sum_{i=1}^{K}\tau_i^2 + \frac{\underline{\nu}_\lambda}{\underline{\mu}_\lambda}}.$$

(b) The cross-country growth data set has a dependent variable which is the average percentage growth in per capita GDP from 1960–1992. To carry out empirical work with this data set, we standardize all the explanatory variables (i.e., subtract off their means and divide by their standard deviations) so as to ensure they are all measured in the same units (i.e., regression coefficients can all be interpreted as measuring the effect of a one standard deviation change in an explanatory variable on the dependent variable). This can be important in the basic LASSO of this question since the assumption of a single parameter, λ, determining the distribution from which the shrinkage parameters for all the coefficients are drawn makes it desirable to have all coefficients being measured in the same units. More sophisticated versions of the LASSO can allow for more flexible types of shrinkage.

For the prior hyperparameters, we set $\underline{\mu}_\lambda = 2$ and $\underline{\nu}_\lambda = 1$ (although the reader may wish to experiment with different prior hyperparameter values). The Gibbs sampler described in part (a) is run for 10 000 burn-in draws followed by 100 000 included draws. Table 16.3 contains posterior means and standard deviations of the regression coefficients along with the posterior means of the shrinkage parameters, τ_i for $i = 1, \ldots, K$. To help gauge the estimated degree of shrinkage in the LASSO prior given in (16.24), remember that the prior standard deviation for a regression coefficient is $\sigma\tau_i$ and we find $E\left(\sigma|y\right) = 0.0082$. The posterior mean for τ_i is given in the table.

Results using the LASSO indicate that most of the 41 regression coefficients are being shrunk to be very close to zero. If we use a rule of thumb where posterior means which are two posterior standard deviations from zero are selected as indicating important explanatory variables, then the LASSO is selecting eight important explanatory variables. It can also be seen that the LASSO is doing a very good job at shrinking unimportant variables in the sense that their coefficients tend to be very small.

To explain in more detail what the LASSO is doing, consider two arbitrarily chosen coefficients (one on an explanatory variable found to be important, one on an unimportant variable). The LASSO prior for the coefficient on the variable GDP level in 1960 has a prior standard deviation of roughly 0.5 (i.e., if we replace the two parameters in $\sigma\tau_i$ by point estimates, then we obtain a value of roughly 0.5). This is a relatively non-informative prior which allocates most of its prior weight in the interval $[-1, 1]$. The estimate of the coefficient is large (-0.979) and many standard deviations away from zero. The OLS estimate of this coefficient is -1.50 so the LASSO prior is imposing some shrinkage, but not much on this coefficient. In contrast, consider the variable Higher education enrollment. The LASSO prior implies a standard deviation of roughly 10^{-6}, implying that almost all of the prior probability for this coefficient is in a small interval near zero. The coefficient on this variable is commensurately small (-7×10^{-5}). Thus, the LASSO can be seen to be automatically choosing a prior for each coefficient, deciding to shrink some of them to be nearly zero but letting others be estimated in a relatively unrestricted fashion.

Exercise 16.9 (Non-parametric regression via variable selection: Smith and Kohn (1996)) Consider a non-parametric regression model of the form

$$y_i = f(x_i) + \epsilon_i, \quad \epsilon_i \overset{iid}{\sim} N(0, \sigma^2), \tag{16.27}$$

$i = 1, 2, \ldots, N$. Suppose that $f(x)$ can be written as a cubic regression spline (e.g., Poirier 1973),

$$f(x) = \delta_0 + \delta_1 x + \delta_2 x^2 + \sum_{j=3}^{J} \delta_j (x - \tau_{j-2})_+^3 = X\delta, \tag{16.28}$$

where $z_+ \equiv \max\{0, z\}$ and $\{\tau_j\}_{j=1}^{J-2}$ denote a collection of known potential *knot* points placed in the interior of x with $\tau_j < \tau_{j+1}$. Note that in this exercise, we do not consider the case where the knot points themselves are unknown (either in number or location), but instead we suppose that f can be approximated reasonably accurately by a large number of potential knot points placed throughout the support of x. See Chib (1998) and Koop and Potter (2005) for related discussion, and Denison, Holmes, Mallick, and Smith (2002) for a more general treatment of the knot points. Alternate approaches to non-parametric regression in various models can be found in, e.g., Koop (2003), Koop and Poirier (2004), Chib (2006), and Koop and Tobias (2006).

Smith and Kohn (1996) considered the problem of estimation of f as a problem of variable selection and proceeded in a manner similar to the SSVS approach of George and McCulloch (1993) described in Exercise 16.7. To this end, let $\theta = [\theta_1 \ \theta_2 \ \cdots \ \theta_{J+1}]$ be an *indicator vector* denoting the columns of X that are to be retained in the model (i.e., $\theta_k = 1$ denotes that the kth column is to be kept and $\theta_k = 0$ denotes that the kth column is to be excluded), and define X_θ as the collection of those columns of X for which the corresponding elements of θ equal one. Let δ_θ denote the set of slope parameters associated with X_θ.

Specify a g-prior for the slope parameters of the form

$$\delta_\theta | g, \theta, \sigma^2 \sim N[0, g^{-1}\sigma^2 (X_\theta' X_\theta)^{-1}], \tag{16.29}$$

Table 16.3: Posterior results using LASSO prior.

Explanatory variable	$E(\tau_i\|y)$	$E(\beta_i\|y)$	$\sqrt{\text{Var}(\beta_i\|y)}$
Primary school enrollment	0.354	0.374	0.185
Life expectancy	0.632	0.953	0.197
GDP level in 1960	0.643	−0.979	0.140
Fraction GDP in mining	0.307	0.261	0.075
Degree of capitalism	0.038	0.027	0.069
No. years open economy	0.454	0.514	0.087
% pop. speaking English	3×10^{-4}	-2×10^{-5}	0.002
% pop. speaking foreign lang.	0.111	0.081	0.098
Exchange rate distortions	6×10^{-4}	-2×10^{-4}	0.005
Equipment investment	0.465	0.537	0.087
Non-equipment investment	0.050	0.037	0.082
Std. dev. of black market premium	3×10^{-4}	-3×10^{-5}	0.002
Outward orientation	4×10^{-4}	-5×10^{-5}	0.003
Black market premium	4×10^{-4}	-1×10^{-5}	0.002
Area	4×10^{-4}	7×10^{-5}	0.001
Latin America	0.003	0.001	0.013
Sub-Saharan Africa	3×10^{-4}	-5×10^{-5}	0.004
Higher education enrollment	4×10^{-4}	-7×10^{-5}	0.003
Public education share	2×10^{-4}	1×10^{-5}	0.001
Revolutions and coups	0.001	2×10^{-4}	0.003
War	4×10^{-4}	9×10^{-5}	0.001
Political rights	4×10^{-4}	3×10^{-5}	0.002
Civil liberties	3×10^{-4}	5×10^{-5}	0.002
Latitude	7×10^{-4}	2×10^{-4}	0.004
Age	2×10^{-4}	1×10^{-5}	0.001
British colony	3×10^{-4}	4×10^{-5}	0.001
Fraction Buddhist	0.307	0.266	0.084
Fraction Catholic	0.079	0.062	0.112
Fraction Confucian	0.468	0.566	0.054
Ethnolinguistic fractionalization	0.001	3×10^{-4}	0.004
French colony	0.005	0.003	0.017
Fraction Hindu	0.002	9×10^{-4}	0.008
Fraction Jewish	4×10^{-4}	1×10^{-4}	0.002
Fraction Muslim	0.473	0.554	0.084
Primary exports	4×10^{-4}	-2×10^{-5}	0.003
Fraction Protestant	0.001	-9×10^{-4}	0.013
Rule of law	0.001	7×10^{-4}	0.009
Spanish colony	0.004	0.003	0.017
Population growth	0.001	3×10^{-4}	0.005
Ratio workers to population	3×10^{-4}	5×10^{-5}	0.001
Size of labor force	0.150	0.106	0.095

and also specify the following priors:

$$p(\sigma^2) \propto 1/\sigma^2, \tag{16.30}$$

$$\theta|\pi = \prod_{j=1}^{J+1} \pi_j^{\theta_j}(1-\pi_j)^{1-\theta_j}. \tag{16.31}$$

For simplicity throughout the remainder of this exercise, assume that $\pi_j = 1/2$ for all j, so that all models are equally likely *a priori*.

(a) Describe a posterior simulator for fitting this non-parametric regression model.

(b) Generate 1500 observations from the following regression model:

$$y_i = 2 + .1x_i - .15x_i^2 + \sin(x_i) + \epsilon_i, \tag{16.32}$$

where the x_i are independently generated from a uniform distribution on $[-2, 2]$ and $\epsilon_i \stackrel{iid}{\sim} N(0, .15)$.

Apply the algorithm derived in part (a) to fit the model. In our solution to this portion of the exercise, we set $g = 1/N = (1500)^{-1}$ and $J + 1 = 12$ (so that there are 12 "optional" variables in total and 9 knot points placed throughout the support of x). We also chose to spread these knots evenly over the interval $[-1.75, 1.75]$. Compare your estimated results to the function used to generate the data.

Solution

(a) To fit this model we directly sample from the joint posterior via the method of composition. Specifically, we sample, in order, from $\theta|y$, $\sigma^2|\theta, y$, and finally $\delta_\theta|\theta, \sigma^2, y$.

Given θ, the regression model takes the form

$$y = X_\theta \delta_\theta + \epsilon.$$

First, note that $y|\theta, \sigma^2$ can be obtained by marginalizing the conditional density $y|\theta, \delta_\theta, \sigma^2$ implied here over the conditional prior for δ_θ. Doing this, we obtain

$$y|\theta, \sigma^2 \sim N\left[0, \sigma^2\left(I_N + g^{-1}X_\theta(X_\theta' X_\theta)^{-1}X_\theta'\right)\right]. \tag{16.33}$$

Using properties of the inverse of a matrix sum of the form $(A + BCD)^{-1}$ (see, e.g., Poirier 1995, p. 627) and an analogous property for a determinant of a similar form, one can show that

$$\begin{aligned}(I_N + g^{-1}X_\theta(X_\theta' X_\theta)^{-1}X_\theta')^{-1} &= I_N - g^{-1}X_\theta\left[g^{-1}X_\theta' X_\theta + X_\theta' X_\theta\right]^{-1}X_\theta' \\ &= I_N - [1/(1+g)]X_\theta(X_\theta' X_\theta)^{-1}X_\theta'\end{aligned}$$

and

$$\begin{aligned}\left|I_N + g^{-1}X_\theta(X_\theta' X_\theta)^{-1}X_\theta'\right| &= |I_N|\left|(X_\theta' X_\theta)^{-1}\right|\left|X_\theta' X_\theta + g^{-1}X_\theta' X_\theta\right| \\ &= (1+g^{-1})^{q_\theta},\end{aligned}$$

where q_θ denotes the number of columns in X_θ. Putting these together, we can write (16.33) as

$$y|\theta, \sigma^2 \propto (1+g^{-1})^{-q_\theta/2} \exp\left(-[1/(2\sigma^2)]y'[I_N - [1/(1+g)]X_\theta(X_\theta' X_\theta)^{-1}X_\theta']y\right). \tag{16.34}$$

To obtain the density $y|\theta$, we must marginalize the conditional density in (16.34) over the prior for σ^2 in (16.30):

$$\begin{aligned} p(y|\theta) &= \int_0^\infty p(y|\theta, \sigma^2)(1/\sigma^2)\, d\sigma^2 \\ &= (1+g^{-1})^{-q_\theta/2} \\ &\quad \times \int_0^\infty (\sigma^2)^{-(N/2+1)} \exp\left(-[1/(2\sigma^2)]y'[I_N - [1/(1+g)]X_\theta(X_\theta' X_\theta)^{-1}X_\theta']y\right) d\sigma^2. \end{aligned}$$

We recognize this integral as the kernel of an

$$IG[N/2, 2(y'[I_N - [1/(1+g)]X_\theta(X_\theta' X_\theta)^{-1}X_\theta']y)^{-1}]$$

density. Using the known form of the normalizing constant of the inverted gamma, and noting that $\pi_j = 1/2$ implies $p(\theta|y) \propto p(y|\theta)$, we obtain

$$p(\theta|y) \propto (1+g^{-1})^{-q_\theta/2}[y'y - [1/(1+g)]y'X_\theta(X_\theta' X_\theta)^{-1}X_\theta' y]^{-N/2}. \tag{16.35}$$

Though this density is not of a standard form, θ is discrete valued. Thus we can calculate the (unnormalized) ordinates for every possible value of θ and then normalize the density to make it proper. This defines the first conditional needed for our posterior simulator.

For the second conditional, we have

$$\begin{aligned} p(\sigma^2|\theta, y) &\propto p(y|\theta, \sigma^2)p(\sigma^2) \\ &= (\sigma^2)^{-[(N/2)+1]} \exp\left(-[1/(2\sigma^2)]y'[I_N - [1/(1+g)]X_\theta(X_\theta' X_\theta)^{-1}X_\theta']y\right), \end{aligned}$$

where the last line follows from our preceding derivation of $y|\sigma^2, \theta$. We recognize this as the following inverted gamma density:

$$\sigma^2|\theta, y \sim IG\left(\frac{N}{2}, 2\left[y'(I_N - [1/(1+g)]X_\theta(X_\theta' X_\theta)^{-1}X_\theta')y\right]^{-1}\right). \tag{16.36}$$

Finally, the complete conditional for δ_θ is as follows:

$$\delta_\theta|\theta, \sigma^2, y \sim N\left([1/(1+g)](X_\theta' X_\theta)^{-1}X_\theta' y, \sigma^2[1/(1+g)](X_\theta' X_\theta)^{-1}\right). \tag{16.37}$$

The posterior simulator is implemented by sampling from $\theta|y$, $\sigma^2|\theta, y$, and $\delta_\theta|\sigma^2, \theta, y$ in (16.35), (16.36), and (16.37), respectively, conditioning on the most recent values of the parameters drawn from the sampler.

(b) We generate 1500 observations as described in part (b) of this exercise. We take 100 draws from the posterior distribution described in part (a). For each draw, we calculate our model's prediction of $f(x)$ over a discrete grid of points throughout the $[-2, 2]$ support.

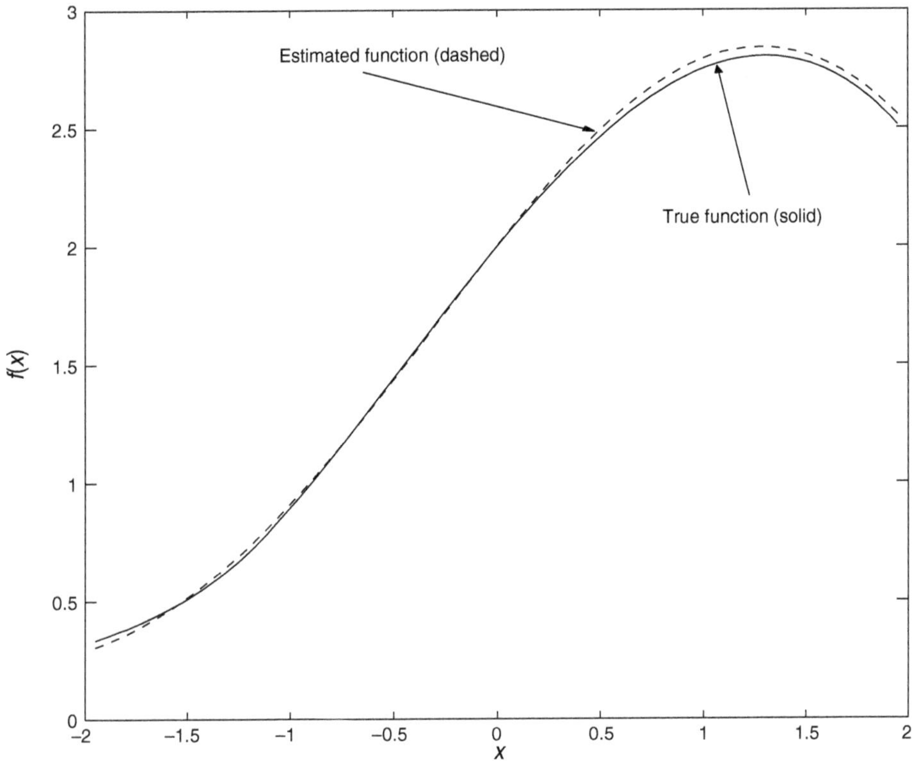

Figure 16.1. "True" and estimated regression functions.

Our final point estimate of f is pieced together as the posterior means of the 100 collected values at each grid point. In Figure 16.1 we present this posterior mean together with the true value of f that was used to generate the data. As one can see, the algorithm performs quite well at recovering the shape of the regression function.

17

Univariate Time Series Methods

The field of time series econometrics is an enormous one and it is difficult to do it justice in only a few chapters. There is a large range of models used with time series data. For univariate time series we have models in the autoregressive moving average (ARMA) class, state space models, models of conditional volatility in the autoregressive conditional heteroscedastic (ARCH) class, and many more. For multivariate time series data, vector autorogressive (VAR) models are the most popular, but many others exist. For both univariate and multivariate specifications there is a growing interest in non-linear alternatives involving thresholds, regime switching, or structural breaks. In addition, new issues arise with time series data such as those relating to the presence of non-stationary data (i.e., unit roots and cointegration). In frequentist econometrics, the presence of unit roots and cointegration cause problems since the asymptotic theory underlying, e.g., estimators and test statistics becomes quite complicated. Bayesian econometrics, which conditions upon the observed data, does not run into these problems. However, subtle issues relating to prior elicitation and identification arise when unit root and cointegration issues are relevant. In this and subsequent chapters, we offer a selection of questions to give the reader a flavor of the Bayesian approach to time series methods. The reader interested in learning more about Bayesian time series methods is referred to Bauwens, Lubrano, and Richard (1999) and Früwirth-Schnatter (2006). We also remind the reader that several of the exercises in Chapter 12 involved time series data: Exercises 12.7 and 12.10 relate to two different structural break models, Exercise 12.15 develops Bayesian methods for the regression model with autocorrelated errors, and Exercise 12.16 describes posterior simulation in a model with moving average errors.

In the present chapter we focus on univariate time series models. The first exercise provides an example of how an autoregressive model can be used in a macroeconomic application. Subsequent exercises show how Bayesian inference is done using various threshold autoregressive (TAR) models. These are a class of popular non-linear time series models which allows for the dynamic properties of a time series to change over time (e.g., to vary over the business cycle).

The remaining exercises in the chapter relate to non-stationary time series. It is worth noting that issues relating to non-stationary time series variables (e.g., unit roots and cointegration) play a large role in frequentist time series econometrics, but a much smaller role in Bayesian econometrics. For the Bayesian, in one sense, there is nothing new in the Bayesian treatment of non-stationary variables. For instance, unit root issues are often addressed in the context of AR (or ARMA) models or the state space models of the next chapter. Cointegration issues are often addressed using restricted versions of VARs (see Chapter 20). In Chapters 12 and 20 we present derivations for AR and VAR models, and these derivations are not dependent on the variables being stationary. However, with non-stationary data, some important contrasts exist between Bayesian and frequentist approaches and some important issues of prior elicitation arise. This considerations motivate the exercises in the latter half of this chapter.

Exercise 17.5, which is based on the classic paper of Sims and Uhlig (1991), illustrates some of the differences between Bayesian and frequentist results with unit root variables. Exercise 17.5 derives the simple finite sample posterior distribution for the AR(1) model with AR coefficient θ. For the reader with no frequentist training in time series, we note that it contrasts sharply with the sampling distribution of the maximum likelihood estimator (MLE). The latter is quite complicated and its asymptotic distribution differs markedly depending on whether $\theta < 1$, $\theta = 1$, or $\theta > 1$. Exercise 17.5 reproduces the enlightening Monte Carlo experiment of Sims and Uhlig (1991) which demonstrates the differences between posterior and sampling distributions in finite samples. These differences persist asymptotically because the convergence of the asymptotic sampling distribution is not uniform (see Kwan 1998). Note also that adding a constant or trend complicates the asymptotic sampling distribution in a non-trivial manner. Most of the remaining questions (see Exercises 17.6, 17.7, and 17.8) discuss various approaches to prior elicitation in the presence of unit roots.

An issue which arises in time series models is the treatment of initial conditions. For instance, in an AR(1) model with data from $t = 1, \ldots, T$, y_0 will appear in the likelihood function. In this chapter we ignore this issue by simply using data from $t = 2, \ldots, T$ and using the (observed) y_1 as the initial condition. With non-stationary time series, treatment of initial conditions can be more important. It is still common to use the approximate (or conditional) likelihood function built from the density $p(y_1, \ldots, y_T|\theta, y_0)$. However, for stationary models it is also possible to obtain the exact likelihood function obtained from the joint density of the sample and the initial condition. Assuming stationarity, we have $y_0 \sim N\left(0, \frac{\sigma^2}{1-\theta^2}\right)$, where σ^2 is the error variance, but if a unit root is present ($\theta = 1$) the variance of this initial condition is undefined. The conditional (on y_0) approach lends itself to analytical results (when using a conjugate prior) and it will be adopted in the following exercises. The exact likelihood function introduces a non-linearity in the autoregressive coefficient and relies on the assumed stationarity of the process. If the initial conditions bring in a lot of information in the likelihood function, they may also produce pathologies when the AR coefficient is near the unit root. The same holds for the constant term. See Bauwens, Lubrano, and Richard (1999, pp. 169–174) for further details.

The reader interested in exploring any of these issues is referred to Bauwens, Lubrano, and Richard (1999). Chapter 6 provides an excellent summary of issues relating to unit roots; cointegration is discussed in Chapter 20. Koop, Strachan, van Dijk, and Villani (2006) surveyed the Bayesian cointegration literature. A few papers that illustrate some of the issues which arise with unit roots include Phillips (1991), Schotman (1994), Sims (1988), and Sims and Uhlig (1991).

Exercise 17.1 (Using the AR(*p*) model to understand the properties of a series) This exercise is based on Geweke (1988b). Let y_t for $t = 1, \dots, T$ indicate observations on a time series variable. y_t is assumed to follow an AR(p) process:

$$y_t = \beta_0 + \beta_1 y_{t-1} + \cdots + \beta_p y_{t-p} + \epsilon_t,$$

where ϵ_t is $iid\ N\left(0, h^{-1}\right)$. Many important properties of y_t depend on the roots of the polynomial $1 - \sum_{i=1}^{p} \beta_i z^i$, which we will denote by r_i for $i = 1, \dots, p$. Geweke (1988b) lets y_t be the log of real GDP, sets $p = 3$, and, for this choice, focuses on the features of interest: $C = \{\beta : \text{two of } r_i \text{ are complex}\}$ and $D = \{\beta : \min|r_i| < 1\}$, where $\beta = (\beta_0, \beta_1, \beta_2, \beta_3)'$. Note that C and D are regions whose bounds are complicated non-linear functions of β_1, β_2, and β_3. If the AR coefficients lie in the region defined by C then real GDP exhibits an oscillatory response to a shock, and if they lie in D then y_t exhibits an explosive response to a shock.

(a) Assuming a prior of the form

$$p\left(\beta_0, \dots, \beta_p, h\right) \propto \frac{1}{h}, \tag{17.1}$$

derive the posterior for β. To simplify things, you may ignore the (minor) complications relating to the treatment of initial conditions. Thus, assume the dependent variable is $y = (y_{p+1}, \dots, y_T)'$ and treat $y_1, \dots, y_p$ as fixed initial conditions.

(b) Using an appropriate data set (e.g., the US real GDP data set provided on the website associated with this book), write a program which calculates the posterior means and standard deviations of β and $\min|r_i|$.

(c) Extend the program of part (b) to calculate the probability that y_t is oscillatory (i.e., $\Pr\left(\beta \in C|y\right)$), the probability that y_t is explosive (i.e., $\Pr\left(\beta \in D|Data\right)$) and calculate these probabilities using your data set.

Solution

(a) This model can be written as a linear regression model in matrix notation as

$$y = X\beta + \epsilon,$$

where $\epsilon = (\epsilon_{p+1}, \ldots, \epsilon_N)'$ and X is the $(T-p) \times (p+1)$ matrix containing an intercept and p lags of the dependent variable. For instance, if $p = 3$,

$$X = \begin{bmatrix} 1 & y_3 & y_2 & y_1 \\ \vdots & \vdots & \vdots & \vdots \\ 1 & y_{T-1} & y_{T-2} & y_{T-3} \end{bmatrix}.$$

Written in this way, it can be seen that (if we condition on the initial observations), the AR(p) model is simply the normal linear regression model. The easiest way to answer this exercise is to note that the prior in (17.1) is the standard non-informative prior for the normal linear regression model and is a limiting case of the natural conjugate prior. Thus, the answer to this exercise is a special case of the answer to Exercise 10.1. To be precise, multiplying the normal linear regression model likelihood in (10.4) by the prior in (17.1) yields the relevant posterior. Manipulations exactly analogous to the solution to Exercise 10.1 can be done to confirm that the posterior for β and h is $NG\left(\overline{\beta}, \overline{Q}, \overline{s}^{-2}, \overline{\nu}\right)$, where $\overline{\nu} = T$,

$$\overline{Q} = \left(X'X\right)^{-1},$$
$$\overline{\beta} = \left(X'X\right)^{-1} X'y,$$

and $\overline{\nu s}^2$ are the standard OLS residuals (denoted SSE in the introductory material of Chapter 10).

Using the properties of the normal-gamma distribution (see Theorem A.8), it follows that the marginal posterior for β is multivariate t:

$$\beta|y \sim t\left(\overline{\beta}, \overline{s}^2\overline{Q}, \overline{\nu}\right). \tag{17.2}$$

(b) From part (a), the posterior for β has a convenient form, and means and standard deviations can be calculated using analytical formulae based on (17.2). That is, using the properties of the t distribution, we have $E\left(\beta|y\right) = \overline{\beta}$ and $\text{Var}\left(\beta|y\right) = \frac{\overline{\nu s}^2}{\overline{\nu}-2}\overline{Q}$. Note that $\min|r_i|$ is a complicated non-linear function of β and no analytical results exist for its posterior mean and variance. However, Monte Carlo integration (see Exercise 11.3) can be done by randomly drawing from (17.2) using a function to calculate the solutions to $1 - \sum_{i=1}^{p} \beta_i z^i = 0$ and, from these, evaluating $\min|r_i|$ at each of the draws. This will produce a random sample from the posterior of $\min|r_i|$ which can be used to calculate its posterior mean and standard deviation (or any other function of its posterior). A program which does this is available on the website associated with this book.

Using the log of the quarterly US real GDP series provided on the website, which runs from 1947Q1 through 2005Q2, we obtain the results in Table 17.1. The Monte Carlo integration program was run for 10 000 replications.

Table 17.1: Posterior results for AR(3) model.

Parameter	Mean	Std. dev.
β_0	0.010	0.004
β_1	1.300	0.066
β_2	−0.196	0.108
β_3	−0.104	0.066
$\min\lvert r_i\rvert$	1.002	0.002

(c) $\Pr(\beta \in C|y)$ and $\Pr(\beta \in D|Data)$ can also be calculated in the Monte Carlo integration program. Formally, since $\Pr(\beta \in C|y) = E[I(\beta \in C|y)]$ and $\Pr(\beta \in D|y) = E[I(\beta \in D|y)]$, where $I(.)$ is the indicator function, the probabilities can be written as expected values of functions of the model parameters. In our computer code, calculating these expected values is equivalent to simply calculating the proportion of draws from the posterior which are in C (or D). Our Monte Carlo integration program calculates $\Pr(\beta \in C|y) = 0.021$ and $\Pr(\beta \in D|y) = 0.132$. Thus, it is very unlikely that real GDP exhibits oscillatory behavior and only slightly more likely that it is explosive.

Exercise 17.2 (The threshold autoregressive model) Dynamics of many important macroeconomic variables can potentially vary over the business cycle. This has motivated the development of many models where different autoregressive representations apply in different regimes. Threshold autoregressive (TAR) models are a class of simple and popular regime-switching models. Potter (1995) provides an early exposition of these models in macroeconomics, and Geweke and Terui (1993) is an early Bayesian treatment. This exercise asks you to derive Bayesian methods for a simple variant of a TAR model.

Consider a two-regime TAR for a time series variable y_t for $t = p+1, \ldots, T$ (where $t = 1, \ldots, p$ are used as initial conditions):

$$\begin{aligned} y_t &= \beta_{10} + \beta_{11} y_{t-1} + \cdots + \beta_{1p} y_{t-p} + \epsilon_t \text{ if } y_{t-1} \leq \tau, \\ y_t &= \beta_{20} + \beta_{21} y_{t-1} + \cdots + \beta_{2p} y_{t-p} + \epsilon_t \text{ if } y_{t-1} > \tau, \end{aligned} \tag{17.3}$$

where ϵ_t is $iid\ N(0, h^{-1})$. We will use the notation $\beta = (\beta_1', \beta_2')'$, where

$$\beta_j = (\beta_{j0}, \beta_{j1}, \ldots, \beta_{jp})', \quad j = 1, 2.$$

For all parts of this question, you may proceed conditionally on the first p observations and, thus, ignore the (minor) complications caused by initial conditions.

(a) Assume that τ is known (e.g., $\tau = 0$) and normal-gamma priors are used (i.e., the joint prior for β and h is $NG(\underline{\beta}, \underline{Q}, \underline{s}^{-2}, \underline{\nu})$); derive the posterior for the model defined by (17.3).

(b) Write a program and carry out Bayesian inference in the TAR model of part (a) for a real GDP growth rate series using a prior of your choice.

(c) Repeat parts (a) and (b) assuming that τ is an unknown parameter.

Solution

(a) The solution to this question follows immediately from noting that the TAR with known τ can be written as a normal linear regression model. That is, analogously to the solution to Exercise 17.1(a), we can write the TAR as

$$y = X\beta + \epsilon,$$

where $y = (y_{p+1}, \ldots, y_T)'$, $\epsilon = (\epsilon_{p+1}, \ldots, \epsilon_N)'$, and X is the $(T-p) \times 2(p+1)$ matrix with tth row given by $[D_t, D_t y_{t-1}, \ldots, D_t y_{t-p}, (1-D_t), (1-D_t) y_{t-1}, \ldots, (1-D_t) y_{t-p}]$, where D_t is a dummy variable which equals 1 if $y_{t-1} \leq \tau$ and equals 0 if $y_{t-1} > \tau$. Thus, we can immediately use the results from Exercise 10.1 to find that the joint posterior for β and h is $NG\left(\overline{\beta}, \overline{Q}, \overline{s}^{-2}, \overline{\nu}\right)$, where $\overline{\nu} = T - p + \underline{\nu}$,

$$\overline{Q} = \left(\underline{Q}^{-1} + X'X\right)^{-1},$$
$$\overline{\beta} = \overline{Q}\left(\underline{Q}^{-1}\underline{\beta} + X'X\widehat{\beta}\right),$$

and

$$\overline{s}^2 = \frac{\underline{\nu}\underline{s}^2 + SSE + \left(\widehat{\beta} - \underline{\beta}\right)' X'X\overline{Q}\underline{Q}^{-1}\left(\widehat{\beta} - \underline{\beta}\right)}{\overline{\nu}}.$$

Note that, in the preceding equation, we are using the same notation defined at the beginning of Chapter 10 where $\widehat{\beta}$ is the standard OLS estimate and SSE the accompanying sum of squared residuals.

(b) A MATLAB program which provides the solution to this part of the exercise is available on the website associated with this book. The basic structure of this program is that it loads in the data, specifies prior hyperparameters, then evaluates the formulae provided in the solution to part (a). For US real GDP growth from 1947Q2 through 2005Q2, we obtain the results shown in Table 17.2 relating to the posteriors of β and $\sigma^2 = \frac{1}{h}$. We set $p = 2$ and use the non-informative variant of the normal-gamma prior. Furthermore, we set τ to the mean of y_{t-1} and thus the two regimes can be interpreted as "below average growth" and "above average growth" regimes.

Table 17.2: Posterior results for TAR model.

Parameter	Mean	Std. dev.
β_{10}	0.572	0.100
β_{11}	0.289	0.129
β_{12}	0.008	0.092
β_{20}	0.213	0.232
β_{21}	0.394	0.130
β_{22}	0.218	0.093
σ^2	0.879	0.083

(c) When τ is treated as an unknown parameter, we need methods of working with the posterior $p(\beta, h, \tau|y)$. This can be done by noting that the rules of conditional probability imply that

$$p(\beta, h, \tau|y) = p(\beta, h|\tau, y)\, p(\tau|y).$$

The first component on the right-hand side of this equation, $p(\beta, h|\tau, y)$, can be analyzed using the methods of part (a). That is, conditioning upon τ is equivalent to assuming it known, and the answer to part (a) shows how to analyze the posterior for β and h for known τ. Hence, we can focus on the second component: $p(\tau|y)$. But, the intuition that conditioning on τ is equivalent to assuming it known can be carried further to provide us with a way of obtaining $p(\tau|y)$. Note first that, for a given value for τ, the marginal likelihood can be calculated in the standard way,

$$p(y|\tau) = \iint L(\beta, h|\tau)\, p(\beta, h|\tau)\, d\beta dh, \tag{17.4}$$

where $L(\beta, h|\tau)$ is the likelihood function for a given value of τ. However, as we have seen from part (a), the TAR model (conditional on τ) is simply a normal linear regression model. Thus, using the normal-gamma natural conjugate prior, standard textbook expressions exist for (17.4) – conditional on τ (see, e.g., Exercise 10.4; Koop 2003, p. 41; Poirier 1995, p. 543). If we use the notation from the solution to part (a), then we can draw on these earlier derivations to write (17.4) as

$$p(y|\tau) = \frac{\Gamma\left(\frac{\overline{\nu}}{2}\right)\left(\underline{\nu}\underline{s}^2\right)^{\frac{\underline{\nu}}{2}}}{\Gamma\left(\frac{\underline{\nu}}{2}\right)\pi^{\frac{T-p}{2}}}\left(\frac{|\overline{Q}|}{|\underline{Q}|}\right)^{\frac{1}{2}}\left(\overline{\nu}\overline{s}^2\right)^{-\frac{\overline{\nu}}{2}}, \tag{17.5}$$

although we stress that X depends on τ (and, thus, so will $\overline{Q}$ and $\overline{s}^2$) and, hence, (17.5) will be different for every possible value of τ.

Since Bayes' theorem implies that

$$p(\tau|y) \propto p(y|\tau)\, p(\tau), \tag{17.6}$$

we can combine (17.5) with a prior for τ in order to obtain the marginal posterior $p(\tau|y)$. Of course, any prior for τ can be used. A common choice is a restricted non-informative one. This treats every possible value for τ as, *a priori*, equally likely, which implies that each regime contains a minimum number of observations (e.g., 15% of the observations).

Note that, even though y_{t-1} is a continuous variable, τ will be a discrete random variable since there are a finite number of ways of dividing a given data set into two regimes. Hence, in practice, posterior inference in the TAR with an unknown threshold can be performed by evaluating (17.5) and, thus, (17.6) for every allowable threshold value. This provides us with $p(\tau|y)$. If interest centers on β and/or h, then we can obtain their posterior properties by taking a weighted average over all possible thresholds, using $p(\tau|y)$ as weights. The validity of this procedure follows from the fact that, if $\tau \in \{\tau_1, \ldots, \tau_{T^*}\}$ denotes the set of possible threshold values, then

$$p(\beta, h|y) = \sum_{i=1}^{T^*} p(\beta, h|\tau = \tau_i, y) \, p(\tau = \tau_i|y) .$$

Thus, insofar as we are willing to use the normal-gamma natural conjugate prior, Bayesian inference in the TAR model can be performed using only textbook analytical results for the normal linear regression model and no posterior simulation is required.

A MATLAB program which extends the program in part (b) to allow for an unknown threshold is provided on the website associated with this book. Here we note one aspect of our program which is commonly used with regime-switching models. The assumption about the errors implies that we have added enough lags to make the errors independent of one another. Thus, $y_t|X_t, \beta, h$ and $y_s|X_s, \beta, h$ are independent of one another for $t \neq s$. This implies that the ordering of rows in our regression model is irrelevant. Thus, we can order all our variables (dependent and explanatory variables) by y_{t-1} without changing the posterior. That is, variables can be ordered so that the first observation of all variables is the one with the lowest value for GDP growth last quarter, the second observation has the second highest value for GDP growth last quarter, etc. If we order our data in this way, then the TAR is equivalent to a structural break (also called changepoint) model (see Exercises 12.7 and 12.10). Such an ordering makes the step "evaluate (17.5) for every allowable threshold" particularly easy and draws out the links between threshold models and structural break models (i.e., a structural break model is a TAR model with the condition $y_{t-1} \leq \tau$ replaced with $t \leq \tau$).

Posterior properties of β and σ^2, using the US real GDP growth data, are provided in Table 17.3. Figure 17.1 plots the posterior of τ. Since we are calculating marginal likelihoods, an informative prior is required. We use a weakly informative prior which reflects our belief that AR coefficients are likely to be well within the stationary region and the error variance is likely to be approximately 1 (since our data is measured as a percentage). However, we are quite uncertain about these prior means and, hence, attach moderately large prior variances to them. Prior hyperparameter values consistent with these beliefs are $\underline{\beta} = 0$, $\underline{Q} = .25I$, $\underline{s}^2 = 1$, and $\underline{\nu} = 5$. In a serious empirical study, the researcher would likely elicit the prior in a more sophisticated manner and/or carry out a prior sensitivity analysis. The posterior properties of β and h are not that different from those found in part (b), despite the fact that we are now averaging over all the thresholds (rather than selecting a single value for the threshold and treating it as known). However, the posterior for the thresholds (see Figure 17.1) is very irregular. Appreciable posterior probability is found for many of the possible thresholds. The posterior mode is roughly the same as the average quarterly growth rate of GDP (0.85%). This threshold value would divide the data into a "below average growth" regime and an "above average growth" regime, as was done in part (a). But many other threshold values also receive some posterior support from the data.

Table 17.3: Posterior results for TAR model with unknown threshold.

Parameter	Mean	Std. dev.
β_{10}	0.542	0.119
β_{11}	0.269	0.139
β_{12}	0.373	0.101
β_{20}	0.249	0.242
β_{21}	0.384	0.127
β_{22}	0.196	0.100
σ^2	0.896	0.083

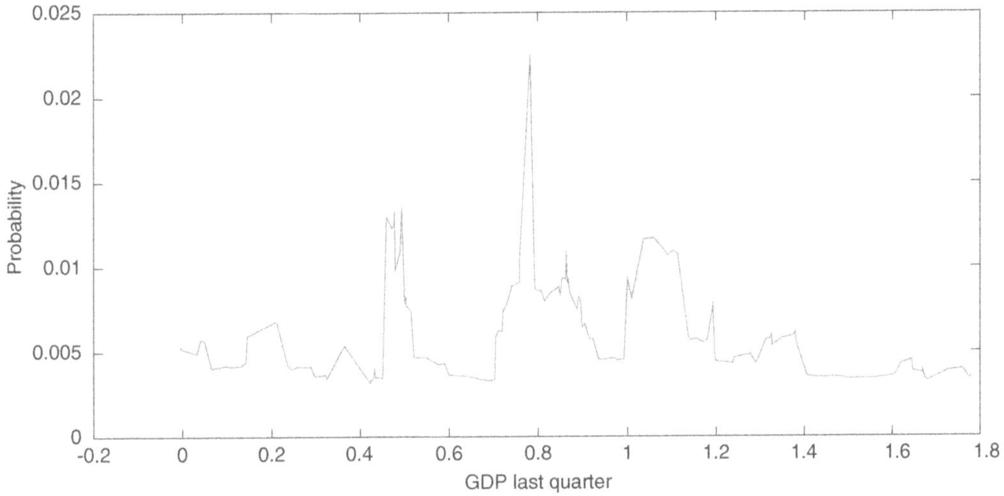

Figure 17.1. Posterior distribution of the threshold parameter τ.

Exercise 17.3 (Extensions of the basic threshold autoregressive model I: Other threshold triggers) There are many extensions of the TAR model which have been found useful in empirical work. In Exercise 17.2, we assumed that the first lag of the dependent variable (last quarter's GDP growth) triggered the regime switch. However, in general, it might be another variable, z, that is the *threshold trigger* and it may take longer than one period to induce the regime switch. Thus, we use the same assumptions and definitions as in Exercise 17.2, except we replace (17.3) by

$$\begin{aligned} y_t &= \beta_{10} + \beta_{11} y_{t-1} + \cdots + \beta_{1p} y_{t-p} + \epsilon_t \text{ if } z_{t-d} \leq \tau, \\ y_t &= \beta_{20} + \beta_{21} y_{t-1} + \cdots + \beta_{2p} y_{t-p} + \epsilon_t \text{ if } z_{t-d} > \tau, \end{aligned} \tag{17.7}$$

where d is the *delay parameter* and z_{t-d} is either an exogenous variable or a function of the lags of the dependent variable.

(a) Assume that d is an unknown parameter with a non-informative prior over $1, \ldots, p$ (i.e., $\Pr(d = i) = \frac{1}{p}$ for $i = 1, \ldots, p$) and that normal-gamma priors are used (i.e., the joint prior for β and h is $NG\left(\underline{\beta}, \underline{Q}, \underline{s}^{-2}, \underline{\nu}\right)$); derive the posterior for the model defined by (17.7).
(b) Using an appropriate data set (e.g., the real GDP growth data set used for the previous question), write a program and carry out Bayesian inference for this model using your results from part (a). Set $p = 4$ and

$$z_{t-d} = \frac{\sum_{d=1}^{p} y_{t-d}}{d},$$

so that (if you are using quarterly real GDP growth data) the threshold trigger is average GDP growth over the last d quarters.

Solution
(a) The solution to this exercise is a straightforward extension of the solution to Exercise 17.2 parts (a) and (c). That is, it follows immediately from noting that, if we condition on τ and d, then this TAR model can be written as a normal linear regression model. Note that, since z_{t-d} is either exogenous or a function of lags of the dependent variable, it can also be conditioned on in the same manner as we condition on X. As in Exercise 17.2(c), we can write the TAR as

$$y = X\beta + \epsilon,$$

where X is the $(T - p) \times 2(p + 1)$ matrix with tth row given by

$$\left[D_t, D_t y_{t-1}, \ldots, D_t y_{t-p}, (1 - D_t), (1 - D_t) y_{t-1}, \ldots, (1 - D_t) y_{t-p}\right],$$

where D_t is now a dummy variable which equals 1 if $z_{t-d} \leq \tau$ and equals 0 if $z_{t-d} > \tau$. Thus, as in the solution to Exercise 17.2(a), the posterior for β and h (now conditional on τ and d) is $NG\left(\overline{\beta}, \overline{Q}, \overline{s}^{-2}, \overline{\nu}\right)$, where $\overline{\beta}$, $\overline{Q}$, $\overline{s}^{-2}$, and $\overline{\nu}$ are defined as in that solution except that X and, thus, the posterior hyperparameters now depend on τ and d.

Analogous to the solution to Exercise 17.2(c), we can write

$$p(\beta, h, \tau, d|y) = p(\beta, h|\tau, d, y)\, p(\tau, d|y).$$

The preceding paragraph describes methods of posterior inference for $p(\beta, h|\tau, d, y)$ and we can focus on $p(\tau, d|y)$. But, also as in Exercise 17.2(c), we can use the facts that

$$p(y|\tau, d) = \iint L(\beta, h|\tau, d)\, p(\beta, h|\tau, d)\, d\beta dh$$

and $p(\tau, d|y) \propto p(y|\tau, d)\, p(\tau, d)$ to note that, by calculating the marginal likelihoods for the normal linear regression model (conditional on τ and d) for every possible value of

Table 17.4: Posterior results for TAR model with unknown threshold and delay.

Parameter	Mean	Std. dev.
β_{10}	0.255	0.226
β_{11}	0.080	0.174
β_{12}	−0.330	0.196
β_{13}	−0.340	0.167
β_{14}	−0.264	0.166
β_{20}	0.557	0.159
β_{21}	0.253	0.087
β_{22}	0.270	0.080
β_{23}	−0.110	0.076
β_{24}	−0.008	0.072
σ^2	0.806	0.076

τ and d, we can build up the posterior $p(\tau, d|y)$. The relevant formula for the marginal likelihood is given in (17.5).
(b) A MATLAB program which extends the program of Exercise 17.2(c) to allow for an unknown delay (and general threshold trigger) is provided on the website associated with this book. Since we are calculating marginal likelihoods, we require an informative prior and use the same weakly informative prior described in the solution to Exercise 17.2(c). As we stressed in that solution, in a serious empirical study the researcher would likely elicit the prior in a more sophisticated manner and/or carry out a prior sensitivity analysis. Posterior properties of β and σ^2, using the US real GDP growth data, are provided in Table 17.4. Figure 17.2 plots the posterior of d. Note that, since different values of d imply different threshold triggers (with different interpretations), the interpretation of the threshold differs across d. Hence, it would make little sense to plot the posterior of τ, and hence we do not do so (although one could plot $p(\tau|y, d)$ for a choice of d). Interestingly, the posterior for d allocates most of the probability to $d = 2$, indicating that it is not last quarter's GDP growth which triggers a regime shift (as the model of Exercise 17.2 implies), but rather GDP growth averaged over the past two quarters. The finding that GDP growth two quarters ago plays an important role in regime shifting in US GDP has been found by others (e.g., Potter 1995).

Note also that the solution to this question can be interpreted as a standard Bayesian posterior analysis where d is an unknown parameter whose posterior we have derived. Alternatively (and equivalently) it can be seen as an example of Bayesian model averaging where we are presenting results (e.g., in Table 17.4) which are averaged over different models where the different models are defined by different threshold triggers. Koop and Potter (1999) is an empirical paper which focuses on the second interpretation.

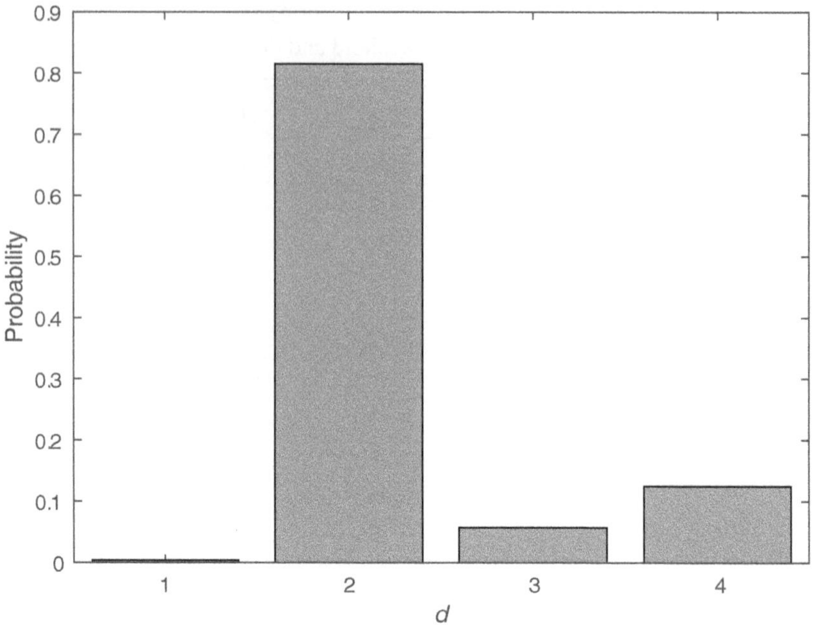

Figure 17.2. Posterior distribution of d.

Exercise 17.4 (Extensions of the basic threshold autoregressive model II: Switches in the error variance) Recently, there has been much interest in the volatility of macroeconomic variables and, in particular, whether the error variance exhibits regime-switching behavior (see, e.g., Sims and Zha 2006). Accordingly, we can extend the models of Exercise 17.2 and 17.3 to

$$\begin{aligned} y_t &= \beta_{10} + \beta_{11} y_{t-1} + \cdots + \beta_{1p} y_{t-p} + \sqrt{h_1^{-1}} \epsilon_t \text{ if } z_{t-d} \leq \tau, \\ y_t &= \beta_{20} + \beta_{21} y_{t-1} + \cdots + \beta_{2p} y_{t-p} + \sqrt{h_2^{-1}} \epsilon_t \text{ if } z_{t-d} > \tau, \end{aligned} \tag{17.8}$$

where all definitions and assumptions are the same as in Exercises 17.2 and 17.3, except that we now assume ϵ_t is $iid\ N(0,1)$.

(a) Assume that d is an unknown parameter with a non-informative prior over $1, \ldots, p$ (i.e., $\Pr(d = i) = \frac{1}{p}$ for $i = 1, \ldots, p$) and normal-gamma priors are used in each regime (i.e., the joint prior for β_j and h_j is $NG\left(\underline{\beta_j}, \underline{Q_j}, \underline{s_j}^{-2}, \underline{\nu_j}\right)$ for $j = 1, \ldots, 2$); derive the posterior for the model defined by (17.8).

(b) Using an appropriate data set (e.g., the real GDP growth data used in the previous exercise), write a program and carry out Bayesian inference for this model using your results from part (a). Set $p = 4$ and

$$z_{t-d} = \frac{\sum_{d=1}^{p} y_{t-d}}{d}.$$

Solution

(a) The posterior for the parameters of this model can be obtained by noting that, conditional on τ and d, the model breaks down into two linear regression models with natural conjugate priors. Thus, standard results (see Chapter 10, Exercise 10.1) for the regression model can be combined to produce a conditional posterior. The unconditional posterior can be obtained using the same methods as in the solution to Exercise 17.3. Precise details follow.

We are interested in the posterior $p(\beta_1, h_1, \beta_2, h_2, \tau, d|y)$, which (given the assumed prior) can be written as

$$p(\beta_1, h_1, \beta_2, h_2, \tau, d|y) = p\left(\beta_1, h_1|y^1, \tau, d\right) p\left(\beta_2, h_2|y^2, \tau, d\right) p(\tau, d|y),$$

where y^j denotes the data in the jth regime for $j = 1, 2$ (which depends on τ and d). But $p\left(\beta_j, h_j|y^j, \tau, d\right)$ is simply the posterior for the normal linear regression model with natural conjugate prior using the data in the jth regime (for $j = 1, 2$). That is, we can write each regime as

$$y^j = X^j \beta_j + \epsilon^j,$$

where y^j and ϵ^j contain all the observations on the dependent variable and errors, respectively, for $j = 1, 2$. The X^j contain an intercept and p lags of the dependent variable for observations in the jth regime. We can immediately use the results from Exercise 10.1 to find that the joint posterior for β_j and h_j (conditional on τ and d) is $NG\left(\overline{\beta_j}, \overline{Q_j}, \overline{s_j}^{-2}, \overline{\nu_j}\right)$, where $\overline{\nu_j} = T_j + \underline{\nu_j}$, T_j is the number of observations in the jth regime,

$$\overline{Q_j} = \left(\underline{Q_j}^{-1} + X^{j\prime} X^j\right)^{-1},$$
$$\overline{\beta_j} = \overline{Q_j}\left(\underline{Q_j}^{-1} \underline{\beta_j} + X^{j\prime} X_j \widehat{\beta_j}\right),$$

and

$$\overline{s_j}^2 = \frac{\underline{\nu_j} \underline{s_j}^2 + SSE_j + \left(\widehat{\beta_j} - \underline{\beta_j}\right)' X^{j\prime} X_j \overline{Q_j} \underline{Q_j}^{-1} \left(\widehat{\beta_j} - \underline{\beta_j}\right)}{\overline{\nu}}.$$

Note that, in the preceding equation, we are adapting our previous notation so that $\widehat{\beta_j}$ and SSE_j are now the OLS estimate and OLS sum of squared residuals, respectively, using data from regime j. This completes our description of $p\left(\beta_1, h_1|y^1, \tau, d\right)$ and $p\left(\beta_2, h_2|y^2, \tau, d\right)$.

In our answer to Exercise 17.3(a) we noted that $p(\tau, d|y) \propto p(y|\tau, d) p(\tau, d)$. Since $p(y|\tau, d)$ was simply the marginal likelihood for the normal linear regression model (conditional on τ and d), we could obtain the requisite posterior by combining standard analytical formula for this marginal likelihood with $p(\tau, d)$. Here we can adopt the same strategy with one slight extension, by noting that the assumptions of our model imply that

$$p(y|\tau, d) = p\left(y^1|\tau, d\right) p\left(y^2|\tau, d\right).$$

Thus, we can calculate marginal likelihoods for the normal linear regression model in each of our two regimes (defined by τ and d) and simply multiply them together to yield the required $p(y|\tau, d)$. As in Exercise 17.3, we must evaluate this marginal likelihood for every possible threshold and delay parameter but, since these are both discrete random variables, this can be done in a straightforward fashion. The relevant formula for the marginal likelihood (see Exercise 17.2) in each regime, adapted to our present notation, is:

$$p\left(y^j|\tau, d\right) = \frac{\Gamma\left(\frac{\overline{\nu}_j}{2}\right)\left(\underline{\nu}_j \underline{s}_j^2\right)^{\frac{\underline{\nu}}{2}}}{\Gamma\left(\frac{\underline{\nu}_j}{2}\right)\pi^{\frac{T_j}{2}}}\left(\frac{|\overline{Q}_j|}{|\underline{Q}_j|}\right)^{\frac{1}{2}}\left(\overline{\nu}_j \overline{s}_j^2\right)^{-\frac{\overline{\nu}_j}{2}}.$$

(b) The MATLAB program which carries out posterior inference in the TAR with regime switching in the error variance is provided on the website associated with this book. We ran this program, using the same weakly informative prior for the coefficients in each regime described in the solution to Exercise 17.2(b), using our US real GDP growth data set.

Table 17.5 presents posterior results for the regression coefficients and error variances in each regime. In this data set, allowing for the regime switching in the errors makes little difference for the AR coefficients (compare Table 17.4 with Table 17.5). However, there is evidence that the error variances in the two regimes are different from one another. In particular, the error variance in the expansionary regime is substantially smaller than the error variance in the recessionary regime.

As a final thought, it is worth noting that the results for Exercises 17.2, 17.3, and 17.4 can be extended in a straightforward manner to the case of many regimes, regimes with different AR lag orders, TAR models where the threshold triggers depend on unknown parameters, TAR models where the threshold trigger in the regression coefficients is different than the trigger for the error variances, etc.

Table 17.5: Posterior results for TAR model with switches in error variance.

Parameter	Mean	Std. dev.
β_{10}	0.589	0.196
β_{11}	0.099	0.188
β_{12}	0.048	0.191
β_{13}	−0.052	0.164
β_{14}	−0.300	0.172
β_{20}	0.494	0.139
β_{21}	0.360	0.072
β_{22}	0.196	0.073
β_{23}	−0.143	0.065
β_{24}	−0.029	0.062
σ_1^2	1.627	0.293
σ_2^2	0.555	0.062

Exercise 17.5 (Sims and Uhlig (1991)) Let y_t for $t = 1, \ldots, T$ represent T observations on a time series variable and set $y_0 = 0$. Assume ϵ_t to be $iid\ N(0, 1)$. The assumption that the variance of ϵ_t is known and equal to unity is merely made for convenience. Consider the AR(1) model

$$y_t = \theta y_{t-1} + \epsilon_t, \tag{17.9}$$

where θ is an unknown parameter.
(a) Given a flat prior, find the posterior distribution for θ.
(b) Using the model of part (a), implement the following experimental design of Sims and Uhlig (1991). Consider 31 values of θ ranging from 0.80 to 1.10 in increments of 0.01. For each value of θ, generate 10 000 random vectors $\epsilon = (\epsilon_1, \ldots, \epsilon_T)'$ each comprising $T = 100$ standard normal random variables. Using (17.9), generate a $T \times 1$ vector y in each case. Thus, 310 000 data series for y are available (i.e., 10 000 series for each of the 31 values for θ).

Now, here is the analysis to perform. For each of these time series, compute $\widehat{\theta}$, which is the posterior mean (and maximum likelihood estimate) of θ. Then, for each of the 31 values for θ, construct a histogram of the $\widehat{\theta}$ corresponding to a particular value for θ using bins: $(-\infty, 0.795)$, $[0.795, 0.805)$, $\ldots$, $[1.095, 1.105)$, $[1.105, \infty)$. Note that this will involve the construction of 31 different histograms. Line up these histograms to produce a surface which is the joint pdf of θ and $\widehat{\theta}$ under a uniform prior defined over the region $[0.80, 1.10]$. Slicing this surface along a given value for θ produces the sampling distribution of $\widehat{\theta}$, the maximum likelihood estimator. Slicing this surface along a given value for $\widehat{\theta}$ produces the posterior distribution for θ corresponding to the realized value of $\widehat{\theta}$. Create the three-dimensional plot described above and carry out a "helicopter tour," examining it from different angles.
(c) Create a two-dimensional plot which slices along $\theta = 1$ to obtain an approximate sampling distribution for the maximum likelihood estimator in the unit root case.
(d) Create a two-dimensional plot which slices along $\widehat{\theta} = 1$ to get the exact posterior distribution for θ at the point $\widehat{\theta} = 1$.

Solution
(a) Note that

$$y_t | y_{t-1}, \ldots, y_1, \theta \sim N\left(\theta y_{t-1}, 1\right).$$

The likelihood function is

$$\begin{aligned} L(\theta) &= \prod_{t=1}^{T} \phi\left(y_t | \theta y_{t-1}, 1\right) \\ &= (2\pi)^{-\frac{T}{2}} \exp\left[-\frac{1}{2}\sum_{t=1}^{T}\left(y_t - \theta y_{t-1}\right)^2\right]. \end{aligned}$$

The maximum likelihood estimate of θ is

$$\widehat{\theta} = \frac{\sum_{t=1}^{T} y_t y_{t-1}}{\sum_{t=1}^{T} y_{t-1}^2}.$$

Noting that

$$\sum_{t=1}^{T} (y_t - \theta y_{t-1})^2 = \sum_{t=1}^{T} \left(y_t - \widehat{\theta} y_{t-1}\right)^2 + \left(\widehat{\theta} - \theta\right)^2 w,$$

where

$$w = \sum_{t=1}^{T} y_{t-1}^2,$$

it can be seen that

$$\begin{aligned} L(\theta) &= (2\pi)^{-\frac{T}{2}} \exp\left[-\frac{1}{2}\left\{\sum_{t=1}^{T} \left(y_t - \widehat{\theta} y_{t-1}\right)^2 + \left(\widehat{\theta} - \theta\right)^2 w\right\}\right] \\ &\propto \phi\left(\theta|\widehat{\theta}, w^{-1}\right). \end{aligned} \quad (17.10)$$

Thus, it can be seen that the posterior distribution of θ is $N(\widehat{\theta}, w^{-1})$.

Note that this exercise is a special case of Exercise 17.1(a). We provide the derivations for this special case since we will use it in the following exercises.

(b, c, and d) A MATLAB program which creates the three figures requested is available on the website associated with this book. The three figures are produced in Figures 17.3, 17.4, and 17.5. With regards to (a), note that Figure 17.3 provides a view from just one

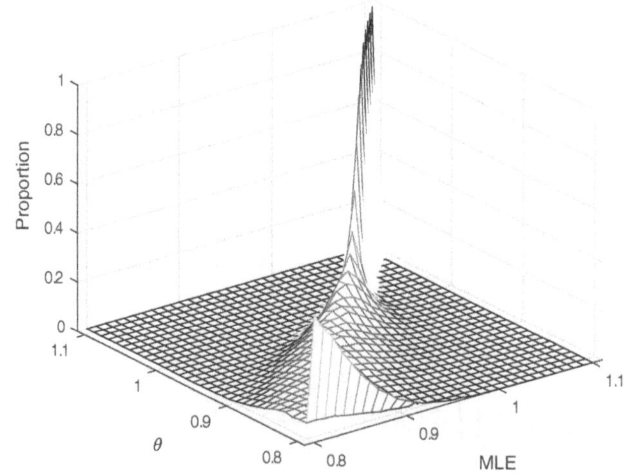

Figure 17.3. Joint histogram involving θ and the MLE.

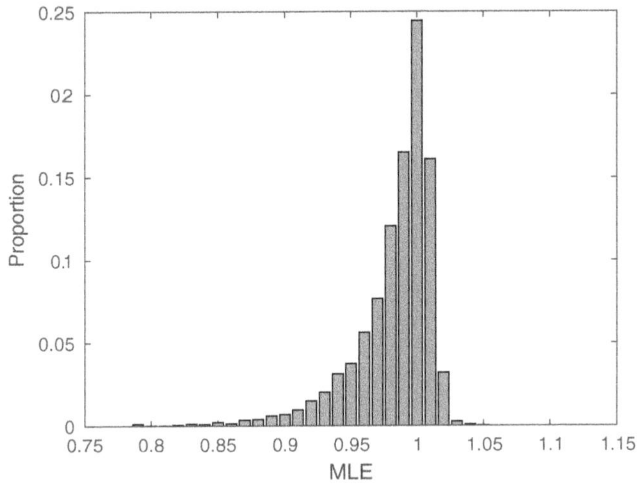

Figure 17.4. Sampling distribution when $\theta = 1$.

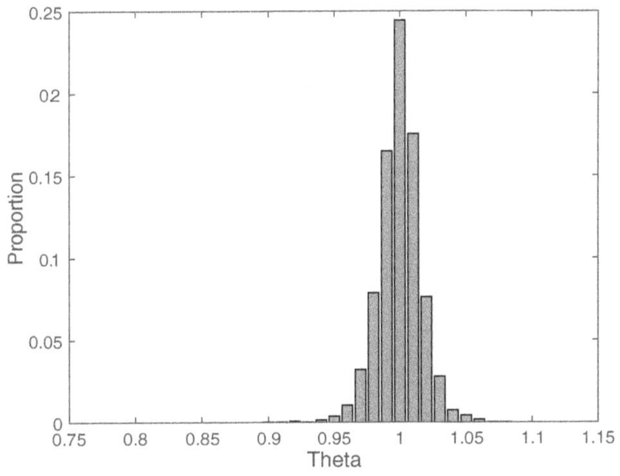

Figure 17.5. Posterior distribution when MLE = 1.

angle. If you have software with the appropriate graphing capabilities (e.g., MATLAB), you can produce Figure 17.3 on the computer screen and then rotate it to obtain a view of any aspect of the distribution you want. This is what Sims and Uhlig (1991) refer to as a "helicopter tour." Note that the small upturn in the histogram for small values of $\widehat{\theta}$ is due to the fact that the graph effectively truncates the posterior at 0.795. That is, the upturn is associated with the bin $(-\infty, 0.795)$, which can receive appreciable posterior support for data sets generated with θ near 0.80. With regards to parts (c) and (d), note that the posterior distribution is symmetric and centered over $\widehat{\theta} = 1$, as we would expect from part (a), but the sampling distribution of the MLE is skewed and downward biased.

Exercise 17.6 (Unit roots and Jeffreys' prior) Let $y = (y_1, \ldots, y_T)'$ and ϵ_t be *iid* $N(0, \sigma^2)$ for $t = 1, \ldots, T$, and assume y_0 is given and σ^2 is unknown. Consider the AR(1) model given in (17.9); find Jeffreys' prior for θ.

Solution

Conditional on y_0, the likelihood function is

$$L(\theta, \sigma^2) = \prod_{t=1}^{T} \phi(y_t | \theta y_{t-1}, \sigma^2)$$

$$= (2\pi\sigma^2)^{-\frac{T}{2}} \exp\left[-\frac{1}{2\sigma^2} \sum_{t=1}^{T} (y_t - \theta y_{t-1})^2\right]. \tag{17.11}$$

Taking second derivatives of the log of (17.11) yields the elements of the Hessian matrix:

$$\frac{\partial^2 \ln L(\theta, \sigma^2)}{\partial \theta^2} = -\frac{1}{\sigma^2} \sum_{t=1}^{T} y_{t-1}^2, \tag{17.12}$$

$$\frac{\partial^2 \ln L(\theta, \sigma^2)}{\partial (\sigma^2)^2} = \frac{T}{2\sigma^4} - \frac{1}{\sigma^6} \sum_{t=1}^{T} (y_t - \theta y_{t-1})^2, \tag{17.13}$$

and

$$\frac{\partial^2 \ln L(\theta, \sigma^2)}{\partial \theta \partial (\sigma^2)} = -\frac{1}{\sigma^4} \sum_{t=1}^{T} (y_t - \theta y_{t-1}) y_{t-1}. \tag{17.14}$$

To compute Jeffreys' prior, we must calculate the negative of the sampling expectation (conditional on y_0) of these quantities.

First, consider (17.12). Noting that (17.9) can be written as

$$y_t = \theta^t y_0 + \sum_{i=0}^{t-1} \theta^i \epsilon_{t-i},$$

it follows that

$$E(y_t^2 | y_0) = E\left(\theta^t y_0 + \sum_{i=0}^{t-1} \theta^i \epsilon_{t-i}\right)^2$$

$$= \theta^{2t} y_0^2 + \sum_{i=0}^{t-1} \theta^{2i} E(\epsilon_{t-i}^2)$$

$$= \theta^{2t} y_0^2 + \sigma^2 \frac{1 - \theta^{2t}}{1 - \theta^2}, \tag{17.15}$$

where the last line uses a formula for the sum of a finite geometric series. In particular, we use the result that $1 + \theta + \theta^2 + \cdots + \theta^n = \frac{1-\theta^{n+1}}{1-\theta}$, which holds provided $\theta \neq 1$. In the unit root case where $\theta = 1$, the analog of (17.15) is

$$E\left(y_t^2|y_0\right) = E\left(y_0 + \sum_{i=0}^{t-1}\theta^i\epsilon_{t-i}\right)^2$$
$$= y_0^2 + \sum_{i=0}^{t-1}E\left(\epsilon_{t-i}^2\right)$$
$$= y_0^2 + t\sigma^2. \tag{17.16}$$

For the case where $\theta \neq 1$, using (17.15), the negative of the expectation (conditional on y_0) of (17.12) is

$$-E\left[\frac{\partial^2 \ln L\left(\theta,\sigma^2\right)}{\partial\theta^2}|y_0\right] = \frac{1}{\sigma^2}\sum_{t=1}^{T}E\left(y_{t-1}^2|y_0\right)$$
$$= \sum_{t=1}^{T}\left[\theta^{2(t-1)}\left(\frac{y_0}{\sigma}\right)^2 + \frac{1-\theta^{2(t-1)}}{1-\theta^2}\right]$$
$$= \left[\left(\frac{y_0}{\sigma}\right)^2\left(\frac{1-\theta^{2T}}{1-\theta^2}\right) + \left(\frac{1}{1-\theta^2}\right)\left(T - \frac{1-\theta^{2T}}{1-\theta^2}\right)\right]. \tag{17.17}$$

For the case where $\theta = 1$, we can use (17.16) to find

$$-E\left[\frac{\partial^2 \ln L\left(\theta,\sigma^2\right)}{\partial\theta^2}|y_0\right] = \frac{1}{\sigma^2}\sum_{t=1}^{T}E\left(y_{t-1}^2|y_0\right) \tag{17.18}$$
$$= \frac{1}{\sigma^2}\sum_{t=1}^{T}\left[y_0^2 + (t-1)\sigma^2\right]$$
$$= T\left[\left(\frac{y_0}{\sigma}\right)^2 + \frac{1}{2}(T-1)\right].$$

Next, consider (17.13) and (17.14). Noting that $\epsilon_t = y_t - \theta y_{t-1}$, the negative of the expectation (conditional on y_0) of (17.13) and (17.14) are, respectively,

$$-E\left[\frac{\partial^2 \ln L\left(\theta,\sigma^2\right)}{\partial\left(\sigma^2\right)^2}|y_0\right] = -\frac{T}{2\sigma^4} + \frac{1}{\sigma^6}\sum_{t=1}^{T}E\left(\epsilon_t\right)^2 \tag{17.19}$$
$$= -\frac{T}{2\sigma^4} + \frac{T}{\sigma^4} = \frac{T}{2\sigma^4}$$

and

$$-E\left[\frac{\partial^2 \ln L\left(\theta,\sigma^2\right)}{\partial\theta\partial\left(\sigma^2\right)}|y_0\right] = -\frac{1}{\sigma^4}\sum_{t=1}^{T}E\left(\epsilon_t y_{t-1}\right) = 0. \tag{17.20}$$

Jeffreys' prior is proportional to the square root of the determinant of the sample information matrix. In our case, for $\theta \neq 1$, Jeffreys' prior, which we denote by $p_P(.)$, is proportional to the square root of the product of (17.17) and (17.19):

$$p_P\left(\theta,\sigma^2\right) \propto \left[\left(\frac{y_0}{\sigma}\right)^2\left(\frac{1-\theta^{2T}}{1-\theta^2}\right)+\left(\frac{1}{1-\theta^2}\right)\left(T-\frac{1-\theta^{2T}}{1-\theta^2}\right)\right]^{\frac{1}{2}}\left[\frac{T}{2\sigma^4}\right]^{\frac{1}{2}}, \quad (17.21)$$

for $\theta \neq 1$.

For $\theta = 1$, the analogous calculation involves (17.18) and (17.19) and yields:

$$\begin{aligned} p_P\left(\theta,\sigma^2\right) &= \left[T\left[\left(\frac{y_0}{\sigma}\right)^2+\frac{1}{2}(T-1)\right]\right]^{\frac{1}{2}}\left[\frac{T}{2\sigma^4}\right]^{\frac{1}{2}} \\ &\propto \frac{T}{\sigma^2}\left[\left(\frac{y_0}{\sigma}\right)^2+\frac{1}{2}(T-1)\right]^{\frac{1}{2}}. \end{aligned} \quad (17.22)$$

The prior given in (17.21) and (17.22) was advocated by Phillips (1991), and the discussion which accompanied this paper reflects its controversial nature. Hence, we use the subscript P for Phillips (rather than Jeffreys) because it is not clear that Jeffreys would have advocated this prior. One controversial aspect about this prior is that it is improper and shoots off to ∞ as $\theta \to \infty$. Note also that, with dependent data (unlike a random sample), there is a crucial difference between the information matrix for a single observation and the information matrix for the entire sample. Here, since the latter is used, sample size, T, and the initial value y_0 appear in Phillips' prior.

Exercise 17.7 (Berger and Yang (1994)) Berger and Yang (1994) tried deriving a reference prior (in the sense of Bernardo 1979) for the model in Exercise 17.5 and found they could only do so when $|\theta| < 1$ but not when $|\theta| \geq 1$. In the end, they advocated use of the following prior density:

$$p_{BY}(\theta) = \begin{cases} \frac{1}{2\pi\sqrt{1-\theta^2}} & \text{if } |\theta| < 1, \\ \frac{1}{2\pi|\theta|\sqrt{\theta^2-1}} & \text{if } |\theta| \geq 1. \end{cases} \quad (17.23)$$

The prior over $|\theta| < 1$ agrees with Jeffreys' prior in the stationary case (see Thornber 1967). Show that $\Pr(|\theta| < 1) = \Pr(|\theta| \geq 1) = \frac{1}{2}$ and, hence, that this prior is proper.

Solution

Using properties of the arcsin function, it follows that

$$\int_0^1 \frac{1}{\sqrt{1-\theta^2}}\,d\theta = \frac{\pi}{2}$$

and, hence, that

$$\begin{aligned} \Pr(|\theta| < 1) &= \int_{-1}^{1} \frac{1}{2\pi\sqrt{1-\theta^2}}\,d\theta \\ &= 2\int_0^1 \frac{1}{2\pi\sqrt{1-\theta^2}}\,d\theta \end{aligned}$$

$$= \frac{1}{\pi} \int_0^1 \frac{1}{\sqrt{1-\theta^2}} d\theta$$
$$= \frac{1}{\pi} \frac{\pi}{2} = \frac{1}{2}.$$

To obtain $\Pr(|\theta| \geq 1)$, define $\gamma = \frac{1}{\theta}$ and consider $d\theta = -\gamma^{-2} d\gamma$. Using the change-of-variable technique,

$$\Pr(|\theta| \geq 1) = \int_{|\theta| \geq 1} \frac{1}{2\pi |\theta| \sqrt{\theta^2 - 1}} d\theta$$
$$= \int_{-1}^{1} \frac{1}{\gamma^2 2\pi |\gamma^{-1}| \sqrt{\gamma^{-2} - 1}} d\gamma$$
$$= \int_{-1}^{1} \frac{1}{2\pi \sqrt{1-\gamma^2}} d\gamma$$
$$= \frac{1}{2}.$$

Therefore, (17.23) integrates to unity and allocates equal prior weight to stationary and non-stationary regions. These properties make (17.23) attractive for testing $|\theta| < 1$ versus $|\theta| \geq 1$.

Exercise 17.8 (Kadane, Chan, and Wolfson (1996)) Using the AR(1) model with known variance of Exercise 17.5, consider using a prior which extends the normal conjugate family to allow a piecewise normal family (where each piece is conditional on a known prior variance, $\underline{h}_i^{-1}$). For example, we could allow one piece to be a normal distribution over the range $(-\infty, 1)$, a second normal distribution might pertain to $(1, \infty)$, and conceivably there might be a lump of prior mass at $\theta = 1$. Then the prior density for θ, given $\underline{h}_i^{-1}$ $(i = 1, 2)$ is

$$p_{\mathrm{KCW}}(\theta) = \underline{\omega}_1 \frac{\phi\left(\theta | \underline{\mu}_1, \underline{h}_1^{-1}\right) I(\theta < 1)}{\Phi\left(\left[1 - \underline{\mu}_1\right] \underline{h}_1^{\frac{1}{2}}\right)} + \underline{\omega}_2 \frac{\phi\left(\theta | \underline{\mu}_2, \underline{h}_2^{-1}\right) I(\theta > 1)}{\Phi\left(\left[1 - \underline{\mu}_2\right] \underline{h}_2^{\frac{1}{2}}\right)} + \underline{\omega}_3 I(\theta = 1), \tag{17.24}$$

where $\Phi(.)$ denotes the cdf of an $N(0,1)$ random variable and $I(.)$ is the indicator function. The hyperparameters are $\underline{\omega}_i$ for $i = 1, 2, 3$ (which are constrained to be non-negative and sum to one), $\underline{\mu}_i$, and $\underline{h}_i$ $(i = 1, 2)$. Show that the posterior distribution is also piecewise normal in the same form with the updated values of the hyperparameters easily obtained. Note: if the error precision is taken to be an unknown parameter with a gamma prior, rather than assumed to be equal to unity, nothing essential changes. The prior is piecewise normal-gamma, as is the posterior.

Solution

One way to approach this problem is to represent the prior in (17.24) hierarchically by adding a component indicator variable, much like the solution to Exercises 15.5 and 15.6. To this end, let $c \in \{1, 2, 3\}$ be a discrete random variable with $\Pr(c = j) = \underline{\omega}_j$, $j = 1, 2, 3$. We can thus write a conditional version of the prior in (17.24) as

$$p_{\text{KCW}}(\theta|c) = \begin{cases} \frac{\phi(\theta|\underline{\mu}_1, \underline{\sigma}_1^2) I(\theta<1)}{\Phi([1-\underline{\mu}_1]\underline{\sigma}_1^{-1})} & \text{if } c = 1, \\ \\ \frac{\phi(\theta|\underline{\mu}_2, \underline{\sigma}_2^2) I(\theta>1)}{1-\Phi([1-\underline{\mu}_2]\underline{\sigma}_2^{-1})} & \text{if } c = 2, \\ \\ I(\theta = 1) & \text{if } c = 3. \end{cases}$$

Thus, marginalized over the prior $p(c)$, it follows that the unconditional prior for θ, $p_{\text{KCW}}(\theta)$, is exactly the same as in (17.24).

We are interested in obtaining $p(\theta|y)$. We know that

$$p(\theta|y) = \sum_{j=1}^{3} p(\theta|c = j, y)\Pr(c = j|y),$$

which shows that the posterior for θ is a mixture of the component densities $p(\theta|c = j, y)$, $j = 1, 2, 3$. For $j = 1, 2$, the posterior densities $p(\theta|c = j, y)$ are truncated normal, following similar logic to that of Exercise 15.7. Specifically,

$$p(\theta|c = 1, y) = \frac{\phi(\theta; \overline{\mu}_1, \overline{\sigma}_1^2)}{\Phi[(1 - \overline{\mu}_1)\overline{\sigma}_1^{-1}]} I(\theta < 1),$$

where

$$\overline{\sigma}_1^2 = (w + \underline{\sigma}_1^{-2})^{-1}, \quad \overline{\mu}_1 = \overline{\sigma}_1^2(w\hat{\theta} + \underline{\sigma}_1^{-2}\underline{\mu}_1), \quad \text{and } w \equiv \sum_{t=1}^{T} y_{t-1}^2.$$

Similarly,

$$p(\theta|c = 2, y) = \frac{\phi(\theta; \overline{\mu}_2, \overline{\sigma}_2^2)}{1 - \Phi[(1 - \overline{\mu}_2)\overline{\sigma}_2^{-1}]} I(\theta > 1),$$

where

$$\overline{\sigma}_2^2 = (w + \underline{\sigma}_2^{-2})^{-1}, \quad \overline{\mu}_2 = \overline{\sigma}_2^2(w\hat{\theta} + \underline{\sigma}_2^{-2}\underline{\mu}_2).$$

Finally, given the point prior employed within the third component,

$$p(\theta|c = 3, y) = I(\theta = 1).$$

Hence, the posterior will be in exactly the same form as the prior in (17.24), where the posterior means and standard deviations within each component are updated using the formulas given here. To finish characterizing $p(\theta|y)$, it remains to calculate the updated posterior weights $\Pr(c = j|y)$, $c = 1, 2, 3$. To this end, we note that

$$\begin{aligned} p(c|y) &\propto p(y|c)p(c) \\ &= \left[\int_{-\infty}^{\infty} p(y, \theta|c)\, d\theta\right] p(c) \\ &= \left[\int_{-\infty}^{\infty} p(y|\theta)p(\theta|c)\, d\theta\right] p(c), \end{aligned}$$

where the last line indicates that the data density does not depend on c, given θ. As shown in Exercise 17.5, the likelihood function $L(\theta)$ can be decomposed into a term involving the least squares residuals and a quadratic form in θ. Specifically, these results implied that

$$p(y|\theta) \propto \exp\left(-(1/2)\sum_{t=1}^{T}(y_t - \hat{\theta}y_{t-1})^2\right) \exp\left[-(1/2)(\theta - \hat{\theta})^2 w\right].$$

When working out the calculations for $p(c|y)$, the term $\exp\left(-(1/2)\sum_{t=1}^{T}(y_t - \hat{\theta}y_{t-1})^2\right)$ moves outside of the integral and is absorbed into the normalizing constant. As such, we can ignore this term when performing the needed calculations. We thus have

$$p(c|y) \propto p(c)\int_{-\infty}^{\infty} \exp\left[-(1/2)(\theta - \hat{\theta})^2 w\right] p(\theta|c)\, d\theta.$$

This expression can be evaluated for each of the three values of c. For the case where $c = 1$, for example, we have (letting $\Psi_1 \equiv \Phi\left([1 - \underline{\mu}_1]\underline{\sigma}_1^{-1}\right)$ for notational simplicity)

$$\begin{aligned} \Pr(c = 1|y) &\propto \frac{\underline{\omega}_1}{\Psi_1}\int_{-\infty}^{\infty}\Bigg(\exp\left[-(1/2)(\theta - \hat{\theta})^2 w\right] \\ &\quad \times [1/\underline{\sigma}_1]\exp\left[-[1/2\underline{\sigma}_1^2](\theta - \underline{\mu}_1)^2\right] I(\theta < 1)\Bigg)\, d\theta \\ &\propto \frac{\underline{\omega}_1}{\Psi_1\underline{\sigma}_1}\exp\left[-(1/2)(\hat{\theta} - \underline{\mu}_1)^2/(\underline{\sigma}_1^2 + w^{-1})\right] \\ &\quad \times \int_{-\infty}^{1} \exp\left[-[1/2\overline{\sigma}_1^2](\theta - \overline{\mu}_1)^2\right] d\theta \\ &\propto \frac{\underline{\omega}_1\overline{\sigma}_1}{\Psi_1\underline{\sigma}_1}\exp\left[-(1/2)(\hat{\theta} - \underline{\mu}_1)^2/(\underline{\sigma}_1^2 + w^{-1})\right] \Phi\left[\frac{(1 - \overline{\mu}_1)}{\overline{\sigma}_1}\right]. \end{aligned}$$

The second line in this derivation follows from completing the square on θ. By similar calculations, we obtain

$$\Pr(c = 2|y) \propto \frac{\underline{\omega}_2\overline{\sigma}_2}{\Psi_2\underline{\sigma}_2}\exp\left[-(1/2)(\hat{\theta} - \underline{\mu}_2)^2/(\underline{\sigma}_2^2 + w^{-1})\right]\left(1 - \Phi\left[\frac{(1 - \overline{\mu}_2)}{\overline{\sigma}_2}\right]\right),$$

where $\Psi_2 \equiv 1 - \Phi\left(\left[1 - \underline{\mu}_2\right] \underline{\sigma}_2^{-1}\right)$. Finally,

$$\Pr(c = 3|y) \propto \underline{\omega}_3 \exp\left(-(1/2)(\hat{\theta} - 1)^2 w\right).$$

These final expressions provide updated formulas for the (unnormalized) component weights. Normalization follows trivially upon dividing each of these quantities by the sum of the unnormalized weights. These results, combined with the derived conditionals $p(\theta|c, y)$ and the formula $p(\theta|y) = \sum_{j=1}^{3} p(\theta|c = j, y)\Pr(c = j|y)$, provide the posterior of interest.

18

State Space and Unobserved Components Models

The preceding chapter focused on time series questions and applications within the class of AR models (or extensions such as the TAR model). Another class of models that are widely used in time series is *unobserved components models*. As their name suggests, these specifications model a time series variable as being made up of different components which are not directly observed by the econometrician. These models have become increasingly popular for modeling macroeconomic time series in particular, and we devote this chapter to questions and applications surrounding these specifications.

Unobserved components models typically decompose a time series into trend and cycle components. This decomposition leads to a structure that falls within a broader class of models called *state space models*, which are used for a huge range of purposes in econometrics, including modeling time variation in parameters and working with missing or mixed frequency data. *Factor models*, which distill the information in large data sets into a lower-dimensional set of factors, are also examples of state space models. State space methods are also used by macroeconomists who work with dynamic stochastic general equilibrium (DSGE) models, since these share a similar structure.

The first part of this chapter contains questions on unobserved components models, concluding with an exercise on dynamic factor models. All of these exercises assume normal errors and specify equations that are linear. However, econometricians are increasingly working with unobserved components models which are non-normal and/or non-linear. The Markov switching model, which forms the basis of one question in this chapter, provides an example of such an extension. In this model, the unobserved states are assumed to evolve according to a Markov process. The *stochastic volatility model* provides another example of such an extension, and we defer coverage of those models until Chapter 19. We begin our review and investigation of unobserved components specifications with the *local level model*.

Exercise 18.1 (The local level model) The simplest unobserved components model is the local level model:

$$y_t = \tau_t + \epsilon_t, \tag{18.1}$$

where ϵ_t for $t = 1, \ldots, T$ are assumed to be *iid* $N(0, \sigma^2)$. The local level (also called the trend component) τ_t is modeled as a random walk:

$$\tau_t = \tau_{t-1} + \eta_t, \tag{18.2}$$

where the η_t for $t = 1, \ldots, T$ are *iid* $N(0, \omega^2)$ and τ_0 is treated as an unknown parameter.

The local level model decomposes y_t into two components: the non-stationary trend component τ_t and the transitory cycle component ϵ_t. The random walk assumption in (18.2) captures the idea that the trend evolves smoothly over time, and that consecutive terms are close to one another. More precisely, the conditional distribution of τ_t given τ_{t-1} and ω^2 is $N(\tau_{t-1}, \omega^2)$. This implies that the prior for τ_t is centered around τ_{t-1}, and ω^2 controls how close these two quantities are. That is, ω^2 controls how smooth the overall trend is. In the limit as ω^2 goes to 0, the local level model reduces to a linear regression with a constant intercept.

The state equation (18.2) implies that τ_t has a stochastic trend – i.e., the unobserved component τ_t can wander widely over time (can trend upward or downward). This trending behavior is stochastic, as opposed to a deterministic trend such as

$$\alpha_t = \alpha + \beta t.$$

In the latter case, the trend α_t is an exact function of time, whereas the stochastic trend τ_t involves a random error term η_t. To see that τ_t exhibits trending behavior and can wander widely, note that by recursive substitution we have

$$\tau_t = \tau_0 + \sum_{s=1}^{t} \eta_s.$$

Hence, the conditional variance of τ_t given the initial τ_0 is

$$\text{Var}(\tau_t \,|\, \tau_0) = t\omega^2,$$

i.e., the variance of the stochastic trend τ_t is increasing linearly with time, which implies that τ_t can wander over an increasing range of values as time increases. This implies y_t has a unit root.

As mentioned above, the local level model is an example of a state space model. More generally, a state space model consists of two modeling levels. In the first level, observations are related to the latent or unobserved variables called states according to the observation (or measurement) equation. In the second level, the evolution of the states is modeled via the state (or transition) equation. In the local level model, the state is τ_t. The observation equation is given by (18.1), and (18.2) is the state equation. In addition,

the system is an instance of a normal linear state model in which both equations are linear in the state τ_t and both the error terms are normal.
(a) Derive a Gibbs sampling algorithm for carrying out posterior inference in the local level model.
(b) Obtain an inflation data series (e.g., an inflation series based on US PCE data from 1959Q1 to 2015Q4 is available on the website associated with this book). Using your Gibbs sampler from part (a), produce an estimate of trend inflation.

Solution
(a) To carry out posterior inference in the local level model in (18.1) and (18.2), we construct a Gibbs sampler to sequentially sample the states $\tau = (\tau_1, \ldots, \tau_T)'$ and the three parameters: the initial state τ_0 and the two variances σ^2 and ω^2. The main challenge is the sampling of the states, which are of dimension T. The states from normal linear state space models are traditionally sampled using methods based on the Kalman filter such as those described by Carter and Kohn (1994), Früwirth-Schnatter (1994), de Jong and Shephard (1995), and Durbin and Koopman (2002). Here we introduce some more recent algorithms which use band matrix routines to sample the states. One main advantage of this recent approach is the simplicity of the derivations. All derivations are based on standard linear regression results derived in Chapter 10. In addition, these new algorithms are more computationally efficient than methods based on the Kalman filter. The following exposition is based on the formulation in Chan and Jeliazkov (2009). See also the discussion on computational efficiency in McCausland, Miller, and Pelletier (2011).

To complete the model specification, we assume the following independent priors for τ_0, σ^2, and ω^2:

$$\tau_0 \sim N(a_0, b_0), \quad \sigma^2 \sim IG(\nu_{\sigma^2}, S_{\sigma^2}), \quad \omega^2 \sim IG(\nu_{\omega^2}, S_{\omega^2}).$$

In this model, the prior on the smoothness parameter ω^2 typically has a large impact on the posterior results. This is because ω^2 is inferred only from the states τ, which are not directly observed. In other words, there are two layers: the data y inform us about τ, which in turn reveal information about ω^2. Consequently, the prior on ω^2 plays a relatively larger role. Here we assume the conventional inverse gamma prior on ω^2.

We can use the following four-block Gibbs sampler to simulate from the joint posterior $p(\tau, \sigma^2, \omega^2, \tau_0 \mid y)$:

1. Draw from $p(\tau \mid y, \sigma^2, \omega^2, \tau_0)$.
2. Draw from $p(\sigma^2 \mid y, \tau, \omega^2, \tau_0)$.
3. Draw from $p(\omega^2 \mid y, \tau, \sigma^2, \tau_0)$.
4. Draw from $p(\tau_0 \mid y, \tau, \sigma^2, \omega^2)$.

To implement the first step, we derive the conditional density of τ:

$$p(\tau \mid y, \sigma^2, \omega^2, \tau_0) \propto p(y \mid \tau, \sigma^2) p(\tau \mid \omega^2, \tau_0).$$

The density $p(y \mid \tau, \sigma^2)$ is referred to as the conditional likelihood (i.e., it is conditional upon τ) and is defined by the observation equation (18.1). This is distinct from the observed-data or integrated likelihood, which integrates out the states:

$$p(y \mid \sigma^2, \omega^2, \tau_0) = \int p(y \mid \tau, \sigma^2) p(\tau \mid \omega^2, \tau_0)\, d\tau.$$

The second density in the integrand, $p(\tau \mid \omega^2, \tau_0)$, is the prior density of τ implied by (18.2). In what follows, we derive explicit expressions for $p(y \mid \tau, \sigma^2)$ and $p(\tau \mid \omega^2, \tau_0)$, and show that the conditional density $p(\tau \mid y, \sigma^2, \omega^2, \tau_0)$ is in fact normal. Then, we discuss an efficient algorithm based on band matrix routines to draw from this high-dimensional density.

Let $y = (y_1, \ldots, y_T)'$ and define ϵ similarly. First, rewrite the observation equation (18.1) in matrix notation:

$$y = \tau + \epsilon,$$

where $\epsilon \sim N(0, \sigma^2 I_T)$, and the conditional likelihood is given by

$$p(y \mid \tau, \sigma^2) = (2\pi\sigma^2)^{-\frac{T}{2}} e^{-\frac{1}{2\sigma^2}(y-\tau)'(y-\tau)}. \tag{18.3}$$

Hence, the local level model is just a linear regression with a matrix of explanatory variables given by $X = I_T$ and regression coefficient vector τ. If we can derive the prior of τ, we can use standard linear regression results to obtain the full conditional density of τ.

To that end, we rewrite the state equation (18.2) as

$$H\tau = \tilde{\alpha}_\tau + \eta, \tag{18.4}$$

where $\tilde{\alpha}_\tau = (\tau_0, 0, \ldots, 0)'$, $\eta \sim N(0, \omega^2 I_T)$, and

$$H = \begin{pmatrix} 1 & 0 & 0 & \cdots & 0 \\ -1 & 1 & 0 & \cdots & 0 \\ 0 & -1 & 1 & \cdots & 0 \\ \vdots & & \ddots & \ddots & \vdots \\ 0 & 0 & \cdots & -1 & 1 \end{pmatrix}.$$

Note that $|H| = 1 \neq 0$, and therefore H is invertible. We claim that $H^{-1}\tilde{\alpha}_\tau = \tau_0 1_T$, where 1_T is a $T \times 1$ column of ones. This can be seen by solving the triangular system $Hz = \tilde{\alpha}_\tau$ for $z = (z_1, \ldots, z_T)'$ by forward substitution. Specifically, the first equation of the system reads $z_1 = \tau_0$. The second equation is $-z_1 + z_2 = 0$, and solving it for z_2 we get $z_2 = \tau_0$. Indeed, the tth equation is $-z_{t-1} + z_t = 0$, and therefore $z_t = z_{t-1}$. We conclude that $z_1 = z_2 = \cdots = z_T = \tau_0$. Since $z = H^{-1}\tilde{\alpha}_\tau$ by construction, we have proved the claim.

The above computation has shown that if we only want the quantity $A^{-1}b$, it is unnecessary to compute the inverse A^{-1}. Instead, we can simply solve $Az = b$ for z. Moreover, if A is a band lower triangular matrix, the number of operations in solving the system is linear in the dimension of the system. Hence, it can be done very quickly even when the dimension is large.

It follows from (18.4) that

$$(\tau \,|\, \omega^2, \tau_0) \sim N(\tau_0 1_T, \omega^2 (H'H)^{-1}),$$

with density

$$p(\tau \,|\, \omega^2, \tau_0) = (2\pi\omega^2)^{-\frac{T}{2}} e^{-\frac{1}{2\omega^2}(\tau - \tau_0 1_T)' H'H (\tau - \tau_0 1_T)}. \tag{18.5}$$

Combining the pdf of this normal prior with the pdf from the normal conditional likelihood yields

$$(\tau \,|\, y, \sigma^2, \omega^2, \tau_0) \sim N(\hat{\tau}, K_\tau^{-1}),$$

where

$$K_\tau = \frac{1}{\omega^2} H'H + \frac{1}{\sigma^2} I_T, \quad \hat{\tau} = K_\tau^{-1} \left(\frac{\tau_0}{\omega^2} H'H 1_T + \frac{1}{\sigma^2} y \right).$$

The proof of this is a simple extension of Exercise 2.3 or a special case of Exercise 10.1 and will not be reproduced here.

The main difficulty of simply sampling from $(\tau \,|\, y, \sigma^2, \omega^2, \tau_0)$ using the normal distribution is that the covariance matrix K_τ^{-1} is a full $T \times T$ matrix, and computing its Cholesky factor is time-consuming – it involves $\mathcal{O}(T^3)$ operations. Fortunately, the precision matrix K_τ is a band matrix, and computing its Cholesky factor involves only $\mathcal{O}(T)$ operations. Hence, it would be useful to have a method to draw from a normal distribution using only the precision matrix. This is described in the following algorithm for a precision sampler.

To generate R independent draws from $N(\mu, K^{-1})$ of dimension n, carry out the following steps:

1. Compute the lower Cholesky factorization $K = BB'$.
2. Generate $Z = (Z_1, \ldots, Z_n)'$ by drawing $Z_1, \ldots, Z_n \sim N(0, 1)$.
3. Return $U = \mu + (B')^{-1} Z$.
4. Repeat Steps 2 and 3 independently R times.

To check that $U \sim N(\mu, K^{-1})$, we first note that U is an affine transformation of the normal random vector Z, so it has a normal distribution. It is easy to check that $E(U) = \mu$. The covariance matrix of U is

$$\text{cov}(U) = (B')^{-1} \text{cov}(Z) \left(B' \right)^{-1\,\prime} = (B')^{-1} (B)^{-1} = (BB')^{-1} = K^{-1}.$$

Hence, U has the desired distribution.

We make a few comments on the computations. As mentioned previously, to compute $\hat{\tau}$, one need not compute the inverse K_τ^{-1}. Instead, we solve the linear system

$$K_\tau z = \frac{\tau_0}{\omega^2} H'H 1_T + \frac{1}{\sigma^2} y$$

for z. Since K_τ is a band matrix, its Cholesky factor is a band triangular matrix. Consequently, solving the above system involves only $\mathcal{O}(T)$ operations. We can similarly calculate $\mu + (B')^{-1} Z$ without computing the inverse of B'.

This type of precision-based algorithm using band matrix routines for drawing a high-dimensional normal random vector is considered by Rue (2001) in the context of Gaussian Markov random fields. Chan and Jeliazkov (2009) and McCausland, Miller, and Pelletier (2011) later derived similar algorithms for normal linear state space models. We will call these algorithms *precision samplers*.

The preceding material developed methods for carrying out Step 1 in the Gibbs sampler. Steps 2 and 3 can be easily implemented, as both $(\sigma^2 \,|\, y, \tau, \omega^2, \tau_0)$ and $(\omega^2 \,|\, y, \tau, \sigma^2, \tau_0)$ can be obtained using standard derivations for regression error variances (see, e.g., Exercises 2.7, 12.6, and 12.9). These are both inverse gamma random variables:

$$(\sigma^2 \,|\, y, \tau, \omega^2, \tau_0) \sim IG\left(\nu_{\sigma^2} + \frac{T}{2}, S_{\sigma^2} + \frac{1}{2}(y-\tau)'(y-\tau)\right),$$

$$(\omega^2 \,|\, y, \tau, \sigma^2, \tau_0) \sim IG\left(\nu_{\omega^2} + \frac{T}{2}, S_{\omega^2} + \frac{1}{2}(\tau - \tau_0 1_T)'H'H(\tau - \tau_0 1_T)\right).$$

Step 4 of the Gibbs sampler can be implemented by recalling that τ_0 only appears in the first state equation,

$$\tau_1 = \tau_0 + \eta_1,$$

where $\eta_1 \sim N(0, \omega^2)$. Given the normal prior $\tau_0 \sim N(a_0, b_0)$, we can again use standard linear regression results to get

$$(\tau_0 \,|\, y, \tau, \sigma^2, \omega^2) \sim N(\hat{\tau}_0, K_{\tau_0}^{-1}),$$

where

$$K_{\tau_0} = \frac{1}{b_0} + \frac{1}{\omega^2}, \quad \hat{\tau}_0 = K_{\tau_0}^{-1}\left(\frac{a_0}{b_0} + \frac{\tau_1}{\omega^2}\right).$$

We summarize the Gibbs sampler for the local level model as follows.

Pick some initial values $\sigma^{2(0)} = s_0 > 0$, $\omega^{2(0)} = o_0 > 0$, and $\tau_0 = t_0$. Then, repeat the following steps from $r = 1$ to R:

1. Draw $\tau^{(r)} \sim p(\tau \,|\, y, \sigma^{2(r-1)}, \omega^{2(r-1)}, \tau_0^{(r-1)})$ (multivariate normal).
2. Draw $\sigma^{2(r)} \sim p(\sigma^2 \,|\, y, \tau^{(r)}, \omega^{2(r-1)}, \tau_0^{(r-1)})$ (inverse gamma).
3. Draw $\omega^{2(r)} \sim p(\omega^2 \,|\, y, \tau^{(r)}, \sigma^{2(r)}, \tau_0^{(r-1)})$ (inverse gamma).
4. Draw $\tau_0^{(r)} \sim p(\tau_0 \,|\, y, \tau^{(r)}, \sigma^{2(r)}, \omega^{2(r)})$ (normal).

(b) In this solution, we decompose the US PCE inflation data into its trend and cyclical components using the local level model and the Gibbs sample derived in part (a). Code which does this is available on the website associated with this book. Note that in

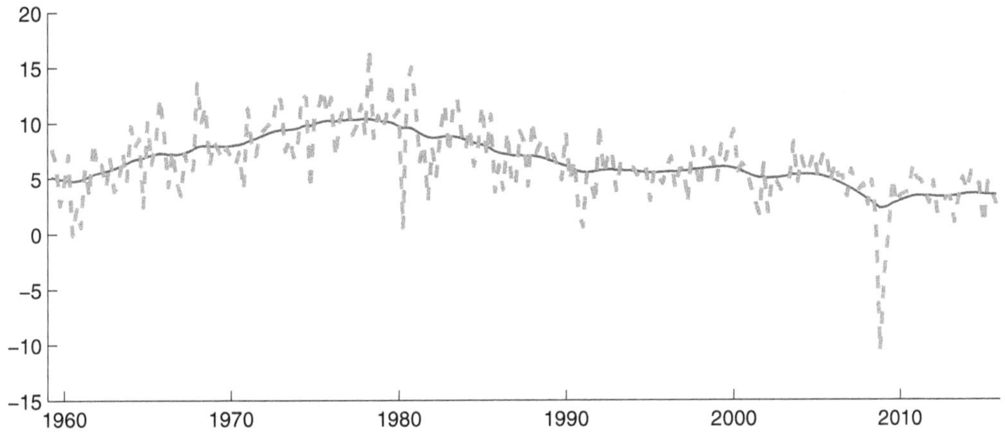

Figure 18.1. Estimated posterior mean of τ_t (solid line) and inflation (dotted line).

MATLAB, the backslash operator \ is used to solve linear systems. This plays a key role in the precision sampler. For example, to solve $\mathbf{Az} = \mathbf{b}$ for $\mathbf{z}$, we can use the command

```
z = A \ b.
```

As mentioned above, prior elicitation about ω^2 is often the most important as it controls the smoothness of the trend component. We set $\nu_{\omega^2} = 3$ and $S_{\omega^2} = 2 \times 0.25^2$, so that the prior mean of ω^2 is 0.25^2. Hence, with high probability, the difference between consecutive trend terms is less than 0.5. For the priors for the other parameters we set $a_0 = 5, b_0 = 100$, and $\nu_{\sigma^2} = 3,\ S_{\sigma^2} = 2$.

Figure 18.1 reports the posterior mean of τ_t based on a sample of 20 000 posterior draws after a burn-in period of 1000. It is evident that the estimate of trend inflation is able to capture the low-frequency movements in the PCE inflation. In particular, it gradually increases from about 5% in the early 1960s to over 10% in the late 1970s. Then it exhibits a steady decline throughout the Great Moderation to between 2% and 3.5% after the Great Recession.

Exercise 18.2 (Estimating the output gap) One common measure of slack in the economy is the output gap, defined as the deviation of the actual output of an economy from its potential or trend output. To estimate the output gap, we need a model for trend output, and unobserved component models are commonly used. Prominent examples include Watson (1986), Clark (1987), and Morley, Nelson, and Zivot (2003). Here we consider the unobserved components model considered by Grant and Chan (2017b), which nests the popular Hodrick–Prescott (HP) filter (see Hodrick and Prescott 1980, 1997).

The trend-cycle decomposition of real output is motivated by the idea that it can be usefully viewed as the sum of two separate components: a non-stationary component that represents the trend and a transitory deviation from the trend. Consider the following decomposition of the log real GDP (y_t):

$$y_t = \tau_t + c_t, \tag{18.6}$$

where τ_t is the trend and c_t is the stationary, cyclical, component.

The cyclical component c_t (which is our measure of the output gap) is modeled as a zero-mean stationary AR(p) process:

$$c_t = \phi_1 c_{t-1} + \cdots + \phi_p c_{t-p} + u_t^c, \tag{18.7}$$

where $u_t^c \sim N(0, \sigma_c^2)$ and the initial conditions are assumed to be zero: $c_0 = \cdots = c_{-1+p} = 0$.

Since trend output is expected to be growing over time, one popular specification for the non-stationary trend τ_t is a random walk with drift:

$$\tau_t = \mu + \tau_{t-1} + \tilde{u}_t^\tau.$$

Here the drift μ can be interpreted as the average growth rate of trend output. Since μ is a constant, this trend specification implies that the trend output is growing on average at a constant rate, which is not supported by the data. For instance, using US real GDP from 1947Q1 to 1998Q2, Perron and Wada (2009) found a break in trend output growth at 1973Q1. Using more recent data, Luo and Startz (2014) and Grant and Chan (2017a) found breaks at 2006Q1 and 2007Q1, respectively.

Here we consider an alternative trend specification that has a time-varying growth rate:

$$\Delta\tau_t = \Delta\tau_{t-1} + u_t^\tau, \tag{18.8}$$

where Δ is the first difference operator such that $\Delta x_t = x_t - x_{t-1}$, $u_t^\tau \sim N(0, \sigma_\tau^2)$, and τ_0 and τ_{-1} are treated as unknown parameters. Since $\Delta\tau_t$ can be interpreted as the trend growth rate at time t, this trend specification implies that the trend growth follows a random walk. As such, by construction this unobserved components model incorporates a stochastic trend growth rate.

(a) Derive a Gibbs sampling algorithm for carrying out posterior inference in this model.

(b) Obtain a real output series (e.g., US real GDP from 1947Q1 to 2015Q4 is available on the website associated with this book) and take its logarithm. Using your Gibbs sampler from part (a), produce an estimate of the output gap.

Solution

(a) Assuming $p = 2$ lags, the model parameters are $\phi = (\phi_1, \phi_2)'$, σ_c^2, σ_τ^2, and $\gamma = (\tau_0, \tau_{-1})'$. We assume the following independent priors:

$$\phi \sim N(\phi_0, V_\phi)1(\phi \in R), \quad \gamma \sim N(\gamma_0, V_\gamma), \quad \sigma_c^2 \sim IG(\nu_{\sigma_c^2}, S_{\sigma_c^2}), \quad \sigma_\tau^2 \sim U(0, b_{\sigma_\tau^2}),$$

where R is the stationarity region. Here we consider a uniform prior for σ_τ^2 instead of the conventional inverse gamma prior, although the latter could be used with minor alterations.

We can use the following five-block posterior sampler to simulate from the joint posterior $p(\tau, \phi, \sigma_c^2, \sigma_\tau^2, \gamma \,|\, y)$:

1. Draw from $p(\tau \,|\, y, \phi, \sigma_c^2, \sigma_\tau^2, \gamma)$.
2. Draw from $p(\phi \,|\, y, \tau, \sigma_c^2, \sigma_\tau^2, \gamma)$.
3. Draw from $p(\sigma_c^2 \,|\, y, \tau, \phi, \sigma_\tau^2, \gamma)$.
4. Draw from $p(\sigma_\tau^2 \,|\, y, \tau, \phi, \sigma_c^2, \gamma)$.
5. Draw from $p(\gamma \,|\, y, \tau, \phi, \sigma_c^2, \sigma_\tau^2)$.

Stack $y = (y_1, \ldots, y_T)'$, and similarly define c, u^c, and u^τ. Then, rewrite the system (18.6), (18.7), and (18.8) in matrix notation:

$$\begin{aligned} y &= \tau + c, \\ H_\phi c &= u^c, \\ H_2 \tau &= \tilde{\alpha}_\tau + u^\tau, \end{aligned}$$

where $\tilde{\alpha}_\tau = (\tau_0 + \Delta\tau_0, -\tau_0, 0, \ldots, 0)'$ and

$$H_2 = \begin{pmatrix} 1 & 0 & 0 & 0 & \cdots & 0 \\ -2 & 1 & 0 & 0 & \cdots & 0 \\ 1 & -2 & 1 & 0 & \cdots & 0 \\ 0 & 1 & -2 & 1 & \cdots & 0 \\ \vdots & \ddots & \ddots & \ddots & \ddots & 0 \\ 0 & \cdots & 0 & 1 & -2 & 1 \end{pmatrix}, \quad H_\phi = \begin{pmatrix} 1 & 0 & 0 & 0 & \cdots & 0 \\ -\phi_1 & 1 & 0 & 0 & \cdots & 0 \\ -\phi_2 & -\phi_1 & 1 & 0 & \cdots & 0 \\ 0 & -\phi_2 & -\phi_1 & 1 & \cdots & 0 \\ \vdots & \ddots & \ddots & \ddots & \ddots & 0 \\ 0 & \cdots & 0 & -\phi_2 & -\phi_1 & 1 \end{pmatrix}.$$

Both H_2 and H_ϕ are band matrices with unit determinant, and therefore they are invertible. Hence, given the parameters, it follows that

$$\begin{aligned} (y \,|\, \tau, \phi, \sigma_c^2) &\sim N(\tau, \sigma_c^2 (H_\phi' H_\phi)^{-1}), \\ (\tau \,|\, \gamma, \sigma_\tau^2) &\sim N(\alpha_\tau, \sigma_\tau^2 (H_2' H_2)^{-1}), \end{aligned}$$

where $\alpha_\tau = H_2^{-1} \tilde{\alpha}_\tau = (\tau_0 + \Delta\tau_0, \tau_0 + 2\Delta\tau_0, \ldots, \tau_0 + T\Delta\tau_0)'$. Then, combining the likelihood function and prior in the preceding equations, we have, using standard linear regression derivations,

$$(\tau \,|\, y, \phi, \sigma_c^2, \sigma_\tau^2, \gamma) \sim N(\hat{\tau}, K_\tau^{-1}), \tag{18.9}$$

where

$$K_\tau = \frac{1}{\sigma_\tau^2} H_2' H_2 + \frac{1}{\sigma_c^2} H_\phi' H_\phi, \quad \hat{\tau} = K_\tau^{-1} \left(\frac{1}{\sigma_\tau^2} H_2' H_2 \alpha_\tau + \frac{1}{\sigma_c^2} H_\phi' H_\phi y \right).$$

Since K_τ is a band precision matrix, we can sample τ efficiently using the precision sampler as described in Exercise 18.1.

To sample ϕ in Step 2, we write (18.7) as

$$c = X_\phi \phi + u^c,$$

where X_ϕ is a $T \times 2$ matrix consisting of lagged values of c_t:

$$X_\phi = \begin{pmatrix} c_0 & c_{-1} \\ c_1 & c_0 \\ \vdots & \vdots \\ c_{T-1} & c_{T-2} \end{pmatrix}.$$

Again, using standard regression results we obtain

$$(\phi \,|\, y, \tau, \sigma_c^2, \sigma_\tau^2, \gamma) \sim N(\hat{\phi}, K_\phi^{-1}) 1(\phi \in R),$$

where

$$K_\phi = V_\phi^{-1} + \frac{1}{\sigma_c^2} X_\phi' X_\phi, \quad \hat{\phi} = K_\phi^{-1}\left(V_\phi^{-1}\phi_0 + \frac{1}{\sigma_c^2} X_\phi' c\right).$$

A draw from this truncated normal distribution can be obtained by the acceptance–rejection method, i.e., we keep sampling from $N(\hat{\phi}, K_\phi^{-1})$ until $\phi \in R$.

Step 3 can be easily implemented since the full conditional distribution of σ_c^2 is inverse gamma:

$$(\sigma_c^2 \,|\, y, \tau, \phi, \sigma_\tau^2, \gamma) \sim IG\left(\nu_{\sigma_c^2} + \frac{T}{2}, S_{\sigma_c^2} + \frac{1}{2}(c - X_\phi\phi)'(c - X_\phi\phi)\right).$$

Next, to implement Step 4, notice that the conditional density of σ_τ^2 is given by

$$p(\sigma_\tau^2 \,|\, y, \tau, \phi, \sigma_c^2, \gamma) \propto (\sigma_\tau^2)^{-\frac{T}{2}} e^{-\frac{1}{2\sigma_\tau^2}\sum_{t=1}^T (\Delta\tau_t - \Delta\tau_{t-1})^2} I(0 < \sigma_\tau^2 < b_{\sigma_\tau^2}),$$

which is not a standard density. However, we can sample from it using a griddy Gibbs step as described in Exercise 11.11.

Lastly, to sample $\gamma = (\tau_0, \tau_{-1})'$, first note that

$$\alpha_\tau = \begin{pmatrix} \tau_0 + \Delta\tau_0 \\ \tau_0 + 2\Delta\tau_0 \\ \cdots \\ \tau_0 + T\Delta\tau_0 \end{pmatrix} = X_\gamma \gamma,$$

where

$$X_\gamma = \begin{pmatrix} 2 & -1 \\ 3 & -2 \\ \vdots & \vdots \\ T+1 & -T \end{pmatrix}.$$

Hence, we have

$$\tau = X_\gamma \gamma + H_2^{-1} u^\tau$$

with $H_2^{-1}u^\tau \sim N(0, \sigma_\tau^2(H_2'H_2)^{-1})$. Then, by standard regression results, we have

$$(\gamma \,|\, y, \tau, \phi, \sigma_c^2, \sigma_\tau^2) \sim N(\hat{\gamma}, K_\gamma^{-1}),$$

where

$$K_\gamma = V_\gamma^{-1} + \frac{1}{\sigma_\tau^2}X_\gamma' H_2' H_2 X_\gamma, \quad \hat{\gamma} = K_\gamma^{-1}\left(V_\gamma^{-1}\gamma_0 + \frac{1}{\sigma_\tau^2}X_\gamma' H_2' H_2 \tau\right).$$

(b) We use the Gibbs sampler of part (a) to produce output gap estimates using the log of US real GDP from 1947Q1 to 2015Q4. The model is given by (18.6), (18.7), and (18.8) with $p = 2$. For the prior, we assume relatively large prior variances with $V_\phi = I_2$ and $V_\gamma = 100I_2$. For the prior means, we set $\phi_0 = (1.3, -0.7)'$ and $\gamma_0 = (750, 750)'$. Note that these values imply that the AR(2) process of the transitory component has two complex roots. Furthermore, we assume the upper bound of the uniform prior on σ_τ^2 to be 0.01 and $\nu_{\sigma_c^2} = 3,\ S_{\sigma_c^2} = 2$.

Figure 18.2 reports the output gap estimates $\{c_t\}$ over the whole sample. The negative estimates generally coincide with the National Bureau of Economic Research (NBER) recession dates, and they are especially large in magnitude during the late 1940s, around 1960, and in the early 1980s. In contrast, the trough of the Great Recession is only about -3.1%. Moreover, the output gap has essentially closed at the end of the sample.

Next, we present the estimated annualized trend output growth rate – the posterior means of $4\Delta\tau_t = 4(\tau_t - \tau_{t-1})$ – in Figure 18.3. It is clear that there is substantial time variation in trend growth over the past six decades. Specifically, the annualized trend growth rate fluctuates between 3.5% and 4% from the beginning of the sample until 1970. It then begins a steady decline and reaches about 3% in the mid 1970s. The estimated trend growth rate remains stable at about 3% from the mid 1970s until 2000, when it starts another gradual decline to about 1.6% in the middle of the Great Recession.

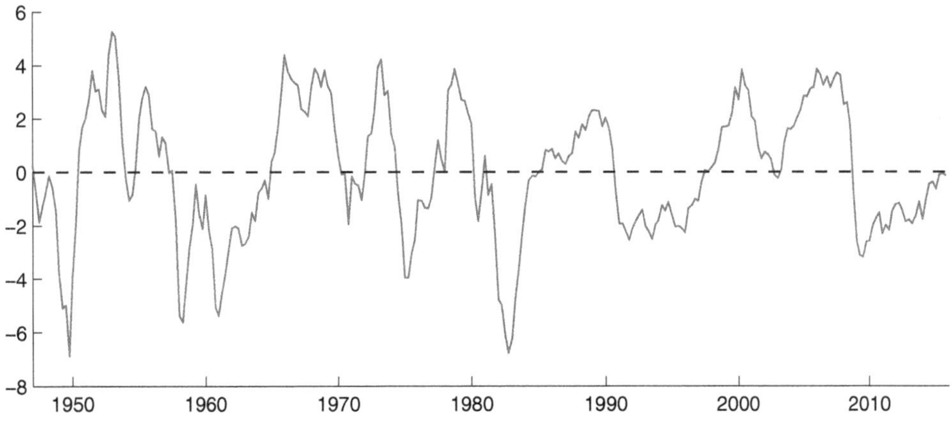

Figure 18.2. Estimate of the output gap.

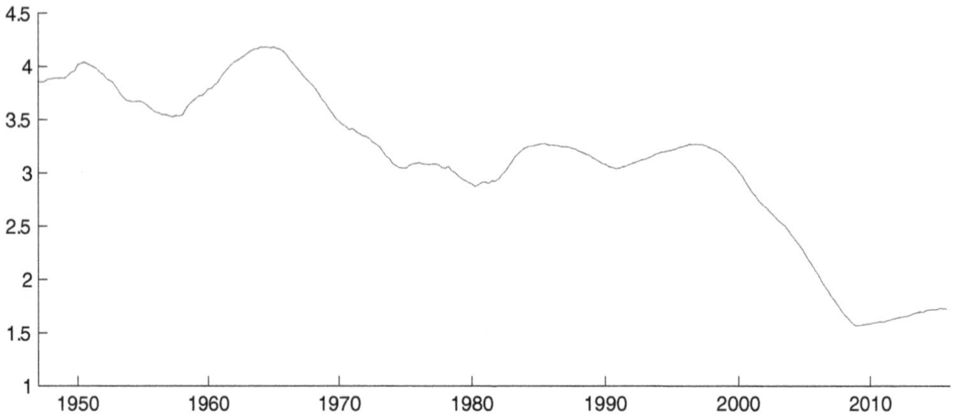

Figure 18.3. Estimate of the annualized growth in trend output $4\Delta\tau_t$.

Exercise 18.3 (The local slope model) This exercise extends the local level model of Exercise 18.1 to allow for a time-varying drift. Specifically, consider the following unobserved components model:

$$y_t = \tau_t + \epsilon_t, \tag{18.10}$$

where $\{\epsilon_t\}$ are assumed to be *iid* $N(0, \sigma_y^2)$. The trend component τ_t is modeled as a random walk with a time-varying drift:

$$\tau_t = \tau_{t-1} + \alpha_t + u_t^\tau, \tag{18.11}$$

$$\alpha_t = \alpha_{t-1} + u_t^\alpha, \tag{18.12}$$

where $\{u_t^\tau\}$ and $\{u_t^\alpha\}$ are *iid* $N(0, \sigma_\tau^2)$ and $N(0, \sigma_\alpha^2)$, respectively, and the initial conditions τ_0 and α_0 are treated as unknown parameters. Since the drift α_t can be interpreted as the slope of the trend and is time varying, the above model is called the local slope model.

It is often of interest to test if the drift α_t is time varying or constant. Formally, a constant drift model is a restricted version of the above model with $\sigma_\alpha^2 = 0$, which implies $\alpha_1 = \cdots = \alpha_T = \alpha_0$. It might appear that the Bayes factor in favor of the unrestricted model against the restricted version with $\sigma_\alpha^2 = 0$ can be obtained using the Savage–Dickey density ratio (see Exercise 6.8),

$$B_{\text{UR}} = \frac{p(\sigma_\alpha^2 = 0)}{p(\sigma_\alpha^2 = 0 \,|\, y)},$$

where the numerator is the marginal prior density of σ_α^2 evaluated at 0 and the denominator is the marginal posterior evaluated at 0. To compute the relevant Bayes factor, one only needs to evaluate two univariate densities at a point, which is often easy to do.

However, this easy approach to calculating the Bayes factor cannot be directly applied in our setting due to two related issues. First, the value 0 is at the boundary of the parameter space of σ_α^2, and therefore the Savage–Dickey density ratio approach is not applicable. Second, the conventional inverse gamma prior for σ_α^2 has zero density at zero and therefore $p(\sigma_\alpha^2 = 0) = 0$.

To overcome these difficulties, we can work with the non-centered parameterization of Früwirth-Schnatter and Wagner (2010). Instead of the error variance σ_α^2, we work with the standard derivation σ_α that is defined to have its support on the whole real line. Using the non-centered parameterization to perform specification checks for models with time-varying parameters is considered in Chan (2018).

Consider the following unobserved components model in the non-centered parameterization:

$$y_t = \tau_0 + \sigma_\tau \tilde{\tau}_t + t\alpha_0 + \sigma_\alpha \sum_{s=1}^{t} \tilde{\alpha}_s + \epsilon_t, \tag{18.13}$$

$$\tilde{\tau}_t = \tilde{\tau}_{t-1} + \tilde{u}_t^\tau, \tag{18.14}$$

$$\tilde{\alpha}_t = \tilde{\alpha}_{t-1} + \tilde{u}_t^\alpha, \tag{18.15}$$

where $\{\tilde{u}_t^\tau\}$ and $\{\tilde{u}_t^\alpha\}$ are mutually independent $N(0,1)$ random variables and $\tilde{\tau}_0 = \tilde{\alpha}_0 = 0$. To see that this is a reparameterization of the model in (18.10), (18.11), and (18.12), let

$$\alpha_t = \alpha_0 + \sigma_\alpha \tilde{\alpha}_t \tag{18.16}$$

$$\tau_t = \tau_0 + \sigma_\tau \tilde{\tau}_t + t\alpha_0 + \sigma_\alpha \sum_{s=1}^{t} \tilde{\alpha}_s. \tag{18.17}$$

Then it is clear that $y_t = \tau_t + \epsilon_t$, and

$$\begin{aligned} \alpha_t - \alpha_{t-1} &= \sigma_\alpha(\tilde{\alpha}_t - \tilde{\alpha}_{t-1}) = \sigma_\alpha \tilde{u}_t^\alpha, \\ \tau_t - \tau_{t-1} &= \alpha_0 + \sigma_\alpha \tilde{\alpha}_t + \sigma_\tau(\tilde{\tau}_t - \tilde{\tau}_{t-1}) \\ &= \alpha_t + \sigma_\tau \tilde{u}_t^\tau. \end{aligned}$$

Hence, it becomes the original model in (18.10)–(18.12).

Früwirth-Schnatter and Wagner (2010) considered a normal prior centered at 0 for σ_α: $\sigma_\alpha \sim N(0, V_{\sigma_\alpha})$. This normal prior on the standard deviation σ_α has two main advantages over the usual inverse gamma prior on the variance σ_α^2.

First, by a change of variable (see, e.g., Kroese and Chan 2014, Section 3.5), we can show that the implied prior for σ_α^2 is $G(\frac{1}{2}, \frac{1}{2V_{\sigma_\alpha}})$. Compared to the conventional inverse gamma prior, this gamma prior has more mass concentrated around small values. Hence, it provides shrinkage: *a priori* it favors the more parsimonious constant-coefficient model. The second advantage is that it is a conjugate prior for σ_α under the non-centered parameterization – it therefore facilitates computation.

The parameter σ_α has support on the real line, but its sign is not identified – its normal prior is symmetric around 0, and changing both the signs of σ_α and $\tilde{\alpha}_t$ does not alter the likelihood value. Consequently, the posterior distribution of σ_α can be bimodal, and care

needs to be taken to sample from the posterior distribution. The preceding derivation and discussion relates to σ_α, but similar considerations hold for σ_τ.
(a) Derive a Gibbs sampler for carrying out posterior inference in this model using the non-centered parameterization and describe how the Savage–Dickey density ratios for $\sigma_\alpha = 0$ and $\sigma_\tau = 0$ can be calculated.
(b) Generate an artificial data set of $T = 250$ observations from the non-centered parameterization of the local slope model. Using this data and the Gibbs sampler from part (a), plot the posteriors of σ_α and σ_τ and calculate the Bayes factor comparing the model with $\sigma_\tau \neq 0$ to the model with $\sigma_\tau = 0$. Also, give the Bayes factor comparing the model with $\sigma_\alpha \neq 0$ to the model with $\sigma_\alpha = 0$.

Solution
(a) The parameters of the local slope model in the non-centered parameterization are $\beta = (\tau_0, \alpha_0, \sigma_\tau, \sigma_\alpha)'$ and σ_y^2. For the Savage–Dickey density ratio identity to hold, the priors under the restricted and unrestricted models need to satisfy a certain condition (see Exercise 6.8). A sufficient condition is that the restricted and unrestricted parameters are independent *a priori*. Accordingly, we assume the following independent priors:

$$\beta \sim N(\beta_0, V_\beta), \quad \sigma_y^2 \sim IG(\nu_{\sigma_y^2}, S_{\sigma_y^2}),$$

where the third and fourth elements of β_0 are zero and V_β is a diagonal matrix. Then, the Gibbs sampler consists of the following steps:

1. Draw from $p(\tilde{\tau}, \tilde{\alpha} \,|\, y, \beta, \sigma_y^2)$.
2. Draw from $p(\beta \,|\, y, \tilde{\tau}, \tilde{\alpha}, \sigma_y^2)$,
3. Randomly permute the signs of $(\tilde{\tau}, \tilde{\alpha})$ and $(\sigma_\tau, \sigma_\alpha)$.
4. Draw from $p(\sigma_y^2 \,|\, y, \tilde{\tau}, \tilde{\alpha}, \beta)$.

As mentioned before, the signs of σ_τ and σ_α are not identified, and the corresponding posterior distributions can be bimodal. Step 3 improves the mixing of the Markov chain by randomly permuting the signs of $(\tilde{\tau}, \tilde{\alpha})$ and $(\sigma_\tau, \sigma_\alpha)$. That is, we draw Z uniformly from 0 to 1. If $Z < .5$, we return $(-\tilde{\tau}, -\tilde{\alpha})$ and $(-\sigma_\tau, -\sigma_\alpha)$; otherwise we keep the draws.

One complication of implementing the first step is that $\tilde{\alpha}_t$ enters the observation equation (18.13) as the sum $\tilde{A}_t = \sum_{s=1}^t \tilde{\alpha}_s$. But it turns out that directly drawing $\tilde{A}_t$ simplifies the computations. To do this, we need the prior of $\tilde{A} = (\tilde{A}_1, \ldots, \tilde{A}_T)'$ implied by (18.15).

First recall that (18.15) implies $H\tilde{\alpha} = \tilde{u}^\alpha$, where $\tilde{u}^\alpha \sim N(0, I_T)$ and H is the first difference matrix, as before. Since $\tilde{A}_1 = \tilde{\alpha}_1$ and $\tilde{A}_t - \tilde{A}_{t-1} = \tilde{\alpha}_t$, we have $H\tilde{A} = \tilde{\alpha}$. Consequently, $\tilde{A} = H^{-1}\tilde{\alpha} = H^{-2}\tilde{u}^\alpha$, and therefore

$$\tilde{A} \sim N(0, (H_2' H_2)^{-1}),$$

where we have used the fact that $H^2 = H_2$ where

$$H_2 = \begin{pmatrix} 1 & 0 & 0 & 0 & \cdots & 0 \\ -2 & 1 & 0 & 0 & \cdots & 0 \\ 1 & -2 & 1 & 0 & \cdots & 0 \\ 0 & 1 & -2 & 1 & \cdots & 0 \\ \vdots & \ddots & \ddots & \ddots & \ddots & 0 \\ 0 & \cdots & 0 & 1 & -2 & 1 \end{pmatrix}.$$

Now, to sample $\tilde{\tau}$ and $\tilde{A}$ jointly, we write (18.13) in terms of $\gamma = (\tilde{\tau}', \tilde{A}')'$:

$$y = \tau_0 1_T + \alpha_0 1_{1:T} + X_\gamma \gamma + \epsilon,$$

where $1_{1:T} = (1, 2, 3, \ldots, T)'$ and $X_\gamma = (\sigma_\tau I_T, \sigma_\alpha I_T)$. Note that X_γ is a sparse but not a band matrix. Hence, computations involving X_γ, though still fast, would not be as fast as those involving band matrices.

Next we derive the prior on γ. Note that (18.14) implies $\tilde{\tau} \sim N(0, (H'H)^{-1})$. Combining the prior on $\tilde{A}$ and using the assumption that $\tilde{\tau}$ and $\tilde{A}$ are independent, we have

$$\gamma \sim N(0, P_\gamma^{-1}),$$

where $P_\gamma = \text{diag}(H'H, H_2'H_2)$. It then follows from standard linear regression results that

$$(\gamma \,|\, y, \beta, \sigma_y^2) \sim N(\hat{\gamma}, K_\gamma^{-1}),$$

where

$$K_\gamma = P_\gamma + \frac{1}{\sigma_y^2} X_\gamma' X_\gamma, \quad \hat{\gamma} = K_\gamma^{-1} \left(\frac{1}{\sigma_y^2} X_\gamma'(y - \tau_0 1_T - \alpha_0 1_{1:T}) \right).$$

Even though X_γ and P_γ are sparse but not band matrices, we can sample γ using the precision sampler algorithm of Exercise 18.1.

Note that (conditional on $\tilde{\tau}, \tilde{\alpha}$) β and σ_y^2 are regression coefficients and a regression error variance, respectively. Thus, standard regression results apply for Steps 2 and 4 in the Gibbs sampler. Finally, given the posterior draws of $\tilde{\tau}$ and $\tilde{\alpha}$, we can recover τ and α using (18.16) and (18.17).

(b) Matlab code for generating a dataset of $T = 250$ observations from the local slope model with $\sigma_\alpha = 0.1$, $\sigma_\tau = 0$, $\alpha_0 = 0.1$, $\tau_0 = 3$, and $\sigma_y^2 = 0.5$ is on the website associated with this book. Code is also provided for the Gibbs sampler of part (a). We ran this code to produce 20 000 posterior draws.

Figure 18.4 plots the histograms of the posterior draws of σ_τ and σ_α. The posterior density of σ_α is clearly bimodal, where the two modes are 0.1 and -0.1, compared to the true value of 0.1. The posterior density of σ_τ is bimodal as well, but it has much more mass around zero. In fact, the estimated Savage–Dickey density ratio $p(\sigma_\tau = 0)/p(\sigma_\tau = 0 \,|\, y)$ is 0.079, implying a Bayes factor of 12.66 in favor of the restricted model with $\sigma_\tau = 0$.

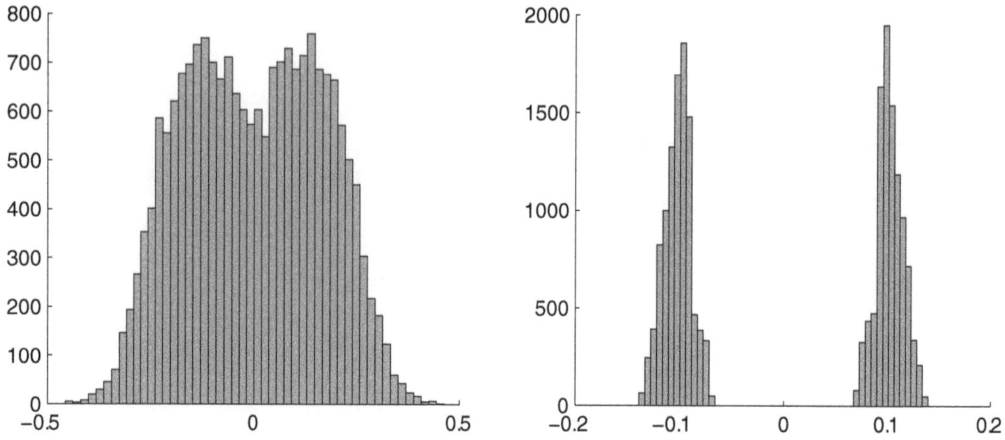

Figure 18.4. Histograms of the posterior draws of σ_τ (left panel) and σ_α (right panel).

In contrast, the estimated Savage–Dickey density ratio $p(\sigma_\alpha = 0)/p(\sigma_\alpha = 0 \,|\, y)$ is, to all intents and purposes, infinity, indicating overwhelming support for the unrestricted model.

Exercise 18.4 (The dynamic factor model) Let $y_t = (y_{1t}, \ldots, y_{nt})'$ be a vector of n dependent variables at time t for $t = 1, \ldots, T$. The dynamic factor model can be written as

$$y_t = \lambda f_t + \epsilon_t, \tag{18.18}$$

$$f_t = \Phi_1 f_{t-1} + \cdots + \Phi_p f_{t-p} + \epsilon_t^f, \tag{18.19}$$

where f_t is a vector of q unobserved latent variables called factors, λ is an $n \times q$ matrix of parameters called factor loadings, $\epsilon_t = (\epsilon_{1t}, \ldots, \epsilon_{nt})'$ is $iid\ N(0, \Sigma)$, and $\epsilon_t^f = (\epsilon_{1t}^f, \ldots, \epsilon_{nt}^f)'$ is $iid\ N\left(0, \Sigma^f\right)$, where Σ^f is assumed to be diagonal. ϵ_t and ϵ_s^f are independent of one another for all s and t. The dynamic factor model is commonly used when n is large and q is small. Thus, a potentially high-dimensional model is reduced to a more parsimonious model where each equation involves only a few right-hand-side variables.

The dynamic factor model requires additional restrictions to ensure identification. A common set of restrictions, which we use in this exercise, is to set Σ to be a diagonal matrix and λ to be a lower triangular matrix with ones on the diagonal. The first of these implies that ϵ_{it} and ϵ_{jt} are uncorrelated with each other for $i \neq j$. Thus, ϵ_{it} is a shock idiosyncratic to equation i and y_{it} is explained by a factor which contains information common to all variables plus this idiosyncratic shock. The second restriction overcomes the lack of identification that arises since $\lambda f_t = \lambda C C^{-1} f_t$ for any non-singular matrix C and, thus, a model with factors f_t and factor loadings λ is equivalent to one with factors $C^{-1} f_t$ and factor loadings λC. By assuming λ to be a lower triangular matrix with ones on the diagonal, we fix both the orientation and the scale of the latent factors.

It is worth noting that other variants of this model are possible and Bayesian inference can be done either as a special case or as a simple extension of the methods described here. The static factor model, popular in finance, arises as the special case where $\Phi_1 = \cdots = \Phi_p = 0$. It is also common to relax the assumption that ϵ_t is independent over time by assuming ϵ_{it} to follow AR processes for $i = 1, \ldots, n$. This is a simple extension of the model used in this exercise.

It is straightforward to develop MCMC methods for Bayesian inference in this model since it is a linear Gaussian state space model. That is, the factors can be interpreted as states and drawn using the precision sampler of Exercise 18.1 (conditional on λ, Φ_1, $\ldots$, Φ_p, Σ). But, conditional on f_t, (18.18) is just a series of n univariate regressions, and standard Bayesian methods for the regression model (e.g. Exercise 10.1) can be used to draw elements of λ and Σ one equation at a time. Finally, conditional on f_t, if $q = 1$ then (18.19) is also a univariate regression and standard Bayesian regression methods can be used to draw the parameters. If $q > 1$, (18.19) has the form of a multivariate regression (see Exercise 2.14) or, equivalently, a vector autoregression (see Chapter 20).

Using a large macroeconomic data set (e.g., the website associated with this book has a large quarterly US data set for 196 variables), carry out Bayesian inference in the dynamic factor model for $q = 1$ and $p = 1$. Plot the factor you extract.

Solution

We use a large macroeconomic data set to extract a common dynamic factor. More specifically, the data is taken from the US Federal Reserve Bank of St. Louis' FRED-QD data set and contains 196 quarterly variables. The sample periods run from 1959Q1 to 2015Q3. All data are transformed to stationarity following the recommendations in the FRED-QD database and then standardized to have mean zero and standard deviation one. The data is available at the website associated with this book. See also McCracken and Ng (2015). Complete details of all the variables in the data set are provided there.

We estimate the dynamic factor model in (18.18)–(18.19) with $q = 1$ latent factor and $p = 1$ lag. In this case the latent factor f_t is a scalar and the factor loading λ is an $n \times 1$ vector with the first element fixed to 1. A Gibbs sampler can be constructed to sequentially sample f_t, λ, Σ, Σ_f, and Ψ_1. All the Gibbs steps are standard and here we only outline the sampling of λ and Σ. Let λ_i denote the ith element of λ and σ_i^2 the ith diagonal entry of Σ. Since Σ is diagonal, we can sample λ_i and σ_i^2 equation by equation. To that end, write (18.18) as

$$\begin{aligned} y_{1t} &= f_t + \epsilon_{1t}, \\ y_{it} &= \lambda_i f_t + \epsilon_{it}, \quad i = 2, \ldots, n, \end{aligned}$$

where $\epsilon_{it} \sim N(0, \sigma_i^2)$. Given these n univariate regressions, we can use standard Bayesian methods for the regression model to draw λ_i and σ_i^2 one equation at a time.

Figure 18.5 reports the estimated dynamic factor f_t over the whole sample. The negative estimates generally coincide with the NBER recession dates. In particular, they are

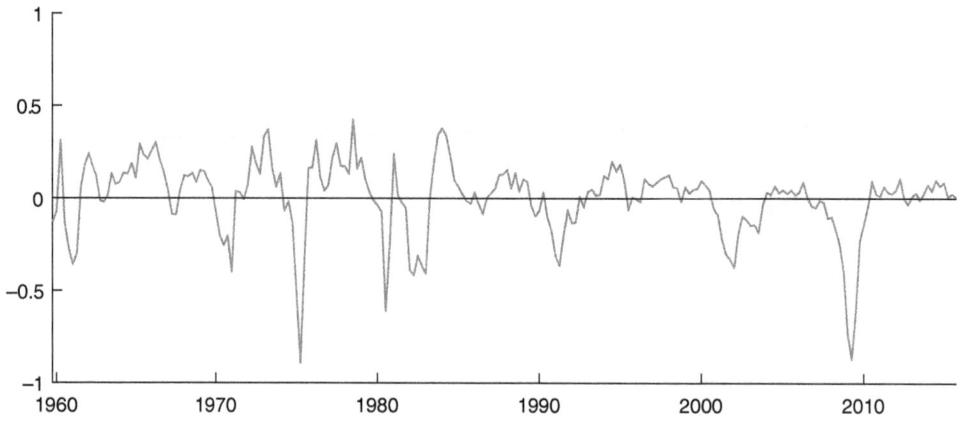

Figure 18.5. Estimate of the dynamic factor.

especially large in magnitude during the Great Inflation of the 1970s, the recession of the early 1980s, and the Great Recession of 2008–2009. Towards the end of the sample the dynamic factor is essentially zero.

Exercise 18.5 (The Markov switching model) Consider a basic version of a Markov switching (or regime-switching or hidden Markov) model, popularized by Hamilton (1989):

$$y_t = \mu_0 + \mu_1 s_t + u_t, \quad u_t \overset{ind}{\sim} N(0, \sigma^2_{s_t}). \tag{18.20}$$

If y_t is GDP growth, then the latent variable s_t denotes the underlying state or regime that the economy is in, and we assume that there are two regimes so that $s_t \in \{0, 1\}\ \forall t$. For identification purposes, we also assume $\mu_1 > 0$ so that state $s_t = 1$ corresponds to the high growth state.

Suppose the following priors are employed:

$$\begin{aligned}
\mu_0 &\sim N(\underline{\mu}_0, \underline{v}_0), \\
\mu_1 &\sim TN_{(0,\infty)}(\underline{\mu}_1, \underline{v}_1), \\
\sigma^2_j &\sim IG(\underline{v}_j, \underline{s}_j), \quad j = 0, 1,
\end{aligned}$$

where TN denotes a truncated normal distribution. Furthermore, suppose the probability of being in state j is described by the Markov process:

$$\begin{aligned}
\Pr(s_t = 0 | s_{t-1} = 0) &= 1 - a, \\
\Pr(s_t = 1 | s_{t-1} = 0) &= a, \\
\Pr(s_t = 0 | s_{t-1} = 1) &= b, \\
\Pr(s_t = 1 | s_{t-1} = 1) &= 1 - b.
\end{aligned} \tag{18.21}$$

For the transition probabilities, the following priors are employed:

$$p(a) \propto a^{\underline{a}_0 - 1}(1-a)^{\underline{a}_1 - 1},$$
$$p(b) \propto b^{\underline{b}_0 - 1}(1-b)^{\underline{b}_1 - 1}.$$

(a) Derive a posterior simulator for fitting this Markov switching model.
(b) Write a program to implement the posterior simulator in part (a) using a real GDP growth data set. The website associated with this book provides quarterly US GDP over the period 1947–2009. Comment on your results.

Solution
(a) The joint posterior of interest is

$$p(\mu_0, \mu_1, \sigma_0^2, \sigma_1^2, a, b, s|y),$$

where $s = (s_1, \ldots, s_T)'$. Conditional on s, the Markov switching model is just a regression with groupwise heteroscedasticity and, hence, standard Bayesian regression methods (see Exercise 12.11) can be used to sample μ_0, μ_1, σ_0^2, and σ_1^2. Conditional on s, sampling from a and b can be straightforwardly done using results from the Bernoulli distribution (see Exercise 2.1). The novelty in employing a Gibbs sampler to fit this model lies in the simulation of the latent states s, and this is what we focus on in this solution.

We follow Chib (1996), who noted that (conditional on all the other parameters in the model, which we denote by θ) s can be sampled jointly in a single step. We first introduce some notation and let

$$S_t = (s_1, s_2, \ldots, s_t) \quad \text{and} \quad S^{t+1} = (s_{t+1}, s_{t+2}, \ldots, s_T),$$

and define Y_t and Y^{t+1} similarly. Thus, S_t is the history of states up to time t and S^{t+1} is the collection of future states.

We begin by noting that we wish to draw from $p(S_T|Y_T, \theta)$, which we write as

$$\begin{aligned} p(S_T|Y_T,\theta) &= p(s_T|Y_T,\theta)p(S_{T-1}|Y_T, s_T, \theta) \\ &= p(s_T|Y_T,\theta) \times \cdots \times p(s_t|Y_T, S^{t+1}, \theta) \times \cdots \times p(s_1|Y_T, S^2, \theta). \end{aligned}$$

The first line of the above derivation follows from the definition of S_{T-1} and writes the joint distribution as a conditional times a marginal. The second line factors the term $p(S_{T-1}|Y_T, s_T, \theta)$ into the component conditional posterior distributions.

In order to generate draws from this posterior conditional, we can work backwards via the method of composition. That is, we can:

1. Draw from $p(s_T|Y_T, \theta)$.
2. Then draw from $p(s_{T-1}|Y_T, S^T = s_T, \theta)$.

3. Then $p(s_{T-2}|Y_T, S^{T-1} = \{s_{T-1}, s_T\}, \theta)$.
4. …
5. Draw from $p(s_1|Y_T, S^2, \theta)$.

With the exception of the term $p(s_T|Y_T, \theta)$ (which we will address later), all of these are of the form

$$p(s_t|Y_T, S^{t+1}, \theta).$$

To evaluate this term, first note that

$$p(s_t|Y_T, S^{t+1}, \theta) = p(s_t|Y_t, S^{t+1}, \theta),$$

since the state s_t does not depend on future Ys given S^{t+1}. In addition,

$$p(s_t|Y_t, S^{t+1}, \theta) \propto p(s_t, S^{t+1}|Y_t, \theta).$$

Finally, since

$$Y^{t+1}|S^{t+1}, s_t, Y_t, \theta$$

does not depend on s_t (given S^{t+1} and θ), we can write

$$p(s_t|Y_t, S^{t+1}, \theta) \propto p(s_t, Y^{t+1}, S^{t+1}|Y_t, \theta).$$

Continuing in this fashion, we obtain:

$$\begin{aligned} p(s_t|Y_t, S^{t+1}, \theta) &\propto p(s_t|Y_t, \theta)p(Y^{t+1}, S^{t+1}|Y_t, s_t, \theta) \\ &= p(s_t|Y_t, \theta)p(s_{t+1}|s_t, \theta)p(Y^{t+1}, S^{t+2}|Y_t, s_t, s_{t+1}, \theta) \\ &\propto p(s_t|Y_t, \theta)p(s_{t+1}|s_t, \theta). \end{aligned}$$

The second line separates s_{t+1} from S^{t+1} and notes that it is independent of everything else given s_t and θ. The final line recognizes that Y^{t+1}, S^{t+2} is conditionally independent of s_t given s_{t+1} and θ.

Since s_t is binary, we obtain

$$\begin{aligned} &\Pr(s_t = 1|Y_T, S^{t+1}, \theta) \\ &\quad = \frac{\Pr(s_t = 1|Y_t, \theta)p(s_{t+1}|s_t = 1, \theta)}{\Pr(s_t = 1|Y_t, \theta)p(s_{t+1}|s_t = 1, \theta) + \Pr(s_t = 0|Y_t, \theta)p(s_{t+1}|s_t = 0, \theta)}. \end{aligned}$$

The terms $p(s_{t+1}|s_t, \theta)$ can be evaluated from the assumed Markov model, as we sample "backwards" (and thus s_{t+1} will be given). As for the term $p(s_t|Y_t, \theta)$, first observe that

$$
\begin{aligned}
p(s_t|Y_{t-1},\theta) &= \sum_{j=0}^{1} p(s_t, s_{t-1}=j|Y_{t-1},\theta) \\
&= \sum_{j=0}^{1} p(s_t|s_{t-1}=j, Y_{t-1},\theta)\Pr(s_{t-1}=j|Y_{t-1},\theta) \\
&= \sum_{j=0}^{1} p(s_t|s_{t-1}=j,\theta)\Pr(s_{t-1}=j|Y_{t-1},\theta),
\end{aligned}
$$

since s_t does not depend on Y_{t-1} given s_{t-1} and θ. The above equation is referred to as the prediction step, as it amounts to predicting the current state s_t given the data available to us at $t-1$.

If $p(s_t|Y_{t-1},\theta)$ is known, we can use it to update our prediction given Y_t. To see this, first note that

$$
\begin{aligned}
p(y_t, s_t|Y_{t-1},\theta) &= p(s_t|y_t, Y_{t-1},\theta)p(y_t|Y_{t-1},\theta) \\
&= p(s_t|Y_t,\theta)p(y_t|Y_{t-1},\theta),
\end{aligned}
$$

which implies that

$$
p(s_t|Y_t,\theta) \propto p(y_t, s_t|Y_{t-1},\theta).
$$

Writing the right-hand side as a conditional times a marginal distribution, evaluating at $s_t = 1$, and normalizing, we obtain

$$
\begin{aligned}
&\Pr(s_t = 1|Y_t,\theta) \\
&= \frac{p(s_t=1|Y_{t-1},\theta)p(y_t|Y_{t-1},s_t=1,\theta)}{p(s_t=1|Y_{t-1},\theta)p(y_t|Y_{t-1},s_t=1,\theta)+p(s_t=0|Y_{t-1},\theta)p(y_t|Y_{t-1},s_t=0,\theta)}.
\end{aligned}
$$

In more complicated versions of the Markov switching model, y_t can depend on elements of Y_{t-1}, though not in the simple model used in this question. Hence, we can proceed as follows:

1. Sample $s_1|Y_0,\theta$ from the discrete distribution:

$$
\Pr(s_1 = 0) = .5, \quad \Pr(s_1 = 1) = .5.
$$

2. Use the update step to calculate $p(s_1|Y_1,\theta)$.
3. Compute $p(s_2|Y_1,\theta)$ from the prediction step.
4. Compute $p(s_2|Y_2,\theta)$ from the update step.
5. …
6. At the last step, calculate $p(s_T|Y_T,\theta)$ and draw s_T from its discrete distribution.

This first part of the process is often termed forward filtering as we cycle through these densities forward in time. We could also draw from $p(s_t|Y_t,\theta)$ for $t = 1,\ldots,T-1$, but this is not what is asked for in this exercise. Instead, we want draws from $p(s_t|Y_T,\theta)$ for

$t = 1, \ldots, T$. Forward filtering allows us to only take an MCMC draw (call it $s_T^{(r)}$) for time T:

$$s_T^{(r)} \sim p(s_T|Y_T, \theta).$$

How can we get the necessary draws of $s_t^{(r)}$ for $t = 1, \ldots, T-1$? By doing backward smoothing according to the following algorithm.

From previous derivations we know that

$$\Pr(s_{T-1} = 1|Y_T, S^T = s_T^{(r)}, \theta)$$
$$= \frac{\Pr(s_{T-1} = 1|Y_{T-1}, \theta)p(s_T = s_T^{(r)}|s_{T-1} = 1, \theta)}{\Pr(s_{T-1} = 1|Y_{T-1}, \theta)p(s_T = s_T^{(r)}|s_{T-1} = 1, \theta) + \Pr(s_{T-1} = 0|Y_{T-1}, \theta)p(s_T = s_T^{(r)}|s_{T-1} = 0, \theta)}.$$

The right-hand side of this expression again depends only on the Markov transition probabilities as well as $p(s_{T-1}|Y_{T-1}, \theta)$, which were calculated in the forward-filtering step using the updating equation. Thus, it is straightforward to take a draw of $s_{T-1}^{(r)}$ given the draw of $s_T^{(r)}$. But given these draws, we can use the analogous formula for s_{T-2} to obtain the necessary draw of $s_{T-2}^{(r)}$. Proceeding backwards in time in this fashion produces the necessary draws.

To summarize, the following strategy can be used to produce draws from $p(S_T|Y_T, \theta)$:

1. Filter the states forward to obtain the (discrete) distributions $p(s_t|Y_t, \theta), t = 1, 2, \ldots, T$.
2. At $t = T$, sample s_T from $p(s_T|Y_T, \theta)$.
3. Given the results from Step 1, sample $s_{-T}|s_T = (s_{T-1}, s_{T-2}, \ldots, s_1|s_T)$ backwards using the formula for $p(s_t|Y_t, S^{t+1}, \theta)$.
4. With the latent states sampled, draw μ, σ^2, a, and b from their (standard) posterior conditional distributions.
5. Repeat for $r = 1, \ldots, R$ draws.

(b) Code which implements the Gibbs sampler of part (a) is provided on the website associated with this book. We use it to model the real growth rate in US GDP over

Table 18.1: Results for heteroscedastic Markov switching model.

Parameter	Posterior mean	Posterior std. dev
μ_0	.72	.077
μ_1	.11	.088
σ_0^2	1.51	.201
σ_1^2	.27	.056
$1-a$	.97	.024
$1-b$	.95	.028

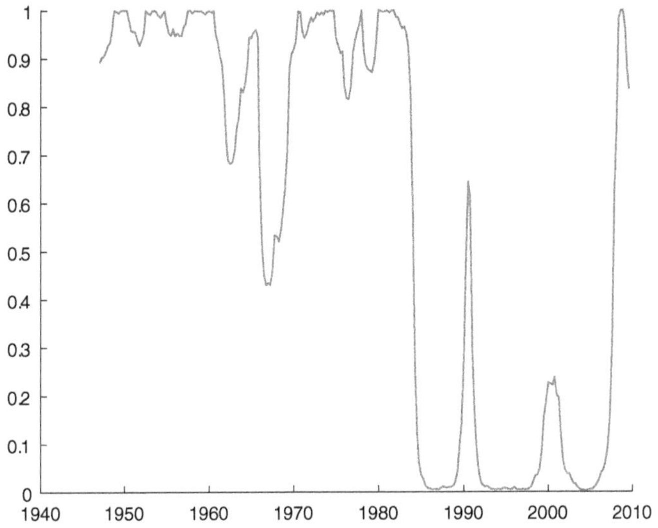

Figure 18.6. Probability of recessionary state.

the period 1947–2009. Table 18.1 presents posterior results and Figure 18.6 plots the probability of being in the recessionary state. Note that persistence within regimes is quite high, and that the difference in error variances between the two regimes is large.

19

Time Series Models for Volatility

In macroeconomic and financial time series, it is often observed that large changes in observations tend to be followed by large changes, while small changes are followed by small changes – the phenomenon that is referred to as volatility clustering. For example, during financial crises movements in financial asset returns tend be large (of either sign), whereas in normal periods the same asset returns might exhibit little time variation.

There are two main econometric approaches to modeling such volatility clustering. The first involves *stochastic volatility models*, where the error variance is time varying in a stochastic fashion. That is, the error variance is a function of past error variances plus a random error. This contrasts with the second class of volatility models where the variance process is a deterministic function of past observations and parameters. Popular examples of the latter class include the autoregressive conditional heteroscedasticity (ARCH) model and its extension, the generalized autoregressive conditional heteroscedasticity (GARCH) model. This chapter contains exercises which allow the reader to understand Bayesian inference in both types of volatility model.

Exercise 19.1 (The stochastic volatility model) The simplest version of a stochastic volatility model assumes that

$$y_t = e^{\frac{1}{2}h_t}\epsilon_t, \tag{19.1}$$

where $\epsilon_t \sim N(0,1)$. It follows that the conditional variance of y_t given h_t is $\text{Var}(y_t \mid h_t) = e^{h_t}$, and hence the conditional variance is time varying. The state h_t is often called the log-volatility. We assume the states $\{h_t\}$ evolve according to a random walk process,

$$h_t = h_{t-1} + u_t, \tag{19.2}$$

where $u_t \sim N(0, \sigma_h^2)$ and is independent of ϵ_t at all leads and lags. The initial condition h_0 is treated as an unknown parameter. It is worth noting that, instead of the random walk process considered in (19.2), many finance applications use a stationary AR(1) process instead. Handling such a case is a simple extension of this exercise.

(a) Develop an MCMC algorithm for Bayesian estimation of the stochastic volatility model.

(b) Extend the MCMC algorithm from part (a) to allow for the measurement equation to have a non-zero mean, and carry out Bayesian estimation of the stochastic volatility model using a data set for the return on a financial asset (e.g., the website associated with this book contains monthly data on the percentage change in the Australian to US dollar exchange rate from January 2005 to December 2012). Plot the posterior mean of h_t and discuss the time-varying pattern of volatility you find.

Solution

(a) This stochastic volatility model is a non-linear state space model where the observation equation, (19.1), is non-linear in the state. The major challenge of Bayesian estimation of this non-linear model is that the joint conditional density of the states $h = (h_1, \ldots, h_T)'$, given the model parameters and the data, is high-dimensional and non-standard. This contrasts with the normal linear state space model where the conditional density of the states is normal and the methods derived and used in Exercises 18.1, 18.2, and 18.3 apply. Consequently, Bayesian estimation using MCMC becomes more difficult. In this solution, we develop an auxiliary mixture sampler (see Kim, Shephard, and Chib 1998) which allows for sampling from the joint conditional posterior of h. Conditional on draws of h, the posteriors of the other parameters, σ_h^2 and h_0, are the same as those of the comparable parameters in the normal linear state space model (see, e.g., Exercise 18.1).

The idea of the auxiliary mixture sampler is to approximate the non-linear stochastic volatility model using a mixture of linear normal models (see Chapter 15 for several exercises on mixture models). An auxiliary latent variable, called a mixture component indicator, is used to write the mixture of normals model and is drawn as part of the MCMC algorithm. Conditional on a draw of the mixture component indicator, the model becomes a normal linear one and standard methods for the normal linear state space model (see Chapter 18) can be used. Details are provided in the remainder of this solution.

We first transform the observation y_t so that the resulting observation equation becomes linear in the log-volatility h_t. More precisely, we square both sides of (19.1) and take the logarithm:

$$y_t^* = h_t + \epsilon_t^*, \tag{19.3}$$

where $y_t^* = \ln y_t^2$ and $\epsilon_t^* = \ln \epsilon_t^2$. In practice, we often set $y_t^* = \ln(y_t^2 + c)$ for some small constant c, say $c = 10^{-4}$, to avoid numerical problems when y_t is close to zero. Then, (19.2) and (19.3) define a linear state space model in h_t. Note, however, that the error ϵ_t^* no longer has a normal distribution (in fact, it follows a log-χ_1^2 distribution) and the machinery for fitting linear normal state space models cannot be directly applied.

To tackle this difficulty, the second step of the auxiliary mixture sampling approach is to obtain an appropriate normal mixture that approximates well the density function of ϵ_t^*, denoted as $f(\epsilon_t^*)$. More precisely, consider the following n-component normal mixture:

$$f(\epsilon_t^*) \approx \sum_{i=1}^{n} p_i \, \phi(\epsilon_t^* \, ; \, \mu_i, \sigma_i^2), \tag{19.4}$$

where $\phi(x \, ; \, \mu, \sigma^2)$ denotes the normal density with mean μ and variance σ^2, and p_i is the probability of the ith mixture component.

We can equivalently write the mixture density in (19.4) in terms of an auxiliary random variable $s_t \in \{1, \ldots, n\}$ that serves as the mixture component indicator:

$$(\epsilon_t^* \mid s_t = i) \sim N(\mu_i, \sigma_i^2), \tag{19.5}$$
$$\Pr(s_t = i) = p_i. \tag{19.6}$$

Using this representation, we have a linear normal model conditional on the component indicators $s = (s_1, \ldots, s_T)'$, and the simulation techniques for normal linear state space models can be used.

The only missing piece is a suitable normal mixture. By matching the moments of the log-χ_1^2 distribution, Kim, Shephard, and Chib (1998) proposed a seven-component normal mixture,

$$f(x) = \sum_{i=1}^{7} p_i \, \phi(x \, ; \, \mu_i - 1.2704, \sigma_i^2),$$

where the values of the parameters of the mixture are given in Table 19.1. We emphasize that these values are fixed and do not depend on any unknown parameters.

Table 19.1: A seven-component normal mixture for approximating the log-χ_1^2 distribution.

Component	p_i	μ_i	σ_i^2
1	0.007 30	−10.129 99	5.795 96
2	0.105 56	−3.972 81	2.613 69
3	0.000 02	−8.566 86	5.179 50
4	0.043 95	2.777 86	0.167 35
5	0.340 01	0.619 42	0.640 09
6	0.245 66	1.795 18	0.340 23
7	0.257 50	−1.088 19	1.262 61

In summary, using the normal mixture approximation in (19.5) and (19.6), the model in (19.3) and (19.2) is now conditionally linear normal given the component indicators $s = (s_1, \dots, s_T)'$.

To complete the model specification, we assume independent prior distributions for σ_h^2 and h_0:

$$\sigma_h^2 \sim IG(\nu_h, S_h), \quad h_0 \sim N(a_0, b_0).$$

Posterior draws from $p(h, s, \sigma_h^2, h_0 \mid y)$ can be obtained via a Gibbs sampler that cycles through the following steps:

1. Sample $(s \mid y, h, \sigma_h^2, h_0)$.
2. Sample $(h \mid y, s, \sigma_h^2, h_0)$.
3. Sample $(\sigma_h^2 \mid y, h, s, h_0)$.
4. Sample $(h_0 \mid y, h, s, \sigma_h^2)$.

The posterior draws obtained are technically from an approximate model, but one can reweight these draws using importance sampling weights to get the exact posterior moments under the original model. However, this step is often skipped in practice as reweighting typically makes little difference; see also the discussion in Kim, Shephard, and Chib (1998).

To implement Step 1, note that given y and h, the errors $\epsilon^* = (\epsilon_1^*, \dots, \epsilon_T^*)'$ are known. It then follows from (19.5) and (19.6) that

$$p(s \mid y, h, \sigma_h^2, h_0) = \prod_{t=1}^{T} p(s_t \mid y_t, h_t, \sigma_h^2, h_0),$$

i.e., the component indicators $\{s_t\}$ are conditionally independent given y, h, and other parameters. Therefore, we can sample each s_t independently.

Since s_t is a discrete random variable that follows a seven-point distribution, it can be easily sampled using a discrete analog of the inverse transform method (see Exercise 11.4 for examples with continuous random variables), provided we can compute $\Pr(s_t = i \mid y_t, h_t, \sigma_h^2, h_0)$ for $i = 1, \dots, 7$. By Bayes' theorem, we have

$$\Pr(s_t = i \mid y_t, h_t, \sigma_h^2, h_0) = \frac{1}{c_t} p_i \, \phi(y_t^* \,;\, h_t + \mu_i - 1.2704, \sigma_i^2),$$

where $c_t = \sum_{j=1}^{7} p_j \, \phi(y_t^* \,;\, h_t + \mu_j - 1.2704, \sigma_j^2)$ is a normalizing constant.

To implement Step 2, recall that we have a normal linear model given the component indicators s. We first rewrite the observation equation (19.3) in matrix notation:

$$y^* = h + \epsilon^*,$$

where $(\epsilon^* \mid s) \sim N(d_s, \Sigma_s)$ with $d_s = (\mu_{s_1} - 1.2704, \dots, \mu_{s_T} - 1.2704)'$, $\Sigma_s = \text{diag}(\sigma_{s_1}^2, \dots, \sigma_{s_T}^2)$, and the fixed parameters $\mu_1, \dots, \mu_7$ and $\sigma_1^2, \dots, \sigma_7^2$ are given in Table 19.1. By a change of variable, we have

$$(y^* \,|\, s, h) \sim N(h + d_s, \Sigma_s).$$

Next, rewrite the state equation (19.2) in matrix form:

$$Hh = \tilde{\alpha}_h + u,$$

where $u \sim N(0, \sigma_h^2 I_T)$, $\tilde{\alpha}_h = (h_0, 0, \ldots, 0)'$, and H is the usual first difference matrix (see Exercise 18.1). Noting that H^{-1} exists and $H^{-1}\tilde{\alpha}_h = h_0 1_T$, we have

$$(h \,|\, \sigma_h^2, h_0) \sim N(h_0 1_T, \sigma_h^2 (H'H)^{-1}).$$

Then, it follows from standard regression results that

$$(h \,|\, y, s, \sigma_h^2, h_0) \sim N(\hat{h}, K_h^{-1}),$$

where

$$K_h = \frac{1}{\sigma_h^2} H'H + \Sigma_s^{-1}, \quad \hat{h} = K_h^{-1}\left(\frac{1}{\sigma_h^2} H'Hh_0 1_T + \Sigma_s^{-1}(y^* - d_s)\right).$$

Since K_h is a band matrix, we can sample h efficiently using the precision sampler described in Exercise 18.1.

Steps 3 and 4 can be done easily, as both conditional distributions are standard. In particular,

$$(\sigma_h^2 \,|\, y, h, h_0) \sim IG\left(\nu_h + \frac{T}{2}, S_h + \frac{1}{2}\sum_{t=1}^{T}(\tau_t - \tau_{t-1})^2\right)$$

and

$$(h_0 \,|\, y, h, \sigma_h^2) \sim N(\hat{h}_0, K_{h_0}^{-1}),$$

where

$$K_{h_0} = \frac{1}{b_0} + \frac{1}{\sigma_h^2}, \quad \hat{h}_0 = K_{h_0}^{-1}\left(\frac{a_0}{b_0} + \frac{h_1}{\sigma_h^2}\right).$$

(b) Adding a constant conditional mean means that (19.1) becomes

$$y_t = \mu + e^{\frac{1}{2}h_t}\epsilon_t, \tag{19.7}$$

where $\epsilon_t \sim N(0, 1)$. The state equation is still given by (19.2). We assume that the prior for this new parameter is given by $\mu \sim N(\mu_0, V_\mu)$.

To estimate the model with the constant conditional mean μ, we simply need an extra block to sample from the conditional density $p(\mu \,|\, y, h)$, and modify the Gibbs sampler discussed in the solution to part (a) by replacing y_t with $y_t - \mu$. Conditional on h, it can be seen that (19.7) can be transformed as

$$e^{-\frac{1}{2}h_t}y_t = e^{-\frac{1}{2}h_t}\mu + \epsilon_{,t}$$

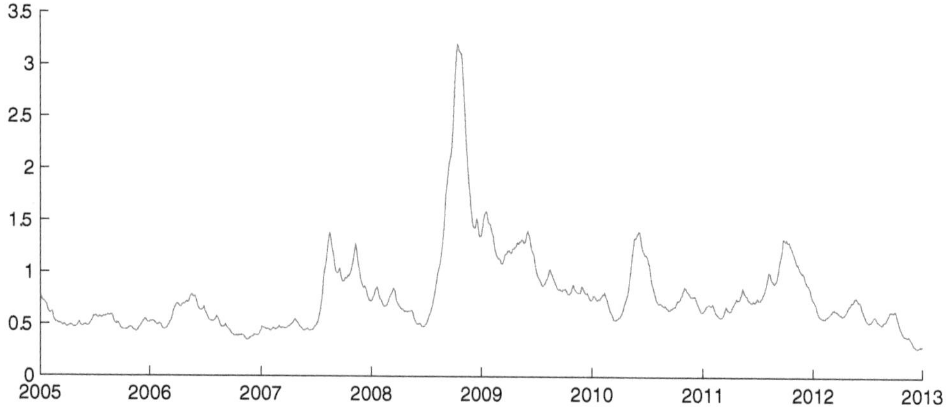

Figure 19.1. Posterior means of the time-varying standard deviations $\{e^{h_t/2}\}$ for the AUD/USD daily returns data.

yielding a regression with dependent variable $e^{-\frac{1}{2}h_t}y_t$, explanatory variable $e^{-\frac{1}{2}h_t}$, and a known error variance. Thus, standard regression derivations imply that

$$(\mu \,|\, y, h) \sim N(\hat{\mu}, K_\mu^{-1}),$$

where $K_\mu^{-1} = V_\mu^{-1} + \sum_{t=1}^T e^{-h_t}$ and $\hat{\mu} = K_\mu^{-1}(\mu_0/V_\mu + \sum_{t=1}^T e^{-h_t}y_t)$.

MATLAB code which implements this MCMC algorithm is available on the website associated with this book. It is worth noting that this code uses a common programming trick to speed up computation. In the code we vectorize the operations in sampling s. In particular, instead of using a "for" loop to sample each s_t at a point in time, we first construct a $T \times 7$ matrix of probabilities, where each row stores the probabilities of s_t belonging to each of the seven components. Then s is sampled jointly. By avoiding the "for" loop, computation is speeded up.

We obtain 20 000 posterior draws after discarding 1000 burn-in draws. Figure 19.1 depicts the posterior means of the time-varying standard deviation. As the figure shows, there is substantial time variation in the volatility. In particular, between 2005 and early 2007, the estimated standard deviation mostly fluctuates around 0.5%. It increases to about 1% in mid 2007 and peaks at 3% during the Great Recession. Although it goes down substantially after 2009, there are times in which it is still much higher than the pre-crisis level.

Exercise 19.2 (The unobserved components stochastic volatility model) In Exercise 18.1 we used an unobserved components model for modeling trend inflation. Specifically, we used the local level model which decomposed the inflation series into a trend and a transitory component. However, a large and growing literature has shown that allowing for stochastic volatility substantially improves inflation forecasts (see, e.g., Clark 2011; Koop and Korobilis 2012; Chan 2013). The unobserved components stochastic volatility

(UC-SV) model adds to the local level model a stochastic volatility process in both state and measurement equations as follows:

$$y_t = \tau_t + \epsilon_t^y,$$
$$\tau_t = \tau_{t-1} + \epsilon_t^\tau,$$
$$h_t = h_{t-1} + \epsilon_t^h,$$
$$g_t = g_{t-1} + \epsilon_t^g,$$

where $\epsilon_t^y \sim N(0, e^{h_t})$, $\epsilon_t^\tau \sim N(0, e^{g_t})$, $\epsilon_t^h \sim N(0, \omega_h^2)$, $\epsilon_t^g \sim N(0, \omega_g^2)$, and the initial conditions τ_0, h_0, and g_0 are treated as unknown parameters.

In this model the inflation series y_t is decomposed into trend inflation τ_t and transitory inflation ϵ_t^y, where both components have time-varying volatility. By comparing the variances of the trend and the inflation gap, we can assess the relative importance of each component in driving the variance of inflation over time.

(a) In Exercise 18.3, the non-centered parameterization of an unobserved components model was introduced and shown to be useful for model comparison using the Savage–Dickey density ratio. Write the UC-SV model in the non-centered parameterization.

(b) Derive an MCMC algorithm for doing Bayesian inference in the model of part (a).

(c) Use your MCMC algorithm from part (b) to carry out Bayesian inference using a time series of inflation (e.g., annualized US CPI inflation from 1947Q1 to 2015Q4 is available on the website associated with this book). In particular, produce estimates of trend inflation and each of the two time-varying volatilities in the UC-SV. Calculate the Bayes factor comparing the unrestricted model to the model with $\omega_h = 0$. Repeat for $\omega_g = 0$.

Solution

(a) To check whether there is time variation in the stochastic volatility processes using Bayes factors, we reparameterize the UC-SV model of Stock and Watson (2007) using the non-centered parameterization discussed in Exercise 18.3. That is, instead of the error variance in the state equation, we work with the standard derivation that is defined to have support on the whole real line. Consequently, we can use the Savage–Dickey density ratio to compare the unrestricted stochastic volatility model against a restricted version in which $\omega_h = 0$ and/or $\omega_g = 0$ and, thus, the volatility in the measurement and/or state equation is constant.

For the UC-SV model, the non-centered parameterization is:

$$y_t = \tau_t + e^{\frac{1}{2}(h_0 + \omega_h \tilde{h}_t)} \tilde{\epsilon}_t^y, \tag{19.8}$$
$$\tau_t = \tau_{t-1} + e^{\frac{1}{2}(g_0 + \omega_g \tilde{g}_t)} \tilde{\epsilon}_t^\tau, \tag{19.9}$$
$$\tilde{h}_t = \tilde{h}_{t-1} + \tilde{\epsilon}_t^h, \tag{19.10}$$
$$\tilde{g}_t = \tilde{g}_{t-1} + \tilde{\epsilon}_t^g,$$

where $\tilde{h}_0 = \tilde{g}_0 = 0$, and $\tilde{\epsilon}_t^y$, $\tilde{\epsilon}_t^\tau$, $\tilde{\epsilon}_t^h$, and $\tilde{\epsilon}_t^g$ are iid $N(0, 1)$.

Using this setup, we can turn off the stochastic volatility in the trend and/or the transitory component by setting $\omega_g = 0$ and/or $\omega_h = 0$, respectively. In their analysis, Stock and Watson (2007) fixed the parameters $\omega_h^2 = \omega_g^2 = 0.2$. In a recent paper, Moura and Turatti (2014) estimated the two parameters while maintaining the assumption that $\omega_h^2 = \omega_g^2 = \omega^2$. Using inflation in the G7 countries, they found that the estimates of ω^2 are statistically different from the calibrated value of 0.2 for a few countries. Here we use an even more flexible specification, estimating both ω_h^2 and ω_g^2 and allowing them to be different.

(b) For the UC-SV model in the non-centered parameterization, the parameters are $\omega_g, \omega_h, \tau_0, h_0$, and g_0, and there are three types of states: $\tau = (\tau_1, \dots, \tau_T)'$, $\tilde{h} = (\tilde{h}_1, \dots, \tilde{h}_T)'$, and $\tilde{g} = (\tilde{g}_1, \dots, \tilde{g}_T)'$.

We assume normal priors for ω_g and ω_h: $\omega_g \sim N(0, V_{\omega_g})$ and $\omega_h \sim N(0, V_{\omega_h})$. In the empirical work of part (c) we set $V_{\omega_h} = V_{\omega_g} = 0.2$ so that the implied prior means are $E(\omega_h^2) = E(\omega_g^2) = 0.2$, which are the same as the calibrated values in Stock and Watson (2007). We further assume that $h_0 \sim N(a_{0,h}, b_{0,h})$, $g_0 \sim N(a_{0,g}, b_{0,g})$, and $\tau_0 \sim N(a_{0,\tau}, b_{0,\tau})$.

Here we highlight two key steps in the Gibbs sampler: sampling τ and $\tilde{h}$ from their conditional posterior distributions. Conditional on these, the posteriors for the other parameters can be derived using simple extensions of derivations in Exercise 18.3 (for ω_g and ω_h) and Exercise 19.1 (for the initial conditions). Thus, we will not reproduce them here.

From Exercise 19.1, recall that $h = h_0 1_T + \omega_h \tilde{h}$ and $g = g_0 1_T + \omega_g \tilde{g}$. Then, it follows from (19.8) that

$$(y \mid \tau, \tilde{h}, h_0, \omega_h) \sim N(\tau, \Omega_h),$$

where $\Omega_h = \text{diag}(e^{h_1}, \dots, e^{h_T})$. Similarly, (19.9) implies that

$$(\tau \mid \tau_0, \tilde{g}, g_0, \omega_g) \sim N(\tau_0 1_T, (H'\Omega_g^{-1}H)^{-1}),$$

where $\Omega_g = \text{diag}(e^{g_1}, \dots, e^{g_T})$ and H is the usual first difference matrix (see Exercise 18.1). Then, by standard linear regression results, we have

$$(\tau \mid y, \tilde{h}, \tilde{g}, \omega_h, \omega_g, \tau_0, h_0, g_0) \sim N(\hat{\tau}, K_\tau^{-1}),$$

where

$$K_\tau = H'\Omega_g^{-1}H + \Omega_h^{-1}, \quad \hat{\tau} = K_\tau^{-1}(H'\Omega_g^{-1}H\tau_0 1_T + \Omega_h^{-1}y).$$

We then use the precision sampler described in Chapter 18 to sample τ.

To sample $\tilde{h}$, we use the auxiliary mixture sampler of Exercise 19.1. Specifically, let $y_t^* = \ln(y_t - \tau_t)^2$ and $\tilde{\epsilon}_t^{y*} = \ln(\tilde{\epsilon}_t^y)^2$ for $t = 1, \dots, T$. Then, it follows from (19.8) that

$$y^* = h_0 1_T + \omega_h \tilde{h} + \tilde{\epsilon}^{y*},$$

where $y^* = (y_1^*, \dots, y_T^*)'$ and $\tilde{\epsilon}^{y*} = (\tilde{\epsilon}_1^{y*}, \dots, \tilde{\epsilon}_T^{y*})'$. As in the solution to Exercise 19.1, we then augment the model with the component indicators $s = (s_1, \dots, s_T)'$ such that, given these indicators, $(\tilde{\epsilon}^{y*} \,|\, s) \sim N(d_s, \Omega_s)$ with d_s and Ω_s obtained from the normal mixture approximation of the log-χ_1^2 distribution (see Table 19.1). We can show that the component indicators are conditionally independent, and we can sample each of them sequentially from a seven-point distribution in the same fashion as in Exercise 19.1.

Next, given s and other parameters, we sample $\tilde{h}$ from the normal distribution

$$(\tilde{h} \,|\, y, \tau, \omega_h, h_0) \sim N(\hat{\tilde{h}}, K_{\tilde{h}}^{-1}),$$

where

$$K_{\tilde{h}} = H'H + \omega_h^2 \Omega_s^{-1}, \quad \hat{\tilde{h}} = K_{\tau}^{-1}(\omega_h \Omega_s^{-1}(y^* - h_0 1_T - d_s)).$$

Again, we use the precision sampler described in Exercise 18.1 to sample from this normal distribution.

The derivation of the conditional posterior of $\tilde{g}$ is basically the same as the derivation for $\tilde{h}$, and will not be given here.

(c) We fit the UC-SV model with quarterly US CPI inflation (transformed to an annual growth rate) from 1947Q1 to 2015Q4. Figure 19.2 reports the posterior means of trend inflation based on a sample of 50 000 posterior draws after a burn-in period of 1000.

Prior to the Great Moderation, estimated trend inflation traces actual inflation very closely. However, since the mid 1980s, the volatility of trend inflation has decreased substantially. In addition, trend inflation itself has exhibited a steady decline from about 5% to less than 2% at the end of the sample.

Next, we report in Figure 19.3 the estimated time-varying standard deviations of the transitory and the trend components. Consistent with Figure 19.2, the variance of trend inflation is high on average before the Great Moderation; in fact, it is higher than the variance of the transitory component throughout the 1970s and early 1980s. Since the

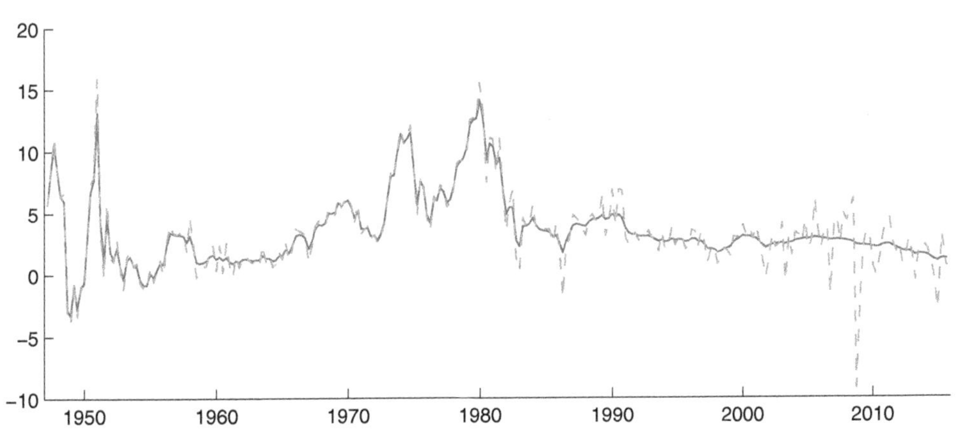

Figure 19.2. Posterior estimates of $\{\tau_t\}$ (solid line) and the CPI inflation rate (dotted line).

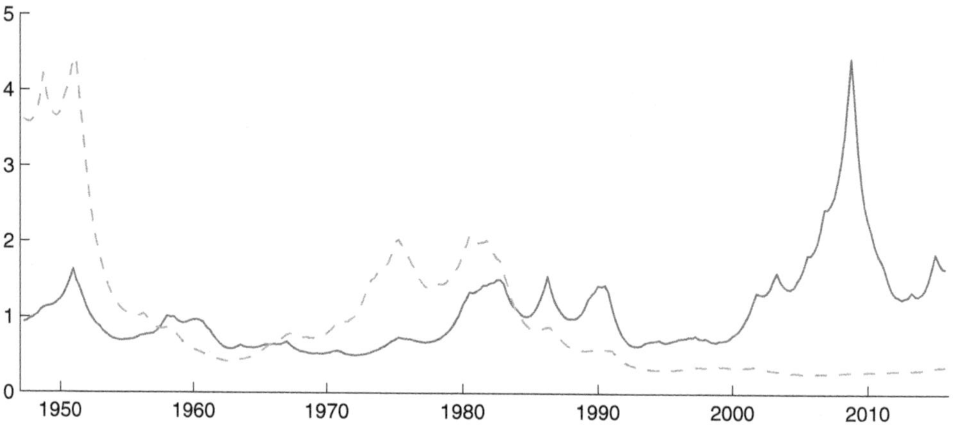

Figure 19.3. Posterior estimates of the time-varying standard deviations of the transitory component $\{e^{h_t/2}\}$ (solid line) and the trend component $\{e^{g_t/2}\}$ (dotted line).

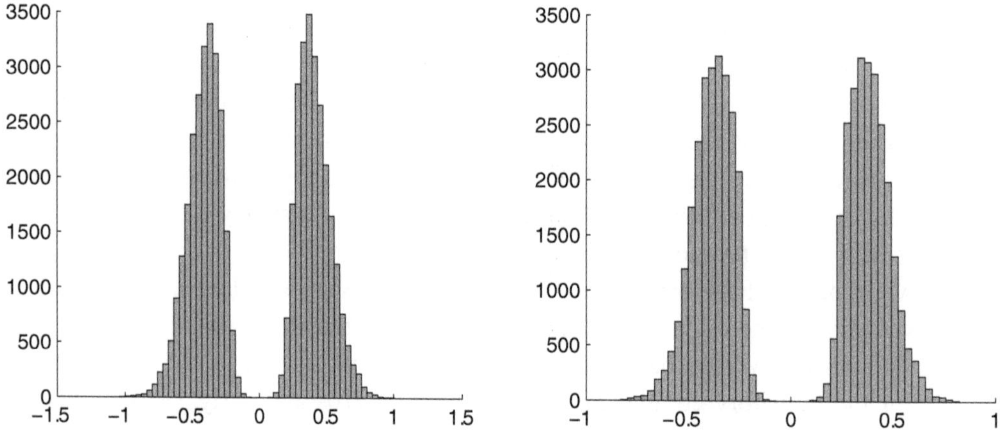

Figure 19.4. Histograms of the posterior draws of ω_h (left panel) and ω_g (right panel).

1980s, however, it has declined substantially and has remained low and stable until the end of the sample.

The volatility estimates presented above suggest that both variances are time varying. This is confirmed by the posterior densities of the standard deviations ω_h and ω_g which, along with their prior densities, can be used to calculate Bayes factors using the Savage–Dickey density ratio. Specifically, Figure 19.4 plots the histograms of the posterior draws of ω_h and ω_g. Both are clearly bimodal and they have virtually no mass at zero. In fact, the log Bayes factor against the restricted model with $\omega_h = 0$ compared to the unrestricted UC-SV model is 94; the corresponding value against the restricted model with $\omega_g = 0$ is 63. In both cases there is overwhelming evidence in support of allowing time-varying volatility.

Exercise 19.3 (Stochastic volatility in mean) In this exercise, we study a stochastic volatility model in which the stochastic volatility has a direct impact on the variable of interest. Originally developed by Koopman and Hol Uspensky (2002) as an alternative to the ARCH in mean model of Engle, Lilien, and Robins (1987), the stochastic volatility in mean model allows the time-varying volatility to enter the conditional mean as an explanatory variable. The stochastic volatility in mean model is widely used in empirical finance to study the relationship between asset returns and their volatility. More recently, it has been used to model macroeconomic data, as in Berument, Yalcin, and Yildirim (2009) for investigating the inflation–inflation uncertainty relationship, and Mumtaz and Zanetti (2013) for examining the impact of monetary shock volatility.

The stochastic volatility in mean model is

$$y_t = \alpha e^{h_t} + x_t'\beta + \epsilon_t^y, \qquad \epsilon_t^y \sim N(0, e^{h_t}), \tag{19.11}$$

$$h_t = h_{t-1} + \epsilon_t^h, \qquad \epsilon_t^h \sim N(0, \sigma_h^2), \tag{19.12}$$

where x_t is a $k \times 1$ vector of covariates, β is the associated $k \times 1$ vector of coefficients, and the errors ϵ_t^y and ϵ_t^h are mutually and serially uncorrelated. The log-volatility is assumed to follow a random walk process, although allowing for a stationary AR(1) process is also commonly done.

This model generalizes the basic stochastic volatility model by allowing for covariates. In particular, the contemporaneous variance e^{h_t} is included as one of the covariates. The associated parameter α captures the impact of volatility, and is often the key parameter of interest.

(a) Develop an MCMC algorithm for doing Bayesian inference in the stochastic volatility in mean model.

(b) Using data on an asset return of your choice and the MCMC algorithm of part (a), estimate the stochastic volatility in mean model. Produce estimates of the volatility and plot the posterior of α. Discuss your results.

Solution

(a) Estimation of the stochastic volatility in mean model is more difficult than the simple stochastic volatility model of Exercise 19.1. This is because now the log-volatility h_t also enters the conditional mean equation, and the auxiliary mixture sampler discussed in Exercise 19.1 cannot be applied to this setting. Consequently, we need to come up with an alternative way to sample the high-dimensional, non-standard distribution of h.

In the original stochastic volatility in mean paper, Koopman and Hol Uspensky (2002) developed a simulated maximum likelihood estimator based on the Kalman filter to fit the model. Specifically, a normal density is constructed to approximate the full conditional density of h. This approximate density is then used to evaluate the integrated likelihood (i.e., the likelihood obtained by integrating out h_t) via importance sampling. Independent draws from this approximate density are obtained using algorithms based on the Kalman filter. Since there are only a few parameters in the stochastic volatility in mean model, one can maximize the likelihood numerically to obtain the maximum likelihood estimates.

Here we want to derive a Bayesian approach and develop an efficient MCMC algorithm for simulating from the joint posterior distribution. As in the simulated maximum likelihood approach, the core of the algorithm is a normal approximation of the conditional density of h. However, we construct the normal approximation differently. Instead of using the Kalman filter, we obtain the approximate density using the Newton–Raphson method based on band matrix algorithms. The latter approach is computationally more efficient as it exploits the special structure of the problem: the Hessian of the log-conditional density of h is a band matrix. Recent papers using band matrix algorithms to obtain approximate densities include Rue, Martino, and Chopin (2009) for non-linear Markov random fields, and McCausland (2012), Chan, Koop, and Potter (2013, 2016) , and Djegnene and McCausland (2014) for non-linear state space models.

It is worth noting that the Bayesian approach can be easily generalized to models with additional features, such as time-varying coefficients (see, e.g., Chan 2017). Due to the modular nature of MCMC algorithms, we can simulate the states in the volatility process and those controlling the time variation in the conditional mean coefficients separately, which reduces the dimension of the problem and makes estimation much easier. In contrast, it is more difficult to generalize simulated maximum likelihood methods to handle multiple non-linear states. For example, in stochastic volatility models with time-varying coefficients, likelihood evaluation would involve simultaneously integrating out both the time-varying coefficients and the stochastic volatility by Monte Carlo methods. This likelihood evaluation step is, in general, computationally intensive.

Let $\gamma = (\alpha, \beta')'$ denote the regression coefficients. We complete the model specification by assuming the following independent priors:

$$\gamma \sim N(\gamma_0, V_\gamma), \quad \sigma_h^2 \sim IG(\nu_h, S_h), \quad h_0 \sim N(a_0, b_0).$$

Posterior draws can be obtained by sequentially sampling from:

1. $p(h \,|\, y, \gamma, \sigma_h^2, h_0)$,
2. $p(\gamma \,|\, y, h, \sigma_h^2, h_0)$,
3. $p(\sigma_h^2 \,|\, y, h, \gamma, h_0)$,
4. $p(h_0 \,|\, y, h, \gamma, \sigma_h^2)$.

Steps 2–4 are standard. Steps 3 and 4 are derived in Exercise 19.1 and Step 2 involves standard regression methods (see, e.g., Chapter 10). Hence, we focus on Step 1. For this, we use an independence chain Metropolis–Hastings algorithm (see Chapter 12) which uses a normal approximation for $p(h \,|\, y, \gamma, \sigma_h^2, h_0)$. We first discuss an efficient way to obtain this normal approximation using the Newton–Raphson method. To that end, we need to obtain the gradient and Hessian of the log-density: $\ln p(h \,|\, y, \gamma, \sigma_h^2, h_0)$.

By Bayes' theorem, we have

$$p(h \,|\, y, \gamma, \sigma_h^2, h_0) \propto p(y \,|\, \gamma, h) p(h \,|\, \sigma_h^2, h_0),$$

and we next derive explicit expressions for the log of the two densities on the right-hand side and take their first and second derivatives. The prior density of h is normal with log-density

$$\ln p(h \,|\, \sigma_h^2, h_0) = -\frac{1}{2\sigma_h^2}(h'H'Hh - 2h'H'Hh_0 1_T) + c_1,$$

where H is the first difference matrix (see Exercise 18.1) and c_1 is a constant independent of h. Hence, the gradient and Hessian of $\ln p(h \,|\, \sigma_h^2, h_0)$ are given by

$$\frac{\partial}{\partial h} \ln p(h \,|\, \sigma_h^2, h_0) = -\frac{1}{\sigma_h^2} H'H(h - h_0 1_T),$$

$$\frac{\partial^2}{\partial h \partial h'} \ln p(h \,|\, \sigma_h^2, h_0) = -\frac{1}{\sigma_h^2} H'H.$$

Next we turn to $p(y \,|\, h, \gamma)$. Let f and G denote, respectively, the gradient and the negative Hessian of $\ln p(y \,|\, h, \gamma)$:

$$f = \frac{\partial}{\partial h} \ln p(y \,|\, h, \gamma), \quad G = -\frac{\partial^2}{\partial h \partial h'} \ln p(y \,|\, h, \gamma).$$

Note that the log conditional likelihood $\ln p(y \,|\, h, \gamma)$ has the form

$$\ln p(y \,|\, h, \gamma) = \sum_{t=1}^{T} \ln p(y_t \,|\, h_t, \gamma).$$

Since h_t only enters the density $p(y_t \,|\, h_t, \gamma)$, the tth element of f is simply

$$f_t = \partial \ln p(y_t \,|\, h_t, \gamma) / \partial h_t$$

and the negative Hessian G is diagonal, where the tth diagonal element is

$$G_t = -\partial^2 \ln p(y_t \,|\, h_t, \gamma) / \partial h_t^2.$$

To provide complete details, note that, for the stochastic volatility in mean model,

$$\begin{aligned}
\ln p(y_t \,|\, h_t, \gamma) = & -\frac{1}{2}\ln(2\pi) - \frac{1}{2}h_t - \frac{1}{2}e^{-h_t}(y_t - \alpha e^{h_t} - x_t'\beta)^2 \\
& -\frac{1}{2}\ln(2\pi) - \frac{1}{2}h_t - \frac{1}{2}\left(\alpha^2 e^{h_t} + e^{-h_t}(y_t - x_t'\beta)^2 - 2\alpha(y_t - x_t'\beta)\right).
\end{aligned}$$

It can be seen that

$$f_t = \frac{\partial}{\partial h_t} \ln p(y_t \,|\, h_t, \gamma) = -\frac{1}{2} - \frac{1}{2}\alpha^2 e^{h_t} + \frac{1}{2}e^{-h_t}(y_t - x_t'\beta)^2,$$

$$G_t = -\frac{\partial^2}{\partial h_t^2} \ln p(y_t \,|\, h_t, \gamma) = \frac{1}{2}\alpha^2 e^{h_t} + \frac{1}{2}e^{-h_t}(y_t - x_t'\beta)^2 > 0.$$

Since G is a diagonal matrix with positive diagonal elements, it is positive definite. Consequently, the Hessian $F(h) = -(H'H/\sigma_h^2 + G)$ is negative definite regardless of the value of h.

Putting these derivations for the prior and likelihood together, the gradient and Hessian of the conditional log posterior, $\ln p(h \,|\, y, \gamma, \sigma_h^2, h_0)$, are:

$$S(h) = \frac{\partial}{\partial h} \ln p(h \,|\, y, \gamma, \sigma_h^2, h_0) = -\frac{1}{\sigma_h^2} H'H(h - h_0 1_T) + f,$$

$$F(h) = \frac{\partial^2}{\partial h \partial h'} \ln p(h \,|\, y, \gamma, \sigma_h^2, h_0) = -\left(\frac{1}{\sigma_h^2} H'H + G\right).$$

Hence, we can implement the Newton–Raphson method. In particular, we can initialize the algorithm with $h = h^{(1)}$ for some constant vector $h^{(1)}$. For $t = 1, 2, \ldots$, use $h = h^{(t)}$ in the evaluation of $S(h)$ and $F(h)$, and compute the Newton–Raphson recursion:

$$h^{(t+1)} = h^{(t)} - F(h^{(t)})^{-1} S(h^{(t)}).$$

This recursion is repeated until some convergence criterion is reached, e.g., when $\|h^{(t+1)} - h^{(t)}\| < \epsilon$ for some predetermined tolerance level ϵ. Note that the Hessian for the stochastic volatility model is globally negative definite. Consequently, the convergence of the Newton–Raphson method is typically very fast.

Now, let $\hat{h}$ be the mode obtained from the Newton–Raphson method and let K_h denote the negative Hessian evaluated at the mode, i.e., $K_h = H'H/\sigma_h^2 + G$. Then we use $N(\hat{h}, K_h^{-1})$ as the proposal density in an independence chain Metropolis–Hastings step. Since the precision matrix is a band matrix, we can use the precision sampler of Exercise 18.1 to obtain draws from $N(\hat{h}, K_h^{-1})$ efficiently.

(b) The solution uses daily excess returns on the S&P 500 index from 2 January 2013 through 31 December 2015. Returns are computed on a continuously compounded basis and expressed in percentages: $R_t = 100 \ln(P_t/P_{t-1})$, where P_t is the S&P 500 index at time t. We use the effective federal funds rate, denoted as i_t, as a proxy for the risk-free rate of return, and the excess returns are defined as $y_t = R_t - i_t$.

MATLAB code which implements the posterior sampler developed in part (a) is available on the website associated with this book. The results are based on 20 000 posterior draws after a burn-in period of 1000. Figure 19.5 plots the posterior estimates of the time-varying standard deviation $\{e^{h_t/2}\}$. The estimates mostly fluctuate between 0.5 and 1, except for the brief episode in the second half of 2015 when the standard deviation peaks at about 2.

The key parameter of interest is α, the regression coefficient on the explanatory variable e^{h_t}. Its posterior mean is -0.204 with a 95% credible interval $(-0.369, -0.048)$. Figure 19.6 depicts the histogram of the posterior draws of α, which has little mass at 0. Using data from 1975 to 1998, Koopman and Hol Uspensky (2002) reported an estimate of -0.023 and an asymptotic 95% confidence interval $(-0.065, 0.019)$. Hence, our estimate has the same sign, but its absolute magnitude is much larger and virtually all of the posterior mass lies in the negative region of the parameter space.

Koopman and Hol Uspensky (2002) explained that the parameter α captures two opposing impacts of volatility on excess returns. On the one hand, the expected component of

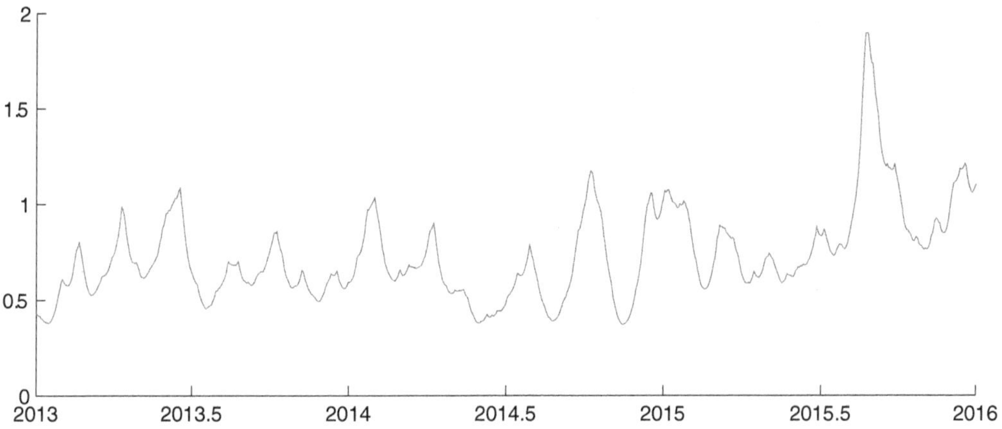

Figure 19.5. Posterior estimates of the time-varying standard deviation $\{e^{h_t/2}\}$.

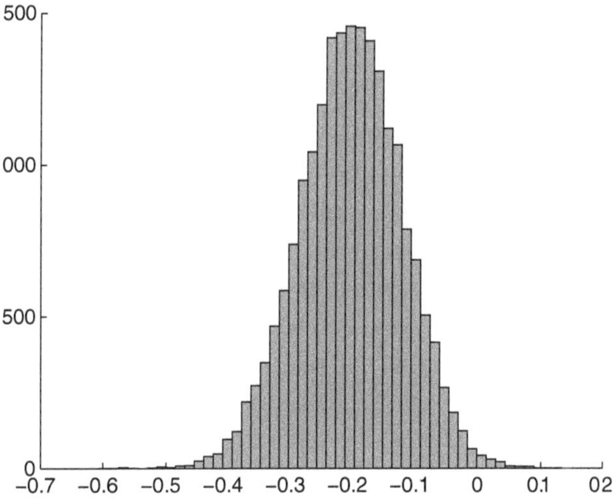

Figure 19.6. Histogram of the posterior draws of α.

volatility could be positively correlated with excess returns if risk-averse investors demand higher expected returns during more volatile periods. On the other hand, unexpected large shocks to the return process induce higher expected volatility in the future. If future cash flows are unchanged, the current stock index should fall. Hence, the unexpected component of volatility should be negatively correlated with excess returns. This is often referred to as the volatility feedback theory. At time t, h_{t+1} captures both the expected and unexpected components of volatility. Hence, our negative estimate of α indicates that the volatility feedback effect dominates.

Exercise 19.4 (Autoregressive conditional heteroscedasticity) If y_t is an observed time series variable and x_t' a $k \times 1$ vector of explanatory variables (for $t = 1, \ldots, T$), then the regression model with ARCH(p) errors is given by

$$y_t = x_t'\beta + \epsilon_t, \tag{19.13}$$

where ϵ_t is $iid\ N\left(0, \sigma_t^2\right)$ and

$$\sigma_t^2 = \alpha_0 + \alpha_1 \epsilon_{t-1}^2 + \cdots + \alpha_p \epsilon_{t-p}^2. \tag{19.14}$$

Since variances must be positive, we must impose the restriction $\alpha_j > 0$ for $j = 0, \ldots, p$. Denote this positivity restriction by

$$P = \{\alpha : \ \alpha_j > 0 \text{ for } j = 0, \ldots, p\},$$

where $\alpha = (\alpha_0, \alpha_1, \ldots, \alpha_p)'$. Furthermore, let the roots of $1 - \sum_{i=1}^p \alpha_i z^i$ be denoted by r_i for $i = 1, \ldots, p$. We will restrict (19.14) to be stationary by imposing $\min|r_i| > 1$. Denote the stationary region as $S = \{\alpha : \ \min|r_i| > 1\}$.

(a) Derive a posterior simulator which carries out Bayesian inference in the normal linear regression model with ARCH errors. Use the following diffuse prior (subject to the positivity and stationarity restrictions):

$$p(\beta, \alpha) \propto I(P)\, I(S). \tag{19.15}$$

As an aside, the interested reader is referred to Geweke (1988a) for a discussion of prior elicitation in ARCH models, including a discussion of several other diffuse priors. You may proceed conditionally on the first p observations and, thus, ignore the (minor) complications caused by initial conditions.

(b) Using an appropriate data set, write a program and carry out Bayesian inference for this model using your results from part (a). The website associated with this book provides a monthly NYSE stock return data set and the solution to this exercise uses this data. This data contains monthly stock returns (exclusive of dividends) from the NYSE from 1952 through 1995. If you are using the NYSE data set, let x_t contain only an intercept and set $p = 4$.

Solution

(a) The posterior is obtained by multiplying prior by likelihood. Using the properties of the normal distribution (and conditioning on $y_1, \ldots, y_p$), the log-likelihood is

$$\begin{aligned}
\ln L(\beta, \alpha) &\propto -\frac{1}{2} \sum_{t=p+1}^{T} \ln\left(\sigma_t^2\right) - \frac{1}{2} \sum_{t=p+1}^{T} \frac{\epsilon_t^2}{\sigma_t^2} \\
&= -\frac{1}{2} \sum_{t=p+1}^{T} \ln\left(\alpha_0 + \alpha_1\left(y_{t-1} - x_{t-1}'\beta\right)^2 + \cdots + \alpha_p\left(y_{t-p} - x_{t-p}'\beta\right)^2\right) \\
&\quad -\frac{1}{2} \sum_{t=p+1}^{T} \frac{(y_t - x_t'\beta)^2}{\alpha_0 + \alpha_1\left(y_{t-1} - x_{t-1}'\beta\right)^2 + \cdots + \alpha_p\left(y_{t-p} - x_{t-p}'\beta\right)^2}.
\end{aligned} \tag{19.16}$$

The difficulty of posterior inference in the ARCH model can be seen in (19.16). The likelihood does not belong in any convenient class of distributions and hence, even with a convenient prior, does not lend itself to analytical results, nor direct Monte Carlo integration, nor Gibbs sampling. Note that, unlike with many other extensions on the regression models, even the conditional posterior for β does not have a simple form. This arises since (19.14) depends on the errors and these depend on β. Thus, β enters not only the conditional mean, but also the conditional variance of the model. Several approaches to posterior simulation are possible (see, e.g., Geweke 1988a; Bauwens, Lubrano, and Richard 1999, Chapter 7). Here we describe a random walk chain Metropolis–Hastings algorithm (see the introductory material to Chapter 12). Let $\theta = (\beta', \alpha')'$, and $\theta^{(r)}$ for $r = 1,\ldots,R$ denote the posterior simulator output. The random walk Metropolis–Hastings algorithm proceeds by generating candidate draws, θ^*, according to

$$\theta^* = \theta^{(r-1)} + z,$$

where z is the increment random variable, which we take to be $N(0, \Sigma)$. These draws are accepted with probability

$$\min\left[\frac{p(\theta = \theta^*|y)}{p\left(\theta = \theta^{(r-1)}|y\right)}, 1\right].$$

If θ^* is accepted then $\theta^{(r)} = \theta^*$, otherwise the posterior simulator sets $\theta^{(r)} = \theta^{(r-1)}$. Note that, since the posterior appears in both the numerator and denominator of the acceptance probability, the integrating constant will cancel out and, hence, we do not need to fully know the posterior, but only its kernel. In our case, the kernel of the posterior is (19.15) times (19.16).

(b) A MATLAB program which implements the random walk chain Metropolis–Hastings algorithm described in the solution to part (a) is available on the website associated with this book. This algorithm requires the selection of Σ. There are many ways of doing this, and some experimentation is typically required to find a value which yields a reasonable acceptance probability. Remember that with the Metropolis–Hastings algorithm you do not want an acceptance probability that is too low, nor too high. If it is too low, then virtually all candidate draws are rejected and the results will, in essence, be based on very few draws. If it is too high, this can be evidence that the random walk chain algorithm is taking candidate draws too close to the current draw. In this case, the algorithm might not be exploring the entire posterior distribution in a reasonable number of draws. Accepting somewhere between a quarter and a half of the draws is often taken as a reasonable benchmark to aim for. We have achieved this by initially setting $\Sigma = cI$ and experimenting with the scalar c until we obtain an acceptance probability that is not very near zero or one. We then use this choice for Σ to produce an estimate of the posterior covariance matrix: $\widehat{\text{Var}(\theta|y)}$. We then set $\Sigma = c\widehat{\text{Var}(\theta|y)}$ and experimented again with different values for c. We finally used $c = 0.5$ in a long run (1000 burn-in replications and 100 000 included replications)

Table 19.2: Posterior results for regression model with ARCH errors.

Parameter	Mean	Std. dev.
β	0.666	0.166
α_0	9.343	1.526
α_1	0.067	0.041
α_2	0.080	0.055
α_3	0.240	0.089
α_4	0.140	0.081

to produce our final results. This choice for Σ resulted in 37.1% of the candidate draws being accepted.

Table 19.2 presents posterior means and standard deviations for the parameters of the ARCH(4) model using the NYSE stock return data.

Exercise 19.5 (Generalized autoregressive conditional heteroscedasticity) In this exercise we consider an extension of the ARCH model discussed in Exercise 19.4, called the generalized autoregressive conditional heteroscedasticity (GARCH) model. Specifically, it generalizes the variance process in (19.13) to include lagged variances:

$$\sigma_t^2 = \gamma_0 + \gamma_1 \epsilon_{t-1}^2 + \cdots + \gamma_p \epsilon_{t-p}^2 + \gamma_{p+1} \sigma_{t-1}^2 + \cdots + \gamma_{p+q} \sigma_{t-q}^2. \tag{19.17}$$

Obviously it includes the ARCH model as a special case with $\gamma_{p+1} = \cdots = \gamma_{p+q} = 0$.

To ensure the variances are always positive, we impose the restrictions $\gamma_j > 0$ for $j = 0, \ldots, p+q$. Denote this positivity restriction by $P = \{\gamma : \gamma_j > 0 \text{ for } j = 0, \ldots, p+q\}$, where $\gamma = (\gamma_0, \gamma_1, \ldots, \gamma_{p+q})'$. For stationarity, we impose the sufficient condition that $\sum_{j=1}^{p+q} \gamma_j < 1$. Denote this stationarity region as $S = \{\gamma : \sum_{j=1}^{p+q} \gamma_j < 1\}$.
(a) Assume the conditional mean equation

$$y_t = \mu + \epsilon_t,$$

where ϵ_t is *iid* $N(0, \sigma_t^2)$ and σ_t^2 is specified in (19.17). Derive a posterior simulator for this GARCH model with $p = 1$ and $q = 1$. To ignore the (minor) complications caused by initial conditions, you may proceed by assuming that $\epsilon_0 = \sigma_{-1}^2 = 0$ and σ_0^2 is a constant.
(b) Using an appropriate data set, write a program and carry out Bayesian inference for this model using your results from part (a). The website associated with this book provides a monthly NYSE stock return data set and the solution to this exercise uses this data.

Solution

(a) We develop a Metropolis–Hastings algorithm to sample from the joint posterior distribution of μ and $\gamma = (\gamma_0, \gamma_1, \gamma_2)'$. To ensure γ satisfies the positivity restriction, we reparameterize the model in terms of $\theta = (\ln \gamma_0, \ln \gamma_1, \ln \gamma_2)'$, and we sequentially draw from the two full conditional distributions $p(\mu|y,\theta)$ and $p(\theta|y,\mu)$. Once we have posterior draws of θ we can exponentiate them to get draws of γ.

We use the following diffuse prior (subject to the positivity and stationarity restrictions):

$$p(\mu,\theta) \propto I(P)I(S).$$

Note that the log-likelihood can be written as

$$\ln p(y|\mu,\theta) = -\frac{T}{2}\ln(2\pi) - \frac{1}{2}\sum_{t=1}^{T}\ln\sigma_t^2 - \frac{1}{2}\sum_{t=1}^{T}\frac{(y_t-\mu)^2}{\sigma_t^2},$$

where the conditional variance process σ_t^2 is given in (19.17) and is a function of both μ and θ.

The full conditional distributions of μ and θ are non-standard, and we use Metropolis–Hastings algorithms to simulate from the posterior. To sample μ, we use a Gaussian proposal with mean $\bar{y}$ and variance s^2/T, where $\bar{y}$ and s^2 are the sample mean and sample variance respectively. For θ, we use a t proposal centered at the mode of $p(\theta|y,\mu)$ with degree of freedom parameters set to 10. The scale matrix is set to be the outer product of the scores, which is guaranteed to be positive definite.

Specifically, the scores are given by

$$\frac{\partial}{\partial\theta}\ln p(y|\mu,\theta) = \frac{1}{2}\sum_{t=1}^{T}\left(\frac{1}{2\sigma_t^2}\left(\frac{(y_t-\mu)^2}{\sigma_t^2}-1\right)\frac{\partial\sigma_t^2}{\partial\theta}\right),$$

where $\partial\sigma_t^2/\partial\theta = (\partial\sigma_t^2/\partial\theta_0, \partial\sigma_t^2/\partial\theta_1, \partial\sigma_t^2/\partial\theta_2)'$ can be obtained recursively as follows. First, initialize

$$\frac{\partial\sigma_1^2}{\partial\theta_0} = e^{\theta_0}, \quad \frac{\partial\sigma_1^2}{\partial\theta_1} = 0, \quad \frac{\partial\sigma_1^2}{\partial\theta_2} = 0.$$

Then, for $t = 2,\dots,T$, set

$$\begin{aligned}
\frac{\partial\sigma_t^2}{\partial\theta_0} &= e^{\theta_0} + e^{\theta_2}\frac{\partial\sigma_{t-1}^2}{\partial\theta_0},\\
\frac{\partial\sigma_t^2}{\partial\theta_1} &= e^{\theta_1}(y_{t-1}-\mu)^2 + e^{\theta_2}\frac{\partial\sigma_{t-1}^2}{\partial\theta_1},\\
\frac{\partial\sigma_t^2}{\partial\theta_2} &= e^{\theta_2}\sigma_{t-1}^2 + e^{\theta_2}\frac{\partial\sigma_{t-1}^2}{\partial\theta_2}.
\end{aligned}$$

(b) A MATLAB program which implements the above Metropolis–Hastings sampler is available on the website associated with this book. We fit the GARCH model using the monthly NYSE stock return data set of Exercise 19.4. The posterior results are based on 20 000 draws after a burn-in period of 1000.

Figure 19.7 reports the estimated σ_t, the standard deviation process under the GARCH model. It is evident from the graph that there is much time variation in the standard

Table 19.3: Posterior results for regression model with GARCH errors.

Parameter	Mean	Std. dev.
μ	0.714	0.167
γ_0	1.10	0.556
γ_1	0.088	0.029
γ_2	0.850	0.051

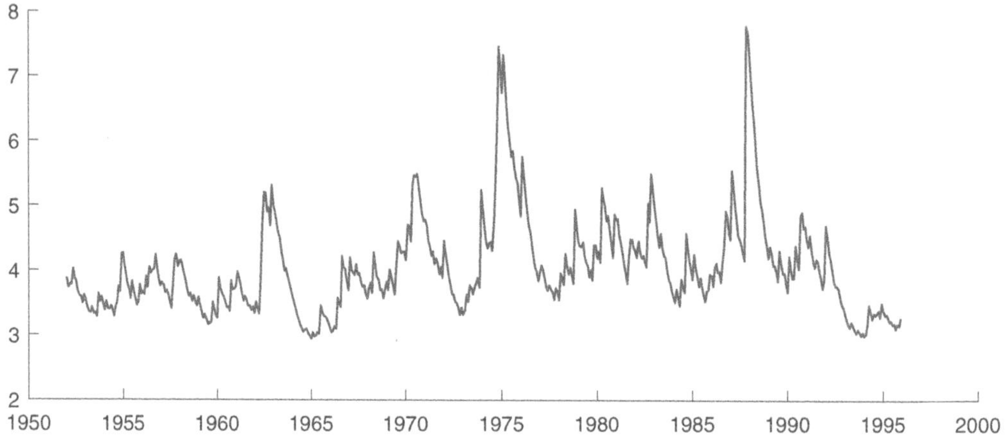

Figure 19.7. Posterior means of the standard deviation process under GARCH σ_t.

deviation process. In particular, the standard deviation of the series was particularly high in the mid 1970s and late 1980s.

Table 19.3 presents posterior means and standard deviations for the parameters of the GARCH model. The estimated conditional mean μ is about 0.714, which is similar to the estimate under the ARCH(4) model in Exercise 19.4. Moreover, the estimated variance process is highly persistent, with the AR(1) coefficient γ_2 estimated to be about 0.85.

20

Multivariate Time Series Methods

Macroeconomists working with time series data are typically interested in the relationships between several variables as opposed to the properties of a single variable. Thus, most macroeconomic models are multivariate instead of being univariate. Accordingly, this chapter contains exercises intended to develop skills in working with popular multivariate time series models.

We will focus on vector autoregressions (VARs) in this chapter. Factor models are also commonly used with macroeconomic and financial applications involving many variables. Since these can be interpreted as state space models, they are covered in Chapter 18. Vector autoregressions have been widely used for macroeconomic forecasting and structural analysis since the seminal work of Sims (1980). In particular, VARs often serve as the benchmark for comparing forecast performance of new models and methods. They are also used to better understand the interactions between macroeconomic variables, often through the estimation of impulse response functions that characterize the effects of a variety of structural shocks on key economic variables. Despite the empirical success of the standard constant-coefficient and homoscedastic VAR, there is much recent work on extending these conventional VARs to models with time-varying coefficients and stochastic volatility. These extensions are motivated by the widely observed structural instabilities and time-varying volatilities in a variety of macroeconomic time series. Accordingly, this chapter also contains exercises on some of these more flexible VARs, including the time-varying parameter VAR and VARs with stochastic volatility.

Vector autoregressions can be over-parameterized, particularly when the number of dependent variables is large. Thus, there is interest in using prior shrinkage to mitigate such concerns. This chapter contains exercises which illustrate several approaches to prior shrinkage that are commonly used with VARs. An alternative way of alleviating over-parameterization concerns is through imposing restrictions on VAR coefficients, and this chapter also contains exercises which show how this can be done. Of particular interest (e.g., due to the presence of cointegration) are restrictions on the rank of the matrix of VAR coefficients. The final exercise in this chapter develops methods for Bayesian inference in the vector error correction model (VECM), which involves such a reduced rank restriction.

Exercise 20.1 (The vector autoregressive model with independent normal-Wishart prior) Suppose $y_t = (y_{1t}, \ldots, y_{nt})'$ is a vector of n dependent variables at time t for $t = 1, \ldots, T$. Then VAR(p) is defined as

$$y_t = b + A_1 y_{t-1} + \cdots + A_p y_{t-p} + \epsilon_t, \tag{20.1}$$

where b is an $n \times 1$ vector of intercepts, $A_1, \ldots, A_p$ are $n \times n$ coefficient matrices, and $\epsilon_t \sim N(0, \Sigma)$. In other words, VAR($p$) is simply a multiple-equation regression where the regressors are the lagged dependent variables. Note that the VAR depends on p initial conditions $y_{-p+1}, \ldots, y_0$. In principle these initial conditions can be modeled explicitly. However, it is common to treat them as fixed (i.e., the first p observations are used as initial conditions and the estimation sample begins with the $(p+1)$th observation). We adopt this strategy in all the VAR questions in this chapter.

VAR(p) can be written as

$$y_t = X_t \beta + \epsilon_t,$$

where $X_t = I_n \otimes [1, y'_{t-1}, \ldots, y'_{t-p}]$ and $\beta = \text{vec}([b,\ A_1,\ \cdots\ A_p]')$. In addition, the observations can be stacked over $t = 1, \ldots, T$ so that VAR(p) can be written as

$$y = X\beta + \epsilon,$$

where $\epsilon \sim N(0, I_T \otimes \Sigma)$.
(a) Derive the likelihood function for the VAR.
(b) Assume that the priors for β and Σ are independent of one another and take the form

$$\beta \sim N(\beta_0, V_\beta), \quad \Sigma \sim IW(\nu_0, S_0), \tag{20.2}$$

where $IW(\cdot, \cdot)$ is the inverse Wishart distribution (see Definition A.6). This is often referred to as the independent normal-Wishart prior. Derive a Gibbs sampler which allows for posterior inference in the VAR.
(c) Use the data set US_macrodata.csv (available on the website associated with this book) which contains US quarterly data on the CPI inflation rate, the unemployment rate, and Fed Funds rate from 1959Q2 to 2007Q4 – the sample ends at 2007Q4 to avoid the periods when interest rate hits the zero lower bound. Estimate a VAR using this data set and the Gibbs sampler derived in part (b). Calculate impulse responses of all variables to a monetary policy shock.

Solution

(a) Since VAR(p) is a multivariate regression model, standard Bayesian derivations used with multivariate normal analysis apply (see Exercise 2.14). In particular, since

$$(y \mid \beta, \Sigma) \sim N(X\beta, I_T \otimes \Sigma),$$

the likelihood function is given by

$$\begin{aligned} p(y \mid \beta, \Sigma) &= |2\pi(I_T \otimes \Sigma)|^{-\frac{1}{2}} e^{-\frac{1}{2}(y-X\beta)'(I_T\otimes\Sigma)^{-1}(y-X\beta)} \\ &= (2\pi)^{-\frac{Tn}{2}} |\Sigma|^{-\frac{T}{2}} e^{-\frac{1}{2}(y-X\beta)'(I_T\otimes\Sigma^{-1})(y-X\beta)}, \end{aligned} \tag{20.3}$$

where the second equality holds because $|I_T \otimes \Sigma| = |\Sigma|^T$ and $(I_T \otimes \Sigma)^{-1} = I_T \otimes \Sigma^{-1}$. Note that the likelihood can also be written as

$$p(y \mid \beta, \Sigma) = (2\pi)^{-\frac{Tn}{2}} |\Sigma|^{-\frac{T}{2}} e^{-\frac{1}{2}\sum_{t=1}^{T}(y_t-X_t\beta)'\Sigma^{-1}(y_t-X_t\beta)}. \tag{20.4}$$

(b) We derive a Gibbs sampler for VAR(p) with likelihood given in (20.3) and priors given in (20.2). Specifically, we derive the two conditional densities $p(\beta \mid y, \Sigma)$ and $p(\Sigma \mid y, \beta)$.

The first step is straightforward, as standard linear regression results apply (see Chapter 10). In fact, we have

$$(\beta \mid y, \Sigma) \sim N(\hat{\beta}, K_\beta^{-1}),$$

where

$$K_\beta = V_\beta^{-1} + X'(I_T \otimes \Sigma^{-1})X, \quad \hat{\beta} = K_\beta^{-1}\left(V_\beta^{-1}\beta_0 + X'(I_T \otimes \Sigma^{-1})y\right),$$

and we have used the result $(I_T \otimes \Sigma)^{-1} = I_T \otimes \Sigma^{-1}$.

Next, we derive the conditional density $p(\Sigma \mid y, \beta)$. We will use the fact that, for conformable matrices A, B, C, we have

$$\text{tr}(ABC) = \text{tr}(BCA) = \text{tr}(CAB).$$

Combining the likelihood in (20.3) with the inverse Wishart prior for Σ, we obtain

$$\begin{aligned} p(\Sigma \mid y, \beta) &\propto p(y \mid \beta, \Sigma)p(\Sigma) \\ &\propto |\Sigma|^{-\frac{T}{2}} e^{-\frac{1}{2}\sum_{t=1}^{T}(y_t-X_t\beta)'\Sigma^{-1}(y_t-X_t\beta)} \times |\Sigma|^{-\frac{\nu_0+n+1}{2}} e^{-\frac{1}{2}\text{tr}(S_0\Sigma^{-1})} \\ &\propto |\Sigma|^{-\frac{\nu_0+n+T+1}{2}} e^{-\frac{1}{2}\text{tr}(S_0\Sigma^{-1})} e^{-\frac{1}{2}\text{tr}\left[\sum_{t=1}^{T}(y_t-X_t\beta)(y_t-X_t\beta)'\Sigma^{-1}\right]} \\ &\propto |\Sigma|^{-\frac{\nu_0+n+T+1}{2}} e^{-\frac{1}{2}\text{tr}\left[\left(S_0+\sum_{t=1}^{T}(y_t-X_t\beta)(y_t-X_t\beta)'\right)\Sigma^{-1}\right]}, \end{aligned}$$

which is the kernel of an inverse Wishart density. Thus, we have

$$(\Sigma \mid y, \beta) \sim IW\left(\nu_0 + T, S_0 + \sum_{t=1}^{T}(y_t - X_t\beta)(y_t - X_t\beta)'\right).$$

We summarize the Gibbs sampler for VAR(p) as follows:

Pick some initial values $\beta^{(0)} = c_0$ and $\Sigma^{(0)} = C_0 > 0$. Then, repeat the following steps from $r = 1$ to R:

1. Draw $\beta^{(r)} \sim p(\beta \,|\, y, \Sigma^{(r-1)})$ (multivariate normal).
2. Draw $\Sigma^{(r)} \sim p(\Sigma \,|\, y, \beta^{(r)})$ (inverse Wishart).

(c) MATLAB code which answers this question and produces the figures below is available on the website associated with this book. The empirical results below use a VAR(2) and set $\beta_0 = 0$, $V_\beta = I$ (except for the diagonal elements of V_β, which correspond to the intercepts in each equation and are set to 10), $\nu_0 = 6$, and $S_0 = I$. In order to identify the monetary policy shocks we order the interest rate last and treat it as the monetary policy instrument.

We first implement the Gibbs sampler described in part (b). Then, given the posterior draws of β and Σ, we compute the impulse-response functions of the three variables to a 100-basis-point monetary policy shock. Thus, the MATLAB code contains several scripts. The main script is VAR.m, which loads the data set and constructs the regression matrix X using the script SURform2.m.

For each of the posterior draws of β and Σ, we use the script construct_IR.m to compute the impulse-response functions of the three variables to a 100-basis-point monetary policy shock. More specifically, we consider two alternative paths: in one, a 100-basis-point monetary policy shock hits the system, and in the other this shock is absent. We then let the two systems evolve according to VAR(p) written as the regression

$$y_t = X_t\beta_t + C\tilde{\epsilon}_t, \quad \tilde{\epsilon}_t \sim N(0, I_3),$$

for $t = 1, \ldots, n_{\text{hz}}$, where n_{hz} denotes the number of horizons and C is the Cholesky factor of Σ. Each impulse-response function is then the difference between these two paths.

The impulse-response functions of inflation, unemployment, and interest rate to a 100-basis-point monetary policy shock are given in Figure 20.1.

By construction, the interest rate increases by 1% on impact, and it gradually goes back to zero over the next 20 quarters. The impact on unemployment is delayed and positive: the unemployment rate rises slowly and reaches a peak of about 0.25% after 3 years on impact.

In contrast, the inflation rate rises shortly after impact, and the effect is positive. The literature often refers to this empirical finding as the price puzzle – a contractionary monetary policy shock should dampen rather than increase inflation. Some argue that this reflects misspecification: some crucial variables are omitted, and both interest rate and inflation are responding to these omitted variables. Alternatively, Primiceri (2005) argues that the monetary policy shocks identified in this context should be interpreted as non-systematic policy actions that capture both policy mistakes and interest rate movements that are responses to variables other than inflation and unemployment.

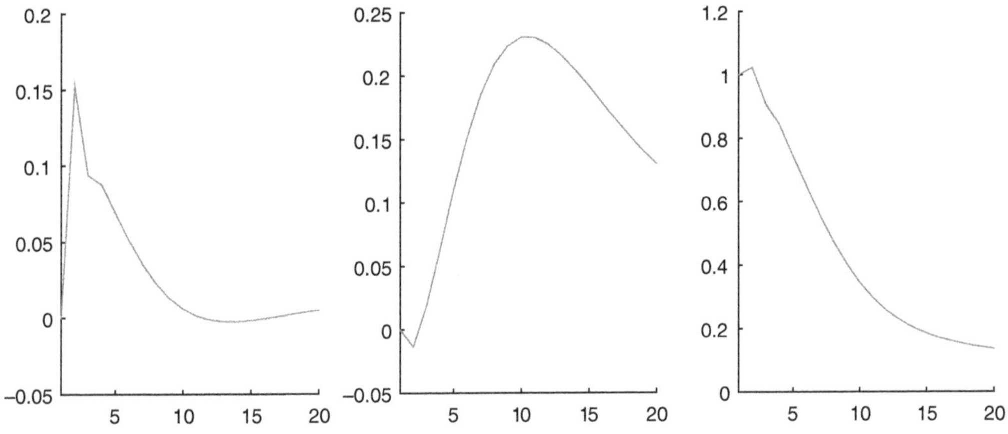

Figure 20.1. Impulse-response functions of inflation (left panel), unemployment (middle panel), and interest rate (right panel) to a 100-basis-point monetary policy shock.

Exercise 20.2 (Vector autoregression with Minnesota prior) For this exercise we use the notation and data set of Exercise 20.1. The reader should refer to that exercise for details of both. The Minnesota prior (see Doan, Litterman, and Sims 1984; Litterman 1986) has traditionally been the most popular prior for Bayesian VARs. It involves a simplification in that Σ is assumed to be a diagonal matrix and replaced with an estimate, $\widehat{\Sigma}$, where $\widehat{\sigma}_{ii} = s_i^2$ (where s_i^2 is the standard OLS estimate of the error variance using an AR model for the ith variable and $\widehat{\sigma}_{ii}$ is the iith element of $\widehat{\Sigma}$). To explain the prior for the vector of VAR(p) coefficients, β, note that some elements correspond to own lags (e.g., in the equation for the first variable in the VAR there are lags of the first variable), some elements correspond to other lags (e.g., in the equation for the first variable in the VAR there are lags of the second and third variables), and some to exogenous or deterministic variables (e.g., the intercept). The Minnesota prior reflects a belief that own lags are more likely to be important explanatory variables than other lags, and more recent lags are likely to be more important than those in the more distant past.

The Minnesota prior assumes $\beta \sim N(\beta_0, V_\beta)$. Consider first the prior mean, β_0. When using stationary variables which exhibit little persistence (e.g., the growth rates of macroeconomic variables) it is common to simply set $\beta_0 = 0$. When working with non-stationary data (e.g., the logs of macroeconomic variables) it is common to set $\beta_0 = 0$ except for the elements corresponding to the first own lag of the dependent variable in each equation. These elements are set to one. Next, consider the prior covariance matrix, V_β, which is assumed to be a diagonal matrix. The Minnesota prior sets the diagonal elements of V_β as follows:

- $\frac{\underline{a}_1}{r^2}$ for coefficients on own lag r for $r = 1, \ldots, p$;
- $\frac{\underline{a}_2 \widehat{\sigma}_{ii}}{r^2 \widehat{\sigma}_{jj}}$ for coefficients on lag r of variable $j \neq i$ for $r = 1, \ldots, p$ in equation i;
- $\underline{a}_3 \widehat{\sigma}_{ii}$ for coefficients on deterministic or exogenous variables in equation i.

The Minnesota prior thus turns a complicated prior elicitation procedure into a much simpler one which requires the researcher to select three scalar prior hyperparameters, $\underline{a}_1$, $\underline{a}_2$, and $\underline{a}_3$. Typically the researcher sets $\underline{a}_1 > \underline{a}_2$. In cases where the number of deterministic terms is small (e.g., if the only such terms are intercepts) then $\underline{a}_3$ is set to a large number, reflecting relatively non-informative prior beliefs.
(a) Derive the posterior for the VAR parameters using the Minnesota prior. Discuss what computational methods can be used to carry out Bayesian inference with this posterior.
(b) Use the data set described in Exercise 20.1(c). Estimate a VAR with the Minnesota prior using this data set.

Solution
(a) This derivation involves working out the posterior for β conditional on $\Sigma = \widehat{\Sigma}$. Note that an identical derivation was done in Exercise 20.1(b) as part of the derivation of the Gibbs sampler in that exercise. Thus, we can simply use our previous derivation to say that

$$(\beta \,|\, y) \sim N(\hat{\beta}, K_{\beta}^{-1}),$$

where

$$K_{\beta} = V_{\beta}^{-1} + X'(I_T \otimes \widehat{\Sigma}^{-1})X, \quad \hat{\beta} = K_{\beta}^{-1}\left(V_{\beta}^{-1}\beta_0 + X'(I_T \otimes \widehat{\Sigma}^{-1})y\right),$$

and the Minnesota prior forms for β_0 and V_β are used. This implies that posterior inference can be done analytically. That is, the posterior mean of the VAR coefficients is $\hat{\beta}$ and the posterior covariance matrix is K_{β}^{-1}. The properties of the normal distribution can be used to calculate other features such as credible intervals.

Thus, there is no need to use any posterior simulation method with the Minnesota prior unless interest centers on non-linear functions of β such as impulse response functions. Monte Carlo integration can be used to carry out posterior inference on features such as impulse response functions. That is, draws can be taken from the normal posterior for β and each transformed to produce an impulse response function. Averages of these draws will converge to the posterior mean of the impulse response function.
(b) MATLAB code (named bvar_minnesota.m) which answers this question is available on the website associated with this book. The results below set $p = 1$, $\underline{a}_1 = 0.5$, $\underline{a}_2 = 0.25$, and $\underline{a}_3 = 100$, and include an intercept. We have also set $\beta_0 = 0$ (although the reader may wish to experiment with other values as the variables do display a fairly high degree of persistence). Table 20.1 presents estimates of the VAR coefficients along with their posterior standard deviations. Each column of the table presents results for one of the three equations in the VAR. If we use the rule of thumb which says that a variable has important explanatory power if its posterior mean is more than two posterior standard deviations from zero, then the first own lag is important in every equation. Beyond this, it is only the unemployment equation which has any important explanatory variables.

Table 20.1: Posterior results using Minnesota prior for the VAR posterior mean (standard deviation in parentheses).

	Inflation	Unemployment	Interest rate
Lag inflation	0.701 (0.057)	0.088 (0.040)	0.212 (0.128)
Lag unemployment	−0.028 (0.022)	0.953 (0.016)	−0.050 (0.050)
Lag interest rate	0.038 (0.013)	0.023 (0.009)	0.927 (0.303)

Exercise 20.3 (Vector autoregression with non-informative prior) VAR(p) is defined in Exercise 20.1, and the reader is referred to that question for definitions and notation. An alternative way of writing the VAR is

$$Y = XA + E, \tag{20.5}$$

where $A = [b, A_1, \ldots, A_p]'$, and Y and E are $T \times n$ matrices with tth rows given by y_t' and ϵ_t', respectively. X is a $T \times k$ matrix with tth rows given by x_t', where $k = 1 + np$. E has a matric-variate normal distribution (see Definition A.12):

$$E \sim MN\left(0, \Sigma \otimes I_T\right).$$

Using a common non-informative prior,

$$p\left(B, \Sigma\right) \propto |\Sigma|^{-\frac{n+1}{2}},$$

derive the posterior of the VAR and discuss Bayesian estimation.

Solution

Using the properties of the matric-variate normal distribution (see Definition A.12), the likelihood function can be obtained as

$$L\left(A, \Sigma\right) \propto |\Sigma|^{-\frac{1}{2}T} \exp\left\{-\frac{1}{2}\mathrm{tr}\left[\Sigma^{-1}\left(Y - XA\right)'\left(Y - XA\right)\right]\right\}.$$

Multiplying this by the prior yields the posterior:

$$p\left(A, \Sigma | Y\right) \propto |\Sigma|^{-\frac{1}{2}(T+n+1)} \exp\left\{-\frac{1}{2}\mathrm{tr}\left[\Sigma^{-1}\left(Y - XA\right)'\left(Y - XA\right)\right]\right\}.$$

But, analogous to derivations for the normal linear regression model (see the introduction to Chapter 10), we can write the term in the exponential in terms of OLS quantities. In particular, if we define

$$\widehat{A} = \left(X'X\right)^{-1} X'Y$$

and

$$S = Y'Y - Y'X\left(X'X\right)^{-1}X'Y,$$

we can use the fact that

$$(Y - XA)'(Y - XA) = S + \left(A - \widehat{A}\right)' X'X\left(A - \widehat{A}\right)$$

to write the posterior as

$$\begin{aligned}
p(A, \Sigma|Y) &\propto |\Sigma|^{-\frac{1}{2}(T+n+1)} \exp\left\{-\frac{1}{2}\mathrm{tr}\left[\Sigma^{-1}\left[S + \left(A - \widehat{A}\right)' X'X\left(A - \widehat{A}\right)\right]\right]\right\} \\
&= |\Sigma|^{-\frac{1}{2}(T+n+1)}\left[\exp\left\{-\frac{1}{2}\mathrm{tr}\left[\Sigma^{-1}S\right]\right\}\right] \\
&\quad \left[\exp\left\{-\frac{1}{2}\mathrm{tr}\left[\Sigma^{-1}\left(A - \widehat{A}\right)' X'X\left(A - \widehat{A}\right)\right]\right\}\right].
\end{aligned}$$

Examining this as a function of Σ^{-1}, it can be seen that the marginal posterior of Σ^{-1} is Wishart. Examining this as a function of A, a matric-variate normal kernel can be found. Thus, we have

$$A|Y, \Sigma \sim MN\left(\widehat{A}, \Sigma \otimes \left[X'X\right]^{-1}\right)$$

and

$$\Sigma^{-1}|Y \sim W\left(S^{-1}, T\right).$$

Thus, Bayesian estimation of the normal VAR with the non-informative prior can be done using analytical results based on OLS quantities. This is the multivariate generalization of the normal linear regression model with a (non-informative version of a) natural conjugate prior (see Chapter 10, Exercise 10.1). Standard results for the natural conjugate prior for the VAR can be used to derive many other results. For instance, the marginal posterior for A is matric-variate t (see, e.g., Bauwens, Lubrano, and Richard 1999, Chapter 9). Kadiyala and Karlsson (1997) discussed a variety of other priors for VAR models. They showed, however, that for most of the priors the researcher may want to use, analytical results are not available. Gibbs sampling is commonly used with such extensions.

Exercise 20.4 (Marginal likelihood of the VAR with a natural conjugate prior) The natural conjugate prior for the VAR is

$$A|\Sigma \sim MN(\underline{A}, \Sigma \otimes \underline{V}), \quad \Sigma \sim IW(\underline{\nu}, \underline{S}),$$

where $\underline{V}$ is a $k \times k$ matrix and we refer the reader to Exercises 20.1 and 20.3 for notation and definitions. The posterior takes the same form:

$$A|\Sigma, Y \sim MN(\overline{A}, \Sigma \otimes \overline{V}), \quad \Sigma|Y \sim IW(\overline{\nu}, \overline{S}),$$

where $\overline{V} = \left(\underline{V}^{-1} + X'X\right)^{-1}, \overline{A} = \overline{V}\left(\underline{V}^{-1}\underline{A} + X'X\widehat{A}\right), \overline{\nu} = \underline{\nu} + T, \overline{S} = \widehat{A}'(X'X)\widehat{A} + \underline{A}'\underline{V}^{-1}\underline{A} + \underline{S} + \widehat{E}'\widehat{E} - \widehat{A}'\overline{V}^{-1}\widehat{A}$, and $\widehat{E} = Y - X\widehat{A}$. The necessary proof is a trivial extension of that done in Exercise 20.3 and so will not be asked for here. Thus, posterior analysis in the VAR with natural conjugate prior can be done analytically. With VARs it is often useful (e.g., for selecting lag length or choosing the optimal values of prior hyperparameters) to know the marginal likelihood. Derive the marginal likelihood for the VAR with natural conjugate prior.

Solution

The marginal likelihood can be obtained by integrating the parameters A and Σ out of the likelihood using the prior. The likelihood is given by

$$Y|A, \Sigma \sim MN\left(XA, \Sigma \otimes I_T\right).$$

To integrate out A, note that $Y = XA + E$ and, conditional on Σ, the two terms in the sum are independent of one another. That is, $Y|\Sigma = XA|\Sigma + E|\Sigma$. $Y|\Sigma$ is the desired distribution and the two right-hand side terms are independent of one another. These are

$$XA|\Sigma \sim MN\left(X\underline{A}, \Sigma \otimes X\underline{V}X'\right),$$
$$E|\Sigma \sim MN\left(0, \Sigma \otimes I_T\right).$$

Adding these two normal terms together gives us

$$Y|\Sigma \sim MN\left(X\underline{A}, \Sigma \otimes \left[I_T + X\underline{V}X'\right]\right).$$

Next, we integrate out Σ using its prior. This can be done using the fact that $Y|\Sigma$ is normal and the prior for Σ is inverse Wishart, and calling on Theorem A.19 of Bauwens, Lubrano, and Richard (1999). This is a multivariate extension of a result proved in Exercise 2.8, and this exercise provides some intuition about how the proof of this theorem is done. The theorem says that if you multiply a matric-variate normal pdf by an inverse Wishart pdf and integrate out the latter, you obtain a matric-variate t distribution. Using Definition A.13, it follows that the pdf of Y (and thus the marginal likelihood) is

$$p(Y) = \frac{\left|\underline{S} + (Y - X\underline{A})'\left(I + X\underline{A}X'\right)^{-1}(Y - X\underline{A})\right|^{-\frac{\underline{\nu}+t}{2}}}{\pi^{\frac{Tn}{2}}\left|(I+X\underline{A}X')^{-1}\right|^{-\frac{n}{2}}\left|\underline{S}\right|^{-\frac{\underline{\nu}}{2}}\prod_{i=1}^{n}\frac{\Gamma\left(\frac{\underline{\nu}+1-i}{2}\right)}{\Gamma\left(\frac{\underline{\nu}+T+1-i}{2}\right)}}.$$

Exercise 20.5 (Stochastic search variable selection in VARs) In Exercise 16.7 we developed stochastic search variable selection (SSVS) methods for the regression model. Exercise 16.7 argued that SSVS methods are a potentially useful way of surmounting over-parameterization and over-fitting concerns which arise when the number of potential explanatory variables is large relative to the number of observations. Vector autoregressions, where each of n equations contains p lags of each of n dependent variables,

also have many potential explanatory variables, and the error covariance matrix, Σ, contains $\frac{n(n-1)}{2}$ free elements. Thus, with large VARs, involving dozens or more dependent variables, there are a huge number of parameters to estimate. Concerns about over-parameterization and over-fitting are likely to be especially severe with VARs. In light of these concerns, you are asked to:
(a) Derive a Gibbs sampling algorithm which allows for Bayesian estimation of the VAR using an SSVS prior (VAR-SSVS).
(b) Using the data set described in Exercise 20.1(c), estimate the VAR-SSVS.

Solution
(a) This solution sets up the prior and derives the posterior conditionals in the same manner as George, Sun, and Ni (2008).

First, we establish notation. VAR(p) is defined as in Exercise 20.1, and we use notation where β is the $K \times 1$ vector of VAR coefficients and Σ is the $n \times n$ error covariance matrix. We work with the Cholesky decomposition

$$\Sigma^{-1} = \Psi\Psi',$$

where Ψ is upper triangular with elements ψ_{ij}. The diagonal elements of the latter matrix are denoted by $\psi = (\psi_{11}, \ldots, \psi_{nn})'$ and the off-diagonal upper triangular elements by $\eta = (\eta_2', \ldots, \eta_n')'$, where $\eta_j = (\psi_{1j}, \ldots, \psi_{j-1,j})'$ for $j = 2, \ldots, n$.

The model is parameterized in terms of β, ψ, and η. Stochastic search variable selection can be interpreted as defining a particular hierarchical prior for these parameters. In particular, the prior for the VAR coefficients is

$$\beta|\gamma^\beta \sim N\left(0, \underline{D}^\beta\right), \tag{20.6}$$

where $\underline{D}^\beta$ is a diagonal matrix with diagonal elements $\underline{d}_i^\beta$ for $i = 1, \ldots, K$, and $\gamma^\beta = \left(\gamma_1^\beta, \ldots, \gamma_k^\beta\right)'$. The SSVS nature of this prior arises by having $\gamma_i^\beta \in \{0, 1\}$ and defining

$$\underline{d}_i^\beta = \begin{cases} \tau_{0i}^2 \text{ if } \gamma_i^\beta = 0, \\ \tau_{1i}^2 \text{ if } \gamma_i^\beta = 1, \end{cases}$$

where τ_{0i}^2 is small and τ_{1i}^2 is large. George, Sun, and Ni (2008) described a semi-default automatic approach to objectively choosing these small and large prior variances. In the empirical illustration of part (b), we choose them subjectively. Thus, if $\gamma_i^\beta = 0$ the corresponding VAR coefficient is shrunk to be close to zero, whereas if $\gamma_i^\beta = 1$ it is estimated in a relatively unrestricted fashion. γ^β is a vector of unknown parameters and, thus, requires a prior. We assume the elements of γ^β to be *a priori* independent of one another, with

$$\Pr\left(\gamma_i^\beta = 0\right) = \underline{p}_i \tag{20.7}$$

and, thus, $\Pr\left(\gamma_i^\beta = 1\right) = 1 - \underline{p}_i$.

The hierarchical prior for η has the same SSVS form, allowing for individual error covariances to be shrunk toward zero or estimated in an unrestricted fashion. In particular, we assume, for $j = 2, \ldots, n$, that

$$\eta_j|\gamma_j^\eta \sim N\left(0, \underline{D}_j^\eta\right), \tag{20.8}$$

where $\underline{D}_j^\eta = \text{diag}\left(\underline{d}_{1j}^\eta, \ldots, \underline{d}_{j-1,j}^\eta\right)$. The vector of SSVS indicator variables, $\gamma_{ij}^\eta \in \{0, 1\}$, is defined as $\gamma^\eta = (\gamma_2^\eta, \ldots, \gamma_n^\eta)'$, where $\gamma_j^\eta = \left(\gamma_{1j}^\eta, \ldots, \gamma_{j-1,j}^\eta\right)'$. Next, we assume that

$$\underline{d}_{ij}^\eta = \begin{cases} \kappa_{0ij}^2 \text{ if } \gamma_{ij}^\eta = 0, \\ \kappa_{1ij}^2 \text{ if } \gamma_{ij}^\eta = 1, \end{cases}$$

where κ_{0ij}^2 is small and κ_{1i}^2 is large. We assume the elements of γ^η to be *a priori* independent of one another, with

$$\Pr\left(\gamma_{ij}^\eta = 0\right) = \underline{q}_{ij}. \tag{20.9}$$

Finally, the error variances are assumed to have gamma priors (independent of one another) and, thus,

$$\psi_{ii}^2 \sim G\left(\underline{a}_i, \underline{b}_i\right) \quad \text{for } i = 1, \ldots, n. \tag{20.10}$$

We next derive a Gibbs sampler involving the posterior conditionals for β, ψ, η, γ^β, and γ^η. We do not provide details of the posterior conditional for β since they are given in the solution to Exercise 20.1, with the prior hyperparameters β_0, V_β of Exercise 20.1 replaced by $0, \underline{D}^\beta$ from (20.6). That is, conditional on γ^β, the SSVS prior for β is a normal prior of exactly the same form as in Exercise 20.1.

Any Bayesian posterior involves multiplying likelihood by prior. To get a conditional posterior for a specific parameter, one fixes all the other parameters and treats the expression as a pdf for the specific parameter. If one follows this strategy for the posterior of γ^β conditional on all the other parameters, things are greatly simplified by noting that γ^β does not enter the likelihood. In fact, it only appears in (20.6) and (20.7). Multiplying the normal form for the former by the Bernoulli form for the latter yields a conditional posterior of a simple form. To be precise, the assumption that γ_i^β is *a priori* independent of γ_j^β for $i \neq j$ means that we can draw the SSVS variable selection indicators independently of one another with probabilities (for $i = 1, \ldots, k$)

$$\Pr\left(\gamma_i^\beta = 0|y, \beta, \eta, \psi\right) = \overline{p}_i,$$

where

$$\overline{p}_i = \frac{\tau_{0i}^{-1} \exp\left(-\frac{\beta_i^2}{2\tau_{0i}^2}\right) \underline{p}_i}{\tau_{0i}^{-1} \exp\left(-\frac{\beta_i^2}{2\tau_{0i}^2}\right) \underline{p}_i + \tau_{1i}^{-1} \exp\left(-\frac{\beta_i^2}{2\tau_{1i}^2}\right) \left(1 - \underline{p}_i\right)};$$

the denominator of this expression ensures that the probabilities sum to one. Furthermore, $\Pr\left(\gamma_i^\beta = 1|y, \beta, \eta, \psi\right) = 1 - \overline{p}_i$.

To obtain the conditional posterior for η, we use notation from Exercise 20.3, write the VAR in matrix form as in (20.5), and let

$$S = (Y - XA)(Y - XA)'$$

be the $n \times n$ sum of squares matrix of the VAR errors with the upper-left $j \times j$ sub-matrix being denoted by S_j, individual elements of S being s_{ij}, and $s_j = (s_{1j}, \ldots, s_{j-1,j})'$. Using the properties of the matric-variate normal distribution, the likelihood function is proportional to

$$|\Psi|^T \exp\left\{\operatorname{tr}\left(-\frac{1}{2}\Psi' S \Psi\right)\right\}.$$

Since Ψ is upper triangular we have $|\Psi|^T = \prod_{i=1}^n \psi_{ii}^T$, and, multiplying out the terms inside the trace operator, we have

$$\sum_{i=1}^n \psi_{ii}^2 v_i + \sum_{j=2}^n \left(\eta_j + \psi_{jj} S_{j-1}^{-1} s_j\right)' S_{j-1} \left(\eta_j + \psi_{jj} S_{j-1}^{-1} s_j\right).$$

Putting these two pieces together we obtain a likelihood proportional to

$$\prod_{i=1}^n \psi_{ii}^T \exp\left\{-\frac{1}{2}\left[\sum_{i=1}^n \psi_{ii}^2 v_i + \sum_{j=2}^n \left(\eta_j + \psi_{jj} S_{j-1}^{-1} s_j\right)' S_{j-1} \left(\eta_j + \psi_{jj} S_{j-1}^{-1} s_j\right)\right]\right\}. \tag{20.11}$$

Note that the likelihood breaks into independent components for each η_j for $j = 2, \ldots, p$, and each has a normal form. The priors given by (20.8) are also normal and independent of one another. It is straightforward to multiply each normal prior by the normal likelihood component for η_j to obtain, for $j = 2, \ldots, p$,

$$\eta_j | y, \beta, \psi \sim N\left(\overline{\mu}_j, \overline{D}_j^\eta\right),$$

where

$$\overline{D}_j^\eta = \left[S_{j-1} + \left(\underline{D}_j^\eta\right)^{-1}\right]^{-1},$$

$$\overline{\mu}_j = -\psi_{jj} \overline{D}_j^\eta s_j.$$

To obtain the posterior conditionals for γ^η we follow the same strategy (and almost identical derivations) as for γ^β and find (for $j = 2, \ldots, n$ and $i = 1, \ldots, j-1$)

$$\Pr\left(\gamma_{ij}^\eta = 0 | y, \beta, \eta, \psi\right) = \overline{q}_{ij},$$

where

$$\overline{q}_{ij} = \frac{\kappa_{0ij}^{-1} \exp\left(-\frac{\psi_{ij}^2}{2\kappa_{0ij}^2}\right) \underline{q}_{ij}}{\kappa_{0ij}^{-1} \exp\left(-\frac{\psi_{ij}^2}{2\kappa_{0ij}^2}\right) \underline{q}_i + \kappa_{1ij}^{-1} \exp\left(-\frac{\psi_{ij}^2}{2\kappa_{1ij}^2}\right) \left(1 - \underline{q}_{ij}\right)};$$

the denominator of this expression ensures that the probabilities sum to one. Furthermore, $\Pr\left(\gamma_{ij}^{\eta}=1|y,\beta,\eta,\psi\right)=1-\overline{q}_{ij}$.

Finally, obtaining draws of ψ can be done by using the independent gamma conditional posteriors for ψ_{jj}^2 for $j=1,\ldots,n$, which are

$$\psi_{ii}^2|y,\beta,\gamma^{\beta}\sim G\left(\overline{a}_i,\overline{b}_i\right),$$

where

$$\overline{a}_i=\underline{a}_i+\frac{1}{2},$$

$$\overline{b}_1=\underline{b}_1+\frac{s_{11}}{2},$$

$$\overline{b}_j=\underline{b}_j+\frac{1}{2}\left\{s_{jj}+s_j'\left[S_{j-1}+\left(\underline{D}_j^{\eta}\right)^{-1}\right]^{-1}s_j\right\}\text{ for } j=2,\ldots,n.$$

The proof is standard since it involves multiplying the gamma prior (20.10) by the normal likelihood in (20.11) and collecting terms involving ψ_{ii}^2. Similar proofs have been given elsewhere, e.g., in Exercise 2.7, and will not be repeated here.

(b) MATLAB code (named VAR_SSVS.m) which answers this question is available on the website associated with this book. The results below set $p=1$ and include an intercept. Prior hyperparameters are set as $\underline{q}_{ij}=\underline{p}_i=\frac{1}{2}$, $\tau_{0i}=\kappa_{0ij}=0.01$, $\tau_{1i}=\kappa_{1ij}=100$, $\underline{a}_i=\underline{b}_i=0.01$ for all i and j, although the reader may wish to experiment with other prior hyperparameter values, including the semi-default automatic values suggested by George, Sun, and Ni (2008, p. 558).

Table 20.2, based on 22 000 draws of which the first 2000 were discarded as the burn-in, presents posterior means, standard deviations, and the posterior inclusion probability (i.e., $\Pr\left(\gamma_i^{\beta}=1|y\right)$ for each $i=1,\ldots,K$). It can be seen that posterior inclusion probabilities are very high for the first own lags in each of the three equations, and their coefficients are similar to the comparable Minnesota prior results in Table 20.1. However, relative to Table 20.1, the remainder of the coefficients have been shrunk toward zero.

Table 20.3 is in the same format as Table 20.2, except that it contains posterior results for Σ. The SSVS algorithm does not apply to the error variances, only the covariances, which is why there are no inclusion probabilities to be reported for the former. It can be seen that there is one covariance, Σ_{21}, that is being shrunk to zero. The VAR-SSVS is providing strong evidence that Σ_{31} and Σ_{32} are non-zero, indicating that the error in the interest rate equation is correlated with the errors of the other two equations.

Exercise 20.6 (Time-varying parameter VAR) In many macroeconomic applications the interrelationships between variables change over time, implying that the VAR coefficients should change; time-varying parameter VAR (TVP-VAR) is a popular model in such cases.

Table 20.2: Posterior results for VAR coefficients using VAR-SSVS.

	Mean	Standard dev.	Inclusion prob.
	Inflation equation		
Lag inflation	0.793	0.049	1.000
Lag unemployment	0.010	0.007	3×10^{-4}
Lag interest rate	0.020	0.009	0.015
	Unemployment equation		
Lag inflation	0.093	0.074	0.595
Lag unemployment	0.969	0.007	1.000
Lag interest rate	0.014	0.010	0.003
	Interest rate equation		
Lag inflation	0.139	0.207	0.329
Lag unemployment	0.003	0.009	1×10^{-4}
Lag interest rate	0.965	0.035	1.000

Table 20.3: Posterior results for Σ using VAR-SSVS.

	Mean	Standard dev.	Inclusion prob.
Σ_{11}	0.177	0.018	—
Σ_{21}	−0.001	0.005	0.053
Σ_{31}	0.112	0.028	1.000
Σ_{22}	0.089	0.009	—
Σ_{32}	−0.142	0.023	1.000
Σ_{33}	0.910	0.090	—

Consider VAR(p) again, but now with time-varying parameters:

$$y_t = a_t + A_{1t}y_{t-1} + \cdots + A_{pt}y_{t-p} + \epsilon_t, \tag{20.12}$$

where $\epsilon_t \sim N(0, \Sigma)$. Define $X_t = I_n \otimes [1, y'_{t-1}, \ldots, y'_{t-p}]$ and $\beta_t = \text{vec}([a_t, A_{1t}, \ldots, A_{pt}]')$ and rewrite the above system as

$$y_t = X_t\beta_t + \epsilon_t.$$

The time-varying parameters β_t are assumed to evolve as a random walk,

$$\beta_t = \beta_{t-1} + u_t, \tag{20.13}$$

where $u_t \sim N(0, Q)$ and the initial conditions β_0 are treated as parameters. In this question, make the simplifying assumption that the covariance matrix Q is diagonal, i.e., $Q = \text{diag}(q_1, \ldots, q_{kn})$ where $k = np + 1$ is the number of explanatory variables in each equation of the TVP-VAR. One can also consider the possibility of a block-diagonal matrix or even a full matrix, but the form of the Gibbs sampler will change slightly. Note that the TVP-VAR is a state space model with measurement equation (20.12) and state equation (20.13).

To complete the model specification, consider independent priors for Σ, β_0, and the diagonal elements of Q:

$$\Sigma \sim IW(\nu_0, S_0), \quad \beta_0 \sim N(a_0, B_0), \quad q_i \sim IG(\nu_{0,q_i}, S_{0,q_i}).$$

(a) Derive a Gibbs sampler which allows for posterior inference in the TVP-VAR.
(b) Using the data set described in Exercise 20.1(c), estimate a TVP-VAR. Carry out an impulse response analysis and discuss whether impulse responses have changed over time.

Solution
(a) The parameters in the TVP-VAR are β_0, Σ, and Q, the states are $\beta = (\beta_1', \ldots, \beta_T')'$, and we derive a Gibbs sampler involving these four blocks.

First, we derive the posterior for β, conditional on the other parameters. Rewrite (20.12) as

$$y = X\beta + \epsilon,$$

where $\epsilon \sim N(0, I_T \otimes \Sigma)$ and

$$X = \begin{pmatrix} X_1 & 0 & \cdots & 0 \\ 0 & X_2 & \cdots & 0 \\ \vdots & \vdots & \ddots & \vdots \\ 0 & 0 & \cdots & X_T \end{pmatrix}.$$

Hence, we have

$$(y \mid \beta, \Sigma) \sim N(X\beta, I_T \otimes \Sigma).$$

So we have reframed the TVP-VAR as a normal linear regression model. Next, we derive the prior of β. To that end, rewrite (20.13) in matrix notation:

$$H\beta = \tilde{\alpha}_\beta + u,$$

where $u \sim N(0, I_T \otimes Q)$, $\tilde{\alpha}_\beta = (\beta_0', 0, \ldots, 0)'$, and

$$H = \begin{pmatrix} I_{nk} & 0 & 0 & \cdots & 0 \\ -I_{nk} & I_{nk} & 0 & \cdots & 0 \\ 0 & -I_{nk} & I_{nk} & \cdots & 0 \\ \vdots & & \ddots & \ddots & \vdots \\ 0 & 0 & \cdots & -I_{nk} & I_{nk} \end{pmatrix}.$$

Note that H is of dimension $Tnk \times Tnk$, and is a multivariate generalization of the usual first difference matrix; $|H| = 1$, and it is therefore invertible. Using a similar argument to Exercise 18.1, one can show that $H^{-1}\tilde{\alpha}_\beta = 1_T \otimes \beta_0$. Therefore, the prior of β is given by

$$(\beta \,|\, \beta_0, Q) \sim N(1_T \otimes \beta_0, (H'(I_T \otimes Q^{-1})H)^{-1}).$$

Thus, the TVP-VAR can also be seen as a multivariate regression with a normal prior, and standard multivariate regression can be used (see, e.g., Exercise 20.1) to derive

$$(\beta \,|\, y, \Sigma, \beta_0, Q) \sim N(\hat{\beta}, K_\beta^{-1}),$$

where

$$K_\beta = H'(I_T \otimes Q^{-1})H + X'(I_T \otimes \Sigma^{-1})X,$$
$$\hat{\beta} = K_\beta^{-1}\left(H'(I_T \otimes Q^{-1})H(1_T \otimes \beta_0) + X'(I_T \otimes \Sigma^{-1})y\right).$$

Since K_β is a band matrix, we can use the precision sampler derived in Exercise 19.1 to sample β efficiently. Alternative algorithms for drawing β involving Kalman filtering and state smoothing methods (e.g., Carter and Kohn 1994) also exist.

The conditional posterior for Σ can be derived using a similar derivation to Exercise 20.1 That is, conditional on β, the TVP-VAR has the same structure as a VAR with known coefficients, and the derivations of Exercise 20.1 can be repeated to show that

$$(\Sigma \,|\, y, \beta, Q) \sim IW\left(\nu_0 + T, S_0 + \sum_{t=1}^{T}(y_t - X_t\beta_t)(y_t - X_t\beta_t)'\right).$$

In a similar vein, conditional on β, the state equations have the same structure as regressions, with the diagonal elements of $Q = \text{diag}(q_1, \ldots, q_{nk})$ having the same role as error variances. Thus, derivations in Exercise 2.7 or 10.1 can be used to show that

$$(q_i \,|\, y, \beta, \beta_0) \sim IG\left(\nu_{0,q_i} + \frac{T}{2}, S_{0,q_i} + \frac{1}{2}\sum_{t=1}^{T}(\beta_{it} - \beta_{i(t-1)})^2\right).$$

Finally, since β_0 only appears in the first state equation,

$$\beta_1 = \beta_0 + u_1,$$

where $u_1 \sim N(0, Q)$. Given the normal prior $\beta_0 \sim N(a_0, B_0)$, we can use standard linear regression results to get

$$(\beta_0 \,|\, y, \beta, Q) \sim N(\hat{\beta}_0, K_{\beta_0}^{-1}),$$

where

$$K_{\beta_0} = B_0^{-1} + Q^{-1}, \quad \hat{\beta}_0 = K_{\beta_0}^{-1}\left(B_0^{-1}a_0 + Q^{-1}\beta_1\right).$$

We summarize the Gibbs sampler for TVP-VAR(p) as follows:

Pick some initial values for $\beta^{(0)}$, $\Sigma^{(0)}$, $Q^{(0)}$, and $\beta_0^{(0)}$. Then, repeat the following steps from $r = 1$ to R:

1. Draw $\beta^{(r)} \sim (\beta \,|\, y, \Sigma^{(r-1)}, Q^{(r-1)}, \beta_0^{(r-1)})$ (multivariate normal).
2. Draw $\Sigma^{(r)} \sim (\Sigma \,|\, y, \beta^{(r)}, Q^{(r-1)}, \beta_0^{(r-1)})$ (inverse Wishart).

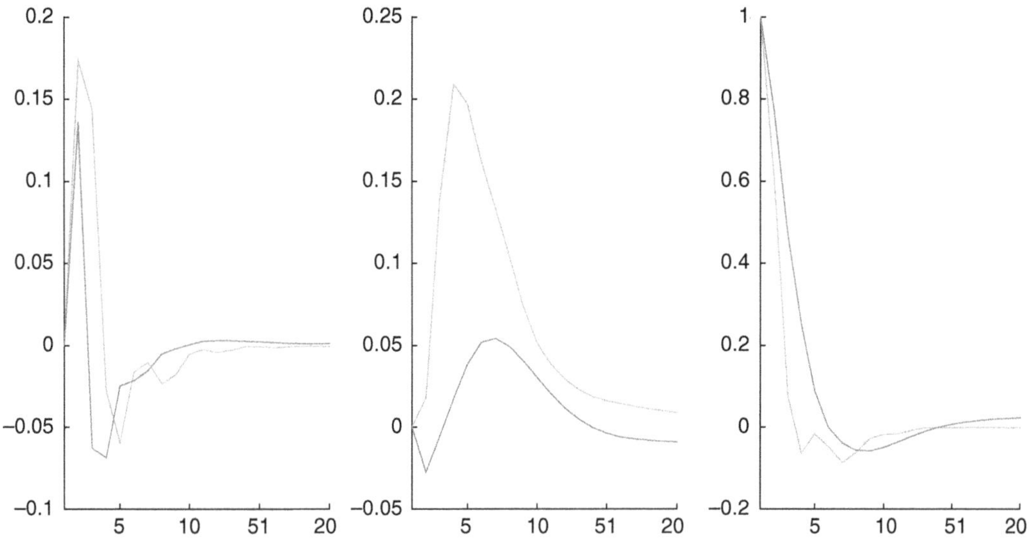

Figure 20.2. Impulse-response functions of inflation (left panel), unemployment (middle panel), and interest rate (right panel) to a 100-basis-point monetary policy shock for 1975Q1 and 2005Q1.

3. Draw $Q^{(r)} \sim (Q \,|\, y, \beta^{(r)}, \Sigma^{(r)}, \beta_0^{(r-1)})$ (independent inverse gammas).
4. Draw $\beta_0^{(r)} \sim (\beta_0 \,|\, y, \beta^{(r)}, \Sigma^{(r)}, Q^{(r)})$ (multivariate normal).

(b) In the empirical example in Exercise 20.1, we estimated a three-variable VAR(2) of inflation, unemployment, and interest rate, and used it to compute impulse response functions to a 100-basis-point monetary policy shock. Given that the sample covers a long period, one might wonder if the responses to the monetary policy shocks were different early in the sample from later in the sample. To address this question, we revisit the Exercise 20.1 example using a TVP-VAR. In particular, we compare the impulse responses associated with the VAR coefficients in 1975 to those in 2005. We use the same data set, lag length, and scheme to identify the monetary policy shock with the TVP-VAR as we did in Exercise 20.1.

The website associated with this book contains MATLAB code which does this. In particular, the MATLAB script VAR_TVP.m implements the Gibbs sampler derived in the solution to part (a). The MATLAB script construct_IR.m calculates the impulse responses.

Figure 20.2 reports two sets of impulse response functions to a 100-basis-point monetary policy shock. The first set is computed using the VAR coefficients at 1975Q1; the second set uses those at 2005Q1. As the figure shows, the impulse-response functions of both inflation and interest rate are very similar across the two time periods, whereas those of unemployment seem to be more different.

We report in Figure 20.3 the mean differences between the two sets of impulse-response functions of the three variables, as well as the associated 90% credible intervals. Despite

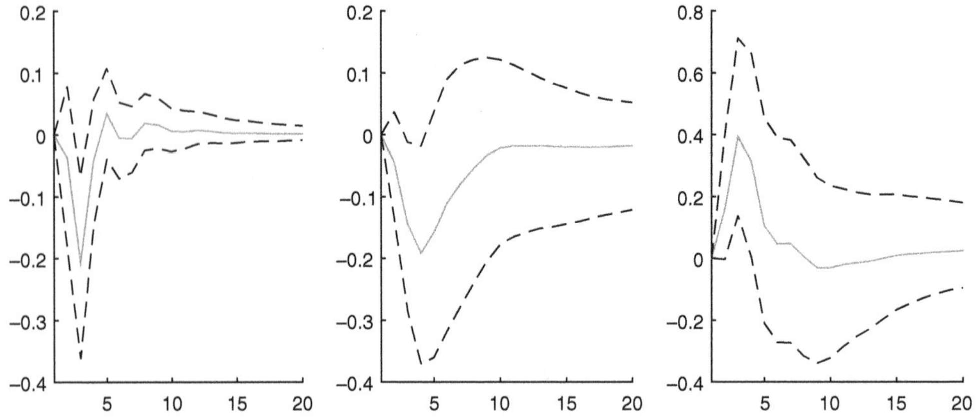

Figure 20.3. Differences between the impulse-response functions of inflation (left panel), unemployment (middle panel), and interest rate (right panel) at 2005Q1 and 1975Q1. The dotted lines are the 5% and 95% quantiles.

some large absolute differences, parameter uncertainty is high and most of the credible intervals contain zero. There seems to be some evidence that the responses of unemployment are different across the two periods, but the evidence is not conclusive.

Exercise 20.7 (Vector autoregression with stochastic volatility) This exercise shows how one can extend the standard VAR with homoscedastic errors to produce a VAR with stochastic volatility (VAR-SV). We start with the constant-coefficient VAR of Exercise 20.1. However, we extend it by allowing the errors to have a time-varying covariance matrix Σ_t:

$$y_t = X_t\beta + \epsilon_t, \quad \epsilon_t \sim N(0, \Sigma_t). \tag{20.14}$$

We want Σ_t to evolve smoothly, while at each time period Σ_t must be a valid covariance matrix, i.e., it is symmetric and positive definite. There are a few approaches to modeling such an evolution, and here we follow the approach in the seminal paper by Cogley and Sargent (2005). They modeled Σ_t as

$$\Sigma_t^{-1} = L' D_t^{-1} L,$$

where D_t is a diagonal matrix and L is a lower triangular matrix with ones on the main diagonal, i.e.,

$$D_t = \begin{pmatrix} e^{h_{1t}} & 0 & \cdots & 0 \\ 0 & e^{h_{2t}} & \cdots & 0 \\ \vdots & \vdots & \ddots & \vdots \\ 0 & 0 & \cdots & e^{h_{nt}} \end{pmatrix}, \quad L = \begin{pmatrix} 1 & 0 & 0 & \cdots & 0 \\ a_{21} & 1 & 0 & \cdots & 0 \\ a_{31} & a_{32} & 1 & \cdots & \vdots \\ \vdots & \vdots & \vdots & \ddots & \vdots \\ a_{n1} & a_{n2} & \cdots & a_{n(n-1)} & 1 \end{pmatrix}.$$

By construction Σ_t is symmetric and positive definite for any values of $h_t = (h_{1t}, \ldots, h_{nt})'$ and $a = (a_{21}, a_{31}, a_{32}, \ldots, a_{n1}, \ldots, a_{n(n-1)})'$. Note that the dimension of a is $m = n(n-1)/2$. Then, each h_{it} is specified independently using a univariate stochastic volatility model (see Exercise 19.1). More precisely, each h_{it} evolves according to the following random walk:

$$h_{it} = h_{i(t-1)} + u_{it}^h,$$

where $u_{it}^h \sim N(0, \sigma_{h,i}^2)$ and h_{i0} is treated as an unknown parameter.

It is worth noting that the parameters in a are restricted to be constant here. Primiceri (2005) considered an extension where these parameters are time varying and modeled as random walks (i.e., both a and β are time varying). The Gibbs sampler for Primiceri's model requires extra blocks relative to the Gibbs sampler derived in this exercise. These can be obtained using standard results for the normal linear state space model (see, e.g., Exercise 20.6).

By construction, $\Sigma_t = L^{-1} D_t (L^{-1})'$, and therefore we can express each element of Σ_t in terms of the elements of D_t and $L^{-1} = (a^{ij})$. More precisely, we have

$$\sigma_{ii,t} = e^{h_{it}} + \sum_{k=1}^{i-1} e^{h_{kt}} (a^{ik})^2, \quad i = 1, \ldots, n,$$

$$\sigma_{ij,t} = a^{ij} e^{h_{jt}} + \sum_{k=1}^{j-1} a^{ik} a^{jk} e^{h_{kt}}, \quad 1 \leq j < i \leq n,$$

where $\sigma_{ij,t}$ is the (i,j) element of Σ_t. Note that the log-volatility h_{1t} affects the variances of all the variables, whereas h_{nt} only affects the last variable.

In addition, despite the assumption of a constant matrix L, this setup also allows for some form of time-varying correlations among the errors. This can be seen via a simple example. Using the formulas above, we have

$$\sigma_{11,t} = e^{h_{1t}}, \quad \sigma_{22,t} = e^{h_{2t}} + e^{h_{1t}} (a^{21})^2, \quad \sigma_{12,t} = a^{21} e^{h_{1t}}.$$

We have used the fact that L^{-1} is a lower triangular matrix with ones on the main diagonal, and therefore $a^{11} = 1$ and $a^{12} = 0$. Now, the (1,2) correlation coefficient is given by

$$\frac{\sigma_{12,t}}{\sqrt{\sigma_{11,t}\sigma_{22,t}}} = \frac{a^{21}}{\sqrt{e^{h_{2t}-h_{1t}} + (a^{21})^2}}.$$

Hence, as long as h_{1t} and h_{2t} are not identical for all t, this correlation coefficient is time varying.

To complete the model specification, use independent priors for β, a, $\sigma^2_h = (\sigma^2_{h,1}, \ldots, \sigma^2_{h,n})'$, and $h_0 = (h_{10}, \ldots, h_{n0})'$:

$$\beta \sim N(\beta_0, V_\beta), \quad a \sim N(a_0, V_a), \quad \sigma^2_{h,i} \sim IG(\nu_{0,h_i}, S_{0,h_i}), \quad h_0 \sim N(b_0, B_0).$$

(a) Derive an MCMC algorithm which allows for posterior inference in this VAR-SV.
(b) Estimate the VAR-SV using the data set described in Exercise 20.1(c) but extended to 2013Q4 so as to investigate whether the Great Recession involved changes in volatilities (this is US_macrodata1.csv on the website associated with this book). Plot the volatilities and discuss your results.

Solution

(a) To estimate the VAR-SV model, we derive a Gibbs sampler that combines standard Bayesian VAR methods (see Exercise 20.1) with methods for drawing the stochastic volatilities. Remember that stochastic volatility models are state space models, and in Exercise 19.1 an auxiliary mixture sampler was derived which allowed for Bayesian estimation of univariate stochastic volatility processes.

The model parameters are β, a, $\sigma^2_{h,i}$, and $h_{0,i}$, and the states are the log-volatilities $h_{i,1:T} = (h_{i1}, \ldots, h_{iT})'$ for $i = 1, \ldots, n$. We derive a five-block Gibbs sampler involving each of these. The two non-standard steps are the sampling of a and $h = (h'_{1,1:T}, \ldots, h'_{n,1:T})'$, and we will describe them in detail below.

We begin with the sampling of a, the lower triangular elements of L. First observe that given y and β, $\epsilon = y - X\beta$ is known. Thus, we can rewrite the model as a system of regressions in which ϵ_{it} is regressed on $\epsilon_{1t}, \ldots, \epsilon_{(i-1)t}$ for $i = 2, \ldots, n$, and $a_{i1}, \ldots, a_{i(i-1)}$ are the corresponding regression coefficients. If we can rewrite the model this way, then we can apply standard linear regression results to sample a.

To be precise, note that

$$L\epsilon_t = \begin{pmatrix} 1 & 0 & 0 & \cdots & 0 \\ a_{21} & 1 & 0 & \cdots & 0 \\ a_{31} & a_{32} & 1 & \cdots & \vdots \\ \vdots & \vdots & & \ddots & \vdots \\ a_{n1} & a_{n2} & a_{n3} & \cdots & 1 \end{pmatrix} \begin{pmatrix} \epsilon_{1t} \\ \epsilon_{2t} \\ \epsilon_{3t} \\ \vdots \\ \epsilon_{nt} \end{pmatrix} = \begin{pmatrix} \epsilon_{1t} \\ \epsilon_{2t} + a_{21}\epsilon_{1t} \\ \epsilon_{3t} + a_{31}\epsilon_{1t} + a_{32}\epsilon_{2t} \\ \vdots \\ \epsilon_{nt} + \sum_{j=1}^{n-1} a_{nj}\epsilon_{jt} \end{pmatrix}$$

$$= \begin{pmatrix} \epsilon_{1t} \\ \epsilon_{2t} \\ \epsilon_{3t} \\ \vdots \\ \epsilon_{nt} \end{pmatrix} - \begin{pmatrix} 0 & 0 & 0 & 0 & 0 & \cdots & \cdots & 0 \\ -\epsilon_{1t} & 0 & 0 & 0 & 0 & \cdots & & \vdots \\ 0 & -\epsilon_{1t} & -\epsilon_{2t} & 0 & 0 & \cdots & & 0 \\ \vdots & & & \ddots & \ddots & & \cdots & 0 \\ 0 & \cdots & 0 & \cdots & 0 & -\epsilon_{1t} & \cdots & -\epsilon_{t(n-1)} \end{pmatrix} \begin{pmatrix} a_{21} \\ a_{31} \\ a_{32} \\ \vdots \\ a_{n(n-1)} \end{pmatrix}.$$

Or, more succinctly,

$$L\epsilon_t = \epsilon_t - E_t a.$$

Noting that $|\Sigma_t| = |D_t|$, we can rewrite the likelihood implied by (20.14) as

$$\begin{aligned} p(y \mid \beta, a, h) &\propto \left(\prod_{t=1}^{T} |D_t|^{-\frac{1}{2}}\right) \exp\left(-\frac{1}{2}\sum_{t=1}^{T} \epsilon_t'(L'D_t^{-1}L)\epsilon_t\right) \\ &= \left(\prod_{t=1}^{T} |D_t|^{-\frac{1}{2}}\right) \exp\left(-\frac{1}{2}\sum_{t=1}^{T} (L\epsilon_t)'D_t^{-1}(L\epsilon_t)\right) \\ &= \left(\prod_{t=1}^{T} |D_t|^{-\frac{1}{2}}\right) \exp\left(-\frac{1}{2}\sum_{t=1}^{T} (\epsilon_t - E_t a)'D_t^{-1}(\epsilon_t - E_t a)\right). \end{aligned}$$

In other words, the likelihood is the same as that implied by the regression

$$\epsilon_t = E_t a + \eta_t, \tag{20.15}$$

where $\eta_t \sim N(0, D_t)$. Therefore, stacking (20.15) over $t = 1, \ldots, T$, we have

$$\epsilon = Ea + \eta,$$

where $\eta \sim N(0, D)$ with $D = \text{diag}(D_1, \ldots, D_T)$. Given the prior $a \sim N(a_0, V_a)$, it then follows that

$$(a \mid y, \beta, h) \sim N(\hat{a}, K_a^{-1}),$$

where

$$K_a = V_a^{-1} + E'D^{-1}E, \quad \hat{a} = K_a^{-1}\left(V_a^{-1}a_0 + E'D^{-1}\epsilon\right).$$

To sample the log-volatility h, we first compute the orthogonalized innovations: $\tilde{\epsilon}_t = L(y_t - X_t\beta)$ for $t = 1, \ldots, T$. It can be seen that $E(\tilde{\epsilon}_t \mid a, h, \beta) = 0$ and

$$\text{cov}(\tilde{\epsilon}_t \mid a, h, \beta) = L(LD_t^{-1}L)^{-1}L' = D_t.$$

Hence, $(\tilde{\epsilon}_{it} \mid a, h, \beta) \sim N(0, e^{h_{it}})$. Therefore, we can apply the auxiliary mixture sampler in Exercise 19.1 to each of the series $\tilde{\epsilon}_{i1}, \ldots, \tilde{\epsilon}_{iT}$ for $i = 1, \ldots, n$. The Gibbs sampler steps for $\sigma^2_{h,i}$ and $h_{0,i}$ for $i = 1, \ldots, n$ are exactly the same as in Exercise 19.1 and will not be repeated here.

To sample β, we rewrite (20.14) as

$$y = X\beta + \epsilon,$$

where $\epsilon \sim N(0, \tilde{\Sigma})$ and $\tilde{\Sigma} = \text{diag}(\Sigma_1, \ldots, \Sigma_T)$ is a block-diagonal matrix. Together with the prior $\beta \sim N(\beta_0, V_\beta)$, we have

$$(\beta \mid y, a, h) \sim N(\hat{\beta}, K_\beta^{-1}),$$

where

$$K_\beta = V_\beta^{-1} + X'\tilde{\Sigma}^{-1}X, \quad \hat{\beta} = K_\beta^{-1}\left(V_\beta^{-1}\beta_0 + X'\tilde{\Sigma}^{-1}y\right).$$

Note that $\tilde{\Sigma}^{-1} = \text{diag}(\Sigma_1^{-1}, \ldots, \Sigma_T^{-1})$ with $\Sigma_t^{-1} = L'D_t^{-1}L$.

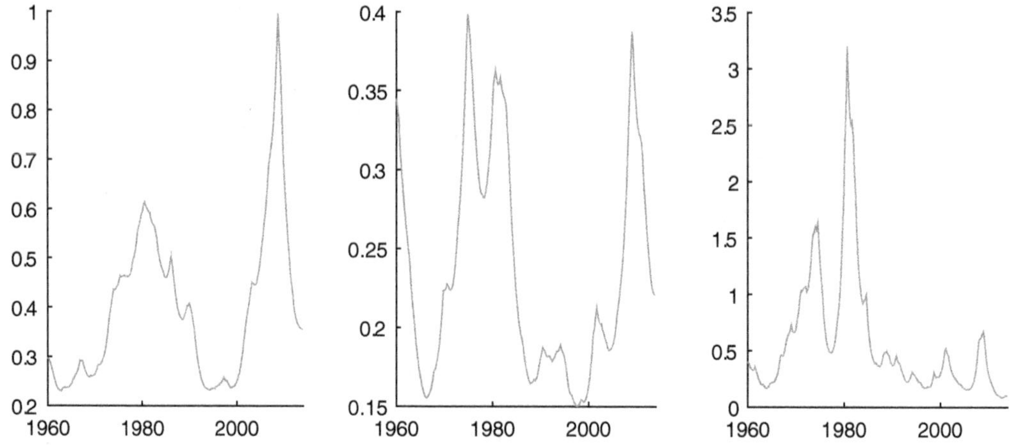

Figure 20.4. Time-varying volatility of the inflation equation (left panel), unemployment equation (middle panel), and interest rate equation (right panel) expressed as standard deviations.

(b) The MATLAB script VAR_SV.m, available on the website associated with this book, contains the Gibbs sampler of part (a) for estimating the VAR-SV model using US quarterly observations on CPI inflation, unemployment, and the interest rate from 1959Q2 to 2013Q4.

Figure 20.4 shows the time-varying volatility of the three equations expressed as standard deviations. The volatility of all three equations decreases substantially in the early 1980s, the timing of which matches the onset of the Great Moderation. The volatility remains low until the Great Recession. These results show that the error variances of all three equations have substantial time variation. Extending the standard VAR with constant variance to one with stochastic volatility is therefore empirically relevant.

Exercise 20.8 (The restricted VAR) In some cases, the researcher may be interested in restricted versions of VAR, where different equations depend on different explanatory variables. For instance, instead of every variable depending on the same number of lags of all variables (as an unrestricted VAR does), the researcher might want to have a different number of lags in each equation and/or each variable depending on lags of only some of the other variables. Discuss how Bayesian inference can be carried out in such a model.

Solution

A VAR with different explanatory variables in each equation is equivalent to a SUR (see Exercise 12.18). In particular, we can write

$$y_{mt} = x'_{mt}\beta_m + \epsilon_{mt},$$

with $t = 1,\ldots,T$ observations for $m = 1,\ldots,M$ variables. y_{mt} is the tth observation on the mth variable, x_{mt} is a k_m-vector containing the tth observation of the vector of explanatory variables relevant for the mth variable, and β_m is the accompanying k_m-vector of regression coefficients.

We can stack all the equations into vectors/matrices as $y_t = (y_{1t}, \ldots, y_{Mt})'$, $\epsilon_t = (\epsilon_{1t}, \ldots, \epsilon_{Mt})'$,

$$\beta = \begin{pmatrix} \beta_1 \\ \cdot \\ \cdot \\ \beta_M \end{pmatrix},$$

$$X_t = \begin{pmatrix} x'_{1t} & 0 & \cdot & \cdot & 0 \\ 0 & x'_{2t} & 0 & \cdot & \cdot \\ \cdot & \cdot & \cdot & \cdot & \cdot \\ \cdot & \cdot & \cdot & \cdot & 0 \\ 0 & \cdot & \cdot & 0 & x'_{Mt} \end{pmatrix},$$

and define $k = \sum_{m=1}^{M} k_m$. Using this notation, we can write the restricted VAR as

$$y_t = X_t\beta + \epsilon_t.$$

We now stack all the observations together as

$$y = \begin{pmatrix} y_1 \\ \cdot \\ \cdot \\ y_T \end{pmatrix},$$

$$\epsilon = \begin{pmatrix} \epsilon_1 \\ \cdot \\ \cdot \\ \epsilon_T \end{pmatrix},$$

$$X = \begin{pmatrix} X_1 \\ \cdot \\ \cdot \\ X_T \end{pmatrix},$$

and write

$$y = X\beta + \epsilon.$$

Thus, ϵ is $N(0, \Omega)$, where Ω is an $NM \times NM$ block-diagonal matrix given by

$$\Omega = \begin{pmatrix} \Sigma & 0 & \cdot & \cdot & 0 \\ 0 & \Sigma & \cdot & \cdot & \cdot \\ \cdot & \cdot & \cdot & \cdot & \cdot \\ \cdot & \cdot & \cdot & \cdot & 0 \\ 0 & \cdot & \cdot & 0 & \Sigma \end{pmatrix}.$$

It can be seen that the restricted VAR can be written as a normal linear regression model with general error covariance matrix (see Exercise 12.12), and the results derived in the solution to that exercise can be directly used. Analytical results do not exist for this model and, thus, we need to think in terms of posterior simulation.

Perhaps the easiest way of developing methods of posterior simulation is to note that, since Ω is a positive definite matrix, a standard theorem in matrix algebra implies that a matrix P exists with the property that $P\Omega P' = I_N$. If we multiply both sides of the regression model by P, we obtain a transformed model:

$$y^* = X^*\beta + \epsilon^*, \tag{20.16}$$

where $y^* = Py$, $X^* = PX$, and $\epsilon^* = P\epsilon$. It can be verified that ϵ^* is $N(0, I_{TM})$. Hence, conditional upon Ω, we have a normal linear regression model with known error covariance matrix. Thus, for suitably chosen priors (e.g., normal or non-informative), $p(\beta|y,\Omega)$ will be normal. If we can find a convenient form for $p(\Omega|y,\beta)$ then a Gibbs sampler can be set up for carrying out posterior inference in this restricted VAR.

A commonly used prior for this model is the independent normal-Wishart prior of Exercise 20.1:

$$p\left(\beta, \Sigma^{-1}\right) = p\left(\beta\right) p\left(\Sigma^{-1}\right),$$

where

$$p\left(\beta\right) = \phi\left(\beta | \underline{\beta}, \underline{V}\right)$$

and

$$p\left(\Sigma^{-1}\right) = f_W\left(\Sigma^{-1} | \underline{H}, \underline{\nu}\right).$$

For prior elicitation, the most important properties of the Wishart are that $E\left(\Sigma^{-1}\right) = \underline{\nu}\underline{H}$ and non-informativeness is achieved by setting $\underline{\nu} = 0$ and $\underline{H}^{-1} = 0_{M\times M}$.

Using this prior, the conditional posteriors $p\left(\beta|y,\Sigma^{-1}\right)$ and $p\left(\Sigma^{-1}|y,\beta\right)$ can be derived in a straightforward fashion using methods presented in solutions to other problems. That is, the fact that $p\left(\beta|y,\Sigma^{-1}\right)$ is normal involves the same proof as in Exercise 10.1 using the transformed model in (20.16). In fact, the proof is a simplified version of our earlier proof since in the transformed model the error covariance matrix is I_{TM} (and, hence, we can use here the Exercise 10.1 proof with h set equal to 1). Repeating the Exercise 10.1 proof and then transforming back to the original model results in

$$\beta | y, \Sigma^{-1} \sim N\left(\overline{\beta}, \overline{V}\right),$$

where

$$\overline{V} = \left(\underline{V}^{-1} + \sum_{t=1}^{T} X_t' \Sigma^{-1} X_t\right)^{-1}$$

and

$$\overline{\beta} = \overline{V} \left(\underline{V}^{-1} \underline{\beta} + \sum_{i=1}^{T} X_t' \Sigma^{-1} y_t \right).$$

The posterior for Σ^{-1} conditional on β can also be derived exactly, as was done in Exercise 11.10, to obtain

$$\Sigma^{-1} | y, \beta \sim W \left(\overline{\nu}, \overline{H} \right),$$

where

$$\overline{\nu} = T + \underline{\nu}$$

and

$$\overline{H} = \left[\underline{H}^{-1} + \sum_{t=1}^{T} (y_t - X_t \beta)(y_t - X_t \beta)' \right]^{-1}.$$

A Gibbs sampler which sequentially draws from the normal $p(\beta | y, \Omega)$ and the Wishart $p\left(\Sigma^{-1} | y, \beta\right)$ can be programmed in a straightforward fashion. As with any Gibbs sampler, the resulting posterior simulator output can be used to calculate posterior properties of any function of the parameters, marginal likelihoods (for model comparison), and/or to do prediction.

Exercise 20.9 (Cointegration and the vector error correction model) Cointegration is an important topic in non-stationary time series econometrics. If cointegration is present among several variables, then it can be shown that a VECM exists which is a restricted version of a VAR(p). That is, if y_t for $t = 1, \ldots, T$ is an $n \times 1$ vector containing observations on n time series variables and ϵ_t is an $n \times 1$ vector of errors, then the VECM is

$$\Delta y_t = \Pi y_{t-1} + \sum_{i=1}^{p-1} \Psi_i \Delta y_{t-i} + \Phi d_t + \epsilon_t,$$

where the matrix of long run multipliers, Π, can be written as $\Pi = \alpha \beta'$ where α and β are both full-rank $n \times r$ matrices, and where $0 \leq r \leq n$ is the number of cointegrating relationships. d_t is a k_d vector containing deterministic terms (e.g., an intercept, deterministic trends, dummy variables, etc.) and Φ is $n \times k_d$. Assume ϵ_t to be $iid\ N(0, \Sigma)$.

Given the interest in cointegration, many authors have derived Bayesian methods for working with the VECM. The present exercise is loosely based on Geweke (1996a). However, before getting into the exercise, a warning is called for. Important statistical issues arise since Π is potentially of reduced rank. A global identification issue can be seen by noting that $\Pi = \alpha \beta'$ and $\Pi = \alpha S S^{-1} \beta'$ are identical for any non-singular S. This indeterminacy is surmounted by Geweke (1996a) by imposing the so-called *linear normalization*, where $\beta = [I_r \ \ B']'$. Even if global identification is imposed, a local identification issue occurs at the point $\alpha = 0$ (i.e., at this point β does not enter the model). As discussed by Kleibergen and van Dijk (1994, 1998), this local identification problem can cause serious problems, when certain non-informative priors are used for posterior computation (e.g., the Gibbs sampler can have an absorbing state) and for Bayesian inference (i.e., the posterior might not integrate to one, and hence is not a valid pdf). The approach of Geweke (1996a) does yield a valid posterior and Gibbs sampler since it imposes the linear normalization and works with informative normal priors. However, there are some drawbacks to this linear normalization (see Strachan and Inder 2004), and normal priors may not be attractive in some empirical contexts. Koop, Strachan, van Dijk, and Villani (2006) surveyed the Bayesian cointegration literature, and the interested reader is referred to this paper for discussion of some of the complications relating to identification and prior elicitation which are ignored in this exercise.

In this exercise impose the linear normalization, and thus work in the parameterization involving α, B, Σ^{-1}, and C, where $C = (\Psi_1 \cdots \Psi_{d-1}\, \Phi)$ is an $n \times k$ matrix with $k = k_d + pn$. Also, let $A = (\alpha\, C)$ and use the following priors (where $f_{MN}(.)$ denotes the matric-variate normal pdf – see Definition A.12):

$$p(A|\Sigma) = f_{MN}\left(A|\underline{A}, \Sigma \otimes \underline{V}_A\right)$$

and

$$p\left(\Sigma^{-1}, B\right) = f_W\left(\Sigma^{-1}|\underline{H}, \underline{\nu}\right).$$

Note that we are using a natural conjugate prior for A and Σ^{-1}, conditional on B, and a non-informative prior for B. In the previous formulae, $\underline{V}_A$ is a $(k+r) \times (k+r)$ positive definite matrix and $\underline{V}_{B1}$ and $\underline{V}_{B2}$ are $r \times r$ and $(M-r) \times (M-r)$ positive definite matrices, respectively.

Derive the conditional posteriors, $p(B|y, A, \Sigma)$, $p(A|y, B, \Sigma)$, and $p\left(\Sigma^{-1}|y, B\right)$, and thus show how a Gibbs sampler can be set up to carry out posterior inference in the VECM.

Solution

The basic idea in developing a Gibbs sampler for the VECM with the prior given in the question is that, conditional on B, the model becomes equivalent to the unrestricted VAR of Exercise 20.4 (or the non-informative prior version of it in Exercise 20.3). Thus, the necessary derivations for A and Σ are basically the same as those in earlier exercises. It is only the derivation of $p(B|y, A, \Sigma)$ which is new. But even this derivation is similar to a previous one since, conditional on A and Σ, the model becomes the same as the restricted VAR of Exercise 20.8. Exact details are provided in the following material.

Let $z_t = \beta' y_{t-1}$, $Z_t = \left(z_t', \Delta y_{t-1}', \ldots, \Delta y_{t-p-1}', d_t'\right)'$. The VECM can be written as

$$\Delta y_t = A' Z_t + \epsilon_t. \tag{20.17}$$

In matrix form we can then write

$$\Delta Y = ZA + E,$$

where ΔY and E are $T \times M$ matrices with tth rows given by $\Delta y_t'$ and ϵ_t', respectively. Z is a $T \times (k+r)$ matrix with tth rows given by Z_t'. E has a matric-variate normal distribution:

$$E \sim MN\left(0, \Sigma \otimes I_T\right).$$

Thus, conditional upon β (or, equivalently, B), the VECM has the same form as a VAR (or a multivariate regression model). Hence, the proof is virtually identical to that provided in Exercises 20.1, 20.2, or 20.3, and we will not provide all the details. Briefly, combining the matric-variate normal likelihood with the normal-Wishart natural conjugate (and treating β as fixed), we obtain the posterior. Writing the posterior in terms of OLS quantities and rearranging yields the normal-Wishart posterior (conditional on β):

$$A|y, \beta, \Sigma \sim MN\left(\text{vec}\left[\overline{A}\right], \Sigma \otimes \overline{V}_A\right)$$

and

$$\Sigma^{-1}|y, \beta \sim W\left(\overline{S}^{-1}, \underline{\nu} + T\right).$$

In the previous formulae we use the notation

$$\overline{V}_A = \left(\underline{V}_A^{-1} + Z'Z\right)^{-1},$$
$$\overline{A} = \overline{V}_A\left(\underline{V}_A^{-1}\underline{A} + Z'Z\widehat{A}\right),$$
$$\widehat{A} = \left(Z'Z\right)^{-1} Z'\Delta Y,$$

and

$$\overline{S} = \underline{H}^{-1} + (\Delta Y - Z\underline{A})'\left[I_T - Z\left(\overline{V}_A^{-1} + Z'Z\right)^{-1} Z'\right](\Delta Y - Z\underline{A})$$

$$\overline{A} = \overline{V}_A\left(\underline{V}_A^{-1}\underline{A} + Z'Z\widehat{A}\right).$$

Thus, $p\left(A|y, B, \Sigma\right)$ follows a matric-variate normal distribution with mean matrix $\overline{A}$ and covariance matrix $\Sigma \otimes \overline{V}_A$, and $p\left(\Sigma^{-1}|y, B\right)$ is Wishart.

It remains to derive $p\left(B|y, A, \Sigma\right)$. To achieve this, it proves useful to write the VECM in another way. Begin by rearranging (20.17) as

$$\Delta y_t - \sum_{i=1}^{p-1} \Psi_i \Delta y_{t-i} - \Phi d_t = \alpha\beta' y_{t-1} + \epsilon_t;$$

denoting the left-hand side of this equation as x_t^*, we obtain

$$x_t^* = \alpha\beta' y_{t-1} + \epsilon_t.$$

Stacking (in the same fashion as earlier in the solution to this exercise), we can write this model as

$$X^* = Y_{-1}\beta\alpha' + E, \tag{20.18}$$

where X^* and Y_{-1} are $T \times M$ matrices with tth rows give by x_t^* and y_{t-1}', respectively. E is as defined previously in this solution.

Intuitively, if α were a square non-singular matrix we could post-multiply both sides of this equation by α'^{-1} and the resulting transformed model would simply be a multivariate regression; standard methods could be used (since we are conditioning on A, x_t^* can be treated as known). This, of course, will not work since α is not a square matrix. However, following Geweke (1996a), we can do something similar. First construct the $M \times M$ matrix (which a standard theorem in matrix algebra tells us is non-singular)

$$C = \left[\alpha^+ \; \alpha^0\right],$$

where α^+ (an $M \times r$ matrix) is the Moore–Penrose generalized inverse of α' (i.e., $\alpha' \alpha^+ = I_r$) and α^0, an $M \times (M-r)$ matrix, is orthogonal to α^+. If we post-multiply (20.18) by C we obtain

$$\left[X^*\alpha^+ \; X^*\alpha^0\right] = \left[Y_{-1}\beta \; 0\right] + \left[E\alpha^+ \; E\alpha^0\right]. \tag{20.19}$$

There is one final issue that needs to be addressed: we are interested in posterior inference on the identified parameter B, rather than β (remember $\beta = [I_r \quad B']'$). But this can be dealt with by imposing the identification restriction and pulling over these elements to the right-hand side of (20.19). We do this by defining the partition

$$Y_{-1} = \left[Y_{-1}^1 \; Y_{-1}^2\right],$$

where Y_{-1}^1 is $T \times r$ and Y_{-1}^2 is $T \times (M-r)$. Write (20.19) as

$$\left[\widetilde{X}_1 \; \widetilde{X}_2\right] = \left[Y_{-1}^2 B \; 0\right] + \left[\widetilde{E}_1 \; \widetilde{E}_2\right], \tag{20.20}$$

where $\widetilde{X}_1 = X^*\alpha^+ - Y_{-1}^1$, $\widetilde{X}_2 = X^*\alpha^0$, $\widetilde{E}_1 = E\alpha^+$, and $\widetilde{E}_2 = E\alpha^0$.

Note that (20.20) is a multivariate normal regression model, except that restrictions are placed on some of the coefficients (i.e., the final r columns of the matrix of explanatory variables are zeros). A multivariate normal regression model with restrictions on the coefficients is a restricted VAR, and Exercise 20.8 shows us how to work with these. Additional details are provided below.

To see the relationship with the restricted VAR most clearly, it is helpful to stack all the columns in (20.20) to put the model in the same form as the solution to Exercise 20.8. Letting $\widetilde{x}_j = \text{vec}\left(\widetilde{X}_j\right)$ and $\widetilde{\epsilon}_j = \text{vec}\left(\widetilde{E}_j\right)$ for $j = 1, 2$ and $b = \text{vec}(B)$, we can write (20.20) as

$$\begin{bmatrix} \widetilde{x}_1 \\ \widetilde{x}_2 \end{bmatrix} = \begin{bmatrix} I_r \otimes Y_{-1}^2 \\ 0 \end{bmatrix} b + \begin{bmatrix} \widetilde{\epsilon}_1 \\ \widetilde{\epsilon}_2 \end{bmatrix} \quad \text{or} \quad \widetilde{x} = \widetilde{Z} b + \widetilde{\epsilon},$$

where $\widetilde{\epsilon}$ is $N\left(0, \widetilde{\Sigma}\right)$ with $\widetilde{\Sigma} = C'\Sigma C \otimes I_T$. In this form it can be explicitly seen that this model has exactly the same format as the restricted VAR of Exercise 20.8. Accordingly, we will not repeat the steps necessary to derive the posterior for b (conditional on A and Σ). Using these previous derivations, we find that

$$b|y, A, \Sigma \sim N\left(\overline{b}, \overline{V}_b\right),$$

where

$$\overline{V}_b = \left[\widetilde{Z}'\left(\widetilde{\Sigma} \otimes I_T\right)\widetilde{Z}\right]^{-1},$$

which, given the particular structure of $\widetilde{Z}$, reduces to

$$\overline{V}_b = \left(\widetilde{\Sigma}^{11}\right)^{-1} \otimes \left(Y_{-1}^{2\prime} Y_{-1}^{2}\right)^{-1},$$

where $\widetilde{\Sigma}^{11}$ is the $r \times r$ upper left hand block of $\widetilde{\Sigma}^{-1}$. Furthermore,

$$\overline{b} = \overline{V}_b \widetilde{Z}'\left(\widetilde{\Sigma} \otimes I_T\right)\widetilde{x}.$$

Thus, Bayesian inference in the VECM with this prior using the linear normalization can be performed using a Gibbs sampler involving only standard distributions (the normal and the Wishart).

Appendix

In this appendix, the pdfs used in the book are defined and some of their properties described. Except for the gamma pdf (which we parameterize in a different way), we follow the notational conventions described in Abadir and Magnus (2002). There are, of course, many other pdfs which arise in other models – Chapter 3 of Poirier (1995) discusses many of these. Probably the most complete source of information on probability distribution is the *Distributions in Statistics* series; see Johnson, Kotz, and Balakrishnan (1994, 1995, 2000) and Johnston, Kotz, and Kemp (1993).

Following standard practice, we introduce two sorts of notation. The first is for the pdf or probability function itself. The second is the symbol "$\sim$" meaning "is distributed as."

Definition A.1 (The uniform distribution) A continuous random variable, Y, has a *uniform distribution* over the interval $[a, b]$, denoted $Y \sim U(a, b)$, if its pdf is given by:

$$f_U(y|a, b) = \begin{cases} \frac{1}{b-a} & \text{if } a \leq y \leq b, \\ 0 & \text{otherwise,} \end{cases}$$

where $-\infty < a < b < \infty$.

Theorem A.1 (Mean and variance of the uniform distribution) If $Y \sim U(a, b)$ then $E(Y) = \frac{a+b}{2}$ and $\text{Var}(Y) = \frac{(b-a)^2}{12}$.

Definition A.2 (The gamma and related distributions) A continuous random variable Y has a *gamma* distribution with mean $\mu > 0$ and degrees of freedom $\nu > 0$, denoted by $Y \sim \gamma(\mu, \nu)$, if its pdf is:

$$f_\gamma(y|\mu, \nu) \equiv \begin{cases} c_\gamma^{-1} y^{\frac{\nu-2}{2}} \exp\left(-\frac{y\nu}{2\mu}\right) & \text{if } 0 < y < \infty, \\ 0 & \text{otherwise,} \end{cases}$$

where the integrating constant is given by $c_\gamma = \left(\frac{2\mu}{\nu}\right)^{\frac{\nu}{2}} \Gamma\left(\frac{\nu}{2}\right)$ and $\Gamma(a)$ is the gamma function (see Poirier 1995, p. 98). It is also common to parameterize the gamma in terms of $\alpha = \frac{\nu}{2}$ and $\beta = \frac{2\mu}{\nu}$, in which case we denote the distribution as $Y \sim G(\alpha, \beta)$. The associated density function under this parameterization is denoted by $f_G(y|\alpha, \beta)$, where

$$f_G(y|\alpha,\beta) \equiv \begin{cases} c_G^{-1} y^{\alpha-1} \exp(-y/\beta) & \text{if } 0 < y < \infty, \\ 0 & \text{otherwise,} \end{cases}$$

and $c_G = \beta^\alpha \Gamma(\alpha)$.
Notes: Distributions related to the gamma include the *chi-square distribution*, which is a gamma distribution with $\nu = \mu$ and denoted by $Y \sim \chi^2(\nu)$, and the *exponential distribution*, a gamma distribution with $\nu = 2$.

The *non-central chi-square distribution*, denoted $\chi^2(\nu, \lambda)$ has the following density function:

$$f(y|\nu,\lambda) = \left[\frac{\exp(-(y+2\lambda)/2)}{2^{\nu/2}}\right] \left(\sum_{k=0}^{\infty} \frac{y^{(\nu/2)+k-1}(2\lambda)^k}{\Gamma(\nu/2+k)2^{(2k)}k!}\right).$$

The mean of the $\chi^2(\nu, \lambda)$ random variable is $\nu + 2\lambda$ and the variance is $2\nu + 8\lambda$.

Theorem A.2 (Mean and variance of the gamma distribution) If $Y \sim G(\alpha, \beta)$ then $E(Y) = \alpha\beta$ and $\text{Var}(Y) = \alpha\beta^2$. If $Y \sim \gamma(\mu, \nu)$, then $E(Y) = \mu$ and $\text{Var}(Y) = 2\mu^2/\nu$.

The *inverted gamma distribution* has the property that, if Y has an inverted gamma distribution, then $\frac{1}{Y}$ has a gamma distribution. In this book we denote the inverted gamma density as $Y \sim IG(\alpha, \beta)$. Though different parameterizations exist (particularly for how β enters the density), we utilize the following form in this text:

$$Y \sim IG(\alpha,\beta) \Rightarrow p(y) = [\Gamma(\alpha)\beta^\alpha]^{-1} y^{-(\alpha+1)} \exp(-1/[y\beta]).$$

The mean of this inverted gamma is $E(Y) = [\beta(\alpha-1)]^{-1}$, for $\alpha > 1$, and the variance is $\text{Var}(Y) = [\beta^2(\alpha-1)^2(\alpha-2)]^{-1}$ for $\alpha > 2$. Further properties of the inverted gamma are given, for example, in Poirier (1995, p. 111).

Definition A.3 (The multivariate normal distribution) A continuous k-dimensional random vector $Y = (Y_1, \ldots, Y_k)'$ has a *normal distribution* with mean μ (a k-vector) and variance Σ (a $k \times k$ positive definite matrix), denoted $Y \sim N(\mu, \Sigma)$, if its pdf is given by:

$$\phi(y|\mu,\Sigma) = \phi(y;\mu,\Sigma) = \frac{1}{2\pi^{\frac{k}{2}}} |\Sigma|^{-\frac{1}{2}} \exp\left[-\frac{1}{2}(y-\mu)'\Sigma^{-1}(y-\mu)\right].$$

In some cases throughout the book we add a subscript to this notation, such as $\phi_k(y|\mu, \Sigma)$, to remind the reader that y is a k-dimensional vector. In other instances we make use of the notation $\phi(y; \mu, \Sigma)$ (typically suppressing the dimensionality subscript) to explicitly denote that μ and Σ are the mean and covariance matrix of y rather than simply arbitrary parameters of the density.

The cumulative distribution function of the multivariate normal evaluated at the point y^* is denoted by $\Phi\left(y^*|\mu,\Sigma\right)$ or, if $\mu = 0$ and $\Sigma = I$, by $\Phi\left(y^*\right)$.

Note: The special case where $k = 1$, $\mu = 0$, and $\Sigma = 1$ is referred to as the *standard normal* distribution.

Theorem A.3 (Marginals and conditionals of the multivariate normal distribution) Suppose the k-vector $Y \sim N\left(\mu,\Sigma\right)$ is partitioned as

$$Y = \begin{pmatrix} Y_{(1)} \\ Y_{(2)} \end{pmatrix},$$

where $Y_{(i)}$ is a k_i-vector for $i = 1, 2$ with $k_1 + k_2 = k$, and μ and Σ have been partitioned conformably as

$$\mu = \begin{pmatrix} \mu_{(1)} \\ \mu_{(2)} \end{pmatrix}$$

and

$$\Sigma = \begin{pmatrix} \Sigma_{(11)} & \Sigma_{(12)} \\ \Sigma'_{(12)} & \Sigma_{(22)} \end{pmatrix}.$$

Then the following results hold:

- The marginal distribution of $Y_{(i)}$ is $N\left(\mu_{(i)},\Sigma_{(ii)}\right)$ for $i = 1, 2$.
- The conditional distribution of $Y_{(1)}$ given $Y_{(2)} = y_{(2)}$ is $N\left(\mu_{(1|2)},\Sigma_{(1|2)}\right)$, where

$$\mu_{(1|2)} = \mu_{(1)} + \Sigma_{(12)}\Sigma_{(22)}^{-1}\left(y_{(2)} - \mu_{(2)}\right)$$

and

$$\Sigma_{(1|2)} = \Sigma_{(11)} - \Sigma_{(12)}\Sigma_{(22)}^{-1}\Sigma'_{(12)}.$$

The conditional distribution of $Y_{(2)}$ given $Y_{(1)} = y_{(1)}$ can be obtained by reversing subscripts 1 and 2 in the previous formulas.

Theorem A.4 (Linear combinations of normals are normal) Let $Y \sim N\left(\mu,\Sigma\right)$ be a k-dimensional random vector and A be a fixed (non-random) $m \times k$ matrix with $\text{rank}\left(A\right) = m$; then $AY \sim N\left(A\mu, A\Sigma A'\right)$.

Definition A.4 (The multivariate t distribution) A continuous k-dimensional random vector $Y = \left(Y_1,\ldots,Y_k\right)'$ has a *t distribution* with mean μ (a k-vector), scale matrix Σ (a $k \times k$ positive definite matrix), and parameter ν (a positive scalar referred to as a *degrees of freedom* parameter), denoted $Y \sim t\left(\mu,\Sigma,\nu\right)$, if its pdf is given by:

$$f_t(y|\mu,\Sigma,\nu) = \frac{1}{c_t}|\Sigma|^{-\frac{1}{2}}\left[\nu + (y-\mu)'\,\Sigma^{-1}\,(y-\mu)\right]^{-\frac{\nu+k}{2}},$$

where

$$c_t = \frac{\pi^{\frac{k}{2}}\Gamma\left(\frac{\nu}{2}\right)}{\nu^{\frac{\nu}{2}}\Gamma\left(\frac{\nu+k}{2}\right)}.$$

Notes: The special case where $k = 1$, $\mu = 0$, and $\Sigma = 1$ is referred to as the *Student t* distribution with ν degrees of freedom. Tables providing percentiles of the Student t are available in most econometrics and statistics textbooks. The case where $\nu = 1$ is referred to as the *Cauchy distribution*.

Theorem A.5 (Mean and variance of the t distribution) If $Y \sim t(\mu, \Sigma, \nu)$ then $E(Y) = \mu$ if $\nu > 1$ and $\text{Var}(Y) = \frac{\nu}{\nu-2}\Sigma$ if $\nu > 2$.

Notes: The mean and variance only exist if $\nu > 1$ and $\nu > 2$, respectively. This implies, for instance, that the mean of the Cauchy distribution does not exist even though it is a valid pdf and, hence, its median and other quantiles exist. Σ is not exactly the same as the variance matrix and, hence, is given another name: the *scale matrix*.

Theorem A.6 (Marginals and conditionals of the multivariate t distribution) Suppose the k-vector $Y \sim t(\mu, \Sigma, \nu)$ is partitioned as in Theorem A.3, as are μ and Σ. Then the following results hold:

- The marginal distribution of $Y_{(i)}$ is $t\left(\mu_{(i)}, \Sigma_{(ii)}, \nu\right)$ for $i = 1, 2$.
- The conditional distribution of $Y_{(1)}$ given $Y_{(2)} = y_{(2)}$ is $t\left(\mu_{(1|2)}, \Sigma_{(1|2)}, \nu + k_1\right)$, where

$$\mu_{(1|2)} = \mu_{(1)} + \Sigma_{(12)}\Sigma_{(22)}^{-1}\left(y_{(2)} - \mu_{(2)}\right),$$

$$\Sigma_{(1|2)} = h_{(1|2)}\left[\Sigma_{(11)} - \Sigma_{(12)}\Sigma_{(22)}^{-1}\Sigma'_{(12)}\right],$$

and

$$h_{(1|2)} = \frac{1}{\nu + k_2}\left[\nu + \left(y_{(2)} - \mu_{(2)}\right)'\Sigma_{(22)}^{-1}\left(y_{(2)} - \mu_{(2)}\right)\right].$$

The conditional distribution of $Y_{(2)}$ given $Y_{(1)} = y_{(1)}$ can be obtained by reversing subscripts 1 and 2 in the previous formulas.

Theorem A.7 (Linear combinations of t distributions are t) Let $Y \sim t(\mu, \Sigma, \nu)$ be a k-dimensional random vector and A be a fixed (non-random) $m \times k$ matrix with rank equal to m; then $AY \sim t(A\mu, A\Sigma A', \nu)$.

Definition A.5 (The normal-gamma distribution) Let Y be a k-dimensional random vector and h a scalar random variable. If the conditional distribution of Y given h is normal and the marginal distribution for h is gamma then (Y, h) is said to have a *normal-gamma distribution*. Formally, if $Y|h, \mu, \Sigma \sim N\left(\mu, h^{-1}\Sigma\right)$ and $h|m, \nu \sim \gamma(m, \nu)$ then $\theta = (Y', h)'$ has a normal-gamma distribution denoted $\theta \sim NG(\mu, \Sigma, m, \nu)$. The corresponding pdf is denoted $f_{NG}(\theta|\mu, \Sigma, m, \nu)$.

Theorem A.8 (Marginal distributions involving the normal-gamma) If $\theta = (Y', h)' \sim NG(\mu, \Sigma, m, \nu)$, then the marginal for Y is given by $Y \sim t\left(\mu, m^{-1}\Sigma, \nu\right)$. By definition, the marginal for h is given by $h \sim \gamma(m, \nu)$.

Definition A.6 (The Wishart and inverse Wishart distributions) Let H be an $N \times N$ positive definite (symmetric) random matrix, A be a fixed (non-random) $N \times N$ positive definite matrix, and $\nu > 0$ a scalar degrees of freedom parameter. Then H has a *Wishart distribution*, denoted $H \sim W(A, \nu)$, if its pdf is given by:

$$f_W(H|A, \nu) = \frac{1}{c_W}|H|^{\frac{\nu-N-1}{2}}|A|^{-\frac{\nu}{2}}\exp\left[-\frac{1}{2}\text{tr}\left(A^{-1}H\right)\right],$$

where

$$c_W = 2^{\frac{\nu N}{2}}\pi^{\frac{N(N-1)}{4}}\prod_{i=1}^{N}\Gamma\left(\frac{\nu+1-i}{2}\right).$$

Note: If $N = 1$, then the Wishart reduces to a gamma distribution (i.e., $f_W(H|A, \nu) = f_G(H|\nu A, \nu)$ if $N = 1$).

An $m \times m$ random matrix Z is said to have an *inverse Wishart distribution* with shape parameter $\alpha > 0$ and scale matrix W if its density function is given by

$$f_{IW}(Z; \alpha, W) = \frac{|W|^{\alpha/2}}{2^{m\alpha/2}\Gamma_m(\alpha/2)}|Z|^{-\frac{\alpha+m+1}{2}}\exp\left[-\frac{1}{2}\text{tr}(WZ^{-1})\right],$$

where Γ_m is the multivariate gamma function and $\text{tr}(\cdot)$ is the trace function. We write $Z \sim IW(\alpha, W)$. For $\alpha > m+1$, $E(Z) = W/(\alpha - m - 1)$.

Theorem A.9 (Means, variances, and covariances relating to the Wishart distribution) If $H \sim W(A, \nu)$ then $E(H_{ij}) = \nu A_{ij}$, $\text{Var}(H_{ij}) = \nu\left(A_{ij}^2 + A_{ii}A_{jj}\right)$ for $i, j = 1, \ldots, N$ and $\text{cov}(H_{ij}, H_{km}) = \nu(A_{ik}A_{jm} + A_{im}A_{jk})$ for $i, j, k, m = 1, \ldots, N$, where subscripts i, j, k, m refer to elements of matrices.

Definition A.7 (The binomial distribution) A discrete random variable Y has a *binomial distribution* with parameters T and p, denoted $Y \sim B(T, p)$, if its probability function is given by:

$$f_B(y|T, p) = \begin{cases} \frac{T!}{(T-y)!y!}p^y(1-p)^{T-y} & \text{if } y = 0, 1, \ldots, T, \\ 0 & \text{otherwise,} \end{cases}$$

where $0 \leq p \leq 1$ and T is a positive integer. The *Bernoulli* distribution is a special case of the binomial when $T = 1$.

Theorem A.10 (Mean and variance of the binomial distribution) If $Y \sim B(T, p)$ then $E(Y) = Tp$ and $\text{Var}(Y) = Tp(1-p)$.

Note: This distribution is used in cases where an experiment, the outcome of which is either "success" or "failure," is repeated independently T times. The probability of success in an experiment is p. The distribution of the random variable Y, which counts the number of successes, is $B(T, p)$.

Definition A.8 (The Poisson distribution) A discrete random variable Y has a *Poisson distribution* with parameter λ, denoted $Y \sim Po(\lambda)$, if its probability function is given by:

$$f_{Po}(y|\lambda) = \begin{cases} \frac{\lambda^y \exp(-\lambda)}{y!} & \text{if } y = 0, 1, 2, \ldots, \\ 0 & \text{otherwise,} \end{cases}$$

where λ is a positive real number.

Theorem A.11 (Mean and variance of the Poisson distribution) If $Y \sim Po(\lambda)$ then $E(Y) = \lambda$ and $\text{Var}(Y) = \lambda$.

Definition A.9 (The multinomial distribution) A discrete N-dimensional random vector $Y = (Y_1, \ldots, Y_N)'$ has a *multinomial distribution* with parameters T and p, denoted $Y \sim M(T, p)$, if its probability function is given by:

$$f_M(y|T, p) = \begin{cases} \frac{T!}{y_1! \cdots y_N!} p_1^{y_1} \cdots p_N^{y_N} & \text{if } y_i = 0, 1, \ldots, T \text{ and } \sum_{i=1}^N y_i = T, \\ 0 & \text{otherwise,} \end{cases}$$

where $p = (p_1, \ldots, p_N)'$, $0 \leq p_i \leq 1$ for $i = 1, \ldots, N$, $\sum_{i=1}^N p_i = 1$, and T is a positive integer.

Definition A.10 (The Dirichlet and beta distributions) Let $Y = (Y_1, \ldots, Y_N)'$ be a vector of continuous random variables with the property that $Y_1 + \cdots + Y_N = 1$. Then Y has a *Dirichlet distribution*, denoted $Y \sim D(\alpha)$, if its pdf is given by:

$$f_D(Y|\alpha) = \left[\frac{\Gamma(a)}{\prod_{i=1}^N \Gamma(\alpha_i)} \right] \prod_{i=1}^N y_i^{\alpha_i - 1},$$

where $\alpha = (\alpha_1, \ldots, \alpha_N)'$, $\alpha_i > 0$ for $i = 1, \ldots, N$, and $a = \sum_{i=1}^N \alpha_i$. The *beta distribution*, denoted by $Y \sim \beta(\alpha_1, \alpha_2)$, is the Dirichlet distribution for the case $N = 2$. Its pdf is denoted by $f_B(Y|\alpha_1, \alpha_2)$.

Note: In the case $N = 2$, the restriction $Y_1 + Y_2 = 1$ can be used to remove one of the random variables. Thus, the beta distribution is a univariate distribution.

Theorem A.12 (Means and variances of the Dirichlet distribution) Suppose $Y \sim D(\alpha)$ where α and a are as given in Definition A.10; then, for $i, j = 1, \ldots, N$,

- $E(Y_i) = \frac{\alpha_i}{a}$
- $\text{Var}(Y_i) = \frac{\alpha_i(a - \alpha_i)}{a^2(a+1)}$
- $\text{cov}(Y_i, Y_j) = -\frac{\alpha_i \alpha_j}{a^2(a+1)}$.

Definition A.11 (The Pareto distribution) A continuous random variable Y has a *Pareto distribution* if its pdf is given by:

$$f_{Pa}(y|\gamma, \lambda) = \begin{cases} \frac{\lambda \gamma^{\lambda}}{y^{\lambda+1}} & \text{if } y \geq \gamma, \\ 0 & \text{otherwise.} \end{cases}$$

Definition A.12 (The matric-variate normal distribution) A $p \times q$ matrix Y of random variables is said to have a *matric-variate normal distribution*, denoted $Y \sim MN(\text{vec}[M], \ Q \otimes P)$, with parameters M (a $p \times q$ matrix), P (a positive definite $p \times p$ matrix), and Q (a positive definite $q \times q$ matrix) if and only if $\text{vec}(Y) \sim N(\text{vec}[M], Q \otimes P)$. Thus, its density is given by:

$$f_{MN}(Y|M, Q \otimes P) = [2\pi^{pq} |P|^q |Q|^p]^{-\frac{1}{2}} \exp\left\{-\frac{1}{2}\text{tr}\left[Q^{-1}(Y - M)' P^{-1}(Y - M)\right]\right\}.$$

Note that vec () takes the columns of a matrix and stacks them in order into a vector.

Definition A.13 (The matric-variate t distribution) A $p \times q$ random matrix Z is said to have a *matric-variate t distribution* with parameters M, P, Q, and ν if its pdf is given by

$$f_{Mt}(Z; M, P, Q, \nu) = \frac{\left|Q + (Z - M)' P (Z - M)\right|^{-\frac{\nu+p}{2}}}{\pi^{\frac{pq}{2}} |Q|^{-\frac{\nu}{2}} \, |P|^{-\frac{q}{2}} \prod_{i=1}^{q} \frac{\Gamma\left(\frac{\nu+1-i}{2}\right)}{\Gamma\left(\frac{\nu+p+1-i}{2}\right)}}$$

and its moments are $E(Z) = M$ and $\text{Var}[\text{vec}(Z)] = \frac{1}{\nu-q-1} Q \otimes P^{-1}$ for $\nu - q - 1 > 0$.

Definition A.14 (The inverse Gaussian distribution) A continuous random variable Y has an *inverse Gaussian distribution* with mean $\mu > 0$ and shape parameter $\lambda > 0$, denoted $invGauss(\lambda, \mu)$, if its pdf is given by

$$f(y|\mu, \lambda) = \left(\frac{\lambda}{2\pi y^3}\right)^{\frac{1}{2}} \exp\left\{\frac{-\lambda (y - \mu)^2}{2\mu^2 y}\right\}$$

for $y > 0$.

Warning: The name "inverse Gaussian" is misleading since y^{-1} does not have a Gaussian (normal) distribution.

Bibliography

Abadir, K. M., R. D. H. Heijmans, and J. R. Magnus (2006). *Statistics*, Econometric Exercises Series, vol. 2, Cambridge University Press, New York.

Abadir, K. M. and J. R. Magnus (2002). Notation in econometrics: A proposal for a standard, *Econometrics Journal*, 5, 76–90.

Achcar, J. A. and A. F. M. Smith (1990). Aspects of reparameterization in approximate Bayesian inference, in: *Bayesian and Likelihood Methods in Statistics and Econometrics* (eds. S. Geisser, J. S. Hodges, S. J. Press, and A. Zellner), North-Holland, Amsterdam, 439–452.

Albert, J. and S. Chib (1993). Bayesian analysis of binary and polychotomous response data, *Journal of the American Statistical Association*, 88, 669–679.

Amemiya, T. (1985). *Advanced Econometrics*, Harvard University Press, Cambridge, MA.

Andrews, D. F. and C. L. Mallows (1974). Scale mixtures of normal distributions, *Journal of the Royal Statistical Society, Series B*, 36, 99–102.

Azzalini, A. and A. Dalla Valle (1996). The multivariate skew-normal distribution, *Biometrika*, 83, 715–726.

Bauwens, L., M. Lubrano, and J.-F. Richard (1999). *Bayesian Inference in Dynamic Econometric Models*, Oxford University Press, Oxford.

Berger, J. (1985). *Statistical Decision Theory and Bayesian Analysis*, 2nd edition, Springer-Verlag, New York.

Berger, J. O. and J. M. Bernardo (1989). Estimating a product of means: Bayesian analysis with reference priors, *Journal of the American Statistical Association*, 84, 200–207.

Berger, J. O. and J. M. Bernardo (1992). On the development of reference priors (with discussion), in: *Bayesian Statistics 4* (eds. J. M. Bernardo, J. O. Berger, A. P. Dawid, and A. F. M. Smith), Oxford University Press, Oxford, 35–60.

Berger, J. O. and L. R. Pericchi (1996). The intrinsic Bayes factor for model selection and prediction, *Journal of the American Statistical Association*, 91, 109–122.

Berger, J. and R. Wolpert (1988). *The Likelihood Principle*, 2nd edition, Institute of Mathematical Statistics, Hayward, CA.

Berger, J. and R.-Y. Yang (1994). Noninformative priors and Bayesian testing for the AR(1) model, *Econometric Theory*, 10, 461–482.

Bernardo, J. M. (1979). Reference prior distributions for Bayesian inference (with discussion), *Journal of the Royal Statistical Society, Series B*, 41, 113–147.

Bernardo, J. M. (2004). Reference analysis, Universitat de Valéncia, unpublished manuscript.

Bernardo, J. and A. F. M. Smith (1994). *Bayesian Theory*, John Wiley and Sons, Chichester.

Berument, H., Y. Yalcin, and J. Yildirim (2009). The effect of inflation uncertainty on inflation: Stochastic volatility in mean model within a dynamic framework, *Economic Modelling*, 26(6), 1201–1207.

Branco, M. D. and D. K. Dey (2002). Regression model under skew elliptical error distribution, *Journal of Mathematical Sciences*, 1, 151–169.

Carlin, B. P., A. E. Gelfand, and A. F. M. Smith (1992). Hierarchical Bayesian analysis of changepoint problems, *Applied Statistics*, 41(2), 389–405.

Carlin, B. P. and T. A. Louis (2000). *Bayes and Empirical Bayes Methods for Data Analysis*, Chapman & Hall / CRC Press, Boca Raton, FL.

Carlin, B. P. and N. G. Polson (1991). Inference for nonconjugate Bayesian models using the Gibbs sampler, *The Canadian Journal of Statistics*, 19, 399–405.

Carter, C. K. and Kohn, R. (1994). On Gibbs sampling for state space models. *Biometrika*, 81, 541–553.

Casella, G. and R. L. Berger (2002). *Statistical Inference*, 2nd edition, Duxbury, Pacific Grove, CA.

Casella, G. and E. George (1992). Explaining the Gibbs sampler, *The American Statistician*, 46, 167–174.

Casella, G., J. T. G. Hwang, and C. Robert (1993). A paradox in decision-theoretic interval estimation, *Statistica Sinica*, 3, 141–155.

Celeux, G., M. Hurn, and C. P. Robert (2000). Computational and inferential difficulties with mixture posterior distributions, *Journal of the American Statistical Association*, 95, 957–970.

Chan, J. (2013). Moving average stochastic volatility models with application to inflation forecast. *Journal of Econometrics*, 176(2), 162–172.

Chan, J. (2017). The stochastic volatility in mean model with time-varying parameters: An application to inflation modeling, *Journal of Business and Economic Statistics*, 35(1), 17–28.

Chan, J. (2018). Specification tests for time-varying parameter models with stochastic volatility, *Econometric Reviews*, 37(8), 807–823.

Chan, J. and I. Jeliazkov (2009). Efficient simulation and integrated likelihood estimation in state space models, *International Journal of Mathematical Modelling and Numerical Optimisation*, 1, 101–120.

Chan, J., G. Koop, and S. M. Potter (2013). A new model of trend inflation, *Journal of Business and Economic Statistics*, 31(1), 94–106.

Chan, J., G. Koop, and S. M. Potter (2016). A bounded model of time variation in trend inflation, NAIRU and the Phillips curve, *Journal of Applied Econometrics*, 31(3), 551–565.

Chan, J. and J. L. Tobias (2015). Priors and posterior computation in linear endogenous variable models with imperfect instruments, *Journal of Applied Econometrics*, 30(4), 650–674.

Chib, S. (1992). Bayes regression for the tobit censored regression model, *Journal of Econometrics*, 51, 79–99.

Chib, S. (1995). Marginal likelihood from the Gibbs sampler, *Journal of the American Statistical Association*, 90, 1313–1321.

Chib, S. (1996). Calculating posterior distributions and modal estimates in Markov mixture models, *Journal of Econometrics*, 75, 79–97.

Chib, S. (1998). Estimation and comparison of multiple change-point models, *Journal of Econometrics*, 86, 221–241.

Chib, S. (2001). Markov chain Monte Carlo methods: Computation and inference, in: *Handbook of Econometrics* vol. 5 (eds. J. J. Heckman and E. Leamer), Elsevier, Amsterdam, 3569–3649.

Chib, S. and B. Carlin (1999). On MCMC sampling in hierarchical longitudinal models, *Statistics and Computing*, 9, 17–26.

Chib, S. and E. Greenberg (1994). Bayes inference in regression models with ARMA(p, q) errors, *Journal of Econometrics*, 64(1–2), 183–206.

Chib, S. and E. Greenberg (1995). Understanding the Metropolis–Hastings algorithm, *The American Statistician*, 49, 327–335.

Chib, S. and I. Jeliazkov (2006). Inference in semiparametric dynamic models for binary longitudinal data, *Journal of the American Statistical Association*, 101, 685–700.

Clark, P. K. (1987). The cyclical component of US economic activity, *The Quarterly Journal of Economics*, 102(4), 797–814.

Clark, T. E. (2011). Real-time density forecasts from Bayesian vector autoregressions with stochastic volatility, *Journal of Business and Economic Statistics*, 29(3), 327–341.

Cogley, T. and Sargent, T. J. (2005). Drifts and volatilities: Monetary policies and outcomes in the post WWII US. *Review of Economic Dynamics*, 8, 262–302.

Cowles, M. and B. Carlin (1996). Markov chain Monte Carlo convergence diagnostics: A comparative review, *Journal of the American Statistical Association*, 91, 883–904.

Cragg, J. G. (1971). Some statistical models for limited dependent variables with application to the demand for durable goods, *Econometrica*, 39, 829–844.

Damien, P., J. C. Wakefield, and S. G. Walker (1999). Gibbs scaling for Bayesian non-conjugate and hierarchical models by using auxiliary variables. *Journal of the Royal Statistical Society, Series B*, 61, 331–344.

de Finetti, B. (1937). Foresight: Its logical laws, its subjective sources, translated from French in: *Studies in Subjective Probability* (eds. H. E. Kyburg, Jr. and H. E. Smokler), Wiley, New York, 1964.

de Jong, P. and N. Shephard (1995). The simulation smoother for time series models, *Biometrika*, 82, 339–350.

Deb, P., M. K. Munkin, and P. K. Trivedi (2006). Bayesian analysis of the two-part model with endogeneity: Application to health care expenditure, *Journal of Applied Econometrics*, 21, 1081–1099.

Denison, D. G. T., C. C. Holmes, B. K. Mallick, and A. F. M. Smith (2002). *Bayesian Methods for Nonlinear Classification and Regression*, Wiley, Chichester.

DiNardo, J. and J. L. Tobias (2001). Nonparametric density and regression estimation, *Journal of Economic Perspectives*, 15, 11–28.

Djegnene, B. and W. J. McCausland (2014). The HESSIAN method for models with leverage-like effects, *Journal of Financial Econometrics*, 13(3), 722–755.

Doan, T., R. Litterman, and C. Sims (1984). Forecasting and conditional projection using realistic prior distributions, *Econometric Reviews*, 3, 1–144.

Durbin, J. and S. J. Koopman (2002). A simple and efficient simulation smoother for state space time series analysis, *Biometrika*, 89, 603–615.

Efron, B. (1973). Discussion, *Journal of the Royal Statistical Society, Series B*, 35, 211.

Engle, R. F., D. M. Lilien, and R. P. Robins (1987). Estimating time varying risk premia in the term structure: The ARCH-M model, *Econometrica*, 55(2), 391–407.

Fair, R. (1978). A theory of extramarital affairs, *Journal of Political Economy*, 86, 45–61.

Fernandez, C., E. Ley, and M. Steel (2001a). Model uncertainty in cross-country growth regressions, *Journal of Applied Econometrics*, 16, 563–576.

Fernandez, C., E. Ley, and M. Steel (2001b). Benchmark priors for Bayesian model averaging, *Journal of Econometrics*, 100, 381–427.

Früwirth-Schnatter, S. (1994). Data augmentation and dynamic linear models, *Journal of Time Series Analysis*, 15, 183–202.

Früwirth-Schnatter, S. (2006). *Finite Mixture and Markov Switching Models*, Springer, New York.

Früwirth-Schnatter, S. and H. Wagner (2010). Stochastic model specification search for Gaussian and partial non-Gaussian state space models, *Journal of Econometrics*, 154, 85–100.

Garthwaite, P. H., J. B. Kadane, and A. O'Hagan (2005). Statistical methods for eliciting probability distributions, *Journal of the American Statistical Association*, 100, 680–700.

Geisser, S. (1984). On prior distributions for binary trials (with discussion), *American Statistician*, 38, 244–251.

Gelfand, A. E. and D. Dey (1994). Bayesian model choice: Asymptotics and exact calculations, *Journal of the Royal Statistical Society, Series B*, 56, 501–514.

Gelfand, A. E., S. Hills, A. Racine-Poon, and A. F. M. Smith (1990). Illustration of Bayesian inference in normal data models using Gibbs sampling, *Journal of the American Statistical Association*, 85, 972–985.

Gelfand, A. E., S. K. Sahu, and B. P. Carlin (1995). Efficient parameterizations for normal linear mixed models, *Biometrika*, 82, 479–488.

Gelman, A., J. B. Carlin, H. Stern, and D. Rubin (1995). *Bayesian Data Analysis*, 2nd edition, Chapman & Hall, London (2004).

George, E. and R. McCulloch (1993). Variable selection via Gibbs sampling, *Journal of the American Statistical Association*, 85, 398–409.

George, E. and R. McCulloch (1997). Approaches for Bayesian variable selection, *Statistica Sinica*, 7, 339–373.

George, E., D. Sun, and S. Ni (2008). Bayesian stochastic search for VAR model restrictions. *Journal of Econometrics*, 142, 553–580.

Geweke, J. (1988a). Exact inference in models with autoregressive conditional heteroskedasticity, in: *Dynamic Econometric Modeling* (eds., E. Berndt, H. White, and W. Barnett), Cambridge University Press, Cambridge.

Geweke, J. (1988b). The secular and cyclical behavior of real GDP in 19 OECD countries, 1957–1983, *Journal of Business and Economic Statistics*, 6, 479–486.

Geweke, J. (1989). Bayesian inference in econometric models using Monte Carlo integration, *Econometrica*, 57, 1317–1339.

Geweke, J. (1991). Efficient simulation from the multivariate normal and Student-t distributions subject to linear constraints, in: *Computer Science and Statistics: Proceedings of the Twenty-Third Symposium on the Interface* (ed. E. Keramidas), Interface Foundation of North America, Inc., Fairfax Station, VA, 571–578.

Geweke, J. (1993). Bayesian treatment of the independent Student-t linear model, *Journal of Applied Econometrics*, 8, S19–S40.

Geweke, J. (1996a). Bayesian reduced rank regression in econometrics, *Journal of Econometrics*, 75, 121–146.

Geweke, J. (1996b). Bayesian inference for linear models subject to linear inequality constraints, in: *Modeling and Prediction: Honoring Seymour Geisser* (eds. W. O. Johnson, J. C. Lee, and A. Zellner), Springer-Verlag, New York, 248–263.

Geweke, J. (1999). Using simulation methods for Bayesian econometric models: Inference, development, and communication (with discussion and rejoinder), *Econometric Reviews*, 18, 1–126.

Geweke, J. (2004). Getting it right: Joint distributions tests of posterior simulators, *Journal of the American Statistical Association*, 99, 799–804.

Geweke, J. (2005). *Contemporary Bayesian Econometrics and Statistics*, Wiley, Hoboken, NJ.

Geweke, J. (2006). Interpretation and inference in mixture models: MCMC is alive, well and simple, University of Iowa, Departments of Economics and Statistics, working paper.
Geweke, J. and M. Keane (2001). Computationally intensive methods for integration in econometrics, in: *Handbook of Econometrics* vol. 5 (eds. J. J. Heckman and E. Leamer), Elsevier, Amsterdam, 3463–3568.
Geweke, J., M. P. Keane, and D. E. Runkle (1997). Statistical inference in the multinomial multiperiod probit model, *Journal of Econometrics*, 80, 125–165.
Geweke, J. and N. Terui (1993). Bayesian threshold autoregressive models for nonlinear time series, *Journal of Times Series Analysis*, 14, 441–454.
Gill, J. (2002). *Bayesian Methods: A Social and Behavioral Sciences Approach*, Chapman & Hall / CRC Press, Boca Raton, FL.
Grant, A. L. and J. C. C. Chan (2017a). A Bayesian model comparison for trend-cycle decompositions of output, *Journal of Money, Credit and Banking*, 49, 525–552.
Grant, A. L. and J. C. C. Chan (2017b). Reconciling output gaps: Unobserved components model and Hodrick–Prescott filter, *Journal of Economic Dynamics and Control*, 75, 114–121.
Greenberg, E. (2013). *Introduction to Bayesian Econometrics*, 2nd edition, Cambridge University Press, New York.
Greene, W. (1999). Marginal effects in the censored regression model, *Economics Letters*, 1, 43–50.
Gujarati, D. (2003). *Basic Econometrics*, McGraw-Hill, Boston, MA.
Hamilton, J. D. (1989). A new approach to the economic analysis of nonstationary time series and the business cycle, *Econometrica*, 57, 357–384.
Hay, J. and R. Olsen (1984). Let them eat cake: A note on comparing alternative models of the demand for medical care, *Journal of Business and Economic Statistics*, 2, 279–282.
Heath, D. and W. Sudderth (1976). De Finetti's theorem on exchangeable variables, *American Statistician*, 30, 188–189.
Heckman, J. (1976). The common structure of statistical models of truncation, sample selection and limited dependent variables and a simple estimator for such models, *Annals of Economic and Social Measurement*, 5, 475–492.
Hodrick, R. J. and E. C. Prescott (1980). Postwar US business cycles: An empirical investigation, Carnegie Mellon University, discussion paper 451.
Hodrick, R. J. and E. C. Prescott (1997). Postwar US business cycles: An empirical investigation, *Journal of Money, Credit, and Banking*, 29(1), 1–16.
Hoeting, J., D. Madigan, A. Raftery, and C. Volinsky (1999). Bayesian model averaging: A tutorial, *Statistical Science*, 14, 382–417.
Jeffreys, H. (1961). *Theory of Probability*, 3rd edition, Clarendon Press, Oxford.
Johnson, N., S. Kotz, and N. Balakrishnan (1994). *Continuous Univariate Distributions*, vol. 1, 2nd edition, John Wiley and Sons, New York.
Johnson, N., S. Kotz, and N. Balakrishnan (1995). *Continuous Univariate Distributions*, vol. 2, 2nd edition, John Wiley and Sons, New York.

Johnson, N., S. Kotz, and N. Balakrishnan (2000). *Continuous Multivariate Distributions*, vol. 1, 2nd edition, John Wiley and Sons, New York.

Johnson, N., S. Kotz, and A. Kemp (1993). *Univariate Discrete Distributions*, 2nd edition. John Wiley and Sons, New York.

Kadane, J., N. Chan, and L. Wolfson (1996). Priors for unit root models, *Journal of Econometrics*, 88, 99–121.

Kadane, J. and J. Dickey (1980). Bayesian decision theory and the simplification of models, in: *Evaluation of Econometric Models* (eds. J. Kmenta and J. Ramsey), Academic Press, New York.

Kadiyala, K. and S. Karlsson (1997). Numerical methods for estimation and inference in Bayesian VAR-models, *Journal of Applied Econometrics*, 12, 99–132.

Kass, R. and L. Wasserman (1995). A reference Bayes test for nested hypotheses and its relationship to the Schwartz criterion, *Journal of the American Statistical Association*, 90, 928–934.

Kass, R. and L. Wasserman (1996). The selection of prior distributions by formal rules, *Journal of the American Statistical Association*, 91, 1343–1370.

Keane, M. (1992). A note on identification in the multinomial probit model, *Journal of Business and Economic Statistics*, 10, 193–200.

Kim, S., N. Shephard, and S. Chib (1998). Stochastic volatility: Likelihood inference and comparison with ARCH Models, *Review of Economic Studies*, 65, 361–393.

Kleibergen, F. and H. K. van Dijk (1994). On the shape of the likelihood/posterior in cointegration models, *Econometric Theory*, 10, 514–551.

Kleibergen, F. and H. K. van Dijk (1998). Bayesian simultaneous equations analysis using reduced rank structures, *Econometric Theory*, 14, 701–743.

Koenker, R. and G. Bassett, Jr. (1978). Regression quantiles, *Econometrica*, 46(1), 33–50.

Koop, G. (2003). *Bayesian Econometrics*, Wiley, Chichester.

Koop, G. and D. Korobilis (2012). Forecasting inflation using dynamic model averaging, *International Economic Review*, 53(3), 867–886.

Koop, G. and D. J. Poirier (1997). Learning about the cross-regime correlation in switching regression models, *Journal of Econometrics*, 78, 217–227.

Koop, G. and D. J. Poirier (2004). Bayesian variants of some classical semiparametric regression techniques, *Journal of Econometrics*, 123, 259–282.

Koop, G. and S. Potter (1999). Dynamic asymmetries in US unemployment, *Journal of Business and Economic Statistics*, 17, 298–312.

Koop, G. and S. Potter (2005). Forecasting and estimating multiple change-point models with an unknown number of change points, Department of Economics, University of Leicester, working paper.

Koop, G., R. Strachan, H. van Dijk, and M. Villani (2006). Bayesian approaches to cointegration, in: *The Palgrave Handbook of Econometrics, Volume 1: Theoretical Econometrics* (eds. T. C. Mills and K. Patterson), Palgrave Macmillan, Basingstoke, Chapter 25.

Koop, G. and J. L. Tobias (2006). Semiparametric Bayesian inference in smooth coefficient models, *Journal of Econometrics*, 134, 283–315.

Koopman, S. J. and E. Hol Uspensky (2002). The stochastic volatility in mean model: Empirical evidence from international stock markets, *Journal of Applied Econometrics*, 17(6), 667–689.

Kozumi, H. and G. Kobayashi (2011). Gibbs sampling methods for Bayesian quantile regression. *Journal of Statistical Computation and Simulation*, 81(11), 1565–1578.

Kroese, D. P. and J. Chan (2014). *Statistical Modeling and Computation*, Springer, New York.

Kwan, Y. K. (1998). Asymptotic Bayesian analysis based on a limited information estimator, *Journal of Econometrics*, 88, 99–121.

Lancaster, T. (2004). *An Introduction to Modern Bayesian Econometrics*, Blackwell Publishing, Oxford.

Leamer, E. (1982). Sets of posterior means with bounded variance priors, *Econometrica*, 50, 725–736.

Leung, S. F. and S. Yu (1996). On the choice between sample selection and two-part models, *Journal of Econometrics*, 72, 197–229.

Li, K. (1998). Bayesian inference in a simultaneous equation model with limited dependent variables, *Journal of Econometrics*, 85, 387–400.

Li, M., D. J. Poirier, and J. L. Tobias (2003). Do dropouts suffer from dropping out? Estimation and prediction of outcome gains in generalized selection models, *Journal of Applied Econometrics*, 19(2), 203–225.

Li, M. and J. L. Tobias (2007). Bayesian analysis of structural effects in an ordered equation system, *Studies in Nonlinear Dynamics and Econometrics*, 10, 1363.

Lindley, D. V. (2004). That wretched prior, *Significance*, 1, 85–87.

Lindley, D. and A. F. M. Smith (1972). Bayes estimates for the linear model, *Journal of the Royal Statistical Society, Series B*, 34, 1–41.

Litterman, R. (1986). Forecasting with Bayesian vector autoregressions – Five years of experience, *Journal of Business and Economic Statistics*, 4, 25–38.

Luo, S. and R. Startz (2014). Is it one break or ongoing permanent shocks that explains US real GDP?, *Journal of Monetary Economics*, 66, 155–163.

Madigan, D. and J. York (1995). Bayesian graphical models for discrete data, *International Statistical Review*, 63, 215–232.

Manning, W., N. Duan, and W. Rogers (1987). Monte Carlo evidence on the choice between sample selection and two-part models, *Journal of Econometrics*, 35, 59–82.

Manning, W., C. Morris, and J. Newhouse (1981). A two-part model of the demand for medical care: Preliminary results from the health insurance experiment, in: *Health, Economics and Health Economics* (eds. J. van der Gaag and M. Perlman), North-Holland, Amsterdam.

McCausland, W. J. (2012). The HESSIAN method: Highly efficient simulation smoothing, in a nutshell, *Journal of Econometrics*, 168(2), 189–206.

McCausland, W. J., S. Miller, and D. Pelletier (2011). Simulation smoothing for state-space models: A computational efficiency analysis, *Computational Statistics and Data Analysis*, 55, 199–212.

McCracken, M. W. and S. Ng (2015). FRED-MD: A monthly database for macroeconomic research. Federal Reserve Bank of St. Louis, working paper 2015-012A.

McCulloch, R., N. G. Polson, and P. E. Rossi (2000). A Bayesian analysis of the multinomial probit model with fully identified parameters, *Journal of Econometrics*, 99, 173–193.

McCulloch, R. and P. E. Rossi (1994). An exact likelihood analysis of the multinomial probit model, *Journal of Econometrics*, 78, 217–228.

McDonald, J. and R. Moffitt (1980). The uses of tobit analysis, *Review of Economics and Statistics*, 62, 318–321.

McLachlan, G. and D. Peel (2000). *Finite Mixture Models*, John Wiley & Sons, New York.

Michael, J. R., W. R. Schucany, and R. W. Haas (1976). Generating random variates using transformations with multiple roots, *The American Statistician*, 30, 88–90.

Morley, J. C., C. R. Nelson, and E. Zivot (2003). Why are the Beveridge–Nelson and unobserved-components decompositions of GDP so different?, *Review of Economics and Statistics*, 85(2), 235–243.

Moura, G. V. and D. E. Turatti (2014). Efficient estimation of conditionally linear and Gaussian state space models, *Economics Letters*, 124(3), 494–499.

Mumtaz, H. and F. Zanetti (2013). The impact of the volatility of monetary policy shocks, *Journal of Money, Credit and Banking*, 45(4), 535–558.

Nandram, B. and M.-H. Chen (1996). Reparameterizing the generalized linear model to accelerate Gibbs sampler convergence, *Journal of Statistical Computation and Simulation*, 54, 129–144.

Neal, R. M. (2003). Slice sampling, *Annals of Statistics*, 31(3), 705–767.

Neyman, J. and E. S. Scott (1948). Consistent estimates based on partially consistent observations, *Econometrica*, 16, 1–32.

Nobile, A. (2000). Comment: Bayesian multinomial probit models with a normalization constraint, *Journal of Econometrics*, 99, 335–345.

Phillips, P. C. B. (1991). To criticize the critics: An objective Bayesian analysis of stochastic trends (with discussion), *Journal of Applied Econometrics*, 6, 333–474.

Perron, P. and T. Wada (2009). Let's take a break: Trends and cycles in US real GDP, *Journal of Monetary Economics*, 56(6), 749–765.

Poirier, D. J. (1973). Piecewise regression using cubic splines, *Journal of the American Statistical Association*, 68, 515–524.

Poirier, D. J. (1995). *Intermediate Statistics and Econometrics: A Comparative Approach*, MIT Press, Cambridge, MA.

Poirier, D. J. (1996). Local Bayes factor approximations, *1996 Proceedings of the American Statistical Association Section on Bayesian Statistical Science*, 334–339.

Poirier, D. J. (1998). Revising beliefs in non-identified models, *Econometric Theory*, 14, 483–509.

Poirier, D. J. (2011). Exchangeability, representation theorems, and subjectivity, in *Handbook of Bayesian Econometrics* (eds. J. Geweke, G. Koop, and H. K. van Dijk), Oxford University Press, Oxford, 40–57.

Poirier, D. J. and A. Melino (1978). A note on the interpretation of regression coefficients within a class of truncated distributions, *Econometrica*, 46, 1207–1209.

Poirier, D. J. and J. L. Tobias (2003). On the predictive distributions of outcome gains in the presence of an unidentified parameter, *Journal of Business and Economic Statistics*, 21, 258–268.

Potter, S. M. (1995). A nonlinear approach to US GNP, *Journal of Applied Econometrics*, 10, 109–126.

Primiceri, G. (2005). Time varying structural vector autoregressions and monetary policy, *Review of Economic Studies*, 72, 821–852.

Raftery, A. E., D. Madigan, and J. A. Hoeting (1997). Bayesian model averaging for linear regression models, *Journal of the American Statistical Association*, 92(437), 179–191.

Ramsey, F. (1926). Truth and probability, in: *The Foundations of Mathematics and Other Logical Essays* (ed. R. B. Braithwaite), Routledge & Keegan Paul, London, 156–198.

Richardson, S. and P. Green (1997). On Bayesian analysis of mixtures with an unknown number of components (with discussion), *Journal of the Royal Statistical Society, Series B*, 59, 731–792.

Ritter, C. and Tanner, M. (1992). Facilitating the Gibbs sampler: The Gibbs stopper and the griddy-Gibbs sampler, *Journal of the American Statistical Association*, 87(419), 861–868.

Rubin, D. (1987). A noniterative sampling/importance resampling alternative to the data augmentation algorithm for creating a few imputations when fractions of missing information are modest: The SIR algorithm, *Journal of the American Statistical Association*, 82, 543–546.

Rubin, D. (1988). Using the SIR algorithm to simulate posterior distributions (with discussion), in: *Bayesian Statistics 3* (eds. J. M. Bernardo, M. H. DeGroot, D. V. Lindley, and A. F. M. Smith), Oxford University Press, Oxford, 395–402.

Rue, H. (2001). Fast sampling of Gaussian Markov random fields with applications, *Journal of the Royal Statistical Society Series B*, 63(2), 325–338.

Rue, H., S. Martino, and N. Chopin (2009). Approximate Bayesian inference for latent Gaussian models by using integrated nested Laplace approximations, *Journal of the Royal Statistical Society Series B*, 71(2), 319–392.

Schotman, P. (1994). Priors for the AR(1) model: Parameterisation issues and time series considerations, *Econometric Theory*, 10, 579–595.

Schwarz, G. (1978). Estimating the dimension of a model, *Annals of Statistics*, 6, 461–464.

Shuster, J. (1968). On the inverse Gaussian distribution function, *Journal of the American Statistical Association*, 63, 1514–1516.

Silverman, B. (1986). *Density Estimation for Statistics and Data Analysis*, Chapman & Hall, London.

Sims, C. A. (1980). Macroeconomics and reality, *Econometrica*, 48, 1–48.

Sims, C. (1988). Bayesian skepticism on unit root econometrics, *Journal of Economic Dynamics and Control*, 12, 463–474.

Sims, C. and H. Uhlig (1991). Understanding unit rooters: A helicopter tour, *Econometrica*, 59, 1591–1600.

Sims, C. and T. Zha (2006). Were there regime switches in US monetary policy?, *American Economic Review*, 96, 54–81.

Smith, A. F. M. and A. E. Gelfand (1992). Bayesian statistics without tears: A sampling–resampling perspective, *The American Statistician*, 46, 84–88.

Smith, M. and R. Kohn (1996). Nonparametric regression using Bayesian variable selection, *Journal of Econometrics*, 75, 317–343.

Stock, J. H. and M. W. Watson (2007). Why has US inflation become harder to forecast?, *Journal of Money Credit and Banking*, 39, 3–33.

Strachan, R. and B. Inder (2004). Bayesian analysis of the error correction model, *Journal of Econometrics*, 123, 307–325.

Tanner, M. and W. Wong (1987). The calculation of posterior distributions by data augmentation, *Journal of the American Statistical Association*, 82, 528–549.

Thornber, H. (1967). Finite sample Monte Carlo studies: An autoregressive illustration, *Journal of the American Statistical Association*, 62, 810–818.

Tibshirani, R. (1996). Regression shrinkage and selection via the Lasso, *Journal of the Royal Statistical Society Series B*, 58(1), 267–288.

Tierney, L. (1994). Markov chains for exploring posterior distributions (with discussion), *Annals of Statistics*, 22, 1701–1762.

Tierney, L. and J. Kadane (1986). Accurate approximations for posterior moments and marginal posterior densities, *Journal of the American Statistical Association*, 81, 82–86.

Tierney, L., R. E. Kass, and J. B. Kadane (1989). Fully exponential Laplace approximations to expectations and variances of nonpositive functions, *Journal of the American Statistical Association*, 84, 710–716.

Tobin, J. (1958). Estimation of relationships for limited dependent variables, *Econometrica*, 26, 24–36.

van Hasselt, M. (2005). Bayesian sampling algorithms for the sample selection and two-part models, working paper, Department of Economics, Brown University.

Vijverberg, W. (1993). Measuring the unidentified parameter of the extended Roy model of selectivity, *Journal of Econometrics*, 57, 69–89.

Wald, A. (1950). *Statistical Decision Functions*, Wiley, New York.

Watson, M. W. (1986). Univariate detrending methods with stochastic trends, *Journal of Monetary Economics*, 18(1), 49–75.

Yang, R. and J. O. Berger (1996). A catalogue of noninformative priors, Technical Report #97-42, Institute of Statistics and Decision Sciences, Duke University.

Yu, K. and R. A. Moyeed (2001). Bayesian quantile regression, *Statistics & Probability Letters*, 54, 437–447.

Zellner, A. (1962). An efficient method of estimating seemingly unrelated regressions and tests for aggregation bias, *Journal of the American Statistical Association*, 57, 348–368.

Zellner, A. (1986a). On assessing prior distributions and Bayesian regression analysis with g-prior distributions, in: *Bayesian Inference and Decision Techniques: Essays in Honour of Bruno de Finetti* (eds. P. K. Goel and A. Zellner), North-Holland, Amsterdam.

Zellner, A. (1986b). Bayesian estimation and prediction using asymmetric loss functions, *Journal of the American Statistical Association*, 81, 446–451.

Zellner, A. (1994). Bayesian and non-Bayesian estimation using balanced loss functions, in: *Statistical Decision Theory and Related Topics V* (eds. S. Gupta and J. Berger), Springer-Verlag, New York.

Zellner, A. and C.-K. Min (1995). Gibbs sampler convergence criteria, *Journal of the American Statistical Association*, 90, 921–927.

Zellner, A. and P. Rossi (1984). Bayesian analysis of dichotomous quantal response models, *Journal of Econometrics*, 25, 365–393.

Index

For EU product safety concerns, contact us at Calle de José Abascal, 56–1°, 28003 Madrid, Spain or eugpsr@cambridge.org.

www.ingramcontent.com/pod-product-compliance
Ingram Content Group UK Ltd.
Pitfield, Milton Keynes, MK11 3LW, UK
UKHW030655060825
461487UK00011B/948

9781108423380